OXFORD MONOGRAPHS IN INTERNATIONAL HUMANITARIAN & CRIMINAL LAW

General Editors

SUZANNAH LINTON

ROBERT CRYER

SALVATORE ZAPPALÀ

Organizing Rebellion

OXFORD MONOGRAPHS IN INTERNATIONAL HUMANITARIAN AND CRIMINAL LAW

The aim of this series is to publish original and innovative books on fundamental, topical, or cutting-edge issues in international humanitarian law and international criminal justice. The primary purpose of the series is to publish books which, in addition to critically surveying existing law, also suggest new avenues for improving the law.

Special attention will be given to works by young scholars.

Organizing Rebellion

Non-State Armed Groups under International Humanitarian Law, Human Rights Law, and International Criminal Law

TILMAN RODENHÄUSER

OXFORD
UNIVERSITY PRESS

OXFORD
UNIVERSITY PRESS

Great Clarendon Street, Oxford, OX2 6DP,
United Kingdom

Oxford University Press is a department of the University of Oxford.
It furthers the University's objective of excellence in research, scholarship,
and education by publishing worldwide. Oxford is a registered trade mark of
Oxford University Press in the UK and in certain other countries

First Edition published in 2018
Impression: 2

Published in the United States of America by Oxford University Press
198 Madison Avenue, New York, NY 10016, United States of America

British Library Cataloguing in Publication Data
Data available

Library of Congress Control Number: 2017958600

ISBN 978–0–19–882194–6

Printed and bound by
CPI Group (UK) Ltd, Croydon, CR0 4YY

To Kurt and Else Rodenhäuser

Foreword

Armed groups are now key players on the international stage, and it is hard to address the horrors of armed conflict without looking directly at the behaviour of these groups. They are involved in armed conflicts, and they are active in multiple contexts outside armed conflict. They may be present in times of tension and internal disturbances, but they also continue to operate after the end of an armed conflict. Today we have to recognize that armed groups affect the lives and well-being of millions of people.

Despite the central role of armed groups and new scholarship devoted to them, foundational questions remain concerning the significance of their structure or organization. At one level it seems that the application of the laws of armed conflict are dependent on the presence of not only a certain intensity of violence, but also a group demonstrating a certain level of organization. The jurisprudence of the International Criminal Tribunal for the former Yugoslavia has shed some light on the matter, but the Tribunal could obviously only address issues that arose before it. The structure and organization of armed groups for the purposes of the application of human rights law and international criminal law is even less well understood.

Dr Rodenhäuser's monograph tackles this terrain, and one of the great merits of the work is his careful consideration of the organization of armed groups both as a matter of public international law and in three inter-related branches of that law—international humanitarian law, human rights law, and international criminal law. As academic scholarship tends more and more towards specialization, much of the writing remains blinkered and limited to a single branch of law or field of specialization. But adopting such a focus would mean that one fails to present the full picture. The actions of armed groups straddle a number of areas. In exploring international humanitarian law, human rights law, and international criminal law, Dr Rodenhäuser has been able to step back, cast his gaze wide, and present us with a multidimensional and wide-angled vision. He identifies points of congruence between the fields, but also instances of tension. He demonstrates command of the subject and admirably navigates between the branches.

In his eminently readable work, Dr Rodenhäuser takes the reader systematically through each field of law and provides a near exhaustive analysis of questions of organization of armed groups that arise therein. In his search for clarity he does not take the easy way out by finding that once a group reaches a certain level of organization we can determine that it has international personality and thus can be the bearer of all the pertinent international legal obligations. Instead he interrogates the rationale and history of each branch of law and finds that the thresholds may be very different, and that even when a threshold is met for a particular branch of law, the power and capacity of the group may determine what obligations are expected of it. His conclusions are based on a careful reading of the drafting of the various texts and he is careful not to lump together all international crimes, all human rights, or even all the international humanitarian law applicable in non-international armed conflict.

Distinctions are drawn between war crimes, genocide, and crimes against humanity, and then again between crimes of commission, omission, and incitement. Similarly he suggests that armed groups fulfilling a governance function in a situation where the state has totally lost control are subject to greater human rights expectations than groups with sporadic control of people or territory. In the context of the law of armed conflict we are taken through the different categories of belligerents, insurgents, rebels, and the newer tests under Additional Protocol II and customary international law. The graduations that are introduced are done to meet the rationale of the field of law under investigation rather than to fit the theories of personality, subjectivity, or what constitutes a function of government. The result is a proposed framework that is both original and intellectually sound.

This timely publication will no doubt be of considerable interest to academics and practitioners alike and will become a key point of reference on issues relating to the organization of armed groups.

Andrew Clapham, Geneva
Sandesh Sivakumaran, Nottingham
November 2017

Series Editors' Preface

The world, as we currently see it, is one in which the state-based paradigm, whilst remaining dominant, rightly or wrongly, does not represent the factual nature of the role of non-state actors, especially in armed conflict situations. In many ways this echoes debates that were had many years ago about the regulation of armed conflicts (then which tended to be called civil wars) where the law of armed conflict/international humanitarian law was, to say the least, underdeveloped. Whilst this has perhaps been somewhat remedied by the development of treaty, and case-law on point (the relationship is, in and of itself, worthy of further study), this is not the whole of the story.

Dr Rodenhäuser's study shows this very clearly. There are other areas of international law that impact on the rights and duties of non-state actors. Whilst it is clear that individuals, be they civilians, members of armed groups, or governmental officials (even within context military or civilian), are bound by international criminal law, it is also the case that the State Responsibility under the Law of Armed Conflict/International Criminal Law is one that has caused considerable controversy, both at the academic and judicial level.

Furthermore, there are considerable questions relating to the rights and duties of states and armed groups (in addition to that of individuals) with respect to, and for, human rights. International human rights law has traditionally dealt with the activities of states, but increasingly, where the state's proverbial writ does not run throughout its territory, non-state actors have (or not) taken on this role, whilst their international responsibility as a group (and for states that may be supporting them) has been unclear.

As such, a study like Dr Rodenhäuser's, that integrates all three areas of law and is based on a very firm understanding of the law, practice, and jurisprudence in the area, is a very welcome addition to the debate in this very controversial part of the law. It is firmly based in the existing law (the *lex lata*), but is also very thoughtful as to how the law ought to develop (the *lex ferenda*). Dr Rodenhäuser's work engages at a very high level with all of the primary and secondary sources that relate to the subject, and their interrelationship.

This is a careful study on areas that are topical, sensitive, and difficult. Dr Rodenhäuser has found a very fine path through the tangled web of the various areas of law involved, looking, in particular at the relationship of individual liability and that of the groups to which such people may be members (and that is, of itself worthy of further debate, although states seem to have little appetite for such discussion).

This study is an outstanding piece of doctrinal analysis of the relevant law on point, but it is also not dry, it shows sensitivity to the broader issues involved, both political and moral, and the relationship of them both to the existing law. It is a scholarly, thoughtful whilst also imaginitive, contribution to the debates on point, grounded in an outstanding understanding of the law, and what surrounds it.

The editors

Acknowledgements

Writing this book has been an enriching, often fascinating, intense but also delightful journey. While it is in the nature of academic research that most of this journey has been rather lonesome, it could not have succeeded without the support and company of colleagues, family, and friends.

First of all, I thank Professor Andrew Clapham for supervising my PhD research, based on which I have written this book. Advice such as 'write the book you want to read', 'keep thinking', or 'Tilman, work on your style by reading authors you think are good' may not be what a young scholar initially hopes for. Yet, it was exactly the advice I needed because instead of giving me concrete instructions to solve a specific problem you made me think and grow myself. From this, I will benefit for a lifetime. It goes without saying that your expertise on this book's substance has been a constant source of challenge and improvement. I also thank Professor Eibe Riedel for encouraging me to embark on this study, Professor Nicolas Michel for being the study's second reader, and Professor Sandesh Sivakumaran for being part of an engaging and challenging PhD jury.

Being based at the Graduate Institute has enabled me to research and work in Geneva's inspiring professional environment (and its beautiful surroundings). I am most grateful to my colleagues and friends at different institutions in Geneva—notably the International Committee of the Red Cross, Geneva Call, and the Graduate Institute—with whom I discussed many ideas and from whom I continue to learn. Your criticism and encouragement have been invaluable. In particular, Jonathan Somer and David Tuck, no matter how busy you were, you never refused to discuss any nitty-gritty legal issue. Moreover, I sincerely thank Ariffadhillah and Professor Mohamad Tay for sharing insights on the working of different armed groups. I am also heavily indebted to Lys Kulamadayil, Patryk Labuda, Elvina Pothelet, and Anne Quintin for countless comments, suggestions, and edits on this study. I know how many evenings you dedicated to improving parts of this work! Furthermore, I sincerely thank Katie Weir and Tina Weadick for proofreading, and the Oxford University Press team for their very professional support in publishing this book. Needless to say, however, the views expressed in this book are those of the author and not necessarily those of any of the mentioned institutions or persons.

Completing this book would not have been possible without the generous financial support of the Graduate Institute of International and Development Studies and the Evangelische Studienstiftung Villigst. Special thanks also go to the Graduate Institute's International Law Department, which financed research trips to Germany and Lebanon to meet representatives from non-state armed groups.

While every journey needs direction and support, company is probably the most important. I am particularly grateful to my parents and sister for their unqualified and unshakable trust. Throughout the past years, you have supported my studies and enabled me to seize opportunities I wished for.

Most profoundly, I thank Lena. Your warmth, humour, trust, intellect, and company have carried me through the past years. It was thanks to you that finalizing this book has been such a pleasant exercise.

Contents

Table of Cases

A. PERMANENT COURT OF INTERNATIONAL JUSTICE AND INTERNATIONAL COURT OF JUSTICE

B. INTERNATIONAL CRIMINAL COURT

C. INTERNATIONAL CRIMINAL TRIBUNAL FOR THE FORMER YUGOSLAVIA

D. INTERNATIONAL CRIMINAL TRIBUNAL FOR RWANDA

E. SPECIAL COURT FOR SIERRA LEONE

F. INTERNATIONAL MILITARY TRIBUNAL AT NUREMBERG AND OTHER POST-WORLD WAR II MILITARY TRIBUNALS

G. REGIONAL HUMAN RIGHTS COURTS

European Court of Human Rights and European Commission of Human Rights

Inter-American Court of Human Rights and Inter-American Commission of Human Rights

African Commission on Human and People's Rights

H. VARIOUS NATIONAL AND INTERNATIONAL CASES

Table of Documents and Resolutions

A. UNITED NATIONS

General Assembly

Resolutions

Reports and other documents

Security Council

Resolutions

Reports and other documents

Human Rights Council/ Commission on Human Rights

Resolutions

Reports and other documents

Treaty Body Documents

Documents related to the establishment of the International Criminal Court

International Law Commission

Other UN Documents

B. INTERNATIONAL COMMITTEE OF THE RED CROSS DOCUMENTS

C. OTHER DOCUMENTS

Table of Treaties

List of Abbreviations

ACHR	American Convention on Human Rights
AFRC	Armed Forces Revolutionary Council
ANSA	Armed non-state actor
APII	Protocol Additional to the Geneva Conventions of 12 August 1949, and relating to the Protection of Victims of Non-International Armed Conflicts (Protocol II)
ARSIWA	Articles on the Responsibility of States for Internationally Wrongful Acts
CAH	Crimes against Humanity
CAT	Convention against Torture and other Cruel, Inhuman or Degrading Punishment
CCL10	Control Council Law No 10
CEDAW	Convention on the Elimination of all Forms of Discrimination against Women
CIL	Customary International Law
CoI	Commission of Inquiry
Common Article 3	Article 3 common to the four Geneva Conventions
CPED	International Convention for the Protection of all Persons from Enforced Disappearance
CPN—M	Communist Party of Nepal–Maoist
CRC	Convention on the Rights of the Child
CRC-OPAC	Optional Protocol to the Convention on the Rights of the Child on the Involvement of Children in Armed Conflict
DRC	Democratic Republic of the Congo
ECHR	European Convention on Human Rights
ECOWAS	Economic Community of West African States
ECtHR	European Court of Human Rights
ESC rights	Economic, social, and cultural rights
FARC	Revolutionary Armed Forces of Colombia
FRPI	Forces de Résistance Patriotique d'Ituri
FSA	Free Syrian Army
GCI	Geneva Convention (I) for the Amelioration of the Condition of the Wounded and Sick in Armed Forces in the Field
GCII	Geneva Convention (II) for the Amelioration of the Condition of Wounded, Sick and Shipwrecked Members of Armed Forces at Sea
GCIII	Geneva Convention (III) relative to the Treatment of Prisoners of War
GCIV	Geneva Convention (IV) relative to the Protection of Civilian Persons in Time of War
HRMMU	United Nations Human Rights Monitoring Mission in Ukraine
IAComHR	Inter-American Commission on Human Rights
IACtHR	Inter-American Court of Human Rights
ICC	International Criminal Court
ICCPR	International Covenant for Civil and Political Rights

ICC Statute	Rome Statute of the International Criminal Court
ICERD	International Convention on the Elimination of all Forms of Racial Discrimination
ICESCR	International Covenant for Economic, Social and Cultural Rights
ICJ	International Court of Justice
ICL	International Criminal Law
ICMW	International Convention on the Protection of the Rights of all Migrant Workers and Members of their Families
ICRC	International Committee of the Red Cross
ICTR	International Criminal Tribunal for Rwanda
ICTR Statute	Statute for the International Criminal Tribunal for Rwanda
ICTY	International Criminal Tribunal for the former Yugoslavia
ICTY Statute	Statute for the International Criminal Tribunal for the former Yugoslavia
IDP	Internally Displaced Person
IHL	International Humanitarian Law
IHRL	International Human Rights Law
ILA	International Law Association
ILC	International Law Commission
IMT	International Military Tribunal
IRA	Irish Republican Army
ISG	Islamic State Group
ISIL	Islamic State of Iraq and the Levant
KLA	Kosovo Liberation Army
LTTE	Liberation Tigers of Tamil Eelam
MRM	Monitoring and Reporting Mechanism on Grave Violations of Children's Rights in Situations of Armed Conflict
NGO	Non-Governmental Organization
NIAC	Non-international armed conflict
NSAG	Non-state armed group
NTC	National Transitional Council
OAG	Organized Armed Group
OHCHR	Office of the United Nations High Commissioner for Human Rights
OISL	OHCHR Investigation on Sri Lanka
PKK	Kurdistan Workers' Party
PTC	Pre-Trial Chamber
RUF	Revolutionary United Front
SCSL	Special Court for Sierra Leone
TRNC	Turkish Republic of Northern Cyprus
UDHR	Universal Declaration on Human Rights
UN	United Nations
UNCESCR	United Nations Committee on Economic, Social and Cultural Rights
UNGA	United Nations General Assembly
UNMISS	United Nations Mission in the Republic of South Sudan
UNSC	United Nations Security Council
UNSG	United Nations Secretary General
UPC/FPLC	Union des Patriotes Congolais/Forces Patriotiques pour la Libération du Congo
VCLT	Vienna Convention on the Law of Treaties

Introduction

Non-state armed groups frequently become parties to armed conflicts, violate human rights, or commit international crimes. As such, this is not news. What has changed, however, is the nature of these groups: while in the late twentieth century armed groups were normally 'clearly defined entities with distinct political and security agendas', today's armed groups are often less structured, fragmented, or operating in loose coalitions and with diverse agendas.[1] Two situations in which the changing nature of non-state armed groups challenged traditional concepts and interpretations of international law provided the impetus for conducting this study. The first one was post-election violence in 2007–08 in Kenya and subsequent prosecutions at the International Criminal Court (ICC). After presidential elections in 2007, violence rocked parts of Kenya. Alleging fraud, supporters of the opposition party committed crimes against perceived supporters of the ruling party. In retaliation, 'groups targeted by the initial attacks . . . directed [attacks] against members of those groups deemed responsible for the initial violence'.[2] A Commission of Inquiry found:

> [P]ost-election violence was more than a mere juxtaposition of citizen-to-citizen opportunistic assaults. These were systematic attacks on Kenyans based on the ethnicity and their political leanings. Attackers organized along ethnic lines, assembled considerable logistical means and traveled [sic] long distances to burn houses, maim, kill and sexually assault their occupants because these were of particular ethnic groups and political persuasion.[3]

The result was more than 1100 persons killed, 3500 injured, and the displacement of 'approximately 350,000'.[4] When in 2010 the ICC prosecutor requested a Pre-Trial Chamber to authorize an investigation into alleged crimes against humanity, the legal issue splitting the Chamber was whether the organizers of these crimes could be considered an organization, as required under article 7(2)(a) of the Rome Statute of the International Criminal Court (ICC Statute). The majority of the

[1] ICRC, *ICRC Strategy 2015–2018* (ICRC 2014) 5.

[2] *Situation in the Republic of Kenya, Decision Pursuant to Article 15 of the Rome Statute on the Authorization of an Investigation into the Situation in the Republic of Kenya, 31 March 2010, Pre Trial Chamber II, ICC-01/09*, ICC, para 105.

[3] Commission of Inquiry into Post-Election Violence, *Report of the Commission of Inquiry into Post-Election Violence (Kenya)* (2008) viii. In more legal terms, Pre-Trial Chamber II found that post-election violence included acts of 'murder, rape and other forms of sexual violence, forcible transfer of population and other inhumane acts'. *Situation in the Republic of Kenya, ICC-01/09*, para 102.

[4] *Situation in the Republic of Kenya, ICC-01/09*, para 131.

Organizing Rebellion: Non-State Armed Groups under International Humanitarian Law, Human Rights Law, and International Criminal Law. Tilman Rodenhäuser.
Published 2018 by Oxford University Press.

Chamber interpreted the organization criterion broadly and authorized the investigation; the dissenting judge argued for a narrow interpretation, which would have prevented the trial from proceeding. Each side received support in subsequent scholarly debate.[5]

The second situation was the escalation of anti-regime protest in Syria into a non-international armed conflict in 2011–12. In response to the Syrian regime's violent suppression of protest, opposition groups armed themselves and increasingly engaged in confrontations with regime forces.[6] When violence escalated in early 2012, the United Nations (UN) Independent International Commission of Inquiry on the Syrian Arab Republic tried to establish whether internal violence amounts to a non-international armed conflict. The Commission stated that while it was

> gravely concerned that the violence in certain areas may have reached the requisite level of intensity, it was unable to verify that the Free Syrian Army (FSA), local groups identifying themselves as such or other anti-Government armed groups had reached the necessary level of organization.[7]

As a result of the inability to find a sufficient degree of organization among various opposition groups, the Commission did not consider international humanitarian law applicable, which meant that, in its view, only human rights law applied in Syria. Following this finding, alleged crimes committed during that period could not be labelled or prosecuted as war crimes. At the same time, however, the Commission argued that 'at a minimum, human rights obligations constituting peremptory international law (ius cogens) bind States, individuals and non-State collective entities, including armed groups'.[8] Thus, while the Commission was unable to verify whether the groups in question were sufficiently organized to become party to an armed conflict, it considered them bound by basic human rights law obligations.

The key legal difficulties in the situations in Kenya 2007–08 and Syria in 2011–12, and reasons for ensuing controversy, define the main questions examined in this book: (1) What is the requisite degree of organization required for non-state armed groups to become party to an armed conflict? (2) What degree of power and organization is required for non-state entities to have obligations under international human rights law (IHRL)? (3) What kind of organizations are able to commit international crimes, or are able to create a context in which individuals commit them?

These questions are relevant beyond the Kenya and Syria examples, and their complexity is not limited to the issues flagged. Armed conflicts involving a variety of groups have erupted in different countries over recent years, including Libya, Yemen, Iraq, the Central African Republic, Ukraine, and the Sahel region. Based on its operational experience in all contemporary conflicts, the International Committee of the Red Cross found that 'a myriad of fluid, multiplying and fragmenting armed

[5] Pertinent legal literature is discussed in Part III of this book.

[6] See Human Rights Council, *Report of the Independent International Commission of Inquiry on the Syrian Arab Republic*, 23 November 2011, A/HRC/S-17/2/Add.1.

[7] Human Rights Council, *Report of the Independent International Commission of Inquiry on the Syrian Arab Republic*, 22 February 2012, A/HRC/19/69, para 13.

[8] ibid para 106.

groups frequently take part in the fighting',[9] contributing to conflicts' growing complexity.[10] Moreover, groups such as Al Qaida or the 'Islamic State Group' (ISG)[11] operate not only in one state's territory or in neighbouring states but across regions and continents, triggering questions of whether they constitute transnational or global armed groups. A similarly global, increasingly discussed, but still not well-understood phenomenon is 'cyber groups', meaning groups participating in armed conflicts but operating primarily or exclusively online.

In conflict and crisis situations, governments often weaken, lose control over parts of their territory and population, and become de facto unable to protect effectively the human rights of persons within their jurisdiction. Instead, people live under the control of non-state entities, or in situations of quasi-anarchy without any authority-wielding actor. For example, in 2016 the Islamic State Group de facto occupied parts of Syrian/Iraqi territory, 'has declared itself a "State", and runs both a civil and a military administration, including the establishment of a "court" system', but blatantly violated international human rights law.[12] Likewise, in 2013 in the Central African Republic, the Séléka armed group ousted a weak central government, and in the ensuing chaos, the Séléka group and other groups labelled Anti-Balaka committed large-scale human rights violations without having government-like structures, or power.[13] Despite the fact that non-state armed groups control territory to varying degrees in states like Afghanistan, Colombia, Mali, Nigeria, or for many years, in Sri Lanka or the Gaza strip, states continue to debate whether and to what extent human rights law applies to such groups. Increasingly, states seem to accept that at least groups exercising control over territory and people have human rights obligations. In contrast, practice and scholarly debate is more controversial regarding possible human rights obligations of groups not controlling territory and population but operating beyond effective state control.

The involvement and relevance of non-state armed groups in crises and armed conflicts is likely to increase. Researchers have identified three trends: first, over recent years the number of groups involved in armed conflicts has quadrupled, and this multiplication is likely to continue; second, the vast majority of armed violence is increasingly taking place outside armed conflicts and non-state armed groups, such as criminal gangs, bear significant responsibility for it; and third, in weak states people are increasingly organizing privately to protect their communities from

[9] ICRC, *International Humanitarian Law and the Challenges of Contemporary Armed Conflicts* (ICRC, 2015) 6.

[10] ibid 5.

[11] Also referred to as 'Islamic State', or 'Islamic State of Syria and the Levant', ISIS, or ISIL.

[12] Human Rights Council, *Report of the Special Rapporteur on the Promotion and Protection of Human Rights and Fundamental Freedoms while Countering Terrorism, Ben Emmerson*, 16 June 2015, A/HRC/29/51, para 30. Similarly, other reports suggest that the ISG has established quasi-state institutions and infrastructure in areas under its control. See International Commission of Inquiry on the Syrian Arab Republic, *Rule of Terror: Living under ISIS in Syria* (14 November 2014) para 16. See also Human Rights Council, *Report of the Independent International Commission of Inquiry on the Syrian Arab Republic*, 13 August 2014, A/HRC/27/60, para 17.

[13] See United Nations Security Council, *The International Commission of Inquiry on the Central African Republic—Final Report*, 22 December 2014, S/2014/928.

different threats, establishing parallel power structures.[14] These trends coincide with a decrease in state power. As the International Committee of the Red Cross stated in its 2015–18 strategy, armed groups 'often operate in the vacuum left by increasingly fragile States, composed of varying combinations of formal and informal armed elements animated by a mixture of motives, including control over natural resources, conduct of criminal activities, and predatory intentions towards the local population'.[15] In this dynamic, the national law of weakened states seems inapt as a legal framework to regulate adequately the activities of actors who are de facto challenging the state's authority and regularly operating beyond state borders. At the same time, opinions differ as to whether and to what extent key fields of contemporary international law on the regulations of violence—international humanitarian, human rights, and criminal law—regulate non-state armed groups' actions.

Legal Framework and Methodology

Broadly speaking, this book's objective is to clarify what kind of armed groups fall under the scope of international humanitarian law, international human rights law, and international criminal law. It aims to show how the three fields of law address non-state armed groups, and to present ways in which the existing legal framework can be interpreted to better accommodate a changing scope of relevant actors.

This book examines each field of law separately but under a common research framework. First, in order to establish whether a field of law can theoretically apply to non-state armed groups, the book examines each field's conceptual and historic origins. Second, it analyses to what extent applicable sources of law—notably treaties and custom—apply to non-state armed groups. Third, the book discusses how pertinent state practice, jurisprudence, expert reports, and literature have applied the law and interpreted the questions of whether and to what extent it addresses armed groups. The author's understanding of how different armed groups organize and operate was further enhanced by discussions with different armed groups' representatives and persons frequently engaging with such groups. Yet, this book does not present detailed case studies; the selection of practical examples was mostly determined by the availability and pertinence of legally relevant information.

Under international humanitarian law (IHL), it is uncontroversial that treaty and customary law apply to armed groups if they become party to a non-international armed conflict.[16] While Additional Protocol II[17] defines criteria according to which

[14] McQuinn and Oliva, *Preliminary Scoping Report—Analyzing and Engaging Non-State Armed Groups in the Field* (2014) 2.

[15] ICRC, *ICRC Strategy 2015–2018* (n 1) 4. See also United States National Intelligence Council, *Global Trends 2025: A Transformed World* (2008).

[16] While no one seriously questions whether IHL binds armed groups, no commonly agreed theory of how IHL treaties bind armed groups exists. See, for instance, Sivakumaran, 'The Addressees of Common Article 3' in Clapham, Gaeta, and Sassòli (eds), *The 1949 Geneva Conventions: A Commentary* (OUP 2015) 415–33; Murray, 'How International Humanitarian Law Treaties Bind Non-State Armed Groups' (2015) 20 Journal of Conflict and Security Law 101–31.

[17] Protocol Additional to the Geneva Conventions of 12 August 1949, and relating to the Protection of Victims of Non-International Armed Conflicts (Protocol II), 8 June 1977 (cited as Additional Protocol II).

a group qualifies as an 'organised armed group' for the purposes of that instrument, article 3 common to the four Geneva Conventions, the ICC Statute, or customary law do not contain similarly explicit definitions: the former refers broadly to 'each Party to the conflict'. There is broad agreement in international practice that each party to an armed conflict needs to have some degree of organization, and international criminal jurisprudence has identified a number of factors indicating whether a group is sufficiently organized. These factors are certainly helpful and enjoy support among many commentators and international organizations.[18] At the same time, they should not be understood as a de facto defintion of what constitutes a party to a non-international armed conflict. Especially when examining conflicts in very different geographical regions, increasingly fractured insurgencies, armed groups operating in different states' territories, or cyber armed groups, the factors that were originally developed by the International Criminal Tribunal for the Former Yugoslavia may not always be helpful. Moreover, there is continuing controversy over very basic questions, such as whether a group must only be sufficiently organized to engage in armed violence, or also to implement basic humanitarian law norms.[19] While the requisite degree of organization of parties to a conflict is examined in a wide range of literature on conflict classification, detailed studies are rare.[20] This book seeks to close this gap by inquiring about the criterion's origins, codifications, interpretations, and application in contemporary practice. It aims to set out an understanding of the requisite degree of organization of non-state parties to an armed conflict that is, on the one hand, sufficiently broad to apply to existing as well as future conflicts, and, on the other hand, precise enough to provide guidance for practitioners and judges engaged in conflict classification.

The legal landscape is significantly different in international human rights law. Traditionally, human rights treaties define rights for individuals and obligations for states; most do not define obligations for non-state entities.[21] Yet, in recent years states in UN fora and human rights mechanisms have increasingly reacted to armed groups' human rights 'violations' or 'abuses'.[22] They have called on groups to respect

[18] eg two recently published commentaries on the Geneva Conventions refer to these factors in their discussion of parties to a non-international armed conflict, and so do most UN reports involving conflict classification and commentators. See, for instance, Moir, 'The Concept of Non-International Armed Conflict' in Clapham, Gaeta, and Sassòli (eds), *The 1949 Geneva Conventions: A Commentary* (OUP 2015) 391–414, paras 38–39; International Committee of the Red Cross, *Convention (I) for the Amelioration of the Condition of the Wounded and Sick in Armed Forces in the Field: Commentary of 2016* (2016) paras 80–81. More examples and practice are discussed in Part I of the book.

[19] eg ICC Trial Chambers took different positions in the Court's first three judgments. See, in particular, *Katanga, Judgment, 7 Mars 2014, Trial Chamber II, ICC-01/04-01/07*, ICC, para 1185; *Bemba Gombo, Judgment pursuant to Article 74 of the Statute, 21 March 2016, Trial Chamber III, ICC-01/05-01/08*, ICC, para 134.

[20] One notable exception is Sivakumaran, *The Law of Non-International Armed Conflict* (OUP 2012) esp 170–80.

[21] Two recent exceptions in which IHRL treaties address obligations directly to armed groups are the 'Optional Protocol to the Convention on the Rights of the Child on the Involvement of Children in Armed Conflict' (CRC-OPAC) and the 'African Union Convention for the Protection and Assistance of Internally Displaced Persons in Africa' (Kampala Convention).

[22] Numerous examples are discussed in Part II of this book. Chapter 6 (Section 6.2.1.3 'Legal semantics: human rights "violations" and "abuses" ') also discusses the use of the terms 'violations' and 'abuses'.

human rights and sometimes also to ensure respect. At the same time, scholarly discussion on the question of human rights obligations of armed groups has increased significantly, with a majority of commentators summarizing recent practice and arguing in favour of further strengthening armed groups' responsibilities under international law. Yet, questions as to the scope of armed groups' human rights obligations, as well as their legal sources, have not yet received much attention.[23] In order to take discussion forward and to provide conceptual underpinning for human rights practice, this book argues that differentiating armed groups according to their degree of power and organization helps to conceptualize and improve understanding of whether, how, and to what extent non-state entities have, or should have, human rights obligations. It aims to show that a differentiated analysis reflects reality and contemporary practice better than a 'one size fits all' approach. It highlights the situations in which human rights obligations of armed groups are needed, allows some conclusions to be drawn on the sources and scope of obligations, and provides a basis for further practice and discussion.

While international criminal law should provide unambiguous definitions of international crimes in order to respect the principle of legality, the question of whether international crimes require state or non-state collective entity involvement has long been debated. This book examines whether non-state entities can create contexts in which individual conduct can amount to international crimes. Simultaneously, such analysis also identifies the requisite degree of organization and capacity required from armed groups to commit international crimes.[24] Regarding war crimes, it is generally agreed that they can be committed in international and non-international armed conflicts, and, to become party to the latter, armed groups need to be sufficiently organized.[25] Likewise, the widely accepted definition of crimes against humanity under article 7(2)(a) ICC Statute requires a 'State or organisational policy' behind the crimes; thus, state involvement is not strictly required. Yet, the ICC Statute does not contain details on the requisite degree of organization of non-state entities behind crimes against humanity. Lastly, at least according to its wording, the universally accepted definition of genocide does not explicitly require any collective entity involvement.

With the establishment of the ICC, states created a court that—if it has the jurisdiction to do so—can prosecute crimes committed anywhere and committed with the involvement of diverse non-state collective entities. Experts expect that in many cases, charges will include crimes against humanity.[26] Yet, judges and

[23] One exception is Katharine Fortin, who recently published a monograph on whether and how IHRL applies to armed groups parties to armed conflicts. She did not, however, examine armed groups not party to armed conflicts, or the scope of possible obligations. See Fortin, *The Accountability of Armed Groups under Human Rights Law* (OUP 2017).

[24] This book does not examine whether international criminal law also applies to legal persons in addition to natural persons. The distinction between 'creating a context for individual crimes' or committing a crime is further discussed in the introduction and conclusion to Part III of this book.

[25] The applicable threshold of organization is similar to that under IHL.

[26] See, eg, Sadat, 'Crimes against Humanity in the Modern Age' (2012) 107 American Journal of International Law 334–77; Kress, 'The ICC's First Encounter with the Crime of Genocide: The Case

experts disagree on which characteristics or degree of organization entities behind crimes against humanity or genocide need to have. Debate in case law and literature mostly turns on the question of whether or not such entities must show certain 'state-like' characteristics, and scholarly debate is—understandably—driven by case law. Examining the definition of crimes against humanity and genocide under the ICC Statute and the ICC *Elements of Crimes*, this book suggests an interpretation of the collective-entity involvement in these crimes based primarily on the crimes' contexts. It identifies different ways of how individuals can commit crimes pursuant to, or in furtherance of a collective policy, and argues that the requisite degree of organization of the entity behind the crime depends on the relation between the criminal act and the organizational policy. In brief, a non-state entity would need a different degree of internal organization and capacity to instigate crimes by private individuals than it would to commit systematic crimes through its own members.

Very limited consideration has been given to the question of whether having a degree of organization sufficient to invite obligations in one field of law would also signify being a sufficiently organized non-state entity in another field. On one occasion, an ICC Pre-Trial Chamber argued that if a collective entity behind crimes against humanity qualifies as a party to an armed conflict, 'inevitably it qualifies as an organisation within the context of Article 7 of the Statute'.[27] Likewise, drawing analogies between different fields of law, commentators suggested: 'If armed groups possess enough international legal personality to be subject to a sliding scale of obligations under international humanitarian law, it seems logical that they should also be subject to international obligations under human rights law.'[28] Based on an examination of the requisite degree of organization under the three fields of law, this book clarifies in which cases such analogies can be validly drawn, and in which cases they may lead to unjustified results.

Structure

Reflecting the three fields of international law under examination, the book is divided into three Parts.

To identify the requisite degree of organization of armed groups under international humanitarian law, Part I starts by examining the way in which the laws of war have traditionally addressed non-state armed groups. Subsequently, it analyses how today's treaty law defines the scope of non-state armed groups party to non-international armed conflicts. The first Part's third chapter ('Organized Armed

against Al Bashir' in Stahn (ed), *The Law and Practice of the International Criminal Court* (OUP 2014) 669–704. See also United Nations General Assembly (UNGA), *International Law Commission: First Report on Crimes against Humanity*, 17 February 2015, A/CN.4/680, para 11.

[27] *Situation in the Republic of Cote d'Ivoire, Decision Pursuant to Article 15 of the Rome Statute on the Authorisation of an Investigation into the Situation in the Republic of Côte d'Ivoire, 3 October 2011, Trial Chamber III, ICC-02/11*, ICC, para 99.

[28] Clapham, *Focusing on Armed Non-State Actors*, in A Clapham and P Gaeta (eds), *The Oxford Handbook of International Law in Armed Conflict* (OUP 2014) 788.

Groups in Contemporary International Practice') identifies three criteria characterizing non-state parties to armed conflicts: they need to be (1) collective entities that are sufficiently organized to (2) ensure respect for fundamental humanitarian norms, and (3) to engage in hostilities. This chapter shows how these criteria can be proved in practice, and discusses the extent to which they apply to specific types of armed groups, such as 'transnational armed groups' or 'cyber armed groups'.

Owing to the continuing controversy over whether non-state groups can have international human rights law obligations, Part II commences by questioning whether, philosophically, human rights should primarily be understood as individual entitlements, or as state obligations. Next, it analyses the extent to which today's state-centred human rights protection system provides adequate human rights protection if states are confronted with armed groups. Subsequently, Chapter 6 'A Three-Pronged Approach to Human Rights Obligations of Non-State Armed Groups' suggests dividing armed groups into three broad categories in order to determine whether and to what extent they can have human rights obligations. These groups are (1) armed groups exercising quasi-governmental authority in defined territory; (2) armed groups exercising de facto control over territory and population; and (3) armed groups not controlling territory and population. For each category of non-state groups, the book presents: the extent of state obligations to prevent human rights violations by such groups; contemporary examples in which human rights mechanisms address the groups' human rights violations; conceptual ideas on how international human rights could bind the groups in question; and suggestions on the possible scope of the groups' human rights obligations.

Part III examines international criminal law, namely the degree of organization of non-state armed groups to commit war crimes, crimes against humanity, or genocide, or to create a context in which individuals can commit such crimes. It does not, however, contain a distinct chapter on war crimes because the necessary degree of organization is similar to the one identified in Part I of the book. Consequently, Part III contains two main sections: one on crimes against humanity and one on genocide. With regard to crimes against humanity, it first examines what—from a conceptual perspective—is the distinct gravity or harm of the crime. It proceeds by analysing the historic development of crimes against humanity, and how different tribunals addressed the question of which kind of armed groups can be involved in it. Afterwards, in Chapter 9 'The "State or Organizational Policy" Requirement for Crimes against Humanity under the Rome Statute of the International Criminal Court', the author examines the 'organisational policy' criterion under article 7(2)(a) ICC Statute and provides an interpretation of the definition's wording, object and purpose, context, as well as subsequent state and jurisprudential practice. With regard to genocide, Chapter 10 'Non-State Entity Involvement in Genocide' first discusses the origin and wording of the crime's definition as found in the Genocide Convention of 1948. Subsequently, it analyses how international jurisprudence has approached the question of whether a collective entity needs to be involved in the commission of the crime, and—if yes—which capacities such entities need.

The book's conclusion identifies similarities and differences between the degrees of organization required from non-state armed groups under the different fields of law. Comparing how the different fields of law address armed groups, it also presents suggestions of how this development is likely to, or should, continue.

Definitions

Outlining the purpose, scope, and methodology of this book also requires clarifications on some of its key notions and concepts.

'Non-state armed groups'

This book examines 'non-state armed groups'. No generic definition of this term exists under international law.[29] Three characteristics of the book's principal subject derive, however, directly from the notion. First, the author analyses groups, meaning collections of people who come together for a certain reason.[30] The precise reason or purpose of why these people unite is immaterial. It is, however, required that the group is distinct from its members.[31] As the International Court of Justice (ICJ) argued in the *Western Sahara* Advisory Opinion, in order to be 'legally an "entity" ' it is essential that the group, whether it is 'composed of States, of tribes or of individuals, is claimed to be a legal entity distinct from its members'.[32] Second, a group needs to be a 'non-state' one. For the purpose of this book, this means that the group is not an organ of a state, not empowered by a state to exercise elements of governmental authority, and not otherwise acting under the instructions, direction, or control of a state.[33] In addition, such groups normally—but not necessarily—operate in contravention of the territorial state's laws. Third, in most cases these groups are armed. This, however, is not a strict or narrowly defined criterion. Being armed should be understood as being capable of engaging in a non-international armed conflict, to commit human rights violations, or to engage in international crimes. The type of arms is not decisive, as long as they serve their purpose. Moreover, being armed is not strictly required. While most groups analysed in this book possess arms

[29] A telling example of this lack of an agreed definition of terms is that in recent years, the UN Security Council has used over nineteen different terms to describe groups that can generally qualify as a 'non-state armed group'. See Burniske, Modirzadeh, and Lewis, *Armed Non-State Actors and International Human Rights Law: An Analysis of the Practice of the UN Security Council and UN General Assembly* (Harvard School of Law Program on Interational Law & Armed Conflict 2017) 9.

[30] See *Oxford Dictionary*, online version, definition of 'group'.

[31] Murray calls this an 'independent will', which he convincingly argues constitutes a strict requirement for any international legal person. See Murray, *Human Rights Obligations of Non-State Armed Groups* (Hart 2016) 79–81.

[32] *Western Sahara, Advisory Opinion, 16 October 1975*, ICJ, para 148. The question of whether a group is a 'collective entity' is examined in detail in Chapter 3 'Organized Armed Groups in Contemporary International Practice'.

[33] In other words, its conduct shall not be attributable to a state under articles 4–10 of the ILC, 'Articles on the Responsibility of States for Internationally Wrongful Acts'. If a group receives support from a state, shares a state's objectives, or is otherwise linked to a state, it continues to be considered 'non-state' as long as its acts cannot be attributable to the state.

and are militarily organized, this is not a sine qua non requirement to be responsible for human rights violations or to be involved in international crimes.

In the course of the following chapters, different terms will be used to refer to different types of non-state armed groups. These include 'armed groups party to an armed conflict', 'organized armed groups', 'armed group', 'collective non-state entities', or 'non-state organizations'. In some cases, different terms are used for stylistic reasons; in most cases, however, the terminology used is chosen in accordance with the field of law under examination. Yet, terminology is in no way essential—unless it has a clearly defined meaning under applicable international law, such as the term 'organised armed group' under Additional Protocol II. The primary purpose of this book is to examine the virtually unrestricted field of non-state armed groups and define to what extent they need to be organized to become legally relevant actors in international humanitarian, human rights, and criminal law. Their name, purpose, or the ways other actors refer to them are not decisive.

'International legal personality'

A related issue is the author's approach to the question of which entities have international legal personality, or are 'subjects of international law'.[34] Generally speaking, the concept of international legal personality 'is employed to distinguish between those social entities relevant to the international legal system and those excluded from it'.[35] In this book, the question of the degree of organization of armed groups required to invite obligations under different fields of law coincides with that of which non-state entities have international legal personality. A hundred years ago, the answer might have been straightforward: 'Since the Law of Nations is a law between states only and exclusively, states only and exclusively are subjects of the Law of Nations'.[36] Non-state armed groups would have been excluded from the international legal system.[37] Yet, at least since 1945, the question of which natural and legal persons have international legal personality has 'given rise to controversy'.[38] While various non-state entities act on the international (legal) stage, there is no

[34] While slight differences exist between the concepts of 'international legal personality' and 'subjects of international law', for the purpose of this book they are treated as synonymous. For discussion of differences, see Portmann, *Legal Personality in International Law* (CUP 2010) 1; Klabbers, *An Introduction to International Law* (CUP 2003) 43.

[35] Portmann, *Legal Personality in International Law* (n 34) 1. In other words, it defines natural and legal persons 'upon whom the law confers rights and imposes duties'. Lauterpacht, 'The Subjects of the Law of Nations' (1947) 45 Law Quarterly Review 438–61, 137.

[36] Oppenheim, *International Law* (Longmans, Green & Co. 1905) 341.

[37] Interestingly, however, such a conclusion would not take into consideration the fact that armed groups recognized as belligerents were, already at that time, subject to international law.

[38] *Reparations for Injuries Suffered in the Service of the United Nations, International Court of Justice, Advisory Opinion, 11 April 1949*, ICJ, 178. As Clapham pointed out, even fifty years after the ICJ's Advisory Opinion, scholarly treatment of the issue has been 'confusing and incomplete', which led Klabbers to diagnosing a 'picture of conceptual helplessness'. Clapham, *Human Rights Obligations of Non-State Actors*, (1st pub and repr, OUP 2006) 59; Klabbers, '(I Can't Get No) Recognition: Subjects Doctrine and the Emergence of Non-State Actors' in Petman and Klabbers (eds), *Nordic Cosmopolitanism* (M Nijhoff Publishers 2003) 351–69, 354.

universal agreement on which persons possess international legal personality, why they do so, and with what consequences.[39] While the objective of this book is not, primarily, to contribute to the issue's doctrinal clarification, it inevitably applies an understanding of which entities may have international legal personality. As even an implicit conception of legal personality arguably 'often determines the starting point of legal analysis and eventually its outcome',[40] a few words on the approach underlying this book are warranted.

This book's approach to international legal personality is based on the ICJ's 1949 Advisory Opinion on *Reparations for Injuries Suffered in the Service of the United Nations*. The Court made three main findings relevant for the present purpose: first, international legal personality, or subjectivity, is not limited to states; second, different subjects exist that 'are not necessarily identical in their nature or in the extent of their rights'; and third, the different persons' 'nature depends upon the needs of the community'.[41] The Court further emphasized: 'Throughout its history, the development of international law has been influenced by the requirements of international life'.[42] Accordingly, this book takes a broad approach to legal personality, which does not restrict international legal persons ex ante to states, or to specific kinds of non-state entities.[43] It does not determine legal personality in the abstract but finds that it depends on the field of law, the specific context in which relevant conduct occurs, and the capacities of the group in question.[44] In this respect, it follows Hersch Lauterpacht, who argued as early as 1947:

> [I]n each particular case the question whether a person or a body is a subject of international law must be answered in a pragmatic matter by reference to actual experience and to the reason of the law as distinguished from a preconceived notion as to who can be subjects of international law.[45]

The ICJ's Opinion did not clarify, however, how non-state entities obtain legal personality. In line with the argument that legal personality should not be defined in the abstract, this book does not assume that legal personality must somehow exist

[39] Nevertheless, over recent years important studies have been published on different ways of understanding international legal personality. See, eg, Portmann, Legal Personality in International Law (n 34); Nijman, *The Concept of International Legal Personality: An Inquiry into the History and Theory of International Law* (TMC Asser Press 2004).

[40] Portmann, *Legal Personality in International Law* (n 34) 19.

[41] *Reparations for Injuries Suffered in the Service of the United Nations* (n 38) 178.

[42] ibid. While this finding was closely linked to international cooperation and the creation of intergovernmental organizations, it should not be interpreted as only applying to this context. It can be argued that 'requirements of international life' do not only require international cooperation but also, eg, the 'strengthening of the international rule of law', for which recognizing international personality of non-state actors is arguably a prerequisite. Nijman, 'Non-State Actors and the International Rule of Law: Revisiting the "Realist Theory" of International Legal Personality' in Noortmann and Ryngaert (eds), *Non-State Actor Dynamics in International Law: From Law-Takers to Law-Makers* (Ashgate 2010) 91–124, 94.

[43] Likewise, Clapham argued that the ICJ's approach is 'quite open-ended'. Clapham, *Human Rights Obligations of Non-State Actors* (n 38) 64.

[44] Daragh Murray refers to this as a 'subject-specific competence'. Murray, *Human Rights Obligations of Non-State Armed Groups* (n 31) 29.

[45] Lauterpacht, 'The Subjects of the Law of Nations' (n 35).

as a prerequisite for addressing entities as bearers of rights or duties.[46] Instead, it is based on the commonly shared assumption that any entity can have international legal personality if international norms apply to it.[47] In practice, however, international law—treaty or custom—rarely addresses non-state armed groups specifically. Instead, it defines general circumstances in which a set of rules binds certain actors. Accordingly, international legal norms can be addressed to armed groups if the armed group meets circumstantial and organizational criteria defined in the field of law in question.[48] For example, the scope of application of international humanitarian law requires the existence of at least two organized conflicting parties; thus, a group needs to have a sufficient degree of organization and operate in a relevant context to become subject to that field of law.

Following the ICJ's finding that different entities can have personality according to the needs of the international community, this book does not consider it controversial that international law can assign norms to state armed groups, which would turn relevant groups into entities with some international legal personality. For example, if states agreed that all armed groups with the factual ability to violate human rights will thereby breach international human rights law and be held responsible, it would be naïve to think that an alleged lack of legal personality would prevent such norms from binding an armed group.

In addition to endorsing the possibility that non-state entities can have international personality, the ICJ argued that being an international person is 'not the same thing' as being a state, and that a non-state entity's 'legal personality and rights and duties are [not] the same as those of a state'.[49] Accordingly, this book considers that different international persons can have different degrees of rights and obligations. As Jan Klabbers phrased it: 'One can have personality in different graduations.'[50] This applies not only to distinct categories of international persons (such as states,

[46] Scholars have suggested different approaches to international legal personality. Portmann suggested five concepts: the 'states only conception', the 'recognition conception', the 'individualistic conception', the 'formal conception', and the 'actor conception'. See Portmann, *Legal Personality in International Law* (n 34). While in the first two, 'personality' depends on the will of states, in the last three, non-state entities need to meet certain criteria to obtain personality. In contrast, Murray argues that none of the approaches taken could explain legal personality. For him, in order to have international legal personality an 'entity must have the capacity to possess direct legal rights or obligations, must actually possess such rights or obligations, and must exist independently'. Murray, *Human Rights Obligations of Non-State Armed Groups* (n 31) 48–50.

[47] As the ILC's first rapporteur on the responsibility of international organizations, Giorgio Gaja, argued: '[A]n entity has to be regarded as a subject of international law even if only a single obligation is imposed on it under international law'. *First Report on Responsibility of International Organizations*, by Mr Giorgio Gaja, Special Rapporteur, 2003, A/CN.4/532, para 15. See also Klabbers, 'The Concept of Legal Personality' (2005) 11 Ius Gentium 35–66.

[48] Examining a group's capacity or organization corresponds with the ICJ's finding that the UN is a subject of international law because it is, inter alia, 'capable of possessing international rights and duties'. *Reparations for Injuries Suffered in the Service of the United Nations* (n 38) 179. Likewise, Murray concludes: 'it is an entity's organisational characteristics that will determine its capacity to possess international rights or obligations'. Murray, *Human Rights Obligations of Non-State Armed Groups* (n 31) 44.

[49] *Reparations for Injuries Suffered in the Service of the United Nations* (n 38) 179. The Court also argued that the UN was in 'possession of a large measure of international personality', which suggests that there can also be small measures of international personality, which still make an entity a legal person.

[50] Klabbers, 'The Concept of Legal Personality' (n 47) 47.

individuals, and non-state collective entities), but also to different groups falling under the broad notion of non-state collective entities (eg armed groups party to an armed conflict, corporations, governmental or non-governmental organizations). Non-state entities, even if armed and opposing a state, are so diverse that considering all of them to be bound by the same set of rules would be inaccurate. A pertinent example is the different obligations that non-state armed groups can have under international humanitarian law. While all parties to an armed conflict are subject to some rules of international humanitarian law and must, accordingly, have some degree of personality, this degree varies: highly organized armed groups with territorial control and the capacity to exercise quasi-governmental powers may, if recognized as belligerents, be bound by a comprehensive set of rules otherwise applicable to armed conflicts between states; groups exercising some territorial control and operating under responsible command may, if applicable, be bound by Additional Protocol II; and groups with rather elementary power and internal organization are bound by article 3 common to the four Geneva Conventions. As a result, the idea that non-state entities can have different degrees of obligations or personality according to their capacities is not a hypothesis but a reality in contemporary international law.

'The degree of organization'

In general terms, this book examines the degree of organization of armed groups. The term 'organization' could be narrowly understood as referring only to groups' internal structures. For the purpose of this book, however, the 'degree of organization' has a broader meaning, which encompasses the group's internal structures and its ability or capacity to engage in pertinent conduct under different fields of law. For example, under international humanitarian law, the requisite degree of organization demands not only a certain command structure but also the ability to engage in hostilities; under human rights law, a group's degree of control over territory and populations is an important criterion; and an entity instigating crimes against humanity or genocide might not need a sophisticated internal structure if it otherwise achieves its purpose.

PART I

THE REQUIRED DEGREE OF ORGANIZATION OF A NON-STATE PARTY TO AN ARMED CONFLICT UNDER INTERNATIONAL HUMANITARIAN LAW

Conflict classification becomes ever more complex. Turmoil or inter-communal tensions escalate into armed conflicts, armed groups fragment increasingly, violence is becoming more and more regionalized, and parties are using new means and methods of warfare.[1] Since it determines whether or not international humanitarian law (IHL) becomes applicable, conflict classification is 'a subject of seminal importance'.[2] As a matter of principle, armed conflicts are fought between two or more parties. International armed conflicts are fought between two or more states.[3] In non-international armed conflicts (NIACs), at least one party must be a non-state entity, and the very notion 'party to the conflict' suggests that a non-state party must be a collective entity. Hence, the suggestion that a party to a NIAC must show a certain degree of organization is largely undisputed: '[t]he difficulty arises not in stating that it must exist, but rather in determining the necessary level [of organization]'.[4] A recent comprehensive study of the laws of NIAC pointed out that 'the element of organisation and the workings of armed groups are only just starting to be understood' because 'insufficient attention has been paid to armed groups, their

[1] For a description of today's conflict environment, see ICRC, *International Humanitarian Law and the Challenges of Contemporary Armed Conflicts* (ICRC, 2015).

[2] Schmitt, 'Classification of Cyber Conflict' (2012) 17 Journal of Conflict and Security Law 245–60, 245.

[3] An international armed conflict can also exist between a state and an armed group if the armed group can be attributed to a state. For further discussion, see ICRC, *Convention (I) for the Amelioration of the Condition of the Wounded and Sick in Armed Forces in the Field: Commentary of 2016* (ICRC 2016); Clapham, 'The Concept of International Armed Conflict' in Clapham, Gaeta, and Sassòli (eds), *The 1949 Geneva Conventions: A Commentary* (OUP 2015) 3–26, paras 40–49.

[4] Moir, *The Law of Internal Armed Conflict* (CUP 2002) 36.

structure, and workings'.[5] The objective of the first part of this book is to examine how the organization requirement developed under IHL, why it is important, how it is defined and interpreted in treaty law and practice, and how it should be understood in contemporary and future conflicts.

Before delving into this analysis, some clarifications and qualifications are necessary. First, for the purpose of IHL, it is irrelevant what different actors call a non-state entity.[6] Instead, it is important whether an entity qualifies as a 'belligerent', a 'Party to the conflict', an 'organised armed group', or 'peoples [that] are fighting against colonial domination and alien occupation and against racist régimes in the exercise of their right of self-determination' as defined under IHL.[7] In this book, the terms 'non-state party to the conflict' or 'organized armed group' are often used interchangeably. However, on some occasions the term 'party to a conflict' depicts a non-state entity that consists of an organized armed group as well as civilian components, or a party that unites different organized armed groups.[8] Second, this book is not concerned with the question of membership of organized armed groups, meaning which individuals form part of a party to the conflict.[9] Nor does Part I focus on the question of how to attribute individual conduct to armed groups, which is addressed in the conclusions to Part III of this book. Instead, the focus is on the structural characteristics that qualify a non-state entity as a party to a NIAC.

The Introduction to this Part also warrants a word of caution. Conflict classification, which necessarily includes a determination of whether a certain entity qualifies as a party to the conflict, is not only controversial but also political. Different interests are at stake, and these interests have changed over time.[10] Some states wish

[5] Sivakumaran, *The Law of Non-International Armed Conflict* (OUP 2012) 210.

[6] While states may call such entities 'criminals', 'terrorists', or 'rebels', these entities see themselves as 'freedom fighters' or 'liberation armies'. From a neutral standpoint, they might be called 'armed non-state actors' or 'non-state armed groups'.

[7] The first term is only defined under customary IHL, the second term is used in article 3 common to the four Geneva Conventions, and the third one in article 1(1) of the Protocol Additional to the Geneva Convention of 12 August 1949, and relating to the Protection of Victims of Non-International Armed Conflicts (Protocol II) (APII) and article 8(2)(f) of the Rome Statute of the International Criminal Court (ICC Statute). The fourth term would qualify a non-state party to an armed conflict as a party to an IAC under article 1(4) API. Groups falling under article 1(4) API are not subject to examination in this chapter.

[8] The former differentiation has been used by the ICRC in its DPH Study. See ICRC, *Interpretive Guidance on the Notion of Direct Participation in Hostilities under International Humanitarian Law* (ICRC 2009). See also Radin, 'Global Armed Conflict? The Threshold of Extraterritorial Non-International Armed Conflicts' (2013) 13 International Law Studies 696–743, 732.

[9] On this issue, see ICRC, *Interpretive Guidance on the Notion of Direct Participation in Hostilities under International Humanitarian Law* (n 8); Boothby, '"And for Such Time": The Time Dimension of Direct Participation of Hostilities' (2010) 42 International Law and Politics 741–68; Sivakumaran, *The Law of Non-International Armed Conflict* (n 5) 359–62.

[10] This Introduction can only provide a very rough overview of the debate. For in-depth discussion, see, eg, McLaughlin, 'Legal-Policy Considerations and Conflict Characterisation at the Threshold between Law Enforcement and Non-International Armed Conflict' (2012) 13 Melbourne Journal of International Law 1–28; Clapham, 'The Concept of International Armed Conflict' (n 3) paras 20–39; International Law Association, 'Final Report on the Meaning of Armed Conflict in International Law' (2010); Blank and Corn, 'Losing the Forest for the Trees: Syria, Law, and the Pragmatics of Conflict Recognition' (2013) 46 Vanderbilt Journal of Transnational Law 693–746; Margulies and Sinnot, 'Crossing Borders to Target Al-Qaeda and Its Affiliates: Defining Networks as Organized Armed Groups in Non-International Armed Conflicts' (2015) 16 Yearbook of International Humanitarian Law 2013

to deny the existence of a NIAC—for example, to have more leeway in suppressing 'troublemakers', to downplay the scale of the crisis, or to deny the non-state adversary any perceived legitimacy.[11] Owing to the rise of international human rights law (IHRL), other states seek to apply IHL at a lower threshold because IHL is generally considered to contain more lenient rules than IHRL on the use of force or the restriction of liberty of individuals.[12] On the humanitarian side, pertinent considerations include that while, in some cases, IHRL is more protective and should apply exclusively, in other cases IHL is more specifically tailored to respond to situations of large-scale violence. For example, the application of IHL grants humanitarian organizations broader humanitarian access, and while IHL applies to all parties to a conflict, many still consider IHRL as not binding non-state entities.[13] Moreover, whereas the Geneva Conventions are universally ratified, important human rights treaties are not.[14] Last but not least, those involved in criminal prosecution may advocate for a low threshold of application because, from a criminal law perspective, the existence of an armed conflict enables the prosecution of war crimes. These political interests can influence how the different actors define the term organized armed group for the purpose of IHL.

Bearing these considerations in mind, this part proceeds as follows. Chapter 1 'Of Rebels, Insurgents, and Belligerents: Non-State Parties in the History of Warfare' examines how the focus of the laws of war changed from being exclusively on states towards including certain state-like non-state entities. In particular, Chapter 1 focuses on the requisite criteria for a non-state entity to qualify as a 'belligerent'. Chapter 2 'Parties to Non-International Armed Conflicts under International Treaty Law' analyses how non-state parties to armed conflicts are defined under international treaty law. First, it shows that despite the drafters' omission of a definition of the notion of a 'Party to the conflict' under article 3 common to the four Geneva Conventions (Common Article 3), read in context the notion suggests characteristics for non-state parties to a conflict. Second, Chapter 2 provides an interpretation of the explicit requirements that qualify non-state entities as 'organised

319–345; Garraway, 'War and Peace: Where Is the Divide' (2012) 88 International Law Studies Series. US Naval War College 93–115; Milanovic, 'The End of Application of International Humanitarian Law' (2014) 96 International Review of the Red Cross 163–88.

[11] On how these concerns were expressed in treaty negotiations, see chapter 2 'Parties to Non-International Armed Conflicts under International Treaty Law'.

[12] eg it would be very difficult to justify extrajudicial killings via a drone unless they can be justified as lawful attacks under IHL. See Kretzmer, 'Rethinking the Application of IHL in Non-International Armed Conflicts' (2009) 42 Israel Law Review 8–45, 24–25. See also ICRC, *International Humanitarian Law and the Challenges of Contemporary Armed Conflicts* (ICRC 2011) 22; Kress, 'Some Reflections on the International Legal Framework Governing Transnational Armed Conflicts' (2010) 15 Journal of Conflict and Security Law 245–74, 261.

[13] On the first point, see Rodenhäuser and Giacca, 'The International Humanitarian Law Framework for Humanitarian Relief During Armed Conflicts and Complex Emergencies' in Breau and Samuel (eds), *Research Handbook on Disasters and International Law* (Edward Elgar 2016) 132–53; on the latter point, see Part II of this book.

[14] eg as of May 2016, 168 states had ratified the International Covenant for Civil and Political Rights (ICCPR), and 164 states the International Covenant for Economic, Social and Cultural Rights (ICESCR).

armed groups' under article 1(1) of APII. Third, it briefly examines whether states established an additional definition of 'organised armed groups' under article 8(2)(c) and (f) of the ICC Statute. Chapter 3 'Organized Armed Groups in Contemporary International Practice' analyses which criteria international practice uses to determine the existence of a non-state party to an armed conflict. Three broad criteria are identified and studied. Based on this analysis, Chapter 3 also discusses under which conditions coalitions of armed groups, transnational armed groups, or cyber armed groups may qualify as a party to a NIAC, and when a non-state party to a conflict ceases to qualify as such.

1

Of Rebels, Insurgents, and Belligerents

Non-State Parties in the History of Warfare

Traditionally, waging war was considered a prerogative of the sovereign, and the laws of war only applied to armed confrontations between kings, or sovereigns.[1] As Oppenheim asserted in 1912: 'To be considered war, the contention must be going on between States.'[2] In the seventeenth and eighteenth centuries, lawyers and philosophers started to recognize the international legal relevance of rebellions,[3] private or mixed wars,[4] or civil wars.[5] In state practice, however, the recognition of belligerency, which reclassified internal violence into 'war' in the international legal sense, only emerged in the early nineteenth century. This Part shows that the traditional state-focus of the laws of war had two main consequences on the slowly emerging recognition of non-state entities as warring parties under international law. First, the criteria that developed in state practice for recognizing a non-state party to a conflict as a belligerent require the non-state party to have state-like characteristics.[6] Second, fundamental principles of the laws of war—such as the equality of belligerents and the principle of distinction—were developed in the context of inter-state conflicts between well-organized armed forces. These principles presuppose that all parties to the conflict—including non-state ones—are collective entities showing certain organizational capacities.

[1] This does not mean that wars involving private entities did not exist as a matter of fact. See, eg, Dinstein, *Non-International Armed Conflicts in International Law* (CUP 2014) 1.

[2] See Oppenheim, *International Law: A Treatise* (2nd edn, Longmans/Green 1912) 62–63. Oppenheim did, however, acknowledge that through recognition of belligerency, a non-state party could become 'a belligerent Power', and 'a civil war becomes war in the technical sense'. ibid 69. For further discussion, see also Milanovic and Hadzi-Vidanovic, 'A Taxonomy of Armed Conflict' in White (ed), *Research Handbook on International Conflict and Security Law: "jus ad bellum, jus in bello", and "jus post bellum"* (Edward Elgar 2013) 256–314, 261–62.

[3] See Ayala, *De jure et officiis bellicis et disciplina militari libri III*, trans Carnegie Institution (Carnegie Institution of Washington 1548–84) 11.

[4] See Grotius, *The Rights of War and Peace, including the Law of Nature and of Nations* (M Walter Dunne 1625) 55.

[5] De Vattel, *The Law of Nations*, trans Joseph Chitty (T & JW Johnson & Co 1758) 287ff.

[6] As shown below, recognition of belligerency did not bring the entire scope of laws of war into force but the scope of applicable rules depended on who—the warring state or a third state—recognized belligerency.

1.1 The Origins of the Statist Focus of the Laws of War

Agreements or codes on rules of war are found in different traditions and, arguably, have existed for as long as war itself.[7] Often, regulations of war were influenced by religions, which differentiated between types of wars. For example, under both Christianity and Islam, restraints on warfare existed for wars among members of the same religion but not for wars against 'non-believers'.[8] The Christian 'just war' concept also distinguished between wars among sovereigns and the oppression of rebellions. Drawing on the writings of Augustine, in the thirteenth century the writer Thomas Aquinas developed three conditions for a war to be just: first, war had to be waged by a sovereign authority; second, it required a just cause in the form of reacting to a wrong; and third, 'it is necessary that the belligerents should have a rightful intention, so that they intend the advancement of good, or the avoidance of evil'.[9] Under his theory of 'just war', Aquinas explicitly excluded the possibility of private individuals waging 'just war' because an individual 'can seek for redress of his rights from the tribunal of his superior'.[10] It was upon the authority to defend the common weal not only against external threats but also against internal disturbances.[11]

In Christian tradition, there was a reason for the particular status of the sovereign: the public authority was considered to rule by the grace of God, and attacking this God-given authority was considered an attack on God himself.[12] In the early sixteenth century, the priest and professor Martin Luther explained in an open letter justifying his harsh stance on the repression of a rebellion of peasants in Germany: 'There stands God's Word, "My son, fear God and the king; if not, thy calamity will come quickly"; and Romans 12, "He that resisteth the ordinance of God, will receive judgment." '[13] For Luther, it was justified to use violence against those who challenged the public authority and thereby the will of God. For him, 'the

[7] For examples of codes regulating warfare by the ancient Greeks and Romans, see Rengger, 'The Jus in Bello in Historical and Philosophical Perspective' in May and Crookston (eds), *War: Essays in Political Philosophy* (CUP 2008) 30–46, 34. For more diverse examples, see Greenwood, 'Historical Development and Legal Basis' in Fleck and Bothe (eds), *The Handbook of International Humanitarian Law* (OUP 2008) 1–38, 15–17; see also Green, *The Contemporary Law of Armed Conflict* (3rd edn, Manchester University Press 2008) 19–21; Harding, 'The Origins and Effectiveness of the Geneva Conventions for the Protection of War Victims' (1973) 13 International Review of the Red Cross 283–90.

[8] For a good analysis of this distinction, see Bartels, 'Timelines, Borderlines and Conflicts' (2009) 91 International Review of the Red Cross 35–67, 41–44.

[9] See Aquinas, *The Summa Theologica*, trans Fathers of the English Dominican Province (2nd edn, Christian Classics 1265–74) Question 40.

[10] ibid.

[11] For a good examination of the three criteria, see Perna, *The Formation of the Treaty Law of Non-international Armed Conflicts* (M Nijhoff 2006) 3–5.

[12] The authority of a city, kingdom, or province was considered 'God's minister'. See Aquinas, *The Summa Theologica* (n 9) Question 40.

[13] Martin Luther, *An Open Letter on the Harsh Book against the Peasants*, found in Marrin (ed), *War and the Christian Conscience: From Augustine to Martine Luther Jr* (Henry Regnery Company 1971) 101–02.

king [shall] be honored and rebels destroyed'.[14] Internal wars were considered to be outside the scope of any regulations of warfare.[15]

During that period, predecessors of the modern laws of war, such as codes of chivalry, applied to wars between Christian princes and the fighting between knights. They did not apply to armed confrontations between a knight and 'ordinary people'.[16] These often-cited early laws of war were not intended to apply to, and had no impact on, what is today called a non-international armed conflict.[17] As Greenwood underlined, these codes were 'intended to apply only to hostilities between Christian princes and [were] seldom applied outside that context'.[18] It was also against this background of inter-state conflicts that in 1762 the Genevan philosopher Rousseau advanced conceptual considerations that underpin the laws of war today. In *The Social Contract*, Rousseau argued:

> [w]ar then is a relation, not between man and man, but between State and State, and individuals are enemies only accidentally, not as men, nor even as citizens, but as soldiers; not as members of their country, but as its defenders. Finally, each State can have for enemies only other States, and not men; for between things disparate in nature there can be no real relation.[19]

While developed with regard to wars between sovereign authorities, these ancient principles of the laws of war suggest a number of basic characteristics that any party to a war must have.[20] First, Rousseau's idea of war as a relation between states and not between individuals suggests that any war requires at least two entities to fight each other—and these entities must signify more than a loosely connected group of individuals. In fact, the fighting must not be attributed to individuals but to organized and identifiable entities.[21] Second, principles such as honour and chivalry implied that both warring parties must be able and willing to respect the laws of

[14] ibid.

[15] In the sixteenth century, the Spanish lawyer Ayala similarly argued that 'a prince has a most just cause of war when he is directing his arms against rebels and subjects who abjure his sovereignty for it is a heinous offense, against both God and the prince, for subjects to resist his authority, all power being from God alone'. Ayala therefore emphasized: 'Now rebels ought not to be classed as enemies, the two being quite distinct, and so it is more correct to term the armed contention with rebel subjects execution of legal process, or prosecution, and not war.' Ayala, *De jure et officiis bellicis* (n 3) 11.

[16] Greenwood, 'Historical Development and Legal Basis' (n 7) 18.

[17] It has been argued that the laws of chivalry did not consider the protection of civilians but rather were aimed at protecting the privileged classes of knights and nobles. See Jochnick and Normand, 'The Legitimation of Violence: A Critical History of the Laws of War' (1994) 35 Harvard International Law Journal 61; Greenwood, 'Historical Development and Legal Basis' (n 7) 17.

[18] Greenwood, 'Historical Development and Legal Basis' (n 7) 18.

[19] Rousseau, *Du contrat social* (Dover Publications 1762) 6. For further discussion, see Greenwood, 'Historical Development and Legal Basis' (n 7) 20.

[20] While some conceptual conclusions can be drawn from Rousseau, it has also been argued that 'their relevance to our modern warfare is open to doubt'. Draper, 'The Development of International Humanitarian Law' in UNESCO and Institut Henry-Dunant (eds), *International Dimensions of Humanitarian Law* (Henry Dunant Institute, UNESCO, M Nijhoff 1988) 67–90, 28; see also Oppenheim, *International Law* (n 2) 64.

[21] Howard argues, eg, that the written and unwritten laws of war in the eighteenth and nineteenth centuries were based on the assumption that war was fought between professional armed forces. See Howard, *The Laws of War: Constraints on Warfare in the Western World* (Yale University Press 1994) 9.

war. The se principles marked the idea of equal rights and obligations of conflicting parties. Considering the impact of these fundamental humanitarian principles on modern humanitarian law, Draper pointed out: 'The humanitarian ideal has inherited those ideas, transformed them and expanded them with a new content'.[22] As shall be seen later in this chapter, these principles left their mark on the criteria that non-state entities have to fulfil to be considered party to an armed conflict.

1.2 The Emerging Idea of Non-State Warring Parties

With the emergence of the Westphalian order, the nature of war shifted from that of armed confrontation between princes to war between sovereign states.[23] The sovereignty-based international system recognized primarily states as subjects of international law, and in principle international law only applied to relations between states but not to states' internal affairs.[24] Non-state entities were not considered subjects of international law.[25] The laws of war would not apply to them. As the eminent Italian jurist Gentilli emphasized even before the conclusion of the 1648 Peace of Westphalia, warring parties that are not sovereign states

> are not properly enemies, even although they conduct themselves as soldiers and commanders and meet the attack of commanders of opposing legions. He is an enemy who has a state, a senate, a treasury, united and harmonious citizens, and some basis for a treaty of peace.[26]

However, this view started to change in the seventeenth and eighteenth centuries. The following paragraphs present the rather progressive views of leading philosophers and lawyers at the time, namely Grotius and de Vattel.

Compared with Gentilli, the Dutch lawyer Grotius advanced an arguably more open view in 1625 to applying the laws of war to non-state groups. For Grotius, the law of nations knew two kinds of public wars: formal and informal ones. While the former was fought between two sovereign entities and according to certain formalities, an informal public war 'may be made without those formalities, even against private persons, and by any magistrate whatever'.[27] Grotius recognized that, at the time, it was disputed whether such less formal wars could be called public wars. For him, however, it seems that if such wars were conducted with the authority of a

[22] Draper, 'The Development of International Humanitarian Law' (n 20) 70.

[23] See Green, *The Contemporary Law of Armed Conflict* (n 7) 26–27.

[24] For further discussion, see Higgins, 'International Law and Civil War' in Luard (ed), *The International Regulation of Civil Wars* (Thames and Hudson 1972) 169–86, 169; Goel, 'An Introduction to Origin, Evolution and Development of International Humanitarian Law' in Doswald-Beck (ed), *International Humanitarian Law: An Anthology* (Lexis Nexis 2009) 1–22, 15; Perna, *The Formation of the Treaty Law* (n 11) 13–14.

[25] See Oppenheim, *International Law* (n 2) 62; see also Wehberg, *La Guerre Civile et le Droit International* (M Nijhoff 1938) 40; Garraway, 'War and Peace: Where is the Divide?' (2012) 88 International Law Studies Series. US Naval War College 94.

[26] Gentilli, *De jure belli libri tres* (Clarendon Press; H Milford 1589) 24–25.

[27] Grotius, 'The Rights of War and Peace' (n 4) 57. Grotius also referred to a war between a State and a non-state entity as a mixed war: 'A mixed war is that which is carried on, on one side by public authority, and on the other by private persons'. Ibid, at 55.

magistrate 'there is no doubt but that such suppressions of tumult are public wars'.[28] Grotius considered rebellions no longer exclusively an internal matter of a state but covered by the law of nations—although the consequences of this finding remained vague.[29] Grotius did not specify whether non-state parties had to fulfil certain criteria to become party to a public war.

In 1758, one of the founding fathers of modern international law, the Swiss de Vattel, was more explicit on this point. In *The Law of Nations*, de Vattel discussed whether 'rebels', 'popular commotion, insurrection, sedition' or 'civil war' fell under the law of nations.[30] For de Vattel, 'rebels' were 'all subjects who unjustly take up arms against the ruler of the society'.[31] 'Popular commotion, insurrection, [and] sedition' were distinguished according to the intensity and widespread nature of the uprising, with insurrection signifying a situation where a public uprising 'infects the majority of the inhabitants of a city or province, and gains such strength that even the sovereign himself is no longer obeyed'.[32] De Vattel considered all of these situations 'state crimes' and although he demanded 'clemency ... [as] a duty in the sovereign' when suppressing such situations, he did not consider the laws of war applicable.[33] This, however, would change in situations of 'civil war', when the party opposing the state 'acquired sufficient strength to give him [the sovereign] effectual opposition, and to oblige him to carry on the war against them according to the established rules'.[34] In these situations, it was 'very evident' for de Vattel that both parties would have to observe the common laws of war.[35] De Vattel argued that this must be the case because

> [a] civil war breaks the bands of society and government, or, at least, suspends their force and effect: it produces in the nation two independent parties, who consider each other as enemies, and acknowledge no common judge. Those two parties, therefore, must necessarily be considered as thenceforward constituting, at least for a time, two separate bodies, two distinct societies. ... On earth they have no common superior. They stand therefore in precisely the same predicament as two nations, who engage in a contest and, being unable to come to an agreement, have recourse to arms.[36]

There are some analogies between De Vattel's considerations and a modern classification of internal violence. For de Vattel, violence by individuals (rebels), 'people who assemble in a tumultuous manner' (popular commotion), commotion that includes acts of violence (sedition), or even more widespread but rather unorganized violence (insurrection) fell below the threshold of a 'civil war'. In order to constitute civil war and be regulated by the laws of war, De Vattel's writings suggest two possible thresholds. First, rather factually, the opposition had to gain sufficient strength

[28] ibid.

[29] Some argue that, for Grotius, natural law applied in internal armed conflicts and thereby influenced the emerging international law applicable to such wars. Johnson, *Ideology, Reason, and the Limitation of War: Religious and Secular Concepts, 1200–1740*, (Princeton University Press 1975) 213; Perna, *The Formation of the Treaty Law* (n 11) 18.

[30] de Vattel, *The Law of Nations* (n 5) paras 289 and 292.

[31] ibid para 288. [32] ibid para 289. [33] ibid para 290. [34] ibid para 292.

[35] ibid para 294. [36] ibid para 293.

to give 'effectual opposition' to the sovereign, which, in turn, required the sovereign to 'carry on the war against them'. Here, the focus is on the military strength of the non-state party and the response by the sovereign. Second, de Vattel's more detailed justification of why the laws of war applied to civil wars suggests that both warring parties must be state-like, namely 'two separate bodies, two distinct societies' having no common superior. Following the second approach, Bartels found that 'the situation described above is similar to those that led about a hundred years later to recognition of the non-state party to conflict as a belligerent'.[37] The criteria for recognizing non-state parties as belligerents are considered next.

1.3 A State-Like Non-State Entity? Recognition of Belligerency

In line with these philosophical considerations, state practice started to change in the nineteenth century and the concept of 'recognition of belligerency' emerged.[38] As Oppenheim explained: 'Through this recognition a body of individuals receives an international position in so far as it is for some parts and in some points treated as though it were a subject of International Law.'[39] Recognition of belligerency could have two effects depending on which state recognized belligerency: when the territorial state recognized the non-state party as a belligerent against which it is engaged in war, the laws of war became applicable between the warring parties.[40] In contrast, when third parties recognized belligerency between a state and a non-state party, the laws of neutrality became pertinent in the relationship between the recognizing state and the parties to the conflict. It did not affect the relationship between the warring parties.[41] State practice shows that no obligation existed for any state to recognize belligerency, irrespective of the intensity of the conflict, the nature of the insurgent party, or the recognition of belligerents by other states.[42] However, if a third state

[37] Bartels, 'Timelines, Borderlines and Conflicts' (n 8) 47.

[38] eg in some cases the US Supreme Court directly cited de Vattel. See The Brig Amy Warwick; The Schooner Crenshaw; The Barque Hiawatha; The Schooner Brilliante (The United States Supreme Court, 1862), in Scott, *Prize Cases Decided in the United State Supreme Court* (Clarendon Press 1923) 1436.

[39] Oppenheim, *International Law* (n 2) 69.

[40] See Pilloud, Sandoz, Swinarski et al, *Commentary on the Additional Protocols of 8 June 1977 to the Geneva Conventions of 12 August 1949* (ICRC; M Nijhoff 1987) para 4345; Sivakumaran, *The Law of Non-International Armed Conflict* (OUP 2012) 16.

[41] As a British Law Officer wrote in 1895, 'the duties imposed upon belligerents by international law are in no sense dependent upon, and have no relation to the action of, neutral Powers which is dictated by their own policy and interests'. Report of the British Law Officers Reid and Lockwood on the fighting between France and the Hovas in Madagascar, see McNair, *International Law Opinions* (CUP 1956) 371; Wehberg, *La guerre civile* (n 25) 83 and 97–98. See also Dinstein, *Non-International Armed Conflicts in International Law* (n 1) 108–11.

[42] For arguments against an obligation on third states to recognize belligerency, see Wehberg, *La guerre civile* (n 25); Lauterpacht, *Recognition in International Law* (CUP 2012) 175–201. See also Falk, 'Janus Tormented: The International Law of Internal War' in Rosenau (ed), *International Aspects of Civil Strife* (Princeton University Press 1964) 185–248, 204–06; Abi-Saab, 'Non-International Armed Conflicts' in UNESCO and Institut Henry-Dunant (eds), *International Dimensions of Humanitarian Law* (M Nijhoff 1988) 217–39, 218; Cullen, *The Concept of Non-International Armed Conflict in International Humanitarian Law* (CUP 2010) 20–21; Sivakumaran, *The Law of Non-International Armed Conflict* (n 40) 16.

recognized a rebelling party prematurely as belligerent, this was considered to be an unlawful intervention in the internal affairs of the state where the rebellion took place.[43] Therefore, certain conditions for the recognition of belligerency by third states developed. These conditions are analysed in the following. In addition, the concepts of insurgency and rebellion in the nineteenth and early twentieth centuries are briefly considered.

1.3.1 Recognition of belligerency in state practice

It is reported that the concept of recognition of belligerency emerged during the South American colonies' and Greek wars of independence in the 1820s.[44] At the time, the legal concepts of insurgency and belligerency 'were almost a *terra incognita*'.[45] For example, in 1825 the British Secretary of State stated broadly that belligerency should be recognized in situations where 'a certain degree of force and resistance [were] attained by a population engaged in a war'.[46] More refined conditions for the recognition of belligerency developed in the context of the American Civil War from 1861–65. In a Prize Court case in 1862, the US Supreme Court inquired generally what situations the laws of war defines as civil war.[47] The Court found that it is not necessary 'that both parties should be acknowledged as independent nations or sovereign States'.[48] Instead, civil wars always begin as insurrections, and the factual circumstances, namely 'the number, power, and organization of the persons who originate and carry it on', may develop an insurrection into a civil war.[49] The Court explained:

> When the party in rebellion occupy and hold in a hostile manner a certain portion of territory; have declared their independence; have cast off their allegiance; have organized armies; have commenced hostilities against their former sovereign, the world acknowledges them as belligerents, and the contest a *war*.[50]

In different cases, the US Supreme Court emphasized three conditions following which the territorial would usually cognize belligerency. These were control over territory, declared and factual independence from the parent state, and hostilities between organized armies. The Court relied on factual conditions that signified war, including the nature and strength of the armed forces involved. It did not require the existence of a state-like political authority on the side of the non-state party.[51]

[43] See Pilloud, Sandoz, Swinarski et al, *Commentary on the Additional Protocols* (n 40) para 4346; Wehberg, *La guerre civile* (n 25) 17–18; Lauterpacht, *Recognition in International Law* (n 42) 176.

[44] See Wehberg, *La Guerre Civile* (n 25) 38.

[45] McNair, *International Law Opinions* (n 41) 327.

[46] Cited in Wehberg, *La guerre civile* (n 25) 20 (original in French, translation by the author).

[47] Prize Courts were courts authorized to decide whether ships were lawfully seized in times of war.

[48] The Brig Amy Warwick; The Schooner Crenshaw; The Barque Hiawatha; The Schooner Brilliante (the US Court, 1862), in Scott, *Prize Cases* (n 38).

[49] ibid. [50] ibid (emphasis in original).

[51] Similarly, in 1877 the US Supreme Court found: 'When a rebellion becomes organized, and attains such proportions as to be able to put a formidable military force in the field, it is usual for the established government to concede to it some belligerent rights' *Williams v Bruffy, 1877, 96 U.S. 176*, US Supreme Court, 179.

In contrast, the US government required additional criteria. Faced with domestic pressure to recognize belligerency in Cuba and to declare neutrality in 1870,[52] US President Grant stated:

The relations between the parent state and the insurgents must amount, in fact, to war in the sense of international law. Fighting, though fierce and protracted, does not alone constitute war; there must be military forces acting in accordance with the rules and customs of war—flags of truce, cartels, exchange of prisoners.

Contrary to the Supreme Court, President Grant required compliance with the laws of war. In addition, he explained:

[T]o justify a recognition of belligerency there must be, above all, a de facto political organization of the insurgents sufficient in character and resources to constitute, if left to itself, a state among nations capable of discharging the duties of a state, and of meeting the just responsibilities it may incur as such toward other powers in the discharge of its national duties.[53]

For the US president, belligerents had to be de facto states.[54]

This view was not undisputed among states. While several South American states recognized the Cuban insurgents as belligerents, despite the fact that the insurgents did not possess an independent government,[55] the Spanish government—for obvious reasons—agreed with the US position. Regarding the second Cuban revolt, in 1897, the Spanish minister of state wrote in a letter to the US government:

The insurgents, as has already been said on another occasion by his Majesty's government, have always been and still are without any real civil government, fixed territory, courts of their own, a regular army, coasts, ports, navy, everything that the principal American writers on international law and statesmen require as preliminary to the discussion of a recognition of belligerency.[56]

This view was also shared by other European states. In the aftermath of the American Civil War—and before the revolts in Cuba—British Law Officers found that the following indicators would signify a state of belligerency:

[T]he length of time during which the contest has existed; the number, order, and discipline of the rebel forces; their subordination to a de facto existing Government, capable of maintaining international relations with foreign States; the acts of the Government against which the rebels are in arms, both with respect to the rebels themselves and to foreign States.[57]

[52] For a good summary of the historic facts of the first revolt in Cuba and debate on the recognition of belligerency, see Wehberg, *La Guerre Civile* (n 25) 31–34.

[53] Text cited in Moore and Wharton, *A Digest of International Law: As Embodied in Diplomatic Discussions, Treaties and Other International Agreements, International Awards, the Decisions of Municipal Courts, and the Writings of Jurists*, Vol I (US Government Printing Office 1906) 194–95.

[54] This requirement is also found in the writing of American commentators. See, eg, Woolsey, 'The Consequences of the Cuban Belligerency' (1896) 5 Yale Law Journal 182–86; Beale, 'The Recognition of Cuban Belligerency' (1896) 9 Havard Law Journal 406–19.

[55] See Wehberg, *La Guerre Civile* (n 25) 33.

[56] Text cited in Moore and Wharton, *A Digest of International Law* (n 53) Vol VI, 152.

[57] Text cited in McNair, *International Law Opinions* (n 41) 143–44.

France was also in favour of a relatively high threshold for recognizing belligerency, requiring belligerents to have both a de facto government and organized armed forces under the command of an authority.[58]

1.3.2 Criteria for the recognition of belligerency

While these excerpts show some commonalities suggesting that certain criteria crystallized in state practice, recognition of belligerency was a political act, necessarily guided by the interests of the recognizing state.[59] Recognition of belligerency was rarely explicit or explained on legal grounds.[60] Nonetheless, eminent jurists assembled in the Institut de Droit International in 1900 adopted a resolution summarizing what they considered the necessary conditions for recognition of belligerency by third states:[61]

- First, insurgents were required to possess 'a given part of the national territory';
- Second, they had to fulfil 'the conditions which must be met to constitute a regular government de facto exercising in that part of the territory the ostensible rights belonging to sovereignty'; and
- Third, their struggle had to be 'conducted by organized forces subject to military discipline and complying with the laws and customs of war'.[62]

Almost fifty years later, Lauterpacht presented another list of cumulative requirements necessary for recognizing belligerency:

> [F]irst, there must exist within the State an armed conflict of a general (as distinguished from a purely local) character; secondly, the insurgents must occupy and administer a substantial portion of national territory; thirdly, they must conduct the hostilities in accordance with the rules of war and through organized armed forces acting under a responsible authority;

[58] Text cited in Zorgbibe, 'Sources of the Recognition of Belligerent Status' (1977) 17 International Review of the Red Cross (1961–1997) 111–27, 121.

[59] As the US Supreme Court argued: '[I]t belongs to the political department to determine when belligerency shall be recognized, and its action must be accepted according to the terms and intention expressed', *The Three Friends, 1897, 166 US 1,* US Supreme Court, 63. See also Sivakumaran, *The Law of Non-International Armed Conflict* (n 40) 13–14; Cullen, *The Concept of Non-International Armed Conflict* (n 42) 17. Nonetheless, as Lauterpacht pointed out: '[R]ecognition is not in the nature of a grant of a favour or a matter of unfettered political discretion, but a duty imposed by the facts of the situation'. Lauterpacht, *Recognition in International Law* (n 42) 175. However, even where a factual assessment was required, it was the interpretation of the facts that would be political.

[60] See Lauterpacht, *Recognition in International Law* (n 42) 176–82; Beale, 'Cuban Belligerency' (n 54) 413.

[61] Contrary to article 8 on the recognition of belligerency by third states, article 4 on recognition by the territorial state does not list any conditions. Indeed, as Moir points out, recognition by the parent state 'was commonly believed to be entirely at the discretion of the government'. Moir, *The Law of Internal Armed Conflict* (CUP) 10.

[62] Institute de Droit International, *Droits et devoirs des Puissances étrangères, au cas de mouvement insurrectionnel, envers les gouvernements établis et reconnus qui sont aux prises avec l'insurrection* (1900) article 8. Translation found in Pilloud, Sandoz, Swinarski et al, *Commentary on the Additional Protocols* (n 40) para 4347.

fourthly, there must exist circumstances which make it necessary for outside States to define their attitude by means of recognition of belligerency.[63]

These conditions reflect state practice, and were also cited by other scholars.[64] At least four criteria can be identified: the intensity of violence; the necessity to recognize belligerency; the existence of a de facto government administrating parts of the territory; and the organized nature of the non-state armed forces. While the first two criteria required a situation that amounted 'in fact to a *war*'[65] and to have an impact on the interests of the recognizing state, the latter two criteria concern the requisite characteristics and abilities of the non-state belligerent. For the purpose of this book, only the latter two criteria require further examination.[66]

The non-state entity needed to be politically and militarily organized. Politically, the insurgent party had to dispose of a 'government de facto exercising ... the ostensible rights belonging to sovereignty'[67] in part of the parent state's territory; in other words, it 'must occupy and administer a substantial portion of national territory'.[68] Expecting insurgents to de facto govern a certain territory and its population brought the non-state party close to having the characteristics of a state.[69] As the American law professor Beale put it in 1895: recognition of belligerency required 'on the part of insurgents an organization purporting to have the characteristics of a state, though not yet recognized as such'.[70] Three points may explain this high

[63] Lauterpacht, *Recognition in International Law* (n 42) 176.

[64] See, eg, Wheaton, *Elements of International Law* (Clarendon Press 1936) 23; McNair, 'Law Relating to Civil War in Spain' (1937) 53 The Law Quarterly Review 471–99, 466–67. The main difference between the two sets of criteria is that Lauterpacht requires that third states may only recognize belligerency when it is necessary for them to define their attitude towards the insurgents. For the purpose of this chapter, there is no need to further elaborate on this requirement. Suffice to note that this requirement was controversial. See Wehberg, *La Guerre Civile* (n 25) 88–92; Sivakumaran, *The Law of Non-International Armed Conflict* (n 40) 13.

[65] Wheaton, *Elements of International Law* (n 64) 30, fn 15.

[66] For discussion of the first two requirements, see McNair, 'Law Relating to Civil War in Spain' (n 64) 476; Sivakumaran, *The Law of Non-International Armed Conflict* (n 40) 12–13; Woolsey, 'The Consequences of the Cuban Belligerency' (n 54) 182. Cullen went as far as concluding that the 'threshold that allowed for an act of recognition by a neutral state was fundamentally determined by [these] two factors'. Cullen, *The Concept of Non-International Armed Conflict* (n 42) 17.

[67] Institute de Droit International, 'Puissances étrangères' (n 62) article 8.

[68] Lauterpacht, *Recognition in International Law* (n 42) 176. For discussion of the minority view holding that non-state belligerents did not need to establish a quasi-government, see Sivakumaran, *The Law of Non-International Armed Conflict* (n 40) 12.

[69] Article 1 of the Montevideo Convention on the Rights and Duties of States proclaims the following: 'The state as a person of international law should possess the following qualifications: (a) a permanent population; (b) a defined territory; (c) government; and (d) capacity to enter into relations with the other states.' While belligerents may not have controlled a population 'permanently' and their territory was not 'defined', if insurgents met the threshold of belligerency they were also close to meeting the four listed criteria for statehood. Nonetheless, recognizing belligerency was different from recognizing statehood, or the legitimacy of a government. See Garner, 'Recognition of Belligerency' (1938) 32 American Journal of International Law 106–13, 111–12; Moir, *The Law of Internal Armed Conflict* (n 61) 5–6.

[70] Beale, 'Cuban Belligerency' (n 54) 407. eg in 1897, the then US President McKinley stated that: 'It is to be seriously considered whether the Cuban insurrection possesses beyond dispute the attributes of statehood, which alone can demand the recognition of belligerency in its favour.' Text cited in Moore and Wharton, *A Digest of International Law* (n 53) Vol I, 198.

threshold. To begin with, recognition of belligerency rendered certain parts of the laws of war applicable, meaning that the conflict would be considered 'as essentially identical to a war between sovereign states'.[71] For the purposes of the laws of war, the non-state belligerent would be treated on a par with the state, which was also deemed 'to be upgrading the legal status of rebels'.[72] In addition, recognizing belligerency brought about a situation in which parts of the laws of nations would govern a formerly internal affair of a state. Such an interference, which de facto recognized that the state was no longer 'maître chez lui'[73] was politically 'very delicate'.[74] States would not take this step lightly. And lastly, it can be assumed that it was only when non-state belligerents governed certain territory that their actions were likely to affect the interests of a third state—for example, by harming or protecting its nationals or property.[75]

Contrary to being politically organized, being militarily organized invoked a requirement inherent in the concept of war. Insurgent armed forces were required to be organized under a responsible authority imposing military discipline, and they needed to conduct hostilities in accordance with the laws of war.[76] First of all, these capacities were necessary to engage in war that would be governed by the laws of nations. Fundamental principles of the laws of war, such as equality of belligerents or distinction, are based on the assumption that two organized entities—as distinct from groups of individuals—confront each other.[77] Moreover, implementing the detailed rules and customs of war, such as those codified in the Hague Regulations of 1907 on the treatment of prisoners of war, required the existence of organized armed forces. In this respect, it can be assumed that the requisite level of military organization required from non-state belligerents resembled the level of organization required under article 1 of the Hague Regulations.[78] This article defined under which conditions the 'laws, rights and duties of war' applied to militias and volunteer corps engaged in wars between states. Thus, entities fulfilling these requirements

[71] Falk, 'Janus Tormented' (n 42) 203.

[72] Sivakumaran, *The Law of Non-International Armed Conflict* (n 40) 9.

[73] Wehberg, *La guerre civile* (n 25) 86.

[74] Opinion of British Law Officers when considering the question whether insurgent vessels shall be treated as pirates or be granted certain belligerent rights. See McNair, *International Law Opinions* (n 41) 333.

[75] See Kalpouzos, *The Applicability of International Law to Armed Conflicts involving Non-State Armed Groups: Between Status and Humanitarian Protection* (unpublished PhD thesis 2011) 56–57.

[76] According to Wheaton, respecting the laws of war at the time meant, inter alia, 'the use of flags of truce, cartels, exchange of prisoners, and the treatment of captured insurgents by the parent State as prisoners of war'. Wheaton, *Elements of International Law* (n 64) 30, fn. 15. On the discussion whether this meant that insurgents actually complied with the laws of war or simply had the ability to comply, see Sivakumaran, *The Law of Non-International Armed Conflict* (n 40) 12.

[77] See Section 1.1 'The Origins of the Statist Focus of the Laws of War'.

[78] Article 1 of the 1907 Regulations Respecting the Laws and Customs of War at Land annexed to the Hague Convention IV states: 'The laws, rights, and duties of war apply not only to armies, but also to militia and volunteer corps fulfilling the following conditions:

1. To be commanded by a person responsible for his subordinates;
2. To have a fixed distinctive emblem recognizable at a distance;
3. To carry arms openly; and
4. To conduct their operations in accordance with the laws and customs of war.'

were deemed sufficiently organized to participate in war as defined and regulated by international law at the time.

1.4 Violence below the Threshold of Belligerency: Rebellion and Insurgency

Two additional concepts from that period need brief consideration: insurgency and rebellion. As one commentator pointed out, international law provided three stages 'for designating the degree of formal *acknowledgment* by third states of the claims made on behalf of the anti-government faction': a first stage in which internal war remained 'fully domesticated ("rebellion")', a second stage where it was 'partially internationalized *on an ad-hoc* basis ("insurgency")', and a third one where the conflict became 'fully internationalized on an *a priori* basis ("belligerency")'.[79] [emphasis in the original] While the laws of war regulated belligerency, they did not regulate 'rebellions' and 'insurgencies'.

1.4.1 Rebels

Traditionally, internal violence not amounting to belligerency was termed 'rebellion'. In accordance with the writings of Gentilli and de Vattel as discussed above, Kotzsch pointed out that 'domestic violence is called rebellion or upheaval so long as there is sufficient evidence that the police force of the parent state will reduce the seditious party to respect the municipal legal order'.[80] Examples of rebellions covered a variety of events, including small but violent protests like the 'Indian language riots' of the 1930s, as well as more general uprisings that were suppressed relatively quickly, such as upheavals in Eastern Europe in 1953 and 1956.[81] While rebels may have shown different degrees of organization, under international law the rebellious bodies were considered 'law-breakers pure and simple' unless states recognized them as either insurgents or belligerents.[82]

1.4.2 Insurgents

In the classification sequence of 'rebellion—insurgency—belligerency', insurgency referred to situations that were more sustained than rebellions but did not amount

[79] Falk, 'Janus Tormented' (n 42) 194; see also Wehberg, *La guerre civile* (n 25) 88; Moir, *The Law of Internal Armed Conflict* (n 61) 4.

[80] Kotzsch, *The Concept of War in Contemporary History and International Law* (Genève: E. Droz 1956) 230. This did not change in the nineteenth and early twentieth centuries, Falk, 'Janus Tormented' (n 42) 198; Wehberg, *La Guerre Civile* (n 25) 42.

[81] For some examples, see Falk, 'Janus Tormented' (n 42) 199. See also McNair, *International Law Opinions* (n 41) 370.

[82] Lauterpacht, *Recognition in International Law* (n 42) 278.

to belligerency.[83] Insurgency constituted a stage when insurgents did not yet fulfil the requirements for the recognition of belligerency but third states felt a need to define their relation to the insurgent party.[84] States did not recognize insurgency in order to bring into force certain pre-defined rights and obligations.[85] All legal consequences of the status of insurgency derived from what was explicitly agreed upon between the recognizing state and the insurgents, meaning that states had significant discretion in deciding what rights to grant to insurgents.[86] Hardly any attempts exist to present clear criteria on requisite degree of organization of insurgent groups. In Lauterpacht's view, 'any attempt to lay down the conditions of recognition of insurgency lends itself to misunderstanding'.[87] Indeed, the two most prominent conflicts during which states recognized insurgency—the second revolt in Cuba between 1895 and 1898 and the Spanish Civil War from 1936–38—are so different that they do not represent good examples for drawing common criteria for the recognition of insurgency.[88] Hence, the defining criterion for when states would recognize insurgency seemed to be the necessity for them to define their relation to the insurgent party—for example, because the insurgents' conduct affected the state's interests.[89] While recognition of insurgency by a third state did not have an effect on the actual fighting, treating rebels as insurgents acknowledged them 'as contestants-at-law, and not as mere law-breakers'.[90]

1.5 An Overly Demanding and Rarely Used Threshold

Under the laws and customs of war applicable before 1949, only the concept of 'recognition of belligerency' provided criteria under which a non-state armed group could become party to a war. To be recognized as belligerents, non-state entities

[83] In the words of Wehberg: 'Un stade intermédiaire apparaît ici, dans lequel les insurgés sont déjà quelque chose de plus que des rebelles, mais n'ont pas encore obtenu les droits de belligérance' (Wehberg, *La Guerre Civile* (n 25) 42).

[84] This was particularly the case when an insurgency had effects on the naval interests of third states. See McNair, 'Law Relating to Civil War in Spain' (n 64) 489; Falk, 'Janus Tormented' (n 42) 199.

[85] See Lauterpacht, *Recognition in International Law* (n 42) 270; Sivakumaran, *The Law of Non-International Armed Conflict* (n 40) 14; Cullen, *The Concept of Non-International Armed Conflict* (n 42) 12–13.

[86] See Lauterpacht, *Recognition in International Law* (n 42) 276.

[87] ibid 276–77. Similarly for Falk, insurgency was a 'catch-all designation' that was at the discretion of states. Falk, 'Janus Tormented' (n 42) 199.

[88] For a comprehensive discussion, see Lauterpacht, *Recognition in International Law* (n 42) 271–74; and Wehberg, *La guerre civile* (n 25) 52–53. Another interesting example of recognition of certain rights without recognizing belligerency was Great Britain's decision not to treat Greek insurgent vessels in 1822 as pirate vessels but to grant them limited rights of belligerency. See ibid 19–20.

[89] Wilson found that: 'There are no requirements for the degree of intensity of violence, the extent of control over territory, the establishment of a quasi-governmental authority, or the conduct of operations in accordance with any humanitarian principles which would indicate recognition of insurgency is appropriate. Indeed, the only criterion for recognition, if one could call it that, is necessity.' Wilson, *International Law and the Use of Force by National Liberation Movements* (Clarendon Press 1988) 24. For practical examples of how states did so in practice, see Fortin, *The Accountability of Armed Groups under Human Rights Law* (OUP 2017) 104–07.

[90] See Higgins, 'International Law and Civil War' (n 24) 170.

were required to have a degree of political and military organization akin to that of states. While the requisite degree of military organization seemed justified by the detailed rules that were rendered applicable, the requirement of disposing of a state-like administration was primarily political and not inherent in the laws of war. In addition to a variety of political and diplomatic considerations, this high threshold for organization was one of the main reasons why states rarely recognized belligerency in practice. As Lauterpacht pointed out, in many cases 'the rebels, although powerful and persistent, may not possess sufficient cohesion to establish governmental agencies of some stability'.[91] While it is probably true that, today, the doctrine of recognition of belligerency 'has declined to the point where recognition of belligerency is almost unknown',[92] it persists, at least, in theory.[93] Nonetheless, commentators have pointed out that when the Spanish Civil War remained—despite its magnitude—unregulated by international law, 'the antiquated and inadequate character of recognition of belligerency became manifest'[94] and demanded the development of fundamental humanitarian rules that would regulate internal armed conflicts based on factual criteria and independent from the often politically motivated recognition of belligerency by states.[95] These new humanitarian rules are found in article 3 common to the four Geneva Conventions (Common Article 3), which is considered next.

[91] Lauterpacht, *Recognition in International Law* (n 42) 183.

[92] United Kingdom Ministry of Defence, *The Joint Service Manual of the Law of Armed Conflict* (MoD 2004) 284. In fact, Sivakumaran found that no formal recognition of belligerency occurred in the twentieth century. Sivakumaran, *The Law of Non-International Armed Conflict* (n 40) 19.

[93] See Dinstein, *Non-International Armed Conflicts in International Law* (n 1) para 338; Akande, 'Classification of Armed Conflicts: Relevant Legal Concepts' in Wilmshurst (ed), *International Law and the Classification of Conflicts* (OUP 2012) 32–80, 50.

[94] Cassese, 'The Spanish Civil War and Customary Law Concerning Internal Armed Conflicts' in Cassese (ed), *Current Problems of International Law* (MVLTA PAVCIS 1975) 287–318, 317.

[95] See also Falk, 'Janus Tormented' (n 42) 191; Cullen, *The Concept of Non-International Armed Conflict* (n 42) 22.

2

Parties to Non-International Armed Conflicts under International Treaty Law

Since 1949, states have adopted three main instruments in which they defined non-international armed conflicts: the four Geneva Conventions, Protocol Additional to the Geneva Conventions of 12 August 1949, and relating to the Protection of Victims of Non-International Armed Conflicts (Protocol II), and the Rome Statute of the International Criminal Court. This chapter examines the requisite degree of organization required for non-state armed groups to become party to an armed conflict, as defined in the different instruments.

2.1 The Notion 'Party to the Conflict' under Common Article 3

In the late nineteenth and the early twentieth centuries, states codified important principles of the laws of war in international treaties. Before the adoption of the Geneva Conventions of 1949, however, none of these treaties formally applied to civil wars.[1] For example, as a treaty among states, the first Geneva Convention of 1864 only applied inter partes; it did not mention civil wars. The view of the then International Committee of the Red Cross (ICRC) president, Gustav Moynier, that this convention was also applicable when states are confronted with 'rebels, barbarians, or those perjuring'[2] was not shared by states. A famous exception to this practice are the 1863 'Instructions for the Government of Armies of the United States in the Field', better known as the 'Lieber Code'. The American law professor Francis Lieber drafted this codification of the modern laws of war on behalf of the government of the United States, which was engaged in a civil war.[3]

[1] One exception was arguably the Martens Clause, contained in the preamble to the 1907 Hague Regulations. See Cullen, *The Concept of Non-International Armed Conflict in International Humanitarian Law* (CUP 2010) 25.

[2] Moynier, *La Croix-Rouge, son Passé et son Avenir* (Sandoz & Thuillier 1882) 219 (original in French, translation by the author).

[3] When Lieber submitted the first draft, he stated: 'I have earnestly endeavored to treat of these grave topics conscientiously and comprehensively; and you, well read in the literature of this branch of international law, know that nothing of this kind exists in any language. I had no guide, no groundwork, no text-book.' Quote found in Baxter, 'The First Modern Codification of the Law of War—Francis Lieber and General Orders No 1 00 - (II)' (1963) 3 International Review of the Red Cross 234–50, 184. For in-depth analyses of the Code and its development, see ibid; Meron, 'Francis Lieber's Code and Principles of Humanity' (1998) 36 Columbia Journal of Transnational Law 269–81, 269.

The Lieber Code was not, however, designed to apply to internal warfare. Rather, Lieber considered the American Civil War akin to a war between states and aimed to codify rules of inter-state warfare.[4] The US government decided to apply them to its civil war.[5] Despite this encouraging example, sufficient momentum to develop international rules applicable to internal warfare was only gained subsequent to the horrors of the Spanish Civil War, the Second World War, and with the emergence of a human rights movement.[6]

The International Red Cross Movement played a key role in this development.[7] In collaboration with national Red Cross Societies and government experts, the ICRC elaborated first drafts of the four Geneva Conventions. While all of the drafts contained an article referring to 'cases of armed conflict not of an international character',[8] none of them listed criteria defining these conflicts.[9] Neither did they refer to the concept of recognition of belligerency. During the ensuing negotiations at the Diplomatic Conference in Geneva in 1949, the meaning of the notion 'armed conflict not of an international character' was 'the burning question, which arose again and again',[10] and it reportedly caused 'the longest single debate of any provision at the Diplomatic Conference of 1949'.[11]

[4] Initially, Lieber did not mention civil war at all in the Code, arguably to avoid the impression that this code would only apply to internal and not to international warfare. In the end, only nine out of 157 rules of the Code were found under the section entitled 'Insurrection—Civil War—Rebellion'. See Meron, 'Francis Lieber's Code' (n 3) 277; Baxter, 'The First Modern Codification of the Law of War' (n 3) 184–85.

[5] Baxter, 'The First Modern Codification of the Law of War' (n 3) 184–85; see also Labuda, 'Lieber Code' in Wolfrum (ed), *The Max-Planck Encyclopedia of Public International Law* (OUP 2012).

[6] See Abi-Saab, 'Non-International Armed Conflicts' in UNESCO and Institut Henry-Dunant (eds), *International Dimensions of Humanitarian Law* (M Nijhoff 1988) 218.

[7] For a more detailed account of these preliminary developments leading to the Diplomatic Conference in Geneva in 1949, see Pictet, *Commentary: I Geneva Conventions of 12 August 1949* (ICRC 1952) 40–43. See also Elder, 'The Historical Background of Common Article 3 of the Geneva Conventions of 1949' (1979) 11 Case Western Reserve Journal of International Law 37–69; Sivakumaran, *The Law of Non-International Armed Conflict* (OUP 2012) 30–39; Moir, *The Law of Internal Armed Conflict* (CUP 2002) 21–23.

[8] See, eg, article 2(4) common to the draft conventions that the XVIIth International Red Cross Conference in Stockholm in 1948 submitted to the Diplomatic Conference in Geneva, reproduced in Federal Political Department (Switzerland), Final Record of the Diplomatic Conference of Geneva of 1949, Vol I (1949).

[9] The draft that the ICRC submitted to the International Red Cross Conference in Stockholm only provided examples of armed conflicts not of an international character, which included 'civil war, colonial conflicts, or wars of religion'. Preux, *Geneva Convention Relative to the Treatment of Prisoners of War: Commentary* (ICRC 1960) 31.

[10] Pictet, *Commentary GCI* (n 7) 49.

[11] Draper, 'Humanitarian Law and Internal Armed Conflicts' (1983) 13 Georgia Journal of International and Comparative Law 253–77, 263. For detailed accounts on the negotiations, see ICRC, *Convention (I) for the Amelioration of the Condition of the Wounded and Sick in Armed Forces in the Field: Commentary of 2016* (ICRC 2016) article 3, paras 7–30; Cullen, *The Concept of Non-International Armed Conflict* (n 1) 27–49; Sivakumaran, *The Law of Non-International Armed Conflict* (n 7) 156–62; Moir, *The Law of Internal Armed Conflict* (n 7) 23–29.

2.1.1 The (non)-definition of 'Party to the conflict' at the 1949 Diplomatic Conference

For states, negotiating the applicability of international law to internal war was sensitive. They feared that regulating the repression of rebellions 'would strike at the root of national sovereignty and endanger national security'[12] or that 'such protection might incite political opponents to take up arms against a legitimate government'.[13] Indeed, at the time, human rights law was still in its infancy, meaning that during non-international armed conflicts not amounting to belligerency, states would not be restrained by international obligations but could act following solely their internal laws and policies. States asserted that '[e]very government had a right to put down rebellion within its borders and to punish the insurgents in accordance with its penal laws'.[14] In this environment, the proposal of adopting regulations applicable in armed conflicts not of an international character felt threatening to many. Others, however, cautioned that '[i]n civil wars there might also be movements for emancipation of a morally creditable character' and that state sovereignty could not be placed above all humanitarian considerations.[15] As a result, diplomats debated a number of different drafts on regulating internal warfare.[16]

The final version of Common Article 3 has a broad scope: the provision applies 'in the case of armed conflict not of an international character occurring in the territory of one of the High Contracting Parties', and binds 'each Party to the conflict'. It contains no explicit definition of the term 'Party to the conflict'. The element defining the 'Party to the conflict' is the 'armed conflict not of an international character' in which that party engages. In other words, determining to what kind of conflict an 'armed conflict not of an international character' refers also determines what entities can be parties to it. Some hints on these questions are found in the drafting history.

2.1.1.1 Basic agreement on what does not constitute an armed conflict

States broadly agreed that not all forms of internal violence could fall under the term 'armed conflict not of an international character'. While some feared that this notion 'may include banditry, uprisings, disorders, rebellion and civil war',[17] a number of states expressed the view that situations of violence between individuals, crime, or riots were excluded from the article's scope.[18] They considered armed conflicts to be more than mere uprisings: 'civil war was a form of conflict resembling international

[12] Federal Political Department (Switzerland), Final Record of the Diplomatic Conference of Geneva of 1949, Vol II, Section B, (1949) 10 (United Kingdom).

[13] ibid 11 (Greece).

[14] ibid 12 (United States of America).

[15] ibid 13 (Mexico). For another good summary of the conflicting interests at stake, see Pictet, *Commentary GCI* (n 7) 43–44.

[16] The different drafts considered by the Special Committee and the Joint Committee tasked to draft a provision that applies to internal armed conflicts are found in Federal Political Department (Switzerland), Final Record, Vol II Section B (n 12) 124–27.

[17] ibid 329 (Burma). See also ibid 94 (Australia).

[18] See ibid 121, as well as 10–15 and 325–39.

war, but taking place inside the territory of a State. It was not a conflict between a number of individuals.'[19] States emphasized that the Geneva Conventions should not apply to 'anarchy, disorder or banditry',[20] or 'action of a State against wrong-doers'.[21] As a result, these situations were not considered armed conflicts; consequently, groups of individuals, rioters, or bandits could not be parties to armed conflicts.

2.1.1.2 Agreement on a threshold lower than 'recognition of belligerency'

Similar agreement did not exist on the question of which situations should fall under the provision. Some commentators concluded that 'there was broad agreement that the threshold required for the application of international humanitarian law [under Common Article 3] would be similar to that traditionally assumed for the recognition of belligerency'.[22] This conclusion is based on some statements made during the conference in which states referred to 'armed conflicts not of an international character' also as 'civil war', and the latter term was generally understood as conflicts that fulfilled the requirements for recognition as belligerency.[23] The argument may find additional support in the ICRC's 1958 commentary, which noted in general terms that armed conflicts not of an international character 'are in many respects similar to an international war, but take place within the confines of a single country'.[24] Following this argument, parties to such conflicts would need to dispose of a state-like degree of political and military organization.[25]

Indeed, during initial discussion on the so-called Stockholm draft, which foresaw the application of all norms of the respective Convention to internal armed conflicts,[26] states suggested a variety of criteria to define the application of the Conventions to armed conflicts not of an international character. Several states supported the criteria that opposition forces 'must be organized military forces belonging to a responsible authority capable of respecting, or enforcing respect for the Convention, in a given territory'.[27] Other states went a step further

[19] ibid 11 (Norway); see also ibid 121.

[20] ibid 11 (Romania); ibid 10 (France).

[21] ibid 11 (Denmark).

[22] Cullen, *The Concept of Non-International Armed Conflict* (n 1) 42; see also Bartels, 'Timelines, Borderlines and Conflicts' (2009) 91 International Review of the Red Cross 66. A better view has been suggested by Sivakumaran, showing that the Joint Committee, to which Cullen refers, used the term civil war as a means to distinguish 'the requisite degree of violence from riots and disturbances', and not to describe 'a situation equivalent to the recognition of belligerency'. Sivakumaran, *The Law of Non-International Armed Conflict* (n 7) 161.

[23] See Cullen, *The Concept of Non-International Armed Conflict* (n 1) 42; see also Bartels, 'Timelines, Borderlines and Conflicts' (n 22) 66.

[24] Pictet, *Geneva Convention IV Relative to the Protection of Civilian Persons in Time of War: Commentary* (ICRC 1958) 36.

[25] See Section 1.3.2 'Criteria for the recognition of belligerency'.

[26] The so-called Stockholm draft provided in article 2(4): 'In all cases of armed conflict not of an international character which may occur in the territory of one or more of the High Contracting Parties, *each of the adversaries shall be bound to implement the provisions of the present Convention.*' See Federal Political Department (Switzerland), Final Record, Vol I (n 8) (emphasis added).

[27] This proposal was advanced by France and received relatively broad support. See Federal Political Department (Switzerland), Final Record, Vol II Section B (n 12) 10–15. Spain, eg, suggested in support

and required either recognition of belligerency by the parent government, or the fulfilment of certain narrow conditions resembling those that were generally required for recognition of belligerency.[28] These conditions were included in the first draft of the Special Committee, which was tasked to find agreement on the provision. This draft required that either the de jure government recognized belligerency, or that the non-state party

> possesses an organized military force, that it is under the direction of an organized civil authority which exercises *de facto* governmental functions over the population of a determinate portion of the national territory, and that it has the means of enforcing the Convention, and of complying with the laws and customs of war.[29]

While such a 'reversion to the classical criteria of recognition of belligerency as the necessary precondition for the application of the full Geneva Convention to the parties engaged in an internal armed conflict ... failed to be adopted',[30] the often-overlooked paragraph 4 of that draft contained an idea that inspired the way forward. It suggested that 'in the case of armed conflicts which do not fulfil the conditions as determined above' the parties to the conflict shall in all circumstances 'act in accordance with the underlying humanitarian principles of the present Convention'.[31] Hence, it suggested a system under which all norms of the respective Convention would apply to a traditional civil war meeting the criteria for recognition of belligerency, while in armed conflicts that did not meet these strict criteria only undefined humanitarian principles would.[32] Both situations were referred to as 'armed conflicts not of an international character'.

The second draft that the Special Committee developed was based on this idea. Contrary to the first approach, which restricted the article's scope of application, the second one left the scope of conflicts undefined and instead limited the applicable provisions. The new approach did not require the non-state party to have state-like characteristics. It demanded broadly that '[i]n the case of armed conflict not of an international character' each party to the conflict shall be bound by a selection of fundamental humanitarian provisions.[33] The delegation of the Union of Soviet Socialist Republics took a related approach in its draft,[34] which the Soviet delegate named a 'Convention in miniature'.[35] Although none of the three different drafts

of the French proposal: 'The Conventions should only be applied in cases where the legal government was obliged to have recourse to the regular military forces against insurgents militarily organized and in possession of a part of the national territory.'

[28] Detailed proposals were presented by the United States of America and by Australia. ibid 12 and 15. The US proposal found explicit support from inter alia China and Canada.

[29] ibid 125, Annex A. [30] Draper, 'Internal Armed Conflicts' (n 11) 264.

[31] Federal Political Department (Switzerland), Final Record, Vol II Section B (n 12) 125, Annex A.

[32] Conflicts not meeting the strict conditions set out in the provision arguably resembled situations previously considered as 'insurgencies'.

[33] See Federal Political Department (Switzerland), Final Record, Vol II Section B (n 12) 125, Annex D and at 126, Annex E.

[34] ibid 127, Annex F. As with the second proposal discussed above, this proposal did not define the scope of armed conflicts not of an international character. Unlike the second proposal, it listed the rules governing non-international armed conflicts in more detail.

[35] ibid 35.

received immediate support from a majority of delegates in the Special Committee, the second approach was finally pursued and informed the new article 3 common to the Four Geneva Conventions as adopted by the Conference.[36]

As a result, the drafting history shows that states did not envisage the strict criteria for recognition of belligerency in order to determine the existence of an 'armed conflict not of an international character' under Common Article 3.[37] It would have been a humanitarian setback if states had agreed to apply only the limited provisions contained in the new article to situations of belligerency formerly regulated by the entire laws and customs of war.[38] This was not the drafters' intention.[39] In order to reach consensus, states discarded the idea of applying all norms of the respective Convention to narrowly defined civil wars. Consequently, the list of indicative criteria that Pictet included in the first ICRC commentary on the new Conventions—which were based on the different suggestions made during the Diplomatic Conference—may not be necessarily 'useful', even if understood as being 'in no way obligatory'.[40] In an internal discussion in the 1950s, the then ICRC president even called them 'obscurities'.[41] In fact, these criteria 'set a far higher threshold of application than is actually required by the Article itself'[42] and can be 'seriously misleading' when considering the lower intensity spectrum of armed conflicts.[43]

The downside of states' deliberate decision not to define parties to non-international armed conflicts (NIAC) and resort instead to 'creative ambiguity'[44] was that '[o]f only one thing one may be sure: There is no consensus as to the application of Article 3 to what are, in comparative terms, the lower levels of violence'.[45] With regard to the parties to these conflicts, Switzerland formulated vaguely that 'armed conflict, as understood in this provision, implies *some form of organization* among the Parties to the conflict'.[46] As will be seen in section 2.1.2 'Non-state

[36] See ibid 339.

[37] See also Elder, 'Historical Background of Common Article 3' (n 7) 53.

[38] Admittedly, an advantage of the new provision would have been that its applicability would no longer depend on recognition by the state party to the conflict but would apply automatically once the threshold was reached.

[39] Resolution 10 adopted at the Conference stated that 'the conditions under which a Party to a conflict can be recognized as a belligerent by Powers not taking part in this conflict, are governed by the general rules of international law on the subject and are in no way modified by the Geneva Conventions'. See Federal Political Department (Switzerland), Final Record, Vol I (n 8) 362 (Resolution 10).

[40] See Pictet, *Commentary GCI* (n 7) 49.

[41] ICRC Archives, A PV JUR.2, Commission Juridique, 20 March 1952, remark by M Boissier.

[42] Moir, *The Law of Internal Armed Conflict* (n 7) 35.

[43] Provost, *International Human Rights and Humanitarian Law* (CUP 2002) 266. The International Criminal Tribunal for the former Yugoslavia (ICTY) and the International Criminal Tribunal for Rwanda (ICTR) considered the criteria 'useful' but not as strict legal conditions. See, eg, *Akayesu, Judgment, 2 September 1998, ICTR-96-4-T*, ICTR, para 619; *Milošević, Decision on Motion for Judgment of Acquittal, 2004, IT-02-54-T*, ICTY, para 19; *Boškoski and Tarčulovski, Judgment, 10 July 2008, Trial Chamber, IT-04-82-T*, ICTY, para 176. See also ICRC, *GCI: Commentary of 2016* (n 11) article 3, paras 69–70; Moir, 'The Concept of Non-International Armed Conflict' in Clapham, Gaeta, and Sassòli (eds) *The 1949 Geneva Conventions: A Commentary* (OUP 2015) para 4.

[44] Sivakumaran, *The Law of Non-International Armed Conflict* (n 7) 161.

[45] Baxter, 'Ius in Bello Interno: The Present and Future Law' in Moore and Friedmann (eds), *Law and Civil War in the Modern World* (The Johns Hopkins University Press 1974) 518–36, 526.

[46] Federal Political Department (Switzerland), Final Record, Vol II Section B (n 12) 335 (emphasis added).

parties falling under Common Article 3', however, broad characteristics of the notion 'Party to the conflict' under Common Article 3 emerge nonetheless from an interpretation of the provision 'in accordance with the ordinary meaning to be given to the terms of the treaty in their context and in the light of its object and purpose'.[47]

2.1.2 Non-state parties falling under Common Article 3

Under Common Article 3, a 'Party to the conflict' must be party to an 'armed conflict not of an international character'. The ordinary meaning of the term 'armed conflict not of an international character' was unclear at the time: the notion only occurred during the travaux préparatoires of the Geneva Conventions and had no predefined meaning.[48] The notion 'armed conflict *not* of an international character' stands in juxtaposition to article 2 common to the four Geneva Conventions defining international armed conflicts. This makes clear that armed conflicts under Common Article 3 must not involve confrontation between two states.[49] Hence, at least one party needs to be a non-state entity.[50] In addition, commentators agree that the ordinary meaning of the notion 'Party to the conflict' intrinsically suggests a 'modicum of organisation'[51] or 'a degree of organisation and control exercised by any wielders of armed force not being a Government agency'.[52] Certain elements defining this 'degree' or 'modicum' of organization are found in the context of Common Article 3.

2.1.2.1 Collective entities with military capacities

First, a party to an *armed conflict* must be a collective entity. While important differences exist between international and non-international armed conflicts,[53] at least when Common Article 3 was adopted the notion of 'armed conflict' was

[47] Article 31 of the Vienna Convention on the Law of Treaties. While rules of treaty interpretation were only codified in 1962, it is agreed that they applied previously as part of customary international law. See ICRC, *GCI: Commentary of 2016* (n 11) introduction, para 16.

[48] See Pictet, *Commentary GCI* (n 7) 49.

[49] As the US Supreme Court held in the *Hamdan* case: 'The term "conflict not of an international character" is used here in contradistinction to a conflict between nations'. *Hamdan v Rumsfeld, 29 June 2006, 548 U. S. 557 (2006)*, US Supreme Court, 630. See also Bianchi and Naqvi, *International Humanitarian Law and Terrorism* (Hart 2011) 103.

[50] It could be argued that given the capital 'P' of 'Party to the conflict' only High Contracting Parties are bound by the obligations. However, as the 1952 ICRC commentary makes clear, this was not the understanding at the 1949 Diplomatic Conference. See Pictet, *Commentary GCI* (n 7) 37. As Moir pointed out, Common Article 3 'was obviously intended to create duties and rights for both States and insurgents'. Moir, *The Law of Internal Armed Conflict* (n 7) 53. See also Murray, 'How International Humanitarian Law Treaties Bind Non-State Armed Groups' (2015) 20 Journal of Conflict and Security Law 125; Sivakumaran, 'The Addressees of Common Article 3' in Clapham, Gaeta, and Sassòli (eds) *The 1949 Geneva Conventions: A Commentary* (OUP 2015) 415–33.

[51] Dinstein, *Non-International Armed Conflicts in International Law* (CUP 2014) para 95.

[52] Draper, *The Geneva Conventions of 1949* (M Nijhoff 2007) 89; see also, eg, ICRC, *International Humanitarian Law and the Challenges of Contemporary Armed Conflicts* (ICRC 2011) 8; Schmitt, 'Classification of Cyber Conflict' (2012) 17 Journal of Conflict & Security Law 255.

[53] See ICRC, *GCI: Commentary of 2016* (n 11) article 3, para 41.

understood as applying to factual circumstances of a 'war'. Based on its observations at the 1949 Conference, the ICRC commented that '[s]peaking generally, it must be recognized that the conflicts referred to in Article 3 are armed conflicts, with armed forces on either side engaged in hostilities—conflicts, in short, which are in many respects similar to an international war'.[54] As war is traditionally understood as confronting entities and not individuals, a non-state party must be a collective entity.[55] This entity needs to have the capacity to bring about, and to engage in, armed violence going beyond 'a mere riot or disturbances caused by bandits'.[56]

2.1.2.2 *The ability to comply with basic humanitarian rules*

Second, such collective entities need to be able to apply fundamental humanitarian rules. The laws of war are traditionally based on the principle of equal obligations among conflicting parties: Common Article 3 prescribes that '*each Party* to the conflict shall be bound to apply' the listed provisions.[57] As Lauterpacht pointed out, 'it is impossible to visualize the conduct of hostilities in which one side would be bound by rules of warfare without benefiting from them and the other side would benefit from them without being bound'.[58] At least traditionally, the applicability of Common Article 3 creates a legal framework 'which enables both sides to know the rules within which they are allowed to operate and to rely on similar conduct by the other side'.[59] Following these considerations, each party to a conflict must have the ability to apply the rules contained in Common Article 3.[60] It would be inconsistent to require all parties to a conflict to apply certain rules if they were not able to do so.[61]

The requirement that all parties must have the capacity to comply with the applicable law sparks at least two questions: what capacities are required from an armed group to implement rules in general; and concretely, what capacity must non-state entities have to implement the obligations listed in Common Article 3? With regard to the first question, the capacity to comply with international humanitarian

[54] Uhler and Coursier, *Commentary GCIV* (n 24) 36.

[55] See Section 1.1 'The Origins of the Statist Focus of the Laws of War'.

[56] Federal Political Department (Switzerland), Final Record, Vol II Section B (n 12) 129. See also Provost, *International Human Rights* (n 43) 267.

[57] See also Pilloud, Sandoz, Swinarski et al, *Commentary on the Additional Protocols of 8 June 1977 to the Geneva Conventions of 12 August 1949* (ICRC) para 4442. For further elaboration, see also Sassòli and Shany, 'DEBATE: Should the Obligations of States and Armed Groups Under International Humanitarian Law Really Be Equal?' (2011) 93 International Review of the Red Cross 425–42, 234.

[58] Lauterpacht, 'The Limits of the Operation of the Law of War' (1953) 30 British Year Book of International Law 206–43, 243.

[59] Pejic, 'Terrorist Acts and Groups: A Role for International Law?' (2005) 75 British Yearbook of International Law 71–100, 86.

[60] The actual implementation of the applicable rules is not, however, a prerequisite for qualifying as a party to the conflict. See *Boškoski and Tarčulovski, IT-04-82-T*, para 205. For further discussion, see Perrin, *Modern Warfare: Armed Groups, Private Militaries, Humanitarian Organizations, and the Law* (UBC Press 2012).

[61] This was also suggested during the drafting conference. France, supported by other states, proposed that parties to an armed conflict must dispose of 'organized military forces belonging to a responsible authority capable of respecting, or enforcing respect for the Convention, in a given territory'. See n 27.

law (IHL) 'presupposes that there is a command structure', which enables the party to train its members, to provide instructions, and to react to possible violations.[62] Indeed, during the 1949 Conference states suggested that non-state parties must act under the command or the directions of an authority.[63] Some states linked the existence of a responsible authority to the ability of a group to respect and to ensure respect for the rules contained in Common Article 3.[64] In addition to being key to implementing the law, a certain command structure also distinguishes a party to a conflict from a loose group of individuals, and it enables the group to conduct military-like operations.[65] Naqvi and Bianchi went as far as to suggest that the idea that non-state parties can be reasonably expected to implement the law 'suggests that a group more akin to a regular armed force is the type of party to the conflict to which common Article 3 was meant to apply'.[66]

Looking concretely at the parties' obligations under Common Article 3, most appear fairly basic, and arguably 'a party to an armed conflict only needs a minimal degree of organisation to ensure their application'.[67] This conclusion is, however, challenged by two requirements: first, parties to a conflict have the positive obligation collect and care for the wounded and sick; and second, Common Article 3 requires that sentences shall only be passed and executions carried out following a judgment by a 'regularly constituted court affording all the judicial guarantees which are recognized as indispensable by civilized peoples'. The obligation to collect and care for the wounded and sick could suggest that only groups with the requisite capacities can be party to armed conflicts, for example, those with the means to evacuate the wounded and facilities to treat them. Yet, as the 2016 ICRC commentary sets out, these are obligations of conduct that have to be performed with due diligence, meaning that the 'exact content depends on the specific circumstances of each case'.[68] In brief, Common Article 3 needs to be understood as requiring 'only what can reasonably be expected under the given circumstances, taking into consideration factors such as the security conditions and the available resources'.[69] Thus, the provision does not define an abstract benchmark but obliges parties to do what

[62] La Rosa and Wuerzner, 'Armed Groups, Sanctions and the Implementation of International Humanitarian Law' (2008) 90 International Review of the Red Cross 327–41, 329.

[63] While some states required a civilian authority (see Federal Political Department (Switzerland), Final Record, Vol II Section B (n 12) 12 (United States)), other states emphasized that a military authority would be sufficient (see ibid 43–44 (France, Uruguay, Norway). During the 1974–77 Diplomatic Conference negotiating APII, Norway opined that '[t]here could not be an armed conflict in the sense of [Common Article 3] except in cases where hostilities broke out between armed forces or other organised groups under responsible command'. Federal Political Department (Switzerland), Official Records of the Diplomatic Conference on the Reaffirmation and Development of International Humanitarian Law Applicable in Armed Conflicts, Vol VIII (1978) 217 (Norway).

[64] See Federal Political Department (Switzerland), Final Record, Vol II Section B (n 12) 120 (France); Pictet, *Commentary GCI* (n 7) 49–50.

[65] The command structure criterion is discussed further in Section 3.3.1 'The crystallization of broad criteria'.

[66] Bianchi and Naqvi, *International Humanitarian Law and Terrorism* (n 49) 107.

[67] *Boškoski and Tarčulovski, IT-04-82-T*, para 197.

[68] ICRC, *GCI: Commentary of 2016* (n 11) para 751, 762.

[69] ibid para 763.

is reasonably possible in the circumstances, including, for example, providing first aid as for own forces, or calling upon civilian medial personnel to collect and care for the wounded.

With regard to the passing of sentences, it seems that if the ability to operate 'regularly constituted courts' in accordance with international law was a requirement sine qua non for any party to a Common Article 3 conflict, most non-state armed groups would be excluded from its scope of application.[70] A convincing approach to avoid this limitation has been suggested by Professor Draper. He argued that Common Article 3 does not restrict internal armed conflicts to those involving only parties that meet this elaborate stage of organization. Rather, article 3(1)(d) 'prevents that Party from attempting to try and punish any persons in its hands' if it cannot do so in accordance with the article.[71] In his view:

> The article binds that Party to the conflict to the extent of its capacity to apply it and at the same time precludes it from asserting rights to undertake activities, such as trials, which it cannot ensure will comply with the standards of civilised peoples.[72]

This approach reflects a sense of realism: first, it will be difficult to know ab initio whether a party will have the material capacity required to implement Common Article 3 in its entirety. And second, such a condition would be overly strict and not supported in practice. In international armed conflicts, a state party's lack of capacity to implement all applicable rules does not affect conflict classification.[73] More specifically, states' and international tribunals' practice shows that the ability to operate 'regularly constituted courts' is not a strict requirement for armed groups to become party to an armed conflict.[74] Hence, in order to become party to an armed conflict not of an international character, armed groups do not need to be able to implement all applicable rules of IHL. For the purpose of conflict classification it is sufficient that they 'be capable of meeting minimal humanitarian requirements',[75] which is normally ensured through a certain command structure.

[70] The question of whether and under what conditions armed groups may conduct trials by 'regularly constituted court, affording all the judicial guarantees which are recognized as indispensable by civilized peoples' has received increasing attention in recent years. See, eg, Somer, 'Jungle Justice: Passing Sentence on the Equality of Belligerents in Non-International Armed Conflict' (2007) 89 International Review of the Red Cross 655–90; Sivakumaran, 'Courts of Armed Opposition Groups' (2009) 7 Journal of International Criminal Justice 489–513; La Rosa and Wuerzner, 'Armed Groups' (n 62); Rodenhäuser, 'International Legal Obligations of Armed Opposition Groups in Syria' (2015) 2015 1 Review of Law 1.

[71] Draper, *The Geneva Conventions of 1949* (n 52) 91.

[72] ibid. See also Sivakumaran, *The Law of Non-International Armed Conflict* (n 7) 186. Interestingly, it is reported that '[i]n the Democratic Republic of the Congo, for instance, some ANSAs [armed non-state actors] were aware of their limited capacities to detain enemy combatants and said they would not detain because they could not do it humanly.' Geneva Call, *Positive Obligations of Armed Non-State Actors: Legal and Policy Issues—Report from the 2015 Garance Talks* (Geneva Call, 2016) 12.

[73] Wilhelm, *Problèmes relatifs à la protection de la personne humaine par le droit international dans les conflits armés ne présentant pas un caractère international* (Brill 1972) 348. This is discussed further with regard to the law of occupation in Section 2.2.2.4 'The capacity to implement the Protocol'.

[74] This requirement is not raised in any of the practice examined later. See Chapter 3 'Organized Armed Groups in Contemporary International Practice'.

[75] Schindler, *The Different Types of Armed Conflicts According to the Geneva Conventions and Protocols* (M Nijhoff 1979) 147.

2.1.2.3 Territorial control?

Third, government-like control over defined territory was among the indicative criteria suggested at the 1949 Conference.[76] While such elevated degree of control might not be necessary, some commentators have argued that in order to carry out the obligations under Common Article 3, the non-state party should be 'in possession of some part of the national territory'.[77] In addition, the 1958 ICRC commentary remarked that in many armed conflicts 'each of the Parties is in possession of a portion of the national territory'.[78] Controlling territory was also among the conditions for recognizing belligerency, although for political rather than military reasons.[79] Indeed, territorial control can be regarded as useful evidence to establish a sufficient degree of organization within the non-state party.[80] However, neither the wording of Common Article 3 nor its context require territorial control as a necessary condition to determine the existence of a non-state party to a NIAC.

2.1.2.4 Interpretation of the threshold 'as widely as possible'?

Fourth, contrary to suggesting additional criteria, in the 1952 ICRC commentary Pictet argued that Common Article 3 'should be applied as widely as possible',[81] possibly implying that the provision could also apply if no armed conflict between two organized parties exists. Understood in that sense, it has been rightly criticized as 'dangerously simplistic',[82] because this seeks 'to expand its scope further than was intended'.[83] Pictet's plea has also been criticized because it would be 'highly improbable' that 'a disorganised group of rioters' would observe basic rules of the laws of war.[84] A better understanding of Pictet's statement is that he aimed to urge parties engaged in violence to apply minimum humanitarian standards irrespective of whether Common Article 3 formally applied, or not. Pictet made this statement at a time when human rights law was still in its infancy, and unless IHL applied, only the state's domestic law regulated internal strife.[85] He appealed to states parties to respect in any situation of internal strife 'a few essential rules which it in fact

[76] The commentary refers to an authority 'acting within a determinate territory', insurgents 'in possession of a part of the national territory', or an insurgent civil authority exercising 'de facto authority over persons within a determinate territory'. Pictet, *Commentary GCI* (n 7) 49.

[77] Draper, *The Geneva Conventions of 1949* (n 52) 90.

[78] Uhler and Coursier, *Commentary GCIV* (n 24) 36.

[79] See Section 1.3.2 'Criteria for the recognition of belligerency'. See also Kalpouzos, 'International Law and Armed Groups' 90–91.

[80] See Sivakumaran, *The Law of Non-International Armed Conflict* (n 7) 181. See also Moir, 'The Concept of Non-International Armed Conflict' (n 43) para 41.

[81] Pictet, *Commentary GCI* (n 7) 50. This plea is only included in the 1952 commentary on the First Geneva Convention and not in the later commentaries on the other three Conventions.

[82] Kress, 'Some Reflections on the International Legal Framework Governing Transnational Armed Conflicts' (2010) 15 Journal of Conflict and Security Law 261.

[83] Bond, *The Rules of Riot: Internal Conflict and the Law of War* (Princeton University Press 1974) 54.

[84] Moir, *The Law of Internal Armed Conflict* (n 7) 37.

[85] See Kretzmer, 'Rethinking the Application of IHL in Non-International Armed Conflicts' (2009) 42 Israel Law Review 18–21.

respects daily, under its own laws, even when dealing with common criminals'.[86] Consequently, while serving as an additional argument not to apply the indicative criteria listed in the 1952 ICRC commentary, this plea cannot mean that IHL as such should apply irrespective of the existence of an armed conflict.

2.1.3 Early state practice following the adoption of Common Article 3

State practice on the application of Common Article 3 during the first decades after its adoption is rare. Some indications of the views of legal experts at the time—government, military, and academic—on which criteria define armed groups as parties to a Common Article 3 threshold are found in an ICRC report of 1962. Considering internal conflicts such as the ones in Guatemala, Nicaragua, Kenya, Algeria, or the Congo, the experts opined that Common Article 3 conflicts exist 'if the hostile action, directed against a legal government, is of a collective character and consists of a minimum amount of organization'.[87] Among the indicative factors for assessing the conflicting parties' degree of organization, the experts included 'the number and framework of the rebel groups [and] their installation or action on a part of the territory'.[88] Other state practice on the application of Common Article 3 during the first decades following the adoption of the Geneva Conventions is, however, 'difficult to find',[89] and, in particular with regard to low-intensity armed conflicts, 'rarely has article 3 been mentioned'.[90] Thus, it is difficult to determine how states interpreted the term 'Party to the conflict' under Common Article 3 in their early practice.

2.1.4 Making sense of Common Article 3's broad wording

At first sight, the elliptical definition of the scope of application of Common Article 3 provides little guidance on the requisite characteristics of parties to an 'armed conflict not of an international character'. As shown above, however, the notion 'Party to the conflict' suggests that any such party must be a collective entity possessing a certain degree of organization. This requirement serves three main purposes: first, internal organization distinguishes parties to a conflict from groups of individuals engaged in unorganized riots or internal disturbances. Second, it enables a group to conduct military-like operations that go beyond crime or sporadic acts of violence. Third, a certain degree of internal organization is a prerequisite for the ability to implement the rules contained in Common Article 3. As a result, a party to a

[86] Pictet, *Commentary GCI* (n 7) 50.

[87] ICRC, *Humanitarian Aid to the Victims of Internal Conflicts. Meeting of a Commission of Experts in Geneva* (ICRC 1962) 82.

[88] ibid 83.

[89] Moir, *The Law of Internal Armed Conflict* (n 7) 68; see also La Haye, *War Crimes in Internal Armed Conflicts* (CUP 2008) 8. More recent state practice is discussed in Chapter 3 'Organized Armed Groups in Contemporary International Practice'.

[90] Junod, 'Additional Protocol II: History and Scope' (1983–84) 33 American University Law Review 29–40, 30. See also Draper, *The Geneva Conventions of 1949* (n 52) 92–93.

non-international armed conflict must be a collective entity having a certain organizational or command structure that allows it to launch military-style operations or armed conflict-like violence, and enables the group to implement the minimum rules of IHL.[91]

Comparing the requisite degree of organization of non-state parties under Common Article 3 to that required for recognition of belligerency, it appears that under Common Article 3 states reduced the necessary degree of organization of non-state parties to the essential capacities required to engage in an armed conflict.[92] The requirement of political organization—such as the existence of a civilian authority exercising control over territory—was avoided. Non-state parties no longer need to be state-like. At the same time, important elements of the requirement to be militarily organized remain. In contrast, the requirement of actual compliance with the law was discarded. Moreover, the ability to implement Common Article 3 requires a lower degree of organization than the capacity to implement the customary laws of international armed conflict (IAC), as rendered applicable by a recognition of belligerency.[93]

The consequences of states' decision to leave the scope of Common Article 3 undefined have been interpreted differently. From a legal perspective, some commentators argued that the 'positive effect of a lack of agreed distinctive criteria is the [resulting] flexibility' which may enable its application to situations not initially considered as falling under the provision.[94] In this respect, the lack of definition 'might even be a blessing in disguise'.[95] At the same time, in practice, this omission also enabled states to interpret the article's applicability in accordance with their political interests, which often meant denying the existence of a NIAC. As Professor Baxter pointed out: 'the first line of defense against international humanitarian law is to deny that it applies at all'.[96] Accordingly, looking at state practice in the 1950s

[91] Schindler confirmed these three criteria based on state practice between 1949 and 1979. See Schindler, *The Different Types of Armed Conflicts* (n 75) 147.

[92] For a comparison between the concept of recognition of belligerency and armed conflicts under Common Article 3, see Schindler, 'State of War, Belligerency, Armed Conflict' in Cassese and Eide (eds), *The New Humanitarian Law of Armed Conflict: Proceedings of the 1976 and 1977 Conferences* (Editoriale Scientifica 1979) 3–20, 147. In this respect, Cullen rightly emphasized: 'Arguably one of the greatest achievements of the common Article is that it lowers the threshold for the application of international humanitarian norms' because '[i]t applies to all situations of non-international armed conflict, including situations of insurgency not reaching the threshold of a civil war'. Cullen, 'Key Developments Affecting the Scope of Internal Armed Conflict in International Humanitarian Law' (2005) 183 Military Law Review, 66–109, 79.

[93] The customary rules of IAC were found, eg, in the Hague Conventions of 1907. As Veuthey pointed out on the relationship between the applicable law and the requisite degree of organization: 'Generally, we can say that the more the rules of protection are detailed and restrictive, the more limited is the definition of the scope of application'. Veuthey, 'Guérilla et Droit Humanitaire' (1983) 65 International Review of the Red Cross 119–142, 352 (original in French, translation by the author). See also Draper, 'Internal Armed Conflicts' (n 11) 264.

[94] Spieker, 'Twenty-Five Years after the Adoption of Additional Protocol II: Breakthrough or Failure of Humanitarian Legal Protection?' (2001) 4 Yearbook of International Humanitarian Law, 129–66, 141.

[95] Moir, *The Law of Internal Armed Conflict* (n 7) 32.

[96] Baxter, 'Some Existing Problems of Humanitarian Law' (1975) 14 Military Law and Law of War Review 298.

and '60s, the ICRC found that the lack of a legal definition of non-international armed conflicts hampered the application of IHL.[97] A new occasion to clarify the scope of application of the laws of non-international armed conflicts arose with the negotiation and adoption of Additional Protocol II to the Geneva Conventions.

2.2 Raising the Bar? 'Organized Armed Groups' under Additional Protocol II

Defining the scope of application of the Additional Protocol II (APII) proved diplomatically challenging.[98] In 1977, states reached agreement only during informal consultations.[99] They agreed that APII shall apply to armed conflicts to which the treaty rules of international armed conflicts do not apply and

> which take place in the territory of a High Contracting Party between its armed forces and dissident armed forces or other organized armed groups which, under responsible command, exercise such control over a part of its territory as to enable them to carry out sustained and concerted military operations and to implement this Protocol.[100]

Article 1(2) APII adds that 'internal disturbances and tensions, such as riots, isolated and sporadic acts of violence and other acts of a similar nature' are not considered armed conflicts and consequently not covered by the Protocol.[101]

Immediately following adoption, some state representatives criticized this provision as a 'retrogressive step',[102] applying only to 'cases of conventional civil war',[103] and thus to a 'very limited number of internal conflicts ... as the conditions laid down are so numerous and so stringent'.[104] Scholars also denounced APII as

[97] ICRC, *Reaffirmation and Development of the Laws and Customs Applicable in Armed Conflicts (Report Submitted to the XXIst International Conference of the Red Cross)* ICRC 1969) 98. See also Forsythe, 'Legal Management of Internal War: The 1977 Protocol on Non-International Armed Conflicts' (1978) 72 American Journal of International Law 272–95, 273–74; Moir, *The Law of Internal Armed Conflict* (n 7) 88.

[98] For comprehensive analyses of the negotiation processes, see Cullen, *The Concept of Non-International Armed Conflict* (n 1) 86–114; Moir, *The Law of Internal Armed Conflict* (n 7) 89–109; Sivakumaran, *The Law of Non-International Armed Conflict* (n 7) 182–92.

[99] Federal Political Department (Switzerland), Official Records of the Diplomatic Conference on the Reaffirmation and Development of International Humanitarian Law Applicable in Armed Conflicts, Vol X (1978) 93–94. No records exist from these consultations.

[100] Article 1(1) APII.

[101] This criterion was not new but reflected what states already agreed on during the 1949 Diplomatic Conference. Indeed, given the apparent gap between the definition of armed conflict under article 1(1) APII and the situations excluded under article 1(2) APII, as well as the drafting history of the provision, it appears that this clause was intended to define the lower threshold of armed conflicts in general, including that of Common Article 3. Abi-Saab, 'Non-International Armed Conflicts' (n 6) 229; Vité, 'Typology of Armed Conflicts in International Humanitarian Law: Legal Concepts and Actual Situations' (2009) 91 International Review of the Red Cross 69–94, 79. See also Moir, 'The Concept of Non-International Armed Conflict' (n 43) para 49.

[102] Federal Political Department (Switzerland), Official Records of the Diplomatic Conference on the Reaffirmation and Development of International Humanitarian Law Applicable in Armed Conflicts, Vol VII (1978) 71 (Cameroon).

[103] ibid 300 (Switzerland).

[104] ibid 101 (Italy); and 71 (Cameroon).

applying only to 'the most intense and characterized civil wars'[105] or to 'conflicts that more resemble traditional interstate conflict'[106] because it 'defines the non-international conflict in such a limited sense that new rules remain inapplicable for most non-international armed conflicts'.[107] It has also been argued that 'Protocol II has seldom been applicable to recent internal conflicts because insurgent groups rarely, if ever, meet the requirements of its Article 1'.[108]

Indeed, unlike Common Article 3, APII contains explicit criteria for its applicability. Under APII, a NIAC must take place 'in the territory of a High Contracting Party between its armed forces and dissident armed forces or other organized armed groups'. Undeniably, this restricts APII to conflicts involving government forces.[109] In addition, APII sets out criteria defining non-state forces. Different views exist on whether the non-state party's degree of organization required under APII differs significantly from that under Common Article 3. While the more prevalent view is that APII 'requires non-governmental forces to have a particularly high level of organisation',[110] Belgium stated at the 1977 Conference that 'the field of application of draft Protocoll II went very little beyond that of Article 3 Common to the Geneva Conventions of 1949'.[111]

After a brief discussion of the broad elements that APII shall apply to 'armed conflicts' involving 'organised armed forces', this section analyses the four requirements that article 1(1) APII requires from organized armed groups.

2.2.1 Armed conflicts between organized armed forces

In general terms, APII applies to non-international 'armed conflicts' between government forces and 'dissident armed forces or other organised armed groups'. In

[105] Abi-Saab, 'Non-International Armed Conflicts' (n 6) 236.

[106] International Law Association, *Final Report on the Meaning of Armed Conflict in International Law* (ILA 2010) 12.

[107] Schindler, The Different Types of Armed Conflicts (n 75) 127; see also Cassese, 'The Status of Rebels under the 1977 Geneva Protocol on Non-International Armed Conflicts' (1981) 30 International and Comparative Law Quarterly 416–39, 418; Meron, 'On the Inadequate Reach of Humanitarian and Human Rights Law and the Need for a New Instrument' (1983) 77 American Journal of International Law 589–615, 599. These views have been followed by more recent publications. See, eg, Moir, *The Law of Internal Armed Conflict* (n 7) 108; Cullen, *The Concept of Non-International Armed Conflict* (n 1) 105–06; La Haye, *War Crimes in Internal Armed Conflicts* (n 89) 46; Quenivet, 'Applicability Test of Additional Protocol II and Common Article 3 for Crimes in Internal Armed Conflict' in Jinks, Maogoto, and Solomon (eds), *Applying International Humanitarian Law in Judicial and Quasi-Judicial Bodies: International and Domestic Aspects* (TMC Asser Press 2014) 31–55, 36. See also Moir, 'The Concept of Non-International Armed Conflict' (n 43) para 5.

[108] Paulus and Vashakmadze, 'Asymmetrical War and the Notion of Armed Conflict—A Tentative Conceptualization' (2009) 91 International Review of the Red Cross, 95–125, 103. The authors do not, however, provide any supporting practice.

[109] In contrast, Common Article 3 also applies to NIAC between armed groups only. See Pilloud, Sandoz, Swinarski et al, *Commentry on the APs (1987)* (n 57) para 4461; Bothe, *New Rules for Victims of Armed Conflicts: Commentary on the Two 1977 Protocols Additional to the Geneva Conventions of 1949*, 2nd edn (M Nijhoff 2013) 718.

[110] Vité, 'Typology of Armed Conflicts' (n 101) 79.

[111] Federal Political Department (Switzerland), Official Records, Vol VII, 291 (Belgium). This view has also been advanced by Sivakumaran, *The Law of Non-International Armed Conflict* (n 7) 190–92.

many cases, dissident armed forces can be presumed to show a similar degree of organization as state armed forces.[112] The term 'organized armed groups', in contrast, covers a broader scope of armed forces. Leaving APII's four defining elements aside, the notions 'armed conflict' and 'organized armed group' encompass basic elements characterizing these groups. Non-state forces under APII must be: (a) a group; (b) organized; (c) armed; and (d) a party to an 'armed conflict'. As set out with regard to Common Article 3, this requires first that non-state forces are a collective entity.[113] Second, the group must be armed and engaged in an armed conflict, which necessarily requires the capacity to orchestrate collective armed violence of certain intensity. Indeed, when negotiating APII, states reemphasized the general understanding that 'organized armed forces carry on hostile activities in arms against the authorities in power',[114] and that 'riots, banditry, isolated acts of terrorism, common crimes, and the like would not be embraced within the definition'.[115] Third, different state experts suggested that organized armed forces must have a disciplinary system sufficient to ensure observance of the rules contained in the Protocol.[116] These basic elements largely reflect the main characteristics of a non-state party under Common Article 3.[117]

A simpler definition of the scope of application than the one eventually adopted was contained in the ICRC's draft protocol presented to the 1974–77 Diplomatic Conference: 'the protocol shall apply to all [non-international] armed conflicts ... taking place between armed forces or other organized armed groups under responsible command'.[118] As Professor Bothe recounts from the negotiations, the ICRC 'tried to maintain the integrity between common Art 3' and APII because the suggested definition 'could be regarded as interpretations of what was meant by an "armed conflict" in common Art 3'.[119] However, many states opposed this draft. In their understanding, the proposed threshold was too low. Several states suggested additional elements allegedly characterizing a party to a non-international armed conflict: they should exercise control over (a substantial part of) territory, be represented by a responsible authority, show actual respect for the rules in question, or be explicitly recognized as belligerent.[120] Other states, as well as the ICRC, countered

[112] See ICRC, *Interpretive Guidance on the Notion of Direct Participation in Hostilities under International Humanitarian Law* (ICRC 2009) 32.

[113] See Section 2.1.2.1 'Collective entitities with military capacities'.

[114] ICRC, *Report of the Work of the Conference (Conference of Government Experts on the Reaffirmation and Development of International Humanitarian Law Applicable in Armed Conflicts)* (ICRC, 1971) paras 170–71. Additional elements that were discussed included the duration of hostilities and their intensity.

[115] ibid para 169.

[116] See ibid para 182 and pp 61, 62, 65.

[117] Yet, states disagreed on other possible elements defining 'organised armed groups'. See ICRC, *Report of the Work of the Conference (Conference of Government Experts on the Reaffirmation and Development of International Humanitarian Law Applicable in Armed Conflicts)* Vol I (ICRC 1972) 70–71.

[118] Federal Political Department (Switzerland), Official Records of the Diplomatic Conference on the Reaffirmation and Development of International Humanitarian Law Applicable in Armed Conflicts, Vol I (1978) 33 (ICRC Draft).

[119] Bothe, *New Rules for Victims of Armed Conflicts* (n 109) 715–16.

[120] Federal Political Department (Switzerland), Official Records of the Diplomatic Conference on the Reaffirmation and Development of International Humanitarian Law Applicable in Armed Conflicts, Vol IV (1978) 6–10 (amendments suggested by Pakistan, Romania, Indonesia, Spain, and

these arguments in order to find a definition that would, in their view, reflect realities of lower intensity internal armed conflicts involving less organized non-state parties.[121]

2.2.2 The explicit requirements of Additional Protocol II

Analysing the compromise formula contained in article 1(1) APII, scholars argued that during the negotiations, proponents of a high threshold 'won the upper hand'[122] and succeeded in inserting an 'exceedingly high' threshold.[123] Some commentators went as far as finding that 'the conditions of application of Protocol II resemble the classical conditions for recognition of belligerency'.[124] However, interpreting article 1(1) in accordance with the ordinary meaning of its terms, in its context, and in light of its object and purpose, reveals that its conditions may not be as high as some have feared.

2.2.2.1 'Responsible command'

According to its ordinary meaning, a 'responsible command' signifies an authority 'exercising control over a group or operation',[125] which comes along with certain obligations and decision-making functions.[126] In the context of APII, this command must exercise authority over an armed group, suggesting that this group must be of a collective nature and not merely isolated individuals.[127] As pointed out with regard to Common Article 3, under IHL a command serves two main purposes: it enables the group (a) to conduct military-like operations, and (b) to ensure respect for applicable rules. Accordingly, the 1987 ICRC commentary stated that 'responsible command' under APII signifies 'an organization capable, on the one hand, of planning and carrying out sustained and concerted military operations, and on the other, of imposing discipline in the name of a de facto authority'.[128]

Opinions vary, however, on the degree of structure and authority that a 'responsible command' implies. Referring to an ICRC statement during the 1977 Conference, Bothe recounts:

> The expression does not mean any armed band acting under a leader. Such armed groups must be structured and possess organs, and must therefore have a system for allocating authority

Brazil). In fact, these suggestions resemble the ones discussed but eventually dismissed during the 1949 Diplomatic Conference with regard to Common Article 3.

121 See, eg, Federal Political Department (Switzerland), Official Records, Vol VIII (n 63) 201–03 (ICRC); 217 (Norway); 218 (New Zealand); 234–35 (Egypt).

122 Cassese, 'The Status of Rebels' (n 107) 418.

123 Meron, 'On the Inadequate Reach of Humanitarian and Human Rights Law and the Need for a New Instrument' (n 107) 599. See also states and commentators cited in nn 102–08.

124 La Haye, *War Crimes in Internal Armed Conflicts* (n 89) 44. See also authors cited in n 158.

125 *Oxford Dictionaries*, online version, definition of 'command'.

126 *Oxford Dictionaries*, online version, definition of 'responsible': '(Of a job or position) involving important duties, independent decision-making, or control over others').

127 See Junod, 'Additional Protocol II' (n 90) 37.

128 Pilloud, Sandoz, Swinarski et al, *Commentary on the APs (1987)* (n 57) para 4463. See also *Akayesu, ICTR-96-4-T*, para 626.

and responsibility: they must also be subject to rules of internal discipline. Consequently, the expression 'organized armed groups' does not imply any appreciable difference in degree of organization from that of regular armed forces.[129]

In contrast, another observer noted that at the Diplomatic Conferences prior to the adoption of the Additional Protocols, '[a]pparently it has been assumed in all quarters that present-day guerrilla warfare is carried out by organized groups endowed with command structures rather than by spontaneous and unorganized uprisings of the civilian population'.[130] Rather following the latter view, the 1987 ICRC commentary finds that a 'responsible command' under article 1(1) APII does 'not necessarily mean that there is a hierarchical system of military organization similar to that of regular armed forces'.[131] Indeed, in light of the provision's context and its object and purpose, it appears that any command system, which enables the group to act collectively, to carry out sustained and concerted military actions, and to implement the Protocol, should satisfy the threshold.

2.2.2.2 Territorial control

Commentators identified the element of territorial control as the 'salient element'[132] of article 1(1) APII, and various states and scholars criticized its inclusion in the article.[133] Most prominently, during the 1974–77 Diplomatic Conference Egypt opined that requiring insurgents to control territory is

> too restrictive in view of the nature of modern, and particularly guerrilla, warfare. In armed conflict situations characterized by high mobility, territorial control continuously changes hands, sometimes alternating between day and night, to the point of becoming meaningless. Other forms of intense armed conflict, such as urban guerrilla armed conflict would not fulfil the requirement of territorial control.

For Egypt, the territorial control requirement would 'severely limit [the Protocol's] real significance and usefulness'.[134] Indeed, compared with the minimalistic wording of Common Article 3, the requirement of territorial control could be considered as the reinsertion of an element that existed for recognition of belligerency but had been abandoned in 1949.

[129] Bothe, *New Rules for Victims of Armed Conflicts* (n 109) 717. For the original statement, see Federal Political Department (Switzerland), Official Records, Vol VIII (n 63) 204.

[130] Rosas, *The Legal Status of Prisoners of War: A Study in International Humanitarian Law Applicable in Armed Conflicts* (Institute for Human Rights Åbo Akademi University 2005) 340. This finding seems pertinent despite the fact that Rosas made it with regard to the status of organized resistance movements in international armed conflicts.

[131] Pilloud, Sandoz, Swinarski et al, *Commentary on the APs (1987)* (n 57) para 4463.

[132] Dinstein, 'Concluding Remarks on Non-International Armed Conflicts' (2012) 88 International Law Studies 399–421, 404.

[133] See Abi-Saab, 'Non-International Armed Conflicts' (n 6) 228; Momtaz, *Le Droit International Humanitaire Applicable Aux Conflits Armés Non Internationaux*, (M Nijhoff 2002) 50; Schindler, *The Different Types of Armed Conflicts* (n 75) 148–49; Moir, *The Law of Internal Armed Conflict* (n 7) 105.

[134] Federal Political Department (Switzerland), Official Records, Vol VIII, 235 (Egypt). Other delegates dismissed the element as being purely political. See ibid 293–94 (Norway).

Article 1(1) APII requires an organized armed group to 'exercise *such control* over a part of its territory *as to enable them* to carry out sustained and concerted military operations and to implement this Protocol' (emphasis added). Exercising territorial control is often considered an element that any armed group under APII has to fulfil. Under this view, 'control by the insurgents over part of the State's territory is a very simple litmus test for the existence of a NIAC [under APII]'.[135] In contrast, it has also been advanced that '[a]s the wording of the provision makes clear, there is no requirement of territorial control in and of itself'. Hence, where a group is able to engage in sustained and concerted military operations and to implement this Protocol, 'the quantum of territory controlled' would not be pertinent as such.[136] Taken to its extreme, this could mean that if an armed group fulfils all other conditions under APII, no territorial control is required at all. While convincing to some extent, this interpretation may overly rely on the wording of the provision at the expense of states' opinions.[137]

According to the 1987 ICRC commentary and subsequent war crime jurisprudence, the word 'such' is key to interpreting this requirement. It limits the requisite territorial control to a quantum that is sufficient to meet the other conditions.[138] This means that territorial control constitutes primarily an 'enabling element',[139] meaning that the amount of territorial control cannot be indicated in the abstract but is determined by the function it serves.[140] A functional interpretation of territorial control informs the quantity of territory under insurgent control and the quality of the power exercised in that territory. As shall be seen next, neither the ability to carry out sustained and concerted military operations, nor the capacity to implement APII, should be interpreted overly strictly as necessarily requiring government-like control over a part of territory. In practice, under APII control over a 'modest area of land' that escaped 'the control of government forces' may suffice.[141]

2.2.2.3 'Sustained and concerted military operations'

As the 1987 ICRC commentary provides, in accordance with its ordinary meaning:

> 'Sustained' (in French the reference is to 'opérations continues') means that the operations are kept going or kept up continuously. The emphasis is therefore on continuity and persistence.

[135] Dinstein, *Non-International Armed Conflicts in International Law* (n 51) rn 147.
[136] Sivakumaran, *The Law of Non-International Armed Conflict* (n 7) 185–86.
[137] The above-discussed statements by states after the adoption of APII suggest that states consider territorial control a strict requirement. In addition, more recently the (government) experts who worked on the 'Tallinn Manual' seemed to consider territorial control a strict requirement under article 1(1) APII. See Schmitt and NATO, *Tallinn Manual on the International Law Applicable to Cyber Warfare* (CUP 2013) Rule 23, para 17.
[138] See Pilloud, Sandoz, Swinarski et al, *Commentary on the APs (1987)* (n 57) para 4466; see also *Akayesu, ICTR-96-4-T*, para 626.
[139] Sivakumaran, *The Law of Non-International Armed Conflict* (n 7) 186.
[140] See Bothe, *New Rules for Victims of Armed Conflicts* (n 109) 718.
[141] Pilloud, Sandoz, Swinarski et al, *Commentary on the APs (1987)* (n 57) para 4467. See also *Akayesu, ICTR-96-4-T*, para 626; Dinstein, *Non-International Armed Conflicts in International Law* (n 51) para 144.

'Concerted' (in French: 'concertées') means agreed upon, planned and contrived, done in agreement according to a plan.[142]

The ability to engage in planned military-like operations is also implicit in the requirement that groups have to operate under a responsible command. The requirement that operations must be 'sustained' could suggest that they have to be 'without interruption'.[143] However, because, in the course of a conflict, hostilities are rarely without interruption, sustained may also be 'an element of duration and means ongoing rather than non-stop'.[144] While the ordinary meaning of the terms 'sustained and concerted' leaves a broad margin of interpretation, the terms might be better understood in their context. Under article 1(2) APII, states excluded 'isolated and sporadic acts of violence' from the Protocol's scope. This suggests that *concerted operations* must be more than *isolated acts*, and that *sustained operations* distinguish armed conflicts from *sporadic violence*. As a result, while some nonetheless argue that sustained and concerted military operations under APII suggest a higher degree of organization than that required under Common Article 3,[145] this interpretation does not necessarily stem from the provision's wording.[146]

As the wording of the article suggests, the ability to carry out sustained and concerted military operations may mean armed groups must have some control over territory. Indeed, the ability to engage in continuing and planned confrontations will often require at least a safe haven where the non-state forces can regroup after battles, store weapons and supplies, and plan their operations. However, it does not demand territorial control going beyond the temporary military control over limited territory.

2.2.2.4 *The capacity to implement the Protocol*

The capacity to implement the Protocol may require a more sophisticated degree of internal organization as well as more stable control over territory. As one commentator analysed:

For respecting a human's fundamental rights, control over a part of the territory may not be necessary. The same cannot hold true for the obligation to care for the wounded and sick or to detain and treat decently persons deprived of their liberty; or to ensure a fair trial to persons

[142] Pilloud, Sandoz, Swinarski et al, *Commentary on the APs (1987)* (n 57) para 4469. As the ICTR summarized: 'In essence, the operations must be continuous and planned' *Akayesu, ICTR-96-4-T*, para 626.

[143] *Oxford Dictionaries*, online version, definition of 'sustained'.

[144] Sivakumaran, *The Law of Non-International Armed Conflict* (n 7) 188.

[145] See *Boškoski and Tarčulovski, IT-04-82-T*, para 197; Cullen, *The Concept of Non-International Armed Conflict* (n 1) 103–05; Graham, 'Defining Non-International Armed Conflict: A Historically Difficult Task' (2012) 88 International Law Studies Series. US Naval War College 44–55, 43.

[146] For arguments in addition to the interpretation suggested above, see Sivakumaran, *The Law of Non-International Armed Conflict* (n 7) 188; see also Milanovic and Hadzi-Vidanovic, 'A Taxonomy of Armed Conflict' in White and Henderson (eds), *Research Handbook on International Conflict and Security Law: 'Jus ad Bellum', 'Jus in Bello', and 'Jus Post Bellum'* (Edward Elgar 2013) 286.

under prosecution. In these cases, territorial control, even if modest, is indispensible in order to establish the minimum necessary in order to apply these provisions.[147]

Likewise, the 1987 ICRC commentary finds that '[t]he threshold for application therefore seems fairly high', which, in the ICRC's view, respected states' views at the Diplomatic Conference and 'a degree of realism'.[148] Indeed, the negotiators of the Protocol were aware of what one of them called 'a very strange automatism': 'if the Second Protocol is only applicable to those conflicts where the other party is able to implement the Protocol[,] with the increase of protective measures, also the field of application is always narrowed'.[149] The result of such an interpretation has been criticized as a 'dangerous circularity ... confusing the issue of the Protocol's threshold with the contents'.[150]

This interpretation is, however, not the only way to read article 1(1) APII. As pointed out with regard to Common Article 3, the required ability to implement the Protocol can also be read as a general requirement to be able to implement IHL, which generally requires a command structure including some kind of disciplinary system. Thus, while APII contains detailed rules on detention and penal prosecutions, the material ability to implement each and every single one of them should not be a strict condition for the applicability of the Protocol as a whole. It is unlikely that the ICRC expected a sophisticated judicial system when it stated in the 1987 commentary that the article 1(1) threshold requires some 'minimum infrastructure' to implement the Protocol.[151] It would also be difficult to assess this ability at an early stage of the conflict, and any assessment of facts would necessarily be controversial. In addition, in other fields of IHL, such as the law of occupation, determining that a state of occupation exists does not require the occupant to be immediately able to implement the entire body of applicable rules.[152]

A better reading would be that with regard to due process guarantees, APII 'does not require courts to be convened; only that persons are not to be sentenced prior to a fair trial'.[153] It has also been argued that articles 5 and 6 APII only become relevant if the armed group takes prisoners, and that 'if an armed group decides not to detain or intern persons and not to sentence individuals, they will be able to implement the Protocol without exercising any territorial control'.[154] The problem with this approach is, however, that it could mean that an APII conflict would have to be

[147] Momtaz, *Le Droit International Humanitaire* (n 133) 50. Original in French, translation by the author. See also Pilloud, Sandoz, Swinarski et al, *Commentary on the APs (1987)* (n 57) para 2266; Junod, 'Additional Protocol II' (n 90) 37.

[148] Pilloud, Sandoz, Swinarski et al, *Commentary on the APs (1987)* (n 57) para 4470.

[149] Comment by Partsch in Cassese and Eide (eds), *The New Humanitarian Law of Non-International Armed Conflict* (Editoriale Scientifica 1979) 117; Bothe, *New Rules for Victims of Armed Conflicts* (n 109) 716.

[150] Moir, *The Law of Internal Armed Conflict* (n 7) 108.

[151] Pilloud, Sandoz, Swinarski et al, *Commentary on the APs (1987)* (n 57) para 4470.

[152] This is the case if one takes a functional approach to occupation. See Ferraro and ICRC, *Occupation and other Forms of Administraion of Foreign Territory* (ICRC 2012) 18; 24–26.

[153] Sivakumaran, *The Law of Non-International Armed Conflict* (n 7) 186.

[154] ibid.

reclassified once it becomes clear that the organized armed group in question is prosecuting individuals but is unable, or no longer able, to guarantee a fair trial.[155] In that case, conflict classification would vary according to the abilities of an organized armed group at a given moment and its actual conduct. This might be conceivable in theory but would be difficult to implement in practice. As a result, while APII has often been read as requiring the material ability to implement each rule contained in the Protocol, article 1(1) can also be understood as primarily requiring a disciplinary system that allows the implementation of at least all rules which do not require state-like infrastructure, such as courts or schools.

2.2.3 A lower threshold than some have feared

The present discussion shows that the degree of organization required from organized armed groups under APII is not necessarily as high as many have suggested or feared. In all cases, the concept of NIAC—be it under Common Article 3 or APII—necessitates that at least two collective entities engage in armed hostilities of certain intensity. Such encounters must be more than isolated or sporadic acts of violence. Engaging in collective military-like violence requires a command structure, which also enables a party to impose discipline among its troops. A command and disciplinary system ensures the ability to implement fundamental humanitarian rules.

Consequently, it has been suggested that the four requirements listed in article 1(1) APII—namely, the responsible command, some control over territory, the ability to conduct concerted and sustained military operations and to implement the Protocol—do not necessarily contain 'any criteria that are not inherent in a non-international armed conflict' under Common Article 3.[156] Strictly speaking, this conclusion can only be maintained if the territorial control requirement is understood purely as an enabling element, without any value in and of itself; and if the ability to implement the Protocol does not require at all times the capacity to implement each and every rule. It is submitted here that even if article 1(1) APII is understood as containing a strict requirement of territorial control, this does not significantly raise the 'organization' requirement of parties to NIAC; rather, it testifies to the relative strength of the non-state party. Compared with Common Article 3, the requirements of operating under a responsible command and having the ability to carry out sustained and concerted military operations as well as to implement APII appear to raise the threshold of application by some degree. However, they do not introduce entirely new elements in the definition of a party to a NIAC.[157]

[155] Dinstein suggests that conflict classifications under APII may change because 'the competence to implement AP/II may be acquired by insurgent organized armed groups and then lost'. Dinstein, *Non-International Armed Conflicts in International Law* (n 51) 47.

[156] Sivakumaran, *The Law of Non-International Armed Conflict* (n 7) 191.

[157] Similarly, Schmitt pointed out that the definition of NIAC under APII only differs from that under Common Article 3 to the extent that 'dissident or other armed forces control territory and its limitation to conflicts involving a State'. Schmitt, 'Cyber Conflict' (n 52) 250.

Article 1(1) APII can hardly be interpreted as requiring 'basically the same conditions as did the recognition of belligerency'.[158] Most significantly, APII does not require the territorial state to recognize belligerency in order to render the Protocol applicable. In addition, the interpretation that APII applies only 'to those conflicts which have reached the scale and intensity of the classical civil war situation, i.e. where two or more political authorities, with virtually de facto governmental authority ... are engaged in armed conflict' is not supported by the wording, context, and object and purpose of the article.[159] Article 1(1) APII focuses primarily on the capacities of the non-state armed forces directly linked to military operations. It does not reinsert the requirement of political organization, which essentially compared organized armed groups to de facto states.[160] As Lotsteen analysed aptly:

> The substantive distinction lies in the fact that upon attaining the objective criteria of belligerency, the insurgents achieve many of the characteristics of an independent state—they become in effect a *de facto* state. This in turn justifies applying to them and to the conflict in which they are involved the body of rules meant to regulate international armed conflicts. On the other hand, the criteria established in Protocol II, while establishing a threshold that is considerably higher than mere civil unrest, is lower than state-to-state warfare.[161]

2.3 Non-State Parties to Armed Conflicts under the Rome Statute of the International Criminal Court

In 1998, states agreed on two definitions of armed conflicts not of an international character under articles 8(2)(d) and (f) of the Rome Statute of the International Criminal Court (ICC Statute). Unlike the thresholds under Common Article 3 and APII, which define the material scope of application of rules of international humanitarian law, articles 8(2)(d) and (f) ICC Statute define the ICC's jurisdiction over war crimes in NIAC. Yet, under these provisions, war crimes are defined as either serious violations 'of article 3 common to the four Geneva Conventions of 12 August 1949' or of 'the laws and customs applicable in armed conflicts not of an international character'.[162] Hence, the definitions of NIACs and their parties under

[158] Provost, *International Human Rights* (n 43) 264; for a similar view, see also Akande, 'Classification of Armed Conflicts' 54; La Haye, *War Crimes in Internal Armed Conflicts* (n 89) 44; Rwelamira, 'The Significance and Contribution of the Protocol Additional to the Geneva Conventions of August 1949' in Swinarski, Petitpierre, Graber et al (eds), *Etudes et essais sur le droit international humanitaire et sur les principes de la Croix-Rouge en l'honneur de Jean Picte* (ICRC; M Nijhoff 1984) 227–36, 234.

[159] Draper, 'The Development of International Humanitarian Law' in UNESCO and Institut Henry-Dunant (eds), *International Dimensions of Humanitarian Law* (Henry Dunant Institute; UNESCO; M Nijhoff 1988) 84. See also Meron, 'On the Inadequate Reach of Humanitarian and Human Rights Law and the Need for a New Instrument' (n 107) 599.

[160] See also Cullen, *The Concept of Non-International Armed Conflict* (n 1) 106–07; Sivakumaran, *The Law of Non-International Armed Conflict* (n 7) 191.

[161] Lotsteen, 'The Concept of Belligerency in International Law' (2000) 166 Military Law Review 109–41, 130.

[162] Article 8(2)(d) ICC Statute; article 8(2)(f) ICC Statute.

the ICC Statute are intrinsically linked to the respective definitions under IHL, and reflect at least some states' views of when the laws and customs of NIAC apply.[163]

Article 8(2)(c) ICC Statute defines war crimes as serious violations of Common Article 3 and applies 'to armed conflicts not of an international character and thus does not apply to situations of internal disturbances and tensions, such as riots, isolated and sporadic acts of violence or other acts of a similar nature.'[164] This definition incorporates the threshold of application of Common Article 3 into the ICC Statute.[165] Hence, parties to armed conflicts falling under article 8(2)(c) ICC Statute need to meet the same threshold as parties to Common Article 3 conflicts.

According to article 8(2)(f) ICC Statute, war crimes listed in article 8(2)(e) can be committed in

> armed conflicts that take place in the territory of a State when there is *protracted armed conflict* between governmental authorities and organized armed groups or between such groups [emphasis added].

Whether this definition refers to armed conflicts similar to the ones defined in article 8(2)(d) or sets out a new threshold is unclear, including the question of whether the capacity of armed groups to meet the article 8(2)(f) threshold is similar to that required under article 8(2)(d), meaning the Common Article 3 threshold. Two issues must be addressed: one, does the term 'organized armed group' under article 8(2)(f) refer to a specific type of non-state entity, such as those defined under article 1(1) APII; and two, does a material difference between articles 8(2)(d) and (f) exist, which would implicate the requisite degree of organization for armed groups to become parties to such conflicts.

2.3.1 'Organized armed groups'

Examining the meaning of the term 'organized armed group' under article 8(2)(f), one commentator suggested that '[t]he term "organized armed group" is defined in Protocol II; it is required that they be "under responsible command and exercise such control over a part of (the) territories to enable them to carry out sustained and concerted military operations" and to abide by the applicable rules'.[166] Indeed, APII contains the term 'organized armed group' and assigns this term a particular meaning. In contrast, the ordinary meaning of this term only requires a collective entity that is sufficiently organized and armed to be able to engage in military-type violence and to implement the applicable rules.[167] The meaning of the term is not

[163] This does not, however, preclude definitions of war crimes from containing jurisdictional limitations that restrict the scope of an armed conflict more than IHL does.

[164] Article 8(2)(d) ICC Statute.

[165] While the negative reference to 'situations of internal disturbances and tensions' is drawn from APII, the exclusion of such situations from the scope of armed conflicts is also implicit in Common Article 3. See Section 2.1.1.1 'Basic agreement on what does not constitute an armed conflict'. See also Schabas, *The International Criminal Court: A Commentary on the Rome Statute* (OUP 2010) 204.

[166] Bothe, 'War Crimes' in Cassese, Gaeta, and Jones (eds), *The Rome Statute of the International Criminal Court: A Commentary* (OUP 2002) 379–425, 423.

[167] See Section 2.2.1 'Armed conflicts between organized armed forces'.

necessarily tied to the threshold defined in article 1(1) APII. Rather, the exact degree of organization required from an organized armed group must be understood in the context of the treaty in which the term is used.

This interpretation is supported by the drafting history of the ICC Statute. During the last days of the 1998 Rome Conference, states discussed a proposal containing a definition of NIACs that was essentially oriented towards article 1(1) APII, including its definition of 'organized armed groups'.[168] This so-called 'Bureau Proposal' received criticism from different states,[169] and the ICRC cautioned:

> The reality is that more and more States are confronted with non-international armed conflicts taking place on their territory involving a number of dissident armed groups fighting against one another, or armed groups fighting against the established Government which either *does not control part of the territory or does not have a proper chain of command.* These types of non-international armed conflicts must also fall under the jurisdiction of the Court.[170]

In the end, states abandoned the APII threshold and agreed on what became article 8(2)(f). The difference between APII and article 8(2)(f) ICC Statute was also recognized in the ICC's first judgment in the *Lubanga* case. Trial Chamber I clarified that article 8(2)(f) 'does not include the requirement in Additional Protocol II that the armed groups need to "exercise such control over a part of [the] territory as to enable them to carry out sustained and concerted military operations"' or operate under a responsible command as defined under APII.[171]

2.3.2 Protracted armed conflicts under article 8(2)(f) ICC Statute

Article 8(2)(f) ICC Statute incorporates almost verbatim the definition of armed conflict under customary international law as crystallized in the '*Tadić* formula' by the International Criminal Tribunal for the former Yugoslavia (ICTY) three years before the Rome Conference.[172] The *Tadić* formula is widely understood as defining the threshold of application of Common Article 3.[173] If article 8(2)(f) contained

[168] See United Nations Diplomatic Conference of Plenipotentiaries on the Establishment of an International Criminal Court, Committee of the Whole—Bureau Proposal (10 July 1998) 7.

[169] See, eg, United Nations, *Official Records of the United Nations Diplomatic Conference of Plenipotentiaries on the Establishment of an International Criminal Court (Vols I–III)* 2002, A/CONF.183/13, 321 (Vol II) (Austria speaking on behalf of the EU); 333 (Vol II) (Sudan); 338 (Vol II) (Finland); 340 (Vol II) (Lithuania); 342 (Vol II) (Romania).

[170] United Nations Diplomatic Conference of Plenipotentiaries on the Establishment of an International Criminal Court, *Information Conveyed by New Zealand—International Committee of the Red Cross: Concerns on Threshold for War Crimes Committed in Non-International Armed Conflicts as Contained in Bureau Proposal* 13 July 1998, A/CONF.183/INF/11 (emphasis added).

[171] *Lubanga Dyilo, Judgment, 14 March 2012, Trial Chamber, ICC-01/04-01/06*, ICC, para 536. See also Dörmann, *Elements of War Crimes under the Rome Statute of the International Criminal Court: Sources and Commentary* (repr, CUP 2004) 386–87.

[172] The *Tadić* formula will be discussed in further detail in Section 3.1 'Broad Criteria for Assessing the Degree of Organization of a Non-State Party to an Armed Conflict'.

[173] See, eg, Pejic, 'The Protective Scope of Common Article 3: More Than Meets the Eye' (2011) 93 International Review of the Red Cross 189–225, 192; Kress, 'The 1999 Crisis in East Timor and the Threshold of the Law on War Crimes' (2002) 13 *Criminal Law Forum* 409–70, 415. The view that the *Tadić* formula defined the lower threshold of Common Article 3 was also held by some states. See United Nations General Assembly (UNGA), *Report of the Ad Hoc Committee on the Establishment of an*

the *Tadić* formula, its threshold would be similar to that of Common Article 3 as contained in article 8(2)(d). However, the formulation inserted in article 8(2)(f) contains one arguably important difference: whereas the *Tadić* formula defines armed conflicts as '*protracted armed violence* between governmental authorities and organized armed groups or between such groups', article 8(2)(f) ICC Statute applies to '*protracted armed conflict* between governmental authorities and organized armed groups or between such groups'.[174] If this slightly different wording signified a material difference between the two thresholds, a contextual interpretation of the term 'organized armed group' could suggest that, under article 8(2)(f), a group would need to be able to engage not only in 'protracted armed violence' but in 'protracted armed conflict'.

The drafting history does not help in determining whether states intended to introduce under article 8(2)(f) a threshold different from that under article 8(2)(d), or 'whether it was simply poor drafting'.[175] The wording of article 8(2)(f) was suggested at the last minute by the Sierra Leonean delegation, and little discussion on the exact formulation is recorded.[176] Taken literally, the 'protracted armed conflict' requirement appears to introduce an explicit element of duration, which would make the article 8(2)(f) threshold slightly higher than that of Common Article 3.[177] Nonetheless, a majority of scholars has argued that the two NIAC thresholds under the ICC Statute should be considered similar.[178] The following reasons were provided: the Sierra Leonean delegation did not intend to introduce a new threshold;[179] the French versions of the *Tadić* formula and article 8(2)(f) are similar;[180] both definitions refer to 'armed conflicts not of an international character', a term that

International Criminal Court, 1995, A/50/22, para 74. This was also recognized in case law—for example, *Tadić, Judgment, 7 May 1997, IT-94-1-T*, ICTY, para 562; *Limaj et al, Judgment, 30 November 2005, IT-03-66-T*, ICTY, para 84.

[174] See *Tadić, Decision on the defence motion for interluctory appeal on jurisdiction, 02 October 1995, Appeals Chamber*, ICTY, para 70 (emphasis added).

[175] Sivakumaran, *The Law of Non-International Armed Conflict* (n 7) 192.

[176] Official Records of the United Nations Diplomatic Conference of Plenipotentiaries on the Establishment of an International Criminal Court (n 169) (Vol II) (Sierra Leone). For in-depth analysis of the drafting history of the provision, see Cullen, 'The Definition of Non-International Armed Conflict in the Rome Statute of the International Criminal Court: An Analysis of the Threshold of Application Contained in Article 8(2)(f)' (2007) 12 Journal of Conflict and Security Law 419–45; Sivakumaran, 'Identifying an Armed Conflict not of an International Character' in Sluiter and Stahn (eds), *The Emerging Practice of the International Criminal Court* (Brill 2009) 361–80.

[177] See, eg, Bothe, 'War Crimes' (n 166) 423. As shall be seen below, in accordance with the ICC Statute's wording, the Court has repeatedly examined whether the NIAC in question was 'protracted'.

[178] Meron, 'The Humanization of Humanitarian Law' (2000) 94 American Journal of International Law 239–78, 260; Spieker, 'The International Criminal Court and Non-International Armed Conflicts' (2000) 13 Leiden Journal of International Law 395–425, 407; Kress, 'War Crimes Committed in Non-International Armed Conflict and the Emerging System of International Criminal Justice' (2001) 30 Israel Yearbook on Human Rights 103, 118; Cullen, 'The Definition of NIAC' (n 1) 419; Sivakumaran, 'Identifying an Armed Conflict not of an International Character' (n 176) 377; Werle and Burghardt, *Principles of International Criminal Law* (2nd edn, TMC Asser Press 2009) 289. See also *Limaj et al, IT-03-66-T*, para 87.

[179] See Sivakumaran, 'Identifying An Armed Conflict' (n 176) 374; Cullen, 'The Definition of NIAC' (n 1) 445.

[180] See Kress, 'The 1999 Crisis in East Timor' (n 173) 419; Sivakumaran, *The Law of Non-International Armed Conflict* (n 7) 194. However, this argument loses some significance due to the fact

is intrinsically linked to Common Article 3;[181] and different thresholds would not contribute to legal clarity and should be avoided.[182] In addition, from a practical point of view, the war crimes under article 8(2)(f) do not necessitate a higher threshold of application than the ones listed in article 8(2)(c).

In their first judgments, ICC Trial Chambers found that 'Article 8(2)(f) of the Statute ... requires the existence of a "protracted" conflict between "organized armed groups" '.[183] In these cases, the protracted nature of the conflicts was uncontroversial.[184] The Trial Chambers held, however, that due to the 'protracted armed conflict' requirement under article 8(2)(f) organized armed groups 'must have a sufficient degree of organisation, in order to enable them to carry out protracted armed violence'.[185] Similarly, Pre-Trial Chamber I argued that article 8(2)(f) 'focuses on the need of the armed group in question to have the ability to plan and carry out military operations for a prolonged period of time'.[186] Accordingly, when establishing whether the different armed groups in the *Lubanga* case were parties to an armed conflict, the Court emphasized each group's ability to engage in 'prolonged hostilities' or to carry out 'sustained military operations'.[187]

As a result, irrespective of whether article 8(2)(f) ICC Statute contains a duration requirement that is not contained in article 8(2)(d), different Trial Chambers found that organized armed groups under article 8(2)(f) must be sufficiently organized to engage in protracted armed violence or conflict. However, they did not provide a general definition of when an armed conflict is protracted. The chambers focused on the ability of the groups to engage in sustained military operations, or protracted hostilities.[188] This could be regarded as a criterion deriving primarily from the 'protracted armed conflict' requirement under article 8(2)(f) ICC Statute. Yet, the idea that all parties to an armed conflict must be able to engage in armed violence going beyond 'isolated or sporadic acts of violence' is implicit in any armed conflict.[189] An armed group would hardly qualify

that the original language of both the *Tadić* judgment and the proposal of Sierra Leone was English, and here the different wording is clear.

[181] See Cullen, 'The Definition of NIAC' (n 1) 440–42.

[182] See Sivakumaran, *The Law of Non-International Armed Conflict* (n 176) 475.

[183] *Lubanga Dyilo, ICC-01/04-01/06*, para 536; *Katanga, ICC-01/04-01/07*, para 1185. See also *Bemba, Decision Pursuant to Article 61(7)(a) and (b) of the Rome Statute on the Charges of the Prosecutor Against Jean-Pierre Bemba Gombo, 15 June 2009, Pre-Trial Chamber II, ICC-01/05-01/08*, ICC, para 235.

[184] In the *Lubanga* case, the ICC established that an armed conflict existed between September 2002 and August 2003. *Lubanga Dyilo, ICC-01/04-01/06*, para 567.

[185] ibid para 536 (emphasis added); *Katanga, ICC-01/04-01/07*, para 1185. It is unclear why the Chamber used the term protracted armed 'violence' instead of 'conflict', especially because the French versions of both judgments use the term 'conflit armé prolongé'.

[186] *Lubanga Dyilo, Decision on the Confirmation of Charges, 29 January 2007, Pre-Trial Chamber I, ICC-01/04-01/06*, ICC, para 234 (emphasis added). See also *Al Bashir, Decision on the Prosecution's Application for a Warrant of Arrest against Omar Hassan Ahmad Al Bashir, 4 March 2009, Pre-Trial Chamber I, ICC-02/05-01/09*, ICC, 60.

[187] *Lubanga Dyilo, ICC-01/04-01/06*, paras 543–46; see also *Bemba Gombo, ICC-01/05-01/08*, para 134.

[188] As Sivakumaran pointed out, these are requirements similar to the ones used by the ICTY in applying the *Tadić* formula. See Sivakumaran, 'Identifying An Armed Conflict' (n 176) 379–80.

[189] See the travaux préparatoires of Common Article 3 as discussed in Section 2.1 'The Notion "Party to the Conflict" under Common Article 3'; article 1(2) APII, and article 8(2)(d) and (f) ICC Statute.

as a party to any armed conflict if it had the capacity to conduct only one military operation, or a short series of isolated strikes. Moreover, in the *Lubanga* and *Katanga* judgments, the Trial Chambers were not clear whether article 8(2)(f) requires the ability to engage in 'protracted armed violence' (English versions), or in 'conflits armés prolongés' (French versions). However, both language versions refer to a similar standard as the *Tadić* formula in the respective language, suggesting that the same requirements apply under article 8(2)(d) and (f).

3

Organized Armed Groups in Contemporary International Practice

In what has been described as a 'seminal declaration'[1] and the 'most authoritative'[2] definition of armed conflicts falling under Common Article 3, the International Criminal Tribunal for the former Yugoslavia (ICTY) Appeals Chamber found in the *Tadić* case in 1995 that, under customary international humanitarian law (IHL),

> [a]n armed conflict exists whenever there is a resort to armed force between States or protracted armed violence between governmental authorities and organized armed groups or between such groups within a State.[3]

Shortly after, the ICTY clarified that based on the *Tadić* formula, two cumulative criteria determine the existence of a non-international armed conflict (NIAC): violence must be sufficiently intense and the parties to the conflict sufficiently organized.[4] The *Tadić* formula and its two criteria have been taken up by subsequent jurisprudence of the ICTY and other tribunals, by different international expert commissions, and states included the *Tadić* formula almost verbatim in the Rome Statute of the International Criminal Court (ICC Statute).[5] It is safe to conclude that this definition of a NIAC reflects customary international law.[6]

[1] Schabas, 'The International Criminal Court' 202.

[2] Dinstein, 'Concluding Remarks on Non-International Armed Conflicts' (2012) 88 International Law Studies 404. Sivakumaran calls it 'widely known and authoritative'; Sivakumaran, *The Law of Non-International Armed Conflict* (OUP 2012) 155.

[3] *Tadić*, para 70.

[4] See *Tadić, IT-94-1-T*, para 562. This two-pronged test has been applied by many ICTY chambers since. See, eg, *Haradinaj et al, Judgment, 3 April 2008, IT-04-84-T, Hamdan v Rumsfeld*, para 49.

[5] See Section 2.3 'Non-State Parties to Armed Conflicts under the Rome Statute of the International Criminal Court'. For accurate summaries of the extent to which the *Tadić* formula was accepted in international practice, see Moir, 'The Concept of Non-International Armed Conflict' in Clapham, Gaeta, and Sassòli (eds), *The 1949 Geneva Conventions: A Commentary* (OUP 2015) paras 7–11; Cullen, *The Concept of Non-International Armed Conflict in International Humanitarian Law* (CUP 2010) 120–22.

[6] The *Tadić* formula is today included in numerous national military manuals as the definition of non-international armed conflicts. See, eg, military handbooks of Australia, Canada, Germany, the Netherlands, Peru, or the United Kingdom (documents on file with the author). The view that this formula represents customary international law is also shared by commentators, see Bothe, 'War Crimes' in Cassese, Gaeta, and Jones (eds), *The Rome Statute of the International Criminal Court: A Commentary* (OUP 2002) 423; Cullen, *The Concept of Non-International Armed Conflict* (n 5) 122; Sivakumaran, *The Law of Non-International Armed Conflict* (n 2) 155; Akande, 'Classification of Armed Conflicts: Relevant Legal Concepts' in Wilmshurst (ed), *International Law and the Classification of Conflicts* (OUP 2012) 51; Milanovic and Hadzi-Vidanovic, 'A Taxonomy of Armed Conflict' in White

The broad acceptance of the *Tadić* formula is, however, also due to its broad and innocuous formulation. Explicitly, the *Tadić* formula contains none of the 'convenient criteria' suggested in the 1952 ICRC commentary on Common Article 3, nor any other criteria inherent in Common Article 3 or listed in article 1(1) of the Protocol Additional to the Geneva Conventions of 12 August 1949, and relating to the Protection of Victims of Non-International Armed Conflicts (Protocol II) (APII).[7] Read in isolation, its wording makes it difficult 'to pinpoint precisely the necessary minimum requirements of organization to be met'.[8] This is aggravated by the fact that structures of armed groups vary widely, which makes it doubtful whether a 'one size fits all' definition of the requisite degree of organization can be found.[9] Accordingly, rather loose interpretations of the degree of organization of non-state armed groups were suggested in case law, requiring armed groups to be 'organized to a greater or lesser degree',[10] to have 'some degree of organization',[11] or to be 'relatively organized'.[12]

Based on these broad definitions, some commentators concluded that 'the necessary degree of organization must not be exaggerated'.[13] Others argued that because some characteristics are not explicitly included in the *Tadić* formula, such as the ability 'to control territory, or to have an organized command in order to implement IHL obligations', they are not required under IHL.[14] These suggestions are convincing in terms of distinguishing the definition required by the *Tadić* formula from the criteria listed in APII. At the same time, the 'organization requirement' should not be downplayed too much. A close examination of international jurisprudence and expert opinions shows that a sufficient degree of organization of armed groups is a strict but often controversial condition for conflict classification, which does require certain capabilities on behalf of the armed group in question. Thus, while it seems

and Henderson (eds), *Research Handbook on International Conflict and Security Law: 'Jus ad Bellum', 'Jus in Bello', and 'Jus Post Bellum'* (Edward Elgar 2013) 283.

[7] See Sections 2.1.2 'Non-state parties falling under Common Article 3' and 2.2.2 'The explicit requirements of Additional Protocol II'.

[8] Kress, 'The 1999 Crisis in East Timor and the Threshold of the Law on War Crimes' (2003) 13 Criminal Law Forum 416.

[9] Different structures or armed groups are further discussed in Section 2.1.2 'Non-state parties falling under Common Article 3'.

[10] *Musema, Judgment, 27 January 2000, Trial Chamber, ICTR-96-13-T*, ICTR, para 248. This seems to be based on an expert view submitted by the International Committee of the Red Cross (ICRC) to the ad hoc tribunals, which stated that 'the term "armed conflict" presupposes the existence of hostilities between armed forces *organised to a greater or lesser extent*'. *Limaj et al, IT-03-66-T*, para 89.

[11] *Limaj et al, IT-03-66-T*, para 89; *Mrkšić et al, Judgment, 5 May 2009, Appeals Chamber, IT-95-13/1-T*, ICTY, para 407.

[12] *Juan Carlos Abella, Decision, 13 April 1998, OEA/Ser.L/V/II.98*, IAComHR, para 152.

[13] Kress, 'The 1999 Crisis in East Timor' (n 8) 416.

[14] Bianchi and Naqvi, 'IHL and Terrorism' 111. Similarly, the final report on the meaning of armed conflict by the International Law Association's Committee on the Use of Force suggested: 'The *Tadić* formulation has no requirement that armed groups … be capable of meeting IHL obligations'. International Law Association (ILA), *Final Report on the Meaning of Armed Conflict in International Law* (ILA 2010) 15. Such a loose interpretation has been adopted by the scholar Boelaert-Suominen, see Boelaert-Suominen, 'Commentary: The Yugoslavia Tribunal and the Common Core of Humanitarian Law Applicable to all Armed Conflicts' (2000) 13 Leiden Journal of International Law 619–53, 634. For a different view supporting the opinion of this author, see Moir, *The Law of Internal Armed Conflict* (CUP 2002) 42.

'universally accepted that a certain level of organization is required on the part of insurgents in order for a NIAC to exist',[15] interpretations of the meaning of 'being organized' differ.

In the following, three broad criteria are identified from international treaty law and practice to determine the requisite degree of organization of non-state parties to NIACs. Non-state parties to NIACs should be a) a collective entity with a certain command structure; b) able to implement basic humanitarian norms; and c) capable of engaging in sufficiently intense violence with their adversary. This chapter also examines under what conditions transnational groups or cyber groups could qualify as parties to a NIAC.

3.1 Broad Criteria for Assessing the Degree of Organization of a Non-State Party to an Armed Conflict

Left with the requirement that non-state parties to an armed conflict must be 'organized armed groups', international tribunals had to narrow down the meaning of being organized. As a first step, ICTY Trial Chambers clarified that organized armed groups 'do not necessarily need to be as organized as the armed forces of a State'.[16] Second, while in an early judgment one chamber found that '[f]actors relevant for this determination' are found in the 1952 ICRC commentary on Common Article 3,[17] the ICTY later emphasized that these criteria are 'neither definitive nor exhaustive'.[18] The tribunal highlighted correctly that the fact that none of these conditions was agreed upon in 1949 'provides a clear indication that no such explicit requirements for the application of Common Article 3 were intended by the drafters of the Geneva Conventions'.[19] Third, the Yugoslavia Tribunal disagreed with the argument that any party to an NIAC needs to meet the requirements listed in article 1(1) APII, emphasizing that 'Additional Protocol II requires a higher standard than Common Article 3'.[20]

Instead, different tribunals—and international practice more widely—examine two explicit questions and one implicit question when establishing the degree of organization of a non-state party to a NIAC: on the one hand, whether the group has the capacity to engage in military-like violence and, on the other hand, whether it is

[15] Moir, *The Concept of Non-International Armed Conflict* (n 5) para 35. See also ILA, *Armed Conflict (Final Report)* (n 14) 28–29. The study presents ample evidence showing that NIAC must involve organized armed groups, meaning that '[v]iolence perpetrated by the assassin or terrorist acting essentially alone or the disorganized mob violence of a riot is not armed conflict'.

[16] *Orić, Judgment, 30 June 2006, IT-03-68-T*, ICTY, para 254; *Boškoski and Tarčulovski, IT-04-82-T*, para 197.

[17] *Tadić, IT-94-1-T*, para 562.

[18] *Milošević, IT-02-54-T*, para 19.

[19] See *Limaj et al, IT-03-66-T*, para 86. For a more detailed argument on this question, see Section 2.1.1 'Basic agreement on what does not constitute an armed conflict'.

[20] See *Limaj et al*, para 89; *Boškoski and Tarčulovski, IT-04-82-T*, paras 196–97. See also *Lubanga Dyilo, ICC-01/04-01/06*, paras 535–36. The Trial Chamber made clear, however, that article 8(2)(f) APII 'does not include the requirement in Additional Protocol II that the armed groups need to "exercise such control over a part of [the] territory as to enable them to carry out sustained and concerted military operations"' or the requirement that the organized armed groups were 'under responsible command'.

able to implement basic rules of IHL. Necessarily, this analysis presupposes that the group in question is a collective entity, meaning that it is more than a loose collection of individuals. The crystallization of these criteria and their application in practice is examined in this section.

3.1.1 The crystallization of broad criteria

In accordance with IHL treaty law, international tribunals took a factual approach to determining the existence of an armed conflict, arguing that the criteria of intensity and organization distinguish 'an armed conflict from banditry, unorganized and short-lived insurrections, or terrorist activities, which are not subject to international humanitarian law'.[21] Considering in general terms what the notion of organization signifies, different chambers suggested two broad rationales. The first one focuses primarily on an armed group's ability to engage in armed violence. As the ICTY argued in the 2008 *Haradinaj et al* judgment, all parties to an armed conflict must be 'sufficiently organized to confront each other with military means'.[22] Similarly, the ICC's Pre-Trial Chamber I and Trial Chamber I in the *Lubanga* case, and Trial Chamber III in the *Bemba* case, argued that an organized armed group under the ICC Statute must 'have a sufficient degree of organisation, in order to enable them to carry out protracted armed violence'.[23]

The second approach concentrates not only on the group's military capacities—which is normally also evident from the intensity criterion—but also on the group's ability to implement fundamental humanitarian norms. In some cases, the ICTY emphasized that 'leadership of the group must, as a minimum, have the ability to exercise some control over its members so that the basic obligations of Common Article 3 of the Geneva Conventions may be implemented'.[24] While some scholars claim that in the *Limaj et al* case the ICTY 'rejected the argument that in order to be bound by IHL a party must be able to implement IHL',[25] it is difficult to find such an explicit dismissal in the judgment.[26] For its part, the International Criminal

[21] *Tadić, IT-94-1-T*, para 562. This approach was confirmed in different cases of the ICTY (see, eg, *Haradinaj et al, IT-04-84-T*, para 38), the ICTR (see, eg, *Rutaganda, Judgment, 6 December 1999, ICTR-96-3-T*, ICTR, para 92) and has been included in the Rome Statute (see Art 8 (2) lit d and f).

[22] *Haradinaj et al, IT-04-84-T*, para 60.

[23] *Lubanga Dyilo, ICC-01/04-01/06*, para 536. *Bemba Gombo, ICC-01/05-01/08*, para 134. Contrary to Trial Chamber II, Trial Chamber III considered the ability to impose discipline an indicative factor only and not a strict criterion.

[24] *Boškoski and Tarčulovski, IT-04-82-T*, para 196; *Đorđević, Judgment, 23 February 2011, Trial Chamber, IT-05-87/1-T*, ICTY, para 1125; *Haradinaj et al, Judgment, 29 November 2012, Trial Chamber, IT-04-84bis-T*, ICTY, para 393.

[25] ILA, *Armed Conflict (Final Report)* (n 14) 20; see also Sivakumaran, *The Law of Non-International Armed Conflict* (n 2) 178–79.

[26] While in para 89 the Chamber states that it does not share the view of the Defence as presented in para 88, it is not clear whether this finding refers to all the Defence's arguments, or, as this author believes, only to the Defence's invocation of APII. Apparently questioning its finding quoted above, in the concluding section the ILA study finds, with regard to the requisite degree of organization in ICTY jurisprudence: 'The underlying theme is that there must be a sufficient level of organisation through a command structure in order for the basic requirements of Common Article 3 to the 1949 Geneva Conventions to be implemented'. ILA, *Armed Conflicts (Final Report)* (n 14) 29.

Tribunal for Rwanda (ICTR) suggested that the requisite 'degree of organisation should be such so as to enable the armed group or dissident forces to plan and carry out concerted military operations, and to impose discipline'.[27] Similarly, the ICC's Pre-Trial Chamber II stressed that armed groups may only become party to an NIAC if they had 'a hierarchical structure which allowed them to act under a responsible command with operational and disciplinary powers'.[28] While dismissing the requirement of a 'responsible command as envisioned by Additional Protocol II',[29] ICC Trial Chamber II similarly emphasized that 'organized armed groups' under the ICC Statute must have a sufficient degree of organization not only to be able to engage in a protracted armed conflict but also 'to be able to implement rules of international humanitarian law applicable' in non-international armed conflicts.[30]

3.1.2 Balancing the broad criteria in practice

The two approaches suggest different interpretations of the notion 'organized armed group'. Under the first approach, the criterion of being organized is understood primarily in terms of the interplay between it and the intensity criterion: armed groups need to be sufficiently organized to engage in intense armed violence. In contrast, the second approach proposes that being organized serves an additional purpose—namely, the ability to implement basic humanitarian obligations. Focusing primarily on the military abilities of the group in question will normally simplify the analysis. A group's ability to engage in protracted armed violence is evident from its operations. Thus, actors with an interest to classify a situation as an armed conflict—for example to justify using force in accordance with an IHL-based 'conduct of hostilities' paradigm and not following an IHRL-based 'law enforcement' paradigm, or in order to prosecute alleged crimes as war crimes—may opt for focusing on the ability to engage in intense violence and less on the internal organization of the armed group.

In contrast, focusing not only on a group's ability to engage in armed violence but also on its internal structures can make classification more demanding. Although the requirement of disposing of a sufficient degree of internal organization to impose discipline and implement basic humanitarian obligations is not particularly high, it is often difficult to determine the internal command structure of non-state armed groups.[31] Such groups may not be established through formal acts and may operate underground, or in remote areas.[32] Normally faced with a militarily superior

[27] *Akayesu, ICTR-96-4-T*, para 626.

[28] *Ntaganda, Decision on the Prosecutor's Application under Article 58, 13 July 2012, Pre-Trial Chamber II, ICC-01/04-02/06*, ICC, para 49.

[29] *Katanga, ICC-01/04-01/07*, para 1186.

[30] ibid para 1185.

[31] On the neccessary capabilities to implement Common Article 3, see section 2.1.2.2 'The ability to comply with basic humanitarian rules'.

[32] See, eg, United Nations (UN) High Commissioner for Human Rights, Democratic Republic of the Congo, 1993–2003: Report of the Mapping Exercise documenting the most serious violations of human rights and international humanitarian law committed within the territory of the Democratic Republic ofthe Congo between March 1993 and June 2003 (2010) para 476; UN Secretary General,

adversary, armed groups also have an interest in keeping their structure and communication secret to protect their operations.[33]

In addition to the cases discussed above, the approach of focusing more on the ability to engage in intense violence than on the ability to implement basic rules of IHL, received some support in recent non-judicial practice, in which a sufficient degree of organization seems to have been inferred from the intensity of violence.[34] Some commentators have taken this approach one step further, arguing that the organization requirement is not important at all:

> The situation should be deemed to be an 'armed conflict' if governmental forces in combating the armed violence apply means and methods incompatible with the right to life, as laid down in fundamental Human Rights instruments, as their *modus operandi.* We also believe that it is of minor importance whether armed groups are 'organized' or not if they are able to conduct armed resistance to such a degree that governmental forces must use military means and methods to achieve their aims.[35]

In a more nuanced manner, others argued that in certain situations 'the best proof of OAG [organized armed group] is in the operational details of violence that members of the group have caused' because their 'sheer ability to mount sustained terrorist attacks is evidence of a "high level of planning and a coordinated command structure"'.[36] Going in a similar direction, it has also been suggested that the

Report of the International Commission of Inquiry on Darfur to the United Nations Secretary-General (2005) paras 127–41.

[33] eg with regard to the Kosovo Liberation Army (KLA), the ICTY found that the 'KLA was effectively an underground organisation, operating in conditions of secrecy out of concern to preserve its leadership, and under constant threat of military action by the Serbian forces. .... In these circumstances it is of no surprise that the organisational structure and the hierarchy of the KLA were confusing, or not known, to outside observers, and that, to some, this suggested a state of confusion'. *Limaj et al, IT-03-66-T,* para 132. The need to keep organizational structures secret has also been emphasized in discussions between the author and armed groups.

[34] eg the Commissions of Inquiry on Darfur found that armed conflicts existed because non-state groups engaged in military-like violence and despite the fact that 'little is known' about the structure of the groups. UN Secretary General, 'Report of the International Commission of Inquiry on Darfur' (n 32) para 131. Similarly, the International Commission of Inquiry of Libya classified the situation under examination as a NIAC despite the explicit finding 'that command structures within the armed opposition forces have been unclear'. Human Rights Council, *Report of the International Commission of Inquiry to investigate all alleged violations of international human rights law in the Libyan Arab Jamahiriya,* 1 June 2011, A/HRC/17/44, para 57. A report on an Expert Meeting at Chatham House concluded that while the Libyan opposition did not have a 'command structure', owing to its important military capabilities the situation amounted to an NIAC. Arimatsu and Choudhury, *The Legal Classification of the Armed Conflicts in Syria, Yemen and Libya* (Chatham House 2014) 38. Similarly, while it seemed difficult to determine the internal structure of armed groups in Syria, the Syria Commission of Inquiry nonetheless classified the situation as an NIAC. See Human Rights Council, *Report of the Independent International Commission of Inquiry on the Syrian Arab Republic,* 15 August 2012, A/HRC/21/50, Annex III. Greater emphasis on a group's ability to engage in combat or other military operations than on its internal command structure can also be seen in the *Abella* case before the IAComHR, *Juan Carlos Abella, OEA/Ser.L/V/II.98,* para 152.

[35] Dahl and Sandbu, 'The Threshold of Armed Conflict' (2006) 45 Military Law and Law of War Review 369–88, 376. For another criticism of the application of the two criteria of 'intensity' and 'organization', see Blank and Corn, 'Losing the Forest for the Trees: Syria, Law, and the Pragmatics of Conflict Recognition' (2013) 46 Vanderbilt Journal of Transnational Law 693–746.

[36] Margulies and Sinnot, 'Crossing Borders to Target Al-Qaeda and Its Affiliates: Defining Networks as Organized Armed Groups in Non-International Armed Conflicts' 16 Yearbook of International

organization requirement would be met if the non-state group is '"armed" to the extent that they have the *capacity* to mount attacks'.[37] In light of the practical difficulties of proving the degree of organization of armed groups, some have cautioned that looking strictly at whether both the organization and the intensity requirement are fulfilled risks 'not seeing the forest for the trees' because too much weight is given to 'technical legalities'.[38] Instead, they suggest that in order to classify a situation as an NIAC, the 'totality of the circumstances' need to be taken into account.[39] Accordingly, it is argued that if the intensity criterion is overwhelmingly satisfied, the organization criterion can to some extent be offset: 'a situation of intense hostilities without significant opposition force organization indicates the exact type of heavy-handed government military response that necessitates humanitarian regulation'.[40] According to that view, reliance on the organizational requirement may even provoke indiscriminate government violence in order to prevent the non-state forces from organizing and to avoid the application of IHL.[41]

The proposal of looking at the intensity and organization requirements together has important merit and is—to some extent—taken up below. At the same time, some of the above views need to be considered with caution. Generally, it is dangerous to argue that armed conflicts exist if a government decides to apply means incompatible with the right to life under human rights law. In practice, this leaves it to the government's discretion which legal regime to apply in a given situation. Granting states larger discretion to use force according to a conduct of hostilities paradigm instead of a law enforcement one as applicable outside armed conflicts might not mitigate violence and suffering.[42] Under international law, a 'heavy-handed government response' to sporadic violence or poorly organized armed elements falls into the category of severe human rights violations, or crimes against humanity, rather than into that of potentially lawful acts of war. Likewise, a single attack by non-state actors may amount to an international crime, or violate human rights law. In contrast, being a party to an armed conflict governed by IHL is not only about applying armed force.[43]

Humanitarian Law 2013 (2015) 319–45, 326. Going in the same direction, Blank and Corn argue: 'Widespread and intense hostilities would offset the requirement to identify significant opposition organization. While some evidence of organization would be necessary, dispersed and nascent movements would satisfy that requirement in the context of such intensity.' Blank and Corn, 'Losing the Forest' (n 35) 741–42.

[37] Arimatsu and Choudhury, *Legal Classification* (n 34) 4 and 18. In fact, the Chatham House report questions whether the requirement that an armed group has a 'command and control structure' is 'appropriate' in situations such as Syria or Libya. For another approach focusing primarily on the intensity of violence, see Arnold, *The ICC as a New Instrument for Repressing Terrorism* (Transnational Publishers 2004).

[38] Blank and Corn, 'Losing the Forest' (n 35) 746. [39] ibid.

[40] ibid 740–41. [41] ibid.

[42] As Garraway puts it, the purpose of such proposals 'is not so much to increase protection but to widen the authority for armed forces to use lethal force'. Garraway, 'Armed Conflicts and Terrorist Organizations' in Herik and Schrijver (eds), *Counter-terrorism Strategies in a Fragmented International Legal Order: Meeting the Challenges* (CUP 2015) 425–32, 443.

[43] See earlier discussion on Common Article 3 in Section 2.1 'The Notion "Party to the Conflict" under Common Article 3'. As Schindler put it, in order to qualify an armed group as party to a NIAC,

Unlike large-scale human rights violations or crimes against humanity, an armed conflict requires two conflicting parties, which have the capacity to engage in armed violence and to respect fundamental humanitarian norms.[44] As the ICRC argued:

> The very logic underlying IHL requires identifiable parties in the above sense [i.e. having a certain level of organization, command structure and, therefore, the ability to implement international humanitarian law] because this body of law—while not affecting the parties' legal status—establishes equality of rights and obligations among them under IHL (not domestic law) when they are at war. The parties' IHL rights and obligations are provided for so that both sides know the rules within which they are allowed to operate and so that they are able to rely on similar conduct by the other side.[45]

Indeed, while the applicability of the laws of war does not depend on reciprocity, imposing obligations on all parties to a conflict if one group cannot implement any rules fails at least halfway.[46] It would also be contrary to the principle of equality of belligerents because although both parties would have obligations, one would effectively be unable to fulfil any.[47] Moreover, some argue that if IHL becomes applicable, it recognizes an 'inherent power to intern' or 'provides a legal basis for internment'.[48] If that view is taken, or if it is agreed that IHL provides more permissive rules on the use of force by all parties to the conflict than human rights law, these permissive aspects of the law should not come into force if the conflicting parties cannot also comply with restrictions IHL imposes on internment or the use of force.

If the primary purpose of IHL is to protect victims of armed conflicts, it seems that '[o]rganization for the purposes of the enforcement of the law is equally as important as, indeed even more important than, organization for the purposes of the intensity of the violence'.[49] Moreover, if the 'organization requirement' for parties to an armed conflict were interpreted as demanding only the ability to engage in sufficiently intense violence, it would be somewhat redundant because this aspect will already be examined as part of proving the intensity of the conflict. Against

'[t]heir armed forces should be under a responsible command and be capable of meeting minimal humanitarian requirements'. Schindler, *The Different Types of Armed Conflicts According to the Geneva Conventions and Protocols* (M Nijhoff 1979) 147. La Haye found that being sufficiently organized to implement basic IHL obligations is 'generally agreed' as a requirement for being party to a NIAC. La Haye, *War Crimes in Internal Armed Conflicts* (CUP 2008) 8.

[44] As discussed in Section 3.3 'Specific Cases', the ability to respect basic IHL norms does not require actual respect for IHL. Instead, the mere ability to respect IHL can also be inferred from a group's ability to respect any kind of rules, such as a code of conduct, or religious law.

[45] ICRC, *International Humanitarian Law and the Challenges of Contemporary Armed Conflicts* (ICRC 2003) 232.

[46] See also Zegveld, *Accountability of Armed Opposition Groups in International Law* (CUP 2002) 140. As Margulies and Sinnot put it: 'it would be unfair to require a disorganised group to observe IHL because it lacks the structure to do so'. Margulies and Sinnot, 'Crossing Borders' (n 36) 324.

[47] For discussion on equality of belligerents in NIAC, see Sassòli and Shany, 'DEBATE: Should the Obligations of States and Armed Groups under International Humanitarian Law Really be Equal?' (2011) 93 International Review of the Red Cross 461–518.

[48] ICRC, *Internment in Armed Conflict: Basic Rules and Challenges (Opinion Paper, November 2014)* (ICRC 2014) 7.

[49] Sivakumaran, *The Law of Non-International Armed Conflict* (n 2) 179.

this background, some scholars found that '[t]here seems to be a general consensus that... [the required level of organization] would enable the parties to carry out the obligations imposed by Common Article 3'.[50] As emphasized above and further discussed below, the ability to implement basic IHL obligations does not require actual compliance with the law but the ability to impose discipline and ensure respect for any given type of rules, be it IHL, religious law, or a sui generis code of conduct.[51]

3.1.3 Avoiding an overly legalistic approach

As a result, three broad criteria can be identified in international practice that provide evidence of the existence of a party to an armed conflict: first, a party to an armed conflict must be a group, meaning that it is a collective entity with a certain degree of internal organization. Second, the group needs to be sufficiently organized to engage in hostilities; and third, it should have the capacity to respect and enforce fundamental IHL norms. These three criteria reflect the requirements identified above under IHL treaty law.[52]

However, practice also shows that it might not always be easy or possible to determine an armed group's internal structure and capacity to ensure respect for fundamental IHL norms. In such situations, the three criteria to determine a group's internal organization should be considered together and might not always be proved

[50] Moir, *The Concept of Non-International Armed Conflict* (n 5) para 36. See also ICRC, *Convention (I) for the Amelioration of the Condition of the Wounded and Sick in Armed Forces in the Field: Commentary of 2016* (ICRC 2016) article 3, para 79. Murray even argued that a 'responsible command' able to ensure 'an armed group's ability to fulfil obligations arising under international humanitarian law' is the single most important factor determining whether a group meets the IHL organization criterion. Murray, *Human Rights Obligations of Non-State Armed Groups* (Hart 2016) 61–67. A little less bold but similarly clear, Pejic found that 'it is widely recognized that a non-state party to a NIAC means an armed group with a certain level of organization that would essentially enable it to implement international humanitarian law. Pejic, 'The Protective Scope of Common Article 3: More than Meets the Eye' (2011) 93 International Review of the Red Cross 190–91. Others have argued that this requirement is found in post-1949 state practice, without, however, providing much support. See Paulus and Vashakmadze, 'Asymmetrical War and the Notion of Armed Conflict—A Tentative Conceptualization' (2009) 91 International Review of the Red Cross 95–125, 98. In any case, there is strong scholarly support for the requirement that basic mechanisms to enforce discipline are indispensible for any party to an armed conflict. See, in addition, eg, Kleffner, 'The Collective Accountability of Organized Armed Groups for System Crimes' in Wilt and Dolman (eds), *System Criminality in International Law* (CUP 2009) 238–69, 243; La Rosa and Wuerzner, 'Armed Groups, Sanctions and the Implementation of International Humanitarian Law' (2008) 90 International Review of the Red Cross 329–30; Provost, *International Human Rights and Humanitarian Law* (CUP 2002) 267.

[51] See Sections 2.1.2.2 'The ability to comply with basic humanitarian rules' and 3.3 'Specific Cases'.

[52] See Chapter 2 'Parties to Non-International Armed Conflicts under International Treaty Law'. With regard to APII, the main difference is the question of territorial control. These three criteria—although stated as indicators—are also found in the ICRC's Opinion Paper,

How is the Term 'Armed Conflict' Defined in International Humanitarian Law? (ICRC 2008) 3.); ICRC, *GCI: Commentary of 2016* (n 50) article 3, para 79. They are also found in the writings of scholars and IHL practitioners. See, eg, Schmitt, 'Classification of Cyber Conflict' (2012) 17 Journal of Conflict & Security Law 255–58; Moir, *The Concept of Non-International Armed Conflict* (n 5) para 36–37; Dröge, 'Get off my Cloud: Cyber Warfare, International Humanitarian Law, and the Protection of Civilians' (2012) 94 International Review of the Red Cross 533–78, 550.

to the same degree. A useful suggestion could be a sliding scale between the group's internal disciplinary structure and ability to implement basic humanitarian norms on the one hand, and the capacity to engage in intense violence on the other hand.[53] The suggestion of balancing to what extent different criteria need to be proved does not mean to dismiss the organization requirement in general, or to reduce the organization criterion to a group's ability to engage in violence. Instead, what is suggested here is that in exceptional cases a sufficient degree of internal organization may be inferred primarily from the group's ability to engage in intense armed violence, even if structures enabling the group to implement fundamental humanitarian norms cannot be proved to the same extent.[54] The idea is to make the reasonable assumption that a group would have a certain command and disciplinary structure if it is able to engage in coordinated and intense military confrontations against an adversary, to recruit and train members, to provide for necessary logistics, and to have structures in place to keep the group united over a certain period of time. However, recognizing the need for some flexibility in the identification of non-state parties cannot displace the fundamental principle that 'unless there is an organised armed group on the other side, one cannot speak of a non-international armed conflict'.[55]

3.2 Assessing the Existence of the Broad Criteria by Means of Specific Indicators

To determine whether non-state entities are sufficiently organized to become party to an NIAC, a variety of indicators has been examined in practice. Unlike the broad criteria set out above, such indicators must not be understood as a strict list of factors that have to be met. These factors help determine whether or not the broad criteria are met. In its case law, the ICTY has examined five groups of factors: (1) the presence of a command structure; (2) the ability to carry out operations in an organized manner; (3) the group's level of logistics; (4) the group's 'level of discipline and its ability to implement the basic obligations of Common Article 3'; (5) and the group's ability to speak with one voice.[56] For their part, ICC Trial Chambers presented the following non-exhaustive list of indicators:

[T]he force or group's internal hierarchy; the command structure and rules; the extent to which military equipment, including firearms, are available; the force or group's ability to

[53] Slightly differently from the approach suggested here but going in the same direction, Margulies and Sinnot argued: 'OAG should not be assessed in a vacuum, but on a sliding scale that also includes the other *Tadić* criterion—intensity'. Margulies and Sinnot, 'Crossing Borders' (n 36) 326.

[54] As Bianchi and Naqvi put it, if 'the group is able to conduct a campaign of [intense] armed violence', 'the lack of organization on the part of the opposing party loses some of its significance'. Bianchi and Naqvi, 'IHL and Terrorism' (n 45) 129.

[55] Pejic, 'Common Article 3' (n 50) 192.

[56] *Haradinaj et al, IT-04-84bis-T*, para 395; *Boškoski and Tarčulovski, IT-04-82-T*, paras 199–203.

plan military operations and put them into effect; and the extent, seriousness, and intensity of any military involvement.[57]

Similar indicators are also used in other practice,[58] and a variety of additional indices has been discussed in jurisprudence.[59]

These factors are useful and enjoy general support among most commentators and actors involved in conflict classification.[60] At the same time, the existence of clear sets of indicators bears the risk of taking these factors as an easy-to-use de facto definition of what constitutes a non-state party to an NIAC, without inquiring further into why these factors are required, which ones are really pertinent, and in what different ways they can be met in practice. For example, reading the factors only in light of early ICTY jurisprudence risks interpreting them with only one type of armed groups in mind, namely those existing in the former Yugoslavia.[61] In practice, whether and how these indicators or indices occur depends on the circumstances in which the armed group in question operates, such as its position vis-à-vis the adversary, the duration of its existence, its logistical and military means, or its cultural background. A weak armed group that faces a powerful state, operates secretly, and applies guerrilla tactics will necessarily organize differently from a powerful armed group that exercises stable and quasi-governmental control over territory. Hence, factors that indicate the existence of an organized armed group in one situation

[57] *Lubanga Dyilo, ICC-01/04-01/06*, para 537. For establishing these factors, the Trial Chamber refers to ICTY jurisprudence. The same list was reproduced in the *Katanga* judgment, see *Katanga, ICC-01/04-01/07*, para 1186; see also *Bemba Gombo, ICC-01/05-01/08*, para 134.

[58] eg the War Report defined 'organized armed groups' as 'those that have a command-and-control structure, typically possess and use a variety of weapons, and control a significant logistical capacity that gives them the capability to conduct regular military operations.' Maslen (ed), *The War Report 2012* (OUP 2013) 10. Similarly, the UN Commission of Inquiry on Libya presented the following factors: 'Examining the nature of the armed group involves considering such factors as whether there is a hierarchical command structure, the extent to which it is able to carry out organised operations (eg organises into zones of responsibility, means of communication); discipline systems, the nature of logistical arrangements and how the group presents itself (eg whether it is capable of involvement in negotiations)'. Human Rights Council, *Report of the International Commission of Inquiry to investigate all alleged violations of the international human rights law in the Libyan Arab Jamahiriya* (n 34) para 64. See also The International Commission of Inquiry on the Central African Republic—Final Report, S/2014/928, para 87.

[59] These include 'the existence of an official command structure, headquarters, uniforms, discrete roles and responsibilities of differing entities, the modes of communication used, ... whether military training is afforded to members of the group, ... [e]xternal relations, such as undertaking negotiations with third parties, ... requiring permits to cross checkpoints, ... the ability to operate within designated zones, control territory, procure, transport, and distribute arms, recruit new members, and co-ordinate actions, ... [t]he existence of internal regulations and disciplinary procedures.' Sivakumaran, *The Law of Non-International Armed Conflict* (n 2) 170–71; see also Akande, 'Classification of Armed Conflicts' (n 6) 52–54. These indices, which are drawn primarily from ICTY and ICC jurisprudence, will be addressed in the following discussion.

[60] See, for instance, Human Rights Council, *Report of the International Commission of Inquiry to investigate all alleged violations of the international human rights law in the Libyan Arab Jamahiriya* (n 34) para 64; UNSC, The International Commission of Inquiry on the Central African Republic—Final Report, UN Doc S/2014/928, 22 December 2014, para 87; ICRC, *GCI: Commentary of 2016* (n 50), paras 422–37; Moir *The Concept of Non-International Armed Conflict* (n 5), paras 38–39.

[61] When the ICTY developed the first set of indicative factors in the *Haradinaj* case, it analysed non-state forces as examined in the *Tadić* case, the *Čelebići* case, or the *Halilović* case, which where highly organized forces linked to state-like entities. Only the Kosovo Liberation Army analyzed in the *Limaj* case constituted a more classical guerrilla force.

should not be interpreted as legal criteria that need to be met in all other situations. When examining conflicts in different geographical regions, increasingly fractured insurgencies, armed groups operating in different states' territories, or cyber armed groups, these factors provide broad guidance but the rationale behind them needs to be thoroughly understood in order to interpret these factors in a context-specific manner.

Instead of focusing primarily in the indicative factors suggested in international jurisprudence, the following sections examine the three criteria established based on IHL treaty law and international practice. Hence, it will be analyzed what it means in practice to 1) be a collective entity; 2) have the ability to ensure respect for fundamental humanitarian norms; and 3) have the capacity to engage in sufficiently intense violence. To be clear, the approach taken in this book is not to dismiss the indicative factors developed in jurisprudence but to build on some of the factors, and it shows how they can be used to prove the three suggested criteria.

3.2.1 Being a collective entity

The concept of war or armed conflict—and, accordingly, IHL—is founded on the idea that at least two adverse parties, that is, collective entities, confront each other.[62] These parties must be identifiable: first, under IHL, members of armed groups lose their civilian status and may be targeted or interned;[63] and second, international law subjects all conflicting parties to certain obligations and may hold them responsible for disrespect of these rules.[64] The prototype of a party to an armed conflict is the state. While it is understandable that some lawyers' analyses of non-state parties are oriented towards the structures of the 'original' subject of international law,[65] it is

[62] See Section 1.1 'The Origins of the Statist Focus of the Laws of War'. See also ICRC, *Challenges Report (2003)* (n 45) 232. As Schmitt points out: 'the organization criterion implies that the actions are best understood as those of a group and not its individual members. This structural requirement is fundamental, for absent structure there is no identifiable enemy to treat as the other party to the conflict.' Schmitt, 'Cyber Conflict' (n 52) 255.

[63] The question of how to define membership in non-state armed groups is subject to continuous debate. See, eg, Dinstein or Watkin arguing for a wide approach to membership (Dinstein, *Non-International Armed Conflicts in International Law* (CUP 2014) 62; Watkin, 'Opportunity Lost: Organized Armed Groups and the ICRC "Direct Participation in Hostilities" Interpretive Guidance' (2010) 42 NYU Journal of International Law and Politics 641–95), or the ICRC arguing for a narrower approach (ICRC, *Interpretive Guidance on the Notion of Direct Participation in Hostilities under International Humanitarian Law* (ICRC 2009)). In addition, the question of whether members of armed groups can be targeted or taken into administrative detention remains subject to debate.

[64] David, 'Internal (Non-International) Armed Conflict' in Clapham and Gaeta (eds), *The Oxford Handbook of International Law in Armed Conflict* (OUP 2014) 353–62, 358. On how international law may hold non-state armed groups (NSAGs) accountable, see Dudai, 'Closing the Gap: Symbolic Reparations and Armed Groups', (2011) 93 *International Review of the Red Cross* 783–808; Kleffner, 'Collective Accountability' (n 50); Sassòli, 'Taking Armed Groups Seriously: Ways to Improve their Compliance with International Humanitarian Law' (2010) 1 Journal of International Humanitarian Legal Studies 5–51; Zegveld, *Accountability of Armed Opposition Groups* (n 46).

[65] eg Ambos and Alkatout argue that 'the respective group's features ought to resemble those of a state as the paradigmatic party to a conflict'. Ambos and Alkatout, 'Has "Justice Been Done"? The Legality of Bin Laden's Killing Under International Law' (2012) 45 Israel Law Review 341–66, 348.

almost a truism that non-state armed groups 'are necessarily always organized differently than State armed forces'.[66] Indeed, in order to understand non-state armed groups and their particular characteristics, a comparison to state armed forces can be rather 'misleading as it skews the notion of organization'.[67] The notion 'organized armed group' is better understood in a functional sense, focusing strictly on what is necessary to become party to an armed conflict under IHL.

One essential feature for the functioning of an organized armed group, that is, its ability to engage in hostilities and to implement the law, is leadership. As Mao Tse Tung pointed out, no matter how small or unorganized a guerrilla force might be, the common 'quality that makes organisation possible' is leadership.[68] In armed forces, leadership is normally exercised through a 'command structure'.[69] Leadership and some kind of command structure distinguish an armed group from loosely connected individuals: 'Normally a member of the group does not act on his own but conforms to the standards prevailing in the group and is subject to the authority of the head of the group.'[70] In armed forces, including non-state ones, leadership can take the form of a 'General Staff' or 'High Command'.[71] Ideally, leadership

> appoints and gives directions to commanders, disseminates internal regulations, organises the weapons supply, authorises military action, assigns tasks to individuals in the organisation, . . . issues political statements and communiqués, and . . . is informed by the operational units of all developments within the unit's area of responsibility.[72]

Whether and to what degree these functions are performed depends, however, on the group's structure. Whereas social science has suggested a variety of 'basic organisational structures'[73] or 'categories' of non-state armed groups,[74] for IHL purposes

[66] Watkin, 'Opportunity Lost' (n 63).
374. Social science research has shown numerous ways of how to understand armed groups as such. See, eg, Weinstein, *Inside Rebellion: The Politics of Insurgent Violence* (CUP 2007); Hoffman, *Inside Terrorism*, rev and expanded edn (Columbia University Press 2006).

[67] Sivakumaran, *The Law of Non-International Armed Conflict* (n 2) 174. It has even been suggested that 'the more nearly the enemy approximates in system to the European model, the less marked is the strategical advantage he enjoys'. Quote from Charles Callwell, found in Sinno, 'Armed Groups' Organizational Structure and their Strategic Options' (2011) 93 International Review of the Red Cross 311–32, 314.

[68] Mao, *On Guerilla Warfare* (US Marine Corps Combat Development Command 1937) chapter I. While Mao likely referred also to ideological leadership, the importance of leadership in non-state armed groups is also stressed in more recent analysis. See, for instance, Gunaratna and Oreg, 'Al Qaeda's Organizational Structure and its Evolution' (2010) 33 Studies in Conflict & Terrorism 1043–78, 1044; Hashim, *Insurgency and Counter-Insurgency in Iraq* (Hurst 2006) 156.

[69] What the term 'command structure' may mean in organized armed groups is further discussed below and should not be understood narrowly. However, as Dinstein points out: 'When divested of any command structure, an armed group will not count as organized.' Dinstein, *Non-International Armed Conflicts in International Law* (n 63) para 132.

[70] *Tadić, Judgment, 15 July 1999, Appeals Chamber, IT-94-1-A*, ICTY, para 120.

[71] See *Boškoski and Tarčulovski, IT-04-82-T*, para 199, referring to the *Limaj et al* and the *Haradinaj et al* cases.

[72] ibid.

[73] Sinno, eg, categorizes armed groups into 'centralized, decentralized, networked, patron–client, multiple, and fragmented' ones. Sinno, 'Armed Groups' (n 67) 316.

[74] Mackinlay, 'The Classification of Insurgent Forces' (2002) 42 The Adelphi Papers 41–92, 43.

armed groups can be broadly considered under two types of command structure: centralized and decentralized.[75] Main characteristics of centralized and decentralized command structures are examined in the next two sections. Moreover, the relationship between such command structures, the IHL notion of 'responsible command', and the criminal law concept of 'command responsibility' are briefly examined. These sections focus mainly on groups operating in the territory of one state. Separate sections analyze 'transnational armed groups', or 'cyber armed groups'.

3.2.1.1 Centralized command structures

Centralized command structures depict armed groups with a hierarchical structure and a functioning chain of command in which central leadership is able to carry out the above-mentioned functions. This structure is largely what prevails in state armed forces, in which fighting forces are divided into different units, such as squads, platoons, companies, battalions, regiments, and brigades. In this structure, each unit has a commander who exercises power over subordinates and is subject to the commands of a superior.[76] Dissident armed forces normally show such hierarchical structures; one commentator aptly described them as 'naturally' possessing 'a built-in structure and hierarchy'.[77] Likewise, a number of armed groups organize under a clear vertical hierarchy. For example, the ICC Pre-Trial Chamber II established with regard to the *Union des Patriotes Congolais/Forces Patriotiques pour la Libération du Congo* (UPC/FPLC) that that group was formally established according to dedicated 'UPC Statuts', operated under the leadership of one president, and 'troops were divided into sectors, brigades, battalions, companies, platoons and sections, headed by subordinate commanders. The UPC/FPLC had staff officers in charge of different matters, including administration, intelligence, operations, logistics and political affairs.'[78]

Prominent examples of other organized armed groups with strong centralized and hierarchical structures include the Lebanese Hezbollah, or the 'Islamic State Group' in Iraq and Syria. The former has been described as having 'a unified leadership structure

[75] Alternatively, these structures have also been called 'pyramidal' and 'horizontal' or 'hierarchical' and 'decentralized'. See Sivakumaran, *The Law of Non-International Armed Conflict* (n 2) 172–74; Hashim, *Insurgency* (n 68) 152.

[76] This structure was outlined by Mao Tse-Tung as follows: 'In an independent guerrilla regiment, there may be ten men per squad, three squads per platoon, three platoons per company, three companies per battalion, and three battalions to the regiment. Two of such regiments form a brigade. Each of these units has a commander, a vice-commander, and a political officer.' Mao, *On Guerilla Warfare* (n 68) chapter V. A number of studies shows that this structure has been followed by a variety of insurgent armed forces. See, eg, Beckett, *Modern Insurgencies and Counter-Insurgencies: Guerrillas and their Opponents Since 1750* (Routledge 2001). For a concrete example of how the structure was implemented in the 'National Democratic Front of the Philippines', see Sivakumaran, *The Law of Non-International Armed Conflict* (n 2) 172–73.

[77] Dinstein, *Non-International Armed Conflicts in International Law* (n 63) para 131. This is also seen in early ICTY case law, in which the armed forces involved in the different wars of secession consisted primarily of former armed forces. *Tadić, IT-94-1-T; Mrkšić et al, IT-95-13/1-T*, paras 407–27.

[78] *Ntaganda, Decision Pursuant to Article 61(7)(a) and (b) of the Rome Statute on the Charges of the Prosecutor Against Bosco Ntaganda, 9 June 2014, Pre-Trial Chamber II, ICC-01/04-02/06*, ICC, paras 13–15.

that oversees the organization's complementary, partially compartmentalized elements'.[79] Leadership is exercised a 'by seven-member Majlis al Shura (Consultative Council)', a Secretary General, and 'sub-councils' for different functions, including military activities.[80] The organization operates under hierarchical control, in which the chain of command goes all the way from the soldiers in the field to the organization's leadership.[81] Similarly, the 'Islamic State Group's' leadership structure in Iraq and Syria reportedly took 'a pyramidal form, with Baghdadi at the top, followed by two deputies, a Shura Council and a cabinet of ministers, and then a council of provincial governors and their individual military commands'.[82] The organization's military hierarchy reportedly operated under 'a clear reporting structure from a local level, through the provincial command, and up to the War Council'.[83]

3.2.1.2 Decentralized command structures

More difficult to determine are command structures of armed groups that operate in a decentralized manner and may consist of 'semi-autonomous or splinter factions operating under an ill-defined leadership structure'.[84] Reportedly, in practice, armed groups combine different command structures according to their needs and operational circumstances.[85] While hierarchical structures can prove more effective than flat 'peer-monitoring' structures and sometimes reflect existing leadership dynamics,[86] analysts also suggest that for non-state armed groups decentralized leadership structures tend to be 'more resilient than centralised ones'.[87] Examining the insurgency in Iraq in the 2000s, one analyst pointed out:

> The decentralized, or networked, organizational structure has been described as 'loose' and 'flat', with fluid or less distinct boundaries between its various subunits. Such organizations have a leadership structure, but it is weak due either to cultural/ environmental factors (i.e. kinship or traditional ties within the leadership) or to the lack of any particular skills that necessarily identify one person over another as designated leader. In Iraq some of the early insurgent groups or cells were made up of family members or neighborhood friends who came together to fight the foreign presence.[88]

Decentralized or horizontal structures encompass a broad variety of more or less organized groups. An example of a notorious armed group that is 'not comparable to an

[79] Addis and Blanchard, *Hezbollah: Background and Issues for Congress* (Congressional Research Center 2011) 10.
[80] ibid.
[81] Hezbollah's hierarchical leadership structure was also explained to the author in an interview with Professor Mohamad Tay.
[82] Lister, 'Assessing Syria's Jihad' (2014) 54 The Adelphi Series 71–98, 75.
[83] ibid 76. For similar accounts on the 'Islamic State Group's' leadership structure, see International Commission of Inquiry on the Syrian Arab Republic, Rule of Terror: Living under ISIS in Syria (OHCHR, 2014) para 13. The transnational dimension of the ISG is further discussed in Section 3.4 'The Degree of Organization of Non-State Parties and the End of NIAC'.
[84] ICRC, *Increasing Respect for International Humanitarian Law in Non-International Armed Conflicts* (ICRC 2008) 11.
[85] Watkin, 'Opportunity Lost' (n 63) 280.
[86] Weinstein, *Inside Rebellion* (n 66) 134.
[87] Sinno, 'Armed Groups' (n 67) 312.
[88] Hashim, *Insurgency* (n 68) 153.

organized army' is allegedly the Taliban.[89] A US Ministry of Defense lawyer described this group as having 'no organized, uniformed military, no strategic military plans, and no formal command and control structure characteristic of a regular military'.[90] Another example is the 'Shining Path' that engaged the government of Peru in a protracted armed conflict in the 1980s and '90s. Reportedly, that group's leadership

> devolved significant power to local committees to organize their own resources, plan actions, and maintain discipline. The Central Committee provided strategic direction, ideological substance, and rigorous guidelines regarding how members should behave; nevertheless Sendero Nacional entrusted its members with decision-making power and operational authority.[91]

These examples show that decentralized leadership structures can prove effective in certain circumstances and do not preclude the ability to engage in significant military action, to implement strict internal codes, or to control territory.

The classification of armed groups as sufficiently organized to become party to an armed conflict proves particularly challenging if violence does not break out between pre-existing groups but develops in a decentralized manner—for example, as a result of mass protest. History shows that 'all guerrilla bands that spring from the masses of the people suffer from lack of organization at the time of their formation';[92] in other words, 'improvised groups of civilians, combining their resources in rebelling against the Government, are likely to be more loosely knit (at least in the early stage of the insurgency)'.[93] This initial lack of organization has recently been accompanied by increased fragmentation amongst armed groups. For example, conflicts in Iraq, Libya, or Syria have been characterized by multiple armed groups emerging independently and participating separately in violence.[94] In addition to practical difficulties in establishing the necessary facts to determine which groups exist and how they are organized, concerns were raised by legal experts that identifying parties to these conflicts poses 'a number of unexpected legal questions', including 'whether too much emphasis is placed on the organizational criterion or whether the problem lay with the indicia of an OAG [organized armed group] rather than with the existence of such a group'.[95]

When mass protests in Libya and Syria were met with intense state violence, UN Commissions of Inquiry (CoI) faced difficulties in identifying the armed groups

[89] See Sivakumaran, *The Law of Non-International Armed Conflict* (n 2) 173.

[90] Parks, 'Combatants' (2009) 85 International Law Studies 248–306, 258.

[91] Weinstein, *Inside Rebellion* (n 66) 150.

[92] Mao, *On Guerilla Warfare* (n 68) chapter I.

[93] Dinstein, *Non-International Armed Conflicts in International Law* (n 63) para 131.

[94] Generally on the phenomenon of increasingly fragmented insurgencies, see Bakke, 'The Problem with Fragmented Insurgencies', *The Washington Post* (13 May 2015). The exact numbers of groups involved in the mentioned conflicts vary. Reports suggest that in '2006 in Iraq there were at one point 18 groups divided into three groupings' (Watkin, 'Opportunity Lost' (n 63) 674); in Libya, estimates of the number of different armed groups active in the conflict ranged 'from 100 to 300' (Human Rights Council, *Report of the International Commission of Inquiry on Libya*, 2 March 2012, A/HRC/19/68 Annex I, para 67); and in Syria, the Carter Center estimated that over the first 2.5 years of the crisis, 'approximately 4,390 armed units and military councils [formed], representing between 68,639 and 85,150 fighters across the country'. The Carter Center, Syria Countrywide Conflict Report #1 (20 August 2013).

[95] Arimatsu and Choudhury, *Legal Classification* (n 34) 17, 40.

involved and determining their degree of organization.[96] Almost one year into the Syria crisis, the CoI found itself 'unable to verify that the Free Syrian Army (FSA), local groups identifying themselves as such or other anti-Government armed groups had reached the necessary level of organization' in order to determine the applicability of IHL.[97] The CoI pointed out that while a number of armed groups identified themselves with the FSA, this did not mean that the 'group has been recognized by the FSA leadership or obeys the command of the FSA leadership abroad'.[98] Similarly, while an early CoI report on Libya could be read as suggesting that opposition forces were united under the 'National Libyan Army' banner,[99] the CoI later clarified that the 'Libyan National Army neither coordinated nor led the military struggle against Qadhafi forces'.[100] These findings, as well as the broader legal debate surrounding conflict classification in Syria, warrant a number of comments.[101]

The concept of NIAC does not require that opposition forces operating in one territory be united under one structure. Rather, NIACs are determined among identifiable parties, and different conflicts can exist between a government and different armed groups, or between such groups if each bilateral relationship meets the organization and intensity requirements. In the Libya crisis, the CoI pointed out that '*thuwar* [anti-Ghadaffi armed groups] brigades were formed autonomously' and owing to 'constraints in telephone and internet communication during the conflict, there was little coordination across regional lines, leading to the development of independent military structures and chains of command'.[102] In addition to such logistical constraints, ideological or religious divides may indicate that certain opposition groups that fight a common enemy are not one group.[103] As the ICTY argued in the *Haradinaj et al* case, the existence of a number of autonomously formed village defence forces each having their own commanders does not turn a situation into one NIAC.[104]

[96] See Human Rights Council, *Report of the International Commission of Inquiry to investigate all alleged violations of international human rights law in the Libyan Arab Jamahiriya* (n 34) para 65.

[97] HRC, *Report of the Independent International Commission of Inquiry on the Syrian Arab Republic*, A/HRC/19/69, para 13.

[98] ibid. Stated differently, a researcher pointed out that 'FSA headquarters does not appear to exercise command over the autonomous groups that fight in its name; however, many of the most important groups who are fighting the regime acknowledge the FSA's leadership, inasmuch as they are able to do so'. Holliday, Syria's Armed Opposition (Institute for the Study of War 2012) 17.

[99] Human Rights Council, *Report of the International Commission of Inquiry on Libya* (n 94) paras 56–57.

[100] ibid Annex I, para 66.

[101] For some legal appreciations of the Syria conflict, see Chatham House, *Classification of Conflicts: The Way Forward* (Chatham House, 2012); Blank and Corn, 'Losing the Forest' (n 35); Grignon, 'The Beginning of Application of International Humanitarian Law: A Discussion of a Few Challenges' (2014) 96 International Review of the Red Cross 139–62; Rodenhäuser, 'International Legal Obligations of Armed Opposition Groups in Syria' (2015) 1 Review of Law 1.

[102] Human Rights Council, *Report of the International Commission of Inquiry on Libya* (n 94) Annex I, para 61. On the fragmentation of the Libya conflict, see also Bassiouni, *Libya from Repression to Revolution: A Record of Armed Conflict and International Law Violations, 2011–2013* (M Nijhoff 2013) 142–43.

[103] eg the Syria CoI pointed out that in addition to the Free Syrian Army, '[s]everal radical Islamic armed groups' emerged in 2012, among them the Al-Qaida-linked 'Al-Nusrah Front'. Human Rights Council, *Report of the Independent International Commission of Inquiry on the Syrian Arab Republic* (n 34) paras 26–31.

[104] See *Haradinaj et al, IT-04-84bis-T*, paras 407–11; *Haradinaj et al, IT-04-84-T*, para 68. Another example of an armed group that initially consisted of largely independent groups of armed men was the National Liberation Army in Macedonia. See *Boškoski and Tarčulovski, IT-04-82-T*, para 286.

In such situations, a NIAC may emerge under at least two scenarios: either as a NIAC involving at least one relatively small party to the conflict, or as a NIAC in which smaller groups form a 'united force' or 'coalition' that becomes party to the NIAC. The main legal consequences of the different scenarios, which may also influence states' and other actors' approach on how to define parties to a NIAC, is the scope of application of IHL: If a conflict is only found to exist with one small party, IHL applies primarily to the relation between the identified parties. The relation between all other actors would continue to be governed solely by international human rights law (IHRL), unless these actions are sufficiently linked to the NIAC.[105] In contrast, if a number of different groups can be found to form one party to a NIAC, IHL would regulate, for example, the use of force or deprivation of liberty vis-à-vis all members of this 'united force' or 'coalition'. Thus, IHL would apply to a broader scope of actors.

The identification of sufficiently organized but relatively small parties to a NIAC

Under the first scenario, violence between one small but sufficiently organized splinter armed group and the adversary armed forces may become sufficiently intense to meet the NIAC threshold. The identification of a NIAC between specific armed forces would render IHL applicable in the entire territory under the parties' control with respect to all acts that show a sufficient nexus to the conflict.[106] This means, for example, that IHL would not only govern the relationship between the two identified parties to the conflict but also that between a party to the conflict and civilians directly participating in hostilities having a nexus with the NIAC.[107] In addition, it has recently been argued that IHL as it relates to NIACs also foresees the possibility that states or organized armed groups become party to an ongoing armed conflict if their actions 'objectively form an integral part of a pre-existing NIAC'.[108] Accordingly, once a conflict between at least two sufficiently organized parties has met the NIAC threshold, IHL would govern a) the relationship between the two

[105] See discussion in the following section.

[106] *Kunarac et al, Judgment, 12 June 2002, Appeals Chamber IT-96-23& IT-96-23/1-A*, ICTY, para 57. For further discussion on the geographical scope of application, see Schöberl, 'The Geographical Scope of Application of the Conventions' in Clapham, Gaeta, and Sassòli (eds), *The 1949 Geneva Conventions: A Commentary* (OUP 2015) 68–83; Pejic, 'Extraterritorial Targeting by Means of Armed Drones: Some Legal Implications' (2015) International Review of the Red Cross 28–31.

[107] On the notion of 'direct participation of hostilities' and the three conditions that turn individual acts into a direct participation, see ICRC, *Interpretive Guidance on the Notion of Direct Participation in Hostilities under International Humanitarian Law* (n 63) 46–64.

[108] The ICRC calls this the 'support-based approach', which developed in the context of multinational military operations. Under this approach, states may become party to an ongoing NIAC even if their action does not itself meet the requisite intensity threshold. What is decisive is that a state's actions make a contribution 'to the collective conduct of hostilities'. The ICRC identified four conditions for applying the support-based approach: '(1) there is a pre-existing NIAC taking place on the territory in which multinational forces are called on to intervene; (2) actions related to the conduct of hostilities are undertaken by multinational forces in the context of the pre-existing conflict; (3) the military operations of multinational forces are carried out in support (as described above) of a party to the pre-existing conflict; and (4) the action in question is undertaken pursuant to an official decision by the troop-contributing country, or the relevant organization to support a party involved in the pre-existing conflict.' ICRC, *International Humanitarian Law and the Challenges of Contemporary Armed Conflicts* (ICRC 2015). The 'support-based approach' was first published in an academic article by ICRC legal advisor Tristan Ferraro. See Ferraro, 'The Applicability and Application of International Humanitarian Law to Multinational Forces' (2013) 95

initial parties, b) the relationship between the initial parties and other groups acting in support of one of the parties, and c) all other acts of individuals that qualify as a direct participation in hostilities, or are otherwise related to the conflict.

This approach is applied in practice. For example, such a differentiated analysis of the fighting at the beginning of the Syria conflict would appear to lie behind the ICRC's finding that in early 2012, armed violence in only two areas, Homs and Idlib, may have reached the NIAC threshold.[109] The ICRC held that 'there is currently a non-international (internal) armed conflict occurring in Syria opposing Government Forces *and a number of organised armed opposition-groups* operating in several parts of the country (including, but not limited to, Homs, Idlib and Hama)'.[110] It would have also helped classify similar situations in Libya. For example, it is reported that in the early stages of armed violence between *thuwar* and government forces in the Libyan city of Misrata, 'there was a core element of organized fighters [about 350–550 combatants] in what was otherwise an unregulated confrontation'.[111] Military operations organized by these fighters, however, often developed into rather 'chaotic' battles, with 'groups of friends arriving independently and organising with fellow fighters as the battle progressed'.[112] According to the approach suggested here, owing to the existence of the 'core element of organized fighters' and sufficiently intense fighting between them and government forces, a NIAC would come into existence and IHL would be applicable.[113] Consequently, IHL would apply to the entire situation, including the relationship between one party to the conflict and non-affiliated fighters that directly participated in hostilities, or between a party to the conflict and a third party—state or non-state in nature—that sufficiently supports the adversary.[114]

International Review of the Red Cross 561–612. There is nothing in the concept that would preclude its application to joint operations of organized armed groups. Instead, the 'equality of belligerents' principle suggests that if such an approach applies to one side of the conflict, it also applies to the other side.

109 See Nebehay, 'Some Syria Violence Amounts to Civil War: Red Cross', *Reuters* (8 May 2012).

110 Statement cited from Maslen (ed), *The War Report 2012* (n 58) 165 (emphasis added). Similarly, the UN CoI stated in June 2012: '*In some areas* the fighting bears the characteristics of a non-international armed conflict. The violence has shifted dramatically from confrontations between protesters and the Government's security apparatus to fighting between its army—together with what appear to be pro-Government militias—and *numerous anti-Government armed groups*' (emphasis added). Human Rights Council, *Oral Update of the Independent International Commission of Inquiry on the Syrian Arab Republic*, 26 June 2012, A/HRC/20/CRP.1, para 104.

111 McQuinn, *After the Fall: Libya's Evolving Armed Groups* (Small Arms Survey 2012) 36.

112 ibid 37.

113 In such situations, it is factually difficult to determine to what extent the intensity of violence in a certain location is attributable only to the 'core group' of fighters. In practice, it is likely that if the core group is sufficiently organized, the assessment of intensity may take the wider situation into account and not only violence strictly attributable to the core group. See also Radin, 'Global Armed Conflict? The Threshold of Extraterritorial Non-International Armed Conflicts' (2013) 13 International Law Studies 724.

114 For further discussion, see Dörmann and Rodenhäuser, 'Contemporary Challenges for International Humanitarian Law' in Crawford (ed), *The International Legal Order: Current Needs and Possible Responses* (Brill 2017) 677–99, 680–82.

The identification of 'united forces' or 'coalitions' as parties to a NIAC

Under a second scenario, independently formed groups may merge into one party to a NIAC. This can happen if different armed groups that are not party to a NIAC join forces and subsequently meet the NIAC threshold jointly.[115] The same principles would also apply if an organized armed group is party to a NIAC and another armed group joins it, or where different existing parties merge into one. The core question is what link must exist between such groups in order to identify them as one party to a NIAC? The clearest one would be if the different groups merge into one hierarchically organized armed group with a central command structure.[116] If this is not the case, different approaches can be suggested. A first one builds on the 'belonging test' as used to determine whether members of non-state militia belong to a party to an international armed conflict and can be considered prisoners of war. A second approach focuses on the question of the degree of control a coalition's leadership must exercise over member groups in order to constitute one party to a NIAC.

The 'belonging test'

The 'belonging test' has been suggested by Melzer. He argues that in a situation in which different armed groups each constitute 'a body having a military structure' that is 'commanded by a "person responsible for his subordinates" ', the decisive link to form one party would be that 'they must "*belong to*" a party to the conflict'.[117] Based on how the term 'belonging to a Party to the conflict' has been understood in the context of determining prisoner-of-war status under article 4(A)(2) of the Third Geneva Convention, Melzer proposes a rather loose link by following the 1960 ICRC commentary. Under this approach, a 'de facto relationship' between the entities would suffice, which 'may find expression merely by tacit agreement, if the operations are such as to indicate clearly for which side the resistance organization is fighting'.[118] In addition, the 'belonging test' would also be met if an 'official declaration' by the party to the conflict would be 'confirmed by official recognition by the High Command' of the individual armed group.[119]

[115] In addition to being sufficiently organized, this would also require a sufficient degree of intensity of violence between the group and an adversary armed force.

[116] See discussion above. This seems to have been the case with the 'Seleka' coalition in the Central African Republic, which shortly after its formation allegedly operated under 'a clear hierarchical military command structure'. International Criminal Court—The Office of the Prosecutor, Situation in the Central African Republic II: Article 53(1) Report (24 September 2014) para 65. In contrast, with regard to the KLA in Kosovo, the ICTY established that it took several months to unite different armed units under a centralized command structure. See *Milutinović et al, Judgment, 26 February 2009, Trial Chamber, IT-05-87-T*, ICTY, paras 821–40.

[117] Melzer, 'The Principle of Distinction between Civilians and Combatants', in Clapham and Gaeta (eds), *The Oxford Handbook of International Law in Armed Conflict* (OUP 2014) 296–331, 314 (emphasis added). This concept has also been hinted at in the ICRC's DPH study. See ICRC, *Interpretive Guidance on the Notion of Direct Participation in Hostilities under International Humanitarian Law* (n 63) 31.

[118] Preux, *Geneva Convention Relative to the Treatment of Prisoners of War: Commentary* (ICRC 1960) 57. This is the test suggested by Melzer. See Melzer, 'The Principle of Distinction between Civilians and Combatants' (n 117) 314–15.

[119] Preux, *Commentary GCIII* (n 118) 57.

It is, however, not entirely clear to which relationship Melzer suggests the 'belonging' test should apply. His suggestion could refer to the relationship between different armed forces to form one party to a conflict, to the question of attributing an already sufficiently organized armed group to a political entity, or to both.[120] For the purpose of determining the requisite link between different armed groups in order to form one party to a conflict, the 'belonging test' can be criticized on two levels. One, there is no legal basis—neither in treaty nor in customary IHL—for using a concept established for the determination of prisoner-of-war status under international armed conflict (IAC) law for the determination of what constitutes a party to a conflict in NIAC.[121] And two, international practice and expert opinions do not support a test as low as the 'belonging test' in NIAC. As shall be seen below, international jurisprudence requires more than a de facto relationship that could express itself merely in fighting a common enemy. In addition, the threshold that different groups form one party based on a declared affiliation is too low. It is generally accepted that sharing 'a common ideology'[122] or '[m]ere "acting toward a collective goal" against the Government is not enough [; . . .] some leadership is essential'.[123]

The 'control test'

A narrower interpretation of when an armed group can be considered as 'belonging' to a party to an international armed conflict is the 'overall control' test suggested by the ICTY Appeals Chamber.[124] Admittedly, the 'overall control' test continues to be controversially discussed in international law, there are no obvious legal sources for applying this concept of the laws of IAC to NIACs, and the question of attributing certain conduct to states for the purpose of state responsibility is different from

[120] On the latter point, it has been suggested: 'The existence of a political leadership is a relevant factor in assessing whether single or multiple parallel NIACs exist in any particular location. If the armed groups operating in a theatre of conflict display a level of loyalty towards the overall objectives articulated by the political leadership, it would seem that although they might be operating separately, their participation in the hostilities would fall under a single NIAC.' Arimatsu and Choudhury, *Legal Classification* (n 34) 41. Yet, the Chatham House experts did not consider mere adherence to a common objective as sufficient for creating one party to a NIAC, which supports the argument made here that political leadership must be more than a shared ideology or goal.

[121] See Heller, 'The Use and Abuse of Analogy in IHL' in Ohlin (ed), *Theoretical Boundaries of Armed Conflict and Human Rights* (CUP 2016); Radin, 'Global Armed Conflict' (n 113) 729–30.

[122] ICRC, *International Humanitarian Law and Terrorism: Questions and Answers* (ICRC 2011). This position is also accepted by the US, which explains that in its fight against Al Qaida and 'associated forces' a 'group that simply embraces al-Qa'ida's ideology is not an "associated force"'. US Department of Defense, *Remarks by the General Counsel of the Department of Defense on the Legal Framework for the United States' Use of Military Force Since 9/11* (US Department of Defense, 10 April 2015).

[123] Dinstein, *Non-International Armed Conflicts in International Law* (n 63) para 95; see also Arimatsu and Choudhury, *Legal Classification* (n 34) 41.

[124] *Tadić, IT-94-1-A*, paras 88–123. The purpose of this chapter does not necessitate an engagement with the continuing discussion on whether the ICTY's 'overall control' or the International Court of Justice (ICJ)'s 'effective control' constitute the correct test for determining state responsibility for acts committed by armed groups. While the ICJ dismissed the overall control test with regard to state responsibility, it left open whether it serves its purpose with regard to conflict classification. See *Case Concerning Application of the Convention on the Prevention and Punishment of the Crime of Genocide (Bosnia and Herzegovina v Serbia and Montenegro), Judgment, 26 February 2007*, ICJ, para 404. For some discussion, see n 4 in the Introduction to Part I.

determining when different armed groups can be considered *one* party to a conflict. Nonetheless, the idea underlying the overall control test has some merit for the present purpose. In the *Tadić* judgment, the ICTY Appeals Chamber emphasized that, under international law, the action of an organized armed group can be attributed to 'a State (or, in the context of an armed conflict, the Party to the conflict)' if the party to which the acts shall be attributed '*has a role in organising, coordinating or planning the military actions* of the military group, in addition to financing, training and equipping or providing operational support to that group'.[125] It is not necessary that the controlling entity issues 'specific orders', or provides 'direction of each individual operation'.[126]

Conceptually, the situation of uniting different armed groups under the banner of one party to an armed conflict is not too different.[127] For example, the 'Kosovo Liberation Army' (KLA) existed as an organization well before the conflict in Kosovo escalated.[128] The question was, however, at what point the violence involving the different KLA-affiliated groups on the ground could be considered acts of the KLA as such, and subsequently, whether the collective entity called KLA met the organizational threshold and was involved in sufficiently intense violence with Serbian armed forces. Similarly, in the Syria crisis, a group of officers who defected founded the FSA in July 2011.[129] Over the following months and years, the same questions as seen regarding the KLA emerged with regard to the FSA, as well as other 'alliances' emerging in Syria.[130] Following the requirements expressed by the ICTY Appeals Chamber, independently formed groups could be considered one party to an armed conflict if an authority within that party—be it an individual, or a command council consisting of members from different groups—'has a role in organising, coordinating or planning the military actions' of the different groups and is involved in 'financing, training and equipping or providing operational support to that group'.

ICTY and ICC jurisprudence considered this issue further. With regard to the KLA, the ICTY found that at the very early stages of the conflict, when KLA-affiliated groups consisted mostly of 'spontaneous and rudimentary military organization[s] at the village level', the 'initial phases of a centralized command structure above the various village commands' were crucial for the KLA to qualify 'as an "organized armed group" under the *Tadić* test'.[131] The Chamber emphasized particularly the '*de facto* authority' consolidated by a 'popular commander' called *Haradinaj*,

[125] *Tadić, IT-94-1-A*, para 137. [126] ibid.

[127] eg referring to article 7 of the ILC 'Draft articles on the responsibility of international organizations' it has been suggested that determining whether an international organization or individual states are parties to a multinational armed conflict would depend on whether the multinational organization exercises 'overall control' over the forces on the ground. See Ferraro, 'IHL and Multinational Forces' (n 108) 590–92.

[128] See, eg, *Haradinaj et al, IT-04-84bis-T*, paras 18–22.

[129] Holliday, 'Syria's Armed Opposition' (n 98) 14–16.

[130] eg in 2014, the Syria CoI reported the 'establishment of permanent or temporary coordination and integration mechanisms, including coalitions and operation rooms'. Human Rights Council, *Report of the independent international commission of inquiry on the Syrian Arab Republic*, 12 February 2014, A/HRC/25/65, para 15.

[131] *Haradinaj et al, IT-04-84-T*, para 89.

who coordinated some activities of different village defence groups.[132] In addition, the KLA smuggled a significant number of weapons into Kosovo, or facilitated the smuggling by different village organizations.[133] To the extent possible, KLA 'professionals' also provided military training for 'KLA soldiers' in different villages.[134] In other case law, the ICTY explained that the leadership's ability to coordinate the operations of groups claiming to be part of it, to divide territory into operation zones, and to organize assistance when one group comes under attack testifies to a degree of organization required to be a party to a conflict.[135] A centralized command structure does not need to be able to command each military operation, or have a functioning reporting system.[136]

In the *Katanga* case, the ICC followed a comparable approach with regard to the 'Ngiti militia', also known as the 'Forces de Résistance Patriotique d'Ituri' (FRPI) active in the 'Walendu-Bindi *collectivité*' in Ituri, Democratic Republic of the Congo. The Chamber had to determine whether the different militia who 'were spread among several camps placed under the authority of various commanders' constituted one 'organized armed group', namely the FRPI.[137] The Chamber answered the question affirmatively, emphasizing vaguely that 'various means of communication and weapons and ammunition were available to them' and its members 'pursued common objectives and conducted joint military operations for a protracted period'.[138] However, when assessing the group's organizational structure in more detail, the Chamber stressed the role played by the 'president' of the movement, called *Katanga*.[139] The Chamber could not establish 'beyond reasonable doubt' that *Katanga* 'was vested ... with effective hierarchical power over all the commanders and combatants of the Ngiti militia'.[140] However, in order to classify the FRPI as an 'organized armed group', the Chamber relied on *Katanga's* 'role as coordinator' that 'testifies to the real military authority he wielded' over the other commanders in the group.[141] This authority was underlined by Katanga's role in facilitating 'the receipt and storage of weapons and ammunition' and his power to allot them to the sub-groups.[142]

While the 'overall control test' emphasizes a state's 'role in organising, coordinating or planning the military actions' of a non-state group as well as a degree of material support, in order to determine whether or not different armed groups form one party to an armed conflict, jurisprudence appears to require a slightly higher threshold. To find a sufficient link between different groups in order to consider them one party to a conflict, there needs to be a uniting element that has been described as 'initial phases of a centralized command' exercising some authority

[132] ibid paras 89 and 67. [133] ibid paras 89 and 76–82. [134] ibid paras 86 and 89.
[135] See *Limaj et al, IT-03-66-T*, paras 95 and 108; *Haradinaj et al, IT-04-84bis-T*, paras 407 and 409; *Milošević, IT-02-54-T*, paras 24–25.
[136] Even if armed groups aim to introduce command and reporting structures, implementation can be challenging if means of communication are limited. See *Haradinaj et al, IT-04-84bis-T*, paras 63, 78–84; *Limaj et al, IT-03-66-T*, para 105.
[137] *Katanga, ICC-01/04-01/07*, para 1209. [138] ibid.
[139] ibid paras 684 and 1359–65. [140] ibid para 1365. [141] ibid paras 1342–43.
[142] ibid para 1362.

beyond the mere coordination of sub-groups.[143] Likewise, interpreting the 'overall control' test under IHL, in the ICRC's view '[t]he notion of overall control does not . . . refer simply to monitoring or checking, but also requires the exercise of some form of authority over the entity in question', meaning that there needs to be a 'relationship of subordination' between the controlling entity and the controlled one.[144]

Based on the notion 'Party to a conflict' under IHL and in line with recent jurisprudence, it is submitted that a party's leadership—whether in the form of one person or a joint council—needs to exercise a degree of both *operational coordination* and *strategic authority*. While operational coordination requires the ability to coordinate military activities and to distribute logistics, strategic authority signifies leadership's de facto authority to determine the overall military objectives and the internal rules that all sub-groups have to follow. If these two elements are fulfilled, a coalition of armed groups can be considered as one collective entity with a certain command structure and the abilities to engage in military violence and to ensure respect for basic IHL. In contrast, it would be difficult to consider different sub-groups as one party to a NIAC if these sub-groups openly oppose or contravene the military strategy or code of conduct determined by the party's overall leadership.

In order to prove sufficient internal structures to qualify as one party to a NIAC, case law of different international tribunals suggest a number of indicative factors that may help prove the existence of one party with a certain command structure. For example, internal regulations that define the group's organizational structure, rules, responsibilities, and a chain of command constitute evidence.[145] In addition, the tribunals placed some emphasis on the existence of headquarters.[146] While headquarters can prove a centralized command structure, organizations may choose not to have one headquarters owing to the high risk of being attacked, or may choose to have different regional headquarters.[147] What constitutes headquarters should, again, be understood functionally. Armed groups regularly established 'control

[143] An element of 'collective coordination ... as an indicator for the organizational criterion' also received support recently from IHL experts. Arimatsu and Choudhury, *Legal Classification* (n 34) 40. eg in Misrata, a number of individuals formed the 'Misratan Military Council' (MMC) as the central 'military authority' of the opposition in that location, without, however, being able to exercise command-and-control functions. Under the overall coordination of the MMC, brigades active in Misrata set up 'control rooms' in which military commanders would coordinate their action and share intelligence. Within the MMC and the control rooms, different commanders participated on a horizontal—not hierarchical—basis. McQuinn, 'After the Fall: Libya's Evolving Armed Groups' (n 111) 17, 41–42.

[144] Ferraro, 'The ICRC's Legal Position on the Notion of Armed Conflict involving Foreign Intervention and on Determining the IHL Applicable to this Type of Conflict' (2015) 97 International Review of the Red Cross 1227–52, 1237 and 1234. The ICRC clarifies, however, that 'the concept of authority referred to is broader and more general than the issuing of orders, and refers rather to general direction and coordination'.

[145] See *Limaj et al, IT-03-66-T*, para 112; *Mbarushimana, Decision on the Confirmation of Charges, 16 December 2011, Pre-Trial Chamber I, ICC-01/04-01/10*, ICC, para 104. eg Macedonia's National Liberation Army's internal regulations are publicly available. See Sivakumaran, *The Law of Non-International Armed Conflict* (n 2) 171.

[146] *Boškoski and Tarčulovski, IT-04-82-T*, para 199; *Haradinaj et al, IT-04-84-T*, paras 64–65.

[147] See *Limaj et al, IT-03-66-T*, para 104. eg the chairman of the Acheh-Sumatra National Liberation Front, Arif Fadhillah, emphasized this point to the author.

rooms' as communication hubs from where to command their operations.[148] In other cases, what was called headquarters was primarily a place to obtain weapons and training.[149] Another frequently assessed indicator is a party's 'ability to speak with one voice'—for example by engaging in political, military, or humanitarian negotiations,[150] or by making public announcements in the name of the party as a whole.[151] The ability to engage externally in the name of a collective entity and to implement the results of negotiations testifies to a degree of internal authority exercised by a party's leadership and proves external recognition thereof.[152] While these indicators are certainly useful, the tribunals' and other international practice show that they should not be interpreted too narrowly and do not constitute a list of strict criteria that each armed group must meet.

3.2.2 Command structures, 'responsible command', and 'command responsibility'

The examination of centralized and decentralized command structures of parties to NIACs warrants the question of how these structures relate to the 'responsible command' concept under IHL. As discussed above, Common Article 3 has often been interpreted as requiring that parties to a NIAC operate under responsible command, and this requirement is explicitly found in article 1(1) APII.[153] Opinions in contemporary practice on whether or not a 'responsible command' constitutes a strict requirement for the existence of an organized armed group under IHL vary. On the one hand, the ICTY Appeals Chamber reasoned that 'it is evident that there cannot be an organized military force save on the basis of responsible command'.[154] Similarly, commentators have argued that 'the notion of responsible command' is 'inextricably linked' with or 'inherent in the idea of organization'.[155] On the other hand, the 'responsible command' notion is not explicitly mentioned among the tribunals' indicative factors for determining a group's degree of organization,[156] and all ICC Trial Chambers dismissed a 'responsible command' as a strict requirement for an organized armed group under article 8(2)(d) and (f) ICC Statute.[157] Similarly,

[148] This has been the case, eg, in Libya and Syria. See McQuinn, 'After the Fall: Libya's Evolving Armed Groups' (n 111) 41–42.

[149] See, eg, *Katanga, ICC-01/04-01/07*, paras 679–81; *Haradinaj et al, IT-04-84bis-T*, para 65.

[150] See *Boškoski and Tarčulovski, IT-04-82-T*, para 203.

[151] See *Haradinaj et al, IT-04-84-T*, para 88.

[152] See *Limaj et al, IT-03-66-T*, para 125; *Đorđević, IT-05-87/1-T*, para 1576.

[153] See Sections 2.1.2 'The ability to comply with basic humanitarian rules' and 2.2.2.1 'Responsible command'.

[154] *Hadžihasanović et al, Decision on Interlocutory Appeal Challenging Jurisdiction in relation to command responsibility, 16 July 2003, Appeals Chamber, IT-01-47-AR72*, ICTY, para 16. For a criticism of the arguments advanced in this decision, see Cullen, *The Concept of Non-International Armed Conflict* (n 5) 148–57.

[155] Sivakumaran, *The Law of Non-International Armed Conflict* (n 2) 174–75; see also La Rosa and Wuerzner, 'Armed Groups' (n 50).

[156] See nn 56–58 and the accompanying text.

[157] See *Lubanga Dyilo, ICC-01/04-01/06*, 536-537; *Katanga, ICC-01/04-01/07*, para 1186.

scholars have raised doubts over whether or not a 'responsible command' is a constitutive element of a party to a NIAC.[158]

This disagreement may to some extent be due to different interpretations of what the notion entails. In the *Hadžihasanović et al* case, the ICTY Appeals Chamber linked 'responsible command' as a characteristic of an organized armed group directly to 'command responsibility' as a mode of individual criminal responsibility because 'the elements of command responsibility are derived from the elements of responsible command'.[159] This finding could be read as suggesting that any armed group must operate under a 'responsible command' that is sufficient to hold the group's leadership individually responsible for acts of subordinates. The essential requirement of the 'command responsibility' concept that could implicate a group's command structure is that the commander or superior needs to exercise effective control over subordinates. Effective control is understood as 'the material ability to prevent and punish the commission' of IHL violations.[160] Applying the concept of command responsibility to alleged crimes committed by an organized armed group, the Special Court for Sierra Leone considered three 'structural factors' to be 'generic features which are critical to facilitating control': 'a functioning chain of command, a sufficiently developed planning and orders process, and a strong disciplinary system'.[161] If these factors were defining elements of an organized armed group under IHL, the threshold of organization would be rather high.[162]

Such narrow interpretation has not been shared by other ICTY Chambers. In the *Limaj et al* case, the Trial Chamber argued:

> While some degree of organisation by the parties will suffice to establish the existence of an armed conflict, this degree need not be the same as that required for establishing the responsibility of superiors for the acts of their subordinates within the organisation, as no determination of individual criminal responsibility is intended under this provision of the Statute.[163]

This reading is further supported by the 1987 ICRC commentary on APII, which found that a 'responsible command' under article 1(1) APII signifies 'some degree of organization ... but this does not necessarily mean that there is a hierarchical system of military organization similar to that of regular armed forces'.[164] Rather, it requires an organization capable of engaging in organized military action and able to enforce

[158] See, eg, Moir, *The Concept of Non-International Armed Conflict* (n 5) paras 43–45. Similarly, the 2016 ICRC commentary does not mention this requirement. See ICRC, *GCI: Commentary of 2016* (n 50) article 3.

[159] *Hadžihasanović et al, IT-01-47-AR72*, para 22.

[160] *Delalić et al, Judgment, 20 February 2001, Appeals Chamber, IT-96-21-A*, ICTY, para 256; see also *Brima et al, Judgment, 20 June 2007, Trial Chamber, SCSL-04-16-T*, SCSL, para 784.

[161] *Brima et al, SCSL-04-16-T*, para 557. Conversely, the ICC held that 'disregard or non-compliance with orders or instructions of the accused' or 'a weak or malfunctioning chain of command' are factors that may indicate a lack of effective control. *Bemba Gombo, ICC-01/05-01/08*, para 190.

[162] For a criticism of the view that a 'responsible command' that gives rise to 'command responsibility' could not exist in horizontally organized armed groups without a chain of command in the classical sense, see Sivakumaran, *The Law of Non-International Armed Conflict* (n 2) 175–76.

[163] *Mrkšić et al, IT-95-13/1-T*, para 407; *Limaj et al, IT-03-66-T*, para 89.

[164] Pilloud, Sandoz, Swinarski et al, *Commentary on the Additional Protocols of 8 June 1977 to the Geneva Conventions of 12 August 1949* (ICRC 1987) para 4463.

internal discipline.[165] As pointed out above, these two broad abilities of organized armed groups derive from IHL treaty law and are broadly accepted in practice.[166] In contrast, equating the 'responsible command' concept for the purpose of conflict classification with the structural requirements for proving 'command responsibility' of group leaders would set the threshold too high and would exclude a number of horizontally organized armed groups.[167] This does not mean, however, that depending on the circumstances commanders of specific units or groups may not exercise effective control over their subordinates.[168]

To sum up, it appears that being a collective entity is the first and fundamentally important criterion for qualifying as a party to an armed conflict. Command structures of conflicting parties may follow traditional centralized structures but may also be decentralized or horizontal in nature. However, being a collective entity is not sufficient to qualify as a party to a NIAC. A collective entity should also have the ability to ensure respect for fundamental humanitarian norms and the capacity to engage in sufficiently intense violence. This does not, however, mean that the entity must be vested with a 'responsible command' that is sufficiently sophisticated to lead to 'command responsibility' of a party's leader for acts of all subordinates. How armed groups may ensure respect for IHL in the absence of a narrowly interpreted 'responsible command' is discussed in the next section.

3.2.3 The ability to ensure respect for fundamental humanitarian norms

A group's ability to ensure respect for fundamental humanitarian norms is largely dependent on the level of discipline within the group. Discipline is commonly understood as 'the practice of training people to obey rules or a code of behaviour, using punishment to correct disobedience'.[169] In armed groups that are party to an armed conflict, discipline serves a number of purposes. Training and obliging members to obey the rules adopted by the party is a prerequisite for ensuring respect for fundamental norms of IHL. It has been rightly emphasized that discipline is required by the 'very logic underlying IHL';[170] in other words, discipline 'is at the very heart of IHL'.[171] While, in practice, respect for IHL is not necessarily a priority

165 See ibid. See also *Akayesu, ICTR-96-4-T*, para 626.

166 See Chapter 2 'Parties to Non-International Armed Conflicts under International Treaty Law'. See also Schmitt, 'Cyber Conflict' (n 52) 255–57; ILA, *Armed Conflicts (Final Report)* (n 14) 28–29.

167 eg while the ICC classified the *Ngiti militia* under its leader *Katanga* as a party to a NIAC, it could not find that 'Katanga was vested . . . with effective hierarchical power over all the commanders and combatants of the Ngiti militia'. *Katanga, ICC-01/04-01/07*, para 1365.

168 See, eg, article 28(a) ICC Statute. For further discussion of the concept of command responsibility in organized armed groups, see Zegveld, *Accountability of Armed Opposition Groups* (n 46) 111–31; Sivakumaran, 'Command Responsibility in Irregular Groups' (2012) 10 Journal of International Criminal Justice 1129–50.

169 Oxford Dictionary, online version, definition of 'discipline'.

170 ICRC, *Challenges Report (2003)* (n 45) 228.

171 Carswell, 'Classification des conflits: le dilemme du soldat' (2009) 91 Revue internationale de la Croix-Rouge 65–85 (translation by the author, the original French text read that discipline 'se trouve au Coeur meme du DIH'). See also Frésard and ICRC, *The Roots of Behaviour in War: A Survey of the Literature* (ICRC 2004) 16–18. Carswell also argues that, normally, only commanders have a more profound knowledge of IHL, and only by imposing orders on their subordinates can IHL be effectively

for armed groups, maintaining discipline among its forces should be. As researchers established, 'lack of discipline among the rank and file wastes resources, alienates potential supporters, and may undermine military efforts'.[172] Moreover, the very survival of the group necessitates that members do not collaborate with the adversary, or 'pursue their own impulses or agendas to the detriment of the organization's goals'.[173] Discipline is also key to implementing planned and coordinated military operations. Thus, the ICTY stressed that the establishment of rules and enforcement mechanisms evidences a 'growing formality and effectiveness of the organizational structure' of an armed group.[174]

Before examining structural factors that may testify to a group's ability to implement basic rules, it must be clear that this examination looks at the group's ability to respect *any kind of rules*—not necessarily IHL. If a group has sufficient structures to require its members to respect a simple code of conduct, or if the group operates under strict unwritten rules, this should be sufficient proof of its ability to also implement basic IHL. Concretely, if a group's code of conduct prescribes attacking members of the group's own constituency, it could similarly include rules prohibiting attacks against other civilians. Likewise, in terms of internal structures, it does not take much to absolutely prohibit torture. There is no objective reason why a basic set of rules applicable and respected within a group could not contain fundamental IHL norms.

Furthermore, determining the ability to implement basic humanitarian rules is not a question of whether a group respects IHL in practice, or adopts a respective policy. On the one hand, a high number of IHL violations can be indicative of a poor disciplinary system and a lack of command. On the other hand, a group can also conduct operations that violate international law in an organized and coordinated manner following a conscious decision by the group's leadership.[175] In fact, the existence of the notion of war crimes recognizes that IHL violations occur in conflicts between organized armed forces.[176] Thus, it is the ability of the group to ensure respect for internal rules more generally that is decisive for the classification of conflict, and not its actual conduct or the question of whether the group's internal rules correspond to IHL. Moreover, as emphasized with regard to Common Article 3 and APII, a party to the conflict does not need to have the capacity to implement every single rule of applicable IHL.[177] In practice, the ability to conduct, for example,

respected. Indeed, this is not only the case with regard to regular armed forces but also, eg, when humanitarian NGOs like Geneva Call train non-state armed groups in IHL they can often only train commanders and superiors and not any soldier. Discipline and respect for IHL will then have to be imposed by them.

[172] Weinstein, *Inside Rebellion* (n 66) 43.

[173] Margulies and Sinnot, 'Crossing Borders' (n 36) 329.

[174] *Limaj et al, IT-03-66-T*, paras 116–17; *Boškoski and Tarčulovski, IT-04-82-T*, para 274.

[175] See *Boškoski and Tarčulovski, IT-04-82-T*, paras 204–05. eg it is reported that the 'Islamic State Group' adopted a policy that 'legalized' rape of certain captured women by its members. See Callimachi, 'ISIS Enshrines a Theology of Rape', *The New York Times* (13 August 2015).

[176] See Bianchi and Naqvi, 'IHL and Terrorism' (n 45) 155.

[177] See Sections 2.1.2.2 'The ability to comply with basic humanitarian rules' and 2.2.2.4 'The capacity to implement the Protocol'.

trials 'affording all the judicial guarantees which are recognized as indispensable by civilized peoples' is not among the criteria that any judicial body has examined for applying Common Article 3. Drawing a strict link between the requisite degree of organization and the scope of the applicable norms would risk augmenting the NIAC threshold in light of the increasing crystallization of IHL norms as custom applicable in all conflicts.[178]

3.2.3.1 Enforcing respect for IHL in armed groups with centralized command structures

Behaviour studies show that structures to ensure respect for internal rules, including IHL, depend on three factors: clear rules; training and orders; and effective sanctions.[179] Similarly, notorious rebel leaders have stressed that guerrillas must internalize the rules of the group, and if 'discipline is violated, it is necessary always to punish the offender, whatever his rank, and to punish him drastically in a way that hurts'.[180] Accordingly, international tribunals have listed 'the existence of internal regulations and whether these are effectively disseminated to members', 'proper training', and 'the establishment of disciplinary rules and mechanisms' as indicators of a group's ability to respect IHL.[181] In practice, numerous examples show that armed groups' elaborate internal regulations—for example, codes of conduct[182]—train their members on military, ideological, and disciplinary issues,[183] or inflict punishment to ensure discipline.[184] Some groups, in particular those with more established structures and control over territory, have also set up military police forces, military courts, and prisons.[185] For example, at the height of the armed conflict in Kosovo, the KLA's disciplinary system included different measures taken at different hierarchical levels of the group, such as subjecting soldiers to 'an oral reprimand, a written critique, a short-term detention sentence, or a referral to the General Staff and to the

[178] In its customary IHL study, the ICRC found that 136 rules apply in non-international armed conflicts, and therefore bind states and non-state conflict parties. On the same issue, see also Sivakumaran, *The Law of Non-International Armed Conflict* (n 2) 25–32, 29.

[179] See Munoz-Rojas and Frésard, 'The Roots of Behaviour in War: Understanding and Preventing IHL Violations' (2004) 86 International Review of the Red Cross 189–206.

[180] Guevara, *Guerilla Warfare*. See quotes from Mao Tse Tung and Guevara in Weinstein, *Inside Rebellion* (n 66) 30.

[181] See, eg, *Boškoski and Tarčulovski, IT-04-82-T*, para 202.

[182] For an assessment of the KLA's internal rules and regulations as well as its military police, see *Limaj et al, IT-03-66-T*, paras 113–15. More generally on the practice of armed groups to adopt codes of conduct, see ICRC, 'A Collection of Codes of Conduct Issued by Armed Groups' (2011) 93 International Review of the Red Cross 483–501.

[183] eg it is reported that the National Resistance Army (NRA) in Uganda constantly trained its members on ideology and the NRA's code of conduct. See Weinstein, *Inside Rebellion* (n 66) 142–44.

[184] See, eg, *Ntaganda, ICC-01/04-02/06*, para 15.

[185] See *Milutinović et al, IT-05-87-T*, para 831. Similarly, the 'Islamic State Group' is reportedly operating a tight disciplinary system with police forces, intelligence, courts, and prisons. See Lister, 'Profiling the Islamic State' (2014) 13 Bookings Doha Center Analysis Paper.

Military Court'.[186] Other groups threatened to expel members who violate the group's rules.[187]

Imposing discipline in a centrally structured group normally follows a hierarchical model: the group's leadership issues rules and orders and the hierarchical structure ensures that they are followed and enforced throughout the group. As seen above, however, groups' structures vary and operating a functioning chain of command and hierarchy is not a strict requirement for qualifying as a party to a NIAC. Similarly, case law does not show that the '"capability of meeting minimum humanitarian requirements" would imply the need for elaborate disciplinary procedures'.[188] For example, in the *Haradinaj et al* case the ICTY considered the KLA in Kosovo sufficiently organized despite the fact that it did not have 'courts, judges, or prisons'.[189] In fact, the tribunal established that during early stages of the insurgency, the 'KLA General Staff had no system for disciplining KLA soldiers', and that imposing discipline through 'zone commanders was ... difficult or impossible, due to lack of organization and regular communication'.[190] Similarly, in the *Limaj et al* case, the tribunal determined that the KLA constituted 'an organised armed group, able to engage in an internal armed conflict' despite the fact that it did not yet have clear internal regulations or a military police.[191]

3.2.3.2 Enforcing respect for IHL in armed groups with decentralized command structures

These findings, however, do not mean that groups are unable to ensure respect for fundamental humanitarian norms without a centralized command or elaborate disciplinary structures. In nascent or decentralized armed groups in which central leadership coordinates military operations but does not have the power to impose discipline in a hierarchical manner throughout the organization, compliance may also be ensured in a decentralized way. The different sub-groups normally form in a 'bottom-up' rather than 'top-down' manner. In one situation, at the lowest level groups of three to five persons came together and formed a fighting unit.[192] In terms of internal discipline, small groups constitute an ideal size because in such groups, control and punishment are easily ensured.[193] Peer pressure or group dynamics may suffice to impose discipline. In order to increase their military effectiveness, small groups normally unite behind commanders. Importantly, in these organically formed groups, the authority of a commander 'is not derived from his rank within the structure of a force, but by his formidable presence'.[194] As the commander of

186 *Đorđević, IT-05-87/1-T*, para 1575.

187 This is reported about 'Al Qaida in Iraq'. See Margulies and Sinnot, 'Crossing Borders' (n 36) 331.

188 Kress, 'The 1999 Crisis in East Timor' (n 8) 417.

189 *Haradinaj et al, IT-04-84-T*, para 69.

190 ibid.

191 *Limaj et al, IT-03-66-T*, paras 94–134.

192 In the Libya conflict, this number 'reflected the limits of transporting fighters by car'. McQuinn, 'After the Fall: Libya's Evolving Armed Groups' (n 111) 33.

193 See Weinstein, *Inside Rebellion* (n 66).

194 Mackinlay, 'The Classification of Insurgent Forces' (n 74) 48.

a powerful battalion in Libya's Misrata pointed out, he did not form his battalion but fighters 'would just follow me back to our base at night'.[195] The larger a group grows, however, the more important formal hierarchies and strict disciplinary structures become.[196] If fighters unite behind a commander and follow the commander's military order, they accept the commander's authority and the rules set out in that group. At that point, a commander exercises some control over the fighters, which is the basic requirement for ensuring respect for fundamental humanitarian norms.

If such groups unite into one party to an armed conflict, meaning that they establish some form of joint leadership exercising operational coordination and strategic authority, the ability to enforce rules often remains primarily with the local commanders. In fact, different sub-groups can form one party to a NIAC even if they each operate under their own explicit or implicit code of conduct, provided that this code is in line with joint rules established by party leadership. It is upon the group leadership to provide rules and objectives for the group as a whole. For example, while it did not have the capacity to disseminate these rules to each individual soldier and was unable to enforce them effectively, early on the KLA General Command adopted a communication pledging to respect the laws of war and distributed this communication together with ICRC IHL booklets among its forces.[197]

A leadership that provides the group's strategy and rules, combined with local or regional commanders who are able to enforce respect for them, corresponds with what the ICTY required to establish the existence of an armed group. In the *Boškoski and Tarčulovski* case, the tribunal found that 'for an armed group to be considered organised, it would need to have *some hierarchical structure* and its leadership requires the *capacity to exert authority over its members*'.[198] In the *Haradinaj et al* case, it further argued that 'leadership of the group must, as a minimum, have the ability to *exercise some control* over its members so that the basic obligations of Common Article 3 of the Geneva Conventions may be implemented'.[199] Similarly, the ICRC argued back in the 1970s that armed groups may qualify as party to a NIAC even if they operate under a 'cellular structure in which commands cannot be given centrally to the whole group'.[200] This decentralized system cannot be too loose, however. A group operating under a decentralized command structure will not qualify as 'genuinely organized' if its units or individual members 'act entirely on their own initiative, in total disregard of a countervailing policy espoused by the armed group'.[201] In other words, rules and strategies designed by a group's overall leadership need to trump sub-groups' codes or regulations.

[195] McQuinn, 'After the Fall: Libya's Evolving Armed Groups' (n 111) 37. Similarly, in the *Haradinaj* case, the ICTY identified Haradinaj as a de facto commander accepted by the people and not as a de jure commander who received his power from the KLA's hierarchy. *Haradinaj et al, IT-04-84-T*, para 67.

[196] See Mao, *On Guerilla Warfare* (n 68) chapter 5; Weinstein, *Inside Rebellion* (n 66) 129.

[197] See *Haradinaj et al, IT-04-84-T*, para 69.

[198] *Boškoski and Tarčulovski, IT-04-82-T*, para 195 (emphasis added).

[199] *Haradinaj et al, IT-04-84bis-T*, para 393 (emphasis added).

[200] See ICRC, *Rules Applicable in Guerrilla Warfare—Paper Submitted the Conference of Government Experts on the Reaffirmation and Development of International Humanitarian Law Applicable in Armed Conflicts* (ICRC 1971) 17.

[201] Dinstein, *Non-International Armed Conflicts in International Law* (n 63) para 140.

3.2.4 The capacity to engage in sufficiently intense violence

Collective and well-disciplined entities may only become party to an armed conflict if they have the capacity to confront their adversary 'with military means';[202] in other words, they must 'develop a sufficient degree of military organisation to conduct hostilities'.[203] In practice, a number of factors is used to determine this capacity. First, as military-type violence is not conducted by uncoordinated individuals but according to military tactics and coordination, the development of 'a unified military strategy', 'operational units [that] coordinate their actions', or 'the effective dissemination of . . . orders and decisions' may testify to the existence of an organization that operates in a military-like manner.[204] Second, the group must be able to conduct operations that contribute to an escalation of violence between the parties. While this can be achieved through 'large scale military operations',[205] this factor depends to some extent on the conflict dynamics. And third, armed groups must possess sufficient logistics to engage in hostilities, including manpower and weapons. In addition, control over territory normally testifies to an elevated degree of military capabilities, and provides a basis from where groups operate. These four aspects are discussed in more detail in the following.

3.2.4.1 Operating in a coordinated manner

Being a party to an armed conflict necessitates a certain command structure, be it centralized or decentralized. This structure enables a group to act 'in a coordinated manner, thereby generally heightening the capability to engage in violence. In military operations, such coordination typically involves mission planning, sharing intelligence and exercising command and control.'[206] The ability to operate according to military strategies and coordination is normally fulfilled where non-state forces consist primarily of, or are led by, dissident military forces.[207] Similarly, a functioning chain of command is a common tool to ensure effective coordination. Yet, in practice, non-state parties to NIACs often do not operate according to patterns similar to those of state armed forces.[208] Especially when militarily inferior, armed groups avoid direct confrontations with state armed forces because they lack the capacity to engage in open hostilities. Weaker groups tend to engage in rather infrequent armed attacks—for example, by ambushing softer targets among the

[202] *Haradinaj et al, IT-04-84-T*, para 60.
[203] ICRC, *Interpretive Guidance on the Notion of Direct Participation in Hostilities under International Humanitarian Law* (n 63) 32.
[204] See *Boškoski and Tarčulovski, IT-04-82-T*, para 200.
[205] ibid.
[206] Schmitt, 'Cyber Conflict' (n 52) 255. Likewise, Watkin points out that whether centrally or horizontally organized 'there is a commonality to fighting wars that requires an organization to consist of commanders, planners, intelligence personnel, and fighters to carry out the military action. There is also a requirement to provide logistical support.' Watkin, 'Opportunity Lost' (n 63) 680.
[207] See, eg, *Bemba, ICC-01/05-01/08*, para 261. See also Human Rights Council, *Report of the International Commission of Inquiry to investigate all alleged violations of international human rights law in the Libyan Arab Jamahiriya* (n 34) paras 36–45, 56; Dinstein, *Non-International Armed Conflicts in International Law* (n 63) para 131.
[208] With regard to the conduct of the Taliban, see, eg, Parks, 'Combatants' (n 90) 258. More generally, see Mao, *On Guerilla Warfare* (n 68).

opponent's security forces and by employing hit-and-run tactics.[209] Another tactic can be the use of improvised explosive devices (IEDs).[210] If such attacks occur as isolated or sporadic acts of violence, followed by periods of calm without major violent confrontations, they do not testify to a sufficient capacity to engage in a NIAC.[211]

3.2.4.2 The ability to provoke an escalation of violence

The classification of armed violence normally changes when armed groups develop the capacity to carry out operations in an increasingly coordinated manner, with higher frequency and longer duration.[212] For example, at the time when armed violence reached the threshold of a non-international armed conflict in Syria, the UN CoI noted that 'sporadic clashes between the armed actors have evolved into continuous combat, involving more brutal tactics and new military capabilities by both sides'.[213] Similarly, the UN CoI on the Central African Republic did not immediately classify the Anti-Balaka group's attacks against civilians and sporadic clashes with their adversary as a NIAC. The classification only changed after the group launched a concerted attack against the capital Bangui and was able to maintain that level of hostilities thereafter.[214] Accordingly, the ICTY emphasized that 'what matters is whether the acts are perpetrated in isolation or as part of a protracted campaign that entails the engagement of both parties in hostilities'.[215]

More frequent and coordinated armed confrontations between parties are likely to change the conflict pattern away from law enforcement methods towards the employment of armed forces under NIAC rules of engagement.[216] The ability of

[209] See *Haradinaj et al, IT-04-84-T*, para 87; *Boškoski and Tarčulovski, IT-04-82-T*, para 276.

[210] See Human Rights Council, *Report of the Independent International Commission of Inquiry on the Syrian Arab Republic* (n 34) para 10.

[211] States made that explicit in article 8(2)(d) and (f) ICC Statute. This is also reflected in findings by the ICTY on the period when KLA violence in Kosovo had not yet reached the level of an armed conflict. See *Haradinaj et al, IT-04-84-T*, paras 98–99.

[212] It appears that the increased frequency and coordination of violent attacks by the KLA against Serbian security forces was a major indicator for the ICTY to qualify the occurring violence as an armed conflict. See ibid paras 98–100. Similarly, in the case of the armed conflict in Darfur, the CoI noted that armed groups took up arms in 2002 but that 'the scale of rebel attacks increased noticeably in February 2003'. For the CoI, this was a clear indication that the conflict was no longer 'a situation of internal disturbances and tensions, riots, or isolated and sporadic acts of violence'. UN Secretary General, 'Report of the International Commission of Inquiry on Darfur' (n 32) para 75.

[213] Human Rights Council, *Report of the Independent International Commission of Inquiry on the Syrian Arab Republic* (n 34) Annex III, para 1.

[214] The International Commission of Inquiry on the Central African Republic—Final Report, S/2014/928, Annex I, para 95.

[215] *Boškoski and Tarčulovski, IT-04-82-T*, para 185. This finding is supported in states' military manuals. See, eg, German Ministry of Defence, *Humanitäres Völkerrecht in bewaffneten Konflikten—Handbuch* (ZDv15/2) (2013) para 210 (translation on file with the author).

[216] This pattern did not only occur in Kosovo and Macedonia but also in Syria, see Human Rights Council, *Report of the International Commission of Inquiry to investigate all alleged violations of international human rights law in the Libyan Arab Jamahiriya* (n 34) paras 21–22. At the same time, the mere fact that the state party decides to employ its armed forces is not decisive for conflict classification as long as armed forces are employed to support law enforcement personnel. See Netherlands, *The Military Manual of the Netherlands* (Dutch Ministry of Defence 2005) para 1007 (translation on file with the author). This has also been implied in ICTY jurisprudence in which the court did not find the kind of

armed groups to increase the number and quality of their armed attacks contributes to a necessary escalation of violence.[217] It seems, however, that the requisite amount of violence that an armed group must be able to engage in cannot be determined in the abstract. It is to some extent relative to the context in which it occurs. For example, it has been pointed out that the international community readily qualified low-intensity armed violence between 'anarchical' armed groups as an armed conflict in Somalia, while a similar degree of violence that involved more sophisticated armed groups in urban areas in South America was not considered an armed conflict.[218] While such classifications may also be politically motivated, it seems nonetheless that an armed group needs more sophisticated operational and logistical capabilities to escalate armed violence if confronted with powerful state security forces than what is required to trigger an armed conflict against a state with weak law-enforcement forces.

3.2.4.3 Sufficient manpower and logistics

In all cases, the ability to engage in sufficiently intense military-like confrontations requires manpower and logistics: a group must be able to recruit members, who need to be armed and possibly trained. In addition, in order to coordinate the armed activities of the group, some means of communication should be available.[219] Sufficient logistics form the backbone of the group's military operations; however, the type and quantity of logistics cannot be determined in the abstract. What is decisive is that they enable the group to engage in sufficiently intense hostilities. For example, the sizes of non-state armed groups vary significantly, and recruitment of fighters takes different forms, ranging from civilians forming or joining armed groups, through foreign fighters, to deserters from other armed forces.[220] Similarly, where modern communication technology is unavailable, or is not used for security reasons, couriers, small radios, mobile phones, or even gunshots may serve groups as ways of coordinating their actions.[221]

armed forces decisive but the rules on the use of force according to which they operated. *Boškoski and Tarčulovski, IT-04-82-T*, paras 244–49.

217 Increasing numbers of armed confrontations, as well as a change in numbers and quality of forces employed by the state, are considered key factors for assessing the intensity of armed conflicts. In addition to the degree of organization of the armed groups involved, a sufficient intensity of violence is the second main requirement for classifying an armed conflict. See, eg, *Boškoski and Tarčulovski, IT-04-82-T*, paras 244–49; *Haradinaj et al, IT-04-84-T*, para 49.

218 See Geiss, 'Armed Violence in Fragile States: Low-intensity Conflicts, Spillover Conflicts, and Sporadic Law Enforcement Operations by Third Parties' (2009) 91 International Review of the Red Cross 127–42, 136.

219 See *Boškoski and Tarčulovski, IT-04-82-T*, para 201.

220 See, eg, Human Rights Council, *Report of the Independent International Commission of Inquiry on the Syrian Arab Republic* (n 34) Annex III, para 10; *Haradinaj et al, IT-04-84bis-T*, paras 43–52. All three forms of 'recruitment' occurred in Syria, while in Kosovo and Macedonia, defectors did not constitute a significant number of recruits. In eastern DRC, armed groups regularly originated as splinter groups from other armed groups. See *Lubanga Dyilo, ICC-01/04-01/06*, paras 80–91.

221 See *Limaj et al, IT-03-66-T*, para 124. Similarly, owing to the lack of other means, in 2003 the FRPI in the Democratic Republic of the Congo communicated by letter, a few short-range radios, and sometimes whistles.

In order to enable the group to engage in hostilities, recruits normally undergo some basic military training. Reportedly, in the case of the KLA this included the following two aspects: 'how to use weapons, [and] how to treat prisoners of war, persons who surrendered, and civilians'.[222] The essential equipment of a fighter is the weapon; however, especially at the beginning of an insurgency, armed groups frequently face supply shortages. Moreover, the available weapons are often inadequate to confront well-equipped armed forces.[223] In such situations, the leadership's ability to improve the supply of weapons and other logistics is key to enhancing the group's operational capacities. Sufficient arms supply has therefore been considered as testifying to an increasing degree of organization.[224] Likewise, the leadership's ability to obtain and distribute sufficient funds and supplies to group members is not only of practical importance but can also help to legitimize its leadership.[225]

3.2.4.4 Control over territory

Another indicator of a group's operational capacity—a proof of strength as compared to the adversary, and a factor that helps the group consolidate its internal organization—is control over territory.[226] Based on an analysis of various conflicts, it has been pointed out that '[a]s a practical matter opposing groups will in most cases control enough territory to organize'.[227] While a group's ability to set up effective government-like infrastructure in the territory it occupies would certainly be evidence of an elevated degree of organization, this is not essential to prove a group's degree of organization.[228] Rather, a group's ability to capture territory is normally a sign of military strength, even if the adversary, owing to its military superiority, retains the possibility to enter territory considered to be under an armed group's control.[229] In addition, territorial control enables the group to regroup after attacks, plan new attacks from a safe haven, and coordinate operations.[230] Territorial control

[222] *Haradinaj et al, IT-04-84-T*, para 86.

[223] eg because of a general shortage of weapons, KLA fighters received weapons such as hunting rifles from the population. See *Limaj et al, IT-03-66-T*, para 122. Similarly, at the beginning of their struggle, the FRPI were only equipped with traditional hunting weapons. See *Katanga, ICC-01/04-01/07*, para 530. In many cases weapons are also obtained locally, in particular through raiding the opponent's stocks. Reportedly, advances on military targets supplied armed groups in Syria with more weapons than had been previously available. See Human Rights Council, *Report of the Independent International Commission of Inquiry on the Syrian Arab Republic* (n 34) Annex III, para 14. Similarly, in the early stages of their struggle, groups in Libya received most of their weapons from defeated opponents, and, at a later stage, they allegedly received supplies from foreign states. See Human Rights Council, *Report of the International Commission of Inquiry to investigate all alleged violations of international human rights law in the Libyan Arab Jamahiriya* (n 34) para 58.

[224] *Limaj et al, IT-03-66-T*, para 122; *Boškoski and Tarčulovski, IT-04-82-T*, para 286. In the conflicts in Iraq and Syria, highly organized armed groups such as the Kurdish People's Defense Units obtained significant amounts of weapons and other equipment from state supporters. Other groups with greater financial means, such as the 'Islamic State Group', also purchased weapons internationlly.

[225] See Human Rights Council, *Report of the Independent International Commission of Inquiry on the Syrian Arab Republic* (n 34) Annex III, para 13.

[226] See also Pilloud, Sandoz, Swinarski et al, *Commentary on the Additional Protocols* (n 164) para 4465.

[227] ILA, *Armed Conflicts (Final Report)* (n 14) 29.

[228] See *Boškoski and Tarčulovski, IT-04-82-T*, para 242.

[229] See *Haradinaj et al, IT-04-84-T*, para 73.

[230] See *Boškoski and Tarčulovski, IT-04-82-T*, para 242; *Haradinaj et al, IT-04-84-T*, para 72.

may thus testify to the group's existing and future capacity to engage in sufficiently intense armed violence. Territorial control is not, however, a strict requirement to qualify an armed group as a party to a NIAC.[231]

3.3 Specific Cases

3.3.1 Transnational armed groups

At least factually, the geographical scope of conflicts is broadening. As the ICRC stated, 'the spillover of conflicts into neighbouring countries, their geographical expanse and their regionalization … appear to have become a distinctive feature of many contemporary armed conflicts'.[232] In part, this is due to 'the multiplication of intervening foreign States *and armed groups*'.[233] Indeed, the intervention of the Lebanese armed group 'Hezbollah' in the Syria conflict contributes to a regionalization of the conflict, as does the intervention of Iranian, Jordanian, Turkish, Russian, or Western states' armed forces. At the same time, the increasing spread of hostilities through entire regions is also due to the expansion of armed groups. Reportedly, after conquering significant territory in Iraq and Syria, the 'Islamic State Group' leader Al-Baghdadi declared in November 2014: 'We announce to you the expansion of the Islamic State to new countries, to the countries of the Haramayn [Saudi Arabia], Yemen, Egypt, Libya, Algeria.'[234] One year later, the US Department of Defense reported 'the first U.S. strike against an ISIL leader in Libya'.[235] According to a report on the threat posed by the ISG to international peace and security, the UN Secretary General found: '[A]s of 15 December 2015, 34 groups from all around the world had reportedly pledged allegiance to ISIL'.[236] Legally, the factual spread of conflict raises the question whether and under what conditions armed groups that operate under the same name in different territories qualify as one party to a NIAC under IHL.

The scope of this chapter does not permit participation in the broad debate on the geographical scope of application of IHL.[237] Instead, the focus lies on the question

[231] See Section 2.1.2.3 'Territorial control?'. See also *Lubanga Dyilo, ICC-01/04-01/06*, paras 536–37; *Katanga, ICC-01/04-01/07*, para 1186.

[232] ICRC, *Challenges Report (2015)* (n 108) 6.

[233] ibid (emphasis added).

[234] Reuters, 'Islamic State Leader Urges Attacks in Saudi Arabia', *Reuters* (13 November 2014); see also Shaheen and Stephen, 'From Syria to Bosnia: Isis and its Affiliates around the World', *The Guardian* (3 July 2015).

[235] US Department of Defense, *Statement from Pentagon Press Secretary Peter Cook on U.S. Strike in Libya* (US Department of Defense, 14 November 2015).

[236] UN Security Council, 'Report of the Secretary-General on the Threat Posed by ISIL (Da'esh) to International Peace and Security and the Range of United Nations Efforts in Support of Member States in Countering the Threat', S/2016/92, 29 January 2016, para 7.

[237] For discussion on this subject, see, eg, Sassòli, *Transnational Armed Groups and International Humanitarian Law* (HPCR Occasional Paper Series, 2006); Schmitt, 'Cyber Conflict' (n 52); Pejic, 'Extraterritorial Targeting' (n 106); Schöberl, 'The Geographical Scope of Application of the Conventions' (n 106). See also ICRC, *GCI: Commentary of 2016* (n 50) article 3, paras 102–32.

of whether and under what conditions non-state armed groups that operate on the territory of multiple states could be considered one organized armed group for the purposes of IHL.[238] This means that the present analysis does not look at the status of individual members of a party to a NIAC that are outside the country in which hostilities take place.[239] Neither does it examine the broader question of whether armed groups, if they do not form one party to a NIAC, may be considered 'associated forces' or 'co-belligerents' of another party to a NIAC.[240] Rather, this section examines the structural links that must exist between armed groups that operate in different states in order to consider them as one transnational organized armed group. After briefly examining different recent approaches that attempt to conceptualize global armed groups, the main parts of this section examine whether the above-suggested categorization of centralized and decentralized command structures applies to transnational armed groups.

3.3.1.1 Different approaches to conceptualizing transnational armed groups

Over the past decade, the debate on the geographical scope of application of IHL was primarily concerned with the US suggestion of a 'global war on terrorism'. In more legal terms, the US claimed to be in an armed conflict with 'Taliban or al Qaida forces'.[241] While both groups are primarily based in Afghanistan and neighbouring Pakistan, attacks in various countries have been committed under the Al Qaida label. Yet, a number of states, as well as the ICRC, have raised doubts whether Al Qaida-affiliated 'bombings in Glasgow, London, Madrid, Bali or Casablanca can

[238] Finding that a transnational armed group could qualify as an organized armed group for the purposes of IHL does not necessarily mean that the entire group becomes party to a NIAC. Commentators have argued that for a NIAC to exist in a non-belligerent state, the criteria of 'organization' and 'intensity' must be fulfilled on the territory of that state. See Pejic, 'Extraterritorial Targeting' (n 106) 38–39.

[239] As the ICRC suggested in its 2015 Challenges Report, the question of which legal regime applies to individual member of armed groups that are outside the state in which hostilities take place may not be similar to 'the legal regime that would be applicable to any use of force against bases established in the territory of a non-belligerent State by a non-State armed group for training and logistical purposes in relation to an ongoing NIAC'. ICRC, *Challenges Report (2015)* (n 108) 16.

[240] For some discussion of this question, see Rodenhäuser, 'Armed Groups, Rebel Coalitions, and Transnational Groups: The Degree of Organization Required from Non-State Armed Groups to Become Party to a Non-International Armed Conflict' (2017) 19 Yearbook of International Humanitarian Law (forthcoming). The concept of 'associated forces' is used in US practice and jurisprudence and follows the concept of co-belligerency as found in IHL of IACs. As defined in a draft 2015 'Authorization for the Use of Military Force' against the Islamic State Group, 'associated forces' means 'organizations fighting for, on behalf of, or alongside ISIL or any closely-related successor entity in hostilities against the United States or its coalition partners'. See 'Obama's Request for Congressional Authorization to Fight the Islamic State: Full Text', *The Washington Post* (11 February 2015); see also US Department of Defense, *Remarks by the General Counsel of the Department of Defense on the Legal Framework for the United States' Use of Military Force Since 9/11* (n 122). For discussion and criticism, see Heller, 'The Use and Abuse of Analogy in IHL' (n 121); Margulies and Sinnot, 'Crossing Borders' (n 36); Lubell, 'The Distinction between International and Non-International Armed Conflicts: Challenges for IHL?' (XVIII Round Table on Current Issues of International Humanitarian Law 2015).

[241] See US Department of Defense, *Remarks by the General Counsel of the Department of Defense on the Legal Framework for the United States' Use of Military Force Since 9/11* (n 122).

be attributed to one and the same party to an armed conflict as understood under IHL'.[242] Similarly, different commentators argued that, on a global scale, Al Qaida appears 'to be a loosely connected, clandestine network of cells'[243] and that 'individual terrorist action all over the globe carried out on the basis of an "Al Qaeda franchise-model" cannot be attributed to Al Qaeda as a non-State party to a non-international armed conflict of global reach'.[244] While there was broad agreement on this factual assessment of Al Qaida, little has been said about which organizational structures would characterize a global armed group.[245]

More recently, focus has shifted from an ill-defined global armed conflict towards determining armed conflicts between specific parties that spread over the territory of multiple states. Different approaches have been suggested. One is based on the assumption that the determinating factor in distinguishing IACs from NIACs 'is the nature and identity of the group(s) and not the territory on which they are based'.[246] Accordingly, the question of whether a NIAC could exist in the territory of more than one state would 'depend on 1) the involvement of qualifying parties, and 2) sufficient intensity with respect to the conflict *as a whole*'.[247] A second approach can be broadly linked to the concept of 'spillover', meaning 'an armed conflict originating within the territory of a State that is waged between government armed forces and one or more organized armed groups ... spills over into the territory of one or more neighbouring States'.[248] In such cases, the conflict continues between the same parties, and IHL remains applicable between them.[249] For the purposes of this chapter, one crucial conclusion drawn from the broad acceptance of the spillover concept is that state borders do not automatically 'cut' a group that in reality operates transnationally into two distinct legal entities.

[242] ICRC, *Challenges Report (2015)* (n 108) 7–8. See also Council of Europe (Venice Commission), *Opinion on the International Legal Obligations of Council of Europe Member States in Respect of Secret Detention Facilities and Inter-State Transport of Prisoners*, 17 March 2006, CDL-AD(2006)009, para 78.

[243] Vité, 'Typology of Armed Conflicts in International Humanitarian Law: Legal Concepts and Actual Situations' (2009) 91 International Review of the Red Cross 93.

[244] Kress, 'Some Reflections on the International Legal Framework Governing Transnational Armed Conflicts' (2010) 15 Journal of Conflict and Security Law 261. See also Sassòli, 'Transnational Armed Groups and International Humanitarian Law' (n 237); Lubell, 'The War (?) against Al-Qaeda' in Wilmshurst (ed), *International Law and the Classification of Conflicts* (OUP 2012) 421–54, 435; Milanovic and Hadzi-Vidanovic, 'A Taxonomy' (n 6) 187; ILA, *Armed Conflicts (Final Report)* (n 14) 25.

[245] eg in the *Hamdan* case, which is often cited as an authority for the theoretical possibility of a global NIAC, the US Supreme Court did not elaborate on this issue. See *Hamdan v Rumsfeld, 548 U. S. 557 (2006)*. Neither do the commentators cited above.

[246] Sivakumaran, *The Law of Non-International Armed Conflict* (n 2) 234.

[247] Schmitt, 'Charting the Legal Geography of Non-International Armed Conflict' (2014) 90 International Law Studies Series. US Naval War College 1, 16. For related views, see also Sivakumaran, *The Law of Non-International Armed Conflict* (n 2) 233–34; Sassòli, 'Transnational Armed Groups and International Humanitarian Law' (n 237) 9; Lubell, 'The War (?)'(n 244) 435.

[248] ICRC, *Challenges Report (2015)* (n 108) 15.

[249] On the spillover concept, see ibid as well as, eg, Milanovic and Hadzi-Vidanovic, 'A Taxonomy' (n 6) 288–93; Akande, 'Classification of Armed Conflicts' (n 6) 55. Recent examples include the spillover of the conflict between the US and the Taliban from Afghanistan into Pakistan, that between Colombia and the FARC into Ecuador, that between Turkey and the PKK into Iraq, or that between Kenya and the Somali Al Shabaab into Kenya.

Opinions vary, however, on the extent to which conflicts can 'spill'. Some assert that 'the continuity of hostilities'[250] or 'the contiguity of land surface between States' are crucial elements of the spillover concept and suggest a geographically narrow reading.[251] Others argue that NIACs can spill beyond adjunct territory if there is sufficient 'nexus' between the violence taking place in the two or more states.[252] According to the first view, the crossing of an often factually invisible border would not hinder the parties to the conflict in continuing to operate as if they were in one state. In the latter case, one decisive aspect of the requisite 'nexus' would be that the two or more sub-groups or units of the non-state party to the conflict are sufficiently linked to qualify as one organized armed group, even if operating in different territories.

Little, if any, state or jurisprudential practice is known that would indicate how states determine a sufficient link between the different components of an alleged transnational armed group. Some US scholars have suggested that 'unlike traditional "internal" armed conflicts, "organization" is not necessarily a condition precedent to the existence' of a transnational armed conflict.[253] Yet, they also recognized that this interpretation is not 'generally representative of a majority of States, international law experts, and international nongovernment organizations with competence in humanitarian law'.[254] Indeed, the ICRC has repeatedly emphasized that, in its view, any geographical spread of a NIAC 'would require, in the first place, the existence of a "unitary" non-State party opposing one or more States'.[255] Following a similar approach, scholars have argued that groups operating in different countries would need to form part of 'the same group',[256] meaning 'a quasi-military organization would be required, not a loose 'terrorism franchise" '.[257] It has been suggested that this requirement is fulfilled if they were 'one and the same, operating within a single command and control structure equally active in the carrying out of the group's military operations against' their adversary.[258]

[250] ICRC, *Challenges Report (2015)* (n 108) 19.

[251] Pejic, 'Extraterritorial Targeting' (n 106) 15.

[252] See, eg, Schmitt, 'Charting the Legal Geography of Non-International Armed Conflict' (n 247) 12; Milanovic, 'The End of Application of International Humanitarian Law' (2014) 96 International Review of the Red Cross 186. The requirement of a sufficient nexus between a targeting operation and an existing conflict has also been advanced by Lubell and Derejko, 'A Global Battlefield?: Drones and the Geographical Scope of Armed Conflict' (2013) 11 Journal of International Criminal Justice 65–88.

[253] Corn and Jensen, 'Transnational Armed Conflict: A "Principled" Approach to the Regulation of Counter-Terro Combat Operations' (2009) 42 Israel Law Review 1–34, 19. Others seem to have simply assumed that Al Qaida on a global scale would qualify as a party to a conflict. See, eg, Blank, 'Defining the Battlefield in Contemporary Conflict and Counterterrorism: Understanding the Parameters of the Zone of Combat' (2010) 39 Georgia Journal of International and Comparative Law 1–38.

[254] Corn, 'Triggering the Law of Armed Conflict?' in Corn (ed), *The War on Terror and the Laws of War: A Military Perspective* (OUP 2015) 68.

[255] ICRC, *Challenges Report (2015)* (n 108) 18. Other commentators seem to base their analyses on the same assumption. See, eg, Moir, *The Concept of Non-International Armed Conflict* (n 5) paras 27.

[256] Sivakumaran, *The Law of Non-International Armed Conflict* (n 2) 233.

[257] Paulus and Vashakmadze, 'Asymmetrical War' (n 50) 117.

[258] Lubell, 'The Distiction between International and Non-International Armed Conflicts: Challenges for IHL?' (n 240).

Determining what signifies a transnational armed group for the purposes of IHL can have important legal and policy implications. If the position is taken that IHL applies without territorial limitations and to all acts and actors sufficiently linked to an armed conflict, finding that different sub-groups are sufficiently connected to form one party to a NIAC in accordance with IHL could mean that IHL applies with regard to all components of that group, wherever located.[259] Following this approach, and subject to *ius ad bellum* restrictions, a party to the NIAC could use force under an IHL framework against all components of that group wherever they are located. In contrast, if different components cannot be proven to form one organized armed group for the purposes of IHL, IHL may not necessarily apply to all components of the group. Hence, using force against such individual groups under a conduct of hostilities paradigm might not necessarily be permitted.

3.3.1.2 Centralized command structures in transnational armed groups

Reportedly, a 'direct command and control' exist(ed) between the 'Islamic State Group' (ISG) in Libya and the group's 'core operation in Iraq and Syria'.[260] This link was primarily based on the alleged leader of the Libyan branch called 'Zubaidi, who headed Islamic State operations in central Iraq prior to going to Libya'.[261] On the one hand, this personal link could be deemed sufficiently strong to determine that the ISG in Libya formed part of the ISG in Syria and Iraq, despite reports that the ISG 'is a hybrid operation in Libya, led partly by foreign fighters and partly by Libyans'.[262] On the other hand, it has been suggested that all parts of the armed group would need to act under 'a centralised military command and a chain of command from top to bottom'.[263] In the view of this author, if the group in Libya was sufficiently organized—either centrally or horizontally—to qualify as an organized armed group for the purposes of IHL, and its leadership was under the direct command and control of ISG headquarters, it would not be necessary to prove a chain of command running all the way from ISG leadership in Syria or Iraq to the ISG rank and file in Libya. If central leadership exercises factual command and control over the commanders of sub-groups or units, and the sub-group's leadership exercises operational coordination and strategic authority over its units, this should suffice to consider the entire sub-group part of the overall organization.

[259] In contrast, if IHL is considered to apply primarily on the territory of belligerent states, including to certain spillover situations, the fact that one group would have different components located in territorially distinct and unconnected places would not necessarily render IHL applicable to all of them.

[260] Unspecified US Department of Defence sources, cited in Chesney, 'The Global War on ISIL and Its Associated Forces' (*Lawforce*, 14 November 2015) <https://www.lawfareblog.com/global-war-isil-and-its-associated-forces> (accessed 2 November 2017).

[261] ibid. [262] ibid.

[263] This standard was suggested by Ambos and Alkatout, 'Has Justice Been Done?' (n 65) 347. Obviously, these authors were unable to find that Al Qaida met this criterion.

3.3.1.3 *Decentralized command structures in transnational armed groups*

The other notorious example of an allegedly global armed group is Al Qaida. Studies on Al Qaida's operations suggest that, as a global network, Al Qaida's structure is best understood in three components:[264]

- The first one is 'core Al Qaida' (CoreAQ) or 'Al Qaeda Senior Leadership', which is based in Afghanistan and Pakistan's 'Federally Administrated Tribal Areas'.[265] Even after 9/11 and the subsequent armed conflict against Al Qaida and the Taliban in Afghanistan, CoreAQ reportedly continued 'to exert some coordination, if not actual command capability, in terms of commissioning attacks, directing surveillance and collating reconnaissance, planning operations, and approving their execution'.[266]
- The second component is a network of Al Qaida-associated organizations that exist(ed) in different parts of the world. Reportedly, before and shortly after 9/11, these organizations were built on 'personal veteran relations' with CoreAQ,[267] and associated groups received 'spiritual guidance ... training, arms, money, and other assistance' from CoreAQ.[268] More recently, the relation between CoreAQ and associated groups became 'more formal', at least to the extent that some of the associated groups changed their names into 'Al Qaeda in the Islamic Maghreb' (AQIM), 'Al Qaeda in the Arabian Peninsula' (AQAP), 'Al Qaeda in Yemen' (AQIY), or 'Al Qaeda in Iraq' (AQI).[269] It has been suggested that these groups 'have strong and traditional operational ties with the Al Qaeda leadership', they 'communicate with Al Qaeda leadership', 'get advice and directions and look to receive approval for their proposals of operations'.[270] In other words, CoreAQ 'controls most of the operational activity' of these groups.[271] It is also reported that CoreAQ appoints senior leaders from its own ranks to head its regional sub-groups, and some sub-group leaders have allegedly joined CoreAQ's leadership.[272] However, others have argued that 'al-Qaeda and other alleged "associated" groups are often only loosely linked, if at all'.[273]

[264] These 'facts' are used to illustrate the subsequent legal argument. The author does not claim that these 'facts' are true—they are not based on legal findings by courts but on studies by individuals or research institutes.

[265] See Rohan and Oreg, 'Al Qaida' (n 68) 1050.

[266] Hoffman, *Inside Terrorism* (n 66) 286. This authority would be exercised by 'Core Al Qaida' members who command high-profile operations globally. Acts committed without such involvement would, however, normally fall under the category of 'roaming terrorists', and their status falls outside the scope of this chapter.

[267] Rohan and Oreg, 'Al Qaida' (n 68) 1051.

[268] Hoffman, *Inside Terrorism* (n 66) 286. This network of associated groups consisted of different Islamist groups from different countries. See Rohan and Oreg, 'Al Qaida' (n 68) 1051.

[269] Rohan and Oreg, 'Al Qaida' (n 68) 1051.

[270] ibid 1053.

[271] ibid.

[272] See Joscelyn, *Osama bin Laden's Files: Al Qaeda's Deputy General Manager in Yemen* (*The Long War Journal*, 2015); Margulies and Sinnot, 'Crossing Borders' (n 36) 333–34.

[273] UN General Assembly, 'Report of the Special Rapporteur on Extrajudicial, Summary or Arbitrary Executions, Philip Alston' (28 May 2010), para 55.

- The third component consists of a variety of groups or individuals that follow Al Qaida's ideology and use its name without being in contact with CoreAQ leadership. Some of them have fought for Al Qaida in the past; others have never met anyone from CoreAQ but can be considered 'homegrown Islamist radicals'.[274] Reportedly, CoreAQ has 'little to do with the activity of local elements that operate on their own initiative and capabilities'.[275]

Reports suggest that similar patterns of relationships between central leadership and different components also exist within the ISG.[276]

Legally, this structure should be assessed as followes: As long as CoreAQ is sufficiently organized, it can be party to a NIAC with different states while present in Afghanistan or Pakistan—just as any other sufficiently armed group can become party to a NIAC. At the other extreme, groups or individuals that operate without any link to the organization, other than sharing a common ideology, would not form one party to a NIAC.[277] Thus, groups and individuals belonging to the third component of the Al Qaida network cannot be considered part of CoreAQ for the purposes of IHL, and neither do groups that pledge allegiance to CoreAQ without creating any further links to the organization.

The more complex case is determining the conditions under which different Al Qaida-associated groups, such as AQAM, AQAP, AQIY, AQI, or the Al Nusra Front in Syria, would form one organized armed group.[278] As suggested above, if all these groups operated under the 'command and control' of CoreAQ, this 'would be an obvious marker'.[279] If that is not the case, one suggestion has been to examine whether one group, such as CoreAQ, 'is in control' of other groups.[280] In addition, 'the level of coordination and participation in each other's operations' has been proposed as 'a partial indicator' for determining whether different groups form one party to a NIAC.[281] Another suggestion has been to develop an additional requirement to determine which groups form one global party to a NIAC, for example, the criterion 'that the affiliated armed group constitute a *threat* to the State party' to the conflict.[282] Yet, this test 'does not reflect current law'[283] and would introduce

[274] Hoffman, *Inside Terrorism* (n 66) 287–88.

[275] Rohan and Oreg, 'Al Qaida' (n 68) 1052–53.

[276] See, eg, UNSC, *Report of the Secretary-General on the threat posed by ISIL (Da'esh) to international peace and security and the range of United Nations efforts in support of Member States in countering the threat*, 29 January 2016, S/2016/92; UNSC, *Report of the Secretary-General on the threat posed by ISIL (Da'esh) to international peace and security and the range of United Nations efforts in support of Member States in countering the threat*, 31 May 2016, S/2016/501; UNSC, *Report of the Secretary-General on the threat posed by ISIL (Da'esh) to international peace and security and the range of United Nations efforts in support of Member States in countering the threat*, 30 September 2016, S/2016/830.

[277] As the US DoD General Council remarked: 'A group that simply embraces al-Qa'ida's ideology is not an "associated force".' US Department of Defense, *Remarks by the General Counsel of the Department of Defense on the Legal Framework for the United States' Use of Military Force Since 9/11* (n 122).

[278] Similar considerations apply to different ISG branches.

[279] Lubell, 'The Distiction between International and Non-International Armed Conflicts: Challenges for IHL?' (n 240).

[280] ibid.

[281] ibid. Regarding the level of control exercised by one group over another, Lubell does not indicate which 'test' (overall control, effective control, or another standard?) he would deem appropriate.

[282] Radin, 'Global Armed Conflict' (n 113) 733.

[283] ibid 734.

an element that is first subjective, second overly vague, and consequently prone to misuse. In addition, if states could determine which groups they consider a threat and therefore a joint enemy force irrespective of whether they form one party under contemporary IHL, could a non-state party likewise decide which group of states it considers a threat and lawfully target them?

The approach suggested here is to apply the same criteria for determining the requisite degree of organization of a transnational armed group as for any non-state party to a NIAC. State or other practice does not suggest differently. This means that a group must be a collective entity with a certain command structure, be able to ensure respect for basic IHL provisions, and having the capacity to engage in sufficiently intense violence. If we assume that the different sub-groups are each sufficiently organized be party to a NIAC, the question is whether they can be considered one collective entity for the purposes of IHL. In theory, this determination should not be different from assessing under what conditions a coalition of armed groups acting in one territory are considered one party to a NIAC. Based on the notion 'Party to the conflict' under IHL and relevant jurisprudence, it is submitted that coordination, possible participation in each other's operations, or material support are not enough. Instead, in addition to operational military coordination, overall leadership would need to exercise strategic authority over sub-groups, meaning that it determines the overarching military strategy as well as core rules.[284]

Looking at how such operational or strategic coordination could operate in practice, Margulies and Sinnot argue that it could consist of two aspects: one, overall leadership should 'guide some or all of the alleged affiliate's choice of targets'.[285] Here, '[o]ngoing correspondence or exchanges of information about targeting or operations' can indicate the requisite operational coordination.[286] And two, leadership should leverage 'money, recruits, training, or expertise' to influence the affiliate's targeting.[287] In addition, in this author's view, exercising military authority would also require the ability to issue key rules applicable to the entire group. However, this does not mean that sub-groups cannot retain certain strategic objectives specific to their local context, or a disciplinary regime and code of conduct in line with their organizational structure and culture. Individual strategies or internal rules need, however, be complemented—and in case of conflict superseded—by directions provided by global leadership. In short, the highest level of strategic authority would no longer be with the sub-group but with the group's global leadership.

As a result, if it can be shown that a group's global leadership unites different organized armed groups under one broad (targeting) strategy including operational and disciplinary rules, is involved in the coordination of at least the sub-groups' major operations, and possibly provides material assistance to the different groups, this alliance of groups could qualify as one party to a NIAC. A fortiori, this is the case if global leadership exercised vertical 'command and control' over all sub-groups. Applying this approach to specific groups necessarily requires a case-by-case analysis

[284] See section 3.3.1.2 'Centralized command structures in transnational armed groups'.
[285] Margulies and Sinnot, 'Crossing Borders' (n 36) 336.
[286] ibid 337.
[287] ibid 336.

of the relationship between each sub-group and the rest of the party. Only following one broad targeting strategy or ideology would not be sufficient. At the same time, an overly narrow focus to identify 'state-like' hierarchical structures should also be avoided. Organizations that are constantly threatened by their adversaries tend to vary their structures with certain flexibility and exercise 'both top-down and bottom-up planning and operational capabilities'.[288] If it cannot be determined that different groups form one organized armed group for the purposes of IHL, they cannot be one party to a NIAC.

3.3.2 Cyber armed groups

Despite the fact that 'no State is known to have publicly qualified an actual hostile cyber operation' as an armed conflict,[289] cyber operations occur increasingly in the context of conventional armed conflicts. In the early 2010s, hackers associated with the label 'Anonymous' conducted cyber operations in relation to armed conflicts between Israel and Hamas in 2012, and in the Ukraine in 2014.[290] Moreover, in 2015 'Anonymous' hackers issued a declaration of war against the 'Islamic State Group': 'Expect massive cyber attacks. War is declared. Get prepared.'[291] Indeed, the cyber world appears particularly fertile for non-state actors. Whereas armed conflicts based on kinetic attacks require a significant level of manpower and number of weapons, some experts caution that in the cyber realm 'non-state actors can leverage the capabilities of IT to produce some of the large-scale effects that can be achieved by large-scale actors'.[292] Engaging in large-scale cyber attacks is also thought to be cheaper than obtaining kinetic weapons of comparable reach.[293] Moreover, the Internet provides armed groups with a readily available means to communicate internally and externally—for example, to recruit new members.[294]

Experts seem to agree that cyber operations may fall under the scope of IHL, including cyber operations that involve non-state parties.[295] Hence, in the absence

[288] Hoffman, *The Myth of Grass-Roots Terrorism* (Foreign Affairs 2008).

[289] ICRC, *Challenges Report (2015)* (n 108) 39.

[290] For further discussion of 'web defacements' or 'denial of service attacks' conducted by these hackers, see Bussolati, 'The Rise of Non-State Actors in Cyberwarfare' in Ohlin, Govern, and Finkelstein (eds), *Cyberwar: Law and Ethics for Virtual Conflicts* (OUP 2015) 102–26, 110.

[291] Video available at:<https://www.youtube.com/watch?v=BAUZnDIWu2I> (accessed 2 November 2017).

[292] Lin, 'Cyber Conflict and International Humanitarian Law' (2012) 94 International Review of the Red Cross 515–31, 521.

[293] See Roberts, 'Cyber Wars: Applying Conventional Laws of War to Cyber Warfare and Non-State Actors' (2014) 41 Northern Kentucky Law Review 535–72, 536.

[294] See, eg, Farwell, 'How ISIS Uses Social Media' (*Politics and Strategy*, 2 October 2014) <https://www.iiss.org/en/politics%20and%20strategy/blogsections/2014-d2de/october-931b/isis-media-9d28> (accessed 2 November 2017).

[295] Addressing NIACs, experts involved in the Tallinn Manual Process found: 'A non-international armed conflict exists whenever there is protracted armed violence, *which may include or be limited to cyber operations*, occurring between governmental armed forces and the forces of one or more armed groups, or between such groups.' [emphasis added] Schmitt and NATO, 'Tallinn Manual' Rule 23. Similarly, states increasingly recognize that international law applies in the cyber context. See references in ICRC, *Challenges Report (2015)* (n 108) 39.

of any state practice to the contrary, IHL would apply to sufficiently intense violence between two or more organized parties, irrespective of which means of warfare they use.[296] Classifying cyber operations as a NIAC would mean that the above-identified IHL criteria would also apply in order to determine whether a certain group qualifies as a party to a conflict: the group in question must be a collective entity, able to engage in sufficiently intense violence against the adversary, and capable of respecting basic norms of IHL. Logically, a group that has proved these qualities in conventional warfare would also qualify as an organized armed group for the purposes of engaging in cyber warfare.[297] The more controversial question is whether or not a group that is only organized online, with members based in different states, and which engages exclusively in cyber operations, could become party to a NIAC. It has been rightly emphasized that because of the 'relatively high threshold required for a non-international armed conflict, it appears this could happen only in the most exceptional cases'.[298] However, many agree that at least in theory 'the failure of members of the group physically to meet does not alone preclude it from having the requisite degree of organization'.[299] This section examines whether and to what extent armed groups that organize exclusively online can qualify as an organized armed group for the purpose of IHL, meaning that they are (1) collective entities, (2) with the ability to implement basic IHL norms, and (3) have the capacity to engage in sufficiently intense cyber violence.

3.3.2.1 'Collective entities' in cyber-space

First of all, parties to a NIAC must be identifiable collective entities showing a certain command structure. Lawyers agree that individual hackers or groups of individuals that loosely cooperate for a certain purpose do not qualify as parties to an armed conflict: 'acting in a collective but otherwise uncoordinated fashion cannot comprise an organized armed group; there must be a distinct group with sufficient organizational structure that operates as a unit'.[300] This criterion excludes the majority of today's cyber operations from the scope of IHL. Reportedly, individuals acting under the flag of 'Anonymous' meet in 'internet relay chats' the type and number of participants in which fluctuate wildly, and where groups are created for specific purposes or operations. In these chats, more experienced hackers suggest targets, provide tools for committing basic cyber attacks, and incite others to participate in

[296] This approach has been taken by experts assembled in the Tallinn Process, as well as by commentators. See Schmitt and NATO, 'Tallinn Manual' (n 295) Rule 23; Dröge, 'Get off My Cloud' (n 52); Schmitt, 'Cyber Conflict' (n 52); Geiss, 'Cyber Warfare: Implications for Non-international Armed Conflicts' (2013) 89 International Law Studies 627–45.

[297] For example, if a party to an ongoing armed conflict engages in cyber-only operations against a third state and violence in this new relationship meets the intensity threshold, this would amount to a NIAC. See also Geiss, 'Cyber Warfare' (n 296) 635.

[298] ibid 629.

[299] Schmitt and NATO, 'Tallinn Manual' (n 295) Rule 23, para 13; Melzer, *Cyberwarfare and International Law* (UNIDIR Resources 2011) 24.

[300] Schmitt and NATO, 'Tallinn Manual' (n 295) Rule 23, para 15.

the attacks.[301] While some participants refer to these chats as 'centralised command and control loci',[302] in most cases the ringleaders do not command the operations. Instead, individual hackers make decisions on whether and how to participate.[303] Thus, one commentator compared leaders of such operations to 'showmen within a circus' who gamble for the support of customers rather than to military commanders leading their forces.[304]

While a 'social movement'[305] such as Anonymous is unlikely to qualify as a distinct group that could become party to an armed conflict, smaller groups with a common purpose and some form of hierarchy can emerge exclusively online. The fact that many cyber operations are amplified through the participation of many unaffiliated activists does not mean that cyber operations may not be attributed to a collective entity in the form of a 'core group' behind the attacks.[306] For example, 'an elite cadre of current and former Anonymous members' formed the 'Ghost Security Group (GhostSec)',[307] which pursues the mission 'to eliminate the online presence of Islamic extremist groups', and maintains a website listing the nicknames of its core members.[308] Such groups could qualify as 'collective cyber entities' that operate under one command structure.

3.3.2.2 Cyber abilities to implement basic IHL norms

In order to form a party to a NIAC, IHL requires such a collective entity to be able to ensure respect for basic humanitarian norms, which normally requires a disciplinary code or directives that are enforced by commanders. Some commentators argue that while orders could be given online, in cyber groups 'the means to enforce such orders are significantly limited'.[309] They conclude that the inability physically to enforce compliance would 'preclude virtually organised groups from qualifying as organised armed groups for the purpose of classifying a conflict as non-international'.[310]

Admittedly, present leadership structures in groups that engage in cyber operations often do not reflect any sort of military-like command and are 'ostensibly flat and leaderless'.[311] However, recent studies suggest that, especially in smaller groups

[301] For more detailed accounts on how Anonymous organizes such attacks, see Bertram, 'Authority and Hierarchy within Anonymous Internet Relay Chat Networks' (2015) 6 Journal of Terrorism Research 15–34; Brooking, 'Anonymous vs The Islamic State', *Foreign Policy* (13 November 2015).

[302] Bertram, 'Internet Relay Chat Networks' (n 301) 17.

[303] See Bussolati, 'The Rise of Non-State Actors' (n 290) 117.

[304] Bertram, 'Internet Relay Chat Networks' (n 301) 29.

[305] ibid 15.

[306] As analysed above, in complex but conventional NIAC, a 'core group' of fighters may form a party to a NIAC and trigger the applicability of the laws of war even if a broader field of individuals participate in the violence.

[307] Brooking, 'Anonymous vs The Islamic State' (n 301).

[308] See <https://ghostsecuritygroup.com> (accessed 3 May 2016).

[309] Geiss, 'Cyber Warfare' (n 296) 636.

[310] Schmitt, 'Cyber Conflict' (n 52) 257. Similarly, Geiss finds that 'the idea that a decentralized virtual group of persons in different locations—possibly dispersed all over the globe—could constitute an organized armed group in the sense of the laws of armed conflict should be dismissed'. Geiss, 'Cyber Warfare' (n 296) 637; Dröge, 'Get off My Cloud' (n 52) 550–51.

[311] Brooking, 'Anonymous vs The Islamic State' (n 301).

of cyber activists, some form of leadership structure does emerge, in which de facto group leaders 'initiated and closed most conversations [i.e. conversations in which specific operations are planned], enforced cultural norms and generally set the tone and pace of any cyber activity'.[312] Enforcement of the group's 'cultural norms' would normally take the form of kicking disobedient persons out of an operation.[313] Such loose group structures among individuals hidden behind nicknames, with implicit social norms, and a maximum punishment of being banned from operations arguably may not suffice to meet the IHL threshold. In contrast, it can also be argued that with the rapid development of online networks, groups emerge with clear leadership structures and internal codes of conduct, as well as more sophisticated non-physical means to enforce discipline. For example, an effective system of detecting violations of internal rules and banning everyone who is not compliant could be considered sufficient to ensure that internal rules are respected. A fortiori, this would be the case if members of such groups could undergo training on the group's code of conduct, and group leaders could enforce compliance in non-physical ways, with punishments such as exclusion; publication of the real identity, location, and past conduct; financial penalties; or cyber violence.

3.3.2.3 *The ability to engage in sufficiently intense cyber violence*

It also remains to be seen whether a cyber-only group would be able to engage in sufficiently intense violence against its adversary. The armed conflict concept is built around the idea of protracted and intense violence between parties. Cyber groups may coordinate their action according to a joint strategy and provide the infrastructure to carry out cyber attacks. What is more questionable at present, however, is whether they are able to engage in violence that resembles an armed conflict.[314] On the one hand, '[t]here is no reason why cyber operations cannot have the same violent consequences as kinetic operations, for instance if they were used to open the floodgates of dams, or to cause aircraft or trains to collide'.[315] On the other hand, an armed conflict does not consist of a series of individual attacks that do not lead to hostilities between two or more parties. Accordingly, it has been emphasized that 'even highly destructive cyber attacks would fail to qualify unless they occurred on a regular basis over time'.[316]

Even more so, an armed conflict—at least in its traditional meaning—requires confrontations between parties and not one-sided attacks against, for example, civilian or governmental infrastructure. Thus, a group would need to have the means to engage in more than 'cyber terrorism'—namely, in 'cyber hostilities'. As one commentator pointed out, as long as such cyber-only acts occur from within a state's

[312] Bertram, 'Internet Relay Chat Networks' (n 301) 28. [313] ibid.

[314] As Schmitt pointed out: 'Cyber operations have the potential for producing vast societal and economic disruption without causing the physical damage typically associated with armed conflict'. Schmitt, 'Cyber Conflict' (n 52) 246.

[315] Dröge, 'Get off My Cloud' (n 52) 551. Dröge finds that 'if such violence is not merely sporadic, it may meet the threshold for a non-international armed conflict'.

[316] Schmitt, 'Cyber Conflict' (n 52) 258.

territory, they will 'most likely be regarded as a criminal threat to be addressed through law enforcement measures'.[317] This perception might, however, change if such acts are committed from outside the victim state's territory and in a context in which law enforcement is more difficult to conduct. Against this background, another commentator suggested that with 'States and non-State actors engaging in ever more destructive and disruptive cyber operations and societies becoming deeply dependent on the cyber infrastructure, state practice accompanied by opinio juris can be expected to result in a lowering of the current threshold' of armed conflict.[318]

To sum up, under IHL as it presently stands, groups that organize online must meet the same broad criteria for becoming party to an armed conflict as those organizing offline. This does not mean, however, that indicative factors that developed in conventional NIAC will be equally applied with regard to cyber conflicts. Findings such as that 'virtual groupings that have no physical infrastructure, such as headquarters, physical meeting points, etc., would be too elusive to qualify as a reference point for the determination of the existence of a non-international armed conflict' may not stand the test of time.[319] Rather, it should not be excluded that collective online entities that develop a certain command structure, have the capacity to impose discipline, and develop means to engage in military-like hostilities with their adversaries become parties to a NIAC. However, as of 2017, the state-of-the-art 'hacktivism' does not seem to meet this threshold.

3.4 The Degree of Organization of Non-State Parties and the End of NIAC

Common Article 3 is silent on how armed conflicts not of an international character end. Similarly, APII only refers at one point to 'the end of the armed conflict',[320] and the 1987 ICRC commentary notes that the lack of a definition of the end of APII's applicability ratione temporis '[l]ogically … means that the rules relating to armed confrontation are no longer applicable *after the end of hostilities*'.[321] Hardly any reports on state practice exist on what 'the end of hostilities' would mean in practice. Adding to this uncertainty, the ICTY's finding in the *Tadić* case that NIACs end when 'a peaceful settlement is achieved'[322] has been criticized as 'too strict a standard',[323] for not providing 'sufficient practical guidance',[324] and bearing the

[317] Melzer, *Cyberwarfare* (n 299) 24. [318] Schmitt, 'Cyber Conflict' (n 52) 260.
[319] Quote from Geiss, 'Cyber Warfare' (n 296) 636. [320] Article 2(2) APII.
[321] Pilloud, Sandoz, Swinarski et al, *Commentary on the Additional Protocols* (n 164) para 4492 (emphasis added).
[322] *Tadić*, para 70.
[323] Bartels, 'From Jus In Bello to Jus Post Bellum: When do Non-International Armed Conflicts End?' in Stahn, Easterday, and Iverson (eds), *Jus post bellum: Mapping the Normative Foundations* (OUP 2014) 297–314, 301.
[324] ICRC, *Challenges Report (2015)* (n 108) 10.

risk of 'introducing a measure of formalism in a determination that should, first and foremost, be driven by facts on the ground'.[325]

Two approaches have been suggested on how to determine the end of a NIAC. The first is based on the 'logical' conclusion that a NIAC ends when its two constituent criteria—the existence of at least two organized parties that engage in sufficiently intense violence—are no longer met.[326] In order to avoid uncertainty on the applicable law due to 'the oscillating intensity of the armed conflict', the ICTY suggested, however, that conflicts should not be declassified lightly.[327] Instead, it is suggested that the absence of the two constitutive criteria should have 'a certain degree of permanence and stability'.[328] The second approach, suggested by the ICRC, requires that either one of the parties has disappeared, or no longer meets the requisite level of organization, or that the hostilities have ceased and 'there is *no real risk of their resumption* even though the level of organization of the parties is still met'.[329] While the two approaches differ on the degree of stability regarding the necessary cease of hostilities, both seem to agree that a conflict would end if one party either disappears, or no longer meets the requisite level of organization.

If one party suffers total defeat, the conflict necessarily ends. This has been the case, for example, with the LTTE in Sri Lanka in 2009, or the Bozizé government in the Central African Republic in 2013.[330] A more difficult situation occurs if conflicts 'are ... of a fluctuating nature' marked by 'instability in the level of organization of the non-State party to the conflict'.[331] For practical reasons, such as legal certainty for the forces involved, a conflict should not be declassified immediately if one party suffers from a temporary drop in logistics that puts its ability to engage in sustained hostilities in question. Similarly, even an important loss of manpower should not lead to a hasty declassification. Logistics and manpower are replaceable. In contrast, the very existence of the group is in question if the group's cohesion and discipline erode 'to an intolerable degree',[332] meaning that the group no longer acts

[325] ibid. The view that determining the end of a NIAC is a factual question and not a formal one is generally accepted by all commentators cited in this section.

[326] See Bartels, 'End of NIACs' (n 323) 303; Milanovic, 'The End of Application of International Humanitarian Law' (n 252) 378–81.

[327] *Haradinaj et al, IT-04-84-T*, para 100. With regard to IAC, see also *Gotovina et al, Judgment, 15 April 2011, Trial Chamber, IT-06-90-T,* ICTY, para 1694. While the ICTY made this finding with regard to the intensity criterion, Venturini argued that this applies similarly to the organization criterion. See Venturini, 'The Temporal Scope of Application of the Conventions' in Clapham, Gaeta, and Sassòli (eds), *The 1949 Geneva Conventions: A Commentary* (OUP 2015) 51–66, para 27.

[328] Milanovic, 'The End of Application of International Humanitarian Law' (n 252) 180.

[329] ICRC, *Challenges Report (2015)* (n 108) 10 (emphasis added). The second prong of this test has also been supported by Jinks, who argued that 'the general applicability of international humanitarian law terminates if active hostilities cease and there is no probability of a resumption of hostilities in the near future'. Jinks, *The Temporal Scope of Application of International Humanitarian Law in Contemporary Conflicts* (Program on Humanitarian Policy and Conflict Research 2003).

[330] See Human Rights Council, *Report of the OHCHR Investigation on Sri Lanka (OISL),* 16 September 2015, A/HRC/30/CRP.2, paras 83–94; The International Commission of Inquiry on the Central African Republic—Final Report, S/2014/928, Annex I, paras 93–94.

[331] ICRC, *Challenges Report (2015)* (n 108) 10.

[332] Chesney, 'Transatlantic Dialogue on International Law and Armed Conflict: When Does LOAC Cease to Apply?'(*Lawfare*, 3 September 2014) <https://www.lawfareblog.com/transatlantic-dialogue-international-law-and-armed-conflict-when-does-loac-cease-apply> (accessed 2 November 2017).

as one but individual members operate entirely on their own initiative, or defect to another group.[333] As a 'fog of uncertainty' regularly surrounds the facts necessary to determine a group's degree of organization,[334] the conclusion that a group no longer meets the requisite level of organization should only be drawn if a clear lack of organization has prevailed for some time.[335]

Moreover, in horizontally structured groups that consist of different sub-groups united by one leader or a leadership council, the loss of leadership exercising *operational coordination* and *strategic authority* would remove the element that qualified the group as one. Again, it should first be assessed whether effective leadership can be swiftly reinstalled. If that is not the case, it will be necessary to examine whether the individual sub-groups qualify individually as parties to a NIAC. This is also required if groups split: each new splinter group should be considered as such. However, in such cases the assessment of the intensity of violence between the splinter groups and their adversaries may not be similar to situations in which a conflict starts anew. Rather, if the new groups continue to be collective entities, able to implement basic norms and engage in sufficiently intense violence, the conflict could either be assumed to continue or the conflict history may inform the intensity assessment.[336] Indeed, in such situations it is unlikely that hostilities will drop with a certain degree of stability, or that they will stop without a real risk of resumption. Moreover, an automatic assumption that conflict ends as soon as one party splits could incite one party to divide itself in order to stop, at least temporarily, the applicability of IHL. Thus, a continuation of the NIAC should be presumed, or the assessment of whether a new NIAC exists between a party to a conflict and a splinter group be adapted so as to match reality.

3.5 Towards a Functional Assessment of the 'Organization Requirement'

Despite the existence of numerous practice-based factors that help in determining the existence of a NIAC and its parties, conflict classification remains challenging. Based on its operational experience, the ICRC stressed in 2015 that

> a myriad of fluid, multiplying and fragmenting armed groups frequently take part in the fighting. Often, their structure is difficult to understand … [and] the opacity or lack of the

[333] See Dinstein, *Non-International Armed Conflicts in International Law* (n 63) para 140.

[334] Chesney, 'Transatlantic Dialogue on International Law and Armed Conflict: When Does LOAC Cease to Apply?' (n 332).

[335] For this assessment, the suggested tests of 'a certain degree of permanence', which show that there is 'no real risk' of a swift restructuring, should be applied.

[336] Depending on the circumstances, one group may continue to exist as a party to the conflict and other groups split off as new entities. Alternatively, the group could split off into a number of district groups. In fact, this situation is not too different from the dismembering of states and questions of state succession. Hence, guidance on this issue could be found in international legal rules on state succession and treaty obligations.

chain of command or control of some groups poses a challenge ... for engaging such groups on issues of protection and compliance with IHL.[337]

Indeed, while the structures of a great number of groups have followed Mao's writings or the model of state armed forces, others form more organically in conflict environments, or consciously decide against any one of the well-known insurgency models. To conclude the analysis of contemporary international practice on the degree of organization required of armed groups to qualify as a party to a NIAC, this chapter argues in favour of a strictly functional interpretation of the legal characteristics constituting a party to a NIAC.

In light of the increasing complexity of today's NIACs, practitioners have cautioned that no strict 'definition would be capable of capturing the factual situations that reality throws up'.[338] Instead, a certain margin of flexibility in conflict classification is needed. Despite these reasonable appeals, in practice and scholarship it seems common to reference the numerous factors that international tribunals have identified as a sort of framework definition setting out the requisite degree of organization of armed groups. However, over-reliance on these indicative factors might set the threshold too high: international courts and tribunals have themselves used these indicative factors rather flexibly.[339] Thus, one does not need to—and maybe should not—'read the modern jurisprudence defining an OAG [organized armed group] as being limited to groups with headquarters, fully functioning logistics, or ironclad discipline'.[340] Instead, a 'more pragmatic approach'[341] may help 'synchronize the applicability of conflict regulation with the reality of armed conflict and actively avoid any law-based disavowal of those realities'.[342]

This being said, the consequences of conflict classification—such as targeting decisions or prosecuting individuals for war crimes—are too important to leave criteria overly vague and to the discretion of the parties, experts, or judges.[343] For this reason, advocacy for an approach that moves too far away from the internationally recognized *Tadić* formula and the indicative factors towards an appreciation of 'a totality of the circumstances' should be considered with caution.[344] International treaty law, practice, and jurisprudence show that parties to a NIAC must be collective entities that are able to engage in sufficiently intense armed violence against an adversary and have the ability to ensure respect for basic humanitarian norms. Assessing the three broad criteria should not be done by comparing non-state entities to state armed forces. Instead, such assessment should focus on which structures and

[337] ICRC, *Challenges Report (2015)* (n 108) 6.

[338] Pejic, 'Status of Armed Conflicts' in Wilmshurst (ed), *Perspectives on the ICRC Study on Customary International Humanitarian Law* (CUP 2007) 77–100, 85.

[339] See the discussion of case law above, in particular the ICTY's *Limaj* and *Haradinaj* cases and the ICC's *Katanga* case.

[340] Margulies and Sinnot, 'Crossing Borders' (n 36) 340.

[341] ibid.

[342] Blank and Corn, 'Losing the Forest' (n 35) 711.

[343] For a discussion of the interests involved in conflict classification, see the Introduction to Part I of this book.

[344] Such an approach has been advanced by Blank and Corn, 'Losing the Forest' (n 35) 731–45.

logistics enable a non-state entity to act jointly, to challenge the adversary militarily, and to establish internal discipline.

The three suggested criteria are cumulative, meaning that no one criterion can be significant enough on its own to satisfy the organization requirement. A strictly organized group that does not have any logistics to engage in armed hostilities can barely be a party to an armed conflict. Similarly, international practice does not consider a mob of rioters, a group of demonstrators, or a disconnected assembly of armed units as one party to a conflict, even if they violently challenge state authorities. At the same time, the three criteria cannot strictly be separated, either. In practice, the conflict's intensity, as well as the ability of a group to engage in hostilities, are often easier to establish than the group's command structure and its ability to implement fundamental humanitarian norms. This is particularly the case 'where the internal structure of the group is loose, or where a clandestine chain of command is at play'.[345] Where such examination is difficult, at least with regard to groups operating in one territory, greater emphasis may be placed on the group's ability to engage in intense armed violence, and a sufficient internal structure inferred from that.[346]

In this functional assessment, the motivation, objectives, or ideology of the parties are irrelevant. Some have argued that groups that are primarily criminally motivated do not fall under the scope of IHL because they do not pursue 'a political objective in the use of force'[347] or 'do not organize themselves to carry out armed conflict with government military forces'.[348] However, many armed groups that fight primarily for a political objective are at the same time pursuing criminal activities, and some criminal organizations may also follow political aims.[349] If the objectives of an armed group were relevant for the qualification of an armed conflict, this would first pose the challenge of discerning what the actual motives of an armed group are, and second, 'open the door to potentially numerous other motivation-based reasons for denial of the existence of an armed conflict'.[350] Hence, the ICTY emphasized that 'the purpose of the armed forces to engage in acts of violence or also achieve some further objective is . . . irrelevant'.[351] As a result, any considerations on the legitimacy of the armed group, its ideals, or its objectives are not pertinent for conflict classification, which must be exclusively based on the functional criteria as set out above.[352]

345 ICRC, *International Humanitarian Law and the Challenges of Contemporary Armed Conflicts* (ICRC 2007) 743.

346 This tendency seems particularly prevalent among Commissions of Inquiry, which do not have the same means at their disposal as courts and do not operate according to the same standards of proof. See Section 3.2 'Assessing the Existence of the Broad Criteria by Means of Specific Indicators'.

347 Hellestveit, *Tribes, Thugs, Terrorists and the Law: Can Non-conventional Armed Violence be Regulated?* (Norwegian Peacebuilding Resource Centre Report, May 2015) 8.

348 ILA, *Armed Conflicts (Final Report)* (n 14) 3.

349 See ICRC, *International Humanitarian Law and the Challenges of Contemporary Armed Conflicts* (Geneva: ICRC 2011) 11; Vité, 'Typology of Armed Conflicts' (n 243); Akande, 'Classification of Armed Conflicts' (n 6) 52.

350 ICRC, *Challenges Report (2011)* (n 349) 11.

351 *Limaj et al, IT-03-66-T*, para 170.

352 See also Maslen (ed), *The War Report 2012* (n 58) 10.

Part I: Conclusion

Analysing the development of the concept of *non-state parties to an armed conflict* from the writings of philosophers in the eighteenth century through international humanitarian law (IHL) treaty law to contemporary practice, three threads can be identified. First, as pointed out by Rousseau almost two and a half centuries ago, one basic principle underlying the laws of war is that war is not a relation between men but between entities. Accordingly, the lawful objective of parties cannot be to harm opponents as individuals but only to overcome the entity for which the individual fights. This necessitates that any party to an armed conflict is a collective, organized entity and not a loosely connected group of individuals. Second, de Vattel already stressed that civil war is fought between two parties who 'acknowledge no common judge' and have no 'common superior' on earth.[1] Thus, the laws of civil war apply to exceptional situations in which at least two entities challenge each other militarily and use means that exceed the methods of law enforcement in a functioning society. As hostilities cannot be completely one-sided, both parties must have sufficient capacity to engage in military-like violence. Third, in these exceptional situations, the key purpose of the laws of war is to reinstall a legal framework that binds all parties to the conflict. The idea that the other party will respect the laws of war is an important incitement for any conflicting party to respect fundamental humanitarian rules. Therefore, non-state entities need to have the ability to implement at least basic legal obligations.

The adoption of the 1949 Geneva Conventions has marked a turning point away from conflict classification primarily based on the subjective and often political recognition of belligerency and towards an assessment based on facts: as an ICRC expert commission stressed in the 1960s, the existence of internal 'conflicts should rest on objective conditions and not be the result of a discretionary appreciation by States ... [T]he existence of an armed conflict, within the meaning of article 3, cannot be denied if the hostile action, directed against the legal government is of a collective character and consists of a minimum amount of organization'.[2] States have discarded the requirements that a non-state party must be recognized as such by their state adversary, that it 'occup[ies] and administer[s] a substantial portion of national territory', or 'conduct[s] the hostilities in accordance with the rules of

[1] de Vattel, *The Law of Nations* (translation by Joseph Chitty) (T & JW Johnson & Co 1758) 239.

[2] ICRC, *Humanitarian Aid to the Victims of Internal Conflicts. Meeting of a Commission of Experts in Geneva* (ICRC 1962) 82.

war'.[3] Today, determining whether a non-state entity qualifies as party to a conflict depends on an assessment of capacities that are functionally required to engage in an armed conflict governed by IHL.

As the first Part of this book has shown, the basic criteria that any party to a non-international armed conflict must be a collective entity with sufficient capacity to engage in intense armed violence against an adversary and the ability to implement basic humanitarian norms are found, implicitly or explicitly, in article 3 common to the four Geneva Conventions, Protocol Additional to the Geneva Conventions of 12 August 1949, and relating to the Protection of Victims of Non-International Armed Conflicts (Protocol II), and the Rome Statute of the International Criminal Court. These are also the broad criteria that international jurisprudence and other practice have used to determine the existence of a non-state party to a conflict. While a number of indicative factors exist that facilitates this determination, those developed by the International Criminal Tribunal for the former Yugoslavia, especially, were based on its own jurisprudence regarding crimes committed in a specific conflict environment. This does not necessarily reduce their usefulness. However, these indicative factors should not be narrowly interpreted or perceived as a de facto definition of a party to a conflict. Armed groups differ in their structures and capacities, ranging 'from those that are highly centralized (with a strong hierarchy, effective chain of command, communication capabilities, etc.) to those that are decentralized',[4] spread from the masses, form varying alliances, operate in different territories, or merely exist in cyber space. A faithful application of the three broad criteria identified in this book provides sufficient flexibility for IHL to respond adequately to continuously changing armed conflicts without leaving its basic principles and achievements behind.

[3] Lauterpacht, *Recognition in International Law* (CUP 2012) 176.

[4] ICRC, *Increasing Respect for International Humanitarian Law in Non-international Armed Conflicts* (ICRC 2008) 11.

PART II

THE REQUIRED DEGREE OF ORGANIZATION OF NON-STATE ARMED GROUPS TO HAVE OBLIGATIONS UNDER INTERNATIONAL HUMAN RIGHTS LAW

Today, literally all crisis or conflict situations raise the issue of how to address human rights violations committed by non-state armed groups.[1] Despite a significant increase in scholarly attention, the questions of whether, under which conditions, and to what extent non-state armed groups have international human rights law (IHRL) obligations remain 'highly controversial'[2] or 'contested as a matter of international law'.[3] In part, this is due to a lack of clarity as to whether states—as the primary lawmakers in international law—want armed groups to have such obligations, and uncertainty as to which sources of international law may bind armed groups.[4] Unlike international humanitarian law (IHL) treaties, which explicitly apply to all parties to a non-international armed conflict, and international criminal law, which sets out obligations for every human being, most IHRL treaties only apply to states and not non-state actors as duty-bearers. Moreover, human rights law has traditionally been understood to impose obligations on states. Consequently, the understanding that non-state armed groups do not have human rights obligations has long been

[1] A number of examples will be discussed in the following chapters. To verify the present finding, a brief look at UN Security Council or Human Rights Council resolutions of the past years suffices.

[2] Bellal, Giacca, and Casey-Maslen, 'International Law and Armed Non-State Actors in Afghanistan' (2011) 93 International Review of the Red Cross 47–79, 48; see also Sivakumaran, *The Law of Non-International Armed Conflict* (OUP 2012) 530.

[3] Human Rights Council, *Report of the International Commission of Inquiry to investigate all alleged violations of international human rights law in the Libyan Arab Jamahiriya*, A/HRC/17/44, para 72.

[4] For recent in-depth studies on this subject, see Fortin, *The Accountability of Armed Groups under Human Rights Law* (OUP 2017); Murray, *Human Rights Obligations of Non-State Armed Groups* (Hart 2016).

prevalent among international lawyers. For example, in 2010, an International Law Association committee concluded: 'consensus appears to be that currently NSAs [non-state actors] do *not* incur direct human rights obligations enforceable under international law'.[5]

At the same time, an increasing number of scholars and human rights experts invokes the possibly binding force of IHRL treaties on armed groups,[6] customary international law obligations and general principles,[7] ius cogens norms,[8] 'general international law',[9] 'customary international legal principles',[10] or 'legitimate expectations of the international community'[11] to argue that armed groups have IHRL obligations. Bellal even concluded that '[t]he important question today is not to be so much "if", but rather "which" obligations are engaged'.[12] Indeed, despite the apparent ambiguity on the source of possible obligations, UN organs, intergovernmental bodies, and human rights mechanisms frequently condemn human rights violations and abuses by armed groups and call upon them to respect human rights.[13] Today's reality, in which a variety of states and armed groups commit acts in complete disregard of their victims' human rights, seemingly forces states and practitioners to move beyond the traditional state-centred focus of IHRL.

In order to conceptualize contemporary practice, to clarify which sources of IHRL could bind non-state armed groups, and to locate possible obligations in the IHRL protection system, this book pursues three main arguments. First, it is shown that, from a philosophical perspective, human rights are best understood as individual entitlements—not primarily as state obligations. Second, this book argues that there is a systemic need for IHRL obligations of armed groups. This need arises

[5] International Law Association, *The Hague Conference (2010): Non-State Actors* (ILA 2010) 17. Interestingly, four years later the same committee found that the 'dominant narrative' contends that non-state armed groups have obligations under IHRL if they exercise effective control over territory. International Law Association, *Washington Conference (2014): Non-State Actors* (ILA 2014) 7.

[6] See Fortin, *The Accountability of Armed Groups under Human Rights Law* (n 4) chapter 8.

[7] Constantinides, 'Human Rights Obligations and Accountability of Armed Opposition Groups: The Practice of the UN Security Council' (2010) 4 Human Rights & International Legal Discourse 89–110, 102–03.

[8] ILA, 'The Hague Conference (2010): Non-State Actors' (n 5) 17.

[9] The term 'general international law' is not defined under international law. Clapham suggests that unlike customary international law such general rules do not come about by 'sustained practice and sense of obligation' but '[t]he obligations arise because the international legal order considers these rights and obligations as generally applicable and binding on every entity that has the capacity to bear them'. Clapham, *Human Rights Obligations of Non-State Actors* (2006) 87.

[10] Human Rights Council, *Report of the Independent International Commission of Inquiry on the Syrian Arab Republic*, 5 February 2013, A/HRC/22/59, para 85.

[11] Commission on Human Rights, *Extrajudicial, Summary or Arbitrary Executions: Report of the Special Rapporteur, Philip Alston*, 27 March 2006, E/CN.4/2006/53/Add.5, para 25.

[12] Bellal, 'Establishing the Direct Responsibility of Non-State Armed Groups for Violations of International Norms: Issues of Attribution' in Gal-Or, Noortmann, and Ryngaert (eds), *Responsibilities of the Non-State Actor in Armed Conflict: Theoretical Considerations and Empirical Findings* (Brill Nijhoff 2015) 304–23, 308. Similarly, Clapham finds: 'We may now be entering a period when some observers may feel the question is no longer "are we there yet?", but rather "have we gone too far?"'. Clapham, 'Human Rights Obligations for Non-State-Actors: Where are We Now?', in Lafontaine and Larocque (eds), *Doing Peace the Rights Way: Essays in International Law and Relations in Honour of Louise Arbour* (Intersentia 2016) 4.

[13] See Sections 6.4–6.6.

factually because states are often unable to protect human rights against violations by armed groups; and *legally*, because states' responsibility for protecting human rights is significantly reduced if they lose control over part of their territory, or have otherwise very limited capacities. Third, recognizing the diversity among armed groups' degree of organization and power, as well as the different contexts in which they operate, this book suggests dividing armed groups into three broad categories for determining possible human rights obligations. These are:

- Groups exercising quasi-governmental authority in defined territory;
- Groups exercising de facto control over some territory and population;
- Groups not exercising control over territory and population.[14]

This categorization avoids treating very different armed groups the same, facilitates the legal analysis of the sources and scope of possible IHRL obligations, and—to some degree—reflects contemporary international practice. It provides a methodological framework to determine at which degree of power and organization an armed group may become subject to different human rights obligations.

Before developing these arguments further, some preliminary issues need to be addressed. This book does not focus on the question of whether or not individuals have human rights obligations.[15] Neither does it look specifically at non-state entities such as corporations, NGOs, or international organizations, which normally operate within the legal framework of states.[16] Moreover, the question of how to attribute wrongful acts committed by non-state groups to states is beyond the purview

[14] Similar categories have been suggested by Bellal, 'Establishing the Direct Responsibility of Non-State Armed Groups for Violations of International Norms: Issues of Attribution' (n 12) 308. For her, these categories reflect 'an emerging practice and certainly not *de lege lata* considerations'. In contrast, Fortin has argued that a difference should be drawn primarily between two categories of armed groups, namely those that exercise control over territory, and those that do not. See Fortin, *The Accountability of Armed Groups under Human Rights Law* (n 4).

[15] For discussion on whether individuals have human rights obligations, see Daes, *Liberté de l'individu en droit: étude des devoirs de l'individu envers la communauté et limitations des droits et libertés de l'homme en vertu de l'article 29 de la Déclaration universelle des droits de l'homme* (Nations Unies 1990); and Rodley, 'Can Armed Opposition Groups Violate Human Rights?' in Mahoney and Mahoney (eds), *Human Rights in the Twenty-First Century: A Global Challenge* (M Nijhoff 1993) 297–318, 304–09.

[16] Their possible human rights obligations are addressed in the general conclusion of this book. For in-depth discussions on possible human rights obligations of these actors, see generally Alston, 'The 'Not-a-Cat' Syndrome: Can the International Human Rights Regime Accommodate Non-state Actors?' in Alston (ed), *Non-State Actors and Human Rights* (OUP 2005) 3–36; Clapham, 'Non-State Actors' in Moeckli, Shah, Sivakumaran et al (eds), *International Human Rights Law* (OUP 2014) 531–49. On possible human rights obligations of corporations, see, eg, Weissbrodt, 'Business and Human Rights' (2005) 74 University of Cincinnati Law Review 55–74; Human Rights Council, *Guiding Principles on Business and Human Rights: Implementing the United Nations 'Protect, Respect and Remedy' Framework*, 21 March 2011, A/HRC/17/31. See also the different briefs submitted to the US Supreme Court in the Kiobel Case, which are available at <http://www.scotusblog.com/case-files/cases/kiobel-v-royal-dutch-petroleum/> (accessed 2 November 2017). On discussions of human rights obligations of international organizations, see Council of Europe Parliamentary Assembly, *Accountability of International Organisations for Human Rights Violations* (Council of Europe 2013); Wilde, 'Understanding the International Territorial Administration Accountability Deficit: Trusteeship and the Legitimacy of International Organizations' 12 International Peacekeeping: The Yearbook of International Peace Operations 155–70.

of this work.[17] The focus of this book is on possible IHRL obligations of non-state armed groups that operate beyond state control and in ignorance of the national legal framework. In the course of the following chapters, reference is made to state obligations and to conduct of the 'de jure government'. The basic understanding behind the use of the two terms is that the de jure government is the actor performing state obligations. However, a distinction between the state and the de jure government is drawn because in some situations, non-state actors engage the state's responsibility, or state obligations bind actors other than the de jure government.[18]

The need for human rights obligations of armed groups is sometimes challenged. For example, it has been argued that because IHL binds non-state armed groups, 'it may not be necessary to extend human rights treaties to them'.[19] This is certainly true with regard to a number of essential rights protections in times of armed conflict, including the prohibition of torture, ill-treatment, arbitrary deprivation of life, or enforced disappearance. However, that conclusion can be questioned on at least two levels.[20] First, IHL only applies in times of armed conflict. In contrast, armed groups exist at all times and may commit human rights violations before the armed conflict threshold is met, or after IHL ceases to apply.[21] Arguably, it is in such situations that there is the greatest need for IHRL obligations of armed groups.[22] Second, even if IHL applies, its material scope is limited. As Giacca points out:

> No rules have been developed to govern the territory under the control of an ANSA [armed non-state actor] in a non-international armed conflict in terms of positive obligations; yet there are many situations where ANSAs with a political structure control and even administer sizeable parts of territory.[23]

[17] While state responsibility is not the primary focus of this work, it will be touched on in Chapter 5 'The Fallacy of Effective Huan Rights Protection under Relevant Treaty Law when Armed Groups Commit Violations'.

[18] For a detailed discussion on de jure and de facto governments, see Seralvo, 'Government Recognition and International Humanitarian Law Applicability in Post-Gaddafi Libya' (2017) 18 Yearbook of International Humanitarian Law 2015 3–41

[19] Zegveld, *Accountability of Armed Opposition Groups in International Law* (CUP 2002) 42. Likewise, to underline that human rights operate primarily between states and their subjects, the ICRC argued in 2011: 'In any event, the vast majority—and probably all—of the human rights obligations that an unsophisticated non-state armed group would be capable of implementing in practice are already binding on it under a corresponding rule of IHL' ICRC, *International Humanitarian Law and the Challenges of Contemporary Armed Conflicts* (ICRC 2011) 14. See also Pejic, 'Conflict Classification and the Law Applicable to Detention and the Use of Force' in Wilmshurst (ed), *International Law and the Classification of Conflicts* (OUP 2012) 80–116, 84.

[20] In addition to arguments presented here, one advantage of applying IHRL in addition to IHL is that there are currently more fora and expert bodies concerned with the implementation of the former. See Clapham, 'Focussing on Armed Non-State Actors' in Clapham and Gaeta (eds), *The Oxford Handbook of International Law in Armed Conflict* (OUP 2014) 766–810, 788.

[21] See Clapham, 'Human Rights Obligations of Non-State Actors in Conflict Situations' (2006) 88 International Review of the Red Cross 491–523, 513; Henckaerts and Wiesener, 'Human Rights Obligations of Non-State Armed Groups: A Possible Contribution from Customary International Law?' in Kolb and Gaggioli (eds), *Research Handbook on Human Rights and Humanitarian Law* (Edward Elgar 2013) 146–69, 153.

[22] See Rodley, 'Non-State Actors and Human Rights' in Sheeran and Rodley (eds), *Routledge Handbook of International Human Rights Law* (Routledge 2013) 523–44, 530.

[23] Giacca, *Economic, Social, and Cultural Rights in Armed Conflict* (OUP 2014) 241. See also Sivakumaran, 'Non-International Armed Conflicts' (n 2) 529–32.

It has been pointed out that IHL may not provide norms regulating various aspects of 'everyday life', such as 'the ability to travel to work, move around freely, access health care, express an opinion freely, gather in public places and be protected from common crime'.[24] Yet, researchers stress that non-state armed groups regularly engage in governance activities, such as 'providing security from violence; developing educational and health facilities; establishing a system of food production and distribution; allocating land and other resources to provide opportunities for civilians to engage in livelihood activities (agriculture, small business, etc.); provide shelter for the displaced; regulating market transactions; taxation of civilians and commercial actors; resolving civil disputes; and addressing other social problems that commonly accompany situation of internal war'.[25]

Moreover, since IHL only applies to acts that are sufficiently linked to the armed conflict,[26] it could be questioned whether all 'governance acts' by armed groups show sufficient nexus to the conflict in order to fall under its scope of application. For example, if an armed group arbitrarily arrests and possibly ill-treats persons living under its control for reasons that are not necessarily related to the conflict—such as ordinary crime—would these acts be covered by relevant IHL norms? On the one hand, it has been argued that acts of law enforcement that are not specifically related to the armed conflict are not covered by IHL.[27] On the other hand, when armed groups take control over territory in the course of an armed conflict, all acts that group commits when controlling or 'governing' such territory and population are inherently linked to the armed conflict and could arguably fall within the scope of application of IHL. While this question warrants further analysis, even in times of armed conflict IHL does not seem to apply to crimes committed by third groups that use the breakdown of law and order to pursue their own criminal agenda.[28] In all cases, it can be concluded that in times of peace and in times of armed conflict, the possible application of IHRL to armed groups can provide an added value.[29]

In order to determine whether and to what extent non-state armed groups have or should have human rights obligations, the present Part is structured as follows. After

[24] Fortin, *The Accountability of Armed Groups under Human Rights Law* (n 4) 51.

[25] Mampilly, 'Insurgent Governance in the Democratic Republic of the Congo' in Krieger (ed), *Inducing Compliance with International Humanitarian Law—Lessons from the African Great Lakes Region* (CUP 2016) 44–78, 44.

[26] As the ICTY put it in the *Boškoski et al* case with regard to war crimes: 'The nexus requirement serves to distinguish war crimes from purely domestic crimes and also prevents purely random or isolated criminal occurrences from being characterized as war crimes. ... In determining whether a nexus between the acts of the accused and the armed conflict exists, reliance may be placed, *inter alia*, upon whether the perpetrator was a combatant, whether the victim was a non-combatant, whether the victim was a member of the opposing party, whether the act may be said to have served the ultimate goal of a military campaign, and whether the crime is committed as part of or in the context of the perpetrator's official duties.' *Boškoski and Tarčulovski, IT-04-82-T*, para 293.

[27] See, for instance, Fortin, *The Accountability of Armed Groups under Human Rights Law* (n 4) 47–51.

[28] For further discussion, see Hellestveit, *Tribes, Thugs, Terrorists and the Law: Can Non-conventional Armed Violence be Regulated?* (Norwegian Peacebuilding Resource Centre Report, May 2015) 2 and 5.

[29] For a detailed study on the 'added value' of applying IHRL to armed groups, see Fortin, *The Accountability of Armed Groups under Human Rights Law* (n 4) chapter 2. See also Murray, *Human Rights Obligations of Non-State Armed Groups* (n 4) 11–12.

presenting, briefly, the classical state-centric view of IHRL, Chapter 4 'Human Rights, Natural Rights, and their Applicability beyond the State–International Relationship' shows that human rights are not intrinsically linked to the relationship between a government and persons under its jurisdiction. Instead, human rights are first and foremost individual entitlements. Chapter 5 'The Fallacy of Effective Human Rights Protection under Relevant Treaty Law when Armed Groups Commit Violations' proceeds by showing that the contemporary state-centric IHRL system inadequately addresses human rights obligations of armed groups: these treaties rarely address armed groups directly and states' positive human rights obligations have certain limits. Building on these findings, Chapter 6 'A Three-Pronged Approach to Human Rights Obligations of Non-State Armed Groups' introduces the suggested three-pronged approach to human rights obligations of non-state armed groups. It examines possible human rights obligations of armed groups exercising quasi-governmental authority in a territory (Section 6.3); armed groups exercising de facto control over territory and population (Section 6.4); and armed groups not controlling territory and population (Section 6.5).

4

Human Rights, Natural Rights, and their Applicability beyond the State–Individual Relationship

A glimpse at different international human rights law (IHRL) treaties is enough to determine that their design follows a common pattern: while many of the rights contained in these treaties are formulated as entitlements of the individual, such as '[e]very human being has the inherent right to life',[1] corresponding obligations are designed for states. It is primarily upon states parties 'to respect and to ensure' these rights, to 'secure' them for everyone, to 'give effect' to them, or to 'take steps . . . with the view to progressively achieving [their] full realization'.[2] Consequently, under these treaties the obligation to uphold the protected rights lies with the state and not with non-state actors. Aside from a very few exceptions, non-state entities are not mentioned as duty-bearers in IHRL treaties.[3] This should not, however, lead to the automatic conclusion that under international law the obligation to respect and protect human rights must always lie exclusively with the state.

4.1 The Classic View: Regulating the Vertical Relationship between Governments and the Governed

According to what some have called the 'orthodox view'[4] or the 'received wisdom',[5] IHRL has traditionally operated between states and persons under their jurisdiction,

[1] Article 6 of the International Covenant on Civil and Political Rights (ICCPR).

[2] See article 2(1) ICCPR and article 1 of the American Convention on Human Rights (ACHR); article 2(1) of the International Covenant on Economic, Social and Cultural Rights (ICESCR); article 1 of the European Convention on Human Rights (ECHR); article 1 of the African Charter on Human and Peoples' Rights (ACHPR).

[3] These exceptions are discussed in Section 5.1 'The Limited Scope of Human Rights Treaties Directly Addressing Armed Groups'.

[4] Nowak and Januszewski, 'Non-State Actors and Human Rights' in Noortmann, Reinisch, and Ryngaert (eds), *Non-State Actors in International Law* (Hart 2015) 113–61, 116.

[5] This term is borrowed from Alston, who used it when referring to the majority view that non-state actors have a very limited role to play in international law. See Alston, 'The "Not-a-Cat" Syndrome: Can the International Human Rights Regime Accommodate Non-State Actors?' in Alston (ed), *Non-State Actors and Human Rights* (OUP 2005) 3–36.

and continues to do so.[6] Indeed, among international lawyers, a certain 'state-centrism … seems to run like a golden thread through the dominant human rights narrative'.[7] According to this narrative—as, for example, argued by Rodley—human rights emerged as 'the historical response to the rise of the modern nation state'.[8] Indeed, it is widely agreed that while the idea of human rights can be found in many cultures, the concept of human rights as enshrined in international law is most directly rooted in philosophical ideas of the age of Enlightenment.[9] During this period, philosophic accounts of human rights and governance—as found, for example, in Locke's 'Two Treatises on Government', or Hobbes' 'Leviathan'—'were undeniably influenced by the events of their time', in particular 'the cruel absolutist rule as well as decades of civil and religious wars'.[10] They were concerned with the relationship between men and a political power.[11] Thus, early human rights documents such as the 'Magna Carta' of 1215, the British 'Bill of Rights' of 1689, the 'Virginia Bill of Rights' of 1776, or the French 'Déclaration des droits de l'homme et du citoyen' of 1789 were designed to regulate the relationship between sovereign states and their subjects.[12] It is argued that as the Western-style nation state spread around the world, so did the state-centric legal concept of human rights.

In addition to the historical support for the concept of human rights defining the relationship between states and their subjects, a number of practical reasons explain IHRL's focus on states as duty-holders.

- First, in modern nation states, the individual is particularly vulnerable to human rights violations committed by the state.[13] Under international law, the sovereign state is the 'legally constituted entity in control of the territory

[6] See, eg, McCorquodale and La Forgia, 'Taking off the Blindfolds: Torture by Non-State Actors' (2001) 1 Human Rights Law Review 189–218, 189; Dinstein, *The Interaction between Customary International Law and Treaties* (Brill 2006) 338; Zegveld, *Accountability of Armed Opposition Groups in International Law* (CUP 2002) 40 and 54; Constantinides, 'Human Rights Obligations and Accountability of Armed Opposition Groups. The Practice of the UN Security Council' (2010) 4 Human Rights & International Legal Discourse 93; Ronen, 'Human Rights Obligations of Territorial Non-State Actors' (2013) 46 Cornell International Law Journal 21–50, 23 and 32.

[7] Nowak and Januszewski, 'Non-State Actors' (n 4) 116.

[8] Rodley, 'Can Armed Opposition Groups Violate Human Rights?' in Mahoney and Mahoney (eds), *Human Rights in the Twenty-First Century: A Global Challenge* (M Nijhoff 1993) 299.

[9] See, eg, Randall, 'The History of International Human Rights Law' in Kolb and Gaggioli (eds), *Research Handbook on Human Rights and Humanitarian Law* (Edward Elgar 2013) 3–34, 5ff.; Tomuschat, *Human Rights: Between Idealism and Realism* (2nd edn, OUP 2008) 7–14; Schabas, *The Universal Declaration of Human Rights: The 'Travaux Préparatoires'* (CUP 2013) lxxi–lxxii; Shestack, 'The Philosophic Foundations of Human Rights' (1998) 20 Human Rights Quarterly 201–34, 207.

[10] Nowak and Januszewski, 'Non-State Actors' (n 4) 130.

[11] See also Lauterpacht, *An International Bill of the Rights of Man* (OUP 2013) 40. He found with regard to natural law, which, for him, formed the basis of human rights: 'Historically the doctrine of natural law is rooted deeply in the claims of freedom against the tyranny of the State and the injustice of its institutions'.

[12] eg one important purpose of the French 'Déclaration des droits de l'homme et du citoyen', as explained in its preamble, was that 'cette Déclaration, constamment présente à tous les Membres du corps social, leur rappelle sans cesse leurs droits et leurs devoirs; afin que les actes du pouvoir législatif, et ceux du pouvoir exécutif, pouvant être à chaque instant comparés avec le but de toute institution politique, en soient plus respectés'.

[13] See Moore, 'From Nation State to Failed State: International Protection from Human Rights Abuses by Non-State Agents' (1999) 31 Columbia Human Rights Law *Review* 82–121, 82.

under its jurisdiction [... having] the sole legitimate right to use force to protect security, maintain law and order, and guarantee the protection of the fundamental rights of its citizens'.[14] If the entity that is tasked to protect the individual 'becomes his assailant', the individual needs international protection.[15]

- Second, the powerful state may not only be a threat to the individual but also the primary protector against violent acts by other private actors.[16] In an ideal world, no international obligations for private actors would be required because all non-state actors are effectively regulated at the national level.[17]
- Third, as an entity with (some) democratic legitimacy, knowledge of local cultural, economic, and social circumstances, and law enforcement machinery, the state is ideally placed to implement human rights protection.[18] The regulation of non-state entities has long been considered 'essentially within the domestic jurisdiction of any state' and therefore beyond the interest of the international community.[19]
- Fourth, international law is traditionally considered as governing the 'relations between independent States'.[20] Hence, when states agreed on international and regional human rights instruments, they defined international obligations of states as sovereigns and as the primary subjects of international law.[21]

In light of the above, it is not surprising that the IHRL treaty system is primarily state-centric. The state was—and still is—considered the central actor in international law, as well as the main threat to and primary protector of the individual. Nonetheless, under this state-centred view of IHRL, arguably one exception exists in 'cases in which a group, usually by virtue of stable control of territory, has the ability to act like a state authority'.[22] Only in this case, IHRL may apply to state-like non-state entities.

[14] Nair, 'Confronting the Violence Committed by Armed Opposition Groups' (1998) 1 Yale Human Rights & Development Law Journal 1–16, 2. See also Cassese, *International Law* (2nd edn, OUP 2005) 73.

[15] Inter-American Commission on Human Rights, *Inter-American Yearbook on Human Rights* (M Nijhoff 1990) 358. See also Tomuschat, 'The Responsibility of other Entities: Private Individuals' in Crawford, Pellet, and Olleson (eds), *The Law of International Responsibility* (OUP 2010) 317–29, 319.

[16] Positive human rights obligations are further discussed in Chapter 5 'The Fallacy of Effective Human Rights Protection under Relevant Treaty Law when Armed Groups Commit Violations'.

[17] Inter-American Commission on Human Rights, *Yearbook* (n 15) 358.

[18] Nowak and Januszewski, 'Non-State Actors' (n 4) 141.

[19] Phrase borrowed from article 2(7) of the Charter of the United Nations. The idea that human rights violations within a state are beyond the legitimate interest of the international community has long disappeared, however. States emphasized during the World Conference on Human Rights in Vienna on 25 June 1993 that 'the promotion and protection of all human rights is a legitimate concern of the international community'.

[20] *Affaire du Lotus, Judgment, 7 September 1927*, PCIJ, 18.

[21] See also Clapham, 'Non-State Actors' in Moeckli, Shah, Sivakumaran et al (eds), *International Human Rights Law* (OUP 2014) 532.

[22] ICRC, *International Humanitarian Law and the Challenges of Contemporary Armed Conflicts* (ICRC 2011) 14–15. See also Rodley, 'Can Armed Opposition Groups Violate Human Rights?' (n 8) 313.

4.2 Human Rights as Individual Entitlements of all Human Beings

IHRL's historical focus on states as duty-holders should not lead to the conclusion that the concept of human rights applies exclusively to the vertical relationship between governments and the governed. The concept of human rights is rooted in the idea of natural law and natural rights, which existed independently from the government–governed relationship.[23] For eminent legal scholars such as Lauterpacht, natural rights were 'of abiding potency and beneficence as the foundation of [human rights'] ultimate validity and as a standard of its approximation to justice'.[24] While Henkin pointed out that today's IHRL is, legally, grounded not so much in natural law as in international instruments adopted by states, for him the political idea of human rights owes much to the idea of natural rights.[25] Thus, when inquiring about the philosophical concept of human rights beyond its codification in international law treaties, it is useful to look closer at the concept of natural rights.

The origins, development, content, and scope of natural law and natural rights are a broad field of research.[26] For the purpose of the present chapter, it suffices to analyse accounts that have been most influential on the development of modern human rights. Locke's theory of natural rights is considered one of the oldest and most significant works in this area.[27] Contrary to Hobbes' pessimistic image of the state of nature and his call for a great and all-powerful Leviathan to protect the individual,[28] Locke, in 1651, provided an account of a state of nature in which 'men' lived in 'a state of perfect freedom to order their actions . . . within the bounds of the law of Nature'.[29] For Locke, in the state of nature man is born

> with a title to perfect freedom, and an uncontrouled enjoyment of all the rights and privileges of the law of Nature, equally with any other man, or number of men in the world.[30]

[23] See Joseph and Castan, *The International Covenant on Civil and Political Rights: Cases, Materials and Commentary* (3rd edn, OUP 2013) 6; Schabas, *The UDHR* (n 9) lxxi; Randall, 'History' (n 9); Shestack, 'Philosophic Foundations' (n 9).

[24] Lauterpacht, *An International Bill* (n 11) 3–4.

[25] See Henkin, *The Age of Rights* (Columbia University Press 1990) 1–2.

[26] For more extensive studies on the issue of natural law and natural rights, see, eg, Passerin d'Entrèves, *Natural Law: An Introduction to Legal Philosophy*, 6th impr. (Hutchinson University Library 1961); Porter, 'From Natural Law to Human Rights: Or, Why Rights Talk Matters' (1999) 14 Journal for Law and Religion 77–96; Shestack, 'Philosophic Foundations' (n 9); Randall, 'History' (n 9).

[27] See also Henkin, *The Age of Rights* (n 25). For an analysis of Grotius', de Victoria's, or de Vattel's accounts of natural rights, see Lauterpacht, *An International Bill* (n 11) 41–49.

[28] For Hobbes, the right of nature was 'the liberty each man hath to use his own power as he will himself for the preservation of his own nature; that is to say, of his own life; and consequently, of doing anything which, in his own judgement and reason, he shall conceive to be the aptest means thereunto'. In order to restrain this state of nature, Hobbes called for a 'great Leviathan' that 'hath the use of so much power and strength conferred on him that, by terror thereof, he is enabled to form the wills of them all, to peace at home, and mutual aid against their enemies abroad'. Hobbes, *Hobbes's Leviathan* (Clarendon Press 1651) chapters XIV and XVII. Hobbes' idea of natural rights and the social contract on which state power was based was rather contrary to the emerging idea of human rights.

[29] Locke, *Two Treatises of Government*, last repr. (Dent 1689) book II, para 4.

[30] ibid book II, para 87.

In Locke's account, infringements of such rights and privileges could be committed by anyone. By nature, 'man' had the power 'to preserve his property, that is, his life, liberty and estate, against the injuries and *attempts of other men*'.[31] This threat is not entirely mitigated if men decide to 'to join and unite into a community'.[32] As Nowak and Januszewski point out, the 'very rationale behind the conclusion of the social contract thus lies in the realisation that individuals can interfere with the enjoyment of the natural rights of others and need a state to ensure coexistence in peace'.[33] If 'man' consents to join a community in order to obtain a 'comfortable, safe and peaceful living', he necessarily gives up some—but not all—of his natural rights, namely what is 'necessary to the ends for which they unite into society'.[34]

For present purposes, Locke's most important idea is that every individual is born free, equal, and independent with certain fundamental rights, which include the right to life, liberty, and property. As these rights existed prior to there being any political power, necessarily they operated vis-à-vis not only a government but also other humans. For Locke, these natural rights existed independently of their codification, and core aspects of the rights prevailed when man entered into a social contract. While far from all Enlightenment philosophers shared Locke's account of natural rights and the social contract,[35] Locke's idea of inalienable individual rights left its mark on some of the most important human rights documents.

When in 1776 the colony of Virginia declared its independence from Great Britain, a 'Constitutional Convention' adopted the 'Virginia Declaration of Rights', which echoes Locke most prominently in its Section 1 by declaring:

> That all men are by nature equally free and independent and have certain inherent rights, of which, when they enter into a state of society, they cannot, by any compact, deprive or divest their posterity; namely, the enjoyment of life and liberty, with the means of acquiring and possessing property, and pursuing and obtaining happiness and safety.

Only weeks later, the idea that all men were endowed with 'inalienable rights', including 'Life, Liberty, and the pursuit of Happiness', was included as 'self-evident' in the United States' 'Declaration of Independence'. Inspired by these declarations, in 1789 during the French Revolution, the 'Assemblée nationale constituante' adopted the 'Déclaration des droits de l'homme et du citoyen'. Like its US predecessor, the French Declaration proclaimed that 'men are born and remain equal in rights', and

[31] ibid (emphasis added). [32] ibid book II, para 95.

[33] Nowak and Januszewski, 'Non-State Actors' (n 4) 130.

[34] Locke, *Two Treatises of Government* (n 29) book II, paras 95 and 99. Rights that 'man' could transfer to society do not include the power 'to destroy his own life, or take away the life or property of another'. ibid book II, para 135.

[35] eg in 1762 in 'The Social Contract', Rousseau provided a theory of a social contract in which the individual aligns itself with the community entirely and without any reservation. Consequently, the individual no longer had his natural freedoms but received benefits from the community, such as collective protection of entitlements that he could formerly only defend individually. So while in principle agreeing with Locke's idea of natural rights, Rousseau believed individuals could give up their rights entirely when joining the social compact. Subsequently, fundamental rights were no longer based on the laws of nature but on the law of the community. Rousseau, *The Social Contract* (Hafner Publishing 1762). See also Kant, *On the Common Saying: That May be Correct in Theory, but it is of No Use in Practice* (CUP 1793).

that '[t]he aim of all political association is the preservation of the natural and imprescriptible rights of man'.

A number of points should be highlighted regarding these declarations. First, their wording shows that these documents drew on the ideas proclaimed by Locke.[36] This suggests that the 'inherent rights of man' enshrined in these early human rights documents were not exclusively focused on the individual–state relationship but also applied in the horizontal relationships between citizens. Second, by their inclusion in these documents, the unwritten natural and inherent rights of men became part of the fundamental laws of these states, which made them part of positive law.[37] Third, the natural law references in these documents had great influence on the constitutions of numerous states in the nineteenth and early twentieth centuries, to the extent that some authors considered them general principles of international law.[38]

At the same time, these declarations left unclear what exactly the inherent rights of men included and how they relate to positive laws of the state.[39] In addition, despite reference to inherent rights of men in different constitutions, the idea of natural rights trumping state law did not, generally speaking, succeed in the nineteenth and early twentieth centuries. Following the dominant legal positivism of the time, many state constitutions recognized the value of inherent rights of individuals but primarily prescribed obligations of the state. This meant that only if corresponding state obligations existed were the human rights of the individual considered 'real rights'.[40] Natural rights, as such, were not imbued with legal value. Owing to the lack of a definition of natural rights in states' positive law, Bentham famously criticized them as 'rhetorical nonsense, nonsense upon stilts', being 'a son that never had a father'.[41]

[36] See Shestack, 'Philosophic Foundations' (n 9) 208; Bates, 'History' in Moeckli, Shah, and Sivakumaran (eds), *International Human Rights Law* (OUP 2014) 15–33, 19; Randall, 'History' (n 9) 8; Tomuschat, *Human Rights* (n 9) 13.

[37] See Lauterpacht, *An International Bill* (n 11) 4 and 23.

[38] For further analysis, see ibid 24–25; Schabas, *The UDHR* (n 9) lxxxix. While inherent rights of man found their way into national constitutions and it seems that agreement emerged on the need to protect them, it is reported that this agreement concerned primarily the moral and political need to protect certain individual rights. It did not express agreement on the philosophical basis of these rights. See McKeon, 'The Philosophic Basis and Material Circumstances of the Rights of Man' in UNESCO (ed), *Human Rights: Comments and Interpretations* (UNESCO 1948) 23–34, 26.

[39] See Randall, 'History' (n 9) 9; Lauterpacht, *An International Bill* (n 11) 27.

[40] Nowak and Januszewski, 'Non-State Actors' (n 4) 131.

[41] Stark (ed), *Jeremy Bentham's Economic Writings: Critical Edition Based on his Printed Works and Unprinted Manuscripts* (transferred to digital printing, Routledge 2010) 334. Marxist authors voiced further criticism, eg, arguing that the idea of natural rights was focused on egoistic men separated from their communities. See Marx, 'On the Jewish Question' in McLellan (ed), *Karl Marx: Early Works* (Basil Blackwell 1844). For further discussion, see Shestack, 'Philosophic Foundations' (n 9) 209–11.

4.3 The Universal Declaration of Human Rights and the Renaissance of 'Natural Rights'

The adoption of the Universal Declaration of Human Rights (UDHR) in 1948 has been described as the renaissance of the natural rights idea, after a period marked by positivism and most heinous human rights violations committed in accordance with the national laws of Nazi Germany.[42] Indeed, states included reference to the 'equal and inalienable rights of all members of the human family' in the preamble to the Declaration.[43] This reference clearly borrows from Locke's writings and the different national declarations discussed above. Moreover, scholars point out that the Declaration's reference to 'human dignity' appears to have been inspired by Kant, and that the UDHR's wording implies that 'the drafters drew from moral philosophy with its demand of reciprocal tolerance and forbearance, and were well aware of the dangers coming from the private side, thus accepting the relevance of horizontal duties'.[44] It has been argued that 'natural rights metamorphosed into internationally recognized "human rights" principles in 1948'.[45] Indeed, the UDHR's wording, historic context, and drafting history suggest that its rights should not be understood as only operating in the vertical relation between the state and its subjects. Instead, they constitute individual entitlements.

Analysing the Declaration's wording, it stands out that the UDHR hardly mentions the state. Scholars have argued that this is 'ostensibly leaving open the question of the duty-holder's identity',[46] and that the UDHR 'clearly enshrines its rights as belonging to all members of the "human family", to "everyone"'.[47] This particular wording can be explained by the historic context of the Declaration.

[42] See Shestack, 'Philosophic Foundations' (n 9) 215. This does not mean that the idea of human rights and an international protection system emerged only during the Second World War. For example, the abolition of the international slave trade, the emergence of international human rights law (IHL), the concept of 'diplomatic protection', and the protection of people in mandated territories and minorities under the League of Nations are ancestors of post-Second World War human rights protection. See, eg, Randall, 'History' (n 9) 10–14; Tomuschat, *Human Rights* (n 9) 22; Burgers, 'The Road to San Francisco: The Revival of the Human Rights Idea in the Twentieth Century' (1992) 14 Human Rights Quarterly 447–77.

[43] Similar clauses are found in the preambles to the ICCPR and the ICESCR.

[44] Nowak and Januszewski, 'Non-State Actors' (n 4) 139. For further discussion of the importance and role of human dignity in IHRL, see also Murray, '*Human Rights Obligations of Non-State Armed Groups* (Hart 2016) 157–58.

[45] Joseph and Castan, *ICCPR* (n 23) 6. This is also supported by the fact that the vast majority of states that negotiated the UDHR came from a natural rights tradition. At the same time, the French delegate at the negotiations of the UDHR emphasized that, despite the fact that states were able to agree on the common ideal and the practical need for human rights protection, 'it was impossible to attain complete agreement on doctrine', meaning the philosophical origin of human rights. United Nations General Assembly, *Draft Universal Declaration of Human Rights: Report of the Third Committee* 9 December 1948, A/777, 865 (France). See also Randall, 'History' (n 9) 17.

[46] Ronen, 'Human Rights Obligations of Territorial Non-State Actors' (n 6) 35.

[47] Grear, '"Framing the Project" of International Human Rights Law: Reflections on the Dysfunctional "Family" of the Universal Declaration' in Gearty and Douzinas (eds), *The Cambridge Companion to Human Rights Law* (CUP 2012) 1–35, 26.

The UDHR was not intended to define state obligations.[48] The UDHR was only one part of an envisaged 'international bill of human rights' consisting of, first, the Declaration proclaiming human rights; second, a convention defining states' corresponding obligations; and third, implementation mechanisms.[49] Still, it has been argued that 'this list of entitlements can be understood as providing for claims towards all possible abusers'.[50]

While for some delegations during the final debates in the UN General Assembly's Third Committee in December 1948 the draft Declaration clearly reflected individual rights and corresponding state obligations,[51] others expressed different ideas on the nature and scope of the UDHR. For example, Chile stated that the UDHR sets out rights and freedoms of the individual, and

> [t]he only nations unable to subscribe to that declaration were States which denied the value of freedom as such and denied that man had rights independently of the form of the State, or which did not believe that man possessed inherent rights that had existed before the formation of social groups.[52]

Similarly, one of the main drafters of the UDHR, René Cassin, explained in the Third Committee:

> The declaration rested on four fundamental pillars: personal rights, relationships between man and his fellow men, public liberties and fundamental political rights, and economic and social rights.[53]

Following Cassin, these rights did not operate exclusively between the state and its subjects but 'they provided safeguards or hope of safeguards, while at the same time also imposing certain limitations upon mankind'.[54] Mankind, in this respect, was to be understood as including states, groups, and individuals.[55] These statements seem to refer to the natural law basis of the proclaimed rights.[56] At the very least, they support the argument that the UDHR contained primarily individual entitlements and did not intend to restrict these rights to only the government–individual relationship.

As a result, the application of the concept of human rights should not be regarded as being restricted to the vertical state–individual relationship. In accordance with

[48] Hakimi, 'State Bystander Responsibility' (2010) 21 The European Journal of International Law 341–85, 346.

[49] See *Draft Universal Declaration of Human Rights: Report of the Third Committee* (n 45) 888 (New Zealand). See also Schabas, *The UDHR* (n 9) xcvii. Against this background, Clapham reminds us that 'the Universal Declaration of Human Rights is written as a proclamation of rights for everyone, the precise obligations of states were not agreed at that time'. Clapham, 'The Rights and Responsibilities of Armed Non-State Actors: The Legal Landscape & Issues Surrounding Engagement' (SSRN 2010) 24.

[50] Nowak and Januszewski, 'Non-State Actors' (n 4) 139.

[51] eg Lebanon expressed the view that following the adoption of the UDHR, 'every Government knew, at present, to what extent exactly it had pledged itself, and every citizen could protest to his Government if the latter did not fulfil its obligations'. *Draft Universal Declaration of Human Rights: Report of the Third Committee* (n 45), 860 (Lebanon). See also ibid 900 (Bolivia).

[52] ibid 863 (Chile). [53] ibid 865 (France). [54] ibid. [55] ibid.

[56] For additional statements emphasizing the character of human rights as basic entitlements of all human beings, see, eg, ibid 867 (Philippines) and 887 (Uruguay).

one of its prominent philosophic underpinnings, namely the natural rights idea, human rights are better understood as individual entitlements, which protect human beings against any attack on inherent rights and dignity. Following this approach, the idea that non-state actors can violate internationally protected human rights and possibly breach an international obligation loses some of its exotic character. As Clapham has suggested,

> the most promising theoretical basis for human rights obligations for non-state actors is first, to remind ourselves that the foundational basis of human rights is best explained as rights which belong to the individual in recognition of each person's inherent dignity. The implication is that these natural rights should be respected by everyone and every entity.[57]

By the same token, finding that the philosophical concept of human rights includes the possibility that non-state actors will violate these rights is not sufficient evidence for the existence of human rights obligations of these actors under international law. Natural rights theory has great value for understanding the concept of human rights, but contrary to the concept of natural rights, 'international human rights are not the work of philosophers, but of politicians and citizens'.[58] In short, it takes more than a philosophical concept to establish international legal obligations. Moreover, as pointed out by Lauterpacht, owing to their controversial reputation, unclear content, and lack of enforcement mechanisms, '[t]he law of nature and natural rights can never be a true substitute for the positive enactments of the law of the society of States'.[59] These positive enactments—namely IHRL treaties—are examined next.

[57] Clapham, 'The Rights and Responsibilities of Armed Non-State Actors' (n 49) 24.

[58] Henkin, *The Age of Rights* (n 25) 6. As summarized by Randall in a common but also contested finding: 'As legal rights, human rights are entitlements "protected by the rule of law", which implies that they form part of positive law. More precisely, so as to be accurately described as *international* human rights, they need to be protected by the *international* legal order. As moral rights, IHR are generally viewed as basic entitlements that belong to every person by virtue of the sole fact of being human.' Randall, 'History' (n 9) 3.

[59] Lauterpacht, *An International Bill* (n 11) 3.

5

The Fallacy of Effective Human Rights Protection under Relevant Treaty Law when Armed Groups Commit Violations

Traditionally, in international treaty law human rights obligations are state obligations. Under international human rights law (IHRL) treaties such as the International Covenant on Civil and Political Rights (ICCPR), it is upon each state party 'to respect and to ensure to all individuals within its territory and subject to its jurisdiction the rights recognized' in the respective treaty.[1] In order to protect the 'inalienable rights of all members of the human family', states developed international treaties in which they take upon themselves the negative duty to respect human rights as well as the positive duty to protect them. This system follows a simple logic:

> Human dignity requires respect from my neighbor as well as from the state. Under the international instruments the state is required not only to respect but to ensure rights, that is, ensure respect for them by private persons.[2]

Indeed, the ability to enjoy most human rights 'would be totally undermined if States had no duties to control human rights abuse in the private sector'.[3]

[1] Article 2(1) International Covenant on Civil and Political Rights (ICCPR). See also the wording of the International Convention on the Elimination of all Forms of Racial Discrimination (ICERD), Convention on the Elimination of all Forms of Discrimination against Women (CEDAW), Convention against Torture and other Cruel, Inhuman or Degrading Punishment (CAT), Convention on the Rights of the Child (CRC), International Convention on the Protection of the Rights of all Migrant Workers and Members of their Families (ICMW), International Convention for the Protection of all Persons from Enforced Disappearance (CPED), and Convention on the Rights of Persons with Disabilities (CRPD). On differences between the scope of the positive obligations included in these treaties as well as their interpretation by states and treaty bodies, see Hakimi, 'State Bystander Responsibility' (2010) 21 The European Journal of International Law 350–52. With regard to regional human rights treaties, see articles 1 and 2 of the American Convention on Human Rights (ACHR); article 1 European Convention on Human Rights (ECHR); Article 1 African Charter on Human and Peoples' Rights (ACHPR). For further discussion on positive obligations under the ECHR, see Mowbray, *The Development of Positive Obligations under the European Convention on Human Rights by the European Court of Human Rights* (Hart 2004); Xenos, *The Positive Obligations of the State Under the European Convention of Human Rights* (Routledge 2012).

[2] Henkin, *The Age of Rights* (Columbia University Press 1990) 8.

[3] Joseph and Castan, *The International Covenant on Civil and Political Rights: Cases, Materials, and Commentary* (3rd edn, OUP 2013) para 1.115. See also Human Rights Committee (HRC), *General Comment No 31: Nature of the General Legal Obligation Imposed on States Parties to the Covenant*, 26 May 2004, CCPR/C/21/Rev.1/Add.13, para 8.

The very existence of states' obligation to protect human rights shows that, at least conceptually, human rights cannot only be violated by states but also by non-state actors. If only states could violate human rights, states' obligation to respect these rights would suffice and no obligation also to protect would be needed. Since non-state actors can infringe individual human rights, the obligation to protect human rights is a necessary component of the international human rights protection system, in which most IHRL treaties contain no obligations for non-state actors. Owing to states' negative and positive human rights obligations, individuals should be fully protected against any human rights violation: international law proscribes states from infringing human rights, and positive obligations require them to proscribe as well as prevent or prosecute human rights violations by non-state actors. As Judge Trindade at the Inter-American Court of Human Rights pointed out: 'nobody is removed from the protection of the Law, even when the applicable law may be different according to the circumstances of each specific case'.[4]

Despite the importance of states' protective human rights obligations, commentators found that their 'concrete content and scope is not unambiguous',[5] meaning that they constitute 'a much greyer area than the extent of a State's "vertical" obligations', that is, its obligation to respect human rights.[6] In fact, for many scholars, human rights protection against violations by armed groups solely based on protective state obligations is not only a 'much greyer area' of IHRL but an essential weakness.[7] This is particularly the case if states have lost control over parts of their territory, are weak, and/or confronted with powerful non-state actors. From a systemic point of view, the potentially resulting lack of human rights protection provides 'the most convincing argument in favour of direct horizontal obligations of armed groups'.[8] Indeed, if the present international human rights protection system

[4] *Miguel Castro Castro Prison v Peru, Judgment (Concurring Opinion of Judge A.A. Cancado Trindade), 2 August 2008*, IACtHR, para 83.

[5] Nowak and Januszewski, 'Non-State Actors and Human Rights' in Noortmann, Reinisch, and Ryngaert (eds), *Non-State Actors in International Law* (Hart 2015) 141.

[6] Joseph and Castan, *ICCPR* (n 3) para 1.110. In this context, a divide between human rights protection in the public sphere (vis-à-vis the state) and in the private sphere (between private individuals) has been criticized, especially with regard to the protection of women. For summaries of the debate, see n 65.

[7] See, eg, Nowak and Januszewski, 'Non-State Actors' (n 5) 319; Kamatali, 'The Application of International Human Rights Law in Non-International Armed Conflicts: From Rhetoric to Action' (2014) 4 Journal of International Humanitarian Legal Studies 220–61, 237; McCorquodale, 'Overlegalizing Silences: Human Rights and Nonstate Actors' (2002) 96 Proceedings of the Annual Meeting (American Society of International Law) 384–88, 93; Tomuschat, 'The Applicability of Human Rights Law to Insurgent Movements' in Fischer and Fleck (eds), *Krisensicherung Und Humanitärer Schutz: Festschrift Für Dieter Fleck* (Berlin: BWV 2004) 573–91; Constantinides, 'Human Rights Obligations and Accountability of Armed Opposition Groups: The Practice of the UN Security Council' (2010) 4 Human Rights & International Legal Discourse 93–94.

[8] Ryngaert, 'Human Rights Obligations of Armed Groups' (2008) 41 Revue Belge De Droit International 355–81, 362. See also Reinisch, 'The Changing International Legal Framework for Dealing with Non-State Actors' in Alston (ed), *Non-State Actors and Human Rights* (OUP 2005) 37–89, 74–75; Cahin, 'Attribution of Conduct to the State: Insurrectional Movements' in Crawford, Pellet, and Olleson (eds), *The Law of International Responsibility* (OUP 2010) 247–56, 523.

had significant gaps or deficiencies in the event of private actors committing human rights violations, additional rules were needed.

In order to determine whether and to what extent protection gaps exist in a primarily state-focused, treaty-based human rights protection system, the present analysis looks at three main issues: first, possible human rights obligations of armed groups directly under IHRL treaties; second, the laws of state responsibility; and third, states' obligation to protect human rights against acts by non-state actors.

5.1 The Limited Scope of Human Rights Treaties Directly Addressing Armed Groups

Normally, IHRL treaties define state obligations. Most do not address non-state actors.[9] Over the past few decades, however, states have also developed treaties at the international and regional levels that directly address non-state armed groups. These are the 'Optional Protocol to the Convention on the Rights of the Child on the Involvement of Children in Armed Conflict' (CRC-OPAC) and the 'African Union Convention for the Protection and Assistance of Internally Displaced Persons in Africa' (Kampala Convention). Owing to the somewhat ambiguous wording of the respective provisions in these treaties, different interpretations exist as to whether they include legal obligations for non-state armed groups, or merely a 'soft moral obligation'.[10]

Article 4 CRC-OPAC provides that

1. Armed groups that are distinct from the armed forces of a State should not, under any circumstances, recruit or use in hostilities persons under the age of 18 years.
2. States Parties shall take all feasible measures to prevent such recruitment and use, including the adoption of legal measures necessary to prohibit and criminalize such practices.
3. The application of the present article under this Protocol shall not affect the legal status of any party to an armed conflict.

The dominant view has been that the use of the words 'should not' instead of 'shall not' in paragraph 1 means that the provision is only suggestive and does not create a legal obligation for armed groups. It is argued that, in combination with paragraph 2, the article remains within the confines of classical IHRL treaties, which only impose legal obligations on states.[11]

[9] For in depth analysis of IHRL treaties, see Fortin, *The Accountability of Armed Groups under Human Rights Law* (OUP 2017) 210–16.

[10] Ryngaert, 'Human Rights Obligations of Armed Groups' (n 8) 364.

[11] See The United Nations Children's Fund, Guide to the Optional Protocol on the Involvement of Children in Armed Conflict (UNICEF 2003); Vandewiele, *Optional Protocol: The Involvement of Children in Armed Conflicts—A Commentary on the United Nations Convention on the Rights of the Child* (M Nijhoff 2006) 42; Bellal, Giacca, and Casey-Maslen, 'International Law and Armed Non-State Actors in Afghanistan' (2011) 93 International Review of the Red Cross 65; Ryngaert, 'Human Rights Obligations of Armed Groups' (n 8) 364–65; Sivakumaran, 'Re-envisaging the International Law of Internal Armed Conflict' (2011) 22 European Journal of International Law 219–64, 248; Henckaerts and Wiesener, 'Human Rights Obligations of Non-State Armed Groups: A Possible Contribution from Customary International Law' in Kolb and Gaggioli (eds), *Research Handbook on Human Rights and Humanitarian Law* (Edward Elgar 2013) 148.

Others have found, however, that article 4(1) CRC-OPAC 'creates distinct obligations for non-state armed groups',[12] or, more cautiously, proposed that other interpretations of the article are possible. Regarding the difference between the words 'should' and 'shall', Clapham has suggested that when addressing an entity that is not party to the protocol, 'should' and 'shall' can both express an obligation. In combination with the formulation that NSAGs should not recruit persons under the age of eighteen 'under any circumstances', he finds that even 'should not' can signify an intention to create a legally binding obligation for non-state armed groups.[13] Likewise, examining the CRC-OPAC and other humanitarian treaties, Yun argues that 'the term "should" in the operative part of treaties always creates legally binding obligations'.[14] It could be added that the savings clause included in paragraph 3 may further indicate that article 4(1) CRC-OPAC includes more than a moral obligation.[15] This textual ambiguity reflects the different views of states in the drafting process. While it is reported that most states believed that the protocol should 'reflect reality in the world today' and address child recruitment by non-state armed groups,[16] there was disagreement as to whether an inter-state treaty could legally bind non-state actors.[17]

Some clarification on how the article should be interpreted is found in subsequent practice. Looking at the practice of the UN Security Council, the UN Special Representative for Children in Armed Conflict, and the UN Secretary General with regard to the monitoring and reporting mechanism on grave violations against children in armed conflict, Bellal, Giacca, and Casey-Maslen argued that such practice 'suggests that armed groups are widely considered to be bound by [article 4(1) CRC-OPAC]'.[18] Accordingly, the UN Commission of Inquiry for Syria stated in 2013:

> Both Government-affiliated militia and anti-Government armed groups were found to have violated the Optional Protocol to the Convention on the Rights of the Child on the involvement of children in armed conflict, to which the Syrian Arab Republic is a party.[19]

[12] Andreopoulos, 'On the Accountability of Non-State Armed Groups', in Andreopoulos, Juviler, and Kabasakal Arat (eds), *Non-State Actors in the Human Rights Universe* (Kumarian Press 2006) 141–63, 153.

[13] Clapham, *Human Rights Obligations of Non-State Actors* (OUP 2006) 75.

[14] Yun, 'Breaking Imaginary Barriers' (2014) 5 Journal of International Humanitarian Legal Studies 213–57, 213, see especially 231–43.

[15] It is questionable why a saving clause would be needed if the article contained only moral obligations for armed groups? Why should a non-legal recommendation have any impact on the legal status of the armed groups? In addition, such clauses are normally used in IHL treaties in which obligations for non-state armed groups are intended. See, eg, Common Article 3 of the Geneva Conventions or article 22(6) Second Protocol to the Hague Convention of 1954 for the Protection of Cultural Property in the Event of Armed Conflict.

[16] See Commission on Human Rights, *Report of the Working group on a draft optional protocol to the Convention on the Rights of the Child on involvement of children in armed conflicts on its fourth session*, 23 March 1998, E/CN.4/1998/102, para 32.

[17] See Commission on Human Rights, *Report of the working group on a draft optional protocol to the Convention on the Rights of the Child on involvement of children in armed conflicts on its sixth session*, 27 March 2000, E/CN.4/2000/74, paras 35–40.

[18] Bellal, Giacca and, Casey-Maslen, 'Armed Non-State Actors in Afghanistan' (n 11) 66. See also Fortin, *The Accountability of Armed Groups under Human Rights Law* (n 9) 229-31.

[19] Human Rights Council, *Report of the independent international commission of inquiry on the Syrian Arab Republic*, A/HRC/22/59, executive summary.

While noting that non-state armed groups cannot become parties to the CRC-OPAC, the Commission argued that the Protocol 'by its terms applies to non-State actors'.[20] Likewise, the Office of the High Commissioner for Human Rights (OHCHR) investigation on Sri Lanka held that the CRC-OPAC 'prohibits the recruitment or use of children under 18 by non-state armed groups'.[21] Accordingly, the armed group Moro Islamic Liberation Front stated publicly that it accepts its 'obligations' under the CRC-OPAC.[22] As a result, while the use of the wording 'should not' instead of 'shall not' may prima facie suggest something less than a legal obligation for non-state armed groups, the wording leaves sufficient scope for the opposite conclusion, which is, in fact, increasingly accepted.[23]

Like the CRC-OPAC, the wording of the Kampala Convention is ambiguous on whether or not it includes direct legal obligations for non-state armed groups. Article 7(5) states that 'Members of armed groups shall be prohibited from …', followed by a number of acts. Article 7(5) includes not only international humanitarian law (IHL)-based obligations but also specific human rights provisions.[24] It has, however, been argued that article 7 addresses 'members of armed groups' and not the groups as such.[25] Also, read together with states' general obligation 'to respect and to ensure respect for the Convention' under its article 3, it can be argued that the Convention does not address armed groups directly but requires states to prohibit members of armed groups from committing certain acts. Moreover, the drafting history of the article shows that possible obligations for armed groups under article 7(5) were controversial.[26]

However, other parts of the Kampala Convention suggest that it does contain obligations for armed groups as such. Article 2(e) states that one of the Convention's objectives is to '[p]rovide for the respective obligations, responsibilities and roles of armed groups, non-state actors and other relevant actors … with respect to the prevention of internal displacement and protection of, and assistance to, internally displaced persons'. Moreover, article 5(11) requires states to 'take measures aimed

[20] ibid 86.

[21] Human Rights Council, *Report of the OHCHR Investigation on Sri Lanka (OISL)*, A/HRC/30/CRP.2, para 658.

[22] MILF Action Plan, cited in Fortin, *The Accountability of Armed Groups under Human Rights Law* (n 9) 230–31.

[23] See also Office of the Special Representative of the Secretary-General for Children in Armed Conflict, *Working Paper No 1: Six Grave Violations Against Children during Armed Conflict* (The Legal Foundation 2013) 11.

[24] Article 7(3) states: 'The protection and assistance to internally displaced persons under this Article shall be governed by international law and in particular international humanitarian law'. However, article 7(5)(c) includes the following prohibition: 'Denying internally displaced persons the right to live in satisfactory conditions of dignity, security, sanitation, food, water, health and shelter; and separating members of the same family'. This goes beyond IHL of non-international armed conflicts (NIACs).

[25] See Bellal, Giacca, and Casey-Maslen, 'Armed Non-State Actors in Afghanistan' (n 11) 166–67; Henckaerts and Wiesener, 'Human Rights Obligations' (n 11) 148.

[26] For further discussion of the drafting history, see Giustiniani, 'New Hopes and Challenges for the Protection of Idps in Africa: The Kampala Convention for the Protection and Assistance of Internally Displaced Persons in Africa' (2009) 39 Denver Journal of International Law and Policy 347–70; Ojeda, 'The Kampala Convention on Internally Displaced Persons: Some International Humanitarian Law Aspects' (2010) 29 Refugee Survey Quarterly 58–66; Fortin, *The Accountability of Armed Groups under Human Rights Law* (n 9) 234–65.

at ensuring that armed groups act in conformity with *their obligations* under Article 7' (emphasis added). This provision suggests that the drafters considered article 7 to contain obligations pertaining directly to armed groups as such. Such a reading finds further support in an 'Explanatory Note' to the Kampala Convention published by the African Union, which states that the Convention outlines 'obligations of Armed Groups in Article 7'.[27]

In light of this analysis, a number of conclusions can be drawn. First, over the past years, states have recognized that, in certain situations, it is necessary for human rights instruments to address not only states but also non-state armed groups. Second, despite the ambiguous wording and conflicting interpretations, both treaties and recent international practice suggest that not only states but also non-state armed groups can have legal obligations under IHRL treaties. Third, the CRC-OPAC and the Kampala Convention address armed groups that are sufficiently organized to be a party to an armed conflict without requiring state-like abilities or control over territory and population.[28] As a result, these treaties show that there is no inherent barrier in human rights law that prevents non-state entities from having IHRL obligations. If states wish to assign human rights obligations to armed groups, they can do so. Yet, even if it is concluded that the CRC-OPAC and the Kampala Convention contain human rights obligations for armed groups, they are materially restricted to specific conduct or specific situations.

5.2 Human Rights Violations by Non-State Entities are Generally Not Attributable to the Territorial State

Before embarking on an analysis of states' positive obligations under IHRL, it should be recalled how the laws on state responsibility regulate states' responsibility for acts committed by non-state armed groups. Generally, under international law 'a State is responsible only for its own conduct, that is to say the conduct of persons acting, on whatever basis, on its behalf'.[29] Elaborating on this principle, the International Law

[27] African Union, Explanatory Note On the African Union Convention for the Protection and Assistance of Internally Displaced Persons in Africa (African Union, 2009) 3.

[28] The CRC-OPAC does not specify under which conditions armed groups qualify as falling under its article 4, but the title of the Protocol arguably restricts its application to armed groups that are sufficiently organized to become party to a NIAC. In contrast, article 1(e) of the Kampala Convention defines armed groups as 'dissident armed forces or other organized armed groups that are distinct from the armed forces of the state'. This does not mean, however, that the scope of the entire treaty is restricted only to situations of armed conflicts. See The United Nations Children's Fund, 'Guide to the Optional Protocol on the Involvement of Children in Armed Conflict' (n 11) 17; Clapham, *The Rights and Responsibilities of Armed Non-State Actors: The Legal Landscape and Issues Surrounding Engagement* (SSRN 2010) 26.

[29] *Case Concerning Application of the Convention on the Prevention and Punishment of the Crime of Genocide (Bosnia and Herzegovina v Serbia and Montenegro)*, para 406. See also Article 2 of the ILC Articles on the 'Responsibility of States for Internationally Wrongful Acts' (from here on, ARSIWA). It is widely accepted that many of the provisions contained in the ILC Articles on State Responsibility form part of customary international law. See, eg, Caron, 'The ILC Articles on State Responsibility: The Paradoxical Relationship Between Form and Authority' (2002) 96 American Journal of International Law 857–73; Cassese, *International Law* (2nd edn, OUP: 2005) 244.

Commission (ILC) Commentary on the Articles on State Responsibility explains that wrongful acts committed by individuals participating in riots or organized insurrectional movements over which the state does not exert effective control are generally not attributable to the state.[30] However, even if non-state conduct may not be attributable to states, states are responsible for breaches of their own obligations in respect of acts committed by non-state actors.[31] The existence of positive obligations has long been recognized in international law. For example, in a finding of an arbitration tribunal concerning damages suffered by a US missionary society in a British colony during a 'native rebellion' in 1898, the tribunal held:

> It is a well-established principle of international law that no government can be held responsible for the act of rebellious bodies of men committed in violation of its authority, where it is itself guilty of no breach of good faith, or of no negligence in suppressing insurrection.[32]

This case concerned the state's obligation to protect foreigners and their property in its territory. It protected state interests, not human rights. Today, however, this principle also applies to states' positive human rights obligations. States have an international obligation to protect any person within their territory or jurisdiction from human rights violations, including those committed by non-state armed groups.[33] As the ILC argued, if a state is in a position to 'adopt measures of vigilance, prevention or punishment in respect of the [insurrectional] movement's conduct'[34] but fails to do so, it engages its international responsibility.

Arguably, two exceptions exist under which the conduct of non-state armed groups becomes attributable to the state.[35] First, under article 10 ARSIWA, a state shall be responsible ex post facto for the conduct of an 'insurrectional movement' that either replaces the government of the state, or 'succeeds in establishing a new State in part of the territory of a pre-existing State'. Given that this principle does not concern the state's responsibility during the insurrection, or its responsibility if the non-state armed group is not successful, it is not further discussed here.[36]

[30] ILC, 'Responsibility of State for Internationally Wrongful Acts (with commentaries)' in *Yearbook of the International Law Commission*, vol II, Part Two, (United Nations 2001) para 2 of the commentary on article 10. Non-attribution of wrongful acts is also recognized as one consequence of the recognition of belligerency: Once the territorial state recognized belligerency, third states would need to address complaints about unlawful acts directly to the belligerent under whose control the acts was committed. See Wheaton, *Elements of International Law*, 42–43.

[31] See ILC, 'Responsibility of State for Internationally Wrongful Acts (with commentaries)' (n 30) para 3 of the commentary on article 10.

[32] *Home Frontier and Foreign Missionary Society of the United Brethren in Christ (United States v Great Britain), Judgment, 18 December 1920*, Arbitral Tribunal, 44.

[33] This is further discussed in Section 5.3 'States' Obligation to Protect Human Rights'.

[34] ILC, 'Responsibility of State for Internationally Wrongful Acts (with commentaries)' (n 30) para 15 of the commentary on article 10.

[35] Arguably, a third exception exists under article 8 ARSIWA, which attributes to the state conduct of persons or groups of persons who are 'in fact acting on the instructions of, or under the direction or control of, that State in carrying out the conduct'. These cases are excluded from this book because entities falling under article 8 ARSIWA are not operating in opposition to the state.

[36] For further discussion of this principle, see Dumberry, 'New State Responsibility for Internationally Wrongful Acts by an Insurrectional Movement' (2006) 17 European Journal of International Law 605–21; D'Aspremont, 'Rebellion and State Responsibility: Wrongdoing by Democratically Elected Insurgents' (2009) 58 International and Comparative Law Quarterly 427–42.

Arguably, a second exception exists under article 9 ARSIWA. This article provides:

The conduct of a person or group of persons shall be considered an act of a State under international law if the person or group of persons is in fact exercising elements of the governmental authority in the absence or default of the official authorities and in circumstances such as to call for the exercise of those elements of authority.

The ILC commentary on the article states that such cases occur only exceptionally—for example, during 'revolution, armed conflict or foreign occupation, where the regular authorities dissolve, are disintegrating, have been suppressed or are for the time being inoperative'.[37] The article's wording does not exclude that acts of non-state armed groups can be attributable to the territorial state if the article's three conditions are met.[38] This interpretation finds some support in the ILC's commentary on article 10, which states that 'the acts of unsuccessful insurrectional movements are not attributable to the State, unless under some other article of chapter II, for example in the special circumstances envisaged by article 9'.[39] Following this line of argument, some scholars have concluded that 'evidence of effective control by, and government-like authority of, armed groups could also engage the responsibility of the State whose authority they supplant, under Article 9 [ARSIWA]'.[40] Fortin elaborated that this could not be the case for any act of the non-state entity but merely for a number of 'impersonal acts' by 'certain groups'.[41]

This interpretation could have the positive outcome of bringing certain conduct of non-state armed groups within the international laws of state responsibility, which may arguably help to avoid a responsibility gap. It has, however, also been recognized that 'international practice and jurisprudence is lacking' to support this interpretation.[42] Indeed, the examples of state practice referred to by the ILC do not support the article's application to insurgent movements that oppose the state. First, the commentary refers to the case of levée en masse under international

[37] ILC, 'Responsibility of State for Internationally Wrongful Acts (with commentaries)' (n 30) para 1 of the commentary on article 9.

[38] These are: 'first, the conduct must effectively relate to the exercise of elements of the governmental authority, secondly, the conduct must have been carried out in the absence or default of the official authorities, and thirdly, the circumstances must have been such as to call for the exercise of those elements of authority'. ibid para 3 of the commentary on article 9. This approach has been suggested, eg, by Cahin, 'The Responsibility of other Entities: Armed Bands and Criminal Groups' in Crawford, Pellet, and Olleson (eds), *The Law of International Responsibility* (OUP 2010) 335. For a thorough examination of the three criteria and a nuanced finding that some acts may be attributed to the state, see Fortin, *The Accountability of Armed Groups under Human Rights Law* (n 9) 250–84.

[39] ILC, 'Responsibility of State for Internationally Wrongful Acts (with commentaries)' (n 30) para 2 of the commentary on article 10.

[40] Ryngaert, 'Human Rights Obligations of Armed Groups' (n 8) 360–61 and 370. Accordingly, Ryngaert suggested that government-like conduct, such as law enforcement measures, by armed groups such as FARC in Colombia or the LTTE in Sri Lanka, could be attributed to the state.

[41] Fortin, The Accountability of Armed Groups under Human Rights Law (n 9) 253–54 and 269. Impersonal acts could consist, eg, of 'acts relating to the resolution of domestic disputes, the registration of births, deaths, and marriages, the administration of basic policing and judicial functions, the provision of healthcare and education, and the provision of telecommunication services in the territory'. It would not include acts relating to the military campaign.

[42] Cahin, 'Responsibility of Other Entities' (n 38) 335; for a remarkable exception, see Fortin, *The Accountability of Armed Groups under Human Rights Law* (n 9) 254–67. This is further discussed below.

humanitarian law. Levée en masse concerns situations in which, faced with the approach of the enemy army, inhabitants spontaneously take up arms and oppose the invading force.[43] They do so in support of the state, or even 'in response to an order by their government' but without being able to organize into regular armed forces.[44] Thus, a levée en masse does not challenge the authority of the territorial state. A second situation on which the article is based is the *Yeager* case before the Iran–United States Claims Tribunal. This case concerned a situation in which local *Komitehs* took up security functions in Iran directly after the Iranian revolution in 1979. The judgment provided the following:

> The Tribunal finds sufficient evidence on the record to establish a presumption that the revolutionary 'Komitehs' or 'Guards' after 11 February 1979 were acting in fact on behalf of the new government, or at least exercised elements of governmental authority in the absence of official authorities, in operations of which the new Government must have had knowledge and to which it did not specifically object.[45]

Hence, the *Komitehs* did not act against the state but conducted security services in a revolutionary situation in which the state was not yet able to provide such services itself.

Other practice referred to in earlier ILC drafts concern cases during the Second World War, in which local administrations fled from an invading force and private persons 'took over, in the interests of the community, the management of certain public concerns'.[46] Similar situations can occur after natural disasters.[47] In addition to the conditions listed in article 9, the essential communality of these situations is 'a normative element in the form of agency', meaning that the private person(s) acted not in opposition to the government but in its interest.[48] In fact, in the commentary on an earlier version of the Articles the then Special Rapporteur Ago explicitly excluded the possibility that acts of insurrectional movements could fall under this article. For Ago, entities that aim to overthrow a government can in no way 'be "in fact exercising elements of the governmental authority" of that State or Government'.[49] Special Rapporteur Crawford, who finalized the ARSIWA, seems to share this view.[50]

43 Article 4(6) of the Geneva Convention III.

44 See Preux, *Geneva Convention Relative to the Treatment of Prisoners of War: Commentary* (ICRC 1960) 67.

45 *Kenneth P Yeager v The Islamic Republic of Iran, Iran–United States Claims Tribunal, Judgment, 1987*, 104.

46 ILC, Draft Articles on State Responsibility with Commentaries thereto Adopted by the International Law Commission on First Reading (1997) para 9 of the draft commentary on article 8 [future article 9].

47 See ibid.

48 ILC, 'Responsibility of State for Internationally Wrongful Acts (with commentaries)' (n 30) para 6 of the commentary on article 9.

49 ILC, 'Chapter II: State Responsibility' *Yearbook of the International Law Commission 1975*, vol II (United Nations 1976) 92, fn 205. However, at one point one ILC member suggested that the article could apply to the conduct of insurrectional movements and his opinion was not opposed by others. See Fortin, *The Accountability of Armed Groups under Human Rights Law* (n 9) 277.

50 See Crawford, *State Responsibility: The General Part* (CUP 2013) 168. In the context of article 9, he argues: 'If the governmental functions in question are exercised by an insurrectionist movement which has not established secure control of the state or which controls only some of its territory,

As a result, there is little evidence that international law holds states directly responsible for governance acts performed by non-state armed groups.[51] It is difficult to imagine that article 9 addresses situations in which an armed group first expels the de jure government from parts of its territory, and if the group then engages in acts of torture or summary executions as part of its governance activities, these acts engage the state's international responsibility. As Fortin has pointed out, this 'would be akin to accusing Iraq of being responsible for the human rights violations committed by the Islamic State on its territory'.[52] Yet, the ILC emphasized that an 'insurrectional movement may itself be held responsible for its own conduct under international law'.[53] Moreover, certain acts performed by entities that exercise quasi-governmental functions may have international legal validity if they are acts of governance performed in the general interest of the inhabitants.[54]

To sum up, when challenged by non-state armed groups, states are only responsible for acts or omissions attributable to them, which normally does not comprise wrongful acts committed by non-state actors.[55] However, there is an exception to this rule: as shall be discussed next, states' obligations include the responsibility to protect human rights against violations by non-state armed groups. A failure to perform this duty would engage a state's international responsibility.

5.3 States' Obligation to Protect Human Rights

In its General Comment No 31 on the legal nature of states' obligations under the ICCPR, the UN Human Rights Committee defined broadly what states' obligation to protect human rights consist of:

> There may be circumstances in which a failure to ensure Covenant rights as required by article 2 would give rise to violations by States Parties of those rights, as a result of States Parties' permitting or failing to take appropriate measures or to exercise due diligence to prevent, punish, investigate or redress the harm caused by such acts by private persons or entities.[56]

Similarly, for the European Court of Human Rights, it is 'common ground' that states have the obligation to put in place 'effective criminal law provisions . . . backed

responsibility will not attach to the state unless the insurrectionist movement succeeds in establishing a new government.'

[51] For a different conclusion and some practice in support, see Fortin, *The Accountability of Armed Groups under Human Rights Law* (n 9) 268–60.

[52] ibid 309.

[53] ILC, 'Responsibility of State for Internationally Wrongful Acts (with commentaries)' (n 30) para 16 of the commentary on article 10.

[54] See generally *Cyprus v Turkey, Judgment, 10 May 2001, Application no 25781/94*, ECtHR, para 96; see also *Legal Consequences for States of the Continued Presence of South Africa in Namibia (South West Africa) Notwithstanding Security Council Resolution 276 (1970), Advisory Opinion, 21 June 1971*, ICJ, para 125. The question of the legal validity of acts performed by non-state entities that govern territory, as well as the question of whether such acts must be recognized by other states, requires further research. For some discussion, see Murray, *Human Rights Obligations of Non-State Armed Groups* (Hart 2016) 128–30.

[55] But see article 10 ARSIWA.

[56] HRC, *General Comment No 31* (n 3) para 8.

up by law enforcement machinery' to protect human rights. States must take 'preventive operational measures' to protect individuals within their jurisdiction from human rights violations.[57] The Inter-American Court of Human Rights explained in more detail that the obligation to protect human rights entails

> the duty of the States Parties to organize the governmental apparatus and, in general, all the structures through which public power is exercised, so that they are capable of juridically ensuring the free and full enjoyment of human rights. As a consequence of this obligation, the States must prevent, investigate and punish any violation of the rights recognized by the Convention and, moreover, if possible attempt to restore the right violated and provide compensation as warranted for damages resulting from the violation.[58]

States' obligation to protect human rights typically takes the form of preventive and retributive measures.[59] As a fundament that enables the state to perform its protective functions, states are required to adopt legislation to give effect to human rights under national law, to set up a law enforcement apparatus that may prevent or otherwise investigate violations, to maintain a justice system that prosecutes alleged human rights violators, and to establish mechanisms that facilitate remedies and reparation for victims.[60] Adopting legislation and setting up law enforcement infrastructure are obligations of result, which means states must not only attempt but actually accomplish these tasks if their responsibility is not to be engaged.[61] Merely establishing such structures is, however, not sufficient. What is also needed is that the government 'conducts itself so as to effectively ensure the free and full exercise of human rights',[62] meaning that it takes 'appropriate measures' and exercises 'due diligence' to address human rights violations by private actors.[63] There cannot be an 'obligation to succeed' in preventing all human rights violations through protective measures.[64] However, states must perform their duty to prevent and to punish human rights violations as diligently as possible in the circumstances.

[57] *Osman v The United Kingdom, Judgment, 28 October 1998, Application no 87/1997/871/1083,* ECtHR, para 115.

[58] *Velasquez Rodriguez v Honduras, Judgment, 29 July 1988,* IACtHR. See also *Zimbabwe Human Rights NGO Forum v Zimbabwe, Judgment, 15 May 2006, 245/02,* AComHPR, paras 143–47.

[59] International Law Association (ILA), *ILA Study Group on Due Diligence in International Law: First Report* (ILA 2014) 16.

[60] For a detailed discussion of these requirements, see Pisillo-Mazzeschi, *Responsabilité de l'état pour violation des obligations positives relatives aux droits de l'homme* (Brill 2008) chapter III.

[61] See ILA, *ILA Study Group on Due Diligence in International Law: First Report* (n 59) 16. Broadly speaking, 'the obligation of result is an obligation to "succeed", while the obligation of diligent conduct is an obligation to "make every effort"'. Pisillo-Mazzeschi, 'The Due Diligence Rule and the Nature of the International Responsibility of States' (1992) 35 German Yearbook of International Law 9–51, 48. As Zegveld pointed out, the obligation to adopt laws against human rights violations by private actors exists at any time and independent of external factors. Zegveld, *Accountability of Armed Opposition Groups in International Law* (CUP 2002) 158.

[62] *Velasquez Rodriguez v Honduras,* para 167.

[63] HRC, *General Comment No 31* (n 3) para 8.

[64] See ILA, *ILA Study Group on Due Diligence in International Law: First Report* (n 59) 16; Nowak and Januszewski, 'Non-State Actors' (n 5) 142.

5.3.1 States' obligation to protect individuals' human rights against violations by non-state armed groups

Human rights law jurisprudence on states' obligations to prevent violent acts of private actors originated with regard to crimes committed by individuals in times of peace.[65] Situations of internal armed conflicts or other confrontations between states and non-state armed groups are arguably different. Philosophically, internal armed conflicts are situations in which the parties to the conflict are independent from each other, enemies, and 'have no common superior'.[66] In such situations, international law foresees distinct obligations for state and non-state parties, that is, IHL. Even if a situation cannot be classified as a non-international armed conflict, it has been suggested that 'the very existence of a flagrant revolution presupposes that a certain set of men have gone temporarily or permanently beyond the power of the authorities'.[67] Consequently, the ILC Commentary on an early draft of the articles on state responsibility found: 'It will rarely be possible to accuse a State of failing in its own obligations of vigilance and protection in relation to the conduct of organs of an insurrectional movement because, most of the time, the actions in question are entirely beyond its control'.[68] Thus, it could be argued that it is practically fruitless to hold a state responsible for failing to adequately protect individuals within its jurisdiction against human rights violations committed by an armed groups.[69]

Initially, human rights treaty bodies' approach on this subject was ambiguous.[70] More recently, however, different treaty bodies have taken a clear stance. For example, in General Comment No 35 on 'Liberty and Security of Person', the Human Rights Committee emphasized that states must 'protect individuals against abduction or

[65] See *Osman v The United Kingdom, Application no 87/1997/871/1083; Velasquez Rodriguez v Honduras*. For an in-depth examination of the historic development of the principle of due diligence, see Hessbruegge, 'The Historical Development of the Doctrines of Attribution and Due Diligence in International Law' (2003–04) 36 NYU Journal of International Law and Politics 265–306; see also ILA, *ILA Study Group on Due Diligence in International Law: First Report* (n 59). States' positive human rights obligations have been discussed especially with regard to the protection against domestic violence and non-discrimination. See, eg, Cook (ed), *Human Rights of Women: National and International Perspectives* (University of Pennsylvania Press 1994); Thomas and Beasley, 'Domestic Violence as a Human Rights Issue' (1995) 58 Alabama Law Review 1119–48; Beate and Eriksson, 'Women's Rights Under International Human Rights Treaties: Issues of Rape, Domestic Slavery, Abortion, and Domestic Violence' (2007) 5 International Journal of Constitutional Law 507–525; Meyersfeld, 'Opuz v Turkey: Confirming the State Obligation to Combat Domestic Violence' (2009) 5 European Human Rights Law Review 684–693; Hasselbacher, 'State Obligations Regarding Domestic Violence: The European Court of Human Rights, Due Diligence, And International Legal Minimums of Protection' (2010) 8 Northwestern Journal of International Human Rights 190–215.

[66] de Vattel (ed), *The Law of Nations* (translation by Joesph Chitty) (T & JW Johnson & Co 1758) para 293.

[67] *Sambiaggio* case, *13 February and 7 May 1903*, Italy–Venezuela Mixed Claims Commission, 513.

[68] ILC, *Yearbook 1975* (n 49) 92. See also Dissenting opinion of Samuel KB Asante in *Asian Agricultural Products Ltd (AAPL) v Sri Lanka*, ICSID Case No ARB/87/3, cited in Barnidge, *Non-State Actors and Terrorism: Applying the Law of State Responsibility and the Due Diligence Principle* (TMC Asser Press 2008) 101.

[69] See, eg, Kamatali, 'Human Rights Law in NIAC' (n 7) 237.

[70] See, eg, *Kurt v Turkey, Judgment, 25 May 1998, Application no 15/1997/799/1002*, ECtHR; *Elcida Arévalo Perez et al v Colombia, 3 November 1989, CCPR/C/37/D/181/1984*, HRC. For discussion of these cases, see Zegveld, *Accountability of Armed Opposition Groups* (n 61) 170–72.

detention by individual criminals or irregular groups, including armed or terrorist groups, operating within their territory'.[71] This is in line with the Committee's previous findings. For example, with regard to 'widespread and indiscriminate attacks against the civilian population'[72] committed by non-state forces in the course of the Algerian civil war in the 1990s, the HRC urged the government to

> adopt effective measures (a) to prevent those attacks and, if they nevertheless occur, to come promptly to the defence of the population; [and] (b) to ensure that proper investigations are conducted by an independent body to determine who the offenders are and to bring them to justice.[73]

Likewise, regional human rights treaty bodies found that states have the obligation to protect individuals 'not only in relation to the power of the State but also with respect to the actions of private individuals, including *any kind of irregular armed groups*.[74] Along the same lines, the African Commission on Human and Peoples' Rights found with regard to human rights violations committed by different forces in the course of a 'civil war' in Chad:

> Even where it cannot be proved that violations were committed by government agents, the government had a responsibility to secure the safety and the liberty of its citizens, and to conduct investigations into murders.[75]

The African Commission came to this conclusion despite the fact that violations were committed in the course of a 'civil war' and the government's assertion that it 'had no control over violations committed by other parties'.[76] The European Commission and the European Court of Human Rights have also heard cases of violations of states' duty to protect individuals from human rights violations allegedly committed by non-state armed groups in situations of internal turmoil or armed conflict.[77]

[71] HRC, *General Comment No 35: Article 9 (Liberty and Security of Person)*, 16 December 2014, CCPR/C/GC/35, para 7.

[72] HRC, *Concluding Observations of the Human Rights Committee: Algeria*, 18 August 1998, CCPR/C/79/Add.95, para 3.

[73] ibid para 6. See also HRC, *Concluding Observations of the Human Rights Committee: Yemen*, 23 April 2012, CCPR/C/YEM/CO/5, paras 16, 24; HRC, *Concluding Observations of the Human Rights Committee: Russian Federation*, 24 November 2009, CCPR/C/RUS/CO/6, para 13; HRC, *Concluding Observations of the Human Rights Committee: The Sudan*, 29 August 2007, CCPR/C/SDN/CO/3, para 9; HRC, *Concluding Observations of the Human Rights Committee: Democratic Republic of the Congo*, 26 April 2006, CCPR/C/COD/CO/3, paras 13, 15.

[74] *Provisional Measures Regarding Colombia: Matter of the Communities of Jiguamiandó and Curbaradó, Order, 7 February 2006*, IACtHR, para 6. (Considerations of the Court) (emphasis added). For similar findings, see also *Provisional Measures Regarding Ecuador: Matter of Pueblo Indígena Sarayaku Order, 6 July 2006*, IACtHR, para 10 (Considerations of the Court). In actual case law, the IACtHR held states responsible for failure adequately to protect civilians against large human rights violations committed by paramilitary non-state groups during an armed conflict. See, eg, *Pueblo Bello Massacre v Colombia, Judgment, 31 January 2006*, IACtHR, paras 139–40.

[75] *Commission Nationale des Droits de l'Homme et des Libertes v Chad, Finding, No 74/92*, AComHPR, para 22.

[76] ibid paras 19 and 21.

[77] See in particular the case of *W v the United Kingdom* regarding the shooting of an individual by an IRA activist during the Northern Ireland crisis (*Mrs W v the United Kingdom, Judgment, 28 February 1983, Application no 9348/81*, EComHR). See also *Belkiza Kaya and others v Turkey, Judgment, 22*

As a result, international practice shows that states are obliged to protect individuals against human rights violations by non-state actors in times of peace and in times of armed conflict. This obligation applies independently of whether violations are committed by individuals or non-state armed groups. In light of the fact that human rights treaty bodies only exercise jurisdiction over complaints against states parties, Zegveld pointed out:

> If international bodies reject positive obligations of states with regard to armed opposition groups, the effect would be that these treaties would provide no protection to civilians against violence committed by armed opposition groups. This may be unacceptable for international bodies whose aim is to safeguard the rights of victims in all situations, including internal conflict.[78]

In addition, a broad scope of states' protective human rights obligation is justified by the state's privileged position as the guarantor of law and order in its territory. In the interest of safeguarding fundamental rights of the individual, states must at all times be obliged to make their best effort to protect human rights.[79]

5.3.2 Limitations on states' responsibility to protect human rights

While appealing on paper and important in many circumstances, state obligations to guarantee human rights will often provide limited protection against violations by non-state armed groups. As emphasized above, the obligation to protect human rights is one of due diligence, which must be determined in light of the state's capacity and the circumstances with which it is confronted. In practice, the very existence of a non-state armed group suggests that the territorial state is unable fully to enforce its authority. This very situation challenges one of the basic assumptions of the state-centric protection system, namely the existence of a strong state 'possessing the necessary resources and political will to implement the human rights project on their own'.[80] Consequently, the state-centred protection system reaches its limits if a state's de jure government is either unable to exercise effective control over its territory or proves incapable of responding effectively to human rights violations by

November 2005, Application nos 33420/96 and 36206/97, ECtHR. In the case of *Ergi v Turkey* regarding the killing of a civilian during alleged fighting between Turkish armed forces and PKK members, the Court found that the state must take 'all feasible precautions against the effect of fighting, including force used by PKK members caught in a government ambush'. *Case of Ergi v Turkey, Judgment, 28 July 1998, Application no 66/1997/850/1057*, ECtHR, para 79.

[78] Zegveld, *Accountability of Armed Opposition Groups* (n 61) 173. Zegveld based her finding on earlier documents and jurisprudence, which partly contradicted this finding but nonetheless led her to a similar conclusion as the one adopted here. See ibid 166–73.

[79] See also Cerone, 'Human Rights on the Battlefield' in Lagoutte, Sano, and Scharff Smith (eds), *Human Rights in Turmoil: Facing Threats, Consolidating Achievements* (M Nijhoff 2007) 97–131, 108.

[80] Nowak and Januszewski, 'Non-State Actors' (n 5) 124. It has also been argued that this system is based on the assumption of the existence of a Western-style nation state that is effectively capable of enforcing the law against any non-state actors. See McCorquodale, 'Non-State Actors and International Human Rights Law' in Clapham (ed), *Human Rights and Non-state Actors* (Edward Elgar 2013) 69–86, 112; Policzer, 'Human Rights Violations and Non-State Armed Groups: A New Framework' (Centre of International Relations Working Papers 2005) 4.

non-state armed groups. The scope of the resulting protection gaps in situations in which the state's de jure government lost parts of its territory to a separatist regime, lost de facto control over some territory, or is otherwise unable to respond effectively to human rights obligations by armed groups shall be discussed in Chapter 6 'A Three-Pronged Approach to Human Rights Obligations of Non-State Armed Groups'.[81]

5.4 The Systemic Need for Direct IHRL Obligations of Armed Groups

It appears that the state-centred human rights protection system based on existing IHRL treaties is ill-prepared for protecting individuals from human rights violations committed by non-state armed groups. To begin with, most IHRL treaties do not contain human rights obligations for non-state actors. Moreover, under international law a state is normally not responsible for human rights violations by private actors unless they can be attributed to it. Thus, the two most direct ways to respond to human rights violations by non-state armed groups are not available. Recognizing that the protection offered by IHRL would be severely limited unless the law provided an obligation to restrain non-state actors, IHRL treaties designate states to protect human rights against any private infringements. This obligation applies to acts committed by individuals and by non-state armed groups.

This system is adequate if a state has a strong law enforcement system able to prevent or otherwise impartially investigate human rights violations by private actors. However, the currently weak condition of many states and the existence of powerful armed groups illustrate that an entirely state-centred human rights protection system no longer fulfils its purpose.[82] Against this background, the former Inter-American Court of Human Rights and International Court of Justice judge, as well as member of the Human Rights Committee, Bürgenthal emphasized:

> Potential violators will obviously not be deterred from engaging in massive human rights abuses in these countries if they know that they will enjoy domestic impunity and that, at most, only the state will be held internationally responsible for their acts.[83]

[81] See Sections 6.3.1 'Limited state obligations to protect human rights in territory under the control of a 'separatist regime'; 6.4.1 'Limited state obligations to protect human rights in territory under de facto control of an armed group', and 6.5.1 'States' obligation to take reasonable measures to prevent and to investigate human rights violations by non-state actors'.

[82] See also Nowak and Januszewski, 'Non-State Actors' (n 5) 124; Bellal, 'Establishing the Direct Responsibility of Non-State Armed Groups for Violations of International Norms: Issues of Attribution' in Noemi Gal-Or (ed), *Responsibilities of the Non-State Actor in Armed Conflict and the Market Place* (Brill Nijhoff 2015) 304; Reinisch, 'Non-state Actors' (n 8) 74–75.

[83] Buergenthal, 'The Normative and Institutional Evolution of International Human Rights' (1997) 19 Human Rights Quarterly 703–23, 718.

Going from the systemic level to the human level, the consequence of this shortcoming is a situation in which many human beings do not enjoy adequate human rights protection, if any. As Ryngaert and Noortmann ask, rather rhetorically:

> [S]hould we tolerate individuals in weak governance zones being left to their own devices, governed as they are by the whim of unaccountable non-state groups?[84]

Obviously, this should not be the case. One avenue to address the limitations of the presently primarily state-focused international protection system is to develop direct IHRL obligations for non-state armed groups, which would complement the obligations of states. While this suggestion is further analysed and developed in Chapter 7 'Conceptual Considerations on the Notion of 'Crimes against Humanity', it is not without risks. It has been cautioned that complementing states' human rights obligations by direct obligations of armed groups could dilute states' duties.[85] Indeed, while impartial human rights experts may strike a clear balance between a state's and a non-state actor's obligations, a state confronted with a non-state armed group might too easily plead that it is objectively not able to fulfil its obligations and that obligations rest primarily on the non-state actor. Moreover, some have also cautioned that if human rights monitoring mechanisms shall in future also examine non-state human rights obligations, this may divert their scarce resources away from their original mandate, which is to examine state compliance with relevant human rights law.[86] Again, the concern is valid: overburdening the current system could effectively weaken it. Thus, when analysing whether IHRL should contain direct obligations for non-state entities, these and other policy considerations need to be kept in mind.

[84] Ryngaert and Noortmann, 'New Actors in Global Governance and International Human Rights Law' (2010) 4 Human Rights and International Legal Discourse 5–14, 13.

[85] eg the UN Working Group on Enforced or Involuntary Disappearances argued that including acts by armed groups under the definition of 'enforced disappearance' under the Convention would 'dilute the responsibility of the State'. Commission on Human Rights, *Report of the Working Group on Enforced or Involutary Disappearances, Addendum: Mission to Colombia*, 17 January 2006, E/CN.4/2006/56/Add.1, para 48; Commission on Human Rights, *Terrorism and Human Rights: Final Report of hte Special Rapporteur, Kalliopi K. Koufa*, 25 June 2004, E/CN.4/Sub.2/2004/40, para 55.

[86] Inter-American Commission on Human Rights, *Inter-American Yearbook on Human Rights* (M Nijhoff 1990) 360.

6

A Three-Pronged Approach to Human Rights Obligations of Non-State Armed Groups

The traditional state-centred approach of international human rights law (IHRL) is not set in stone.[1] Instead, in order to remain relevant, IHRL needs to adapt to the changing needs and concerns of the international community, which, in recent years, include addressing a great number of serious human rights violations by state and non-state actors. Seemingly responding to this need, addressing non-state armed groups directly on human rights issues has become increasingly accepted in the international community over the past two decades.[2] While the mandate of classical human rights protection institutions, such as regional human rights courts or United Nations (UN) treaty bodies, continue to be restricted to state violations, a number of other human rights protection mechanisms have broadened their focus to address human rights violations by non-state armed groups (NSAGs). Likewise, the issue of human rights obligations of non-state actors is increasingly receiving scholarly attention.[3] The main objective of the following sections is to conceptualize

[1] As Nowak and Januszewski phrased it: '[I]nternational human rights law must be conceived as a dynamic and ever-evolving process, rather than a static system resilient to evolution and unable to adapt to new circumstances.' Nowak and Januszewski, 'Non-State Actors and Human Rights' in Noortmann, Reinisch, and Ryngaert (eds), *Non-State Actors in International Law* (Hart 2015) 124. Higgins put it more generally: in international law, norm development occurs 'as much through the force of circumstance as through any conscious intellectual circumstances'. Higgins, *Problems and Process: International Law and How we Use it* (Clarendon Press 1994) 54.

[2] A number of recent examples is discussed in the following sections. For good studies of UN practice in the 1990s and the 2000s, see, eg, Tomuschat, 'The Applicability of Human Rights Law to Insurgent Movements' in Fischer and Fleck (eds), *Krisensicherung und Humanitärer Schut: Festschrift für Dieter Fleck* (BWV 2004) 573–91; Constantinides, 'Human Rights Obligations and Accountability of Armed Opposition Groups: The Practice of the UN Security Council' (2010) 4 Human Rights & International Legal Discourse 89–110; Henckaerts and Wiesener, 'Human Rights Obligations of Non-State Armed Groups: A Possible Contribution from Customary International Law?' in Kolb and Gaggioli (eds), *Research Handbook on Human Rights and Humanitarian Law* (Edward Elgar 2013) 146–69. Good discussions of individual situations are also included in Clapham, *Human Rights Obligations of Non-State Actors* (OUP 2006); Bellal, Giacca, and Casey-Maslen, 'International Law and Armed Non-State Actors in Afghanistan' (2011) 93 International Review of the Red Cross 47–79; Ryngaert, 'Human Rights Obligations of Armed Groups ' (2008) Revue Belge De Droit Internationale 355–81.

[3] For some earlier writings on human rights obligations of armed groups, see Rodley, 'Can Armed Opposition Groups Violate Human Rights?' in Mahoney and Mahoney (eds), *Human Rights in the Twenty-First Century: A Global Challenge* (M Nijhoff 1993) 297–318; Buergenthal, 'The Normative and Institutional Evolution of International Human Rights'(1997) 19 Human Rights Quarterly 703–23; Alston, 'The "Not-a-Cat" Syndrome: Can the International Human Rights Regime Accommodate

recent state and other international practice.[4] Before delving into the analysis, however, an introductory section will elaborate on the suggested three-pronged approach and address some methodological questions.

6.1 Basic Idea behind a Three-Pronged Approach

In order to be subject to international law obligations, an armed group must be a collective entity, meaning that it needs to be a 'legal entity distinct from its members'.[5] Such a collective entity needs to have some kind of internal structure, which links members to the group; in contrast, a loose assembly of individuals does not form an armed group for the purposes of international law. These structures can be referred to as command structures, which might be vertical or horizontal in nature.[6] Thus, it does not require a traditional hierarchy as found in government institutions, or armed forces. Armed groups can also operate under flat hierarchies in which the members of groups operate on an equal level.[7] If the group as such shall be subject to human rights obligations, the group should also have the means to ensure respect for the applicable rules; otherwise, the purpose of imposing such obligations would be lost ab initio. This does not mean that the group actually needs to respect IHRL in practice, or recognize its validity or applicability. Instead, the group needs to be able to enforce discipline within the group in order to ensure respect for any kind of rule. In this respect, any group able to enforce its own code of conduct or religious laws can also be considered able to enforce fundamental human rights.[8] As shall be seen in this chapter, the scope of possible IHRL obligations should take a group's capacities into account.

Beyond the basic features of being a collective entity able to ensure respect for basic rules, possible human rights obligations of non-state armed groups should be determined depending on the group's degree of power and organization, as well as the circumstances in which the group operates. It is suggested that obligations are analysed best on a spectrum, meaning that the scope of possible obligations corresponds to a group's degree of power and organization.[9] For analytical purposes

Non-State Actors?' in Alston (ed), *Non-State Actors and Human Rights* (OUP 2005) 3–36; Clapham, *Human Rights Obligations of Non-State Actors* (n 2).

[4] This book focuses primarily on resolutions adopted by states in UN fora, and on reports prepared by UN institutions and experts for intergovernmental fora. Examination of national state practice—eg national jurisprudence or domestic pronouncements of state leaders—is beyond the scope of this work. As it is unclear to what extent the practice and opinio juris of armed groups contributes to the formation of international law, statements and practice of armed groups are cited only to prove that a number of groups is able and ready to respect and protect human rights.

[5] *Western Sahara, Advisory Opinion, 16 October 1975,* ICJ, para 148.

[6] See Section 3.3.1 'Transnational armed groups'.

[7] Hashim, *Insurgency and Counter-Insurgency in Iraq* (Hurst 2006) 153.

[8] For more detailed discussion of these points, see Section 3.3.2 'Cyber armed groups'.

[9] Similarly, Clapham suggests that 'the extent of [non-state armed groups' (NSAGs')] obligations depends on what kind of non-state actor they are, the context in which they are operating, and any relevant promises made by them. In other words the scope of their obligations depends on their capacity, context, and commitments.' Clapham, 'Human Rights Obligations for Non-State Actors. Where are We Now?' in Lafontaine and Larocque (eds) *Doing Peace the Right Way. Essays in International Law and Relations in Honour of Louise Arbour* (Intersentia forthcoming) 1. Also

it is convenient to divide this spectrum into three categories.[10] The three suggested categories are:

- groups exercising quasi-governmental authority in defined territory;
- groups exercising de facto control over territory and population;
- groups not exercising control over territory and population.

Recognizing that possible obligations should exist on a scale, and dividing armed groups into three broad categories, reflects a reality in which the degree of organization and power among non-state armed groups varies widely.[11] It avoids demanding a local and poorly organized armed group without control over territory and population to live up to the same standards as a state-like non-state entity.[12] Instead, it proposes a model in which every armed group is assumed to be sufficiently organized to respect certain baseline obligations, which are complemented by additional obligations that groups with greater capacities will have to fulfil. In this respect, the scope of an armed group's obligations is likely to vary throughout the 'life span' of the group. This also means that the scope of possible obligations established for groups with a low degree of power and organization applies a fortiori to groups with greater capacities. For example, if armed groups not exercising control over territory and population are

advocating a differentiated approach to the scope of human rights obligations of armed groups, Giacca emphasized that the content of human rights obligations of NSAGs could 'be determined by a number of indicia', including: 'the level of organization of the ANSAs; an identifiable political structure; the level of control of the ANSAs [armed non-state actors] over the territory; the capacity to administer the territory; the duration of the authority exercised in the territory; and a level of stability in the territory'. Giacca, *Economic, Social, and Cultural Rights in Armed Conflict* (OUP 2014) 270–71.

[10] Dividing armed groups into three categories is inspired by an approach suggested by Bellal, who suggested based on an analysis of recent practice: '[H]uman rights law obligations of non-State armed groups *would be determined on a sliding scale:* 1. When a non-State armed group controls and *defacto* 'administers' a territory the scope of its human rights law obligations would be akin to the one of a State; 2. When the group does not possess a *defacto State-like* structure, but nonetheless controls a territory, it would still be bound by some human rights obligations, although it is not so clear at this point which ones; 3. Finally, there are situations where the structure of the armed group is very loose and where there is no effective control of territory, at least not in a stable manner.' Bellal, 'Establishing the Direct Responsibility of Non-State Armed Groups for Violations of International Norms: Issues of Attribution' in Noemi Gal-Or (ed), *Responsibilities of the Non-State Actor in Armed Conflict and the Market Place* (Brill Nijhoff 2015) 308–09.

[11] For example, in an International Committee of the Red Cross (ICRC)-led consultation process on the treatment of persons deprived of liberty in non-international armed conflicts (NIACs), states cautioned: '[T]he capacity of non-State parties to NIACs can vary immensely, making it difficult to identify a set of consistent expectations with regard to detention. Non-State parties to a NIAC range from hierarchically complex, well-financed armed groups that exercise control over large swathes of territory at one extreme, to minimally organized, poor, and mobile groups at the other.' ICRC, *Strengthening International Humanitarian Law Protecting Persons Deprived of their Liberty—Draft Resolution and Concluding Report* (ICRC 2015) 37.

[12] Scholars have invoked the argument that non-state armed groups are often unlikely to have the capacity to comply with IHRL as an argument to dismiss the applicability of IHRL to these groups. See, eg, Moir, *The Law of Internal Armed Conflict* (CUP 2002) 194; Pejic, 'Conflict Classification and the Law Applicable to Detention and the Use of Force' in Wilmshurst (ed), *International Law and the Classification of Conflicts* (OUP 2012) 84. The approach suggested here may be able to address this apparent diversity among armed groups.

bound by peremptory human rights obligations, these obligations also bind groups with de facto or quasi-governmental control over territory and population.

Similar obligations for all armed groups would not be justified from a systemic point of view either. One of the core arguments made in this book is that IHRL obligations of armed groups are necessary in order to avoid significant human rights protection gaps. These gaps vary according to the de jure government's control over its territory and its capacities to prevent and investigate human rights violations. In many situations, at least some human rights are adequately protected or provided for by the de jure government. For example, if the de jure government continues to provide sufficient public services, such as health care or education, in territory otherwise under the de facto control of a non-state armed group, there is no need for an obligation on armed groups to provide these services. In contrast, if an armed group establishes itself as the de facto authority in a territory and ousts all government institutions, the obligation to provide services may devolve to the non-state armed group. In all cases, strong arguments exist to suggest that every armed group that acts beyond effective government control should respect certain fundamental human rights.[13] As a result, not only the varying capacities of armed groups but also the very different contexts in which they operate necessitate a differentiated approach to determining whether and to what extent non-state actors have human rights obligations.

Categorizing the broad spectrum of armed groups into three broad clusters is certainly a simplification of reality. In practice, it will be difficult to draw exact lines between the three suggested groupings. Likewise, in particular the category of groups exercising de facto control over some territory and population will contain armed groups with very different capacities. Such groups range from those that have just secured military control over a village to groups that exercised territorial control for years without having been able to set up governance infrastructure. Nonetheless, as is seen below, the suggested categories can be used as analytical tools that reflect reality to some extent, can facilitate legal analysis, and allow specific conclusions to be drawn on the nature and scope of IHRL obligations of different categories of armed groups. In particular, instead of looking only at armed groups on a spectrum, the present model provides a bottomline at which groups should have a basic but defined scope of obligations, and an endpoint at which state-like groups have human rights obligations akin to those of states. The complex task of calibrating the amount of obligations to the degree of organization and power of the armed group is primarily required between these two fixed points.

In this book, armed groups are divided according to whether and to what extent they control territory and population. For the purpose of human rights protection, the relationship between an armed group and human rights bearers, namely individuals, is essential. During crises and conflict situations, however, control over territory is a criterion that is often easier to determine than a group's effect on people.

[13] See Section 6.5 'Human Rights Obligations of Groups Not Controlling Territory and Population' below.

Moreover, especially when examining the degree of power of armed groups and their ability to administer or govern a population, including by establishing relevant infrastructure, de facto control over territory appears to be a prerequisite for exercising certain powers. Thus, control over individuals, populations, and territory are all relevant factors when examining possible IHRL obligation of armed groups. When speaking of 'groups exercising quasi-governmental authority in defined territory', in this book control over population in that territory is assumed. In other cases, this book speaks explicitly of 'control over territory and population'.

6.2 Preliminary Considerations on Evaluating State and UN Practice

Before entering an in-depth analysis on whether and to what extent non-state armed groups have human rights obligations, some methodological questions need clarification. As the following sections draw heavily on UN resolutions and documents produced by UN human rights mechanisms, the first question is what legal weight such practice has. This includes the issue of the extent to which this practice contributes to the formation of customary international law. Moreover, the legal significance of the semantic differentiation between state 'violations' of IHRL and non-state armed groups' 'abuses' of IHRL are discussed. The second issue that merits some preliminary words is the author's assumption that the IHRL protection system should be 'effective'. In the present context, this means that if the state-centred IHRL protection system does not correspond to reality and presents significant gaps, this necessitates human rights obligations for non-state actors.

6.2.1 The legal value of UN reports and resolutions

6.2.1.1 UN mandate-holder or human rights expert reports

Owing to their mandate to report on human rights violations committed in crisis situations and armed conflicts, UN commissions of inquiry and other human rights experts have been at the forefront of exploring the material scope of IHRL. As is seen in the following sections, many of their reports address human rights violations by non-state armed groups. This practice raises the question of the reports' legal significance.

UN expert reports do not constitute a traditional source of international law.[14] They could, however, be considered akin to 'judicial decisions', or 'the teachings of the most highly qualified publicists' and therefore be a 'subsidiary means for the determination of rules of law'.[15] In this respect, the application of international law in such reports may provide 'useful evidence of what the law is'.[16] Indeed, the role

[14] For a list of traditional sources of international law, see article 38 of the Statute of the International Court of Justice.

[15] Article 38 (d) Statute of the International Court of Justice.

[16] Brierly and Clapham, *Brierly's Law of Nations: An Introduction to the Role of International Law in International Relations* (7th edn, OUP 2012) 66.

of UN commissions of inquiry, fact-finding missions, or other mandate-holders is primarily to establish facts and to evaluate them in light of applicable international law.[17] Whether a commission or expert report is considered useful evidence of the current state of international law depends on a number of factors, including the quality of the legal arguments. With regard to the application of IHRL to non-state armed groups, UN experts are in a delicate position because IHRL treaties only exceptionally contain such obligations. Thus, possible human rights obligations of armed groups must stem primarily from unwritten sources of law. However, no tribunal or other authority has conducted a thorough analysis of state practice and *opinio juris* that mandate-holders could refer to in order to prove that such obligations exist. Neither have mandate-holders themselves conducted this research.

At present, the result is that most reports cite previous UN reports, resolutions, and sometimes scholarly writing as proof of an 'increasing acceptance' of IHRL obligations of armed groups.[18] Schoiswohl criticized the often peripheral remarks presented on the question of the legal basis of such obligations, and suggested that 'torn between legal reality and moral necessity', UN human rights documents and reports, in particular, 'appear reluctant to diminish the argumentative force of their assertions by digging too deep into legal substance'.[19] Likewise, Fortin noted that the simple reference to an increasing acceptance of IHRL obligations of some armed groups is seemingly 'repeated as a "formula" phrase that then gives the Commission of Inquiry a licence to apply human rights law to the armed group in question'.[20]

Indeed, UN human rights reports rarely provide in-depth legal analysis of the possible sources and scope of IHRL obligations of armed groups. Notwithstanding these deficiencies, such omissions do not mean that obligations do not exist. Lack of theoretical legal justifications might also be due to reports' focus on practice and the limited resources at their disposal. Moreover, references to previous UN reports may have particular weight because the different human rights mechanisms operate under state supervision.[21] As one former Special Rapporteur on extrajudicial, summary, or arbitrary executions explained, an expert committee's or mandate-holder's interpretation of the law is, in most cases, 'explicitly endorsed by the parent

[17] For further detail, see Program on Humanitarian Policy and Conflict Research (HPCR), *HPCR Advanced Practitioner's Handbook on Commissions of Inquiry: Monitoring, Reporting, and Fact-Finding* (Harvard Humanitarian Initiative 2015) 19–43.

[18] eg, the UN Commission of Inquiry on Libya only referenced a UN Secretary General Panel of Experts Report on Sri Lanka as support for this finding, which itself only vaguely referred to some UN practice as support. See Human Rights Council, *Report of the International Commission of Inquiry to Investigate all Alleged Violations of International Human Rights Law in the Libyan Arab Jamahiriya*, 1 June 2011, A/HRC/17/44, para 72; United Nations Secretary General (UNSG), *Report of the Secretary General's Panel of Experts on Accountability in Sri Lanka* (UNSG, 31 March 2011) para 188.

[19] Schoiswohl, 'De Facto Regimes and Human Rights Obligations—The Twilight Zone of Public International Law' (2001) 9 Austrian Review of International and European Law 45–90, 46–47. Although Schoiswohl made this finding in 2001, it remains relevant today.

[20] Fortin, *The Accountability of Armed Groups under Human Rights Law* (OUP 2017) 343–45.

[21] To what extent such UN practice is distinguished from the practice of states in UN fora remains contested and cannot be discussed in this study. For some discussion, see International Law Commission, *Third Report on Identification of Customary International Law*, by Michael Wood, Special Rapporteur, 27 March 2015, A/CN.4/682, paras 68–79.

body [consisting of states] noting or approving the report'.[22] Consequently, such reports gain legal significance compared with the writings of scholars or reports of non-governmental organizations (NGOs). In addition, owing to the specific diplomatic context in which UN mandate-holders and human rights expert reports are presented, they necessarily inform and possibly influence discussions of human rights violations and abuses among states in international fora. Clearly phrased reports may convince diplomats, who are rarely international law experts, to condemn human rights violations of armed groups and call on them to respect IHRL. UN as well as NGO reports can influence states' views and practice on this matter, which, in turn, will inform lawyers' analysis of international law.

6.2.1.2 The formation of customary international law and state practice in international organizations

When reports on human rights violations by non-state armed groups are submitted to intergovernmental bodies such as the Security Council or the Human Rights Council, states consider such reports, take note, welcome, or otherwise endorse them, make statements with regard to the situation at stake, and might adopt resolutions. Such practice expresses states' opinio juris and constitutes practice relevant for the formation of norms of customary international law.[23] As the ninth edition of Oppenheim's *International Law* states: 'the concentration of state practice now developed and displayed in international organizations and the collective decisions and the activities of the organizations themselves may be valuable evidence of general practices accepted as law in the fields in which those organizations operate'.[24] Thus, states' pronouncements on legal questions during international debates and in resolutions adopted by UN organs should be considered when analysing whether norms of customary international law develop.[25]

The more delicate question is whether contemporary state practice and opinio juris suffice to determine that customary IHRL obligations exist for non-state armed groups.[26] As is seen in the following sections, the question is not whether a unitary

[22] United Nations Commission on Human Rights (UNGA), *Report of the Special Rapporteur on Extrajudicial, Summary or Arbitrary Executions*, 16 August 2007, A/62/265, para 53. For further discussions, see Alston, Morgan-Foster, and Abresch, 'The Competence of the UN Human Rights Council and its Special Procedures in Relation to Armed Conflicts: Extrajudicial Executions in the "War on Terror"' (2008) 19 European Journal of International Law 183–209.

[23] See, eg, Crawford, *Brownlie's Principles of Public International Law* (8th edn, OUP 2012) 192–93; Brierly and Clapham, *Law of Nations* (n 16) 61.

[24] Jennings and Watts, *Oppenheim's International Law*, Vol 1 (9th edn, OUP 2008) 31.

[25] For further discussion to what extent resolutions adopted in international fora contribute to the formation of customary international law, see International Law Commission, *Third Report on Identification of Customary International Law* (n 21) paras 45–54. See also International Law Commission, *Identification of Customary Law*, 30 May 2016, A/CN.4/L.872.

[26] This book does not examine to what extent the practice of non-state armed groups is relevant for the formation of customary international law. For recent scholarship on this question, see Sassòli, 'Taking Armed Groups Seriously: Ways to Improve their Compliance with International Humanitarian Law' (2010) 1 Journal of International Humanitarian Legal Studies 5–51; Sivakumaran and Roberts, 'Lawmaking by Non-state Actors: Engaging Armed Groups in the Creation of International

body of customary norms exists that binds states and all kinds of armed groups in the same way.[27] Rather, it would need to be determined which norms, or group of norms, bind non-state armed groups in light of their capacity and the context in which they operate. While a thorough examination of state practice and opinio juris would be a legitimate endeavour in its own right, it is beyond the scope of this book.[28] In other words, this book will not present a firm legal finding on whether or not possible IHRL obligations of armed groups have developed into customary law. It suffices to recall that numerous scholars raise doubts as to whether contemporary practice is sufficiently consistent and coherent to establish a rule of customary international law.[29] It has been argued that 'further evidence from a larger variety of practice, in particular from States, would be necessary in order to reach a firm conclusion in this respect'.[30] Likewise, frequent participants in international fora such as the Human Rights Council report that far from all states support the idea that non-state armed groups have IHRL obligations.[31]

At the same time, the standard of when opinio juris and state practice suffice to turn a rule into customary international law remains debated and its application varies. In principle, state practice needs to be 'extensive and virtually uniform' as well as sufficiently representative to 'show a general recognition that a rule of law or legal obligation is involved'.[32] However, in practice, the International Criminal

Humanitarian Law', (2011) 37 Yale Journal of International Law 107–52; Fortin, *The Accountability of Armed Groups under Human Rights Law* (n 20) 324–34.

[27] For further discussion of how customary international law applies differently to different international legal persons, see Murray, 'How International Humanitarian Law Treaties Bind Non-State Armed Groups' (2015) 20 Journal of Conflict and Security Law 101–31; Fortin, *The Accountability of Armed Groups under Human Rights Law* (n 20) 204–05.

[28] A recent, yet not comprehensive, study of United Nations Security Council (UNSC) and UNGA practice has concluded: 'It is not currently possible to state, however, that either of these principal UN organs has taken sufficient steps to formally endow ANSAs with human-rights obligations in general under international law.' Burniske, Modirzadeh, and Lewis, *Armed Non-State Actors and International Human Rights Law: An Analysis of the Practice of the UN Security Council and UN General Assembly* (Harvard School of Law Program on International Law & Armed Conflict 2017) 27.

[29] See, eg, Rodley, 'Non-State Actors and Human Rights' in Sheeran and Rodley (eds), *Routledge Handbook of International Human Rights Law* (Routledge: 2013) 523–44; Ronen, 'Human Rights Obligations of Territorial Non-State Actors' (2013) 46 Cornell International Law Journal 50; Kamatali, 'The Application of International Human Rights Law in Non-International Armed Conflicts: From Rhetoric to Action' (2014) 4 Journal of International Humanitarian Legal Studies 220–61.

[30] Henckaerts and Wiesener, 'Human Rights Obligations' (n 2) 161.

[31] eg, Breitegger reports with regard to Human Rights Council debates on Libya and possible IHRL obligations of the Transitional National Council: 'Especially Argentina, Chile and Lebanon made the legal argument that IHRL does not bind non-state armed groups. Other states, including China, Nigeria (on behalf of the African Group), Brazil, Russia, Algeria, Indonesia, Botswana and Guatemala were opposed to calling on the Transitional National Council (TNC) to respect IHRL, as this may imply an implicit political recognition of the TNC as the new legal government of Libya.' Breitegger, 'The Legal Framework Applicable to Insecurity and Violence Affecting the Delivery of Health Care in Armed Conflicts and other Emergencies', 95 International Review of the Red Cross 83–127, para 93 and accompanying text. See also Kleffner, 'The Applicability of the Law of Armed Conflict and Human Rights Law to Organised Armed Groups' in Kleffner and de Wet (eds), *Convergence and Conflicts of Human Rights and International Humanitarian Law in Military Operations* (Pretoria University Law Press 2014) 49–66, 60–61.

[32] *North Sea Continental Shelf (Federal Republic of Germany v Netherlands), Judgment, 20 February 1969,* ICJ, para 74. The criteria that state practice 'has to be virtually uniform, extensive

Tribunal for the former Yugoslavia (ICTY) did not present an exhaustive study to determine that individual criminal responsibility extends to violations of international humanitarian law (IHL) of non-international armed conflicts,[33] and it has been questioned whether the International Court of Justice (ICJ) applies a coherent methodology to identify rules of customary international law.[34] In light of often inconclusive, insufficient, or sometimes contradictory state practice and opinio juris, former ICJ Judge Simma and Professor Paulus argued that if international judicial bodies find the existence of a rule of customary law, 'there is always an element of innovation'.[35] In some cases, rules are deduced from state practice and opinio juris, in some cases from existing norms or principles, and in some cases they may simply be 'asserted'.[36] Moreover, as custom is necessarily identified by humans, some degree of subjectivity or political motives are involved. As a result, a variety of factors influences scholars', commissions', or tribunals' findings of whether human rights obligations of armed groups form part of customary IHRL. If one were to conclude that, at present, most or even all armed groups do not have any IHRL obligation, the least that can be said is that increasing practice of calling non-state armed groups to respect fundamental norms of IHRL 'indicate[s] the direction that international law may be headed'.[37]

6.2.1.3 Legal semantics: human rights 'violations' and 'abuses'

Adding to the complexity of the issue, in the practice of inter-governmental and non-governmental organizations, acts of non-state armed groups are often referred to as human rights 'abuses' instead of human rights 'violations'. In contrast, with regard to IHL, under which it is uncontroversial that armed groups have legal obligations,

and representative' have also been used in the ICRC's customary IHL study. See Doswald-Beck and Henckaerts, *Customary International Humanitarian Law* (CUP 2005) xlii–xlv.

[33] See *Tadić, Decision on the Defence Motion for Interlocutory Appeal on Jurisdiction*, 2 October 1995, Appeals Chamber, ICTY, paras 128–37.

[34] See Talmon, 'Determining Customary International Law: The ICJ's Methodology between Induction, Deduction and Assertion' (2015) European Journal of International Law 417–43; Pellet, 'Shaping The Future Of International Law: The Role of the World Court in Law-Making' in Arsanjani, Cogan, Sloane et al (eds), *Looking to the Future—Essays on International Law in Honor of W Michael Reisman* (M Nijhoff 2010) 1065–84; Benvenisti, 'Customary International Law as a Judicial Tool for Promoting Efficiency' in Benvenisti and Hirsch (eds) *The Impact of International Law on International Cooperation: Theoretical Perspectives* (CUP 2004) 85–116.

[35] Simma and Paulus, 'The Responsibility of Individuals for Human Rights Abuses in Internal Conflicts: A Positivist View' (1999) 93 American Journal of International Law 302–16, 313.

[36] See Talmon, 'Determining Customary International Law' (n 34) 441–42.

[37] McCorquodale and La Forgia, 'Taking off the Blindfolds: Torture by Non-State Actors' (2001) 1 Human Rights Law Review 216. For a finding that customary rules have in fact crystallized, see Constantinides, 'Obligations and Accountability of Armed Opposition Groups' (n 2) 102–03. More carefully, based on their study of UN practice, Burniske, Modirzadeh, and Lewis have concluded: 'The trend in the UN Security Council, in short, is toward increasing recognition that (at least certain) ANSAs have a role in helping to ensure that human rights are not abused.' However, they do not find that current practice suggests that the UNSC will in future recognize general human rights obligations of armed groups under international law. Burniske, Modirzadeh, and Lewis, *Armed Non-State Actors and International Human Rights Law* (n 28) 28.

resolutions condemn rather consistently armed groups' 'violations'. Arguably, this different wording is legally significant. In 1996, a group of UN Special Rapporteurs and chairpersons of human rights mechanisms emphasized that a 'distinction should be made between citing such groups as human rights violators and the adverse effects their action might have on the enjoyment of human rights'.[38] For these experts, non-state groups can commit crimes but, in order to avoid either relativizing state obligations or providing excuses for state violations, the term 'human rights violations' should be reserved for state conduct.[39] Likewise, Amnesty International explained more recently:

> While human rights treaties are directly binding as a matter of international law only on states, when a group such as the Taliban engages in conduct that would constitute a violation of human rights if it were perpetrated by a state, Amnesty International condemns the acts as human rights abuses.[40]

This could suggest that the term 'violation' refers to the breach of a legally binding norm, whereas other actors commit crimes under national or international law, or human rights 'abuses', without violating IHRL as such.

As is seen in the expert reports discussed in this work, a great number of UN human rights experts does not share the view that non-state armed groups cannot violate IHRL. In addition, it is questionable whether states see more than a linguistic or political significance in the use of different terms. To be clear, in UN fora such as the Security Council or the Human Rights Council, states seemingly agreed to the 'unwritten convention' of calling acts by non-state actors human rights 'abuses' instead of 'violations'.[41] However, at least three facts suggest that the legal weight of this practice should not be overrated. First, while this difference is drawn in most resolutions, the use of the different terms is not consistent.[42] Moreover, only some states use this distinction in their official statements at the UN; many states simply

[38] Commission on Human Rights, *Report of the Meeting of Special Rapporteurs/Representatives/Experts and Chairpersons of Working Groups of the Speical Procedures of the Commission on Human Rights and of the Advisory Service Programme*, 1996, E/CN.4/1997/3, para 44.

[39] ibid, at para 47. For related arguments on why 'disappearances' committed by states should be distinguished from 'kidnappings' committed by non-state actors, see Report of the Working Group on Enforced or Involutary Disappearances, *Addendum: Mission to Colombia*, 17 January 2006, E/CN.4/2006/56/Add.1, paras 46–48.

[40] Amnesty International, *'The Hands of Cruelty': Abuses by Armed Forces and Taliban in Pakistan's Tribal Areas* (Amnesty International 2012) 36–37. Nonetheless, Amnesty International has adopted a practice of calling upon armed groups 'to respect the human rights recognized under international law'.

[41] This 'unwritten convention' is clearly apparent in the Security Council's recent resolutions on, eg, Afghanistan, Somalia, the Democratic Republic of the Congo, Syria, or Mali, or in Human Rights Council resolutions on the Islamic State Group's conduct in Syria, Iraq, or Libya, Boko Haram's conduct in Nigeria, and the 2015 crisis in Burundi.

[42] In recent resolutions on the Central African Republic (CAR), the Security Council strongly condemned 'the continued violations of international humanitarian and human rights law . . . perpetrated by armed groups'. United Nations Security Council, *Resolution 2031 (2011)*, 21 December 2011, S/RES/2031, para 14. This was repeated subsequently in resolution 2088 (2013). For other examples, see Constantinides, 'Obligations and Accountability of Armed Opposition Groups' (n 2) 96–102. In the Human Rights Council, eg in resolutions 23/18 and 24/34 on the Central African Republic, states condemned 'all human rights violations ... by armed groups'. Similarly, resolution S-14/1 on Cote d'Ivoire or resolution 20/17 on Mali condemn 'human rights violations' of armed groups. For additional examples, see also Giacca, *Economic, Social, and Cultural Rights in Armed Conflict* (n 9) 250, n

speak of human rights violations by armed groups.[43] This suggests that a number of states does not consider the linguistic difference particularly significant. Second, in Security Council resolutions, states regularly call on government forces and armed groups to respect their obligations under IHRL.[44] Similar demands have been issued by states in the Human Rights Council, even where the resolution otherwise sticks to the 'abuse' language.[45] Such demands do not seem to establish new obligations, but recall existing ones. Thus, they appear to be based on the assumption that non-state armed groups are bound by some IHRL norms.[46] Third, in at least one situation, the Security Council has not only called on armed groups to respect certain norms of IHRL but has also established a 'Sanctions Committee' that can impose travel bans and economic sanctions on

> individuals and entities designated by the Committee as: . . . (b) involved in planning, directing, or committing acts that violate international human rights law or international humanitarian law, as applicable, or that constitute human rights abuses or violations.[47]

89; Burniske, Modirzadeh, and Lewis, *Armed Non-State Actors and International Human Rights Law* (n 28). Likewise, the UN Secretary General is not consistent on this issue. In a 2016 report on the Islamic State Group, one headline is 'grave human rights violations', and the following sentence refers to 'appalling human rights abuses'. United Nations Secretary General, *Report of the Secretary-General on the Threat Posed by ISIL (Da'esh) to International Peace and Security and the Range of United Nations Efforts in Support of Member States in Countering the Threat*, 29 January 2016, S/2016/92, para 9.

[43] eg, in Security Council debates on resolution 2042 (2012) and resolution 2165 (2014) on Syria, only Australia applied the violations/abuse language. Other states, such as Argentina, simply expressed the view that resolution 2165 (2014) sends 'a clear message to all of the parties without exception recalling their obligations under international humanitarian law and international human rights law'. United Nations Security Council, *The Situation in the Middle East*, 14 July 2014, S/PV.7216. Likewise, following the Security Council's adoption of a resolution condemning 'gross, systematic and widespread abuses of human rights' by the Islamic State Group, the United Kingdom simply commended the Council for not standing 'idle in the face of terrorism and violations of human rights'. United Nations Security Council, *Threats to International Peace and Security Caused by Terrorist Acts*, 15 August 2014, S/PV.7242. In the Human Rights Council, it is striking that during the Council's Special Session on the Situation in Central African Republic the vast majority of states expressed their concern with human rights violations committed by different—mostly non-state—parties in the crisis. In the Special Session on the Islamic State Group, a number of states condemned human rights violations committed by the Islamic State Group and associated groups, while especially Western states paid attention to distinguishing between IHL violations and IHRL abuses. Records of the 20th and the 22nd Special Sessions are available online at <http://webtv.un.org> (accessed 6 November 2017).

[44] eg, regarding conduct by state and non-state actors in Afghanistan, in particular the 'Taliban, Al Qaida and other extremist groups', the Council called 'for all parties to comply with their obligations under international humanitarian and human rights law'. United Nations Security Council, *Resolution 1943 (2010)*, 13 October 2010, S/RES/1943 (2010). The Council repeated this call in most subsequent resolutions on Afghanistan. The Security Council addressed similar demands—this time in the operative part of the resolution and under chapter VII—to all parties of the Darfur conflict in Sudan. United Nations Security Council, *Resolution 2063 (2012)*, 31 July 2012, S/RES/2063 (2012) para 13. A pattern of using the term 'human rights abuses' while at the same time calling on armed groups to 'comply' with their 'obligations' under IHRL, was also identified by Fortin. See Fortin, *The Accountability of Armed Groups under Human Rights Law* (n 20) 340–41.

[45] See, eg, resolution S8/1 on the Democratic Republic of the Congo, resolution S22/1 on ISIS, or resolution 23/1 on Syria.

[46] For a similar conclusion, see Tomuschat, 'Insurgent Movements' (n 2); Clapham, *Human Rights Obligations of Non-State Actors* (n 2) 501.

[47] United Nations Security Council, *Resolution 2134 (2014)*, 28 January 2014, S/RES/2134 (2014) para 37.

Under this mechanism, different members of armed groups have been sanctioned.[48] It is difficult to consider that the Security Council would establish sanctions for individuals or groups for 'human rights abuses' if such acts were not considered violations of international law.

In line with these observations, a New York diplomat confirmed to this author that the Security Council acts on the assumption that non-state actors have certain international legal obligations and that compliance with human rights standards is expected. According to this diplomat, the term 'abuses' merely reflects a linguistic arrangement to distinguish between different actors. Following a similar reading, the International Commission of Inquiry on the Central African Republic cited the Security Council's condemnation of 'human rights violations and abuses, committed by armed groups' as support for the conclusion that there is a 'general understanding that non-state groups that exercise de facto control over territory must respect human rights in their activities'.[49] Similarly, Tomuschat concluded that 'there can be no doubt that "human rights abuses" boils down to nothing else than violations of human rights'.[50] Indeed, it is highly questionable whether states' condemnation '*in the strongest possible terms* [of] the continued, widespread and grave abuses of human rights'[51]—as, for example, committed by the Islamic State Group (ISG)—does not refer to violations of the law but, instead, merely to 'transgressions of some moral code'.[52]

As a result, state practice in the UN Security Council and Human Rights Council suggest that a number of states consider non-state armed groups to be bound by some IHRL norms.

Reference to human rights 'abuses' instead of 'violations' does not necessarily mean that armed groups are not legally bound by IHRL; however, it could suggest a difference between obligations of states and those of armed groups. Indeed, states are bound by applicable IHRL treaties as well as customary law, and they have the obligation to respect, protect, and fulfil human rights. By contrast, non-state armed groups do not normally have obligations under human rights treaties. Moreover, as shall be argued, even under customary international law there is no uniform set of IHRL norms that binds all armed groups in the same way. Possible obligations depend on groups' degree of power and organization, as well as the circumstances in which they operate. Therefore, when states speak of human rights abuses by armed groups and violations by states, this can also be understood as a way of emphasizing the different obligations the two kinds of entities hold.[53] As Alston argued:

[48] See Consolidated United Nations Security Council Sanctions List, available at <https://scsanctions.un.org/fop/fop?xml=htdocs/resources/xml/en/consolidated.xml&xslt=htdocs/resources/xsl/en/consolidated.xsl> (accessed 25 November 2017).

[49] Human Rights Committee, *The International Commission of Inquiry on the Central African Republic—Final Report*, S/2014/928.

[50] Tomuschat, 'Insurgent Movements' (n 2) 581.

[51] Human Rights Council, *Technical Assistance and Capacity-Building in Strengthening Human Rights in Iraq in the Light of the Abuses Committed by Daesh and Associated Terrorist Groups*, 8 April 2015, A/HRC/RES/28/32, para 1.

[52] Clapham, 'Where are We Now?' (n 9) 6.

[53] In contrast, the uniform reference to IHL 'violations' by all parties to the conflict reflects the principle of 'equality of belligerents', which requires that state and non-state parties to a NIAC have similar

The international community does have human rights expectations to which it will hold [... non-state armed groups], but it has long been reluctant to press these demands directly if doing so would be to 'treat it like a State'.[54]

This difference may also explain the recent practice of states to demand all parties to a conflict to respect IHRL 'as applicable', which leaves the determination of the scope of applicable norms open.[55]

6.2.2 The principle of effectiveness and the protection of human rights

The traditional approach of addressing human rights obligations exclusively to states and not to non-state armed groups is not only at odds with reality but also disregards the limits of states' protective human rights obligations. As a matter of fact, the international human rights protection system needs to be adapted in order to correspond to reality and have a 'real world' impact. This idea is often expressed in the principle of effectiveness.[56] When looking at a legal order, or, for the purposes of this book, at the IHRL protection system, the principle of effectiveness requires, in the words of Hans Kelson, that 'a legal order, as a whole, must be by and large effective in order to be valid'.[57] In other words, the principle of effectiveness operates to avoid that a 'schism emerges between the normative order and the facts on the ground'.[58] It has been argued that the principle of effectiveness has influenced the structure of international law 'by systematically connecting the world of law to its ability to display effects in the world of facts and vice versa'.[59] While the importance of this principle has diminished to some extent, due to the emergence of fundamental universal values that resist and restrain the legal effect of facts,[60] the gist of the principle

obligations under IHL. For discussion on the principle, see Sassòli and Shany, 'DEBATE: Should the Obligations of States and armed Groups under International Humanitarian Law Really be Equal?' (2011) 93 International Review of the Red Cross 425–42.

[54] United Nations Commission on Human Rights, *Extrajudicial, summary Summary or arbitrary Arbitrary executionsExecutions: : Report of the Special Rapporteur*, Philip Alston, E/CN.4/2006/53/ Add.5, para. 26. The concern of states not to grant non-state entities any legal status by subjecting them to certain legal norms beyond the status as addressee of these norms is also apparent in IHL treaties, as well as in the above discussed Convention on the Rights of the Child–Optional Protocol to the Convention on the Rights of the Child (CRC—OPAC) and the Kampala Convention.

[55] See, eg, UN Security Council resolutions S/Res/2254 (2015), S/Res/2258 (2015), or S/Res/2259 (2015).

[56] As Taki put it: '[I]f international law is not to be mere speculation, but to be significantly efficacious, it has to come to terms with reality to some extent.' Taki, 'Effectiveness' in Wolfrum and Max-Planck-Institut für Ausländisches Öffentliches Recht und Völkerrecht (Heidelberg) (eds), *The Max-Planck Encyclopedia of Public International Law* (OUP 2012) para 1.

[57] Kelsen, *Principles of International Law* (Rinehart & Co 1952) at 414. In addition to the system dimension of the principle, the principle of effectiveness may operate at the norm level. Here, the principle can be invoked to support an interpretation that aims at an effective solution of an issue; or it reflects the requirement that for certain norms 'factual elements [need] to be taken into account for legal consequences to arise'. Zappalà, 'Can Legality Trump Effectiveness in Today's International Law?' in Cassese (ed), *Realizing Utopia: The Future of International Law* (OUP 2012) 105–17, 105; see also Taki, 'Effectiveness' (n 56).

[58] Fortin, *The Accountability of Armed Groups under Human Rights Law* (n 20) 242.

[59] Zappalà, 'Can Legality Trump Effectiveness in Today's International Law?' (n 57) 107.

[60] eg, prior to the prohibition of the use of force, states could acquire territory by effectively occupying and annexing it. While in such cases the effectiveness of the situation created a legal right, today

remains important. In order to be effective and continue to be valid, the human rights protection system needs to be readapted to reality.

Concretely, today's IHRL protection system should address the increasing schism between, on the one hand, a protection system that is largely focused on states and, on the other hand, a factual situation in which states are unable to protect or fulfil human rights when they lose control over territory, or are otherwise incapable of preventing and investigating human rights violations by non-state armed groups. In fact, as Fortin argued, realizing that the contemporary IHRL protection system is often ineffective when states are confronted with non-state armed groups is a 'fundamental part of understanding how and why armed groups may bear obligations under international law in particular circumstances'.[61] Invoking IHRL obligations of armed groups and holding them accountable for violations would, in many situations, simply recognize reality: if a non-state armed group is effectively controlling territory and population, or is operating beyond effective state control, human rights obligations should be directly addressed to the group. Addressing only the state as the primary human rights duty-bearer would be ineffective.

6.3 Human Rights Obligations of Groups Exercising Quasi-Governmental Authority in Defined Territory

The first category of non-state armed groups analysed here consists of groups exercising quasi-governmental authority in a territory.[62] Some scholars have referred to such groups as '*de facto* regimes'.[63] However, no internationally agreed definition exists of this term. In order to avoid confusion about definitions, this work does not use the term '*de facto* regime' but refers to non-state armed groups exercising quasi-governmental authority in defined territory.[64] Quasi-governmental authority

the prohibition of the use of force trumps the effectiveness of the situation. See Taki, 'Effectiveness' (n 56) para 13.

[61] Fortin, *The Accountability of Armed Groups under Human Rights Law* (n 20) 201.

[62] As explained above, exercising quasi-governmental authority in a territory necessarily implies exercising such control over population living in the territory.

[63] This term apparently originated in German scholarship, most notably in the work of Jochen Abraham Frowein. See Frowein, *Das De Facto-Regime im Völkerrecht: Eine Untersuchung zur Rechtsstellung 'nichtanerkannter Staaten' und ähnlicher Gebilde*, (C Heymann 1968). For Frowein, an important consequence of qualifying a non-state entity as a de facto regime would be that states treat such entities 'as partial subjects of international law', meaning vested with certain rights and obligations. See Frowein, 'De Facto Regime' in Wolfrum and Max-Planck-Institut für Ausländisches Öffentliches Recht und Völkerrecht (Heidelberg) (eds), *The Max-Planck Encyclopedia of Public International Law* (OUP 2012) para 3.

[64] The term 'de facto regime' is used to refer to a broad range of non-state entities— from those having all characteristics of states to armed groups that exercise government-like functions for a short period. For a list of state-like entities, see Frowein, 'De Facto Regime' (n 63) para 1. For Heintze, however, it seems that the term 'de facto regime' also applies to non-state entities in situations 'where several armed groups exercise regional power as the central government disintegrates' and to some entities which broadly fit under the term 'insurgents'. Heintze, 'Are De Facto Regimes Bound by Human Rights?' in Institute for Peace Research and Security Policy at the University of Hamburg (ed), *Yearbook on the Organization for Security and Co-operation in Europe (OSCE)* (Nomos 2010) 267–76, 272. See

can be exercised during times of peace or armed conflict. The defining characteristic of groups exercising quasi-governmental authority is that they 'in fact govern a specific territory'[65] and its people, meaning that they have at least temporarily 'ousted the parent sovereign from its sphere of effective governance, and thus represent the sole... authority for a given region'.[66] Often, these entities have 'consolidated their positions over a longer period of time',[67] and the manner in which they exercise authority has been described as 'State-like'[68] or 'quasi-state'.[69] In other words, such groups take over 'all the functions of a sovereign government, in maintaining law and order, instituting and maintaining courts of justice, adopting or imposing laws regulating the relations of the inhabitants of the territory to one another and to the government'.[70]

In order to analyse whether and to what extent such groups have or should have IHRL obligations, this section—as well as Sections 6.4 'Human Rights Obligations of Groups Exercising De Facto Control over Territory and Population' and 6.5 'Human Rights Obligations of Groups Not Controlling Territory and Population'—proceed in four steps. First, it examines the extent of the state's de jure government's obligation to protect human rights in parts of its territory under the quasi-governmental control of an armed group. This is done to identify if a gap in human rights protection exists. Section 6.3.2 'Contemporary international practice' shows that, in such situations, states and human rights experts have directly invoked human rights obligations of armed groups. As practice provides little theoretical justification for such findings, Section 6.3.3 'Conceptual considerations' presents conceptual considerations of how armed groups with quasi-governmental capacities could be bound by IHRL. Section 6.3.4 'The scope of obligations' examines the possible scope of these groups' IHRL obligations.

6.3.1 Limited state obligations to protect human rights in territory under the control of a 'separatist regime'

As examined above, under IHRL treaties states have the obligation to respect, protect, and fulfil human rights. It has been argued that in situations in which a state loses control over parts of its territory, human rights obligations become 'temporarily inoperative' or 'dormant as a matter of law' with regard to persons living in these

also Rudolf, 'Non-State Actors in Areas of Limited Statehood as Addresses of Public International Law Norms on Governance' (2010) 4 Human Rights and International Legal Discourse 127–44, 134–36.

[65] Frowein, 'De Facto Regime' (n 63) para 3.

[66] Schoiswohl, 'De Facto Regimes' (n 19) 52.

[67] Heintze, 'De Facto Regimes' (n 64) 269.

[68] Schoiswohl, 'De Facto Regimes' (n 19) 50.

[69] Heintze, 'De Facto Regimes' (n 64) 269. Yet, these entities are normally not recognized as states by a majority of other states. Frowein explains in this respect: 'Because of the imperfect nature of international law no possibility exists of clarifying whether entities have the quality of States even though they are not recognized as such.' Frowein, 'De Facto Regime' (n 63) para 2.

[70] UK House of Lords, The *Arantzazu Mendi* case, Judgment, 23 February 1939, cited in Schoiswohl, 'De Facto Regimes' (n 19) 51.

territories.[71] Such conclusions could, for example, be justified by a finding that the circumstances of the case preclude wrongfulness on the part of a state, or because its failure to protect human rights was caused by force majeure.[72] This section examines how loss of territorial control to an armed group with quasi-governmental capacities affects states' human rights obligations. Section 6.5 'Human Rights Obligations of Groups Not Controlling Territory and Population' below analyses in more detail which measures states generally have to take to prevent and prosecute human rights violations by private actors.

The suggestions that states' human rights obligations become temporarily inoperative or dormant warrant closer examination. The starting point for determining the territorial scope of application of an international treaty is article 29 of the Vienna Convention on the Law of Treaties. It provides that, unless otherwise indicated, 'a treaty is binding upon each party in respect of its entire territory'. No contrary indications are found in IHRL treaties: states parties shall respect and protect the rights of persons within its territory or subject to its jurisdiction,[73] the latter being 'presumed to be exercised normally throughout the State's territory'.[74] The European Court of Human Rights (ECtHR) found, however, that:

> [t]his presumption may be limited in exceptional circumstances, particularly where a State is prevented from exercising its authority in part of its territory. That may be as a result of military occupation by the armed forces of another State which effectively controls the territory concerned, acts of war or rebellion, or the acts of a foreign State supporting the installation of a separatist State within the territory of the State concerned.[75]

[71] Zegveld, *Accountability of Armed Opposition Groups in International Law* (CUP 2002) 208–10; Kleffner, 'Organized Armed Groups' (n 31) 55.

[72] As defined in article 23 of the ILC Articles on State Responsibility, a case of *force majeure* precludes wrongfulness in the case of 'the occurrence of an irresistible force or of an unforeseen event, beyond the control of the State, making it materially impossible in the circumstances to perform the obligation'. This does not apply if the situation is due to conduct of the state invoking it, or if the state assumed the situation. As highlighted in the commentary, 'Mixed claims commissions have frequently cited the unforeseeability of attacks by rebels in denying the responsibility of the territorial State for resulting damage suffered by foreigners.' International Law Commission, *Responsibility of State for Internationally Wrongful Acts (with Commentaries)* 2001, para 7 on article 23. For further discussion on the *force majeure* principle and human rights protection, see Doswald-Beck, *Human Rights in Times of Conflict and Terrorism* (OUP 2011) 39–41; Zegveld, *Accountability of Armed Opposition Groups* (n 71) 217–18; Kleffner, 'Organized Armed Groups' (n 31) 55. Another possibility, which has not yet been dealt with in practice, could be to invoke the impossibility of performance of treaty obligations or a fundamental change of circumstances (articles 61 and 62 of the ILC Articles on State Responsibility). See Giacca, *Economic, Social, and Cultural Rights in Armed Conflict* (n 9) 117.

[73] See article 2(1) of the International Covenant for Civil and Political Rights (ICCPR), article 1 of the European Convention on Human Rights (ECHR), and article 1(1) of the American Convention on Human Rights (ACHR). On a clarification of the ICCPR's formula 'within its territory and subject to its jurisdiction', see Human Rights Committee, *General Comment No 31: Nature of the General Legal Obligation Imposed on States Parties to the Covenant*, 26 May 2004, CCPR/C/21/Rev.1/Add.13, para 10.

[74] *Ilaşcu and others v Moldova and Russia, Judgment, 8 July 2004, Application no 48787/99*, ECtHR, para 312. Similarly, the Office of the United Nations High Commissioner for Human Rights (OHCHR) stressed with regard to the situation in Eastern Ukraine at the end of 2014 that despite the fact that the territory was under control of non-state armed groups, 'it should be recalled that the Government of Ukraine remains responsible for protecting human rights of residents in all its territory'. Office of the United Nations High Commissioner for Human Rights, *Report on the Human Rights Situation in Ukraine* (OHCHR, 15 December 2014) para 87.

[75] *Ilaşcu and others v Moldova and Russia* (n 74) para 312. References to case law omitted.

The types of situation referred to in this non-exhaustive list should be understood as including cases in which a non-state armed group succeeds in setting up a separatist regime in part of a state's territory. For the ECtHR, the decisive criterion seems to be that 'another State or separatist regime exercises effective control' over the area in which the human rights violation occurs.[76]

The European Court examined the extent of such limitations on the state's jurisdiction for the purpose of human rights protection in the *Ilașcu v Moldavia and Russia* case. In that case, Moldavia was accused of not taking adequate measures to protect individuals from human rights violations committed by the separatist authorities of the Transdniestria region. The Court found that even if the state is de facto prevented from exercising its authority, it does not cease to have jurisdiction under the European Convention on Human Rights (ECHR) over parts of its territory that are temporarily governed by 'a local authority sustained by rebel forces or by another State'.[77] While recognizing that the scope of the state's jurisdiction is limited, the court held:

> However, even in the absence of effective control over the Transdniestrian region, Moldova still has a positive obligation under Article 1 of the Convention to take the *diplomatic, economic, judicial or other measures that it is in its power* to take and are in accordance with international law to secure to the applicants the rights guaranteed by the Convention.[78]

In the Court's opinion, this involves the obligation to take measures to re-establish control over territory and to ensure respect for human rights in these territories.[79] The scope of states' positive human rights obligations is, however, reduced to measures possible in the circumstances.[80] Necessarily, what a state can achieve by diplomatic, economic, legal, or other means if it lost control over parts of its territory is limited. As is seen in the examination of practice below, depending on the circumstances such measures may include the initiation of criminal investigations or economic measures to ensure basic standards of living.

Until now, the European Court only accepted states' limited responsibility if this 'was compensated by the finding that another Convention State exceptionally exercised jurisdiction outside its territory and thus had full responsibility under the Convention'.[81] The Court emphasized 'the need to avoid a vacuum in Convention protection'.[82] This could suggest that the ECtHR will only allow for such limitations if another Convention state can be found responsible.[83] Yet, the Court clarified that such limitations may also apply with regard to territory 'under the effective control

[76] *Sargsyan v Azerbaijan, Judgment, 16 June 2015, Application no 40167/06,* ECtHR, para 140.

[77] *Ilașcu and others v Moldova and Russia* (n 74) para 333.

[78] ibid, at para 331. This approach was confirmed in *Catan and others v Moldova and Russia, Judgment, 19 October 2012, Applications nos 43370/04, 8252/05 and 18454/06,* ECtHR, paras 109–110 (emphasis added).

[79] See *Ilașcu and others v Moldova and Russia* (n 74) paras 339–341.

[80] In the words of the Court, the state's obligations must not be interpreted in a way 'to impose an impossible or disproportionate burden'. ibid, at para 332. This is discussed in more detail below.

[81] *Sargsyan v Azerbaijan* (n 76) para 148.

[82] ibid.

[83] See Larsen, '"Territorial Non-Application" of the European Convention on Human Rights' (2009) 78 Nordic Journal of International Law 73–93, 84–85.

of another entity',[84] which could be 'armed forces of another State' or *'a separatist regime'*.[85] What seems decisive is that a local authority—sustained by a non-state armed group or a third state—established effective control over the territory and its population. If, at the same time, one of the core objectives of the Court is 'to avoid a vacuum in Convention protection', the logical conclusion of the Court's approach would be that, in such situations, human rights obligations will need to devolve to the non-state 'separatist regime'.

Different UN human rights mechanisms have taken a largely similar approach to states' human rights obligation vis-à-vis persons living within their jurisdiction but in areas beyond the de jure government's control. Early Human Rights Committee findings could suggest that, in such situations, states may be released from their human rights obligations.[86] However, in recent observations, the Committee has taken a more nuanced stance. One example has been the Committee's observations on Georgia's obligations with regard to the Abkhazia and Tskhinvali/South Ossetia regions. While these regions have effectively been under the quasi-governmental authority of a non-state entity, the Committee found:

> The State party should continue to take all possible measures, without discrimination, to enhance protection under the Covenant for the population of these regions by the Abkhazia and Tskhinvali Region/South Ossetia de facto authorities.[87]

Likewise, the UN Committee on Economic, Social, and Cultural Rights did not release the government of Iraq from its human rights obligations vis-à-vis persons living in territory controlled by the ISG. The Committee recognized that owing to a lack of effective territorial control, the state party is 'unable to ensure that the Covenant rights are fully implemented in the entirety of its territory'.[88] Yet, it reminded the government of its primary responsibility to protect human rights within its territory, which requires that 'it must strive to the extent possible to meet its obligations under the Covenant by resorting to all measures compatible with international law'.[89]

To sum up, the European Court's approach, as well as that taken by different UN human rights mechanisms, show that while states may not be able to ensure the full scope of human rights in territory under the quasi-governmental authority

[84] *Sargsyan v Azerbaijan* (n 76) para 149.

[85] ibid, at para 148 (emphasis added).

[86] eg, looking at the human rights situation in Cyprus in 1994, the UN Human Rights Committee stated that owing to the hostile occupation of part of the state's territory for two decades, the government of Cyprus 'is not in a position to exercise control over all of its territory and consequently cannot ensure the application of the Covenant in areas not under its control'. Human Rights Committee, *Consideration of Reports Submitted by States Parties under Article 40 of the Covenant—Comments of the Human Rights Committee*, 3 August 1994, CCPR/C/79/Add.39, para 3.

[87] Human Rights Committee, *Concluding Observations of the Human Rights Committee: Georgia*, 15 November 2007, CCPR/C/GEO/CO/3, para 6.

[88] UN Committee on Economic, Social, and Cultural Rights, *Concluding Observations on the Fourth Periodic Report of Iraq*, 27 October 2015, E/C.12/IRQ/CO/4, para 5.

[89] ibid. This approach also underlies the Committee against Torture's observations regarding the same situation, which are further discussed below. See Committee against Torture, *Concluding Observations on the Initial Report of Iraq*, 14 August 2015, CAT/C/IRQ/CO/1, para 11.

of a non-state party, their human rights obligations do not become legally inoperative or dormant, as such. Neither have such situations been considered as cases of force majeure.[90] Instead, human rights mechanisms require states to protect and to fulfil human rights to the extent possible in the circumstances. This may include documenting human rights violations to enable future prosecutions, or permitting the delivery of humanitarian assistance to territory beyond its control.[91] Thus, even where a state lost control over parts of its territory and population, it needs to be determined on a case-by-case basis 'to what extent a minimum effort was nevertheless possible and whether it should have been made'.[92] With regard to the delicate question of the scope of states' positive obligations, it has been rightly analysed that 'the very limited case law and practice do not indicate what specific measures the state should take in order to comply with international obligations', which leaves a wide margin of discretion to the state on the measures to take.[93] However, owing to the limited practical impact that states may achieve through diplomatic, economic, or legal measures, their positive human rights obligations appear insufficient to ensure effective human rights protection for persons living under the quasi-governmental control of armed groups. As shall be seen below, in such circumstances, different human rights mechanisms demand for human rights obligations to be increasingly addressed to non-state entities.[94] Importantly, such obligations need to exist in parallel with the state's obligation, meaning that a non-state entity's human rights obligations do not release the state from its own human rights obligations.[95]

6.3.2 Contemporary international practice

The aim of this section—and of the related Sections 6.4.2 'Contemporary international practice' and 6.5.2 'Contemporary international practice'—is not to provide a comprehensive study of state and other international practice in order to make a firm determination of whether customary human rights law exists that binds armed groups in the respective circumstances. Instead, the objective here is to look for indications of how states and human rights experts have responded to situations

[90] In fact, as Giacca points out, with regard to such situations, '[i]t is important to point out that governments have generally not expressly invoked *force majeure*, not even implicitly'. Giacca, *Economic, Social, and Cultural Rights in Armed Conflict* (n 9) 123.

[91] On the latter point, see ibid, at 124–25.

[92] *Ilaşcu and others v Moldova and Russia* (n 74) para 334.

[93] Giacca, *Economic, Social, and Cultural Rights in Armed Conflict* (n 9) 127.

[94] The idea of holding different entities responsible for a specific human rights obligation is well established at least in ECtHR case law; eg, in the *Ilaşcu* case, the Court found Moldavia responsible for violating its obligation to protect human rights under its jurisdiction, and Russia for controlling the entity that committed the actual violations. See *Ilaşcu and others v Moldova and Russia* (n 74) paras 454, 464. For further discussion, see Murray, *Human Rights Obligations of Non-State Armed Groups* (Hart 2016) 178–80.

[95] Under international law, different actors can have parallel obligations with regard to the same situation or conduct. For discussion, Clapham, *Human Rights Obligations of Non-State Actors* (n 2) 348; Nowak and Januszewski, 'Non-State Actors' (n 1); Hakimi, 'State Bystander Responsibility' (2010) 21 The European Journal of International Law 341–85.

in which non-state armed groups commit human rights violations in different contexts.

A first situation in which a non-state armed group exercised quasi-governmental authority in a defined territory was Hamas's rule in the Gaza strip.[96] In 2009, different UN Special Rapporteurs argued in a joint report on the 'Human Rights Situation in Palestine and other Occupied Arab Territories' that

> it is worth recalling that non-State actors that exercise government-like functions and control over a territory are obliged to respect human rights norms when their conduct affects the human rights of the individuals under their control.[97]

In particular, Hamas was found responsible for not respecting the right to food and not investigating any allegations of arbitrary or extrajudicial killings of Palestinian civilians by its forces.[98] These findings were repeated and elaborated on in the so-called 'Goldstone Report', in which experts emphasized that although Hamas could not sign IHRL treaties, 'the Gaza authorities have an obligation to respect and enforce the protection of the human rights of the people of Gaza, inasmuch as they exercise effective control over the territory'.[99] The authority's duty to prevent and to prosecute violations of IHRL and IHL committed 'within its area of de facto governmental authority' was further emphasized in subsequent reports.[100] Accordingly, for the experts, Hamas's IHRL obligations comprise the negative one to respect and the positive one to protect human rights. Such findings were made in addition to Israel's obligations as an occupying power[101] and the Palestinian Authority's obligation to

[96] For the purpose of this book, it is assumed that Hamas is distinct from the Palestinian Authority and does not represent the Palestinian state. It considers a period when Hamas did not form part of a unity government. The author is, however, aware of the ongoing controversy on this issue.

[97] Human Rights Council, *Human Rights Situation in Palestine and other Occupied Arab Territories*, 29 May 2009, A/HRC/10/22, para 22; see also Human Rights Council, *Report of the Detailed Findings of the Independent Commission of Inquiry Established Pursuant to Human Rights Council Resolution S-21/1*, 24 June 2015, A/HRC/29/CRP.4, para 45. In a footnote to this paragraph, the experts refer to a report of a group of special mandate-holders, who found with regard to Hezbollah in Lebanon that a non-state armed group should respect human rights if it 'exercises significant control over territory and population and has an identifiable political structure'. Human Rights Council, *Mission to Lebanon and Israel (Report of Different Special Rapporteurs)*, 2 October 2006, A/HRC/2/7, para 19. This finding was reiterated in Human Rights Council, *Report of the Detailed Findings of the Independent Commission of Inquiry Established Pursuant to Human Rights Council Resolution S-21/1*, above, para 45. It was also reiterated in different OHCHR reports on the Occupied Palestinian Territories. See, eg, A/HRC/8/17; A/HRC/16/71; A/HRC/19/20; or A/HRC/22/35.

[98] Human Rights Council, *Human Rights Situation in Palestine and other Occupied Arab Territories*, 29 May 2009, A/HRC/10/22, paras 50 and 96.

[99] Human Rights Council, *Human Rights Situation in Palestine and other Occupied Arab Territories: Report of the United Nations Fact-Finding Mission on the Gaza Conflict*, 25 September 2009, A/HRC/12/48, para 1369. At another point in the report, the experts found 'it is *clear* that non-State actors that exercise government-like functions over a territory have a duty to respect human rights' (emphasis added). ibid, at para 310.

[100] ibid, at para 1682. This obligation was reiterated in Human Rights Council, *Report of the Detailed Findings of the Independent Commission of Inquiry Established Pursuant to Human Rights Council Resolution S-21/1* (n 97) para 683.

[101] Human Rights Council, *Human Rights Situation in Palestine and other Occupied Arab Territories: Report of the United Nations Fact-Finding Mission on the Gaza Conflict* (n 99) para 302. These obligations were found to apply 'to the extent that the measures it [Israel] adopts affect the enjoyment of human rights of the residents of the Gaza Strip'.

investigate human rights violations in Gaza '[i]n line with their legal obligations [to] take urgent measures to rectify this long-standing impunity'.[102]

A second pertinent example occurred in Libya in 2011. When peaceful demonstrations against the rule of Muammar al-Gaddafi escalated into an armed conflict and opposition groups took control over more and more territory, some groups established the National Transitional Council (NTC) as a political and military authority.[103] While the degree of quasi-governmental authority exercised by the NTC was far less elaborate and stable than Hamas's authority in Gaza, the legal reasoning applied with regard to the NTC was the same.[104] A UN Commission of Inquiry noted that although the extent to which IHRL binds non-state actors remains 'contested as a matter of international law, it is increasingly accepted that where non-state groups exercise de facto control over territory, they must respect fundamental human rights of persons in that territory'.[105] The Commission went on to explain that because the NTC

> has been *exercising de facto control over territory akin to that of a Governmental authority*, it will examine also allegations of human rights violations committed by its forces.[106]

As in the Gaza report, the Commission examined violations of the obligations to respect and to protect human rights.[107] This approach was received positively by states. In the Human Rights Council, states welcomed the work of the Commission of Inquiry and urged 'all parties concerned to respect applicable international law, in particular international human rights law and international humanitarian law'.[108] Likewise, further into the crisis, states in the Security Council strongly condemned 'all violations of applicable human rights and international humanitarian law'[109] and encouraged the NTC to protect the Libyan population and to 'prevent further abuses and violations of human rights and international humanitarian law and to

[102] Human Rights Council, *Report of the Detailed Findings of the Independent Commission of Inquiry Established Pursuant to Human Rights Council Resolution S-21/1* (n 97) para 666.

[103] Different states recognized the NTC almost instantly as the 'sole representative of all Libya'. See Human Rights Council, *Report of the International Commission of Inquiry to Investigate all Alleged Violations of International Human Rights Law in the Libyan Arab Jamahiriya* (n 18) para 41.

[104] eg, Bellal raises reasonable doubts as to whether the NTC really qualified as a de facto authority. See Bellal, 'Establishing the Direct Responsibility of Non-State Armed Groups for Violations of International Norms: Issues of Attribution' (n 10) 314–17.

[105] Human Rights Council, *Report of the International Commission of Inquiry to Investigate all Alleged Violations of International Human Rights Law in the Libyan Arab Jamahiriya* (n 18) para 72; see also Bassiouni, *Libya from Repression to Revolution: A Record of Armed Conflict and International Law Violations, 2011–2013* (M Nijhoff 2013) 301.

[106] Human Rights Council, *Report of the International Commission of Inquiry to Investigate all Alleged Violations of International Human Rights Law in the Libyan Arab Jamahiriya* (n 18) para 72 (emphasis added).

[107] eg, with regard to attacks on migrant workers and sexual violence committed by civilians in areas under NTC control, the report found that such acts raise 'issues of failures to protect from non-State violence', ibid, at 217.

[108] Human Rights Council, *Situation of Human Rights in the Libyan Arab Jamahiriya*, 14 July 2011, A/HRC/RES/17/17, paras 4 and 6.

[109] In that paragraph, the Security Council referred explicitly to violence against African migrants and minorities, which were reportedly committed by non-state armed groups. United Nations Security Council, *Resolution 2009 (2011): Libya*, 16 September 2011, S/RES/2009 (2011), para 5.

put an end to impunity'.[110] Invoking obligations of the NTC was done in addition to calls upon 'the Libyan authorities to promote and protect human rights'.[111] The approach of evaluating the conduct of armed groups 'who exercise government-like functions and control' under IHRL has been taken throughout the crisis, lead to several reports on human rights violations of armed groups,[112] and has been taken 'note [of] with apprechiation' by states in the Human Rights Council.[113]

A third example has been the ISG's de facto occupation of territory in Syria and Iraq. As UN Special Rapporteur Emmerson pointed out, the ISG 'controls large swathes of territory in which millions of individuals live; it has declared itself a "State", and runs both a civil and a military administration, including the establishment of a "court" system'.[114] For Emmerson, in this situation '[t]he threshold for ISIL to be bound by human rights obligations has clearly been met'.[115] Likewise, the UN Committee against Torture deplored 'the severe human rights violations committed by the so-called Islamic State of Iraq and the Levant (ISIL) and associated armed groups'.[116] Fully aware of the systematic denial of 'basic human rights and freedoms'[117] by the ISG,[118] states in the Security Council unanimously deplored and condemned 'in the strongest terms the terrorist acts of ISIL and its violent extremist ideology, and its continued gross, systematic and widespread abuses of human rights and violations of international humanitarian law'.[119] However, acting under chapter VII, the Council did not call upon the ISG to respect and to protect human rights but simply to 'cease all violence and terrorist acts'.[120] Only in a

[110] ibid. [111] ibid, at para 7.

[112] See, eg, Human Rights Council, *Investigation by the Office of the United Nations High Commissioner for Human Rights on Libya: Detailed Findings*, 15 February 2016, A/HRC/31/CRP.3, para 29.

[113] Human Rights Council, *Technical Assistance and Capacity-Building to Improve Human Rights in Libya*, 20 April 2016, A/HRC/RES/31/27, para 30.

[114] Human Rights Council, *Report of the Special Rapporteur on the Promotion and Protection of Human Rights and Fundamental Freedoms while Countering Terrorism*, Ben Emmerson, 16 Jube 2015, A/HRC/29/51, para 30. Similarly, other reports suggest that the ISG has established quasi-state institutions and infrastructure in areas under its control. See International Commission of Inquiry on the Syrian Arab Republic, 'Rule of Terror: Living under ISIS in Syria', para 16. See also Human Rights Council, *Report of the Independent International Commission of Inquiry on the Syrian Arab Republic*, 13 August 2014, A/HRC/27/60, para 17.

[115] Human Rights Council, *Report of the Special Rapporteur on the Promotion and Protection of Human Rights and Fundamental Freedoms while Countering Terrorism*, Ben Emmerson (n 114)) para 30. For Emmerson: 'This means, at a minimum, that ISIL is bound under international law to respect core human rights obligations, such as the right to life, the absolute prohibition of torture, cruel, inhuman and degrading treatment, the prohibition of slavery and the prohibition of enforced disappearance, as well as the right to freedom of thought, conscience and religion.'

[116] UN Committee against Torture, *Concluding Observations on the Initial Report of Iraq*, 7 September 2015, CAT/C/IRQ/CO/1, para 11.

[117] International Commission of Inquiry on the Syrian Arab Republic, 'Rule of Terror: Living under ISIS in Syria' (n 114) para 74.

[118] These crimes have also been reported on prior to the 'Rule of Terror' report. See Human Rights Council, *Report of the Independent International Commission of Inquiry on the Syrian Arab Republic* (n 114).

[119] United Nations Security Council, *Resolution 2170 (2014)*, 15 August 2014, S/RES/2170 (2014), para 1.

[120] ibid, at para 4. One possible explanation for states' less human rights-oriented approach could be that states did not consider the ISG primarily as an entity exercising quasi-governmental authority

non-binding Human Rights Council resolution did states urge 'all parties to comply with applicable international humanitarian law and human rights law'.[121]

Seemingly recognizing the lack of control exercised by the Government of Iraq over ISG-held territory, the Human Rights Council only urged 'the Government of Iraq to investigate all alleged abuses and violations of human rights and violations of international humanitarian law'.[122] Providing some detail on the scope of this obligation, the UN Committee against Torture recommended that the Government:

> Continue to keep thorough documentation on the victims of inhuman treatment in areas not under governmental control, on the type of violations of the Convention against them and the damage inflicted, as well as the identity, if possible, of the alleged perpetrators, so that the State party can fully exercise its duties under the Convention when effective control is re-established and ensure that those found responsible are prosecuted and held accountable.[123]

Thus, states' calls on all parties to respect IHRL were made to complement the continuing but limited obligations of the de jure government to protect human rights.

The idea that IHRL binds non-state entities that exercise quasi-governmental authority finds additional support in human rights jurisprudence. For example, in the *Sadiq Shek Elmi v Australia* case, the Committee against Torture had to examine whether conduct of certain non-state armed groups in Somalia could constitute an act of torture under article 1 of the Convention against Torture (CAT). Under the Convention, the act of torture requires 'the consent or acquiescence of a public official or other person acting in an official capacity'—a formulation chosen to exclude any similar acts when committed by private actors.[124] Finding that some of the armed groups in Somalia 'exercise certain prerogatives that are comparable to those normally exercised by legitimate governments', the Committee held that 'the members of those factions can fall, for the purposes of the application of the Convention, within the phrase "public officials or other persons acting in an official capacity" contained in article 1'.[125] Likewise, in the *R v Zardad* case before the UK

over people and territory but as a terrorist organization committing international crimes. This perception was, eg, different with regard to the NTC in Libya. See United Nations Security Council, *Threats to International Peace and Security Caused by Terorist Acts*, 15 August 2014, S/PV.7242. Records of the Human Rights Council's 22nd Special Session on the *Human Rights Situation in Iraq in Light of Abuses Committed by the Islamic State in Iraq and the Levant and Associated Groups* are available online at <http://webtv.un.org> (accessed 6 November 2017). Such hesitations of states in situations in which they consider non-state armed groups 'terrorists' have also been pointed out by Philip Alston. See United Nations Commission on Human Rights, *Extrajudicial, Summary or Arbitrary Executions: Report of the Special Rapporteur*, Philip Alston (n 54) para 26.

[121] Human Rights Council, *S-22/1: The Human Rights Situation in Iraq in the Light of Abuses Committed by the So-Called Islamic State in Iraq and the Levant and Associated Groups*, 3 September 2014, A/HRC/RES/S-22/1, para 2.

[122] Human Rights Council, *Technical Assistance and Capacity-Building in Strengthening Human Rights in Iraq in the Light of the Abuses Committed by Daesh and Associated Terrorist Groups* (n 51) para 2.

[123] UN Committee against Torture, *Concluding Observations on the Initial Report of Iraq* (n 116) para 11.

[124] See McCorquodale and La Forgia, 'Taking off the Blindfolds' (n 37)192. However, there were also states that argued against this narrow scope and suggested including obligations for non-state entities comparable to government authority. See ibid, at 194–97.

[125] *Sadiq Shek Elmi v Australia, CAT/C/22/D/120/1998.*

Central Criminal Court, Judge Treacy argued that acts of torture under the CAT can be committed with the consent or acquiescence of a non-state group that 'acquired a sufficient degree of control, permanence, authority or organization to fulfill criteria sufficient for it to be recognised as an authority wielding official or quasi-official powers'.[126]

These examples underline that there is support for the assertion—as made by different UN human rights expert commissions—that it is 'increasingly accepted' that non-state armed groups exercising quasi-governmental authority in a defined territory have obligations under IHRL.[127] Yet, probably for factual and for diplomatic reasons, the link between IHRL obligations and quasi-governmental abilities is not always made explicitly. While UN mechanism reports or resolutions rarely provide details on the scope of the territorial state's continuing obligation to protect and fulfil human rights in such territory, practical restrictions are at least implicitly recognized. Adding to the apparent lack of clarity in the international community's response to human rights obligations of armed groups exercising quasi-governmental authority, states do not normally specify which source of law could bind non-state armed groups. Moreover, they rarely define the scope of IHRL they find applicable. These questions are considered next.

6.3.3 Conceptual considerations

Conceptually, there is little doubt that armed groups exercising quasi-governmental authority in a territory should be bound by IHRL. As Rodley pointed out, if an entity exercises 'effective power', demands for respect of IHRL reflect the

> spirit of both the conceptual scope of human rights and the rationale behind the international law approach to them ... [because] the individual [would be] at the mercy of a government or of another power over whose actions the government is impotent.[128]

Experts at a meeting held by the Geneva Academy of International Humanitarian Law and Human Rights agreed with that approach, emphasizing that the vertical

[126] *R v Zardad Judgment, 7 April 2004,* UK Central Criminal Court, para 36.

[127] Another pertinent situation occurred in Yemen after a coalition of Houthi fighters and fighters linked to former president Saleh took control over most population centres in the country in 2014/2015. An OHCHR report stated that 'non-State actors that exercise government-like functions and de facto control over a territory are increasingly considered to be bound by international human rights obligations', a Security Council Panel of Experts report found that these groups 'violated international human rights law', and the Human Rights Council called upon 'all parties in Yemen to respect their obligations under international human rights law'. See Human Rights Council, *Situation of Human Rights in Yemen,* 7 September 2015, A/HRC/30/31, para 24; United Nations Security Council, *Final Report of the Panel of Experts on Yemen Established Pursuant to Security Council Resolution 2140 (2014),* 26 January 2016, S/2016/73, para. 144; Human Rights Council, *Technical Assistance and Capacity-Building for Yemen in the Field of Human Rights,* 12 October 2015, A/HRC/RES/30/18, para 3.

[128] Rodley, 'Can Armed Opposition Groups Violate Human Rights?' (n 3) 313. The principle idea is also maintained in Murray's 'de facto control theory', which builds on the traditional approach but expands it in light of current contemporary human rights threats posed by non-state armed groups. See Murray, *Human Rights Obligations of Non-State Armed Groups* (n 94) chapter 5, in particular at 151. See also Kleffner, 'Organized Armed Groups' (n 31) 57.

power relationship in such situations would reproduce the '*raison d'être* of human rights law' and justify its application.[129] In addition, if non-state armed groups control territory and exercise quasi-governmental functions they can be assumed to have the 'administrative and logistical capacity' to comply with human rights law.[130] While there seems to be 'broad agreement among experts'[131] on this basic idea, less agreement exists on two related issues. First, how could IHRL bind non-state armed groups, meaning which source of international law could apply to them and why? And second, if these groups were bound by IHRL, would all or only some rules apply?

6.3.3.1 Binding non-state armed groups by IHRL treaties

The question of how international law can bind armed groups has been discussed extensively—yet not conclusively—with regard to IHL.[132] Scholars have suggested different approaches, which may also inform the debate on potential IHRL obligations of armed groups. This section only examines approaches that apply directly to armed groups; it does not consider theories arguing that armed groups are bound through possible obligations of their members.[133] Moreover, while some have claimed that under international law armed groups would need to agree to possible human rights obligations,[134] this section is based on the widespread understanding that '[t]he rule that any obligation requires the consent of the party concerned has long been abandoned'.[135] The first three pertinent approaches invoke a possible binding effect of international treaties on (non-state) third parties; a fourth one relies on customary international law.

[129] Geneva Academy of International Humanitarian Law and Human Rights, *Rules of Engagement—Protecting Civilians through Dialogue with Armed Non-State Actors* (Geneva Academy 2011) 25.

[130] ICRC, *Strengthening Legal Protection for Persons Deprived of their Liberty in Relation to Non-International Armed Conflict* (ICRC 2012) 5–6.

[131] Geneva Academy of International Humanitarian Law and Human Rights, *Rules of Engagement—Protecting Civilians through Dialogue with Armed Non-State Actors* (n 129) 25.

[132] For a comprehensive list, ICRC, *Convention (I) for the Amelioration of the Condition of the Wounded and Sick in Armed Forces in the Field: Commentary of 2016* (ICRC 2016) article 3, para 155–58.

[133] For a comprehensive discussion on such approaches, see Fortin, *The Accountability of Armed Groups under Human Rights Law* (n 20) 187–98; Giacca, *Economic, Social, and Cultural Rights in Armed Conflict* (n 9) 237.

[134] Ryngaert, 'Human Rights Obligations' (n 2) 374–75.

[135] Tomuschat, 'Insurgent Movements' (n 2) 587. This does not mean that international treaties bind states without their consent. However, states are not required to consent to customary rules being binding on them, including newly independent states that had no say in the development of such rules. Similarly, under IHL there is little controversy on the fact that customary rules bind all parties to the conflict irrespective of their prior consent. For further discussion on this issue, see Rodenhäuser, 'Human Rights Obligations of Non-State Armed Groups in other Situations of Violence: The Syria Example' (2013) 3 Journal of International Humanitarian Legal Studies 263–90, 278–79; Murray, *Human Rights Obligations of Non-State Armed Groups* (n 94) 94–101; Clapham, 'Focussing on Armed Non-State Actors' in Clapham and Gaeta (eds), *The Oxford Handbook of International Law in Armed Conflict* (OUP 2014) 770.

A binding effect of human rights treaties on non-state armed groups

In order to explain how IHL treaties bind non-state armed groups, it has been argued that in accordance with articles 34–36 of the Vienna Convention on the Law of Treaties, international treaties can create obligations for third parties if the treaty intends to bind them, and if the third party explicitly accepts the obligations.[136] However, this approach would have only limited effect in practice because it depends on the non-state armed group's acceptance of the obligations. To overcome this obstacle, it has been shown that states can also create obligations for non-state entities without their consent.[137] For example, it is undisputed that states created obligations for all individuals under international criminal law. Consequently, states should also be able to create IHRL obligations for collective non-state entities. Akin to IHL treaties, IHRL treaties could bind armed groups if states intend them to do so.

While the 'third-party-obligations' approach is crucial to explain how IHL treaties create obligations for non-state armed groups, their effect with regard to IHRL is limited. As seen above, most obligations under human rights treaties are exclusively addressed to states and are not intended to create obligations for non-state armed groups. Thus, the question of how these treaties bind non-state armed groups does not emerge. Only if we accept that treaties such as the Convention on the Rights of the Child–Optional Protocol to the Convention on the Rights of the Child (CRC-OPAC) or the Kampala Convention contain direct obligations for armed groups—similar to IHL treaties, for example—could this approach be used at all. Nonetheless, the idea that states create norms of international law that bind non-state entities is equally important to understand how other sources of international law, such as custom, bind armed groups.[138]

Another approach to explain how IHL binds armed groups is called the theory of 'legislative jurisdiction' or 'prescriptive jurisdiction'. This theory explains obligations of armed groups based on the state's competence to legislate for all natural and legal persons under its jurisdiction.[139] It argues that if a state ratifies an international treaty that foresees obligations for persons under its jurisdiction, international

[136] This argument was made by Cassese with regard to the question of whether or not IHL treaty provisions bind non-state armed groups. See Cassese, 'The Status of Rebels under the 1977 Geneva Protocol on Non-International Armed Conflicts' (1981) 30 International & Comparative Law Quarterly 416–39. For discussion, see eg Sivakumaran, 'Binding Armed Opposition Groups' (2006) 55 International & Comparative Law Quarterly 369–94, 377–79; Murray, 'How International Humanitarian Law Treaties Bind Non-State Armed Groups' (n 27) 9–18; Fortin, *The Accountability of Armed Groups under Human Rights Law* (n 20) 179–85.

[137] See Murray, 'How International Humanitarian Law Treaties Bind Non-State Armed Groups' (n 27) 18–21; 27–28; Clapham, 'Focussing on Armed Non-State Actors' (n 135) 778.

[138] For discussion on the question to what extent armed groups' practice is relevant for the formation of customary international law, see n 166 below.

[139] For more detailed discussions of this theory, see, eg, Kleffner, 'The Applicability of International Humanitarian Law to Organized Armed Groups' (2011) 93 International Review of the Red Cross 443–61, 445–49; Murray, 'How International Humanitarian Law Treaties Bind Non-State Armed Groups' (n 27); Sivakumaran, 'Binding Armed Opposition Groups' (n 136) 381–93; Abi-Saab, 'Non-International Armed Conflicts' in UNESCO and Institut Henry-Dunant (eds), *International Dimensions of Humanitarian Law* (M Nijhoff 1988) 231; Pilloud, Sandoz, Swinarski et al, *Commentary on the Additional Protocols of 8 June 1977 to the Geneva Conventions of 12 August 1949* (ICRC 1987) para 4444.

law obligations can become binding on armed groups. This could be the case if international treaties intend to bind armed groups and have direct effect within a state's jurisdiction, or if international treaties are translated into national legislation that binds armed groups.[140] With regard to IHRL, it has been argued that treaties bind non-state armed groups indirectly through states' positive obligation to protect human rights against violations committed by private persons, which includes prescribing such violations through national law.[141] While this could explain how IHRL binds armed groups or their members through national law, it does not explain how IHRL treaties may bind armed groups directly. As a result, most approaches that may explain how IHL treaties bind non-state armed groups have limited merit to explain how IHRL could bind them.

Human rights treaty obligations devolving with territory

A third approach to explain how IHRL treaties could bind non-state armed groups exercising quasi-governmental authority is to invoke the idea that human rights treaty obligations devolve with territory. Under this approach, it is argued that IHRL treaties that apply in a state would bind a non-state armed group if it exercises quasi-governmental authority over territory and its people.[142] Demanding entities that effectively govern territory to respect the internationally protected rights of persons under its control would be an expression of the principle of effectiveness, meaning that the factual situation would significantly influence the applicable legal framework.[143] Moreover, this idea can be based on two arguments, the first looking at the continuity of obligations, the second at the continuity of rights.

The first argument invokes the continuity of human rights obligations for successor governments or states. With regard to successor governments within a state, the applicable principle is that international law treaties bind states as entities and not a specific government.[144] Thus, a change in government does not change the

[140] As argued above, with regard to IHRL the former approach would have limited effect because IHRL treaties rarely provide direct obligations for armed groups. Moreover, Clapham remarks with regard to the prospect of states transforming international law into binding law within their jurisdiction: 'While some states do this some of the time for some obligations, we cannot really reliably infer that the outlawed group as such is considered to be bound simply by the act of a state's ratification of a treaty.' Clapham, 'Focussing on Armed Non-State Actors' (n 135) 778.

[141] See Kleffner, 'Organized Armed Groups' (n 139) 52–53.

[142] This approach has also been invoked to explain the applicability of IHL to armed groups; eg, with regard to Common Article 3, the ICRC argued in the 1958 commentary on GCIV: '[T]he responsible authority at their head exercises effective sovereignty, it is bound by the very fact that it claims to represent the country, or part of the country'. Uhler and Coursier, *Geneva Convention Relative to the Protection of Civilian Persons in Time of War: Commentary* (ICRC 1958) 37. In addition, Giacca argued that: 'This approach is consistent with the principle of effectiveness under international law and with the law of state responsibility.' Giacca, *Economic, Social, and Cultural Rights in Armed Conflict* (n 9) 235. Moreover, Murray argues that a binding effect of IHRL treaties on armed groups with de facto control would also be consistent with a modern interpretation of IHRL treaty texts that, prima facie, only address obligations to states. See Murray, *Human Rights Obligations of Non-State Armed Groups* (n 94) 164–68.

[143] For details on the principle of effectiveness, see Section 6.2.2 'The principle of effectiveness and the protection of human rights' above.

[144] For discussion of this principle, see Brierly and Clapham, *Law of Nations* (n 16) 155–56.

international obligations of the governing entity within a state. This principle could be extended to situations in which a non-state armed group establishes a government in only part of a state's territory. As Nair pointed out in 1961 with regard to international law treaties in general: 'since treaties are made on behalf of the State, and bind the State as a whole, all treaties already in existence when an insurrection breaks out are necessarily binding on the insurgent community'.[145]

The idea that IHRL treaties in force in a territory bind any new governing entity finds further support in international law's approach to the applicability of human rights treaties in situations of state succession, meaning if a separatist entity establishes a new state. While it is often argued that new states do not inherit treaty obligations of the state from which they split, recent state practice may suggest that human rights treaties constitute an exception to this rule.[146] Indeed, strong arguments exist for a continuity of human rights obligations in cases of state succession.[147] As ICJ judge Weeramantry emphasized, human rights treaties do not infringe the state's sovereignty and are not primarily concerned with state interests.[148] Thus, their continuation does not impose an undue burden on the new state's sovereign rights or interests.[149] Instead, these treaties are better understood as mostly codifying individual rights that exist independently from the Convention in question, and reflect an interest of the international community.[150]

This leads to the second part of the argument. As shown above, human rights are best understood as rights of the individual, meaning that they 'inherently belong to individuals and are key to individual dignity'.[151] From a naturalist point of view, human rights exist 'independently of, and before, the State'.[152] In this respect, IHRL treaties have a rather declaratory function, not creating but rather confirming

[145] McNair, *The Law of Treaties* (Oxford: Clarendon Press 1961) 676.

[146] Kamminga, 'State Succession in Respect of Human Rights Treaties', (1996) 7 European Journal of International Law 469–48. For a different view, see Rasulov, 'Revisiting State Succession to Humanitarian Treaties: Is there a Case for Automaticity?' (2003) 14 European Journal of International Law 141–70.

[147] In addition, certain treaties regulating the use of territory, and arguably multilateral treaties, bind successor states. See Cullen and Wheatley, 'The Human Rights of Individuals in De Facto Regimes under the European Convention on Human Rights' (2013) 13 Human Rights Law Review 691–728; Murray, *Human Rights Obligations of Non-State Armed Groups* (n 94) 135–36.

[148] *Case concerning Application of the Convention on the Prevention and Punishment of the Crime of Genocide (Bosnia and Herzegovina v Serbia and Montenegro)— Seperate Opinion of Judge Weeramantry, 11 July 1996,* ICJ, 645–47.

[149] This argument applies a fortiori to non-state entities. While the idea that a new state is a sovereign entity and does not inherit obligations exists to protect the state's sovereignty, this argument does not apply to non-state entities, which are not sovereigns or equal to states.

[150] See *Case concerning Application of the Convention on the Prevention and Punishment of the Crime of Genocide (Bosnia and Herzegovina v Serbia and Montenegro)—Seperate Opinion of Judge Weeramantry* (n 148) 647–48.

[151] Human Rights Council, *Report of the Special Rapporteur on the Promotion and Protection of Human Rights and Fundamental Freedoms while Countering Terrorism*, Ben Emmerson (n 114) para 30. For further discussion, see Chapter 4 'Human Rights, Natural Rights, and their Applicability beyond the State–Individual Relationship' above.

[152] See *South West Africa (Ethiopia v South Africa), Judgment, Dissenting Opinion of Judge Tanaka, 18 July 1966,* ICJ, 297.

existing rights, which apply irrespective of IHRL treaties.[153] If the spirit of the international law approach to human rights is to protect the individual from any authority that effectively governs a territory and its people, every authority must be bound to respect and to protect human rights. Even if the naturalist view is not followed, it would be precarious for individuals and contrary to the object and purpose of human rights law if individuals lose human rights protection if the entity under whose authority they live changes. As Tomuschat argued, if human rights belong to the people in the territory, 'it would seem logical to conclude that it is irrelevant who exercises governmental authority in that territory'.[154] This continuity in human rights protection is especially needed in situations of internal turmoil or armed conflict.[155]

To some extent, this approach finds support in the UN Committee on Human Rights' understanding of the continuity of state obligations under the International Covenant for Civil and Political Rights (ICCPR). The Committee held:

> The rights enshrined in the Covenant belong to the people living in the territory of the State party. .... [O]nce the people are accorded the protection of the rights under the Covenant, such protection devolves with territory and continues to belong to them, notwithstanding change in government of the State party, including dismemberment in more than one State or State succession or any subsequent action of the State party designed to divest them of the rights guaranteed by the Covenant.[156]

The ECtHR hinted at a similar direction. In the *Cyprus v Turkey* case, the Court considered whether legal procedures offered by the de facto regime governing northern Cyprus (the Turkish Republic of Northern Cyprus, TRNC) could be considered 'domestic remedies' under the ECHR. The Court argued that '[l]ife goes

[153] See ibid. Whether human rights treaties are only declaratory or also create human rights is disputed. Schabas holds the view that even the rights enshrined in the Universal Declaration of Human Rights (UDHR) did not all exist previously. Schabas, *The Universal Declaration of Human Rights: The 'Travaux Préparatoires'* (CUP 2013) lxxi–lxxii.

[154] Tomuschat, 'Insurgent Movements' (n 2) 588. Likewise, as ICJ Judge Weeramantry argued, if human rights treaties ceased to apply in the case of state succession

> the strange situation would result of the people within a State, who enjoy the full benefit of a human rights treaty, such as the International Covenant on Civil and Political Rights, and have enjoyed it for many years, being suddenly deprived of it as though these are special privileges that can be given or withdrawn at the whim or fancy of Governments. Populations once protected cease to be protected, may be protected again, and may again cease to be protected, depending on the vagaries of political events. Such a legal position seems to be altogether untenable, especially at this stage in the development of human rights.

Case concerning Application of the Convention on the Prevention and Punishment of the Crime of Genocide (Bosnia and Herzegovina v Serbia and Montenegro)—Seperate Opinion of Judge Weeramantry (n 148) 649.

[155] *Case concerning Application of the Convention on the Prevention and Punishment of the Crime of Genocide (Bosnia and Herzegovina v Serbia and Montenegro)— Seperate Opinion of Judge Weeramantry* (n 148) 650–51. For a good elaboration of this point, see Fortin, *The Accountability of Armed Groups under Human Rights Law* (n 20) 275–76.

[156] Human Rights Committee, *General Comment No 26: Continuity of Obligations*, 8 December 1997, CCPR/C/21/Rev.1/Add.8/Rev.1, para 4. For a doctrinal discussion on this approach, see Cullen and Wheatley, 'The Human Rights of Individuals in De Facto Regimes under the European Convention on Human Rights' (n 147) 720–22.

on in the territory concerned for its inhabitants', that 'life must be made tolerable and be protected by the de facto authorities', and that the Court cannot ignore acts of the de facto authorities.[157] Otherwise, it would be 'stripping the inhabitants of the territory of all their rights whenever they are discussed in an international context, which would amount to depriving them even of the minimum standard of rights to which they are entitled'.[158] While this case was particular because Turkey was considered responsible for acts of the TRNC, the Court seemingly invoked the idea that human rights belong to people and that even (unlawful) quasi-governmental authorities must respect and protect them.

Again, a potential difficulty with this line of argument could be that IHRL treaties are not addressed to 'territorial authorities with quasi-governmental capacities' but to states, which in international law are first and foremost represented by their de jure governments. This obstacle might not be insurmountable, however. As Murray argues with reference to the 'evolutionary principle' as identified by the International Court of Justice, treaties should be interpreted 'in light of the reality of the contemporary international legal order'.[159] Therefore, 'the effectiveness of international law, and the effective protection of individuals' human rights' require that these treaties bind not only de jure governments but also 'entities filling the role of a vertical authority'.[160] This (re)interpretation would also be supported by the treaties' object and purpose, which is to protect the individual.[161] Such evolutionary and teleological interpretation is not without precedent. Famously, in the *Tadić* case, the International Criminal Tribunal for the former Yugoslavia (ICTY) Appeals Chamber gave significant weight to realities in 'modern inter-ethnic armed conflicts' and the object and purpose of IHL in finding that not only nationality but also 'allegiance to a party' are decisive in determining who is a protected person under the Fourth Geneva Convention.[162] Accordingly, IHRL treaties' wording of binding 'States Parties' could be interpreted as applying to the de jure government and to any other entity that controls part of the state's territory in a quasi-governmental manner.

As a result, the idea that human rights belong primarily to human beings and that corresponding treaty obligations devolve with territory and bind any entity exercising quasi-governmental authority therein provides a strong argument for IHRL obligations of non-state armed groups.[163] However, even if this idea were followed, under IHRL treaty law the applicable norms would be limited to those to which the territorial state is party; treaties that do not apply in a certain territory cannot devolve with it. A necessary addition—or an alternative, if the treaty law approach is

[157] *Cyprus v Turkey, Application no 25781/94*, para 96. [158] ibid.

[159] Murray, *Human Rights Obligations of Non-State Armed Groups* (n 94) 266.

[160] ibid. [161] ibid, at 266–68. [162] *Tadić, IT-94-1-A* (n 33) para 166.

[163] However, the question of how international law treats situations in which non-state armed groups succeed states in exercising quasi-governmental authority over territory remains subject to debate and sparks a number of unanswered questions. One of these questions would be whether and under what procedure armed groups could derogate from pertinent treaty obligations. For some discussion, see Rudolf, 'Non State Actors' (n 64) 139–41. Rudolf noted that limited evidence exists that states actually used this reasoning when calling upon armed groups to respect human rights.

not followed—would be to argue that if armed groups 'exercise sovereignty [... they] must observe human rights as a matter of customary law'.[164] This leads to the fourth approach on how to bind non-state armed groups to IHRL, namely by means of customary international law.

6.3.3.2 Binding non-state armed groups by customary IHRL

In addition to possible IHRL treaty obligations, human rights obligations could also stem from unwritten sources of international law, i.e. customary IHRL or human rights principles.[165] With regard to the practical impact of the norms, it has been argued that non-state armed groups might be more likely to comply with a rule established by the international community than a rule applicable because of the treaty-making or legislative power of the state they are opposing.[166]

Undoubtedly, non-state parties to armed conflicts are bound by customary rules of IHL.[167] As the UN International Commission of Inquiry on Darfur argued:

> [A]ll insurgents that have reached a certain threshold of organization, stability and effective control of territory, *possess international legal personality and are therefore bound by the relevant rules of customary international law* on internal armed conflicts referred to above [i.e. basic IHL rules].[168]

As seen in the statement, a key aspect of whether an armed group can be bound by customary IHL is that the group possesses 'international legal personality'. The question of under which conditions armed groups have sufficient 'international legal

[164] Heintze, 'De Facto Regimes' (n 65) 272. The question of whether or not such groups exercise 'sovereignty', or rather 'authority', is disputed among scholars. See Tomuschat, 'Insurgent Movements' (n 2) 587; Ryngaert, 'Human Rights Obligations' (n 2) 358; Kleffner, 'Organized Armed Groups' (n 31) 451–54.

[165] This argument is often invoked by scholars; eg, Clapham asserts that 'international human rights principles are increasingly considered applicable to armed non-state actors'. Clapham, 'Focussing on Armed Non-State Actors' (n 135) 789. Likewise, Chinkin noted: 'Non-state actors that cannot be treaty parties may be held to be bound by customary international law.' Chinkin, 'Sources' in Moeckli, Shah, and Sivakumaran (eds), *International Human Rights Law* (OUP 2010) 103–23, 112. See also Heintze, 'De Facto Regimes' (n 64) 268.

[166] Different commentators emphasized this point with regard to IHL. See Kleffner, 'Organized Armed Groups' (n 139) 446; Clapham, *The Rights and Responsibilities of Non-State Actors: The Legal Landscape and Issues Surrounding Engagement* (SSRN 2010) 23. Yet, this argument is also limited. Traditionally, unwritten sources of international law such as custom depend on state *opinio juris* and practice. While the ICTY suggested that practice by non-state armed groups could at least be considered with regard to customary IHL, others consider the legal significance of non-state practice unclear. See Doswald-Beck and Henckaerts, *Customary International Humanitarian Law* (n 32) xxxvi. For further discussion on this issue, see, fe, Murray, 'How International Humanitarian Law Treaties Bind Non-State Armed Groups' (n 27) 7–8. Fortin, *The Accountability of Armed Groups under Human Rights Law* (n 20) 324–34.

[167] See *Prosecutor v Sam Hinga Norman—Decision on Preliminary Motion Based on Lack of Jurisdiction (Child Recruitment), 2004,* Special Court for Sierra Leone, para 22. For discussion, see Murray, 'How International Humanitarian Law Treaties Bind Non-State Armed Groups' (n 27) 6–7; Kleffner, 'Organized Armed Groups' (n 31) 454–56; Sivakumaran, 'The Addressees of Common Article 3' in Clapham, Gaeta, and Sassòli (eds), *The 1949 Geneva Conventions: A Commentary* (OUP 2015) 415–33.

[168] United Nations Secretary, *Report of the International Commission of Inquiry on Darfur to the United Nations Secretary-General* (United Nations 2005) para 172 (emphasis added).

personality' to be addressees of customary IHRL remains debated.[169] Importantly, as pointed out in the introduction to this study, international legal personality is not a 'one-size' concept. The International Court of Justice pointed out that recognizing legal personality of a non-state entity 'is not the same thing as saying that it is a State, which it certainly is not, or that its legal personality and rights and duties are the same as those of a State'.[170] Thus, international legal personality exists on a spectrum, meaning that the scope of personality and corresponding rights and obligations vary according to the capacity of the addressee and the context in which it operates.[171] On this spectrum, a non-state armed group that is able to establish quasi-governmental authority in a defined territory is probably as sophisticated and as state-like as a non-state entity can become. This means that its capacity to comply with IHRL obligations should also be state-like. Moreover, owing to the territorial state's limited obligations to protect and to fulfil human rights vis-à-vis individuals living under the authority of an armed group exercising quasi-governmental authority, direct obligations for the group are urgently needed. Therefore, Section 6.3.4 'The scope of obligations' argues that the scope of IHRL obligations of such groups should be broad rather than narrow.

6.3.4 The scope of obligations

Condemnation by the international community of human rights violations or abuses committed by non-state armed groups exercising quasi-governmental authority in a territory is not new.[172] Despite the increasing frequency of such condemnations or calls upon armed groups to respect applicable IHRL, pertinent statements, resolutions, or reports do not seem to follow a clear legal reasoning and do not invoke a consistent body of norms. This is mostly for three reasons. First, IHRL treaty law does not provide a binding set of rules applicable to non-state armed groups, which could be referred to. Second, the scope of customary IHRL remains disputed. And third, the relevant resolutions or reports are normally concerned with human rights violations in specific geographic or thematic contexts. Thus, their objective is not to establish a generally applicable set of norms that bind certain categories of non-state armed groups. Nonetheless, based on the conceptual considerations above, this

[169] For detailed discussion, see Fortin, *The Accountability of Armed Groups under Human Rights Law* (n 20); Murray, *Human Rights Obligations of Non-State Armed Groups* (n 94) part 1.

[170] ICJ, *Reparations for Injuries Suffered in the Service of the United Nations*, Advisory Opinion, 11 April 1949, 179.

[171] With regard to the idea that legal personality exists on a spectrum, see the Introduction to this book.

[172] eg, in 2002 the Security Council called on armed groups in the Eastern Democratic Republic of the Congo (DRC) as 'the de facto authorities in the regions affected to ensure the protection of civilians and the rule of law'. See United Nations Security Council, *Resolution 1417 (2002): Democratic Republic of the Congo*, 14 June 2002, S/RES/1417 (2002), para 5. Similarly, when the Taliban governed most of Afghanistan, the Security Council condemned 'the continuing grave violations of the human rights of women and girls, including all forms of discrimination against them, in all areas of Afghanistan, particularly in areas under the control of the Taliban'. United Nations Security Council, *Statement by the President of the Security Council*, 7 April 2000, S/PRST/2000/12.

section argues that non-state armed groups exercising quasi-governmental authority in a territory should be bound by a broad set of IHRL obligations. Depending on which source of law is applied, these should consist of all IHRL treaty obligations applicable in the territory, and/or of customary IHRL.

If the approach is followed that human rights and corresponding obligations devolve with territory and bind the entity that effectively governs territory and population, this would mean that the full scope of human rights obligations applicable to the territorial state would also apply to the new governing entity. In this case, a state-like non-state armed group could be bound by obligations deriving from a variety of IHRL treaties, including civil and political, as well as economic, social, and cultural rights. Likewise, it would be incumbent on the group to respect, protect, and fulfil the rights in question.[173] While this encompasses a broad scope of obligations, it is not a utopian demand. If a group is able to establish quasi-governmental authority to sustain its de facto rule in a certain territory, this will also enable the group to comply with IHRL. For example, Hamas authorities in Gaza have been described as being firmly in charge of the legislative, executive, and judicial sector, which not only enabled it to establish undisputed authority in its territory, but also to provide social services and economic policies.[174] Likewise, the ISG established quasi-governmental structures in the core territory under its effective control, and was able to provide law and order as well as social welfare services.[175] As a result, these non-state entities have sufficient capacity to respect, protect, and fulfil a broad scope of human rights obligations, including implementing a welfare, health-care, or education system.[176]

In addition, customary rules of IHRL could bind non-state armed groups. Determining the scope of applicable norms of customary IHRL is, however, complicated. Unlike under IHL, where the ICRC suggested a partly controversial but generally appreciated list of customary IHL norms,[177] no such list exists under IHRL. Consequently, some commentators have called for the broad application of 'the human rights catalogue … regardless of the type of the entity in question'.[178]

[173] For discussion on how the obligations to respect, protect, and fulfil could apply to armed groups and what the different obligations would entail, see Murray, *Human Rights Obligations of Non-State Armed Groups* (n 94) 181–97.

[174] See, eg, Berti, 'Non-State Actors as Providers of Governance: The Hamas Government in Gaza between Effective Sovereignty, Centralized Authority, and Resistance' (2015) 69 Middle East Journal 9–31; Mukhimer, *Hamas Rule in Gaza* (Palgrave Macmillan 2013).

[175] See Malik, 'The ISIS Papers: Leaked Documents Show How Isis is Building its State, *The Guardian* (7 December 2015).

[176] For further examples and discussion of non-state armed groups implementing economic, social, and cultural rights, see Giacca, *Economic, Social, and Cultural Rights in Armed Conflict* (n 9) 269–70. See also Fortin, *The Accountability of Armed Groups under Human Rights Law* (n 20) 164–68. For a number of practical examples of armed groups respecting and fulfilling the right to education, see Somer, *Education and Armed Non-State Actors: Towards a Comprehensive Agenda* (Protect Education in Insecurity and Conflict 2015).

[177] For discussion on the ICRC customary IHL study, see, eg, Wilmshurst (ed), *Perspectives on the ICRC Study on Customary International Humanitarian Law* (CUP 2007); Bellinger and Haynes, 'A US Government Response to the International Committee of the Red Cross Study Customary International Humanitarian Law' (2007) 89 International Review of the Red Cross 443–71.

[178] Ronen, 'Non-State Actors' (n 29) 32.

A more precise approach could be to apply the civil, political, economic, social, and cultural rights as set out in the Universal Declaration of Human Rights (UDHR).[179] As Schabas suggested with regard to 'quasi-States and analogous entities': '[N]obody would challenge the application of the Universal Declaration of Human Rights to its territory.'[180] Indeed, it is today broadly accepted that a number of human rights found in the UDHR forms part of customary international law, or reflects general principles of international law.[181]

Some human rights experts have pursued this approach. For example, the UN Special Rapporteur for extrajudicial, summary, or arbitrary executions, Philip Alston, argued:

> Human rights norms operate on three levels—as the rights of individuals, as obligations assumed by States, and as legitimate expectations of the international community. .... [A non-state armed group] does not have legal obligations under ICCPR, but it remains subject to the demand of the international community, first expressed in the Universal Declaration of Human Rights, that every organ of society respect and promote human rights.[182]

Referring to previous academic writings of Alston, it has been suggested that, for him, 'legitimate expectations' signify customary law obligations.[183] Indeed, based on this theoretical statement, Alston argued that 'it is especially appropriate and feasible to *call for an armed group to respect human rights norms* when it "exercises significant control over territory and population and has an identifiable political structure" '.[184] Thus, Alston did not refer to standards, expectations, or responsibilities, but to legal 'human rights norms'.[185]

[179] This avenue was taken, eg, in the 'Goldstone Report' regarding Hamas in Gaza. See Human Rights Council, *Report of the United Nations Fact-Finding Mission on the Gaza Conflict*, 25 September 2009, A/HRC/12/48, para 1371.

[180] Schabas, *The Universal Declaration of Human Rights* (n 153) cxxii.

[181] See, eg, ibid, at cxix–cxx; Hannum, 'The Status of the Universal Declaration of Human Rights in National and International Law' (1995) 25 Georgia Journal of International and Comparative Law 287–398, 340; Meron, *Human Rights and Humanitarian Norms as Customary Law* (Clarendon Press 1989) 88; Lillich, 'The Growing Importance of Customary International Human Rights Law' (1996) 25 Georgia Journal of International and Comparative Law 1–30; Baderin and Ssenyonjo (eds), *International Human Rights Law: Six Decades after the UDHR and Beyond* (Ashgate 2010) 6. A precise determination of which rights form part of customary international law is, however, lacking. For a tentative assessment, see Hannum, 'The Status of the Universal Declaration of Human Rights' 231–43.

[182] United Nations Human Rights Commission, *Extrajudicial, Summary or Arbitrary Executions: Report of the Special Rapporteur*, Philip Alston (n 54) para 25.

[183] See Fortin, *The Accountability of Armed Groups under Human Rights Law* (n 20) 354–55. This suggestion is based on an article in Alston and Simma, in which they cite an author who argued that the UDHR contains 'obligations characteristic of customary international law', Simma and Alston, 'The Sources of Human Rights Law: Custom, Jus Cogens, and General Priniples' (1988) 12 Australian Yearbook of International Law 82–108, 91. For a different view arguing that legitimate expectations do not signify legal obligations, see Ryngaert, 'Human Rights Obligations' (n 2).

[184] United Nations Human Rights Commission, *Extrajudicial, Summary or Arbitrary Executions: Report of the Special Rapporteur*, Philip Alston (n 54) para 26 (emphasis added).

[185] For further discussion on the relationship between such legitimate expectations and customary international law, Henckaerts and Wiesener noted: 'The question of whether such a legitimate expectation exists is closely related to the existence of a rule of customary international law. It may be argued that the existence of a legitimate expectation that armed groups respect human rights law supports or forms the basis of a customary law rule to the effect that human rights law binds armed groups.' Henckaerts and Wiesener, 'Human Rights Obligations' (n 2) 158. However, Henckaerts and Wiesener concluded cautiously that

Accordingly, as seen in Alston's remarks and the discussion of contemporary international practice as well as possible treaty obligations of armed groups, armed groups with quasi-governmental capacities also have the capacity to comply with a broad range of human rights obligations.[186] Going in the same direction, the Office of the High Commissioner for Human Rights stressed:

> It is increasingly considered that under certain circumstances non-State actors can also be bound by international human rights law and can assume, voluntarily or not, obligations to *respect, protect and fulfil* human rights.[187]

In addition to its practicability,[188] this approach 'seems justifiable if we accept that the people living under the control of an armed group must be protected as much as possible'.[189] It can likewise be justified in relation to a state's obligations if exercising extraterritorial control over territory, which comprise 'the entire range of substantive rights'.[190] Yet, it is less clear to what extent such an approach would be accepted by states. If an armed group was required to protect and to fulfil human rights, including through their progressive realization, this implies that the armed group may also adopt legislation on various issues. Undoubtedly, especially the territorial state is unlikely to accept such competencies of non-state armed groups on its territory.[191] In order to address the issue, Murray has made the following useful suggestion:

> [A]rmed group activity [should] be evaluated by analogy to the status quo ante bellum requirement established by the law of belligerent occupation. This provision is intended to preserve the territory's unique tapestry of laws, customs and culture, while ensuring its continuing independent viability, thereby acknowledging the temporary nature of occupation and the occupant's lack of sovereignty.[192]

in order to find that customary rules of IHRL applicable to non-state groups exist, 'it would still be necessary to collect further evidence from a larger variety of practice, in particular from States'. ibid, at 157. See also Kamatali, 'Human Rights Law in NIAC' (n 29). For a view holding that such custom exists, see Constantinides, 'Obligations and Accountability of Armed Opposition Groups' (n 2) 102–03; Hessbruegge, 'Human Rights Violations Arising from Conduct of Non-State Actors' (2005) 11 Buffalo Human Rights Law Review, 40–41.

[186] To some extent echoing the idea of 'legitimate expectations', the ICRC pointed out that if non-state armed groups exercise 'stable control of territory [and have] the ability to act like a state authority' they would also have de facto recognized 'human rights *responsibilities*'. ICRC, *International Humanitarian Law and the Challenges of Contemporary Armed Conflicts* (ICRC 2011) 15 n 10.

[187] Office of the United Nations High Commissioner for Human Rights, *International Legal Protection of Human Rights in Armed Conflict* (OHCHR 2011) 21 (emphasis added).

[188] As the International Law Association (ILA) suggested, 'there seem to be few practical obstacles in implementing the negative obligation to respect human rights (that is, refrain from violations) and a potential positive obligation to ensure their protection in areas under their control'. International Law Association, *Washington Conference (2014): Non-State Actors* (ILA 2014) 14.

[189] Bellal, Giacca, and Casey-Maslen, 'Armed Non-State Actors in Afghanistan' (n 2) 71.

[190] *Cyprus v Turkey* (n 157) para 77.

[191] See Hampson, 'Other Areas of Customary Law in Relation to the Study' in Wilmshurst and Breua (eds), *Perspectives on the ICRC Study on Customary International Humanitarian Law* (CUP 2007) 55–56. Underlining this point, Hampson asked pertinently: 'Does Colombia, for example, really accept that the FARC [Revolutionary Armed Forces of Colombia] can legitimately criminalize opposition to itself on the part of individuals living in areas under their control?'

[192] Murray, *Human Rights Obligations of Non-State Armed Groups* (n 94) 191.

6.4 Human Rights Obligations of Groups Exercising De Facto Control over Territory and Population

The second category of armed groups consists of those exercising de facto control over territory and population without having established quasi-governmental authority. This means that their control over territory and its population is less stable or protracted, and the groups have not been able to establish significant public administration or governance infrastructure.[193] Such situations are likely to occur during armed conflicts when an armed group's territorial control is recent, the group is struggling to defend the territory against government forces, or its resources are primarily focused on the armed struggle.[194] Situations in which armed groups exercise varying degrees of de facto control over territory and people also exist outside armed conflicts.[195] As different examples cited in this and Chapter 5 'The Fallacy of Effective Human Rights Protection under Relevant Treaty Law when Armed Groups Commit Violations' show, however, situations may gradually develop from 'de facto control over territory and population' to 'quasi-governmental authority'.[196] Groups are likely to establish some form of governance structure when control over territory stabilizes.[197] As one researcher pointed out, however: 'a sufficient period of relatively stable territorial control is a precondition for any insurgency attempting to contruct a civilian governance system'.[198] Such governance systems are established for different reasons, such as to gain support from the local population, to underline

[193] See also Kleffner, 'Organized Armed Groups' (n 31) 453.

[194] This was the situation, eg, in Syria in 2012 and the beginning of 2013 when armed groups only started to establish de facto control over territory and were unable to unite under one leadership structure. See Human Rights Council, *Report of the Independent International Commission of Inquiry on the Syrian Arab Republic*, A/HRC/21/50, 60–63; Human Rights Council, *Report of the Independent International Commission of Inquiry on the Syrian Arab Republic*, A/HRC/22/59, paras 12–28. In contrast, it is reported that when the Free Aceh Movement took control over parts of the Indonesian Aceh region between 1999 and 2003, the group almost immediately established government-like structures that were planned and designed during the on-going struggle and partly based on traditional societal structures. This was reported to the author in an interview with Arif Fadhillah, chairperson of the Acheh-Sumatra National Liberation Front.

[195] While the question of whether such situations amount to armed conflicts is often disputed, Murray provides the following examples for situations of de facto control outside armed conflicts: the Naxalites control over certain districts in India; Boko Haram's control over districts of Nigeria prior to 2013; gang control over parts of cities in Mexico or Brazil; the control of the Communist Party of Nepal—Maoist (CPN—M) control over parts of Nepal; or the control of the Irish Republican Army (IRA) over certain communities in Northern Ireland. Murray, *Human Rights Obligations of Non-State Armed Groups* (n 94) 142–45.

[196] For a number of additional examples of where armed groups exercised control over territory and populations, see ibid, at 1-6.

[197] eg, in the course of the Syrian conflict the 'Islamic State Group' consolidated control over different parts of Syria where they ruled with 'harsh governance methods ... based on the establishment of order through a combination of brutality and the provision of essential services, including security and employment'. See Human Rights Council, *Report of the Independent International Commission of Inquiry on the Syrian Arab Republic* (n 114) paras 16–17.

[198] Mampilly, 'Insurgent Governance in the Democratic Republic of the Congo' in Krieger (ed), *Inducing Compliance with International Humanitarian Law—Lessons from the African Great Lakes Region* (CUP 2016) 48.

their claim to independence, statehood, or being the legitimate representatives of the people, or simply because the group sees the necessity to respond to the needs of the population.[199] Consequently, it may not always be possible to draw a clear line between these two categories.

In situations in which non-state armed groups exercise control over territory and population without having established quasi-governmental authority and institutions, de facto they constitute the highest military authority in the territory under their control. Yet, because they do not have quasi-governmental infrastructure, in some instances the de jure government continues to provide some public administration functions or services. For example, during the early stages of the Syria armed conflict, reportedly the government continued to pay public officials, including teachers, who performed their functions in areas held by non-state armed groups. The Damascus government also continued to provide electricity and water.[200] Likewise, during the first months of the Ukraine conflict the Kiev government continued to operate public institutions and pay social services in areas controlled by armed groups. Even after withdrawing its institutions and most services, it continued to supply gas and electricity.[201]

From an international law prespective, such situations are highly complex. As is discussed in Section 6.4.1 'Limited state obligations to protect human rights in territory under de facto control of an armed group', even when loosing some control over territory the state continues to be responsible for protecting and fulfilling human rights—albeit to a limited extent. Thus, in order to avoid a protection gap, non-state armed groups should have human rights obligations in accordance with the degree of control they exercise and their capacities.

6.4.1 Limited state obligations to protect human rights in territory under de facto control of an armed group

As pointed out with regard to states' human rights obligations vis-à-vis persons living within their jurisdiction but in areas under the quasi-governmental control of an armed group, IHRL treaties apply throughout a state's territory even if the state has temporarily lost control over parts of it.[202] UN human rights mechanisms, as well as the ECtHR, recognized, however, that if a state no longer effectively controls parts of its territory, this affects its ability to implement IHRL in these areas. The ECtHR restricted its finding on limited state responsibility to situations in which non-state armed groups succeed in establishing 'a local authority', or a 'separatist regime' that

[199] For a discussion of groups' motivations to establish governance structures, see ibid, at 46; Fortin, *The Accountability of Armed Groups under Human Rights Law* (n 20) 43–47.
[200] See Fortin, *The Accountability of Armed Groups under Human Rights Law* (n 20) 169.
[201] See Office of the United Nations High Commissioner on Human Rights, *Report on the Human Rights Situation in Ukraine* (n 74) para 48.
[202] See Section 6.3.1 'Limited state obligations to protect human rights in territory under the control of a "separatist regime" 'above. The scope of states' protective obligations to prevent and prosecute human rights violations by armed groups is discussed in Section 6.5.1 'States' obligation to take reasonable measures to prevent and to investigate human rights violations by non-state actors' below.

is 'sustained by rebel forces, or by another State'.[203] This might not include cases in which the state loses military control temporarily without having its entire governance infrastructure removed from an area. However, in non-international armed conflicts, control over territory frequently changes, becomes disputed among the parties to the conflict, and the state may no longer be able to exercise 'effective control'[204] or face 'difficulties ... in restoring and ensuring law and order'.[205] In such situations, the state's ability to protect and fulfil human rights is severely restricted, despite the fact that state institutions sometimes continue to provide certain basic services, such as education, health, and welfare.

Despite the ECtHR restriction of its finding to specific circumstances, the approach of demanding states to take those measures that can reasonably be expected in the circumstances should be instructive. Indeed, even if states lose control over territory and population only temporarily, and militarily rather than in an out-right manner, this may still constitute 'exceptional circumstances' in which the state is prevented from exercising part of its authority in its entire territory.[206] In such situations, the state's human rights obligations should not be determined in the abstract but in accordance with the states' remaining capacity to protect and to fulfil human rights of persons in areas beyond its effective control. As Giacca pointed out, this is 'a question of degree, [which] would depend on the circumstances of the cases with regard to a number of factors, including the level of stability of the territory controlled either by a foreign power or by a non-state entity'.[207]

This approach finds support in UN human rights mechanism practice. For example, in its concluding observations on the Democratic Republic of the Congo in 2006, the Human Rights Committee took note of the fact that the state did not exercise effective control in the eastern regions of the country, but nonetheless reminded the government that 'the provisions of the Covenant and all the obligations thereunder apply to the territory in its entirety'.[208] Thus, with regard to violations committed by non-state actors, the Human Rights Committee recommended the government to 'take all necessary steps to strengthen its capacity to protect civilians in the zones of armed conflict'[209] and to inquire into violations reported to it, prosecute and punish those responsible, and grant effective reparations.[210] For its part, the UN Committee on Economic, Social, and Cultural Rights (UNCESCR) stressed in its concluding observations on Colombia that even in times of armed conflict, the Covenant requires the 'protection and promotion of all economic,

[203] *Ilaşcu and others v Moldova and Russia* (n 74) para 333.
[204] Human Rights Committee, *Concluding Observations of the Human Rights Committee: Democratic Republic of the Congo*, CCPR/C/COD/CO/3, para 4.
[205] Human Rights Committee, *Concluding Observations of the Human Rights Committee: Yemen*, CCPR/C/YEM/CO/5, para 16.
[206] *Ilaşcu and others v Moldova and Russia* (n 74) para 312.
[207] Giacca, *Economic, Social, and Cultural Rights in Armed Conflict* (n 9) 125.
[208] Human Rights Committee, *Concluding Observations of the Human Rights Committee: Democratic Republic of the Congo* (n 204) para 4.
[209] ibid, at para 13.
[210] ibid, at para 15. See also *Human Rights Committee, Concluding Observations of the Human Rights Committee: Yemen* (n 205) para 24.

social and cultural rights ... to the best of [the state's] ability under the prevailing adverse conditions'.[211] In that Committee's view, this includes taking 'all necessary measures ... to prevent the recruitment of children by illegal armed groups'.[212]

While the UNCESCR did not mention the human rights situation in areas beyond government control in its observations on Ukraine in 2014, other UN mechanisms did. For example, the Committee against Torture recommended the de jure government to 'keep thorough documentation on the victims of inhuman treatment in areas not under governmental control ... so that the State party can fully exercise its duties under the Convention when effective control is re-established'.[213] Moreover, the United Nations Human Rights Monitoring Mission in Ukraine (HRMMU) emphasized that 'the Government of Ukraine remains responsible for protecting human rights of residents in all its territory, including those territories in the East of Ukraine which remains held by armed groups'.[214] Concretely, with regard to the government's decision to withdraw state institutions from areas held by non-state armed groups, the HRMMU argued that stopping the provision of basic services, such as pensions, based on the recipients' place of residence 'violates international law'.[215]

As a result, different human rights mechanisms have clarified that states' human rights obligations apply throughout a state's territory, including with regard to areas over which a state has lost control. The scope of these obligations is, however, reduced to measures that can be reasonably expected in the circumstances. Given the great variety of practical circumstances in which states lose control over territory, the scope of obligations must be context-specific and determined on a case-by-case basis. For example, if the state continues to operate public institutions in areas temporarily held by armed groups, it retains the obligation to ensure the provision of basic services. Likewise, if the state continues to have law enforcement personnel on the ground, it has been suggested that it must take steps to prevent human rights violations and investigate alleged violations, to the degree possible. Yet, despite the continuing nature of human rights obligations, states' practical ability to prevent and to investigate human rights violations, or to ensure the enjoyment of basic economic, social, and cultural rights, would seem to be severely limited if the state lost control over territory. As is seen in Section 6.4.2 'Contemporary international practice', in such situations UN fora and human rights experts increasingly call upon non-state armed groups to respect human rights of persons under their de facto control.

[211] UN Committee on Economic, Social, and Cultural Rights, *Concluding Observations of the Committee on Economic, Social and Cultural Rights: Colombia*, 7 June 2010, E/C.12/COL/CO/5, para 7.

[212] ibid, at para 16. See also Human Rights Committee, *Concluding Observations of the Human Rights Committee: Yemen* (n 205) para 24.

[213] Committee against Torture, *Concluding Observations on the Sixth Periodic Report of Ukraine*, 12 December 2014, CAT/C/UKR/CO/6, para 11.

[214] Office of the United Nations High Commissioner for Human Rights, *Report on the Human Rights Situation in Ukraine* (n 74) para 87.

[215] United Nations Office of the High Commissioner for Human Rights, *Report on the Human Rights Situation in Ukraine* (OHCHR, 13 September 2015) para 100.

6.4.2 Contemporary international practice

UN reports on recent conflicts provide support for the argument that IHRL contains human rights obligations for non-state armed groups exercising de facto control over territory and population. For example, when the Syria crisis escalated into a non-international armed conflict during the first months of 2012, a UN Commission of Inquiry found that armed groups had gained strength and established sanctuaries in parts of the country.[216] At that time, it did not seem that these groups exercised quasi-governmental functions in such sanctuaries. Reportedly, it was only at a later stage that 'the local military powers have evolved into the semblance of a state—complete with a police force, judiciary (or Sharia council), and whatever means of income generation is available'.[217] At a time when groups did not yet exercise quasi-governmental authority, the UN Commission of Inquiry argued that armed groups 'must ... respect the fundamental human rights of persons forming customary international law (CIL), in areas where such actors exercise *de facto* control'.[218] States in the Human Rights Council welcomed the report, and 'strongly condemn[ed] ... any human rights abuses by armed opposition groups'.[219] This was done in addition to a '*call* upon the Syrian authorities to meet its responsibility to protect the Syrian population'.[220]

The findings of the HRMMU point in the same direction. Examining the human rights situation during the start of the armed conflict in Eastern Ukraine, the HRMMU identified a widening protection gap. This gap was caused by a demise of state security in combination with armed groups' increasing occupation of key public infrastructure without, however, 'undertaking any governing responsibilities'.[221] Despite the fact that non-state groups organized an independence referendum and aimed to create a territory called 'Novorossia', reportedly their control over territory and government infrastructure was not stable, but regularly changed hands during government security operations.[222] In this situation, the HRMMU identified 'serious human rights concerns ... in areas under the control of armed groups'.[223] While using careful language, such as that armed groups committed 'criminal activity resulting in human rights abuses', the Monitoring Mission also stated unambiguously that different acts 'in violation of international law ... [were] carried out by the armed groups'.[224] Later on, the Mission stated more concretely:

[216] Human Rights Council, *Report of the Independent International Commission of Inquiry on the Syrian Arab Republic* (n 194) para 26.

[217] The Carter Center, *Syria Countrywide Conflict Report #2* (Carter Center, 20 November 2013). It is questionable, however, whether most of these groups would qualify as 'exercising quasi-governmental authority' as defined in this book.

[218] Human Rights Council, *Report of the Independent International Commission of Inquiry on the Syrian Arab Republic* (n 194) annex II, para 10.

[219] Human Rights Council, *Situation of Human Rights in the Syrian Arab Republic*, 17 October 2012, A/HRC/RES/21/26, paras 1 and 4.

[220] ibid, at para 9.

[221] Office of the United Nations High Commissioner for Human Rights, *Report on the Human Rights Situation in Ukraine* (OHCHR, 15 June 2014) para 175.

[222] ibid, at paras 2 and 174. [223] ibid, at para 6. [224] ibid, at para 154.

Without prejudice to their legal status, armed groups are also obliged to respect the rights of residents who remained in areas under their control. These include protecting a minimum level of the enjoyment of economic and social rights, at the very least by facilitating humanitarian access.[225]

As shown above, the HRMMU invoked these obligations in addition to the de jure government's obligation to protect and to fulfil human rights obligations 'in all its territory'.[226]

A borderline example between the exercise of 'de facto control over territory' and 'quasi-governmental authority' has been the more than twenty-five years of 'Liberation Tigers of Tamil Eelam' (LTTE) control over parts of Sri Lanka. Reportedly, in the early years of the conflict, the government continued to provide public security though police and justice institutions in LTTE-held territory.[227] As its control over territory stabilized, the LTTE set up 'pseudo-state institutions', which provided a number of public services through 'its own police, jails, courts, immigration department, banks and some social services'.[228] However, an Office of the United Nations High Commissioner for Human Rights (OHCHR) Investigation on Sri Lanka also remarked that '[p]aradoxically, Colombo-appointed Government Agents continued to work in LTTE controlled areas, even to the end of the conflict to deliver government services such as health and education'.[229] With regard to this situation, a UN Panel of Experts asserted:

> [I]t is now increasingly accepted that non-state groups exercising *de facto* control over a part of a State's territory must respect fundamental human rights of persons in that territory.[230]

In such circumstances, it would be reasonable to require the state to provide education and health in accordance with its human rights obligations. Practially, however, the state's ability to enforce law and order in LTTE-controlled areas was limited.[231]

An emphasis on a link between human rights obligations of armed groups and their control over territory and population is also found in the Security Council's approach to human rights violations by armed groups—for example, as committed by different rebel groups in eastern parts of the Democratic Republic of the Congo.[232]

[225] Office of the United Nations High Commissioner for Human Rights, *Report on the Human Rights Situation in Ukraine,* 15 December 2014, para 54.

[226] ibid, at para 87.

[227] See Mampilly, *Rebel Rules—Insurgent Governance and Civilian Lifeduring War* (Cornell University Press 2011) 109. For a good analysis of different aspects of LTTE rule in Sri Lanka, see Fortin, *The Accountability of Armed Groups under Human Rights Law* (n 20) 168.

[228] United Nations Secretary General, *Report of the Secretary General's Panel of Experts on Accountability in Sri Lanka* (n 18) para 33. See also Human Rights Council, *Report of the OHCHR Investigation on Sri Lanka (OISL)*, A/HRC/30/CRP.2, para 151.

[229] Human Rights Council, *Report of the OHCHR Investigation on Sri Lanka (OISL)* (n 229) para 152.

[230] United Nations Secretary General, *Report of the Secretary General's Panel of Experts on Accountability in Sri Lanka* (n 19) para. 188.

[231] eg, prosecuting cases of extrajudicial killings was severely hampered in situations where suspects escaped into LTTE-controlled areas, which the government's police were unable to enter. See United Nations Commission on Human Rights, *Extrajudicial, Summary or Arbitrary Executions: Report of the Special Rapporteur*, Philip Alston (n 54) para 34.

[232] For a good analysis, see Constantinides, 'Obligations and Accountability of Armed Opposition Groups' (n 2) 101–02.

To sum up, situations of armed conflicts in which armed groups exercise de facto control over at least some territory include a broad range of factual scenarios. The size of territory and its nature—rural areas, villages, or major cities—vary, and so does the capacity of armed groups to govern territory under their de facto control through law enforcement and public administration infrastructure. Likewise, the degree of the de jure government's ability to protect and to fulfil human rights vis-à-vis individuals in such territories is highly context-dependent. What these situations have in common, however, is that the state has lost at least its position as the factual authority in that territory and is unable to enforce its laws against the will of the non-state armed group. In such situations, it has been argued that it is 'increasingly accepted' or a 'widely accepted understanding'[233] that non-state armed groups have certain human rights obligations. The question of the nature and scope of these obligations is discussed in Section 6.4.3 'Conceptual considerations'.

6.4.3 Conceptual considerations

If we return to what many hold to be the essence of human rights law, namely the protection of individuals from a government or other authorities, prima facie this concept also encompasses non-state armed groups that de facto control territory and population. After all, when gaining control over territory, an armed group establishes itself as the de facto highest authority. In such territory, the armed group constitutes the greatest threat to individuals' rights and should be the peoples' primary protector. Yet, commentators have interpreted this authority–subject relationship differently. Following a narrow reading, it has been argued that by merely taking control over territory these groups may not exercise 'effective power' in a government-like manner and consequently fall outside the 'human rights equation'.[234] In contrast, the OHCHR's view is that:

> the application of human rights standards to non-State actors is particularly relevant in situations where they exercise some degree of control over a given territory and population. . . .. Indeed, the assumption of international human rights responsibilities by non-State actors is seen as a pragmatic recognition of the realities of a conflict, without which rights holders would lose out on any practicable claim to their human rights.[235]

The High Commissioner's argument is even more convincing if human rights are understood primarily as individual entitlements that may not be violated and less as state obligations vis-à-vis their subjects.[236]

[233] See, eg, Human Rights Committee, *The International Commission of Inquiry on the Central African Republic —Final Report* (n 49) para 41.

[234] See Rodley, 'Non-State Actors' (n 29) 532.

[235] United Nations Office of the High Commissioner for Human Rights, *International Legal Protection of Human Rights in Armed Conflict* (n 187) 25.

[236] See, eg, Philip Alston in United Nations Human Rights Commission, *Extrajudicial, Summary or Arbitrary Executions: Report of the Special Rapporteur*, Philip Alston (n 54) para 27; Clapham, *Human Rights Obligations of Non-State Actors* (n 2) 25–58.

Accepting that non-state armed groups exercising de facto territorial control have some IHRL obligations necessarily poses the question of the obligations' source. As discussed above, few IHRL treaties contain human rights obligations for armed groups—most do not. Yet, if IHRL treaty obligations are considered to devolve with territory, IHRL treaties applicable in a territory could bind a group that exercises de facto territorial control.[237] Persons living under the de facto control of non-state armed groups should not be deprived of their human rights.[238] While the 'continuation of rights' argument applies to the present situation, it is less clear to what extent the 'continuation of obligation' argument does. On the one hand, if an armed group exercises de facto control over territory and population, the most effective option might be to require this entity to respect the IHRL treaties applicable in the territory under its control. On the other hand, the principle of the continuation of treaty obligations has been developed with regard to situations in which either a new government takes power in an existing state, or a new state is established in accordance with international law. While this principle might also be applied where armed groups exercise quasi-governmental authority in a defined territory, situations in which groups only exercise some degree of military control over territory are different. For example, as, in many cases, both the de jure government and the armed groups would need to have some human rights obligations, it could not be argued that all treaty obligations would devolve to the non-state armed group. Rather, the group should only assume some obligations complementing those of the state. Moreover, as discussed in further detail below, armed groups without state-like abilities may not be able to comply with the broad scope of IHRL treaty obligations.

An alternative source of human rights obligations is customary IHRL.[239] As explained above,[240] to this end it must be determined whether armed groups exercising de facto control over territory and population have sufficient 'international legal personality' to be bound by certain IHRL norms.[241] It has been argued that international law recognizes some legal personality on the part of armed groups if they become party to a non-international armed conflict (NIAC). For example, if Common Article 3 applies to groups as a matter of treaty law, this would subject the group 'to direct cognition by the international legal order'.[242] Moreover, territorial control has been identified as an 'indicator of an armed group's "legal personality" under international law'.[243] Thus, it can be argued that if an armed group gains de facto control over parts of a state's territory and population in the course of an armed

[237] For further discussion, see Section 6.3.3.1 'Binding non-state armed groups by IHRL treaties' above.

[238] United Nations Office of the High Commissioner for Human Rights, *International Legal Protection of Human Rights in Armed Conflict* (n 187) 25.

[239] As seen above, this view was explicitly taken by the UN Commission of Inquiry on Syria. See Human Rights Council, *Report of the Independent International Commission of Inquiry on the Syrian Arab Republic* (n 194) annex II, para 10.

[240] See section 6.3.3.2 'Binding non-state armed groups by customary IHRL' above.

[241] ibid.

[242] Murray, 'How International Humanitarian Law Treaties Bind Non-State Armed Groups' (n 27) 9.

[243] Fortin, *The Accountability of Armed Groups under Human Rights Law* (n 20) 343.

conflict, it is likely to have sufficient legal personality to bear not only customary IHL but also customary IHRL obligations.[244] In addition, Tomuschat argued:

> A movement struggling to become the legitimate government of the nation concerned is treated by the international community as an actor who, already at his embryonic stage, is subject to the essential obligations and responsibilities every State must shoulder in the interest of a civilized state of affairs among nations.[245]

The rather vague references to 'essential obligations and responsibilities',[246] or to 'fundamental human rights of persons'[247] that may include 'a minimum level of the enjoyment of economic and social rights'[248] lead to the question of the scope of these obligations.

6.4.4 The scope of obligations

As previously remarked, international practice rarely defines which human rights norms bind armed groups. While groups with state-like capacities and exclusive control over territory should be expected to respect, protect, and fulfil a wide scope of IHRL, this might not be the case for armed groups exercising de facto control over territory and population during an armed conflict. These groups' capacity to protect or to fulfil human rights might be low, for example, because their internal organization is primarily designed to engage in hostilities and maintain discipline. Moreover, if such groups exercise military control over territory, the territorial government may still be providing certain services to the population—sometimes including maintenance of law and order—and continue to have some IHRL obligations vis-à-vis the individuals living under the armed group's control. Consequently, the armed group's limited capacities combined with the state's continuing IHRL obligations suggest a narrower scope of obligations as compared to armed groups that exercise quasi-governmental authority. In this respect, the idea that all obligations binding the state authorities under IHRL treaty law devolve to the non-state de facto authorities might be too broad: the group has not established itself as an entity akin to a new government. Likewise, it might not be feasible to require these groups to respect, protect, and fulfil the full scope of customary IHRL.[249]

[244] This argument could justify IHRL obligations that are analogous to IHL obligations. However, the argument that an armed group has sufficient personality to bear IHL obligations would not necessarily mean that it also has sufficient personality to bear a broad scope of IHRL obligations.

[245] Tomuschat, 'Insurgent Movements' (n 2) 587. While this finding could be understood as limited to groups that indeed seek to become the legitimate government of a nation and establish ab initio government-like infrastructure, the different contexts with regard to which Tomuschat made this finding does not suggest a narrow reading. See ibid, at 577–85.

[246] ibid, at 587.

[247] United Nations Secretary General, *Report of the Secretary General's Panel of Experts on Accountability in Sri Lanka* (n 19) para 188.

[248] Office of the United Nations High Commissioner on Human Rights, *Report on the Human Rights Situation in Ukraine* (n 225) para 54.

[249] As Murray emphasized, 'Subjecting armed groups to obligations that they are incapable of fulfilling will not only contradict the principle of effectiveness, but it may also affect groups' perceptions in relation to the credibility of international law itself, undermining respect for other binding obligations.' Murray, *Human Rights Obligations of Non-State Armed Groups* (n 94) 172.

A first approach that takes into account the group's capacity and responds to some needs of the population under its control could be requiring armed groups to respect norms of IHRL that are equally found in IHL of NIAC.[250] The principal strength of this approach is that if a group can be expected to comply with a norm under one field of international law, it can similarly do so under another field of law. Moreover, IHL was designed for conflict situations in which territorial control shifts between the parties and therefore takes this challenge into account. Indeed, different examples exist in which the Security Council or other UN bodies call on armed groups to respect IHL and IHRL, and limit their examination of facts to violations of norms that exist in both fields.[251] If the view is taken that IHL applies to all acts committed by armed groups when occupying territory, this approach would provide limited additional protection. In contrast, if it was concluded that governance acts by armed groups do not fall within the scope of IHL, the approach of applying IHRL norms that also exist in IHL would at least extend IHL protections to all acts that would be prohibited under IHL but arguably fall outside its scope of application.[252] In that case, IHRL could regulate a group's use of force in law enforcement operations in territory under its control. Moreover, a group would be prohibited from arbitrarily detaining or ill-treating persons living in territory under its control for reasons unrelated to the conflict, such as stealing or domestic violence. Likewise, intra-party violence such as torture or rape would undoubtedly be prohibited.[253]

A second approach could focus on a number of essential customary IHRL obligations. These could consist, first, of non-derogable civil and political rights, which apply in any situation, including armed conflicts.[254] Arguably, most also constitute peremptory norms of international law.[255] These basic civil and political

[250] See Rodley, 'Can Armed Opposition Groups Violate Human Rights?' (n 3) 312. Indeed, it can be argued that respect of IHL, which protects civilians and civilian objects, goes a long way in simultaneously protecting the human rights of persons under an armed group's control.

[251] A case in point was also the approach taken by the UN Secretary General's Panel of Experts on Accountability in Sri Lanka. In the report, the experts explained that they had not addressed 'human rights violations beyond those that it has characterized as violations of international humanitarian law'. United Nations Secretary General, *Report of the Secretary General's Panel of Experts on Accountability in Sri Lanka* (n 19) para 243.

[252] IHL regulates conduct that has a nexus to the conflict. See *Kunarac et al, IT-96-23& IT-96-23/1-A*, para 57. The question of the requisite nexus between a crime and an armed conflict is normally discussed in the international criminal law context. See, eg, Mettraux, *International Crimes and the 'Ad Hoc' Tribunals* (OUP 2006); Werle, *Principles of International Criminal Law* (TMC Asser Press 2005); Cryer, Hakan, Robinson et al, *An Introduction to International Criminal Law* (CUP 2014) 232 et sec.

[253] See also Clapham, 'Where are We Now?' (n 9) 5. For discussion of whether IHL applies to intra-party violence, see Rodenhäuser, 'Squaring the Circle? Prosecuting Sexual Violence against Child Soldiers by their "Own Forces" '(2016) Journal of International Criminal Justice 171–93.

[254] See article 4(2) ICCPR, article 27(2) ACHR, article 15(2) ECHR, article 4(2) Arab Charter on Human Rights, ECHR. For further discussion, see Human Rights Committee, *General Comment No 29: States of Emergency (article 4)*, 31 August 2001, CCPR/C/21/Rev.1/Add.11, para 3; Rodenhäuser, 'Fundamental Standards of Humanity: How International Law Regulates Internal Strife' (2013) 26 Journal for International Law of Peace and Armed Conflict 121–130.

[255] For further discussion on peremptory norms or jus cogens, see Section 6.5.4 'The scope of obligations' below.

rights need to be complemented by economic, social, and cultural rights (ESC rights). As the UN Committee on Economic, Social, and Cultural Rights argued:

> [E]ven in a situation of armed conflict, fundamental human rights must be respected [.....] [B]asic economic, social and cultural rights, as part of the minimum standards of human rights, are guaranteed under customary international law and are also prescribed by international humanitarian law.[256]

However, it remains unclear which ESC rights form part of customary IHRL.[257] Depending on the scope of customary IHRL, the added value of such obligations could be limited if similar obligations apply under applicable IHL.[258] Yet, it seems that the scope of customary ESC rights is broader than that foreseen in IHL with regard to NIACs.[259] Thus, requiring armed groups to comply with customary IHRL—for example, as found in the UDHR—could be legally sound and add a layer of protection in practice.[260]

However, it may not always be feasible to require armed groups with de facto control over territory and population to respect, protect, and fulfil all customary human rights. For example, groups might be factually unable to protect human rights, or to work towards their progressive realization—even if they install themselves as the de facto authority in a territory. Nonetheless, any group can at least be required not to interfere with, to facilitate the individual's enjoyment, and sometimes also to provide for certain human rights.[261] They can respect civil and political rights.[262] In practice, this could mean that such groups should be required to abstain from obstructing existing educational systems or humanitarian relief, facilitate the latter's delivery, or provide basic services for detainees.[263] Thus, they should be held

[256] UN Committee on Economic, Social, and Cultural Rights, *Concluding Observations of the Committee on Economic, Social and Cultural Rights: Israel*, 26 June 2003, E/C.12/1/Add.90, para 31.

[257] For detailed discussion of this question, see Giacca, *Economic, Social, and Cultural Rights in Armed Conflict* (n 9) 260–64.

[258] eg, customary IHL requires all parties to 'allow and facilitate rapid and unimpeded passage of humanitarian relief for civilians in need' and foresees special respect and protection for vulnerable groups, such as women, children, the elderly, or disabled. See rules 55, 134, 135, 138 of the ICRC Customary IHL Study. See Doswald-Beck, L and J-M Henckaerts, *Customary International Humanitarian Law* (CUP 2005). Moreover, eg, article 3(a) APII requires that children 'shall receive an education'. These rights to food or to education are also regulated under IHRL, see articles 11 and 13 of the International Covenant for Economic, Social, and Cultural Rights (ICESCR).

[259] See Giacca, *Economic, Social, and Cultural Rights in Armed Conflict* (n 9) 260–64.

[260] Murray suggests a broader approach, arguing that norms as found in the ICCPR and the ICESCR should apply because of their nature as erga omnes obligations. See Murray, *Human Rights Obligations of Non-State Armed Groups* (n 94) 145–48.

[261] For discussion of what the obligation to respect may entail, see ibid, at 183–86. For a contrary view emphasizing that all human rights compliance requires the 'existence of an organisational apparatus exercising public functions and capable of securing human rights', see Ronen, 'Non-State Actors' (n 29) 27.

[262] This is obvious for the prohibition of torture, extrajudicial deprivations of life, or freedom of movement. In contrast, the prohibition of arbitrary detention or the right to a fair trial require some infrastructure to be implemented. Without entering into details, approaches to respect these rights could be to implement them with the means at the group's disposal, meaning, eg, bringing persons before tribunals established by the group respecting the requisite fair-trial guarantees. If the group lacks this infrastructure, it should not detain persons except to the extent permissible under IHL.

[263] Yet, as scholars highlighted, restricting obligations to a duty to respect might be too strict. Armed groups will also be able to comply with basic elements of the obligation to fulfil—eg, by facilitating access

accountable if they do not comply with these basic obligations. For instance, the UN International Commission of Inquiry on the Central African Republic held that 'forcible transfer of population and the destruction of houses ... clearly constitute violations of the right to adequate housing', and that the sectarian violence committed by both parties to the conflict 'put in great jeopardy' the 'rights to food, water and access to health services'.[264]

Just as states' human rights obligations decrease if they lose territorial control and the necessary means to protect and fulfil human rights, the scope of human rights obligations of armed groups should increase in accordance with their degree of power and capacity.[265] As seen in the examples above, groups exercising de facto control over territory and population range from those that have just conquered a village to those that have occupied certain territory for years without being able to establish quasi-governmental infrastructure. This diversity means that the scope of IHRL obligations of armed groups cannot be static but varies according to the group's capacities and the circumstances in which it operates. To put it simply: the greater the degree of control over territory and population, and the greater the group's capacities, the greater should be its human rights obligations. Such an interpretation of the application of a potentially sophisticated body of law in difficult circumstances has, for example, been suggested by the ICRC with regard to the application of the laws of occupation. The ICRC argues:

> The law of occupation comprises both negative and positive obligations. Negative obligations, such as the prohibition to deport protected persons outside the occupied territory, apply immediately, whereas positive obligations, the vast majority of them being obligations of means, would take effect over time according to the level of control exerted, the constraints prevailing in the initial phases of the occupation, and the resources available to the foreign forces.[266]

In analogy, a model would make sense under which the obligation to respect customary IHRL applies at all times, and obligations to protect and to fulfil human rights become progressively applicable. Like states, armed groups should take steps

to food or health care. As Giacca argued, 'it could be reasonable to expect that entity to ensure at least the right of access to the existing health facilities on a non-discriminatory basis, or that it provides essential drugs. However, it would be difficult to expect the entity to adopt and implement a territorial "public health strategy and plan of action" addressing the health concerns of the whole population .....' Giacca, *Economic, Social, and Cultural Rights in Armed Conflict* (n 9) 244–45. Likewise, Murray points out that armed groups should be required to fulfil human rights by facilitating or calling for humanitarian relief, or by providing basic services for detainees. Murray, *Human Rights Obligations of Non-State Armed Groups* (n 94) 189–90. See also Fortin, *The Accountability of Armed Groups under Human Rights Law* (n 20) 59–62.

264 Human Rights Committee, *The International Commission of Inquiry on the Central African Republic—Final Report* (n 49) paras 517–18.

265 The idea that human rights obligations can be 'divided and tailored' according to the circumstances has received support in human rights law jurisprudence. See Luban, 'State Criminality and the Ambition of International Criminal Law' in Isaacs and Vernon (eds), *Accountability for Collective Wrongdoing* (CUP 2011) 61–91; International Court of Justice, *Legal Consequences of the Construction of a Wall in the Occupied Palestinian Territories (Advisory Opinion), International Court of Justice, Advisory Opinion, 9 July 2004,* ICJ, para 112.

266 ICRC, *GCI: Commentary of 2016* (n 132) article 2, para 131.

to protect and to fulfil human rights 'to the maximum of [their] available resources' to ensure at least 'minimum essential levels' of every applicable human right.[267]

6.5 Human Rights Obligations of Groups Not Controlling Territory and Population

The third category of armed groups consists of those not controlling territory and population, either de facto or in a quasi-governmental manner. In principle, the scope of groups falling within this category could comprise any group that violates individuals' human rights, such as ordinary criminals, terrorist groups, the mafia, or organized armed groups engaged in a non-international armed conflict without exercising territorial control. Such groups operate in times of peace or in times of armed conflict. In times of armed conflict, non-state parties to the conflict are bound by IHL, which requires all parties to respect certain fundamental humanitarian guarantees. Commentators rightly emphasize that IHRL obligations of armed groups are especially relevant in crisis situations where IHL does not apply; these can be categorized broadly as internal disturbances and tensions, including violence prior to an armed conflict, or post-conflict situations.[268] Thus, this section looks especially at situations outside armed conflicts, or acts not necessarily being sufficiently linked to a conflict in order to exclude that possible obligations stem from IHL.

6.5.1 States' obligation to take reasonable measures to prevent and to investigate human rights violations by non-state actors

If states exercise control over their entire territory, they have the obligation to respect, protect, and fulfil human rights as required under applicable treaty and customary law. Human rights violations by private actors engage primarily states' obligation to protect human rights. This obligation comprises different measures. In addition to prohibiting private human rights violations and establishing a law enforcement infrastructure, protective duties include preventing violations, investigating them if they occur, prosecuting the perpetrators, and providing redress for the victims.[269] Among these different aspects of states' obligation to protect human rights, 'it is inescapable to conclude that the quintessence of protection concerns the *prevention* of

[267] UN Committee on Economic, Social, and Cultural Rights, *General Comment No 3: The Nature of States Parties' Obligations (article 2, para 1)*, 14 December 1990, E/1991/23, para 10.

[268] See discussion in the introduction to Part II of this book.

[269] See Human Rights Committee, *General Comment No 31: Nature of the General Legal Obligation Imposed on States Parties to the Covenant* (n 73) para 8; *Osman v The United Kingdom, Application no 87/1997/871/1083*, para 115. These obligations are also found in the 'Basic Principles and Guidelines on the Right to a Remedy and Reparation for Victims of Gross Violations of International Human Rights Law and Serious Violations of International Humanitarian Law' as adopted by the General Assembly in 2006. See United Nations General Assembly, *Basic Principles and Guidelines on the Right to a Remedy and Reparation for Victims of Gross Violations of International Human Rights Law and Serious Violations of International Humanitarian Law*, 16 December 2006, A/Res/60/147.

human rights violations'.[270] Thus, the main focus of this section is on the scope of state's obligation to prevent human rights violations. The obligation to investigate shall also be briefly examined. These obligations also apply—to the extent feasible—if states no longer control all of their territory.

6.5.1.1 The obligation to prevent human rights violations

The classic test to determine whether a state complies with its obligation to prevent human rights violations has been developed by the ECtHR in the *Osman* case with regard to the right to life. The European Court held that in order to determine a violation, it must be established that:

> the authorities *knew or ought to have known* at the time of the existence of a *real and immediate risk* to the life of an identified individual or individuals from the criminal acts of a third party and that they *failed to take measures within the scope of their powers* which, judged reasonably, might have been expected to avoid that risk.[271]

At the same time, the European Court emphasized that human rights violations are often unpredictable, that states retain 'operational choices' in terms of 'priorities and resources', and that positive obligations should not be interpreted as imposing 'an impossible or disproportionate burden on the authorities'.[272]

While this test was originally developed in the ECHR's *espace juridique*, the Inter-American Court of Human Rights applied the *Osman* test in its own jurisprudence and the UN Human Rights Committee used related criteria.[273] Subsequent practice and scholarship also suggests that the test applies not only to threats to the right to life but also, more generally, to states' obligation to prevent human rights violations.[274] The *Osman* test consists of three determinative factors: first, the state

[270] Xenos, *The Positive Obligations of the State under the European Committee of Human Rights* (Routledge 2012) 97.

[271] *Osman v The United Kingdom* (n 269) para 116 (emphasis added).

[272] ibid. Moreover, measures must be in accordance with states' other human rights obligations.

[273] See, eg, *Pueblo Bello Massacre v Colombia, Judgment, 31 January 2006,* IACtHR, para 123; *González et al ('Cotton Field') v Mexico, Judgment, 16 November 2009,* IACtHR, para 280. Back in 1990, the Human Rights Committee found in the *William Eduardo Delgado Páez v Colombia* situation that '[i]t cannot be the case that, as a matter of law, States can ignore known threats to the life of persons under their jurisdiction. .... States parties are under an obligation to take reasonable and appropriate measures to protect them.' *William Eduardo Delgado Páez v Colombia, 23 August 1990, CCPR/C/39/D/195/1985,* para 5.5. In contrast, the African Commission's jurisprudence is less coherent. In a first case, it suggested a relatively high test for state responsibility, requiring that the state 'can be held complicit where it fails systematically to provide protection of violations from private actors who deprive any person of his/her human rights', meaning that it 'condones a pattern of abuse through pervasive non-action'. Single human rights violations by private individuals would not suffice to engage the state's responsibility. *Zimbabwe Human Rights NGO Forum v Zimbabwe, 245/02,* para 160. Later, it seems to change its jurisprudence towards the '*Osman* test', explaining that a state is required to take 'tangible measures to prevent the immediate risks of perpetration of the said acts'. *Association of Victims of Post Electoral Violence & INTERIGHTS v Cameroon, Judgment, 25 November 2009, 272/03,* AComHPR, para 90.

[274] The Inter-American Court of Human Rights (IACtHR) did not formulate the test in a manner restricted to the right to life. See *Pueblo Bello Massacre v Colombia* (n 273) para 123; *González et al ('Cotton Field') v Mexico* (n 273) para 280. See also Joseph and Castan, *The International Covenant on Civil and Political Rights: Cases, Materials, and Commentary* (3rd edn, OUP 2013) paras 1.112–1.113;

had or should have had knowledge of, second, a real and immediate risk of a human rights violation caused by a non-state actor and, third, failed to take reasonable measures within its power to avoid the risk. There is little doubt that non-state armed groups can pose a real and immediate risk to individuals' human rights.[275] It cannot, however, be expected that states will foresee every armed attack by non-state forces in fragile security situations when the risk of attacks is generally high.[276] Yet, states cannot pretend they did not know of a risk, or ignore indications. Case law suggests that even during armed conflicts a state's responsibility is engaged if it fails to act in situations where a threat was reasonably foreseeable.[277]

If the state knows, or ought to have known, of an immediate and real risk posed by a non-state armed group, IHRL requires the state to take 'reasonable'[278] or 'appropriate'[279] measures, within its power, to avoid the risk being realized. What is reasonable or appropriate in specific circumstances requires an analysis of the situation at stake, including the seriousness of the threat, the right to be protected, and the capacities of the state, as well as its priorities and resources.[280] Therefore, in deciding which measures to take, IHRL leaves a margin of appreciation to the state.[281]

and Pisillo Mazzeschi, *Responsabilité de l'Etat pour Violation des Obligations Positives Relatives aux Droits de l'Homme* (Brill 2008) 407–08; Krähenmann, 'Positive Obligations in Human Rights Treaties' (PhD thesis 2012) 371–72. But see Zegveld, *Accountability of Armed Opposition Groups* (n 71) 193–94. At the time, she argued that this standard would only apply to cases with government acquiescence or involvement.

275 A number of indicators exists to determine such risk. See, eg, *Kilic v Turkey, Judgment, 28 March 2000, Application no 22492/93,* ECtHR, para 65; *Mahmut Kaya v Turkey, Judgment, 28 March 2000, Application no 22535/93,* ECtHR; *Case of Ergi v Turkey, Applciation no 66/1997/850/1057,* para 80.

276 See, eg, *Belkiza Kaya and others v Turkey, Application nos 33420/96 and 36206/97,* paras 80–85. As Krähenmenn asserts: 'The threshold to hold states accountable for abuses committed by rebel forces is high since under normal circumstances the state authorities were neither aware nor should have been aware of a "real and immediate" risk against particular individuals despite the increased risk due to a general situation of violence.' Krähenmann, 'Positive Obligations in Human Rights Law during Armed Conflicts' in Kolb and Gaggioli (eds), *Research Handbook on Human Rights and Humanitarian Law* (Edward Elgar 2013) 170–87, 175, particularly n 110.

277 See *Pueblo Bello Massacre v Colombia* (n 273) paras 134–40. A 'should-have-known' standard was also applied by the ICJ with regard to states' obligation to prevent genocide. See *Case concerning Application of the Convention on the Prevention and Punishment of the Crime of Genocide (Bosnia and Herzegovina v Serbia and Montenegro)* (n 148) paras 436 and 438. For further discussions, see Doswald-Beck, *Human Rights in Times of Conflict and Terrorism* (n 72) 180–84; Vermeulen, *Enforced Disappearance: Determining State Responsibility under the International Convention for the Protection of all Persons from Enforced Disappearance* (Intersentia 2012) 420; Zegveld, *Accountability of Armed Opposition Groups* (n 71) 191–92.

278 The standard of reasonableness forms part of the *Osman* test as applied in human rights jurisprudence. See n 273 above.

279 United Nations General Assembly, *Basic Principles and Guidelines on the Right to a Remedy and Reparation for Victims of Gross Violations of International Human Rights Law and Serious Violations of International Humanitarian Law* (n 269) para 3(a).

280 See Hakimi, 'State Bystander Responsibility' (n 95) 373 and 380; Kamminga, '"Due diligence" Mania: The Misguided Introduction of an Extraneous Concept into Human Rights Discourse' (2011) Maastricht Faculty of Law Working Paper No 2011/07, 3; International Law Association, *ILA Study Group on Due Diligence in International Law: First Report* (ILA 2014) 3.

281 See *Plattform Ärzte für das Leben v Austria, Judgment, 21 June 1988, Application no 10126/82,* ECtHR. Courts normally judge the overall appropriateness of a state's action. See *Mrs W v the United Kingdom, Application no 9348/81,* paras 13–15; *Kilic v Turkey* (n 275) para 75; *Belkiza Kaya and others v Turkey* (n 276) para 82; *Ituango Massacres v Colombia, Judgment, 1 July 2006,* IACtHR, paras 134–35; *Pueblo Bello Massacre v Colombia* (n 273) para 138. As Hakimi pointed out correctly: 'According states

Among the different pertinent factors to determine whether reasonable action was taken, the biggest variable is the state's capacity to prevent effectively armed groups from committing human rights violations. Inevitably, this capacity 'varies greatly from one State to another',[282] and positive human rights obligations cannot require states to perform operations that are impossible or disproportionate.[283] Especially in situations of turmoil or conflict, security forces might be challenged by non-state actors on different fronts,[284] and the size or the nature of territory in which armed groups operate can make effective government responses difficult.[285] Moreover, as the UNCESCR emphasized in its concluding observations on Afghanistan in 2010, if a state

> has been ravaged by armed conflicts for over three decades, in which it has experienced destruction of institutions and infrastructure [this] is seriously impeding the implementation of the rights enshrined in the Covenant.[286]

As a result, even if a state knows of a real and immediate threat of human rights violations, it may be objectively unable take effective preventive measures.

Outside armed conflict, human rights protection is especially weak in states with poor governance and security structures.[287] If states are fragile, the human rights situation is often marked by the authorities' inability 'to effectively perform one or other of the basic state functions—namely to provide security and ensure well-being and the rule of law'.[288] It has been argued that, in such situations, human rights 'can offer at best peripheral protection'.[289] Indeed, in the extreme situation in which state

some discretion makes sense because states are, in the first instance, best situated to assess and respond to particular instances of abuse. Given the range of possible circumstances and measures, international law cannot possibly specify the measures that states must take in every obligation-to-protect scenario. But the obligation would be meaningless if states had complete discretion to define their own conduct.' Hakimi, 'State Bystander Responsibility' (n 95) 372.

[282] *Case concerning Application of the Convention on the Prevention and Punishment of the Crime of Genocide (Bosnia and Herzegovina v Serbia and Montenegro)* (n 148) para 431.

[283] *Osman v The United Kingdom* (n 269) para 116. At the same time, the African Commission on Human and Peoples' Rights stressed that 'this need not be inconsistent with maintaining some minimum requirements'. *Zimbabwe Human Rights NGO Forum v Zimbabwe* (n 273) para 155. See also *Ilaşcu and others v Moldova and Russia* (n 74) para 334.

[284] See *Pueblo Bello Massacre v Colombia* (n 273) para 134.

[285] See United Nations Commission on Human Rights, *Report of the Special Rapporteur on Extrajudicial, Summary or Arbitrary Executions, Philip Alston: Mission to the Democratic Republic of the Congo*, 14 June 2010, A/HRC/14/24/Add.3, para 20. Looking at the situation in the eastern Democratic Republic of the Congo, he emphasized: 'The difficulties in achieving such civilian protection cannot be overstated. They include difficult terrain, sometimes inaccessible villages, severe resource constraints, and rebels bent on destruction.'

[286] Committee on Economic, Social, and Cultural Rights, *Concluding Observations of the Committee on Economic, Social and Cultural Rights—Afghanistan*, 7 June 2010, E/C.12/AFG/CO/2-4, para 12.

[287] Developing states, or those whose capacities are temporarily restrained, in certain circumstances cannot be held to the same standard as a strong state with well-developed and functioning justice and law-enforcement institutions. For treaty body practice on this point, see Hakimi, 'State Bystander Responsibility' (n 95) 375.

[288] Geiss, 'Armed Violence in Fragile States: Low-Intensity Conflicts, Spillover Conflicts, and Sporadic Law Enforcement Operations by Third Parties' (2009) 91 International Review of the Red Cross 130.

[289] Thürer, 'The "Failed State" and International Law' (1999) 81 International Review of the Red Cross 731–61, 9. See also Zegveld, *Accountability of Armed Opposition Groups* (n 71) 210.

institutions have collapsed, or are unable to exercise control over parts of the territory, the state's ability to protect human rights is largely ineffective.[290] Still, states have to protect human rights to the extent possible in the circumstances.[291] In this respect, Hakimi rightly concluded:

> Defining reasonableness in part based on capacity would enjoin all states to make concerted efforts to restrain abusers, without requiring them to do that which they genuinely cannot.[292]

As a result, although the capacity of a government appears to be 'generally accepted as a valid factor in determining due diligence',[293] pleading incapacity cannot easily relieve states of their human rights obligations. As the International Court of Justice argued with regard to the obligation to prevent genocide, states have the obligation to make 'the best effort within their power' to prevent such events.[294]

6.5.1.2 The obligation to investigate alleged human rights violations

Realistically, states are not always in a position to prevent human rights violations committed by non-state armed groups. As Doswald-Beck aptly analysed with regard to human rights protection during armed conflicts:

> [T]he fact that many people are likely to be attacked means that specific means of protection for particular unnamed individuals may not be the relevant issue, but rather whether subsequent behavior by the authorities, in particular lack of investigation, showed a lack of appropriate effort.[295]

As part of their positive obligations in cases of gross human rights violations, states have the duty to 'investigate violations effectively, promptly, thoroughly and impartially and, where appropriate, take action against those allegedly responsible in accordance with domestic and international law'.[296] Like a state's obligation to

[290] Nonetheless, even in such extreme situations international practice suggests that states—as the bare minimum of the obligation to protect human rights—have to develop the requisite structures and abilities to resume their protective functions. See, eg, United Nations Security Council, *Preliminary Report of the International Commission of Inquiry on the Central African Republic, Submitted Pursuant to Security Council Resolution 2127 (2013)*, 26 June 2014, S/2014/373, paras 120 and 124; see also Human Rights Committee, *Concluding Observations of the Human Rights Committee: Democratic Republic of the Congo* (n 204).

[291] See also Zegveld, *Accountability of Armed Opposition Groups* (n 71) 183; Hakimi, 'State Bystander Responsibility' (n 95); International Law Association, *ILA Study Group on Due Diligence in International Law: First Report* (n 280). For criticism of the due diligence standard, see Kamminga, '"Due Diligence" Mania: The Misguided Introduction of an Extraneous Concept into Human Rights Discourse' (n 280).

[292] Hakimi, 'State Bystander Responsibility' (n 95) 376.

[293] International Law Association, *ILA Study Group on Due Diligence in International Law: First Report* (n 280) 31.

[294] Consequently, the ICJ dismissed Serbia's claim of incapacity to prevent genocide. See *Case concerning Application of the Convention on the Prevention and Punishment of the Crime of Genocide (Bosnia and Herzegovina v Serbia and Montenegro)* (n 148) para 438.

[295] Doswald-Beck, *Human Rights in Times of Conflict and Terrorism* (n 72) 183–84.

[296] United Nations General Assembly, *Basic Principles and Guidelines on the Right to a Remedy and Reparation for Victims of Gross Violations of International Human Rights Law and Serious Violations of International Humanitarian Law* (n 269) para 3(b). In case law, human rights bodies have elaborated on a number of requirements that investigations and prosecutions have to fulfil. See, eg, *Velasquez*

prevent human rights violations, the obligation to investigate and to prosecute them requires the application of 'all available legal means'.[297] In this respect, human rights mechanisms have appreciated 'the difficult circumstances'[298] faced by a country during internal armed conflicts and that such situations may impede 'the search for conclusive evidence in the domestic criminal proceedings'.[299] Thus, while states' obligation to investigate human rights violations is relatively broad and applies as a sort of secondary layer of protection in situations where the state has been unable to prevent violations, it is also dependent on the circumstances and the state's capacities. In certain situations, a state may be effectively unable to conduct meaningful investigations, or the state's limited capacities are unlikely to produce a meaningful outcome.[300]

To sum up, in order to protect individuals from human rights violations by private actors, states have an obligation to prevent and to investigate such acts. These are obligations of conduct, which have to be fulfilled with due diligence. Thus, it is not expected that states are able to prevent every crime, or always to lead successful investigations. Demanding absolute protection would be unrealistic. Instead, states have to make the best effort within their power that can be reasonably expected in the circumstances. One of the major shortcomings of this system is that it depends on the state's 'degree of effectiveness'.[301] This means that a functioning state is likely to be able to provide sufficient security for people under its jurisdiction, or to investigate crimes and prosecute those responsible. In contrast, in a number of circumstances, the best efforts of a weak, dysfunctional, or failing state may not be sufficient to provide a minimum degree of protection for individuals threatened by non-state armed groups, especially if confronted with a powerful armed group.[302] As argued in Sections 6.3 'Human Rights Obligations of Groups Exercising Quasi-Governmental Authority in Defined Territory' and 6.4 'Human Rights Obligations

Rodriguez v Honduras, Judgment, 29 July 1988, IACtHR, paras 176–81; *Pueblo Bello Massacre v Colombia* (n 273) paras 142-150; *Case of Ergi v Turkey* (n 275) paras 82–85; *Case of Yasa v Turkey, Judgment, 2 September 1998, Application no 63/1997/847/1054,* ECtHR, paras 98–104; *Kilic v Turkey* (n 275) paras 78–83. For more detailed discussions, see Doswald-Beck, *Human Rights in Times of Conflict and Terrorism* (n 73) 184–88; Krähenmann, 'Positive Obligations' (n 274) 414–18; Zegveld, *Accountability of Armed Opposition Groups* (n 71) 196–204.

[297] *Pueblo Bello Massacre v Colombia* (n 273) para 143. See also *Ramsahai and others v The Netherlands, Judgment, 15 May 2007, Application no 52391/99,* ECtHR, para 324.

[298] *Pueblo Bello Massacre v Colombia* (n 273) para 146.

[299] *Yasa v Turkey* (n 296) para 104. As Zegveld pointed out, such circumstances can also include state structures and judicial institutions that were implicated during armed conflict, 'threats against the judicial branch and witnesses, a high number of crimes, and the lack of cooperation by victims and witnesses'. Zegveld, *Accountability of Armed Opposition Groups* (n 71) 197.

[300] eg, examining human rights violations by different non-state armed groups in the Central African Republic, a UN Commission of Inquiry had to recognize that the state had disintegrated to an extent that it no longer had 'functioning criminal investigation, prosecution and judicial institutions' in order to meet its human rights obligations. Human Rights Council, *Preliminary Report of the Independent Expert on the situation of Human Rights in the Central African Republic, Marie-Thérèse Keita Bocoum,* 30 May 2014, A/HRC/26/53, para 34.

[301] Zegveld, *Accountability of Armed Opposition Groups* (n 71) 208.

[302] In such cases, a state's inability cannot be demonstrated by failure to investigate one crime. Instead, it would require a continuous failure of the state to address human rights violations by armed groups.

of Groups Exercising De Facto Control over Territory and Population', this is a fortiori the case if states lose control over territory. Sections 6.5.2 'Contemporary international practice'–6.5.4 'The scope of obligations' shows that, in practice, it becomes increasingly necessary to require non-state actors to respect IHRL, even if they do not exercise significant de facto control over territory and population.

6.5.2 Contemporary international practice

Most situations in which UN organs or expert commissions address armed groups' human rights violations or abuses are situations of armed conflicts in which the non-state armed group exercises at least some control over territory and population. However, the international community has also responded to situations in which armed groups operate in circumstances not amounting to an armed conflict, or in which groups operate in a territory in which a non-international armed conflict takes place but commit human rights violations that are unrelated to the conflict. In such situations, the only source of international law that could provide obligations for the armed group is IHRL. IHL is either not applicable, or does not regulate the conduct in question. A prominent example of the first type of situation occurred during the first year of the Syria crisis, in 2011/2012. While armed groups started to challenge the government's authority, they did not exercise control over territory and were not considered sufficiently organized to become party to an armed conflict. In this situation, a UN Commission of Inquiry held:

> at a minimum, human rights obligations constituting peremptory international law (ius cogens) bind States, individuals and non-State collective entities, including armed groups. Acts violating ius cogens—for instance, torture or enforced disappearances—can never be justified.[303]

States in the Human Rights Council explicitly welcomed the Commission's report as well as its recommendations, which included 'that all armed groups ensure respect for and act in accordance with international human rights law'.[304] Likewise, in the course of escalating violence between government and non-state groups in Burundi in 2015, states on the UN Security Council strongly condemned 'violations and abuses of human rights committed in Burundi both by security forces and by militias and other illegal armed groups'.[305] In its final report, the United Nations

[303] Human Rights Council, *Report of the Independent International Commission of Inquiry on the Syrian Arab Republic*, A/HRC/19/69, para 106.

[304] See Human Rights Council, *Situation of Human Rights in the Syrian Arab Republic*, 10 April 2012, A/HRC/RES/19/22, para 1. Interestingly, when this author asked a Commission member how states reacted to these findings, the Commission member could not remember any opposition to this statement or related findings on human rights violations committed by opposition groups.

[305] United Nations Security Council, *Resolution 2248 (2015)*, 12 November 2015, S/RES/2248 (2015). The resolution calls upon all parties 'to reject any kind of violence'. However, it only calls upon the government 'to respect, protect and guarantee all human rights and fundamental freedoms for all'. Similar calls were not addressed to non-state armed groups. For a similar condemnation by states in the Human Rights Council, see Human Rights Council, *Preventing the Deterioration of the Human Rights Situation in Burundi*, 17 December 2015, A/HRC/RES/S-24/1.

Independent Investigation on Burundi recommended that 'non-state actors must prioritize the protection of civilians and refrain from human rights abuses'.[306]

While in these situations the government was still exercising control over most of its territory and continued exercising authority, a somewhat different situation occurred in the Central African Republic in 2013. In late 2012, an armed conflict broke out between a coalition of armed groups, called Séléka, and government forces. In March 2013, Séléka took power and its leaders formed the state's new government. However, with regard to the government's capacity to protect human rights, an OHCHR report noted:

> The country is exhausted and divided. What little infrastructure there was outside Bangui has been destroyed by ex-Séléka and the State's ability to maintain law and order, which was already limited, has been wiped out. The State has virtually ceased to exist in Bangui and the provinces; there is no rule of law.[307]

In reaction to Séléka's taking of power, former members of the armed forces and self-defence groups formed the anti-balaka coalition. These groups were poorly organized, had no 'credible chain of command', no 'political leadership', and operated mostly autonomously, sometimes exercising control over 'specific territory'.[308] Reportedly, between the formation of different anti-balaka groups around June 2013 and up to at least December 2013, the situation did not amount to a NIAC, meaning that IHL did not apply to the situation.[309]

From March 2013 onwards, different groups allegedly committed severe human rights violations,[310] which sparked international reaction. States on the Security Council repeatedly condemned the 'widespread human rights violations and abuses, perpetrated by armed groups', called for individual criminal responsibility, and urged the transitional authorities to exercise their primary responsibility to protect civilians and ensure accountability.[311] Likewise, states on the Human Rights Council demanded an 'immediate halt to all human rights violations and abuses and acts of violence by all parties, and the strict observance of all human rights and fundamental freedoms'.[312] It is not clear to what extent the different armed groups

[306] Human Rights Council, *Report of the United Nations Independent Investigation on Burundi (UNIIB) Established Pursuant to Human Rights Council Resolution S-24/1*, 20 September 2016, A/HRC/33/37 para 153.

[307] Human Rights Council, *Report of the United Nations High Commissioner for Human Rights on the Situation of Human Rights in the Central African Republic*, 19 February 2014, A/HRC/25/43, para 54.

[308] International Commission of Inquiry on the Central African Republic, *Preliminary Report of the International Commission of Inquiry on the Central African Republic, Submitted Pursuant to Security Council Resolution 2127 (2013)*, 26 June 2014, S/2014/373, paras 40-44. See also United Nations Secretary General, *Report of the Secretary-General on the Central African Republic Submitted Pursuant to Paragraph 22 of Security Council Resolution 2121 (2013)*, 15 November 2013, S/2013/677, paras 5–10.

[309] See Human Rights Committee, *The International Commission of Inquiry on the Central African Republic—Final Report* (n 49) paras 39; 82–101.

[310] ibid, at paras 44–50.

[311] United Nations Security Council, *Resolution 2127 (2013)*, 5 December 2013, S/RES/2127 (2013), paras 17–18. See also United Nations Security Council, *Resolution 2121 (2013)*, S/Res/2121 (2013).

[312] Human Rights Council, *Situation of Human Rights in the Central African Republic and Technical Assistance in the Field of Human Rights*, 21 January 2014, A/HRC/RES/S-20/1, para 2.

operating in the Central African Republic, especially the different groups referred to as anti-balaka in 2013, exercised de facto control over territory and population. It is also debated at what point the situation constituted an armed conflict. Nonetheless, states on the Human Rights Council reminded 'all parties of their responsibilities under international human rights law'.[313]

A third relevant example is the occupation of Mali's north in 2012 through different armed groups, which declared the establishment of the 'State of Azawad'.[314] While some groups installed themselves as the new authorities and implemented some form of law and order,[315] a variety of non-state groups operated in northern Mali. In this situation, states on the Human Rights Council condemned

> the human rights violations and acts of violence committed in northern Mali, in particular *by the rebels, terrorist groups and other organized transnational crime networks*, including the violence perpetrated against women and children, the killings, hostage-takings, pillaging, theft and destruction of religious and cultural sites, as well as the recruitment of child soldiers.[316]

States demanded an immediate halt to these acts and 'strict respect for all human rights and fundamental freedoms'.[317] The Security Council echoed these demands by '*[c]ondemning strongly* the abuses of human rights committed in the north of Mali by armed rebels, terrorist and other extremist groups' and demanding under chapter VII that 'all groups in the north of Mali cease all abuses of human rights and violations of international humanitarian law'.[318] While some non-state actors in northern Mali exercised control over territory and people, not all 'terrorist groups' and 'organized crime networks' did. Moreover, it is questionable whether acts of the latter two had a sufficient nexus to the armed conflicts in the territory.

In addition to these country-specific reports and resolutions, the UN Security Council has considered fundamental human rights violations of very different armed groups in the context of the 'Monitoring and Reporting Mechanism on grave violations of children's rights in situations of armed conflict' (MRM). Analysing the listing of state forces and non-state armed groups in the annex of the Secretary-General's *Reports on Children in Armed Conflict* as a party committing grave violations of children's rights, commentators found that, in order to be listed, 'a degree of control of territory or a level of de facto authority over a population' does

[313] ibid. This demand and the reminder to all parties of their responsibilities under international human rights law was repeated in subsequent resolution 27/28. See Human Rights Council, *Technical Assistance and Capacity-Building in the Field of Human Rights in the Central African Republic*, 3 October 2014, A/HRC/RES/27/28, paras 1–2.

[314] This state was, however, not recognized by other states and immediately rejected by the Economic Community of West African States (ECOWAS) and the African Union. See Human Rights Council, *Report of the United Nations High Commissioner for Human Rights on the Situation of Human Rights in Mali*, 2013, A/HRC/22/33, para 10.

[315] ibid, at executive summary.

[316] Human Rights Council, *Human Rights Situation in Mali*, 17 July 2012, A/HRC/RES/20/17, para 2 (emphasis added).

[317] ibid, at para 3.

[318] United Nations Security Council, *Resolution 2071 (2012): Mali*, 12 October 2012, S/RES/2071 (2012), para 5.

not seem to be required.[319] While the title of the MRM suggests that only armed groups party to an armed conflict would fall under the scope of the mechanism, the actual lists of groups that commit such violations explicitly includes groups that operate in undefined 'other situations'.[320] If groups are not party to an armed conflict, IHL does not apply to them. Consequently, the only reference point for potential legal obligations towards children is IHRL.[321] This practice further strengthens the impressions that at least states in the Security Council consider certain fundamental obligations to be binding on any non-state armed group, irrespective of whether it qualifies as a party to an armed conflict, de facto controls territory, or exercises quasi-governmental authority.[322]

To sum up, a number of similarities between these different situations can be identified. While international law and practice places the primary duty to respect, protect, and fulfil human rights on states, in certain situations states complement this primary responsibility by demanding that non-state armed groups respect human rights. In order to be subject to such demands, it is not required for an armed group to exercise control over territory or population. Neither are findings limited to armed conflict situations, in which it could be argued that IHRL obligations only restate applicable IHL. Rather, a key commonality of the above situations is that the territorial authority was unable to exercise effectively its obligation to protect individuals from human rights violations committed by these groups. This was the case either because the groups in question gained sufficient strength to operate beyond state control, or because the state no longer had the capacity to fulfil its obligations. Consequently, if the state is unable to protect the most fundamental human rights of people within its territory, international human rights protection

[319] Bellal, Giacca, and Casey-Maslen, 'Armed Non-State Actors in Afghanistan' (n 2) 73.

[320] United Nations Security Council, *Children and Armed Conflict: Report of the Secretary General*, 15 May 2014, A/68/878–S/2014/339, 50. Indeed, from the outset the Security Council made clear that by listing such groups in a report it 'does not seek to make any legal determination as to whether situations … are or are not armed conflicts within the context of the Geneva Conventions and the Additional Protocols thereto, nor does it prejudge the legal status of the non-State parties involved in these situations'. See United Nations Security Council, *Resolution 1612*, 26 July 2005, S/RES/1612, para 8 (preamble). The 2014 annex lists the Philippine armed groups 'Abu Sayyaf Group' and 'Bangsamoro Islamic Freedom Fighters', but it is unclear whether they are parties to non-international armed conflicts governed by IHL. See Children and Armed Conflict: Report of the Secretary General, ibid, 50. For past examples of situations in which the classification of conflicts was disputed, see Clapham, *Human Rights Obligations of Non-State Actors* (n 2) 512–13.

[321] The Secretary General's report that developed the six grave violations against children refers not only to applicable IHL and international criminal law (ICL) but also to different IHRL instruments, such as the CRC, the CRC-OPAC, International Labour Organization Convention 182 concerning the Prohibition and Immediate Action for the Elimination of the Worst Forms of Child Labour (1999), or the African Charter on the Rights and Welfare of the African Child (1999). See United Nations Security Council, *Children and Armed Conflict: Report of the Secretary-General*, 9 February 2005, A/59/695–S/2005/72, para 70. With regard to the recent inclusions of attacks against schools and hospitals, Giacca noted that this 'is not only an advancement of the operationalization of the IHL prohibition to attack hospitals, schools, and other civilian objects, but also clear progress in the operationalization of the right to education and the right to health during the course of military operations on the agenda of the Security Council'. Giacca, *Economic, Social, and Cultural Rights in Armed Conflict* (n 9) 253.

[322] See also Clapham, *Human Rights Obligations of Non-State Actors* (n 2) 545.

needs to apply to other actors in order to promote and work towards universal respect for human rights.[323]

6.5.3 Conceptual considerations

It is difficult to fit the relationship between individuals and armed groups without territorial control or de facto governmental authority within the parameters of the traditional 'human rights equation', meaning the relationship between a governing authority and individuals under its control.[324] Rather, recent practice of UN human rights experts and states in UN organs suggests that human rights may also operate outside the traditional equation. The main reason for this conceptual change appears to be a simple and convincing one: a purely state or authority-focused understanding of human rights no longer adequately responds to human rights violations in the twenty-first century.

6.5.3.1 Justifying human rights obligations outside the government–individual relationship

One approach to conceptualizing human rights obligations of armed groups without control over territory and population could be to invoke human rights obligations in the same way as a state's extraterritorial obligations when the state does not control territory: if armed groups do not exercise territorial control in the area where the alleged violations are committed, they would need to exercise physical control over the victim.[325] Accordingly, non-state armed groups could have human rights obligations vis-à-vis persons that are de facto under their 'power or effective control' despite the fact that the group operates within a territory under the general control and jurisdiction of another entity.[326] To some extent, this approach safeguards the authority–individual relationship underlying the traditional human

[323] This forms part of the Human Rights Council's mandate. See United Nations General Assembly, *Basic Principles and Guidelines on the Right to a Remedy and Reparation for Victims of Gross Violations of International Human Rights Law and Serious Violations of International Humanitarian Law* (n 269) para. 158.

[324] As discussed above, this term has been used by different authors to express the vertical relationship between those exercising effective power and those at their mercy. See, eg, Rodley, 'Can Armed Opposition Groups Violate Human Rights?' (n 3) 313; Zegveld, *Accountability of Armed Opposition Groups* (n 71) 149. See also Commission on Human Rights, *Extrajudicial, Summary or Arbitrary Executions: Report of the Special Rapporteur*, 22 December 2004, E/CN.4/2005/7, para 76.

[325] See *Öcalan v Turkey, Judgment, 12 March 2003, Application no 46221/99,* ECtHR, para 93. In this case the ECtHR argued that although arrested by Turkish authorities and initially held in Kenya, 'directly after he had been handed over by the Kenyan officials to the Turkish officials the applicant was under effective Turkish authority and was therefore brought within the "jurisdiction" of that State'. This was the case because Öcalan was under Turkey's 'authority and control' despite the fact that they operated extraterritorially.

[326] Human Rights Committee, *General Comment No 31: Nature of the General Legal Obligation Imposed on States Parties to the Covenant* (n 73), para 10. In this General Comment the Human Rights Commission explained that states parties 'must respect and ensure the rights laid down in the Covenant to anyone within the power or effective control of that State Party, even if not situated within the territory of the State Party'.

rights equation, and commentators suggested that this 'could be a way forward'.[327] However, the approach might be both too narrow and too broad at the same time. On the one hand, it limits human rights obligations to a narrow scope of situations in which an armed group exercises physical control over an alleged victim. On the other hand, this concept could be very broad by theoretically encompassing any situation of kidnapping by a group of criminals.

Another approach is to leave the traditional 'human rights equation' aside and to focus instead on the question of whether, in a given situation, the protection of human dignity necessitates addressing human rights obligations to armed groups. This approach can be based on two closely related arguments. First, the rationale behind human rights is the protection of the inherent dignity of all human beings: 'the essential rights of man are not derived from one's being a national of a certain state, but are based upon attributes of the human personality'.[328] These rights are not granted to the individual by the state but are inherent in being a human.[329] They must be protected against any violation.[330] Second, in the IHRL protection system, the enjoyment of human rights nonetheless depends on their protection by a state or another entity. However, as analysed above, states' obligation to protect human rights of individuals under their jurisdiction depends to some extent on the state's capacity and power. Consequently, if the state's capacity to protect human rights is severely limited, the effectiveness of the IHRL protection system and the aim of avoiding a protection gap or vacuum underlines a need for human rights obligations of non-state armed groups. In other words, effective human rights protection necessitates human rights obligations for armed groups if the state is genuinely unable to exercise its protective functions.[331] Indeed, in such cases, it is not necessarily the nature of control exercised by the group but its 'ability to conduct certain activity in relation to that territory or population, coupled with the state's inability to reasonably impose its will' that should be decisive.[332]

This approach corresponds with recent state practice. The examples from Syria, Burundi, the Central African Republic, or Mali show that states in UN organs called for armed groups to respect human rights in situations where the state was unable to respond to human rights violations and protect its citizens. The idea that effective international human rights protection necessitates human rights obligations of non-state entities applies a fortiori to situations where armed groups control territory and

[327] Bellal, Giacca, and Casey-Maslen, 'Armed Non-State Actors in Afghanistan' (n 2) 71.

[328] ACHR, preamble. See also UDHR, preamble.

[329] As Judge Tanaka pointed out: 'A State or States are not capable of creating human rights by law or by convention; they can only confirm their existence and give them protection.' *South West Africa (Ethiopia v South Africa)*, Judgment, Dissenting Opinion of Judge Tanaka, 18 July 1966, ICJ,, 297.

[330] For further discussion, see Chapter 4 'Human Rights, Natural Rights, and their Applicability beyond the State–Individual Relationship' above.

[331] In practice, this would normally be proved not by single cases in which a state is unable to exercise its protective duties but by a continuous failure to do so. See also Murray, *Human Rights Obligations of Non-State Armed Groups* (n 94) 148–49.

[332] ibid, at 145. Murray focused primarily on the notion of control, but argued that this notion needs to be interpreted in a flexible manner to address situations in which state and armed groups exercise control concomitantly.

populations, or exercise quasi-governmental functions. At the same time, this approach may also explain why states on the Human Rights Council do not equate all acts of terrorism or extremism with human rights abuses or violations but condemn instead 'their detrimental effects on human rights'.[333] As long as a state's government is able to protect its citizens adequately against human rights violations, states may not see a need for the government's obligation to protect human rights to be complemented by direct obligations for armed groups.

6.5.3.2 Legal sources binding armed groups without control over territory and population

IHRL obligations of armed groups without territorial control obviously cannot devolve with territory. Likewise, at present, they can only stem exceptionally from IHRL treaty law.[334] Thus, the source of these obligations must lie in either customary IHRL or human rights principles, which may apply to international legal persons. The question of at what point an armed group has sufficient international legal personality to be subject to fundamental IHRL obligations remains, however, unclear. As discussed above, if the armed group is not party to an armed conflict, IHL treaty law does not apply and would not recognize some form of international personality of the group. Likewise, territorial control would not be present as an indicator for legal personality.[335] Nonetheless, following the approach presented in the paragraphs above, armed groups could have sufficient personality to possess fundamental human rights obligations if two factors are present: they need to have the ability to respect basic human rights obligations, and there needs to be a systemic necessity to impose obligations on them. With regard to the first factor, it has rightly been suggested that 'in order to respect some fundamental norms ... the capacity requirement should be low'.[336] With regard to the second factor, it appears that effective IHRL protection requires fundamental IHRL obligations for non-state entities if the state is unable to protect individuals against human rights violations committed by that group.[337]

[333] See, eg, Human Rights Council, *Effects of Terrorism on the Enjoyment of Human Rights*, 9 April 2015, A/HRC/RES/28/17, para 1.

[334] As pointed out above, IHRL treaties are focused on states and only provide for certain limited obligations for non-state armed groups.

[335] See discussion in Section 6.4.3 'Conceptual considerations' above.

[336] Kleffner, 'Organized Armed Groups' (n 31) 274. While Kleffner made this argument with regard to customary IHL, it similarly applies to IHRL.

[337] Analysing under which conditions armed groups have international legal personality under IHL, Fortin argues that in addition to the capacity or organization of the group itself, an 'international element' must be present. According to Fortin, 'this international element may be satisfied by demonstrating a combination of the following factors: either that the armed group is operating in the context of a non-international armed conflict, *that the parent State has reduced capacities, has lost control over a portion of territory*, that the situation is such to merit the attention of the international community as a whole or that the interests of a third State are involved'. Likewise, Fortin also concludes that the international legal capacity to have IHRL obligations depends on the capacity of the armed group and on a second element, which could derive from 'the level of atrocities committed by the armed group (e.g. are they widespread or systematic?), the *incapacities of the parent State* or the involvement of the

Moreover, in recent international practice, the UN Commission of Inquiry on Syria and the United Nations Mission in the Republic of South Sudan suggested that a particular form of customary IHRL could bind armed groups, namely peremptory human rights law, or ius cogens. Both argued that peremptory human rights obligations 'bind States, individuals and non-state entities, including armed groups'.[338] Indeed, as the ICTY held with regard to the prohibition of torture, the recognition of a norm as an ius cogens prohibition

> is designed to produce a deterrent effect, in that it signals to all members of the international community and the individuals over whom they wield authority that the prohibition of torture is an absolute value from which nobody must deviate.[339]

Likewise, the Court of First Instance of the European Communities argued that ius cogens should be understood as 'a body of higher rules of public international law binding on all subjects of international law . . . and from which no derogation is possible'.[340] On the one hand, the finding that certain basic IHRL norms bind states, individuals, and all other legal persons provides a strong argument for human rights obligations of armed groups. On the other hand, it does not explain at what point armed groups would become 'subjects of international law', or 'members of the international community' bound by this set of norms. Instead, similar considerations to the ones discussed above would need to apply. As also shown in Section 6.5.4 'The scope of obligations', however, reference to peremptory IHRL norms provides a body of human rights obligations that any armed group is able to respect and that the international community has an undisputed interest to protect.

6.5.4 The scope of obligations

Different factors suggest that the scope of possible IHRL obligations of armed groups without control over territory and population should be rather narrow. With regard to the groups' capacity, it is unlikely that they have institutions or other infrastructure that would allow them to protect or to fulfil most human rights.[341] It would be unrealistic to expect armed groups to establish law and order in a territory over which they do not exercise control, or to develop strategies to ensure food security or the public health of the population. Moreover, if the state's government continues to exercise control over the territory in question, it is the government's sovereign obligation to protect and to fulfil human rights. Thus, there is no systemic need to assign

international community'. Fortin, *The Accountability of Armed Groups under Human Rights Law* (n 20) 387 (emphasis added).

[338] Human Rights Council, *Report of the Independent International Commission of Inquiry on the Syrian Arab Republic* (n 303) para 106; United Nations Mission in the Republic of South Sudan (UNMISS), *Conflict in South Sudan: A Human Rights Report*, 8 May 2014, para 18.

[339] UN Committee on Economic, Social, and Cultural Rights, *Concluding Observations of the Committee on Economic, Social and Cultural Rights: Colombia* (n 211) para 154.

[340] *Kadi v Council and Commission, Judgment, 21 September 2005, T-315/01,* The Court of the First Instance of the European Communities, para 226.

[341] As pointed out in Section 6.4.4 'The scope of obligations', any armed group might be able to facilitate human rights as part of the obligation to fulfil.

human rights obligations to armed groups, except for the obligation not to interfere with fundamental human rights. As a political science researcher put it: 'Insurgents who fight using hit-and-run tactics can only affect civilian livelihoods for the worse, as governance remains the preserve of the incumbent.'[342] Still, any armed groups should have the capacity to respect fundamental human rights, meaning an internal structure able to ensure that its members abstain from violating them.[343] As a result, a realistic minimum that any armed group can be required to comply with could be the obligation to respect customary civil and political, as well as economic, social, and cultural rights.[344] As argued above, a reference list of such rights is found in the UDHR.

A more limited subset of customary human rights norms would be those recognized as ius cogens.[345] Invoking peremptory human rights norms limits the applicable norms to the most basic rights that every group would be able to respect and which form the necessary basis for enjoying all other rights.[346] Yet, no universally agreed list of peremptory human rights norms exists.[347] The Human Rights Committee suggested the prohibition of the following acts as ius cogens: arbitrary deprivation of life; torture or cruel, inhuman, or degrading treatment or punishment; hostage-taking; collective punishments; arbitrary deprivations of liberty; and ignorance of fundamental principles of fair trial.[348] UN human rights experts further suggested the prohibition of enforced disappearance, sexual violence and slavery, and the recruitment and use of children in hostilities.[349] Most of these norms also correspond with the basic prohibitions found in Common Article 3, which reflect 'elementary considerations of humanity'.[350] While it is unlikely that states would agree on a precise list of peremptory human rights standards, it appears from UN reports and resolutions that the above-cited norms are the most relevant protections

[342] Mampilly, 'Insurgent Governance in the Democratic Republic of the Congo' (n 198) 56.

[343] See discussion in Section 6.4.4 'The scope of obligations' above.

[344] For further discussion on the scope of rights this would entail, see Section 6.4.4 'The scope of obligations' above.

[345] In addition to the UN reports on Syria and South Sudan cited above, this suggestion was made by the International Law Association. See International Law Association, *The Hague Conference (2010): Non-State Actors* (ILA 2010) 17.

[346] For the idea of 'basic rights', see Shue, *Basic Rights: Subsistence, Affluence, and US Foreign Policy* (Princeton University Press 1980) 13–34.

[347] See also United Nations General Assembly, *Report of the International Law Commission: Annex, Jus Cogens (Mr Dire D Tladi)*, 2014, A/69/10.

[348] Human Rights Committee, *General Comment No 29: States of Emergency (article 4)* (n 254) para 11. In its commentary on the Articles on State Responsibility, the ILC held: 'Those peremptory norms that are clearly accepted and recognized include the prohibitions of aggression, genocide, slavery, racial discrimination, crimes against humanity and torture, and the right to self-determination.' International Law Commission, *Responsibility of State for Internationally Wrongful Acts (with commentaries)* (n 72) para 5 of the commentary on article 26.

[349] See UNMISS, *Conflict in South Sudan: A Human Rights Report* (n 338) para 18. Further indications could be drawn from the rights listed in article 2 of the Turku Declaration of Minimum Humanitarian Standards.

[350] *Case concerning Military and Paramilitary Activities in and against Nicaragua (Nicaragua v United States of America), International Court of Justice, Judgment, 27 June 1986,* International Court of Justice, para 218.

for individuals threatened by armed groups, and, unfortunately, also the most frequently violated ones.

It has been suggested that a list of non-derogable or peremptory human rights norms could consist of prohibitions of the acts underlying crimes against humanity or genocide.[351] Indeed, the prohibition of crimes against humanity and genocide are broadly considered as ius cogens.[352] Applying that argument to possible human rights obligations of armed groups, Fortin suggests that 'the law on "crimes against humanity" provides a valuable legal affirmation of the fact that individuals, and armed groups committing crimes against humanity are violating human rights'.[353] At first sight, this 'appears only logical' because the secondary international criminal law norms on crimes against humanity and genocide also protect primary IHRL norms.[354] Yet, this approach has also been criticized for 'putting the cart before the horse': while secondary norms, such as those defining individual criminal responsibility for individuals committing crimes against humanity, are normally based on primary norms prohibiting such conduct in the first place, a lack of primary obligations might not be compensated for by secondary norms.[355]

Moreover, rules on individual criminal responsibility could provide an argument for binding obligations for individuals but not for collective entities.[356] In addition, concluding from the international legal prohibition of crimes against humanity an obligation not to commit the individual underlying acts may not be sound ratione materie. Under international criminal law, crimes against humanity do not apply to human rights violations as such—only if they are committed in particular contexts.[357] It is not the underlying act but the context that makes these acts an international crime. This essential characteristic of crimes against humanity or genocide would not be considered if a simple analogy between the criminalization of certain acts as international crimes and human rights obligations of armed groups were drawn. At the same time, if a large scale or systematic attack against a civilian population is ongoing, all individuals are practically prohibited from committing human rights violations as refelcted in article 7(1) of the Rome Statute of the International Criminal Court (ICC Statute) if these acts were committed as part of the ongoing attack and with knowledge thereof.

To sum up, whether owing to an obligation of armed groups to respect customary IHRL, human rights obligations constituting peremptory international law (ius cogens), or fundamental considerations of humanity, in international practice a body

351 See Hessbruegge, 'Conduct of Non-State Actors' (n 185) 41–44; Giacca, *Economic, Social, and Cultural Rights in Armed Conflict* (n 9) 258.

352 See n 348 above. For an interpretation of which prohibitions the rather minimalist wording of Common Article 3 comprises, see ICRC, *GCI: Commentary of 2016* (n 132).

353 Fortin, *The Accountability of Armed Groups under Human Rights Law* (n 20) 321. For further analysis, see ibid, at chapter 10.

354 Kleffner, 'Organized Armed Groups' (n 31) 56.

355 ibid. However, this would lead to a paradoxical result under which acts are criminalized but not prohibited under international law. In the present author's view, this cannot be right.

356 ibid, at 56–57.

357 This point is discussed in great detail in Part III of this book.

of IHRL might cristallize which binds armed groups even if they do not control territory and population. Such development would reaffirm the importance of individual human rights protection in times when it is most needed. Moreover, by invoking a number of fundamental human rights norms vis-à-vis state and non-state actors and at all times, the international community underlines and defends certain international core values that have developed over recent decades.

Part II: Conclusion

'Where are the good old days when everyone knew that human rights violations can only be committed by states against individuals?'[1] Gone, replaced by a complex reality in which an exclusive focus on states as duty-bearers under international human rights law (IHRL) no longer provides an adequate model to address numerous human rights violations by non-state armed groups. Instead, states in United Nations (UN) organs or intergovernmental fora, as well as human rights experts, increasingly address demands to respect IHRL directly to armed groups. In order to conceptualize this development, this book raised three main arguments: (1) Contrary to the 'received wisdom', human rights may not only apply to the authority–individual relationship. Conceptually, they can also be understood as applying to the horizontal relationships between private actors. (2) While under IHRL treaty law it is primarily upon states to protect individuals against human rights violations by private actors, this obligation is limited if the state loses control over parts of its territory, or is otherwise unable to fulfil its obligations. In order to avoid a protection gap, IHRL obligations should be directly assigned to armed groups. (3) Contemporary international practice suggests that this requires a differentiated approach, taking account of the different nature and capacity of non-state armed groups. Assigning IHRL obligations to armed groups needs to complement and not substitute state obligations under the traditional state-centred human rights protection system.

For the purpose of determining the need for IHRL obligations of non-state armed groups, possible sources of such obligations, and their scope, the degree of possible obligations of armed groups should be understood as existing on a spectrum. For analytical purposes, they can be best examined under three broad categories, meaning if certain signposts are placed on the spectrum. First, if armed groups are able to exercise quasi-governmental control in a defined territory, they factually resemble states. Thus, they should be required to respect, protect, and fulfil a broad scope of IHRL obligations towards persons under their control, either based on the territorial state's treaty obligations that devolve to the group, or based on customary IHRL. Second, groups that exercise de facto control over territory and population but are not able to establish state-like infrastructure should at least respect customary IHRL vis-à-vis persons under their control. In addition, possible obligation to protect and to fulfil human rights should depend inter alia on the extent to which the de jure government continues to provide such functions. Third, in situations in which armed groups do not exercise control over territory or population but the de

[1] Reinisch, 'The Changing International Legal Framework for Dealing with Non-State Actors' in Alston (ed), *Non-State Actors and Human Rights* (OUP 2005) 37.

jure government is nonetheless unable to prevent or to investigate groups' human rights violations, non-state armed groups should be required to respect fundamental human rights.

Under the suggested model, armed groups' human rights obligations would depend on their capacity as well as on the context in which they operate. Indeed, obligations should vary according to the group's infrastructure and the degree of power they exercise over persons under their control. Consequently, determining the exact scope of possible obligations requires a case-by-case assessment of these factors. The three-pronged model developed here, however, presents rather clear benchmarks: it provides a bottomline category in which all groups should have one set of basic obligations, and a category of groups with quasi-governmental authority, which should have state-like human rights obligations. The challenge of relating the exact scope of human rights obligations with the concrete capacities and operational circumstances of the armed group in question arises only with regard to the broad category of groups exercising some de facto control over territory and population.

Despite numerous examples of states and human rights experts calling on armed groups to respect IHRL, practice remains somewhat unclear on the nature and scope of possible human rights obligations. Likewise, debate among international law scholars continues. While some analysts claim that non-state armed groups exercising control over territory and population are bound by customary IHRL, more cautious commentators raised doubts over whether opinio juris and state practice are sufficient at this stage. Indeed, states' traditional concern that addressing non-state armed groups in human rights language may grant these groups certain legitimacy continues to spark objections to recognizing any legal obligations of these groups. This is especially the case if non-state armed groups are considered 'terrorists', which many states tend to regard as criminals, pure and simple. Nonetheless, the variety of state practice in UN bodies and expert views discussed in this book demonstrates a remarkable change from the beginning of the 1990s, when UN Human Rights Special Mandate Holders still felt that reporting on killings committed by armed groups 'would be inappropriate, given their legal status'.[2] Recent state and human rights expert practice of addressing human rights obligations to armed groups indicates in which direction international human rights law develops.

Engaging armed groups on human rights protection involves numerous challenges. Yet, recent examples show that some armed groups have committed publicly to respect and to protect human rights, and have adopted internal rules and procedures.[3] For instance, the 'Free Syrian Army' declared in 2016 that it shall 'treat Syrian citizens in areas under our control in accordance with international human rights treaties'.[4] Even at a much earlier stage, it commanded all its fighters to adhere to a code of conduct requiring them to 'respect human rights in accordance

[2] Report of the Special Rapporteur on Extrajudicial, Summary or Arbitrary Executions, A/62/265, para 40.

[3] Prominent examples of such public commitments are Geneva Call's 'Deeds of Commitment' signed by armed groups. The obligations included in these deeds are based primarily on international humanitarian law (IHL) but also on IHRL.

[4] Free Syrian Army, New Battalions Sign the Code of Conduct (2012).

with our legal principles, our tolerant religious principles, and the international laws governing human rights'.[5] Likewise, the Sudanese 'Justice and Equality Movement' (JEM) announced in 2008 that it will do its 'utmost to guarantee the protection of civilian populations in accordance with the principles of human rights'.[6] In 2010, it established a 'JEM Committee for Human Rights' with the mandate to conduct '[i]mmediate and periodic reviews of JEM directives relating to observation of Human Rights and Rights of Children and their harmonization with relevant international Conventions and ethos'.[7]

Thus, engaging armed groups on human rights protection can lead to concrete measures with the potential to fill international protection gaps and enhance the security and well-being of individuals. In other words, 'deeper engagement up to and including limited recognition of insurgent governance systems should be considered by those concerned with improving the welfare of populations trapped within contemporary conflict zones'.[8] Recognizing that armed groups have sufficient capacity to respect at least fundamental human rights, and that meaningful human rights protection necessitates direct engagement with these armed groups can, however, only be a first step. Additional measures are needed: states should unambiguously require all armed groups to respect human rights; pertinent obligations need to be spelled out clearly and with some sort of involvement of armed groups; international actors need to further develop their approaches to engage armed groups on such obligations; and (quasi-) judicial enforcement mechanisms should address these groups directly.

[5] Free Syrian Army, Declaration (2016).

[6] Justice and Equality Movement, Statement by the Opposition Movements (2008).

[7] Justice and Equality Movement, Establishment of a JEM Committee for Human Rights (2010).

[8] Mampilly, 'Insurgent Governance in the Democratic Republic of the Congo' in Krieger (ed), *Inducing Compliance with International Humanitarian Law: Lessons from the African Great Lakes Region* (CUP 2016) 77.

PART III

THE REQUIRED DEGREE OF ORGANIZATION OF NON-STATE ENTITIES TO COMMIT INTERNATIONAL CRIMES OR TO CREATE CONTEXTS IN WHICH INDIVIDUALS COMMIT THEM

In its present form, international criminal law (ICL) criminalizes the conduct of natural persons,[1] irrespective of whether they are private individuals, state officials, or members of non-state entities.[2] It is not concerned with states' or non-state entities' international responsibility.[3] Seemingly, ICL applies to crimes 'committed by men, not by abstract entities'.[4] This is, however, only half the truth. A closer look at international crimes as defined in the Rome Statute of the International Criminal Court (ICC Statute) reveals that, in most cases, these crimes require collective entity involvement: the crime of aggression can only be committed by states;[5] war crimes assume the existence of an armed conflict involving at least two conflicting parties;[6] crimes against humanity require a 'State or organizational policy' behind the

[1] See article 25(1) of the Rome Statute of the International Criminal Court (ICCSt), article 6 of the Statute of the International Criminal Tribunal for the former Yugoslavia (ICTY Statute), and article 5 of the Statute of the International Criminal Tribunal for Rwanda (ICTR Statute).

[2] See article 27 ICC Statute, article 7(2) ICTY Statute, and article 6(2) ICTR Statute.

[3] See Cassese, *International Criminal Law* (2nd edn, OUP 2008) 11–13. For some discussion, see Luban, 'State Criminality and the Ambition of International Criminal Law' in Isaacs and Vernon (eds), *Accountability for Collective Wrongdoing* (CUP 2011) 61–91. An emphasis on the distinction between individual and state responsibility is also found in article 25(4) ICC Statute.

[4] Famously, the International Military Tribunal (Nuremberg) held in its 1946 judgment: 'Crimes against International Law are committed by men, not by abstract entities, and only by punishing individuals who commit such crimes can the provisions of International Law be enforced.' *International Military Tribunal (Nuremberg), Judgment, 1 October 1946*, 55.

[5] Article 8*bis* ICC Statute. As the crime of aggression requires state involvement and cannot be committed by non-state entities, it is not further analysed in this book.

[6] Article 8 ICC Statute.

crimes;[7] and, in most cases, the crime of genocide involves a 'context of a manifest pattern of similar conduct', which normally requires a collective entity to be behind it.[8] Under these definitions, collective entities do not commit the crimes but their involvement is necessary to create a context in which individuals commit international crimes.[9]

When international crimes were first adjudicated following World War II, trials concerned crimes committed on behalf of states. In contrast, since the 1990s, international criminal tribunals have prosecuted crimes committed with the involvement of states and non-state entities. Accordingly, while the question of whether or not different international crimes require state involvement are addressed in this book, that question is no longer controversial and is not the book's primary focus. Instead, it examines *which kind of entities* have a sufficient degree of power and organization to create contexts in which international crimes can be committed. The requisite degree of power and organization of a non-state entity behind international crimes should not be determined in the abstract—for example, by referring to the undefined quality of being 'state-like' as a 'one-size-fits-all' solution. Instead, characteristics of collective entities involved in war crimes, crimes against humanity, or genocide need to be inferred in concreto from the crimes' definitions under international law. Accordingly, this study applies a functional approach under which the degree of organization of a collective entity behind an international crime is determined by what is needed to enable the commission of the crime.

Before delving into the analysis, this part's scope needs some clarification. This study is limited to core international crimes, or international crimes proper, as listed in the ICC Statute. It does not examine transnational crimes, such as terrorism or human trafficking.[10] Moreover, the present study is not concerned with the question of whether or not international criminal responsibility of collective non-state entities exists. In line with contemporary ICL, it examines primarily what kinds

[7] Article 7(2)(1) ICC Statute.

[8] Preparatory Commission for the International Criminal Court, *Elements of Crimes*, 2000, PCNICC/2000/1/Add.2, 6-7. In contrast to the other listed crimes, genocide can, in exceptional cases, also be committed by an individual acting alone. This is further discussed in Chapter 10 'Non-State Entity Involvement in Genocide' below.

[9] International crimes have also been described as 'system crimes'. According to Cassese: 'What is notable is that this conduct [an international crime] is either (a) linked to an international or internal armed conflict or, absent of such a conflict, (b) has a political or ideological dimension, or is somehow linked or otherwise connected to (instigated, influenced, tolerated, or acquiesced in) the behaviour of State authorities or organized non-state groups or entities.' Cassese, *International Criminal Law* (n 3) 54. For further discussion, see Röling, 'The Significance of the Laws of War' in Cassese (ed), *Current Problems of International Law: Essays on UN Law and on the Law of Armed Conflict* (A Giuffrè 1975) 133–55, 138–39; van der Wilt and Nollkaemper (eds), *System Criminality in International Law* (CUP 2009).

[10] As Boister explains, unlike international criminal law in the narrow sense, transnational criminal law 'does not create individual penal responsibility under international law. TCL [transnational criminal law] is an indirect system of interstate obligations generating national penal laws. The suppression conventions impose obligations on state parties to enact and enforce certain municipal offences.' Boister, '"Transnational Criminal Law"?' (2003) 14 European Journal of International Law 953–76, 962. See also Cryer, 'The Doctrinal Foundations of International Criminal Law' in Bassiouni (ed), *International Criminal Law* (M Nijhoff 2008) 107–28, 108–10; Gaeta, 'International Criminalization of Prohibited Conduct' in Cassese (ed), *The Oxford Companion to International Criminal Justice* (OUP 2009) 63–74, 63–64.

of non-state entities can create contexts in which individuals commit war crimes, crimes against humanity, or genocide.[11] This does not mean, however, that findings on which non-state entities are sufficiently organized and powerful to constitute the entity behind an international crime are not also relevant if that entity's responsibility is in question. They are. If an armed group has sufficient capacity to develop a policy to attack a civilian population and implements this policy in a systematic manner, not only individual perpetrators of criminal acts but also the entity as such should be considered responsible.[12] The link between a collective entity's involvement in a crime and its possible collective resonsibility are addressed briefly at the end of Part III. In order to incorporate individual and collective responsibility, this book refers not only to 'groups able to create a context in which individuals can commit international crimes' but also to 'groups with sufficient capacity to commit or instigate certain crimes', or simply 'groups behind the crimes'.

This part does not contain an examination of the requisite degree of organization of armed groups to become party to an armed conflict, which is a necessary contextual element for the commission of war crimes. Instead, it is submitted that similar findings apply as determined in Part I of this book, which examined the requisite degree of organization of non-state armed groups to become party to an armed conflict. While ICL and international humanitarian law (IHL) are different fields of law, each having their own purpose and objectives, with regard to war crimes the two fields are inherently linked.[13] War crimes are essentially the criminalization of certain grave violations of IHL. As Bothe put it, 'Rules concerning the punishment of war crimes are secondary rules in relation to the primary rules concerning behaviour which is prohibited in case of an armed conflict.'[14] Indeed, war crimes are regularly defined with direct reference to IHL—namely, either as 'violation of the laws and customs of war',[15] or as violations of particular obligations as defined in IHL treaties.[16] Thus, war crimes can only be committed if an armed conflict exists and IHL applies. Consequently, the requisite degree of organization of an armed group to become party to an armed conflict creating the context of war crimes must

[11] For discussion on the collective criminal responsibility of non-state entities, see, eg, Clapham, 'Extending International Criminal Law beyond the Individual to Corporations and Armed Opposition Groups' (2008) 6 Journal of International Criminal Justice 899–926; Clapham, 'Focussing on Armed Non-State Actors' in Clapham and Gaeta (eds), *The Oxford Handbook of International Law in Armed Conflict* (OUP 2014) 807–08. Fortin, 'The Accountability of Armed Groups under Human Rights Law' (OUP 2017) 296–303.

[12] For recent developments in this respect, see United Nations General Assembly (UNGA), *Report of the International Law Commission*, 18 August 2016, A/71/10, 281.

[13] For a comprehensive analysis of differences between the two fields, see Sassòli, 'Humanitarian Law and International Criminal Law' in Cassese (ed), *The Oxford Companion to International Criminal Justice* (OUP 2009) 111–20.

[14] Bothe, 'War Crimes' in Cassese, Geta, and Jones (eds), *The Rome Statute of the International Criminal Court: A Commentary* (OUP 2002) 381.

[15] See, eg, article 228 of the Peace Treaty of Versailles; article 6(b) of the Nuremberg Charter; article 5(b) of the Tokyo Charter; article 3 ICTY Statute, article 8(2)(b) and (e) ICC Statute. For a definition of when an international humanitarian law (IHL) violation constitutes a war crime in non-international armed conflict (NIAC), see *Tadić, Judgment, 7 May 1997, Trial Chamber, IT-94-1-T,* International Tribunal for the former Yugoslavia, para 94.

[16] See, eg, article 2 ICTY Statute, article 4 ICTR Statute, article 8(2)(a) and (c) ICC Statute.

be similar to a group's degree of organization necessary to become party to a conflict governed by IHL.

As a result, the ICL part of this book examines two main issues: first, the degree of organization required from non-state groups to constitute an entity behind crimes against humanity; and second, whether collective-entity involvement is needed for the commission of genocide and, if so, what degree of organization is needed.

Non-State Entity Involvement in Crimes against Humanity

Crimes against humanity (CAH) are generally understood as certain severe human rights violations if committed as part of a widespread or systematic attack directed against a civilian population. At the time of their first codification in 1945, CAH were considered state crimes. Over the past decades, however, the scope of CAH has broadened. In Yugoslavia, crimes committed on behalf of state-like entities, such as the 'Serb Autonomous Regions', were prosecuted as CAH; in Sierra Leone, crimes by different poorly organized non-state parties to the armed conflict fell within this category; and cases before the International Criminal Court (ICC) include numerous CAH charges against members of different armed groups. While it is no longer controversial that CAH do not require state involvement, the 'outer limits of crimes against humanity' continue to be debated.[17] Public discourse seems to be pushing the boundaries: allegations of CAH have arisen with regard to crimes committed under the instigation or direction of networks or groups supporting opposing political parties and ethnicities during post-election violence in Kenya in 2007–2008, regarding crimes by groups of fighters in the early days of the Syria crisis,[18] and following recent terrorist attacks in European capitals.[19] Some have even suggested that the mass killing committed by a mentally disturbed individual in Norway in 2011 amounted to a crime against humanity,[20] while one commentator, in a provocative post, argued that under a broad definition of CAH, the 2011 London riots could be international crimes.[21]

[17] This notion is borrowed from Kress, 'On the Outer Limits of Crimes against Humanity: The Concept of Organization within the Policy Requirement: Some Reflections on the March 2010 ICC Kenya Decision' (2010) 23 Leiden Journal of International Law 855–73. Likewise, DeGuzman finds that the contextual elements of CAH 'are subject to considerable controversy', and Jalloh argues that it is 'not entirely clear what is the distinguishing characteristic or feature of a crime against humanity that moves it from the realm of the domestic to the international'. DeGuzman, 'Crimes against Humanity' in Schabas and Bernaz (eds), *Routledge Handbook of International Criminal Law* (Routledge 2011) 121, 121; Jalloh, 'What Makes Crimes against Humanity Crimes against Humanity?' (2013) 28 American University International Law Review 381–441, 385.

[18] Human Rights Watch, '"You Can Still See their Blood"—Executions, Indiscriminate Shootings, and Hostage Taking by Opposition Forces in Latakia Countryside (Human Rights Watch 2013).

[19] See Kress, 'Actes de Terrorisme: Nouvelles Formes de Crimes contre l'Humanité?' (manuscript with the author 2016).

[20] See BBC, 'Norway: Police Ponder New Anders Behring Breivik Charge' (BBC, 11 July 2011).

[21] See Schabas, 'London Riots: Were they Crimes against Humanity?' (15 August 2011) http://humanrightsdoctorate.blogspot.ch/2011/08/london-riots-were-they-crimes-against.html accessed 2 November 2017.

In this respect, the fairly broad definition of CAH under international law, including the ICC Statute, might be both a blessing and a curse. On the one hand, CAH apply to a variety of criminal acts and do not require a nexus to an armed conflict.[22] Thus, they can encompass heinous human rights violations during internal disturbances preceding armed conflicts, or mass violence that never escalates into an armed conflict, such as certain cases of post-election violence.[23] On the other hand, the vague codifications of the crime make a precise determination of the crime's scope challenging for international criminal lawyers, which might challenge the need for legal clarity.

Defining the material scope of CAH under contemporary international law is a legal endeavour with important political ramifications. This is particularly true with regard to the question of which kind of entities—a state, a non-state actor with quasi-governmental capacities, a party to an armed conflict, or any group or organization—may constitute an entity behind CAH. As one commentator analysed,

> the gist of the issue is how to reconcile the call for the broadest possible protection of human rights by way of ICL [international criminal law] (here crimes against humanity) with legitimate concerns as to the principle of strict construction and a possible loss of significance or 'downgrading' of crimes against humanity.[24]

In other words, leaving aside strictly legal arguments, at the policy level a very broad interpretation of possible entities behind CAH could enable the prosecution of different non-state actors for a variety of widespread or systematic acts of violence against a civilian population. However, opening the definition of CAH to an overly broad scope of acts could effectively weaken states' acceptance of and support for ICL. For example, states may not agree to apply internatinal justice tools to acts of violence that might—in their view—be best prosecuted at the national level and that may not amount to the 'most serious crimes of concern to the international community as a whole'.[25]

Focusing on the ICC, it has been argued that the current debate on the question of the entity behind CAH 'is nothing less than a struggle to shape the future jurisdiction and direction of the Court'.[26] Indeed, opponents of a wide interpretation of non-state entity involvement under article 7(2)(a) ICC Statute argue that this might 'broaden the scope of possible ICC intervention almost indefinitely',[27] 'infringe on state sovereignty',[28] overstretch the Court's resources, or lead to greater selectivity in the selection of cases.[29] In contrast, while sharing some of the concerns, others

[22] On the question of whether CAH require an armed conflict nexus, see Schabas, *The International Criminal Court* (1st edn, OUP 2010) 144–47; Cassese, *International Criminal Law* (n 3) 108; *Tadić, IT-94-1-T* (n 15) para 141.

[23] For an empirical study of CAH jurisprudence over the past decades, see Sadat, 'Emerging from the Shadow of Nuremberg'.

[24] Ambos, *Treatise on International Criminal Law* (OUP 2013) 75.

[25] Preamble to the ICC Statute.

[26] Sadat, 'Emerging from the Shadow of Nuremberg' (n 23) 335.

[27] *Situation in the Republic of Kenya, Dissenting Opinion of Judge Hans-Peter Kaul, 31 March 2010, Judge Kaul, ICC-01/09,* ICC, para 10.

[28] ibid.

[29] See ibid; Jalloh, 'Situation in the Republic of Kenya' (2011) 105 American Journal of International Law 546; Hansen, 'The Policy Requirement in Crimes against Humanity: Lessons from and for the Case

argue that 'prosecutorial overreaching, interstate politics, and judicial efficiency' are important issues, but the material definition of a crime is not the place to address them.[30] Indeed, defining the material scope of CAH under international law is relevant not only for cases before the ICC but also for national prosecutions. Thus, it should not be guided by tribunal-specific institutional considerations.

In order to determine which kinds of non-state armed groups can constitute an entity behind CAH under contemporary international law, this part proceeds as follows. In a first chapter, it considers the question conceptually, meaning how different legal philosophers define the crime's scope. The second chapter examines considerations of crimes by non-state armed groups in the historical development of CAH and discusses different CAH cases before the former Yugoslavia and Sierra Leone tribunals. The third and main chapter analyses the definition of CAH under article 7 ICC Statute, in particular the requirement that CAH need to be committed 'pursuant to or in furtherance of a State or organizational policy'. It argues that determining which types of organizations can provide the required policy depends on whether the policy merely instigates or also directs the crimes. Accordingly, the requisite capacity should not be determined in the abstract but by the capacity needed to realize CAH in different circumstances.

of Kenya' (2011) 43 George Washington International Law Review, 31–35. In Hansen's view, this might infringe the ICC's deterrent effect because not all deserving situations can be prosecuted, and could make it prone to increased criticism for 'political' decisions.

[30] Sadat, 'Emerging from the Shadow of Nuremberg' (n 23) 377. Indeed, questions of gravity and subsidiarity are regulated under article 17 ICC Statute. Moreover, the ICC Prosecutor has some discretion in the selection of cases. See article 53 ICC Statute.

7

Conceptual Considerations on the Notion of 'Crimes against Humanity'

Codifications of crimes against humanity (CAH) in international law instruments provide definitions of the crime and set out its legal elements. Yet, these definitions differ,[1] and interpretations of the crime's different elements vary. The question of the nature of the entity behind CAH, especially, remains disputed and accomplished jurists have suggested conflicting replies. In light of this disagreement and in order to clarify the concept and rationale of CAH beyond international law definitions, Part III of the book starts by examining how legal philosophers explain 'what is crime against humanity'.[2] It focuses particularly on different positions as to whether non-state entities can commit CAH, and—if yes—which kind of entities. The understanding of CAH developed in this chapter provides a conceptual account of the crime and its possible perpetrators and serves to underpin the legal analysis in subsequent chapters.

7.1 A Distinction between Ordinary Crimes and Crimes against Humanity

The term 'crimes against humanity' elicits the impression that the crimes committed are more serious than other crimes, meaning they affect and concern all human beings. However, why should the crime of murder be more shocking when committed as a crime against humanity than when committed as a crime under domestic law? If there is something commonly called 'humanity', why should 'humanity' be harmed more by one murder than by another? As in the case of war crimes and

[1] See article 5 of the Statute for the International Criminal Tribunal for the former Yugoslavia (ICTY Statute), article 3 of the Statute for the International Criminal Tribunal for Rwanda (ICTR Statute), and article 7 of the Rome Statute of the International Criminal Court (ICC Statute).

[2] This phrase is borrowed from Vernon, 'What is Crime against Humanity?' (2002) 10 Journal of Political Philosophy 231–49. The present analysis remains, however, restricted to philosophical approaches that are not too far detached from the law. As Chehtman argued, aptly, 'On the one hand if a philosophical conception of CAH is to provide us with useful insights into existing practice, it cannot be entirely divorced from legal practice and political discourse. On the other hand, we cannot take legal practice and political discourse as a given and develop a conception of CAH as merely a rationalization of their fundamental traits. Any theoretical account of CAH that is worth pursuing must also provide a critical bite on the legal practice.' Chehtman, 'Contemporary Approaches to the Philosophy of Crimes against Humanity' (2014) 14 International Criminal Law Review 813–35, 814.

Organizing Rebellion: Non-State Armed Groups under International Humanitarian Law, Human Rights Law, and International Criminal Law. Tilman Rodenhäuser. © Tilman Rodenhäuser, 2018. Published 2018 by Oxford University Press.

genocide, certain criminal acts—such as murder or torture—qualify as CAH and therefore as international crimes if they are committed in a particular context. Thus, the distinctive character of CAH derives from something other than the underlying criminal act. Accordingly, Macleod suggested:

> Any definition of the crime, then, will have to pass what we might term the Arendt Test: does the definition successfully capture and account for the gap between this crime and other lower-order crimes?[3]

In order to draw this distinction, the very term 'crimes against humanity' suggests that the particular character of CAH could be explained by determining under what conditions 'humanity' is harmed by certain crimes. According to its ordinary usage, the term 'humanity' has two meanings: first, it can be understood as 'humaneness', referring to core human values found in all human beings; and second, humanity can stand for 'humankind', meaning a community of all human beings.[4]

7.1.1 Crimes against humanity as inhumane crimes or especially heinous human rights violations

In the context of CAH, 'humanity' can undoubtedly be understood as 'humaneness': these crimes are certainly '*particularly odious offences* in that they constitute a serious attack on human dignity or a grave humiliation or degradation of one or more persons'.[5] They are 'unimaginable atrocities'.[6] Understood in this sense, CAH correspond to large-scale human rights violations.[7] Accordingly, Renzo suggested that instead of focusing only on collective violations of human rights, CAH should also encompass some 'individual violations of human rights' because even individual acts listed under CAH 'deny their victims the status of human being'.[8] Renzo advanced that every human being has certain pre-institutional basic rights emanating from and protecting his or her human dignity.[9] In order to protect these rights

[3] Macleod, 'Towards a Philosophical Account of Crimes against Humanity' (2010) 21 European Journal of International Law 281–302, 292.

[4] The Oxford Dictionaries, online version, defines 'humanity' first as 'human beings collectively' or second as 'the quality of being humane'. For a broader discussion of the two meanings of humanity, see Vernon, 'What is Crime against Humanity' (n 2) 238–40; Luban, 'A Theory of Crimes against Humanity' (2004) 29 Georgetown Law Faculty Publications and Other Works, 86–91.

[5] Cassese, *Cassese's International Criminal Law* (2nd edn, OUP 2008) 98.

[6] Preamble to the ICC Statute.

[7] As Cassese pointed out, 'While ICL [international criminal law] concerning war crimes largely derives from, or is closely linked with, IHL [international humanitarian law], ICL concerning crimes against humanity is to a great extent predicated upon international human rights law.' Cassese, *Cassese's International Criminal Law* (3rd edn, OUP 2013) 92. For further elaboration of this point, see Fortin, *The Accountability of Armed Groups under Human Rights Law* (OUP 2017) 307–21.

[8] Renzo, 'Crimes against Humanity and the Limits of International Criminal Law' (2012) 31 Law and Philosophy 443–76, 448; see also Renzo, 'A Criticism of the International Harm Principle' (2010) 4 Criminal Law and Philosophy 267–82.

[9] Renzo does not include all human rights in this category but only those rights that Henry Shue identified as a prerequisite to enjoy all other rights. See Renzo, 'Crimes against Humanity' (n 8) 450–52. On the idea of basic rights as differentiated from the larger category of human rights, see Shue, *Basic Rights: Subsistence, Affluence, and US Foreign Policy* (Princeton University Press 1996) 13–34.

and human status, CAH should include violations of rights that amount to a denial of human status, irrespective of their perpetrator.[10]

With this suggestion, Renzo consciously departed from established definitions of CAH. His approach would enhance human rights protection by criminalizing any violation of a restricted number of human rights—including violations committed by private individuals or members of armed groups. However, equating CAH with grave human rights violations or ordinary crimes might miss the particular quality of the crime, which turned CAH into an international crime even before the Universal Declaration of Human Rights was adopted. It was not individual attacks on isolated persons but systematic attacks on whole populations that triggered this development and justify universal criminal jurisdiction regarding these crimes.[11] In international law, states draw a distinction between human rights violations and CAH.[12] Making CAH over-inclusive also risks diminishing 'the strength of moral condemnation attached to labelling something an international crime',[13] and could eventually weaken international criminal law (ICL) in its entirety.[14] Thus, CAH should be something more than grave human rights violations.

7.1.2 Crimes against humanity as harm to 'humankind'

If particularly inhumane acts form part of CAH but do not define the crime's distinct character, the distinguishing element of CAH could be that such crimes harm humankind understood as a community of all human beings. This view finds support in the preamble of the Rome Statute, which states that unimaginable atrocities 'deeply shock the conscience of humanity', and that most serious crimes 'concern … the international community as a whole'. Likewise, in post-World War II jurisprudence a British Court argued that CAH are 'committed whenever the victim suffers prejudice as a result of the National Socialist rule of violence and tyranny *to such an extent that mankind itself was affected thereby*'.[15] The criminal law theory underlying this approach can be explained by analogy with domestic law: in civil cases, only the victim and the perpetrator are parties. If certain community values are violated, which is normally the case in criminal cases, the state represents the community interest in their suppression and becomes a party in the case. With regard to CAH, it can be argued that some crimes are so grave that humankind has an

[10] See Renzo, 'Crimes against Humanity' (n 8) 449–52.

[11] See Chehtman, *The Philosophical Foundations of Extraterritorial Punishment* (OUP 2010) 291; Macleod, 'Philosophical Account' (n 3).

[12] eg, while states agree that universal jurisdiction exists for CAH and many accept the International Criminal Court's (ICC's) jurisdiction over such crimes, states have not agreed to establish a 'World Court of Human Rights'. On the idea of a World Court of Human Rights, see Nowak and Kozma, *A World Court of Human Rights* (2009) <http://www.udhr60.ch>, accessed 13 November 2017.

[13] Fisher, 'The Distinct Character of International Crime: Theorizing the Domain' (2009) 8 Contemporary Political Theory 44–67, 48.

[14] See May, *Crimes against Humanity: A Normative Account* (CUP 2005) 107.

[15] Decision of the Supreme Court of the British Zone dated 26 October 1948, (unofficial translation), quoted from *Tadić, Judgment, 7 May 1997, Trial Chamber, IT-94-1-T*, ICTY, para 260 (emphasis added).

interest in their suppression.[16] The question is, which crimes inflict such harm on humankind?

For Hannah Arendt, mankind is affected by CAH because these crimes constitute an attack upon diversity among humans, 'that is, upon a characteristic of the "human status" without which the very words "mankind" or "humanity" would be devoid of any meaning'.[17] She emphasizes that, compared with crimes under domestic law, 'an altogether different order is broken and an altogether different community is violated'.[18] For Arendt, CAH, such as the extermination of Jewish people, harm humankind because they reduce diversity among human beings.[19] Following a related but broader approach, Macleod argues that humankind—understood as a '*grand-être*'—has an interest in a stable international order, in respect for the human status of every human being, and has a conscience that can be shocked.[20] For Macleod, crimes damaging humanity's interests or shocking its conscience affect every human being and justify external judicial intervention.[21] While some argue that reference to 'the conscience of humanity', or humanity's 'common bonds' or interests is 'beautiful and forceful, but ... too sweeping',[22] it does not seem too far-fetched to identify certain common interests. In this respect, May argued, 'International law is premised on the idea that all political communities have a strong interest in peace and in the protection of basic human rights.'[23] Such common interests are, for example, reflected in the Charter of the United Nations, or the ICC Statute.

To sum up, CAH can be characterized as grave human rights violations and particularly inhumane acts that, at the same time, violate elementary interests of humankind. As the International Law Commission stated:

> The concept of 'crimes against humanity' is generally seen as having two broad features. First, the crime is so heinous that it is viewed as an attack on the very quality of being human. Second, the crime is so heinous that it is an attack not just upon the immediate victims, but

[16] See Luban, 'A Theory of Crimes against Humanity' (n 4) 88–89; Vernon, 'What is Crime against Humanity' (n 2) 242; May, *Normative Account* (n 14) chapter 3; Duff, *Antony Duff, Answering for Crime: Responsibility and Liability in the Criminal* Law (Hart 2007), cited in Chehtman, 'Contemporary Approaches to the Philosophy of Crimes against Humanity' (n 2) 827–28.

[17] Arendt, *Eichmann in Jerusalem: A Report on the Banality of Evil* (revised and enlarged edn, Penguin Books 1994) 269.

[18] ibid, at 272.

[19] From a legal perspective, Arendt's approach can be criticized for not distinguishing adequately between genocide and CAH. Her theory reflects, rather, reasons why genocide constitutes an international crime. As Luban notes, 'Arendt uses the term "crime against humanity" to refer to genocide, which is perfectly natural in everyday usage, but in legal terms confuses two distinct crimes with different elements.' Luban, 'A Theory of Crimes against Humanity' (n 4)116 n 107.

[20] See Macleod, 'Philosophical Account' (n 3) 292–94. For Macleod, humanity's conscience should be understood as 'a disposition to react to certain events in a certain manner and to form certain judgements'. ibid, at 299.

[21] See ibid, at 299–301. For some criticism, see Chehtman, 'Contemporary Approaches to the Philosophy of Crimes against Humanity' (n 2) 822–23.

[22] Wilt, 'Crimes against Humanity: A Category Hors Concours in (International) Criminal Law?' in Van Beers, Corrias, and Werner (eds), *Humanity across International Law and Biolaw* (CUP 2014) 25–41, 32.

[23] May, 'Humanity, International Crime, and the Rights of Defendants' (2006) 20 Ethics & International Affairs 373–82.

also against all humanity, and hence the entire community of humankind has an interest in its punishment.[24]

Although this account of CAH convinces from a philosophical perspective, it leaves lawyers with the difficult questions of defining which values or interests can be attributed to humanity as a *grand-être*, what exactly shocks its conscience, and at what point the requisite threshold of harm would be met.[25]

7.2 Crimes against Humanity as Group Crimes

One approach to conceptualizing what harms or shocks humanity is to consider CAH as 'group crimes', meaning that CAH are committed by groups and against groups. Characterizing CAH as group crimes would reflect two of CAH's defining legal elements, namely that such crimes must be widespread (against a victim group) or systematic (committed by a group).[26] The following analysis is divided into a first part, examining why CAH must target victim groups, and a second part, on the group character of the perpetrators.[27]

7.2.1 Crimes against humanity as crimes against groups (populations)

In order to determine what distinguishes CAH from ordinary crimes, Luban, Vernon, and May suggest that CAH are not targeted against individuals but against

[24] International Law Commission, *First Report on Crimes against Humanity*, A/CN.4/680, para 27; see also *Erdemović, Sentencing Judgement, 20 October 1995, Trial Chamber, IT-96-22-T*, ICTY, para 28; Luban, 'A Theory of Crimes against Humanity' (n 4) 92; Kuschnik, 'Humaneness, Humankind and Crimes against Humanity', (2010) 2 Goettingen Journal of International Law 501–30, 510; Jalloh, 'What Makes Crimes against Humanity Crimes against Humanity?' (2013) 28 American University International Law Review 381–441.

[25] Macleod leaves this point open, stating: , 'Although it may be implausible to claim that the *grand-être* has an interest in any one individual, or is seriously harmed by one murder, it certainly can be said to have an interest in large blocks of it'. Macleod, 'Philosophical Account' (n 3) 298—99. May points exactly to this problem by emphasizing that it would be particularly difficult to determine indicators that show that humanity's conscience is shocked. See May, *Normative Account* (n 14) 84.

[26] See May, *Normative Account* (n 14) 83. Following along the same lines, criminologists have found that 'genuinely international criminality' shows specific constants, namely 'its collective and organizational dimension as well as its political nature'. Chouliaras, 'A Strategic Choice: The State Policy Requirement in Core International Crimes' (2015) 28 Leiden Journal of International Law 953–75, 968.

[27] The analysis is primarily based on the work of three legal, political science, and philosophy scholars: Luban's idea of CAH as attacks on the human being's nature as a 'political animal', Vernon's state-focused account of CAH, and May's 'international harm principle'. In his 'normative account' of CAH, May develops two key principles on why CAH amount to international crimes. For May, the 'international harm principle' justifies international prosecution of individual perpetrators of CAH. In addition, the 'security principle' provides a moral argument as to why such crimes justify international prosecutions, which would otherwise violate the territorial state's sovereignty. See May, *Normative Account* (n 14) chapters 4 and 5. For discussion and criticism of these accounts, see, eg, Altman, 'The Persistent Fiction of Harm to Humanity' (2006) 20 Ethics & International Affairs 367–72; Chehtman, 'Contemporary Approaches to the Philosophy of Crimes against Humanity' (n 2); Wilt, 'Crimes against Humanity: A Category Hors Concours in (International) Criminal Law?' (n 22).

groups.[28] According to Luban, human beings are 'political animals' in the sense that although human beings are individualistic, they need to live in groups. These groups constantly pose a threat to the human being's individuality and its individual interests. In order to mitigate this threat, humans form political organizations to regulate social interaction. Owing to its nature as a political animal, a human being needs to live in groups governed by a certain political structure.[29] For Luban, attacks on groups constitute CAH because they attack both natural characteristics of the political animal: first, these crimes harm the individual not as an individual but as a member of a population. Thereby, they deny the victim's individual value and identity. May adds that by disregarding the individuality of the human being, such crimes constitute an 'assault on what is common to all humans and hence to all of humanity'.[30] Second, these crimes target groups. Since human beings naturally have to live in groups, such attacks target this essential need of the human being.[31] As Vernon points out, since living in communities reduces humans' vulnerability, attacking a community leaves the individual especially vulnerable and renders CAH particularly harmful.[32] May suggests further that the international community should care if humans are targeted for reasons of group affiliation 'that are beyond their autonomous agency',[33] and he emphasizes that if groups are attacked, 'there is a much greater likelihood that the harm will be spread throughout a population rather than focused exclusively on a particular victim'.[34]

In addition to providing a philosophical argument as to why certain crimes harm some of humanity's key interests, characterizing CAH as crimes targeting populations or communities points to two important legal characteristics: first, focusing on victim groups excludes the commission of isolated crimes targeted against particular individuals from the scope of CAH. Second, attacks on groups can be expected to result in many victims, meaning that fundamental rights violations occur on a large scale.[35] Importantly, however, none of these accounts requires that crimes are committed on discriminatory grounds. Instead, groups should be understood as populations, defined, for example, by living in one geographical area.[36]

7.2.2 Groups as perpetrators of the crime

The second element the three authors emphasize is that CAH are normally committed by groups, namely by states or state-like entities. Following a Hobbesian

[28] These groups are not as narrowly defined as victim groups of genocide, or groups defined by race, colour, sex, language, religion, or social origin. Rather, with regard to CAH, groups should be understood as populations, which can also be loosely defined, eg, by living in one area.
[29] See Luban, 'A Theory of Crimes against Humanity' (n 4) 113–14.
[30] May, *Normative Account* (n 14) 85.
[31] See Luban, 'A Theory of Crimes against Humanity' (n 4) 116–17.
[32] See Vernon, 'What is Crime against Humanity?' (n 2) 244. This characteristic of CAH resembles the 'political animal' idea that Luban developed two years later.
[33] May, *Normative Account* (n 14) 85.
[34] ibid, at 86.
[35] For further discussion of these elements, see Section 9.2.4.2 'The required degree of organization as deduced from the contextual elements of CAH'.
[36] See Luban, 'A Theory of Crimes against Humanity' (n 4) 105–06.

approach, Luban explains this point as follows: as a political animal the human being needs to live in politically organized communities, which are entrusted with protecting individuals on their territory. If such entities turn against groups under their control, they invert their role and pervert their raison d'être. For Luban, 'the leitmotif binding together all the legal features [of CAH] is that of politics gone horribly wrong'.[37] Likewise, Vernon advances that CAH constitute 'an abuse of state power involving a systematic inversion of the jurisdictional resources of the state'.[38] May argues that focus on crimes by states or state-like entities follows the idea that, in such situations, a governing entity first violates its protective responsibilities, and second, is unlikely to prosecute its own crimes.[39] For Luban, humankind has an interest in repressing violence by politically organized groups against other groups in the same society.[40] The three experts agree that, in such situations, humanity should take on the role of the sovereign and prosecute the crime.[41]

The argument is pursuasive that crimes committed by states or state-like entities against individuals under their control harm humanity: if a governing entity—acting under a fig leaf of legitimacy or legality—perverts its governance responsibilities and turns against groups under its control, the protection of the victims warrants at least judicial intervention by the international community. This state-focused approach to CAH reflects the origin of the crime and the historic fact that CAH have often been committed by states against their citizens.[42] Moreover, the notion that CAH are committed with the involvement of collective entities and not by isolated individuals is a characteristic of the international legal definition of CAH. Yet, contrary to these assertions, it is submitted that a focus on crimes by states or state-like entities against persons under their control is too narrow. A state-focused account does not include situations in which a non-state entity is not state-like but commits a large-scale attack against a victim population, and the territorial authority is unable to prevent or halt the crimes. Moreover, a narrow approach to states and their relationship with individuals under their control may not account for state crimes committed extraterritorially.[43] For the purpose of this chapter, it is only necessary to elaborate on the first point.

[37] ibid, at 109. [38] Vernon, 'What is Crime against Humanity?' (n 2) 242.

[39] May, *Normative Account* (n 14) 88. Likewise, Chouliaras stressed the 'flagrant assault on the most fundamental human rights, accompanied in principle by impunity' as a key characteristic of CAH. Chouliaras, 'A Strategic Choice: The State Policy Requirement in Core International Crimes' (n 26) 955.

[40] Luban, 'A Theory of Crimes against Humanity' (n 4) 138.

[41] See Vernon, 'What is Crime against Humanity?' (n 2) 242–43. See also May's 'Security Principle', *Normative Account* (n 14) chapter 4.

[42] For further discussion of the history of CAH, see Chapter 8 'The Historical Development of Crimes against Humanity and Jurisprudence of the Rwanda, Former Yugoslavia, and Sierra Leone Tribunals'. As May has pointed out, 'Typically, there is no weak or non-existent State, but rather . . . the problem is often that a State is too strong, perceiving itself to be so strong that it can attack segments of its own population.' May, *Normative Account* (n 14) 81.

[43] See Ambos, *Treatise on International Criminal Law* (OUP 2013) 47.

7.3 Expanding the Concept of CAH to Non-State Entities

Discussion so far has shown that in addition to being large-scale crimes targeting populations, CAH are distinguished from ordinary crimes by the societal context in which they occur. This section argues first that this societal context cannot be restricted to situations in which states are directly responsible for large-scale crimes, but should also encompass widespread crimes committed by non-state entities against populations deprived of protection. Second, it examines which non-state entities could be responsible for such crimes.

7.3.1 Crimes against humanity as large-scale crimes against populations deprived of protection

The societal context of CAH could be construed narrowly as 'states assaulting their people'. Yet, at a more abstract level, the key characteristic defining such situations should not necessarily be active state involvement but that a population is attacked in a context in which it is deprived of protection by the governing entity.[44] If this deprivation of protection is one element turning certain large-scale crimes into CAH, logically states and state-like entities are the predominant perpetrators of this crime. However, victim populations find themselves in a similar situation if the governing entity is either unwilling or unable to prevent or halt large-scale human rights violations by non-state entities.[45] As Sadat emphasized, '"chaos, anarchy, [and] a collapse of State authority" may be precisely the kind of situation in which the victims of atrocity crimes' need international protection.[46] The victims are left at the mercy of perpetrators of severe and large-scale human rights violations without protection at the national level. In van de Wilt's words:

> The oppression by the state of its own population—or its impotence to shield the population against oppression by other powerful groups— bereaves that people of a vital capacity and simultaneously arouses the concern of all humanity, because the essential destruction of the political realm reflects upon all of us.[47]

This understanding of CAH does not negate the role of the state or a state-like entity in the commission of the crime: CAH may occur if the governing entity

[44] While many recognize this aspect, some argue nonetheless that it should restrict CAH to state-sponsored crimes. See, eg, Chouliaras, 'A Strategic Choice: The State Policy Requirement in Core International Crimes' (n 26) 955.

[45] The state's unwillingness to intervene may also be considered as state involvement. See Preparatory Commission for the International Criminal Court, *Elements of Crimes*, 2 November 2000, PCNICC/2000/1/Add.2, 5.

[46] Sadat, 'Crimes against Humanity in the Modern Age' (2012) 107 *American Journal of International Law* 334–77, 370.

[47] Wilt, 'Crimes against Humanity: A Category Hors Concours in (International) Criminal Law?' (n 22) 35.

either violates or is unable to fulfil its obligation to protect individuals under its jurisdiction.[48]

The suggested approach justifies why certain crimes can be considered to cause harm to humanity. Moreover, it corresponds with theories of why some crimes invite international prosecution.[49] Scholars have argued that if the prohibition of international crimes is to be effective, there must be an alternative forum to the courts of a state that is 'responsible for perpetrating, instigating or allowing them, or simply unable to do anything about them'.[50] In order to justify why an external actor should be permitted to prosecute crimes committed under the jurisdiction of a state, these scholars invoke a functional approach to sovereignty.[51] Accordingly, some scholars argue that if 'a government perpetrates or permits the violation of the basic rights of its people, third parties—in this case, other states in the international community—have a moral right, if not a duty, to interfere'.[52] Arguably, in such situations, the state forfeits its right to oppose intervention by international bodies.[53] The extent to which such situations justify unsolicited third-party intervention by armed force continues to be debated. However, the idea that certain large-scale crimes—whether committed by states or non-state actors—grant every state the right to prosecute the alleged perpetrators irrespective of where the crime was committed is well established as the principle of universal jurisdiction.[54]

In summary, a combination of elements explains CAH's status as an international crime. To start with, CAH consist of fundamental human rights violations. However, to distinguish CAH from ordinary crimes, two elements are decisive: first, CAH are large-scale crimes committed against a group or population. By directing a crime against a group or population, its perpetrators deny the individual value of the victims, threaten human beings' need to live in communities, and threaten a much wider group of persons than individual crimes. Second, CAH are particularly harmful and spark the interest of humanity because they are committed in situations in which the victims are deprived of any protection by the territorial authority. This can be the case either because state or governing-entity agents commit or condone the crime, or because the entity in power is unable to protect the victim

[48] This broader approach to potential perpetrators of CAH finds some support in May's normative account of CAH. He finds that for acts to amount to crimes against humanity 'there is a third option (not properly part of the international harm principle) that can be met if the state whose subject allegedly committed the crime is either too weak to prosecute or ineffectual in doing so'. Unfortunately, May explicitly excludes this aspect from his analysis and does not elaborate further on it. May, *Normative Account* (n 14) 92. See also Wilt, 'Crimes against Humanity: A Category Hors Concours in (International) Criminal Law?' (n 22) 27.

[49] For a discussion of different grounds of international jurisdiction, see Sadat, 'Crimes against Humanity in the Modern Age' (n 46) 370.

[50] Chehtman, 'Contemporary Approaches to the Philosophy of Crimes against Humanity' (n 2) 833.

[51] May summarizes this approach as follows: 'Sovereignty is premised on the willingness and ability of a State to protect its subjects.' May, *Normative Account* (n 14) 68.

[52] Altman and Wellman, 'A Defense of International Criminal Law' (2004) 115 Ethics 35–67, 45–46.

[53] May, *Normative Account* (n 14) 68.

[54] See The Princeton Principles on Universal Jurisdiction, (2001); International Law Association, *Final Report on the Exercise of Universal Jurisdiction in Respect of Gross Human Rights Offences* (ILA 2000).

population against large-scale crimes by a non-state entity. As Ambos underlined, the rationale for criminalizing certain crimes as CAH under international law 'is the extreme *gravity* of certain crimes, which is usually accompanied by the unwillingness or inability of national criminal systems to prosecute them'.[55] Following this understanding of CAH, the range of potential perpetrators of the crimes cannot be restricted to states or state-like entities, but includes a variety of non-state actors. Section 7.3.2 'Characteristics of groups able to commit crimes against humanity' examines whether general characteristics exist that define perpetrators of CAH.

7.3.2 Characteristics of groups able to commit crimes against humanity

Scholars have suggested different characteristics of groups able to commit CAH. If CAH were considered crimes by entities with an obligation to protect human rights of individuals under their jurisdiction, the analysis would require an examination of which entities have such protective obligations.[56] As discussed above, however, this should not be a condition sine qua non to define possible perpetrators of CAH. Coming from a state-focused account of CAH, Vernon and May suggest the following characteristics for perpetrators: they should have state-like resources at their disposal in order to commit crimes on a certain scale and sustain them, have the institutional capacity to declare certain acts right or wrong, and exercise territorial control 'to immobilize a group and also to deny it external help'.[57] Moreover, the entity behind the crime should be able to involve larger parts of society as perpetrators, to plan the crimes with the aim of harming more than an individual, and be able to evade prosecution for its crimes.[58] In the following, it is shown that none of these characteristics necessarily restricts the range of perpetrators to states or state-like entities.

Looking at the capacity of the potential perpetrators of CAH, it is undisputed that non-state entities can commit most severe acts of violence and can direct such attacks against groups or populations. As crimes in countries such as Sierra Leone have shown, it does not take state-like resources to commit grave and large-scale crimes, and neither is it necessary to involve larger parts of society as perpetrators.[59] Similarly, non-state entities can develop group dynamics and forms of leadership under which they determine for their members what is right and what is wrong, and morally exclude potential victims from their group.[60] It is also questionable whether

[55] Ambos, *Treatise on International Criminal Law* (n 43) 56.

[56] For an in-depth analysis of this question, see Section 6.3 'Human Rights Obligations of Groups Exercising Quasi-Governmental Authority in Defined Territory'.

[57] Vernon, 'What is Crime against Humanity?' (n 2) 243.

[58] See May, *Normative Account* (n 14) 88.

[59] eg, in Sierra Leone, members of the Armed Forces Revolutionary Council committed crimes against humanity with relatively limited resources and with no effective territorial control or state-like governmental infrastructure. See *Brima et al, Judgment, 20 June 2007, SCSL-04-16-T,* SCSL, para 238.

[60] On a study of group behaviour in armed groups, Frésard and ICRC, *The Roots of Behaviour in War: A Survey of the Literature* (ICRC 2004) 46–86. See also Kleffner, 'The Collective Accountability of Organized Armed Groups for System Crimes' in Van de Wilt and Nollkaemper (eds), *System Criminality in International Law* (CUP 2009) 244–45.

territorial control is a necessary condition. The immobilization of people is not a strict element of CAH, but large-scale crimes can also be committed against people who are able to flee. As cases of forced displacement show, the flight of victims can be one aim of CAH.[61] The denial of external help appears important for the commission of CAH but does not restrict it to state crimes: if the state is unable to protect its citizens against large-scale crimes and does not call for external assistance, the victims of the crime are trapped in their home territory and denied any external protection in the same way as if the state committed the crimes itself.[62] As a result, while many of these elements characterize groups typically responsible for CAH—namely, states or state-like entities—they do not exclude other non-state entities from the scope of potential perpetrators.

Luban suggests an additional element. He restricts perpetrators of CAH to 'politically organized groups acting under color of policy'.[63] This definition contains two elements: perpetrators must be 'politically organized', and act under a policy. The policy suggestion effectively excludes individual perpetrators acting independently of any organization. Instead, acting under a policy links individual acts to the authors of the policy. It underlines the character of CAH as crimes committed by groups.[64] In principle, nothing excludes non-state entities from adopting such a policy. In contrast, it is less clear why a group needs to be 'politically organized'. Haque has argued that 'politically organized groups' can commit CAH because it is particularly unlikely that the state will prosecute members of these groups.[65] For Haque, '[p]olitically organized groups are appropriate targets for international law because they [. . .] are uniquely capable of co-opting the state to either assist or ignore group violence'.[66] Unfortunately, Haque does not clarify what makes a group 'politically organized' as opposed to groups organized in any other manner. The decisive criterion appears to be that the state is unwilling to halt the group's crimes, or to administer justice, either because it acquiesces to the crime or the organized group is powerful enough to co-opt the state. It would only

[61] eg, in the Darfur region, state forces and militias are alleged to have committed CAH. These crimes did not require the immobilization of the victims but consisted, inter alia, of enforced displacement. Displacement can be both internal and across international borders and is, by definition, not the immobilization of a population but its mobilization. See United Nations Secretary General, *Report of the International Commission of Inquiry on Darfur to the United Nations Secretary-General* paras 633–38.

[62] As much as the principle of non-intervention under international law prohibits external intervention in cases of state violence, it prohibits intervention in case of non-state violence unless the state invites a third party to intervene, or the UN Security Council authorizes intervention.

[63] Luban, 'A Theory of Crimes against Humanity' (n 4) 97.

[64] As Chouliaras argues, analysing international crimes 'should look for the structural conditions that trigger criminality, meaning it should focus on the political motivation and social organization of violence. . . .. The study of organizational, as opposed to individual, etiological factors and the employment of the concepts of organizational goals, structure, and process will redefine core international crimes as instances of organizational and not simply individual deviance.' Chouliaras, 'A Strategic Choice: The State Policy Requirement in Core International Crimes' (n 26) 971.

[65] See Haque, 'Group Violence and Group Vengeance: Toward a Retributivist Theory of International Criminal Law' (2005) 9 Buffalo Criminal Law Review 303–04.

[66] ibid, at 304.

be a small step to add groups operating in situations in which the state is unable to protect its citizens.[67]

To sum up, CAH signify large-scale crimes committed in accordance with a group policy and taking place in a societal context in which the territorial state is either actively or passively involved in the crime, or unable to prevent or halt it. With regard to the element that CAH are mass-atrocities targeting a victim population, a non-state entity would need to be able to develop and promulgate a policy that directs crimes against a victim group. It also needs to be sufficiently organized and equipped to execute this policy, meaning that it has the capacity to instigate or sustain large-scale human rights violations. With regard to the societal context of CAH, at least two scenarios are conceivable. On the one hand, perpetrators would either need to constitute themselves as the governing authority, or be capable of co-opting the governing authority, in order to enable the commission of large-scale crimes and avoid prosecution. On the other hand, irrespective of the non-state entity's capacity, CAH can also be committed if the state is simply unable to fulfil its protective obligations towards the victim population. While the former case requires a certain political power on the part of the non-state entity, in the latter case it is the incapacity of the state that enables the commission of the crime. The territorial state would need to be dysfunctional to the extent that it is unable to prevent or to halt the crimes. Thus, instead of concentrating on the nature of the entity behind the crimes, it might be 'more convincing to develop a concept of crimes against humanity while downplaying the focus on the entity behind these crimes'.[68]

[67] See Fisher, 'The Distinct Character of International Crime' (n 13) 60. She argues that 'a rebel group or faction of society with particular aims' can commit CAH.

[68] Ambos, *Treatise on International Criminal Law* (n 43) 47.

8

The Historical Development of Crimes against Humanity and Jurisprudence of the Rwanda, Former Yugoslavia, and Sierra Leone Tribunals

In international law, the notion 'crimes against humanity' emerged as a reaction to state crimes. Its first use dates back to 1915, when the governments of Great Britain, France, and Russia condemned Turkish massacres against the Armenian population in the Ottoman Empire as 'crimes of Turkey against humanity and civilization'.[1] After World War I, the idea underlying crimes against humanity (CAH) was included in the peace treaty with Turkey, the Treaty of Sevres, which envisaged prosecution of those 'responsible for the massacres committed during the continuance of the state of war on territory which formed part of the Turkish Empire'.[2] This phrase referred to large-scale crimes committed by Turkey against its citizens. However, the Treaty of Sevres never entered into force.[3] No reference to CAH was included in the Treaty of Versailles.[4] As an international crime, CAH were first codified in the

[1] A quote of the original note is found in Schwelb, 'Crimes against Humanity' (1946) 23 British Year Book of International Law 181. See also Cassese, *Cassese's International Criminal Law* (3rd edn, OUP 2013) 84–85. The idea of 'laws of humanity' dates back to the St Petersburg Declaration of 1868 or earlier dates, and was first codified in the preamble to the 1907 Hague Convention Respecting the Laws and Customs of War on Land. See Triffterer (ed), *Commentary on the Rome Statute of the International Criminal Court: Observers' Notes, Article by Article* (2nd edn, CH Beck 2008) 166; Paust, Bassiouni, and Scharf, *International Criminal Law: Cases and Materials* (4th edn, Carolina Academic Press 2012) 703; Schwelb, 'Crimes against Humanity' (above) 180.

[2] Article 230 Treaty of Sevres, concluded on 10 August 2020 between Allied Powers and the Ottoman Empire.

[3] Replacing the Treaty of Sevres, the Treaty of Lausanne entered into force in 1923, but did not contain a provision on the prosecution of war crimes or crimes against humanity. For further discussion of these early documents, see Schwelb, 'Crimes against Humanity' (n 1) 179–83; Bassiouni, *Crimes against Humanity: Historical Evolution and Contemporary Application* (CUP 2011) 86–98.

[4] Articles 227 and 228 of the Treaty of Versailles (concluded on *28 June 1919 between Allied Powers and Germany*) included 'supreme offence against international morality and the sanctity of treaties' and 'acts in violation of the laws and customs of war'. The treaty did not include reference to violations of the laws of humanity as recommended by the Commission on the Responsibility of the Authors of the War and on Enforcement of Penalties.

Charter of the International Military Tribunal (Nuremberg Charter) in 1945, which aimed to prosecute the 'major war criminals of the European Axis countries'.[5]

This chapter analyses how CAH developed from when they were first codified in 1945 until their adjudication in the 1990s and early 2000s, focusing on whether the different definitions and interpretations of CAH were exclusively state-focused or also encompassed crimes by non-state actors.[6]

8.1 Crimes against Humanity in the Nuremberg Charter and in Post-World War II Jurisprudence

CAH were first codified in article 6(c) of the Nuremberg Charter.[7] This article defined CAH as:

> murder, extermination, enslavement, deportation, and other inhumane acts committed against any civilian population, before or during the war; or persecutions on political, racial or religious grounds in execution of or in connection with any crime within the jurisdiction of the Tribunal, whether or not in violation of the domestic law of the country where perpetrated.

Owing to its historical context, and as stated in the article's chapeau, the aim of the Nuremberg Tribunal was to prosecute persons 'acting in the interests of the European Axis countries'.[8] Thus, Schabas highlighted that the Tribunal's jurisprudence over CAH was limited to offenders acting 'in the interest of a state'.[9] This conclusion is corroborated by the article's requirement that CAH must be committed in 'execution of or in connection with any crime within the jurisdiction of the Tribunal'.[10] Crimes within the Tribunal's jurisdiction were crimes against peace and

[5] Article 6 Nuremberg Charter (Agreement for the Prosecution and Punishment of the Major War Criminals of the European Axis, 1945). While Bassiouni finds that CAH were an emerging custom by 1919 but only found its definition in positive international law in 1945 (see Bassiouni, *Crimes against Humanity* (n 3) 147). Cassese doubted that CAH formed part of customary international law before 1945 (see Cassese, *International Criminal Law* (2nd edn, OUP 2008) 106–09).

[6] For comprehensive but more general accounts of the history of CAH, see, eg, Bassiouni, *Crimes against Humanity* (n 3); International Law Commission, *First Report on Crimes against Humanity*, A/CN.4/680, paras 28–39; Werle and Jessberger, *Principles of International Criminal Law* (OUP 2014) 328–32; Ambos, *Treatise on International Criminal Law* (OUP 2013); Cassese, *Cassese's International Criminal Law* (n 1) 84–90.

[7] A similar definition is found in article 5 of the International Military Tribunal for the Far East Charter. Yet, charges of crimes against humanity were not levelled at any suspect before the Tokyo Tribunal.

[8] Justice Jackson, who was involved in the negotiations of the Nuremberg Charter on behalf of the President of the United States of America, made this desire clear when he reported, 'Our case against the major defendants is concerned with the Nazi master plan, not with individual barbarities and perversions which occurred independently of any central plan.' Justice Jackson, *Report to the President on Atrocities and War Crimes* (1945), available at <http://avalon.law.yale.edu/imt/imt_jack01.asp> (accessed 25 November 2017).

[9] Schabas, *Unimaginable Atrocities: Justice, Politics, and Rights at the War Crimes Tribunals* (OUP 2012) 128.

[10] While the semicolon in the English text suggests that the nexus to other crimes only applies to persecution-type crimes, it has been convincingly argued that this was not how the drafting states intended to define it. The understanding that the nexus to other crimes applied to all crimes defined under article 6(c) was explicitly clarified in the Berlin Protocol of 6 October 1945. For detailed discussion, see

war crimes—two crimes that could only be committed with state involvement.[11] This nexus requirement served primarily to protect states from prosecution for acts unrelated to World War II, which they would have considered infringements of the principle of non-intervention.[12] The material definition of CAH under article 6(c) did not, however, foresee that only state actors could commit CAH. Neither did it explicitly require the involvement of the state. Essentially, article 6(c) defined CAH as certain odious crimes when 'committed against any civilian population'.[13] This wording is very broad and does not provide much information on which elements characterize CAH and who the possible perpetrators may be.

The International Military Tribunals' judgment of 1946 remained vague on legal elements of CAH.[14] Still, foreshadowing the core elements of CAH as later included in its various definitions, the Tribunal held that Germany's 'policy of terror was certainly carried out on a vast scale, and in many cases was organized and systematic'.[15] More guidance on the question of which actors can commit CAH is found in the jurisprudence of the military tribunals established by the Allied powers in occupied Germany, which adjudicated cases under the Control Council Law No 10 (CCL10).[16] Most cases focused on crimes committed by Nazi officials. Yet, the military tribunals also adjudicated crimes committed by different private actors, and expressed diverse views on the legal elements of CAH.

Schwelb, 'Crimes against Humanity' (n 1) 192–95; Bassiouni, *Crimes against Humanity* (n 3) 121–26. See also *International Military Tribunal (Nuremberg) Judgment, 1 October 1946*, 468.

[11] See Schabas, 'State Policy as an Element of International Crimes' (2007) 98 Journal of Criminal Law and Criminology 961.

[12] For further discussion on this point, see Bassiouni, *Crimes against Humanity* (n 3) 136; Ambos and Wirth, 'The Current Law of Crimes against Humanity: An Analysis of UNTAET Regulation 152000' (2002) 13 Criminal Law Forum 1–90, 5. Arguably, this limitation was only of a jurisdictional nature because international law no longer shielded states from judicial intervention in cases of mass atrocities. See *The United States of America v Josef Altstötter, et al (Justice case), Judgment, 4 December 1947*, United States Military Tribunal, 979–82.

[13] The clarification that the international criminalization of CAH is independent from the crime's legality under domestic law does not add any substantive element to the definition of CAH either.

[14] Leila Sadat commented that '[f]rom a legal standpoint, the judgment of the International Military Tribunal was a disappointment' and that 'one of the most unfortunate legacies of the IMT [International Military Tribunal] judgment is that it failed to provide any criteria that could be used to distinguish crimes against humanity either from war crimes or from ordinary municipal crimes, such as torture, murder, or rape'. Sadat, 'The Interpretation of the Nuremberg Principles by the French Court of Cassation: From Touvier to Barbie and Back Again' (1994) 32 Columbia Journal of Transnational Law 309–10.

[15] *International Military Tribunal (Nuremberg), Judgement, 1 October 1947, 468.*

[16] Article 2(1)(c) CCL10 defined CAH as: 'Atrocities and offenses, including but not limited to murder, extermination, enslavement, deportation, imprisonment, torture, rape, or other inhumane acts committed against any civilian population, or persecutions on political, racial or religious grounds whether or not in violation of the domestic laws of the country where perpetrated.' Contrary to article 6(c) of the Nuremberg Charter, the definition of CAH in CCL10 did not require a nexus to other crimes in the definition of CAH. Nonetheless, as the Nuremberg Charter was an integral part of the CCL10, most jurisprudence based on CCL10 maintained the focus on crimes committed with a nexus to either war crimes or crimes against peace (see, eg, *The United States of America v Carl Krauch, et al (IG Farben*

In the *Justice* case against members of the Reich Ministry of Justice and the German judiciary, the United States Military Tribunal III expressed a state-centric view on CAH. It found that article 2(1)(c) CCL10:

> provides for punishment of crimes committed against German nationals only where there is proof of conscious participation in systematic *government organized or approved procedures* amounting to atrocities and offenses of the kind specified in the act and committed against populations or amounting to persecutions on political, racial, or religious grounds.[17]

In the Tribunal's view, 'governmental participation is a material element of the crime against humanity. Only when official organs of sovereignty participated in atrocities and persecutions did those crimes assume international proportions.'[18] Hence, the Tribunal stated in unequivocal terms that state involvement was a necessary requirement for CAH.

Yet, the Tribunal's interpretation of CAH's scope did not exclude crimes committed by non-state actors. In the *Flick* and the *IG Farben* cases, managers of private enterprises were charged with CAH inter alia for the 'enslavement of concentration camp inmates, including German nationals'.[19] Although the Tribunal did not find the industrials on trial responsible for designing the Third Reich's slave-labour programme, the Tribunal decided that the use of slave labour in their private factories amounted to CAH.[20] Likewise, in a number of cases against individuals who denounced Jews or political opponents to German authorities, tribunals found that private actors can commit CAH if acting in accordance with a state policy.[21] Thus, already at an early stage in the history of CAH, tribunals held that CAH were not restricted to crimes of state officials but could also be committed by private individuals if following a state policy.

An even broader understanding of CAH was expressed in an obiter dictum in the *Einsatztruppen* case, in which US Military Tribunal II held:

> Crimes against humanity are acts committed in the course of wholesale and systematic violation of life and liberty. It is to be observed that insofar as international jurisdiction is concerned, the concept of crimes against humanity does not apply to offenses for which the criminal code of any well-ordered state makes adequate provision. *They can only come within the purview of this basic code of humanity because the state involved, owing to indifference, impotency or complicity, has been unable or has refused to halt the crimes and punish the criminals.*[22]

case), United States Military Tribunal, Judgment, 30 July 1948). For an exception, see *The United States of America v Otto Ohlendorf, et al (Einsatzgruppen case), United States Military Tribunal, Judgment, 10 April 1948*. Moreover, analysing German jurisprudence based on CCL10, Ambos and Wirth argue that German tribunals did not require a war nexus but some link to an authority in order to distinguish CAH from ordinary crimes. Ambos and Wirth, 'The Current Law of Crimes against Humanity' (n 12) 6.

[17] *The United States of America v Josef Altstötter, et al (Justice case)* (n 12) 982 (emphasis added).

[18] ibid, at 984.

[19] *The United States of America v Friedrich Flick et al (Flick case), United States Military Tribunal, Judgment, 22 December 1947*, 1193; *The United States of America v Carl Krauch et al (IG Farben case)* (n 16) 1166.

[20] See *The United States of America v Carl Krauch et al (IG Farben case)* (n 16) 1186.

[21] See Cassese, *International Criminal Law* (n 5) at 116.

[22] *The United States of America v Otto Ohlendorf et al (Einsatzgruppen case)* (n 16) 498 (emphasis added).

Contrary to the finding in the *Justice* case, in this case the tribunal did not consider active state involvement a condition sine qua non for the commission of CAH. Instead, it focused on two elements: first, the crimes must be large-scale and systematic; and second, the territorial state needs to be unable or unwilling to halt or prosecute them. This statement did not limit the potential perpetrators of CAH to state officials or persons acting in accordance with a state policy, but suggested that CAH can also be committed without direct state involvement.

In summary, the definition of CAH under the Nuremberg Charter and post-World War II jurisprudence focused on crimes committed by Nazi Germany and not on crimes by non-state entities. Still, jurisprudence by different military tribunals found that non-state actors can commit CAH pursuant to a state policy. Moreover, at least in the *Justice* case, the Tribunal left open the possibility that CAH could be committed without direct state involvement if the territorial state is unwilling or unable to halt and prosecute the crimes.[23] Accordingly, in an attempt to define CAH following the Nuremberg case law, the United Nations War Crimes Commission held in 1948:

> Isolated offences did not fall within the notion of crimes against humanity. As a rule systematic mass action, *particularly if it was authoritative*, was necessary to transform a common crime, punishable only under municipal law, into a crime against humanity, which thus became also the concern of international law.[24]

Following this definition, state action was not a material element of CAH.[25] Instead, the decisive elements of CAH were that crimes be committed in a systematic manner and on a mass scale.

8.2 The International Law Commission's Codification of Crimes against Humanity

In 1947, one of the first tasks states entrusted to the newly established International Law Commission (ILC) was to formulate the principles of international law recognized in the Nuremberg Charter and the 1946 judgment, and to prepare a 'draft code of offences against the peace and security of mankind'.[26] While in the

[23] Paust went as far as arguing there was no requirement for the act being committed to be 'in furtherance of some state or organizational policy'. Paust, 'The International Criminal Court does not have Complete Jurisdiction over Customary Crimes against Humanity and War Crimes' (2010) 43 John Marshall Law Review 686–87.

[24] Commission des Crimes de Guerre des Nations Unies, *History of the United Nations War Crimes Commission and the Development of the Laws of War* (His Majesty's Stationery Office 1948) 179 (emphasis added).

[25] State action could be read into the reference to 'authoritative' mass action. However, being 'authoritative' was not a strict criterion.

[26] United Nations General Assembly (UNGA), Formulation of the Principle Recognized in the Charter of the Nuremberg Tribunal and in the Judgment of the Tribunal, 21 November 1947, A/Res/177(II).

1950s the ILC's draft codes reflected closely the Nuremberg Charter's definition of CAH, in the early 1990s the Commission adopted broader definitions of the crime.

8.2.1 The 1951 and 1954 drafts of the *Code of Offences against the Peace and Security of Mankind*

In the 'Nuremberg Principles'[27] of 1950 and in the first draft *Code of Offences against the Peace and Security of Mankind* of 1951, the ILC followed closely the Nuremberg Charter's definition of CAH. In accordance with the Military Tribunals' jurisprudence on non-state perpetrators of CAH as discussed above, article 2(10) of the 1951 draft Code stated that inhumane acts can be committed both by 'the authorities of a State or by private individuals', provided that the acts be connected to war crimes or crimes against peace.[28] Three years later, the ILC did not include this nexus requirement in the 1954 draft Code. In order to differentiate 'any inhuman act committed by a private individual' from CAH, the ILC specified that CAH consist of '[i]nhuman acts ... by the authorities of a State or by private individuals acting at the instigation or with the toleration of such authorities'.[29] This suggests that non-state individuals can commit CAH for non-official purposes and not acting in accordance with a state policy, as long as the acts are condoned by the territorial state. Thus, passive state involvement would suffice. Still, at the time, some academic commentators criticized a definition of CAH that necessarily requires some state involvement for being inconsistent with other definitions of international crimes, because states had decided just a few years earlier not to require any state involvement for the crime of genocide.[30]

8.2.2 The 1991 and 1996 *Draft Code of Crimes against the Peace and Security of Mankind*

Owing to states' disagreement on the definition of the crime of aggression, further work on a draft Code was postponed for almost three decades.[31] When in 1991 the ILC adopted a revised *Draft Code of Crimes*, it no longer included an explicit provision on CAH, but termed the corresponding offence 'systematic or mass violations of human rights'.[32] Under article 21 of the 1991 *Draft Code*, any

[27] International Law Commission, *Principles of International Law Recognized in the Charter of the Nürnberg Tribunal and in the Judgment of the Tribunal* (United Nations 1950) article 2(10).

[28] International Law Commission, *Draft Code of Offences against the Peace and Security of Mankind* (United Nations 1951).

[29] UNGA, *Draft Code of Offences against the Peace and Security of Mankind*, 4 December 1954, A/Res/897(IX), article 2(11).

[30] See Johnson, 'The Draft Code of Offences against the Peace and Security of Mankind' (1955) 4 International and Comparative Law Quarterly 465.

[31] UNGA, 4 December 1954, A/Res/897(IX) (n 29). The ILC was only asked to resume its work on a draft code in 1981, see UNGA, Draft Code of Offences against the Peace and Security of Mankind, 10 December 1981, A/Res/36/774.

[32] International Law Commission, *Draft Code of Crimes against the Peace and Security of Mankind with Commentaries* (United Nations 1991) article 21.

individual could be charged for this crime if he or she committed certain 'violations of human rights ... in a systematic manner or on a mass-scale'. Some have argued that reference to 'human rights violations' suggests that 'state involvement may have been viewed as a sine qua non' for CAH.[33] Yet, according to the ILC's commentary, perpetrators of this crime were not limited to state actors.[34] The commentary explained that 'the article does not rule out the possibility that private individuals with *de facto* power or organized in criminal gangs or groups might also commit the kind of systematic or mass violations of human rights covered by the article'.[35] Thus, in the ILC's view, this crime could not be committed by isolated individuals, but required some kind of authority or group behind the underlying acts.[36]

Scholars criticized the 1991 draft for various reasons.[37] However, it does not seem that states voiced major concerns with the formulation of CAH in the 1991 draft.[38] Accordingly, five years later, the ILC included the essence of the 1991 *Draft Code* in article 18 of 1996 *Draft Code of Crimes*. This provision defined 'crimes against humanity' as certain crimes 'when committed in a systematic manner or on a large scale and instigated or directed by a Government or by any organization or group'. In its commentary, the ILC argued:

> The instigation or direction of a Government or any organization or group, which may or may not be affiliated with a Government, gives the act its great dimension and makes it a crime against humanity imputable to private persons or agents of a State.[39]

As a result, the ILC did not limit CAH to crimes committed with active or passive state involvement. In the Commission's view, certain heinous human rights violations could amount to CAH if committed in a widespread or systematic manner by any individual acting at the instigation or under the direction of a state or non-state collective entity.[40] The ILC only excluded crimes committed by individuals acting on their 'own initiative' and according to their 'own criminal plan'. The ILC did not

[33] Schabas, *Unimaginable Atrocities* (n 9) 136.

[34] However, the commentary admits that states, 'in view of their official position, have far-reaching factual opportunity to commit the crimes covered by the draft article'. International Law Commission, *Draft Code* (n 32) para 5 on article 21.

[35] ibid.

[36] This point was emphasized by the ILC in its commentary on the 1996 Draft Articles. See International Law Commission, *Draft Code of Crimes against the Peace and Security of Mankind (with Commentary)* (United Nations 1996) para 5 on article 18. See also Ambos, *Treatise on International Criminal Law* (n 6) 53.

[37] Bassiouni criticizes the 1991 draft for violating the principle of legality and for not adequately distinguishing 'conduct that is wholly within the national criminal jurisdiction of a given state and conduct that constitutes an international crime irrespective of national law'. Bassiouni, *Crimes against Humanity* (n 3) 179–80. Similarly, Tomuschat hints at a number of weaknesses in the drafting of the provision. Tomuschat, 'Crimes against the Peace and the Security of Mankind and the Recalcitrant Third State' in Dinstein and International Legal Colloquium on War (eds), *War Crimes in International Law* (M Nijhoff 1996) 49–50. See also Schabas, *Unimaginable Atrocities* (n 9) 135–36.

[38] *Tadić, Judgment, 7 May 1997, Trial Chamber, IT-94-1-T*, ICTY, para 665.

[39] International Law Commission, *Draft Code* (n 36) para 5 on article 18.

[40] As Jalloh argued, in the ILC's view 'the hallmarks of such offenses lie in their widespread or systematic nature' and not in the nature of the perpetrators. Jalloh, 'What Makes Crimes against Humanity Crimes against Humanity?' (2013) 28 American University International Law Review 405.

require the 'organization or group' behind CAH to have state-like characteristics. Instead, what seemed decisive is that the entity is able to instigate or direct large-scale or systematic crimes. While the ability to direct widespread or systematic crimes would, arguably, require some kind of command or control relationship between the group and the individual perpetrators, this is not the case if the group merely instigates the crimes.[41]

The ILC draft articles cannot, however, be taken as an authoritative restatement of positive international law.[42] Still, the opinion of international law experts drafting definitions of international crimes at the request of the United Nations is significant.[43] Therefore, international and national courts have referred to the ILC's *Draft Codes* when establishing material elements of CAH.[44] The ILC's work has been especially important because state practice on the question of what constitutes CAH was very limited at the time.[45] Relevant national CAH cases are discussed in Section 8.3 'The Need for State Involvement as Found in National Jurisprudence'.

8.3 The Need for State Involvement as Found in National Jurisprudence

In the period between the Nuremberg Trials and the establishment of the tribunals for the former Yugoslavia and Rwanda, national CAH trials prosecuted crimes committed by agents of Nazi Germany during World War II. For example, the *Eichmann* case before the District Court of Jerusalem in 1961 adjudicated crimes committed by a German state official. In this case, the Court did not (need to) consider whether state involvement was a requirement for the commission of CAH.[46] In contrast, the Dutch Supreme Court in the *Menten* case, the Supreme Court of Canada in the *Finta* case, and French Courts in the *Touvier* and *Barbie* cases pronounced themselves on the question of whether state involvement was a material element of

[41] This argument is further developed in Section 9.2 'Different Organizational Capacities as Suggested in the *Elements of Crimes* and in ICC Jurisprudence' below.

[42] The ILC's mandate is to 'initiate studies and make recommendations for the purpose of encouraging the progressive development of international law and its codification'. UNGA, Establishment of an International Law Commission, GA/Res/174(II), 21 November 1947.

[43] It must be noted, however, that the members of the ILC serve on the commission in a private capacity. International Law Commission, *Observations of the International Law Commission on the Review of the Multilateral Treaty-Making Process, Submitted Pursuant to General Assembly Resolution 32/48* (United Nations 1979). In this respect, the ILC's reports or opinions cannot be regarded as expressing an opinio juris.

[44] See, eg, *Tadić, IT-94-1-T* (n 38) paras 647–48; *Sivakumar v Canada (Minister of Employment and Immigration), Canadian Federal Court, Judgment, 4 November 1993; Situation in the Rebublic of Kenya, Decision Pursuant to Article 15 of the Rome Statute on the Authorization of an Investigation into the Situation in the Republic of Kenya, ICC, 30 March 2010, ICC-01/09*, para 91.

[45] The limited amount of national case law from the period is discussed in Section 8.3 'The Need for State Involvement as Found in National Jurisprudence'.

[46] For a more detailed discussion of the case, see Paust, Bassiouni, and Scharf, *International Criminal Law: Cases and Materials* (n 1) 713–18.

CAH. As is seen in the following paragraphs, unlike the ILC, most national Courts suggested that state involvement was a material element of CAH.

In the *Menten* case, Menten—a Dutch member of Nazi Germany's 'Schutzstaffel'—was accused of war crimes and crimes against humanity, as defined in article 6(b) and (c) of the Nuremberg Charter, for killing Jews in Podhorodce.[47] Found guilty of the alleged crimes, Menten appealed the Rotterdam District Court's judgment by arguing inter alia that CAH must 'form part of a system based on terror and/or constitute a link in a consciously pursued state policy'.[48] On appeal, the Dutch Supreme Court held in 1981:

The concept of crimes against humanity also requires—although this is not expressed in so many words in the above definition—that the crimes in question form part of a system based on terror or constitute a link in a consciously pursued policy directed against particular groups of people.[49]

While the Supreme Court required a 'system based on terror' or policy behind CAH, it did not state that CAH must be committed pursuant to a *state* policy. Yet, this omission may also be coincidental because, in the *Menten* case, the existence of a terror system and a state policy was undisputed.

In the *Finta* case before the Supreme Court of Canada, Finta, a former member of the Hungarian Gendarmerie, faced allegations of CAH under section 7(3.76) of the Canadian Criminal Code.[50] In 1994, the Supreme Court held that criminal acts as established in the definition of CAH must be 'undertaken in pursuance of a policy of discrimination or persecution of an identifiable group or race'.[51] Referring only to the opinion of Professor Bassiouni, the Court concluded that, at the time, 'State action or policy' were contextual elements required for the commission of CAH.[52] In France, in the cases of the former head of Nazi Germany's Gestapo in Lyon, Barbie, and a member of the *Milice française* which collaborated with Nazi Germany, Touvier, the French *Court de Cassation* had to interpret article 6(c) of the Nuremberg Charter. The highest French court defined CAH in 1985 as:

inhumane acts and the persecutions which, *in the name of a State practicing a hegemonic political ideology*, have been committed in a systematic fashion, not only against persons because

[47] *Public Prosecutor v Menten, District Court of Amsterdam, Judgment, 14 December 1977*, International Law Reports, Vol 75, 332.

[48] *Public Prosecutor v Menten, Dutch Supreme Court, Judgment, 13 January 1981*, International Law Reports, Vol 75, 361.

[49] ibid, at 362–63.

[50] This law defined CAH as follows: '"crime against humanity" means murder, extermination, enslavement, deportation, persecution or any other inhumane act or omission that is committed against any civilian population or any identifiable group of persons, whether or not it constitutes a contravention of the law in force at the time and in the place of its commission, and that, at that time and in that place, constitutes a contravention of customary international law or conventional international law or is criminal according to the general principles of law recognized by the community of nations'.

[51] *Regina v Finta, Ontario Court of Appeal, Canada, Judgment, 24 March 1994*, Supreme Court Reports, 814.

[52] ibid, at 823.

they belong to a racial or religious group, but also against the adversaries of this policy, whatever the form of their opposition.[53]

Thus, in the view of the French *Court de Cassation*, state involvement constituted a material element of CAH.

In summary, in all four cases the national courts required—more or less explicitly—state involvement for the commission of CAH. Different reasons may explain these conclusions, which divert at least from later ILC reports. First, the courts had to apply a definition of CAH as recognized in the 1940s. As seen above, at that time, CAH under the Nuremberg Charter were at least jurisdictionally limited to state crimes. Second, the courts were not concerned with the question of whether CAH could also be committed without state involvement: the Nazi state policy behind all crimes was uncontroversial.[54] Still, the arguments or sources on which some Courts based their findings can be challenged: in the *Finta* case, the Canadian Court only cited one legal scholar as proof of a state policy requirement.[55] Moreover, the French Court's interpretation of article 6(c) of the Nuremberg Charter as requiring acts 'in the name of a State practicing a hegemonic political ideology' was without precedent in international jurisprudence.[56] Thus, while this limited amount of national case law required state involvement for CAH committed in 1945, it reveals little about the state of customary international law at the time of the pronouncements.

As a result, in the first half of the twentieth century, state crimes shocked the conscience of humanity and required international judicial intervention. In 1945, the recognition as international crimes of acts committed by states against their own citizens was an equally courageous and controversial step in lifting the veil over state sovereignty.[57] In the words of the British Chief Prosecutor Shawcross at the Nuremberg Tribunal, it signified that under international law, the state's 'omnipotence' has limits and that the 'individual human being ... is not disentitled to the protection of mankind when the state tramples upon his rights in a manner which outrages the conscience of mankind'.[58] Against this background and in the context of Nazi Germany's crimes, the first codification of CAH and jurisprudence

[53] *Fédération Nationale des Déportés et Internés Résistantes et Patriotes and Others v Barbie, French Court de Cassation, Judgment, 20 December 1985*, International Law Reports, Vol 78, 137 (emphasis added).

[54] While in the *Touvier* case a lower court held that Touvier, supporting the Vichy regime in France, did not act in the name of a state practising a hegemonic political ideology, the French *Court de Cassation* found that Touvier acted in the interest of the Nazi State. See *Touvier, French Court de Cassation, Judgment, 27 November 1992*, International Law Reports, Vol 100, 341.

[55] Although Bassiouni has written extensively on CAH and is a well-recognized expert in this field, the mere reference to the writing of a legal scholar is not a convincing argument of a material element of a crime. See Mettraux, 'The Definition of Crimes against Humanity and the Question of a "Policy" Element' in Sadat (ed), *Forging a Convention for Crimes against Humanity* (CUP 2011) 166.

[56] See Sadat, 'The Interpretation of the Nuremberg Principles by the French Court of Cassation' (n 13) 360.

[57] This is the case, even though in 1945 CAH were restricted to crimes linked to war crimes or crimes against peace. They did not include crimes without such nexus.

[58] Quote found in Schwelb, 'Crimes against Humanity' (n 1) 198.

on Nazi crimes concerned state crimes only. Following this historical development, some have argued that the purpose of an international criminalization of CAH 'is to protect civilian populations against victimization by state agents in furtherance of or as part of a state policy'.[59] Despite this state-centric focus during the immediate post-World War II period, others did challenge the exclusive concentration on state crimes. For example, the French Advocate General asked, in the *Barbie* case:

> Are there not forces and organizations whose powers might be greater and whose actions might be more extensive than those of certain countries represented institutionally at the United Nations? Care is required because other methods of total abuse of the human condition could equal in horror, albeit from other aspects, those of which we have just spoken [i.e. crimes of states]. Certain forms of international terrorism are surely in the process of giving us just such an example.[60]

Indeed, between 1945 and the early 1990s, at least in the ILC's view, the scope of CAH broadened and state involvement was abandoned as an element of CAH. The Commission argued instead that CAH require the instigation or direction of the underlying acts by either a state or a non-state group or organization. This progressive development of the law corresponds with changes in many societies since 1945, in which not only states but also non-state entities commit atrocities. The importance of including crimes committed under the direction or at the instigation of non-state actors was paramount in the prosecutions of different actors in the former Yugoslavia and Sierra Leone in the 1990s.

8.4 Crimes against Humanity by Non-State Armed Groups in the Jurisprudence of the Rwanda, Former Yugoslavia, and Sierra Leone Tribunals

The jurisprudence of the International Criminal Tribunal for the former Yugoslavia (ICTY), the International Criminal Tribunal for Rwanda (ICTR), and the Special Court for Sierra Leone (SCSL) has contributed tremendously to the process of clarifying the definition of CAH under international law.[61] While most crimes adjudicated by the ICTR were committed pursuant to a state policy, the ICTY and the SCSL had to decide cases in which members of non-state groups were charged with CAH. In these cases, the question of 'the entity behind CAH' became pertinent.

[59] Bassiouni, *Crimes against Humanity* (n 3) 117.

[60] Quote found in Paust, Bassiouni, and Scharf, *International Criminal Law: Cases and Materials* (n 1) 722.

[61] See, generally, Mettraux, 'Crimes against Humanity in the Jurisprudence of the International Criminal Tribunals for the Former Yugoslavia and for Rwanda' (2002) 43 Harvard International Law Journal 237–316; Ambos and Wirth, 'The Current Law of Crimes against Humanity' (n 12); Bassiouni, *Crimes against Humanity* (n 3) 182–99.

8.4.1 State involvement was not a material element of CAH in the ICTR's jurisprudence

The ICTR Statute is mute on the question of whether CAH must be instigated or directed by a state or non-state entity. Article 3 of the ICTR Statute defines CAH as specific acts 'when committed as part of a widespread or systematic attack against any civilian population on national, political, ethnic, racial or religious grounds'. The question of state involvement in the large-scale crimes committed between April and July 1994 in Rwanda is, however, uncontroversial. Early on, the ICTR found an anti-Tutsi policy designed by the Rwandan state pursuant to which crimes were committed.[62] Yet, in the ICTR's view, CAH would not necessarily require state involvement. For example, in the *Akayesu* case, the Tribunal argued that CAH require a policy 'involving substantial *public or private resources*' and that '[t]here was no requirement that this policy must be adopted formally as the policy of a state'.[63] Likewise, in subsequent case law, the ICTR emphasized that while customary international law requires, arguably, a state policy behind CAH, state involvement is not required under the ICTR statute and 'the Tribunal's jurisdiction covers both State and non-State actors'.[64] Accordingly, in the *Kayishema and Ruzindana* case, the Tribunal held:

> As *Prefect*, Kayishema was a State actor. As a businessman Ruzindana was a non-State actor. To have jurisdiction over either of the accused, *the Chamber must be satisfied that their actions were instigated or directed by a Government or by any organisation or group*.[65]

As a result, in accordance with the ILC's view, the ICTR did not restrict CAH to crimes committed pursuant to a state policy, but stated that non-state organizations or groups could be entities able to instigate or direct CAH under its statute as well as under customary international law.[66]

8.4.2 CAH committed by non-state armed groups in ICTY jurisprudence

Like the ICTR Statute, the ICTY Statute does not specify whether CAH require involvement of a state or non-state entity.[67] Still, the Tribunal had to adjudicate crimes committed at the instigation or under the direction of states and non-state

[62] See *Akayesu, Judgment, 2 September 1998, Trial Chamber, ICTR-96-4-T,* ICTR, paras 93–111.

[63] ibid, at para 580.

[64] *Kayishema et al, Judgment, 21 May 1999, Trial Chamber, ICTR-95-1-T,* ICTR, para 126.

[65] ibid (emphasis added).

[66] In both judgments, the Tribunals referred explicitly to the ILC Draft Codes. See *Akayesu, ICTR-96-4-T* (n 62) n 145; *Kayishema et al, ICTR-95-1-T* (n 64) para 125. The Appeals Chamber of the two ad hoc tribunals explained with regard to the ICTY Statute that unless it is clear from the text of the Statute, its provisions 'must be interpreted in light of, and in conformity with, customary international law'. *Tadić, IT-94-1-A* (n 38) para 287. The same finding applies to the interpretation of the ICTR Statute.

[67] Article 5 ICTY Statute defines CAH as certain crimes 'when committed in armed conflict, whether international or internal in character, and directed against any civilian population'.

entities. In the Yugoslavia context, the nature of the non-state entities behind alleged crimes varied. On the one hand, the Tribunal heard cases against members of entities exercising quasi-governmental powers, namely groups governing so-called 'Serb Autonomous Regions' proclaimed after the disintegration of the Federal Socialist Republic of Yugoslavia.[68] On the other hand, at a later stage, the Tribunal also adjudicated cases against members of the Kosovo Liberation Army (KLA). The KLA did not consist of dissident armed forces and was not the effective territorial authority, but was characterized 'as a guerrilla force engaged in limited combat with superior, conventional military forces'.[69] Early on, the Tribunal held that although CAH 'need not be related to a policy established at State level, in the conventional sense of the term, they cannot be the work of isolated individuals alone'.[70] In the ICTY's view, CAH require some sort of planning by a collective entity behind the crimes to distinguish them from more random and isolated crimes.[71] Sections 8.4.2.1 'The dismissal of a state-involvement criterion in the *Tadić* case' and 8.4.2.2 'Characteristics of entities behind CAH as found in the *Limaj et al* case' examine which kind of armed groups the ICTY considered as entities behind CAH—first in the *Tadić* case, and then in the *Limaj et al* case.

8.4.2.1 The dismissal of a state-involvement criterion in the Tadić *case*

The ICTY's initially rather swift finding that CAH require a policy behind the crimes but that such policy does not need to be a state policy was further developed in the *Tadić* case. Examining 'the nature of the entity behind the policy', a Trial Chamber argued that 'the traditional conception was, in fact, not only that a policy must be present but that the policy must be that of a State, as it was the case in Nazi Germany'.[72] Recognizing that customary international law can change over time, however, the Chamber held:

> [T]he law in relation to crimes against humanity has developed to take into account forces which, although not those of the legitimate government, have *de facto* control over, or are able to move freely within, defined territory.[73]

Accordingly, in the Chamber's view, CAH did not require involvement of a de jure state, but a policy distinguishing CAH from 'isolated, random acts of individuals'[74]

[68] *Tadić, IT-94-1-T* (n 38) paras 97–103.

[69] *Limaj et al, Judgment, 30 November 2005, Trial Chamber, IT-03-66-T,* ICTY, para 195.

[70] *Nikolić, Review of Indictment Pursuant to Rule 61 of the Rules of Proceedure and Evidence, 20 October 1993, Trial Chamber, IT-94-2-R61,* ICTY, para 26.

[71] See also Robinson, 'Crimes against Humanity: A Better Policy on "Policy"' in *The Law and Practice of the International Criminal Court* (OUP 2014) 705–31, 708. In Robinson's view, 'The *Tadić* Decision equated the policy element with the requirement recognised by the ILC in the 1996 draft Code of Crimes, that an attack must be "instigated or directed by a Government or by any organization or group".'

[72] *Tadić, IT-94-1-T* (n 38) para 654.

[73] ibid.

[74] ibid, at para 653.

could also be that of a non-state entity. To support this finding, the Chamber mentioned that the prosecution argued—without objection from the defence—that CAH cannot only be committed on behalf of entities exercising control over territory but also 'by a terrorist group or organization'.[75]

Accordingly, in the *Tadić* case, the Trial Chamber suggested different types of non-state groups as the possible 'entity behind the policy': first, groups exercising de facto control over territory; second, groups able to move freely within territory; and third, possibly terrorist groups or other organizations. The first type of non-state entity seemingly refers to groups exercising de facto control over territory in a state-like manner. In Ambos's view, it encompasses entities exercising 'the *highest de facto* authority in the given territory [which] can—within limits—control all other holders of power and all individuals'.[76] For him, 'it also seems to be clear that it must be in a position akin, or at least similar to, a state; that is, it must possess similar capacities of organization and force'.[77] Indeed, this could be what the chamber had in mind when examining crimes committed on behalf of an entity governing a 'Serb Autonomous Region'. However, equalling '*de facto* control over territory' with being 'state-like' is a narrow interpretation, which can be challenged: in practice, de facto control over territory can hardly be equated with having a state-like degree of institutional organization.[78] Contrary to a possibly high threshold of de facto territorial control, the ability of a group to move freely within a defined territory can be fulfilled by various non-state entities—even if they do not have sufficient capacity to control territory, or to act in a state-like manner. Effectively, this requirement is dependent on the strength of the territorial authority, meaning that a group with relatively low capacities can be able to move freely in a territory if the territorial authority is unable to intervene. Reference to terrorist groups or other organizations is even broader and may include a variety of non-state groups.

In sum, the ICTY held that under customary international law, CAH are not restricted to state crimes. The ICTY's *Tadić* judgment could be read as following the ILC's inclusion of 'any organization or group' as the possible entity behind CAH. Yet, as Kress points out, the '*ratio decidendi* of the 1997 *Tadić* decision is the assimilation of organizations with territorial control to states for the purpose of the policy requirement of crimes against humanity'.[79] Indeed, the Chamber only explicitly pronounced itself on groups exercising de facto control over territory. At the same

[75] ibid, at para 654. The Tribunal found that this assertion reflected recent statements on CAH, and cited, inter alia, the ILC *Draft Code of Crimes* of 1991 (n 32) and 1996 (n 36), as well as a case before a United States Court of Appeal. *Tadić, IT-94-1-T* (n 38), at para 655.

[76] Ambos, *Treatise on International Criminal Law* (n 6) 72.

[77] ibid.

[78] See discussion on the *Limaj* case below. Practice examples of armed groups exercising control over territory without being state-like are discussed in Section 6.4 'Human Rights Obligations of Groups Exercising De Facto Control over Territory and Population'.

[79] Kress, 'On the Outer Limits of Crimes against Humanity: The Concept of Organization within the Policy Requirement: Some Reflections on the March 2010 ICC Kenya Decision' (2010) 23 Leiden Journal of International Law 869.

time, by means of obiter dictum, the Tribunal left 'open the possibility that other organizations might meet the test as well'.[80] In a number of subsequent cases, the ICTY applied a test under which it required the entity behind CAH to exercise territorial control. For example, in the *Kupreškić et al* case, the tribunal found that a policy behind CAH can be state-sponsored, part of a governmental policy, or part of a policy by 'an entity holding de facto authority over a territory'.[81] The issue of what minimum requirements an entity behind CAH must fulfil and how to interpret the territorial control requirement came up again in the *Limaj et al* case with regard to crimes allegedly committed by members of the KLA.

8.4.2.2 Characteristics of entities behind CAH as found in the Limaj et al *case*

Contrary to earlier ICTY cases in which the Tribunal adjudicated crimes committed with the involvement of states or state-like entities, with regard to the Kosovo conflict the ICTY was confronted with alleged crimes committed with the involvement of a non-state entity that did not resemble a state. The KLA was an armed resistance group with limited internal organization, which had long operated underground and was only beginning to mount an open insurgency.[82] While the ICTY considered the KLA sufficiently organized to be a party to a non-international armed conflict, it stressed that the conflict was 'fluid in nature', with territorial control changing between the parties.[83] It characterized the KLA as 'a non-state actor with extremely limited resources, personnel and organization'.[84] The accused were charged with committing CAH in the form of ill-treatment, torture, and murder allegedly of detainees.[85]

While in the *Tadić* case the Tribunal examined 'the nature of the entity behind the *policy*', the ICTY Appeals Chamber had dismissed the policy requirement for CAH in the *Kunarac* case.[86] Thus, in the *Limaj et al* case, the Chamber examined the question of the entity behind CAH as part of its discussion of whether an 'attack on a civilian population' existed.[87] At the outset, the Tribunal reiterated its previous jurisprudence by stressing that the contextual element of CAH serves to 'exclude single, random or limited acts from the domain of crimes against humanity',[88] meaning crimes that are 'merely the workings of individuals acting pursuant to haphazard or individual design'.[89] After finding that the KLA's crimes were not widespread, the Chamber examined whether there was a policy behind them that could indicate a systematic character.[90] The Chamber argued—referring

[80] Robinson, 'Defining Crimes against Humanity at the Rome Conference' (1999) 93 American Journal of International Law 43–57, 50; See also Kress, 'On the Outer Limits of Crimes against Humanity' (n 79) 869.

[81] *Kupreškić et al, Judgment, 14 January 2000, Trial Chamber, IT-95-16-T,* ICTY, para 552.

[82] *Limaj et al, IT-03-66-T* (n 69) paras 45–52.

[83] ibid, at para 195.

[84] ibid, at para 191.

[85] ibid, at para 229.

[86] *Kunarac et al, IT-96-23& IT-96-23/1-A,* para 98.

[87] *Limaj et al, IT-03-66-T* (n 69) paras 189–91.

[88] ibid, at para 194.

[89] ibid, at para 212.

[90] The Chamber underlined that a policy is 'most often' found where there is 'significant State action and where formal channels of command can be discerned'. ibid.

to the *Tadić* case—that 'an organisational unit must demonstrate in order to have sufficient competence to formulate a policy [...] a level of *de facto* control over territory'.[91] Considering the facts of the case, the tribunal concluded that the KLA's ability to erect roadblocks, to develop civilian structures, and examples of command and control in its ranks indicated 'increasing control over, and the ability to move within, much of Kosovo'.[92]

On the one hand, the Chamber reiterated the '*de facto* control over territory' standard. On the other hand, in the *Limaj et al* case, this finding was significantly restricted in scope: first, the tribunal did not require territorial control as a general condition for the ability of non-state entities to commit CAH. Neither did it require such control for widespread crimes. Territorial control was only found to be a requirement for the 'competence to formulate a policy'; and this policy was considered indicative of but not legally required for systematic attacks against a civilian population. Therefore, the Chamber's reasoning suggests that systematic crimes without a policy, or widespread crimes, could amount to CAH even if the entity behind the crimes did not control any territory. Second, the Chamber did not seem to equate '*de facto* control over territory' with being state-like. It considered the criterion met by proving that the KLA had some degree of de facto territorial control in a situation in which military engagements were fluid in nature, with 'reversals of territorial acquisitions'.[93] The KLA did not have state-like infrastructure at its disposal.

In addition, the tribunal's reasoning for defining de facto territorial control as a requirement for 'sufficient competence to formulate a policy' can be questioned. Why should de facto territorial control be necessary in order to formulate a policy behind CAH, which serves primarily to exclude individual ordinary crimes from the scope of CAH?[94] Likewise, to what extent are examples of command and control in the ranks of a group proof of territorial control? Rather, de facto control over, or the ability to move freely within, territory might enable a group to execute a policy and launch an attack reaching the required scale and organization of CAH. Command and control in the group's ranks indicate the group's ability to enforce a policy. Thus, territorial control and command-and-control structures appear to be attributes that might enable an entity to implement a large-scale or systematic attack, but it is unclear why territorial control should be a strict requirement for a group's ability to formulate a policy behind CAH.[95]

[91] ibid, at para 213. [92] See ibid, at para 214. [93] ibid.

[94] ibid, at para 212. Note that a policy was not regarded as a legal element of CAH but as 'an important indication that the acts in question are not merely the workings of individuals acting pursuant to haphazard or individual design, but instead have a level of organisational coherence and support of a magnitude sufficient to elevate them into the realm of crimes against humanity'.

[95] Concretely, from the Chamber's reasoning it is unclear why territorial control would be a prerequisite for the KLA's policy to 'target those individuals thought to be collaborating with the Serbian forces'. ibid, at para 216.

In fact, the Chamber's line of argument could also suggest a different assessment of what kind of non-state groups may constitute an entity behind CAH. In order to prove an attack against a civilian population, the Chamber argued:

> Due to *structural factors and organisational and military capabilities*, an 'attack directed against a civilian population' will most often be found to have occurred at the behest of a State. Being the *locus of organised authority* within a given territory, able to *mobilise and direct military and civilian power*, a sovereign State by its very nature possesses the attributes that permit it to *organise and deliver an attack* against a civilian population; it is States which can most easily and efficiently *marshal the resources to launch an attack* against a civilian population on a 'widespread' scale, or upon a 'systematic' basis.[96]

In this statement, the Chamber emphasized the state's factual capabilities and not its legal powers as a territorial sovereign as key characteristics enabling the commission of CAH. This focus on an entity's capabilities is further supported by the Chamber's argument that criminal acts require 'a level of organisational coherence and support of a magnitude sufficient to elevate them into the realm of crimes against humanity'.[97]

If the Chamber's above portrayal of state capacities is considered crucial to an entity's ability to commit CAH, the following elements can be deduced: the entity should be the 'organised authority within a given territory' with sufficient 'organisational and military capabilities' in order to 'mobilise and direct military and civilian power' and to 'marshal the resources' to launch a widespread or systematic attack against a civilian population.[98] These criteria can be summarized as follows: first, the group must have sufficient capacity to organize a widespread or systematic attack; and second, it must have the power—arguably, including territorial control—and material resources to execute it.[99] As a result, if a non-state entity is able to acquire enough resources to orchestrate crimes of sufficient scale and establishes an internal structure or degree of organization that enables it to implement a pattern of crimes going beyond isolated acts of individuals, this group seems sufficiently organized to be the entity behind CAH.

To sum up, while the ICTY repeatedly reiterated that CAH may not be committed by individuals pursuant to 'haphazard or individual design', it remains unclear from its case law under which conditions non-state entities can qualify as an

[96] ibid, at para 191 (emphasis added). Cassese notes with regard to this statement that it is 'acceptable to the extent that it is intended merely to reflect what happens in practice, not as the formulation of a legal requirement (plainly, a widespread or systematic attack on the population can be carried out by non-state groups or paramilitary units with the acquiescence of state authorities or in circumstances where such authorities lack the effective power to put an end to such attacks)'. Cassese, *International Criminal Law* (n 5) 101.

[97] *Limaj et al, IT-03-66-T* (n 69) para 212.

[98] ibid, at para 191.

[99] This categorization serves the aim of structuring the requirements for groups to commit CAH. It is not strict, meaning that it should not be understood in a way that the widespread commission of a crime is not also related to the organized nature of the perpetrators; or, that the systematic commission of CAH does not also depend on the capacity and the resources of the perpetrators (see *Blaškić, Judgment, 3 March 2000, IT-95-14-T,* ICTY, para 203).

entity behind CAH. As long as the Tribunal considered the existence of a policy to be a material element of CAH, arguably it determined de facto territorial control to be a prerequisite for formulating a policy and therefore for committing CAH. However, in later case law, the Tribunal considered the policy element, and seemingly also the territorial control requirement, to be merely indicative of the systematic character of the crime. At least in the ICTY's view, no policy element and no territorial control by the entity behind the crime would be required for widespread crimes. Thus, under ICTY jurisprudence, CAH cannot be limited to crimes committed with the involvement of entities exercising de facto territorial control. An alternative approach could be to focus on the entity's capacity to organize and commit crimes with sufficient organizational coherence and magnitude to amount to an attack against a civilian population. This approach emphasizes the entity's de facto capabilities that are immediately relevant for the commission of CAH.

8.4.3 The capacity-oriented approach in the SCSL's jurisprudence

The question of which entities can commit CAH also emerged in cases before the SCSL.[100] For example, in the *Brima et al* case, the accused were sergeants or staff sergeants of the Armed Forces Revolutionary Council (AFRC), a non-state armed group consisting of former members of Sierra Leone's armed forces and party to a non-international armed conflict in Sierra Leone.[101] During the indictment period, AFRC forces were first part of a military government, meaning that at that time their crimes were 'state-sponsored'.[102] During this period, AFRC and allied Revolutionary United Front forces controlled most of the country.[103] This changed after AFRC forces came under military attack by multinational forces, had to withdraw from Sierra Leone's capital Freetown, and lost governmental power. From there on, the AFRC was a non-state entity and 'faced with the challenge of more limited resources and poorer organisational capacity'.[104] Following withdrawal from Freetown, AFRC troops moved through Sierra Leone but no longer resembled a state army. According to the SCSL, their 'organization and control remained minimal'.[105] Without elaborating much on whether CAH require the involvement of specific kinds of entities, the Court found crimes committed during this period beyond reasonable doubt to be widespread and systematic.[106] The SCSL established that even at that time the AFRC was able to implement policies or plans to attack civilians.[107]

[100] The definition of CAH in the SCSL Statute did not indicate whether CAH require involvement of a state or non-state entity.
[101] See *Brima et al, SCSL-04-16-T*, paras 249–53. See ibid.
[102] ibid, at para 225. [103] ibid. [104] ibid, at para 266.
[105] ibid, at paras 176–77. [106] ibid, at para 224.
[107] Two examples of such policies were 'Operation Pay Yourself' and 'Operation Spare No Soul', both brutally attacking the civilian population. ibid, at para 238.

Despite the lack of detailed discussion, the SCSL's conclusions suggest that CAH are not state crimes but can be committed with the involvement of non-state entities. The accused in the pertinent cases were members of armed groups party to a prolonged non-international armed conflict. Owing to the complete breakdown of law and order in many parts of the country, they were able to move freely within, and often controlled, large parts of the territory.[108] Yet, the SCSL did not explicitly require control over territory or state-like features to find an armed group capable of committing a widespread or systematic attack against a civilian population. In the *Brima et al* case, the SCSL held that while 'limited resources' and 'poorer organisational capacity' may lead to 'practical difficulties' in proving the widespread or systematic nature of an attack, it does not preclude it.[109] For the SCSL, the decisive requirements were that the armed groups had the capacity to commit widespread or systematic crimes, and that the attacks were directed against a civilian population.[110] Thus, the SCSL followed a capacity-oriented approach, which was already hinted at in ICTY jurisprudence.

[108] ibid, at para 237. While the Revolutionary United Front (RUF) and the AFRC controlled large parts of the territory, the activities of the so-called 'Civil Defence Forces' were more restricted to territory under their control.

[109] ibid.

[110] ibid, at paras 210–26. This strict focus on a disjunctive widespread or systematic test is also found in the *Fofana and Condewa* case concerning another non-state armed group. In this case, the SCSL satisfied itself that the crimes committed were widespread and so did not investigate any other elements regarding the nature of the group behind the crimes. However, in this case, no substantial investigation was required because the alleged crimes were not directed against a civilian population and therefore were not CAH. See *Fofana and Kondewa Judgment, 9 October 2007, Trial Chamber, SCSL-04-14-T,* SCSL, paras 692–93; *Taylor, Judgment, 18 May 2012, SCSL-01-01-T,* SCSL, para 558.

9

The 'State or Organizational Policy' Requirement for Crimes against Humanity under the Rome Statute of the International Criminal Court

The codification of crimes against humanity under article 7 of the ICC Statute (ICC Statute) is the most widely accepted definition of the crime.[1] Reportedly, reaching agreement on a definition of crimes against humanity (CAH) required significant diplomatic efforts at the Rome Conference in 1998.[2] Yet, almost two decades later, this definition seems to be crystallizing into customary international law, which may also influence other international and national tribunals' jurisprudence.[3] Under article 7 ICC Statute:

> 'crime against humanity' means any of the following acts [criminal acts listed under article 7(1)(a)–(k)] when committed as part of a widespread or systematic attack directed against any civilian population, with knowledge of the attack.

Article 7(2)(a) of the ICC Statute adds:

> 'Attack directed against any civilian population' means a course of conduct involving the multiple commission of acts referred to in paragraph 1 against any civilian population, pursuant to or in furtherance of a *State or organizational* policy to commit such attack; (emphasis added)

[1] International Law Commission, *First Report on Crimes against Humanity*, A/CN.4/680, para 121.

[2] This was especially the case because there was no agreed definition of CAH in positive international law, and the existing definitions applied in other tribunals were not uniform. See Robinson, 'Crimes against Humanity: Reflections on State Sovereignty, Legal Precision and the Dictates of the Public Conscience' in Lattanzi and Schabas (eds), *Essays on the Rome Statute of the International Criminal Court* (il Sirente 2000) 139–69, 141. For Ambos, article 7 of the Rome Statute of the International Criminal Court (ICC Statute) 'represents both a "codification" and a "progressive development" of international law'. Ambos, *Treatise on International Criminal Law* (OUP 2013) 49.

[3] The ICC Statute is formulated in a way that emphasizes that it is not declarative of customary international law. See Schabas, *Unimaginable Atrocities: Justice, Politics, and Rights in the War Crimes Tribunals* (OUP 2012) 144; Bassiouni, *Crimes against Humanity: Historical Evolution and Contemporary Application* (CUP 2011) 202. However, the International Law Commission (ILC) has argued that 'with the passage of time and the adherence of a large number of States to the Rome Statute, it seems likely that Article 7 is having an effect in crystalizing customary international law'. For a similar view and additional authorities, see Robinson, 'The Draft Convention on Crimes against Humanity: What to Do with the Definition?' in Bergsmo and Song (eds), *On the Draft Crimes against Humanity Convention* (Torkel Opsahl Academic EPublisher 2014) 105.

Under the ICC Statute, any natural person—state official, member of an armed group, or civilian—can commit CAH in his or her official or private capacity if the acts are sufficiently connected to the widespread or systematic attack against a civilian population, and if the perpetrator had knowledge of the attack.[4] In order to exclude isolated or sporadic acts of violence from the scope of CAH, any such attack has to be 'pursuant to or in furtherance of a State or organizational policy'. As this requirement shows, unlike previous definitions of CAH, the ICC Statute explicitly requires CAH to be committed with the involvement of a state or an organization.[5] The key question for the purposes of this book is which entities qualify as an organization behind the policy under article 7(2)(a) ICC Statute.

This question is of paramount importance for the International Criminal Court (ICC), which some commentators predict will become a '"crimes against humanity" court'.[6] Indeed, a great majority of situations before the ICC involve CAH charges, including against non-state actors.[7] In these situations, the Court faces at least three different types of entities behind alleged CAH: states, non-state parties to an armed conflict, and non-state organizations not involved in an armed conflict and not exercising quasi-governmental authority.[8] In the young jurisprudential history of the Court, Pre-Trial Chamber II's decision to authorize investigations into post-election violence in Kenya in 2007–2008 triggered a controversy on the question of what kinds of non-state entities may constitute an 'organization' under article 7(2)(a) ICC Statute.[9] In the Kenya situation, the entities behind the alleged crimes were not parties to an armed conflict, nor state-like entities exercising quasi-governmental authority, but in one case a 'Network' involving politicians, youth leaders, tribal elders, farmers, and businessmen,[10] and in the other one a 'criminal organization'.[11]

[4] For further discussion of the nexus and knowledge requirements, see *Katanga, Judgment, 7 March 2014, Trial Chamber II,* ICC-01/04-01/07, ICC, paras 1124–25. The crimes must not in and of themselves constitute a widespread or systematic attack. See Cassese, *International Criminal Law* (2nd edn, OUP 2008) 116. Triffterer (ed), 'Commentary on the Rome Statute of the International Criminal Court: Observers' Notes, Article by Article' (2nd edn, CH Beck 2008) 176.

[5] This point is further discussed in Section 9.1.2 'The ordinary meaning of organization' below.

[6] Sadat, 'Emerging from the Shadow of Nuremberg' 377.

[7] As of March 2016, eight of the ten situations before the ICC involve charges of CAH. Out of these eight situations, five involve allegations of crimes committed with the involvement of non-state armed groups.

[8] While most cases involving non-state actors concern situations in which members of parties to an armed conflict commit CAH, a notable exception is the Kenya situation, in which violence did not amount to an armed conflict. Likewise, in the Libya situation, only CAH are charged—although against state actors.

[9] See *Situation in the Republic of Kenya, Decision Pursuant to Article 15 of the Rome Statute on the Authorization of an Investigation into the Situation in the Republic of Kenya, 31 March 2010, Pre-Trial Chamber II, ICC-01/09,* ICC. For some discussion, see Werle and Burghardt, 'Do Crimes against Humanity Require the Participation of a State or a "State-Like" Organization?' (2012) 10 Journal of International Criminal Justice 1151–70; Hansen, 'The Policy Requirement in Crimes against Humanity: Lessons from and for the Case of Kenya' (2011) 43 George Washington International law Review 1–41; Sadat, 'Emerging from the Shadow of Nuremberg' (n 6); Rodenhäuser, 'Beyond State Crimes: Non-State Entities and Crimes against Humanity' (2014) 27 Leiden Journal of International Law 913–28. Additional views are discussed in this chapter.

[10] See *Ruto et al, Decision on the Confirmation of Charges Pursuant to Article 61(7)(a) and (b) of the Rome Statute, 23 January 2012, Pre-Trial Chamber II, ICC-01/09-01/11,* ICC.

[11] See *Muthaura et al, Decision on the Confirmation of Charges Pursuant to Article 61(7)(a) and (b) of the Rome Statute, 23 January 2012, Pre-Trial Chamber II, ICC-01/09–02/11,* ICC.

The objective of this chapter is to determine which types of non-state entities fall under the notion 'organization' under article 7(2)(a) ICC Statute. In accordance with article 21(1)(a) ICC Statute, as well as general rules on treaty interpretation as found in the Vienna Convention on the Law of Treaties (VCLT), Section 9.1 'The Meaning of Organization under Article 7(2)(a) ICC Statute as Interpreted under General Rules of Treaty Interpretation' interprets the term 'organization' 'in good faith in accordance with the ordinary meaning to be given to the terms of the treaty in their context and in the light of its object and purpose'.[12] Section 9.1 also briefly considers the Statute's preparatory works. Building on the suggestion that the meaning of 'organization' is understood best in its context in the ICC Statute, Section 9.2 'Different Organizational Capacities as Suggested in the *Elements of Crimes* and in ICC Jurisprudence' analyses what capacity is needed from a non-state entity to develop an organizational policy which is sufficiently effective to realize a course of conduct involving multiple criminal acts against a civilian population. This part considers in particular the degree of organization the ICC's *Elements of Crimes* suggest for an organization behind CAH, as well as the Court's practice in the application of its Statute.[13]

9.1 The Meaning of Organization under Article 7(2)(a) ICC Statute as Interpreted under General Rules of Treaty Interpretation

In order to provide some historical background on the definition of CAH under the ICC Statute, this section starts by briefly analysing how the drafters understood the notion 'state or organizational policy' in the definition of CAH. In the main part of this section, the notion 'organization' is interpreted in accordance with its ordinary meaning, its context, and in the light of its object and purpose.

9.1.1 The meaning of organization during the ICC Statute's preparatory works

The definitions of CAH in the Nuremberg Charter and the ad hoc tribunals' statutes reflected to some extent the factual circumstances of the situations to which they applied.[14] In contrast, when states negotiated the definition of CAH

[12] Article 31(1) Vienna Convention on the Law of Treaties.

[13] According to article 21(1)(a) ICC Statute, the Court shall apply the Element of Crimes 'in the first place' together with the Statute and the Rules of Procedure and Evidence. This conforms to article 31(3)(a) VCLT. Moreover, under article 21(2) ICC Statute and in accordance with article 31(3)(b) VCLT, the Court's jurisprudence shall be considered in the interpretation of the Statute.

[14] Although the requirement of a nexus to an armed conflict had been abandoned by the International Law Commission (ILC) in 1954, and CAH were widely considered to apply in times of war and in times of peace, article 5 ICTYSt contains the restriction that CAH can only be 'committed in armed conflict'. While not containing the armed conflict requirement, under article 3 ICTRSt, CAH had to be part of an attack 'on national, political, ethnic, racial or religious grounds'. Considering these two particularities of the ad hoc tribunals' statutes, Bassiouni finds, 'The formulations of the CAH provisions in the statutes of the ICTY [International Criminal Tribunal for the former Yugoslavia] and the International Criminal Tribunal for Rwanda [ICTR], like those of their predecessors, were tailored to fit the situations

under the ICC Statute, they had to find a definition that applied to a variety of situations. The key element distinguishing CAH from ordinary crimes is the context in which they are committed.[15] For states, defining this context under the ICC Statute meant defining the threshold at which the new court could be authorized to intervene in what were formerly states' internal affairs. Therefore, the 'Preparatory Committee on the Establishment of an International Criminal Court' left the exact definition of the contextual elements of CAH to the diplomatic conference in Rome.[16] At the Rome conference, the main issue with regard to the definition of CAH was whether an attack against a civilian population must be 'widespread and systematic' (cumulative) or 'widespread or systematic' (alternative) in order to constitute CAH.[17] A number of states expressed concern that if the context of CAH under article 7(1) only required a 'widespread *or* systematic attack', isolated crimes or waves of crimes, which are normally addressed under domestic criminal law and do not constitute CAH, could fall under the definition.[18] Other states argued that this concern was adequately addressed by the requirement that such acts must be committed as part of an 'attack against any civilian population'.[19] Compromise was achieved thanks to Canada's proposal to define 'attack directed against any civilian population' under article 7(2)(a) ICC Statute as requiring, inter alia, a 'state or organizational policy'.[20]

to which they were to apply. Thus, the formulations were tailored to fit the facts. Consequently, these formulations were not necessarily drafted with a view toward future application …'. Bassiouni, *Crimes against Humanity* (n 3) 188; see also Werle, *Principles of International Criminal Law* (2nd edn, TMC Asser Press 2009) 291.

[15] This is clear from the concept and history of CAH (see Parts II and III of this book), as well as from its legal definition. See Robinson, 'The Elements of Crimes against Humanity' in Lee (ed), *The International Criminal Court: Elements of Crimes and Rules of Procedure and Evidence* (Transnational Publishers 2001) 58.

[16] See Schabas, *The International Criminal Court: A Commentary on the Rome Statute* (1st edn, OUP 2010) 143. The final draft of the crime of CAH as agreed by the Preparatory Committee did not contain any specification of the potential perpetrators of CAH. Preparatory Committee on the Establishment of an International Criminal Court, *Report of the Working Group on the Defintion of Crimes*, 1997, A/AC.249/1997/L.5. In an early draft of a definition of CAH for the statute of an international criminal court, the chairperson of the preparatory commission presented a 'Compilation of proposals and suggestions with regard to the definition of crimes against humanity'. Only one of these suggestions explicitly required that CAH are committed according to a 'public policy'. All other suggestions did not limit the scope of potential entities behind CAH. See Preparatory Committee on the Establishment of an International Criminal Court, *Definition of Core Crimes: Chairman's Informal Texts and Compilation of Proposals and Suggestions with Regard to the Definition of Core Crimes*, 1996, A/AC.249/CRP.9/Add.4, 13.

[17] For a good account of states' interests at the Rome Conference, see Robinson, 'The Elements of Crimes against Humanity' (n 15) 57.

[18] See Official Records of the United Nations Diplomatic Conference of Plenipotentiaries on the Establishment of an International Criminal Court (Vol I-III) A/CONF.183/13, Vol II, 150 para 90 (Great Britain) or 151 para 108 (Thailand). See also Robinson, 'Crimes against Humanity' (n 2) 161.

[19] See Robinson, 'Crimes against Humanity: A Better Policy on "Policy" ' in *The Law and Practice of the International Criminal Court* (OUP 2014) 708.

[20] See Triffterer (ed), 'Commentary on the Rome Statute' (n 4) 234. According to Darryl Robinson, who was part of the Canadian Delegation, the Canadian proposal was explicitly based on the ILC's definition of CAH under the 1996 *Draft Articles*, and the ICTY's interpretation of CAH in the *Tadić* case,

This addition was intended to exclude random or isolated acts from the scope of CAH.[21]

Reportedly, the question of the entity behind CAH was barely debated in Rome.[22] Some states criticized the 'state or organizational policy' requirement as constituting 'an unacceptable threshold that in no way reflected contemporary realities or international law'.[23] More explicitly, Sri Lanka stated that, in its view, the state or organizational policy requirement was also 'intended to cover the 'policy of non-governmental entities'.[24] However, these statements—as well as the rest of the Official Records from the Rome Conference—provide no indication on which kind of non-state entities qualify as an 'organization' able to provide a policy under article 7(2)(a) ICC Statute. Against this background, the personal recollections of some of the negotiators may provide further insights. For example, Leila Sadat recalls that the term 'organization'

> was intended at least to address actions taken by various non-State entities in a case involving a state's disintegration into component parts as well as situations in which no clear central authority exists, including attacks on civilians by non-State actors.[25]

Darryl Robinson, who was a member of the Canadian delegation and reportedly 'one of the leading negotiators on Article 7',[26] recounts the following:

> Although the ILC and the ICTY referred to instigation by a 'government, organization or group', the delegations at the Rome Conference referred only to the policies of a state or organization, feeling that, if there is in fact a difference between the terms 'organization' and 'group', then the higher degree of organization connoted by the former term would be indispensable for the instigation or direction of a crime against humanity.[27]

In summary, the drafting history of article 7 ICC Statute, as well as recollections by some negotiators, confirms that states intended to include crimes committed with the involvement of both states and non-state entities in the definition of CAH.[28] The

which included non-state groups as entities behind CAH. See Robinson, 'Crimes against Humanity: A Better Policy on "Policy"' (n 19) 708–09.

21 See Sadat, 'Emerging from the Shadow of Nuremberg' (n 6) 370.

22 This has been reported to the author by one of the negotiators of the definition of CAH at the Rome Conference.

23 Official Records of the United Nations Diplomatic Conference of Plenipotentiaries on the Establishment of an International Criminal Court (Vol. I-III) (n 18) 345 (Congo); see also 328 (Jamaica).

24 ibid, at 288 (Sri Lanka). For additional discussion, see Jalloh, 'What Makes Crimes against Humanity Crimes against Humanity?' (2013) 28 American University International Law Review 414–15.

25 Sadat, 'Emerging from the Shadow of Nuremberg' (n 6) 43.

26 Kress, 'On the Outer Limits of Crimes against Humanity: The Concept of Organization within the Policy Requirement: Some Reflections on the March 2010 ICC Kenya Decision' (2010) 15 Journal of Conflict and Security Law 868.

27 Robinson, 'Crimes against Humanity' (n 2) 163.

28 For an opposing but isolated opinion of a person participating in the Rome Conference, see Bassiouni, *The Legislative History of the International Criminal Court* (Transnational Publishers 2005) 151–52.

travaux préparatoires do not, however, provide clear indications of which kind of non-state entities may qualify as an organization under article 7(2)(a) ICC Statute.

9.1.2 The ordinary meaning of organization

Article 7(2)(a) ICC Statute requires that an act amounting to CAH must be committed pursuant to or in furtherance of a 'State or organizational policy'. Plain English language is not entirely clear on whether 'organizational' refers to an organization as an entity behind the crime, or to the manner in which the acts are committed. Reference to other authentic treaty languages shows that a policy of an organization is required.[29] According to its ordinary meaning, the word 'organization' means 'an organized group of people with a particular purpose, such as a business or government department'.[30] Reference to an 'organization' or 'organized group' also suggests that it is not an instant assembly of persons or a group that meets randomly but a more stable entity. Drawing on the ordinary meaning of the word 'organization', as well as on article 2(a) of the United Nations Convention against Transnational Organized Crime, Judge Kuniko Ozaki argued that an organization under article 7(2)(a) ICC Statute should be understood as:

> at a minimum: (i) a collectivity of three or more persons; (ii) existing for a certain period of time, which, at least, transcends the period during which the policy was formed and implemented; (iii) with a particular aim or purpose, whether it is criminal or not, and (iv) with a certain structure.[31]

Yet, an organization does not require any formal legal status, particularly not one associated with statehood.[32] Similarly, a required number of persons, or the required degree of organization—such as whether the organization must have an established hierarchy or certain resources at its disposal—cannot be determined based on the ordinary meaning of the word.

9.1.3 A contextual interpretation of organization

The finding that an organization does not have to be a state is further supported by a contextual interpretation. While Bassiouni has argued that 'the words "organizational

[29] The French version requires 'la politique d'un État ou d'une organisation' and the Spanish version 'la politica de un Estado o de una organización'. For a more comprehensive assessment of this question, see *Situation in the Republic of Kenya, ICC-01/09* (n 9) n 82.

[30] Oxford Dictionaries, online version, defintion of 'organization'. For an ordinary French meaning, see *Katanga, ICC-01/04–01/07* (n 4) para 1119.

[31] *Bemba Gombo (Seperate Opinion Kuniko Ozaki) Judgment, 21 March 2016, Trial Chamber III, ICC-01/05–01/08*, ICC, para 29. Additional potentially relevant factors suggested by Judge Kuniko Ozaki include 'whether the group has an established internal hierarchy; whether the group exercises control over part of the territory of a state; the group's infrastructure and resources; and whether the group is part of a larger group, which fulfils some or all of the abovementioned criteria'. Such factors are not based on the ordinary meaning and are discussed in Section 9.2 'Different Organizational Capacities as Suggested in the *Elements of Crimes* and in ICC Jurisprudence' below.

[32] See also *Situation in the Republic of Kenya, ICC-01/09* (n 9) para 90.

policy" refer to the policy of an organ of the state',[33] others suggest that the formulation 'State or organizational policy' would be redundant if both terms referred to a state policy.[34] Following the latter view, Pre-Trial Chamber II held that 'had the drafters of the Statute intended to exclude non-state actors from the term "organization", they would not have included this term in article 7(2)(a) of the Statute'.[35] Examining what kind of organizations may develop such a policy, Judge Kaul argued that the juxtaposition of the terms 'state' and 'organization' indicates that the two entities have something in common, suggesting that an organization should be one that 'may act like a State or has quasi-State abilities'.[36] Werle and Burghardt, in contrast, argue that it 'contradicts linguistic and grammatical rules to assume from the use of the conjunction "or" that the second of the juxtaposed terms (here "organization") must share definitional characteristics with the first (here "state")'.[37] Likewise, Bartels and Fortin consider Kaul's view 'particularly unreasonable' because it would not correspond to the fact that a variety of non-state armed groups, and not only state-like ones, commit atrocities of an international dimension.[38]

A better approach for a contextual interpretation is to consider the meaning of organization in the wider context of CAH under the ICC Statute. This context includes the crime's underlying acts and the widespread or systematic 'attack directed against any civilian population', the latter being defined in article 7(2)(a). With regard to the underlying acts,[39] it appears that most crimes do not require capacities other than those available to ordinary criminals or non-state parties to an armed conflict. In contrast, the crime of 'apartheid' requires inhumane acts 'committed in the context of an institutionalized regime of systematic oppression and domination', and 'enforced disappearance' consists, inter alia, of 'the arrest, detention or abduction of persons by, or with the authorization, support or acquiescence of, a State or a political organization'.[40] Thus, a non-state entity able to commit the crime of apartheid would need to have the institutional capacity to establish a regime of systematic repression; in other words, it would need to exercise quasi-governmental authority in a territory. Moreover, the crime of enforced disappearance needs at least authorization, support, or acquiescence of a 'political organization'. In the context

[33] Bassiouni, 'The Legislative History' (n 28) 152.

[34] See *Situation in the Republic of Kenya, ICC-01/09* (n 9) para 45. Likewise, Trial Chamber II argued in the *Katanga* case, that 'the organisation is not the State, as the text uses the conjunction "or" to denote that the concepts are and must remain distinct'. *Katanga, ICC-01/04–01/07* (n 4) para 1117.

[35] *Situation in the Republic of Kenya, ICC-01/09* (n 9) para 92.

[36] See *Situation in the Republic of Kenya, ICC-01/09* (n 9) para 51. Yet, commonality cannot be the constitutive elements of statehood under international law.

[37] Werle and Burghardt, 'Do Crimes against Humanity Require the Participation of a State or a "State-Like" Organization?' (n 9) 1156.

[38] Bartels and Fortin, 'Law, Justice and a Potential Security Gap: The "Organization" Requirement in International Humanitarian Law and International Criminal Law' (2015) Journal of Conflict & Security Law 17. See also Werle and Jessberger, *Principles of International Criminal Law* (OUP 2014) 344. Moreover, the criterion of being 'state-like' is unhelpful because it lacks precise legal meaning. While it is normally understood as suggesting a high threshold for non-state entities to qualify as an organization, it is not clear on which criteria this assessment is based.

[39] These acts are listed in article 7(1)(a)–(k) and defined in article 7(2)(b)–(i) ICC Statute.

[40] Article 7(2)(h), (i) ICC Statute.

of enforced disappearances, the term 'political organization' is also likely to refer to quasi-governmental capacities.[41] Yet, while such high degrees of power and organization are needed for these two specific crimes, they are not generally needed to commit other crimes amounting to CAH.

Looking at the contextual elements of CAH, under article 7(2)(a) ICC Statute the 'organizational policy' is linked to the commission of the attack. An organization must at least be able to provide a policy, pursuant to or in furtherance of which a course of conduct involving the multiple commission of certain acts against any civilian population are committed. This raises the question of whether it suffices that an organization simply adopts and promotes a policy to commit the attack, or whether the organization also needs to implement the policy. In the first case, the organization could be one that merely instigates crimes committed by others. In the latter case, implementation of the policy could mean that the organization needs to have the capacity to organize and implement the attack with its own resources. The different implications of these options are further discussed in section 9.2 'Different Organizational Capacities as Suggested in the *Elements of Crimes* and in ICC Jurisprudence' below. Before that, Section 9.1.4 'A teleological interpretation of organization' considers which conclusions on the entity behind CAH can be drawn from the object and purpose of the criminalization of CAH under the ICC Statute.

9.1.4 A teleological interpretation of organization

According to the preamble to the ICC Statute, the Court shall be concerned with 'unimaginable atrocities that deeply shock the conscience of humanity'.[42] With the adoption of the Statute, states aim to protect certain international values, namely 'the peace, security and well-being of the world'.[43] The main objective of the Statute is that 'the most serious crimes of concern to the international community as a whole must not go unpunished'[44] and 'to put an end to impunity for the perpetrators of these crimes'.[45] This section does not aim to deduce the meaning of 'organization' from the ICC Statute's broad objectives. Instead, it addresses arguments claiming that limitations on the scope of entities falling under the term 'organization' derive from (i) the ICC Statute's focus on particularly grave crimes and its objective to further world peace and security; or (ii) the purpose to end impunity.

9.1.4.1 Unimaginable atrocities that deeply shock the conscience of humanity and the objective to protect international values

The ICC Statute's preamble underlines that in prosecuting alleged international crimes, the ICC shall focus on particularly 'grave' and 'most serious crimes' that

[41] For in-depth discussion, see Giorgou, 'State Involvement in the Perpetration of Enforced Disappearance and the Rome Statute' (2013) 11 Journal of International Criminal Justice 1001–21.

[42] ICC Statute, preamble, para 2. [43] ibid, para 3. [44] ibid, para 4.

[45] ibid, para 5.

'shock the conscience of humanity'.[46] Unfortunately, these specifications are rather vague and do not adequately serve as legal determinants of which conduct they cover. In particular, they do not restrict the scope of potential perpetrators, but emphasize that the gravity or scale of the crimes shall be decisive. Likewise, the Court's objective to protect the peace, security, and well-being of the world is broad and does not specify whether any specific kind of entity will need to be involved in the crimes. In fact, by including widespread or systematic attacks against any civilian population in the ICC Statute, states qualified such acts ipso facto as heinous atrocities threatening international peace and security.[47] Accordingly, Werle and Burghardt conclude that there is no 'normatively valid argument' that justifies restricting the perpetrators of CAH if the acts in question meet the definition of CAH under article 7 ICC Statute.

In contrast, in a dissenting opinion on Pre-Trial Chamber II's decision to authorize investigations in the Kenya situation, Judge Kaul strongly advocated for a more restrictive interpretation of the organization behind CAH under the ICC Statute. Kaul argued that to adopt and implement a policy behind CAH, a 'private entity must have the means and resources available to reach the gravity of systemic injustice in which parts of the civilian population find themselves'.[48] Where he drew the line, however, was in defining what the required 'systemic injustice' caused by CAH is; in other words, 'What is the underlying rationale or raison d'être of crimes against humanity?'.[49] Analysing the emergence of CAH as an international crime since 1945, Kaul correctly finds that, after World War II, it was systematic mass crimes by sovereign states against civilian populations that led to the international criminalisation of CAH. In Kaul's view, not the mere scale of the crimes but 'the presence of a policy element elevated those crimes to the international level'.[50] Drawing from history, Kaul concluded:

> If leaders of a state who normally have the duty to uphold the rule of law and to respect human rights engage in a policy of violent attacks against a civilian population it is the community of states which must intervene and prevent, control and repress this threat to the peace, security and well-being of the world.[51]

From this line of argument two main points can be distilled: first, the crimes must follow a policy. With the adoption of the ICC Statute, this point ceased to be controversial. Second, what makes CAH especially heinous is the particular relationship between the perpetrators and the victims, namely that the perpetrators violate their obligation to respect and to protect the human rights of the victims on a mass scale.

Different commentators praised Judge Kaul's dissenting opinion.[52] Yet, limiting the entity behind CAH to states or state-like entities with an obligation to protect

[46] This gravity requirement is further emphasised in article 17(1)(a) ICC Statute.

[47] See Werle and Burghardt, 'Do Crimes against Humanity Require the Participation of a State or a "State-Like" Organization?' (n 9) 1166; see also Werle and Jessberger, *Principles of International Criminal Law* (n 38) 344.

[48] *Situation in the Republic of Kenya, ICC-01/09* (n 9) para 66.

[49] ibid, at para 56.

[50] See ibid, at paras 59–61, quote at 60.

[51] ibid, at para 63.

[52] See, eg, Kress, 'On the Outer Limits of Crimes against Humanity' (n 26) 862; Schabas, *Unimaginable Atrocities* (n 3) 144.

human rights of the victims is overly restrictive. Admittedly, the argument that CAH are international crimes because they constitute a 'systematic inversion of the jurisdictional resources of the state' might convince at first sight.[53] Different scholars advanced the idea that the criminalization of CAH aims to protect human rights, which arguably only apply between the individual and a state or some 'authority or power'.[54] Moreover, in a world of sovereign states, which exercise control over persons under their jurisdiction, the risk of mass crimes is especially high when a territorial authority turns against its population.[55] Yet, while Judge Kaul's historical analysis is correct, the factual circumstances of CAH in the past should not necessarily be regarded as material elements of today's definition of CAH.[56] Equally strong arguments exist against a restrictive 'human rights protection' or 'governmental power'-focused approach.

First, while CAH have an apparent link to human rights protection,[57] international criminal law and human rights law are two distinct fields. CAH as international crimes are distinct from human rights violations.[58] As the International Law Commission (ILC) put it, 'In the case of crimes against humanity, the composite act is a violation separate from the individual violations of human rights of which it is composed.'[59] Crimes under international criminal law are also not limited to crimes committed by entities traditionally considered bound by human rights law.[60] For example, there is no doubt that any non-state party to an armed conflict can commit war crimes even if there may be doubts over whether the party

[53] Vernon, 'What is Crime against Humanity?' (2002) 10 Journal of Political Philosophy 243.

[54] See Ambos and Wirth, 'The Current Law of Crimes against Humanity: An Analysis of UNTAET Regulatuion 152000' (2002) Criminal Law Journal Forum 30–31; Ambos, 'Crimes against Humanity and the International Criminal Court' in Sadat (ed), *Forging a Convention for Crimes against Humanity* (CUP 2011) 279–304, 283. Abrams and Ratner also advanced the idea that the 'emphasis on some form of official action—though not necessarily that of the recognized government—remains more justifiable because of the focus of human rights and humanitarian law on protecting individuals from those with power over them'. Ratner and Abrams, *Accountability for Human Rights Atrocities in International Law: Beyond the Nuremberg Legacy* (3rd edn, OUP 2009) 79.

[55] As Vernon argues, in such situations the victims are deprived of any hope for protection from that state. They depend on an intervention by the international community. See Vernon, 'What is Crime against Humanity?' (n 53) 243.

[56] See also deGuzman, 'The Road from Rome: The Developing Law of Crimes against Humanity' (2000) 22 Human Rights Quarterly 370.

[57] See Schabas, *The International Criminal Court* (n 16) 139; Cassese, *International Criminal Law* (n 4) 99; Meron, *The Humanization of International Law* (M Nijhoff 2006) 266.

[58] For further conceptual arguments, see Section 8.1 'Crimes against Humanity in the Nuremberg Charter and in Post-World War II Jurisprudence' above.

[59] International Law Commission, *Responsibility of State for Internationally Wrongful Acts (with Commentaries)* (United Nations 2001) 34.

[60] Werle and Burghardt underline this point with a national-law analogy: 'In the same way that, on the national level, it is not only violations of constitutionally protected individual rights attributable to the state that are punishable, crimes under international law are also not limited to violations of human rights by states.' Werle and Burghardt, 'Do Crimes against Humanity Require the Participation of a State or a "State-Like" Organization?' (n 9) 1164; Robinson, 'Essence of Crimes against Humanity Raised by Challenges at ICC' (*EJIL: Talk!* 27 September 2011) <http://www.ejiltalk.org/essence-of-crimes-against-humanity-raised-by-challenges-at-icc/> accessed 13 November 2017.

has human rights obligations. In addition, human rights obligations are not necessarily restricted to state-like entities.[61]

Second, as argued in Chapter 7 'Conceptual Considerations on the Notion of 'Crimes against Humanity' above, limiting CAH conceptually to crimes with the involvement of a state or state-like entity is based on a narrow understanding of the crime's 'harm to humanity'. CAH do not harm humanity because a state or an entity exercising territorial power commits the crimes in question. CAH are particularly heinous crimes which require international (judicial) intervention because large-scale crimes are committed against a population in a context in which the entity normally tasked to protect the victims is unwilling or unable to halt or to redress the crimes.[62] If 'the highest *de facto* authority in the territory'[63] is unwilling or unable to protect the victims of mass crimes, it is difficult to see why—all other facts being equal—a widespread or systematic attack against a civilian population by a non-state group without state-like capacities poses less of a threat to international peace and security than similar acts committed by states.[64]

Third, confining CAH to crimes committed with the involvement of states or state-like entities would exclude heinous crimes that otherwise meet the elements of CAH. Today, a variety of non-state actors commit atrocities factually resembling CAH without having state-like characteristics.[65] As Hansen argues, a statist approach to CAH is 'based on a Eurocentric understanding of mass violence where only the state (or entities that resemble a state) is seen as capable of adopting and implementing policies to conduct such violence'.[66] By referring to the situations currently before the ICC, he finds that these are:

> all testimonies of how in the *absence* of efficient and legitimate state structures, rebel groups, clan leaders, and other non-state actors—and sometimes state agencies acting on behalf of particular leaders, rather than according to a policy of the state—may organize extremely serious abuses against the civilian population.[67]

Likewise, Werle and Jessberger emphasize that a state-focused approach based on crimes committed in Europe 'cannot simply be transposed onto other political and

[61] On this point, see Part II of this book.

[62] See Section 7.3 'Expanding the Concept of CAH to Non-State Entities' above. This argument seems to be supported by Cassese, who argued, 'Plainly, a widespread or systematic attack on the population can be carried out by non-state groups or paramilitary units with the acquiescence of state authorities or in circumstances where such authorities lack the effective power to put an end to such attacks.' Cassese, *International Criminal Law* (n 4) 101, n 4.

[63] Ambos and Wirth, 'The Current Law of Crimes against Humanity' (n 54) 27.

[64] Crimes committed by a non-state armed group can amount to CAH if there is a policy of deliberate tolerance by the territorial state. (see ibid, at 31.) This assumes a functioning state, or a state strong enough to intervene. This is not, however, always the case in situations where crimes factually amounting to CAH occur.

[65] See Bassiouni, *Crimes against Humanity* (n 3) 52 and 97. Similarly, Sadat argues that limiting CAH to crimes of states 'does not respond to the terrible suffering of today's victims of CAH nor does it accurately describe the modern law of CAH'. Sadat, 'Emerging from the Shadow of Nuremberg' (n 6) 6.

[66] Hansen, 'The Policy Requirement in Crimes against Humanity' (n 9) 37.

[67] ibid. See also Jalloh, 'What Makes Crimes against Humanity Crimes against Humanity?' (n 24) 416.

cultural contexts'.[68] Accordingly, Trial Chamber II argued in the *Katanga* case that interpreting 'organisation' as requiring 'quasi-state characteristics' would not 'further the Statute's goal of prosecuting the most serious crimes':

> To so conceive the organisation would in effect exclude any entities that may have undertaken a widespread or systematic operation involving the multiple commission of acts under article 7(1) of the Statute pursuant to or in furtherance of their policy, on the sole ground that they are insufficiently hierarchical to be considered, in theory, as capable of pursuing or enforcing a policy whose aim is such an attack.[69]

This argument is closely linked to the ICC's objective to end impunity for core crimes.

9.1.4.2 Ending impunity

The ICC's aim is not to prosecute and end impunity for state crimes but for 'the most serious crimes of concern to the international community as a whole'.[70] If crimes factually amounting to CAH are committed with the involvement of a non-state organization, and if the territorial state is unwilling or unable to prosecute the crimes, the aim to end impunity necessitates ICC intervention. Admittedly, state involvement heightens the risk of impunity. As Schabas argues:

> Over the decades, one important justification for prosecuting crimes against humanity as such has been the fact that these atrocities generally escape prosecution in the state that normally exercises jurisdiction, under the territorial or active personality principles, because of the state's own involvement or acquiescence.[71]

Yet, as the Kenya situation before the ICC shows, the argument that crimes by non-state actors that are not state-like are generally prosecuted domestically does not reflect reality.[72] Therefore, achieving the ICC's objective of effectively addressing core crimes and ending impunity should not be hampered by invoking a particular interpretation of a crime's object and purpose, in particular if such interpretation is not supported by other means of treaty interpretation.[73]

To sum up, interpreted in accordance with its ordinary meaning, context, and object and purpose, the term 'organizational policy' in article 7(2)(a) ICC Statute is not limited to policies by states or state-like organizations. Requiring a 'state or organizational policy' underlines that the 'organization' is not a state. Likewise, the object and purpose of the ICC Statute do not necessitate a state-focused interpretation of

[68] Werle and Jessberger, *Principles of International Criminal Law* (n 38) 345. See also Sadat, 'Emerging from the Shadow of Nuremberg' (n 6) 336.

[69] *Katanga, ICC-01/04–01/07* (n 4) para 1122.

[70] ICC Statute, preamble, para 4.

[71] Schabas, *Unimaginable Atrocities* (n 3) 149–50.

[72] The argument that international prosecution of crimes by non-state actors that are not state-like is generally not necessary has been advanced by Schabas among others, see ibid, at 150.

[73] As the ILC has emphasized, 'When a treaty is open to two interpretations one of which does and the other does not enable the treaty to have appropriate effects, good faith and the objects and purposes of the treaty demand that the former interpretation should be adopted.' United Nations, *Yearbook of the International Law Commission*, Vol II (United Nations 1966) 219.

the entity behind CAH. Instead, any crime that shocks the conscience of humanity, poses a threat to the peace and security of mankind, and is likely to go unpunished should fall under the Court's jurisdiction if it falls under its jurisdiction ratione materie. In principle, this requires a factual assessment of the alleged crimes independent of whether the entity behind the crimes exercised territorial control, had quasi-governmental powers, or owed human rights obligations to the victims. In order to determine more precisely which characteristics an 'organization' behind CAH must have, the word's ordinary meaning suggests that it consists of a group of persons vested with a minimum of structure and stability in order to achieve a common purpose. Moreover, read in its context, an organization should at least be able to provide a policy pursuant to or in furtherance of which a course of conduct involving the multiple commission of crimes against any civilian population is committed.

To a certain extent, this capacity-oriented approach has been included in the *Elements of Crimes* and finds support in ICC jurisprudence.

9.2 Different Organizational Capacities as Suggested in the *Elements of Crimes* and in ICC Jurisprudence

Under article 7(2)(a) ICC Statute, the notion 'State or organizational policy' suggests that the organization behind CAH is linked to the policy pursuant to or in furtherance of which the attack against a civilian population is committed. States took this view when agreeing on the *Elements of Crimes*:[74] they specified 'that "policy to commit such attack" requires that the State or organization *actively promote or encourage* such an attack against a civilian population'.[75] In a footnote to this specification, the *Elements of Crimes* state:

> A policy which has a civilian population as the object of the attack *would be implemented by State or organizational action*. Such a policy may, in exceptional circumstances, be *implemented by a deliberate failure to take action*, which is consciously aimed at encouraging such attack. The existence of such a policy cannot be inferred solely from the absence of governmental or organizational action.[76]

Accordingly, the *Elements of Crimes* suggest as least three possible ways of how the entity behind CAH might be involved.

- First, it could be an entity that promotes and encourages the attack, meaning that the entity instigates the attack without being directly involved in its

[74] According to article 9 ICC Statute, the *Elements of Crimes* 'shall assist the Court in the interpretation and application of articles 6, 7 and 8'.

[75] Preparatory Commission for the International Criminal Court, *Elements of Crimes*, 2 November 2000, PCNICC/2000/1/Add.2, 9 (emphasis added).

[76] ibid, at 9, n 6 (emphasis added). As Ambos reports, 'This contradictory text is the result of a compromise achieved during the Fourth Session (13 to 31 March 2000) of the Preparatory Commission ("PrepCom").' Ambos, *Treatise on International Criminal Law* (n 2) 71.

execution. The entity's action would consist of instigating the crimes, which could be accompanied by the provision of political and/or logistical support to the perpetrators. The criminal acts defined under article 7(1)(a–k) ICC Statute would be committed by individuals or groups not belonging to the organixation behind the policy.

- Second, the organization behind the policy could implement the policy though its own action in a narrower sense, meaning that the entity's agents commit the acts constituting the attack. This means that the organization needs to have itself sufficient resources—manpower, logistics, and internal structures—to implement multiple criminalized acts against a civilian population.
- Third, a policy could also be implemented by inaction, meaning that the entity tolerates the attack. At first sight, this could simply mean that the state or organization would have to decide to do nothing.

Each of these options has different implications for the requisite degree of power and organization of the entity behind the policy, which are examined in Sections 9.2.2 'An organization tolerating an attack against a civilian population'–9.2.4 'An organization implementing the policy through its own actions'. First, however, the brief Section 9.2.1 'The policy behind CAH' recalls the main characteristics of a policy behind CAH.

9.2.1 The policy behind CAH

Article 7 ICC Statute is the first international definition of CAH explicitly requiring a 'State or organizational policy' as a legal element of the crime.[77] The wording of article 7(2)(a) clarifies that a policy cannot be any policy, but must be one 'to commit such attack'.[78] As seen from the drafting history of article 7, as well as from the International Criminal Tribunal for the former Yugoslavia's (ICTY's) *Tadić* case, the policy requirement serves primarily to exclude isolated or random crimes by individuals.[79] Likewise, different Pre-Trial Chambers (PTCs) have held that 'an attack which is planned, directed or organised—as opposed to spontaneous or isolated

[77] While different views exist on whether a policy is a legal element of CAH under customary international law, for the purpose of this book—and with regard to the fact that states explicitly included this element in the ICC Statute—the policy requirement is considered a legal element of CAH. The question of whether a policy constitutes a legal element of CAH under customary international law has been discussed in jurisprudence and doctrine, and the ad hoc tribunals finally dismissed the policy requirement from the legal definition of CAH under customary international law. Two reference articles that reflect academic controversy are Schabas, 'State Policy as an Element of International Crimes' 98 The Journal of Criminal Law & Criminology 953–82 and Mettraux, 'The Definition of Crimes against Humanity and the Question of a "Policy" Element' in Sadat (ed), *Forging a Convention for Crimes against Humanity* (CUP 2011) 142–76. The two most important references in jurisprudence are *Tadić, Judgment, 7 May 1997, IT-94-1-T*, ICTY, para 653 and *Kunarac et al, Appeals Chamber Judgment, 12 June 2002, IT-96-23 & IT-96-23/1-A*, ICTY, para 98. See also International Law Commission, *Third Report on Identification of Customary International Law*, by Michael Wood, Special Rapporteur' (27 March 2015) para 140.

[78] This excludes policies pursuing aims other than the commission of crimes. See *Ruto et al, ICC-01/09–01/11* (n 10) para 213.

[79] See *Tadić, IT-94-1-T* (n 77) para 653; *Gbagbo, Decision on the Confirmation of Charges against Larent Gbagbo, 12 June 2014, Pre-Trial Chamber I, ICC-02/11–01/11*, ICC, para 214. See also

acts of violence—will satisfy the policy criterion'.[80] While planning, directing or organizing could set the threshold rather high, Robinson suggests emphasizing the policy's function of excluding 'random acts of individuals acting on their own criminal initiatives': 'to be an "attack", the acts must be directed, instigated or encouraged by some source *other than individuals* acting independently', which in his view signifies a policy.[81] A policy does not need to be formally adopted but can be inferred from how crimes are committed.[82] As Ambos puts it, 'an implicit or *de facto* policy is sufficient'.[83] In essence, the policy behind CAH interlinks the underlying crimes, guides the attack, and thereby distinguishes CAH from ordinary crimes.[84] In addition, as the Trial Chamber argued in the *Katanga* case, the policy behind the crimes 'refers essentially to the fact that a State or organisation intends to carry out an attack against a civilian population, whether through action or deliberate failure to take action'.[85] Thus, the policy also links the attack to the entity behind it.

However, the existence of a policy behind CAH does not mean that the attack is also 'systematic',[86] which normally refers to its 'organized nature', showing 'patterns of crimes, in the sense of non-accidental repetition of similar criminal conduct on a regular basis'.[87] The difference between an attack following a policy and one that is systematic becomes clearer if the ordinary meaning of 'policy' is compared with that of 'plan', which underlies a systematic attack. Whereas a plan is 'a detailed proposal for doing or achieving something', a policy is 'a course or principle of action adopted or proposed by an organization or individual'.[88] Accordingly, while a

Robinson, deGuzman, Jalloh et al, *Amicus Curiae Observations of Professors Robinson, deGuzman, Jalloh and Cryer, ICC-02/11-01/11* (ICC 2013) paras 22–23.

[80] *Gbagbo, ICC-02/11–01/11* (n 79) para 215.

[81] Robinson, 'Crimes against Humanity: A Better Policy on "Policy"' (n 19) 710.

[82] See *Katanga, ICC-01/04–01/07* (n 4) para 1109. As the Trial Chamber argued 'in the majority of situations amenable to the Court, some aspects of the policy pursued against a civilian population will only crystallise and develop as actions are set in train and undertaken by the perpetrators'. See also *Situation in the Republic of Kenya, ICC-01/09* (n 9) para 87; *Tadić, IT-94-1-T* (n 77) para 653; *Kupreškić et al, Judgement, 14 January 2000, IT-95-16-T*, ICTY, para 551. For a detailed analysis of this question, see Robinson, deGuzman, Jalloh et al, *Amicus Curiae Observations of Professors Robinson, deGuzman, Jalloh and Cryer, ICC-02/11–01/11* (n 79) paras 17–36.

[83] Ambos, *Treatise on International Criminal Law* (n 2) 70.

[84] See Ambos, 'Crimes against Humanity' (n 54) 286; *Katanga, ICC-01/04–01/07* (n 4) para 1114.

[85] *Katanga, ICC-01/04–01/07* (n 4) para 1108.

[86] As different ICC Chambers have highlighted, while the policy element and the systematic character of CAH are to some extent related, 'that does not mean that the terms "policy" and "systematic" are to be considered synonymous'. ibid, at para 1111. For further discussion of this point, see Robinson, 'Crimes against Humanity: A Better Policy on "Policy"' (n 19) 713–14.

[87] Initially, different pre-trial chambers found that one element of a state or organizational policy is that 'the attack must be thoroughly organised and follow a regular pattern', which effectively equates the policy element with the systematic character of CAH. See, eg, *Ntaganda, Decision on the Prosecutor's Application under Article 58, Pre-Trial Chamber, 13 July 2012, ICC-01/04–02/06*, ICC, para 24. Likewise, some commentators have suggested that the definition of attack under article 7(2)(a) ICC Statute comes close to requiring the crimes to be widespread and systematic. See, eg, Clark, 'History of Efforts to Codify Crimes against Humanity: From the Charter of Nuremberg to the Statute of Rome' in Sadat (ed), *Forging a Convention for Crimes against Humanity* (CUP 2011) 8–27, 21. However, other Chambers argued convincingly that this is too high a threshold. See *Gbagbo, ICC-02/11–01/11* (n 79) para 223; see also *Katanga, ICC-01/04–01/07* (n 4) para 1123.

[88] See Oxford Dictionaries, online version, definitions of 'plan' and 'policy'.

policy is normally of a more general character and aims broadly to eliminate, persecute, or weaken a certain community, the systematic nature of the attack is found in planned and repeated action implemented against a civilian population.[89] This difference is reflected in case law. For example, in the *Ruto et al* case, the allegedly systematic nature of the attack was shown by the concrete pattern according to which the crimes were committed.[90] In contrast, the policy had a more general objective, namely to 'punish and expel from the Rift Valley those perceived to support PNU [Party of National Unity], namely, Kikuyu, Kamba and Kisii civilians'.[91] Similarly, in the *Ntaganda* case, the systematic nature of the attack was proven by the concrete pattern of the attack,[92] whereas the policy behind the attack was found to be one of ethnic cleansing with a broader objective in mind.[93]

Having set out key characteristics of a policy behind CAH, Sections 9.2.2 'An organization tolerating an attack against a civilian population'–9.2.4 'An organization implementing the policy through its own actions' show how the different ways in which the policy relates to the crimes underlying CAH determine the requisite degree of organization of the entity behind the policy.

9.2.2 An organization tolerating an attack against a civilian population

The *Elements of Crimes* suggest that, exceptionally, a policy can be one of tolerating an attack against a civilian population. Such a policy would be 'implemented by a deliberate failure to take action, which is consciously aimed at encouraging such attack'.[94] This means that the entity behind the policy would not use its own resources to orchestrate a widespread or systematic attack against a civilian population but it would enable such an attack by abstaining from acting. Ambos provides the following example to illustrate the implementation of this kind of policy:

> Take the case of the large-scale killing of inhabitants in a certain area by private groups in order to get hold of its natural resources, accompanied by an official failure to stop these crimes from occurring. The government's motive for inaction could be that the victims of

[89] See *Katanga, ICC-01/04–01/07* (n 4) para 1113.

[90] The 'perpetrators approached the target locations simultaneously, in large numbers, and from different directions, by vehicles or on foot, or both'. *Ruto et al, ICC-01/09–01/11* (n 10) para 179.

[91] ibid, at para 181.

[92] The Pre-Trial Chamber found reasonable grounds to believe that the crimes were systematic because 'the perpetrators employed similar means and methods to attack the different locations: they approached the targets simultaneously, in large numbers, and from different directions, they attacked villages with heavy weapons, and systematically chased the population by similar methods, hunting house by house and into the bushes, burning all properties and looting'. *Ntaganda, ICC-01/04–02/06* (n 87) para 31.

[93] The Court found reasonable grounds to believe that 'the organization promoted a policy aimed at targeting "non-originaires" civilians of Ituri, mainly Lendu, in order to expel them from the territory, eliminate them, systematically loot and burn their properties, with the ultimate goal of occupying the territory and creating the "Etat Indépendant de l'Ituri"'. ibid, at para 27.

[94] *Elements of Crimes* (n 75) 9, n 6 (emphasis added). As Ambos reports, 'This contradictory text is the result of a compromise achieved during the Fourth Session (13 to 31 March 2000) of the Preparatory Commission ("PrepCom").' Ambos, *Treatise on International Criminal Law* (n 2) 71.

the attack are opponents of the government and thus the private groups would be doing the government's 'dirty work'.[95]

Considering an entity's capacity to adopt a policy of tolerance or inaction, it could be argued that this requires essentially nothing else from the entity behind CAH than to decide not to do anything. If this was strictly applied to non-state organizations, it would set the organizational threshold low: essentially any group of persons could adopt such policy. The better view is that a deliberate failure to take action can only amount to a policy behind CAH if the entity adopting this policy is either a state or has quasi-governmental capacities. Only deliberate inaction by an entity that would otherwise have the responsibility and capacity to protect the victims will enable and possibly guide the crimes.[96] In contrast, if an entity without such capacities decides not to take action, such a policy would not affect the situation. In international law, the obligation to protect individuals from crimes normally stems from human rights law. Consequently, the scope of entities behind a policy of tolerance would be limited to states and non-state organizations with quasi-governmental capacities having the obligation to protect human rights of individuals under their control.[97]

9.2.3 An organization actively promoting or encouraging an attack

In a second scenario, an entity's policy could promote and instigate CAH without any other involvement in the crime. The *Elements of Crimes* state that 'it is understood that "policy to commit such attack" requires that the State or organization actively promote or encourage such an attack against a civilian population'.[98] Accordingly, Trial Chamber II suggested in the *Katanga* case that this 'presupposes that the organisation in question has sufficient means to promote or encourage a campaign involving the multiple commission of acts referred to in article 7(2) of the Statute'.[99] While the Chamber seemingly continued by arguing that an organization needs to have sufficient capacity to carry out the attack itself, this is not the only way to interpret the 'organizational policy' requirement.[100] If a policy behind CAH is essentially a tool to exclude spontaneous or isolated acts of violence from the crime's scope, to connect the individual acts, to guide the attack, and to link the

[95] Ambos, '*Treatise on International Criminal Law' Law* (n 2) 70.

[96] For similar conclusions, see Ambos, 'Crimes against Humanity' (n 54) 425–26; Werle and Jessberger, *Principles of International Criminal Law* (n 38); Jalloh, 'What Makes Crimes against Humanity Crimes against Humanity?' (n 24).

[97] See Section 6.3 ' Human Rights Obligations of Groups Exercising Quasi-Governmental Authority in Defined Territory'. See also Ambos, *Treatise on International Criminal Law* (n 2) 71.

[98] *Elements of Crimes* (n 75) 9.

[99] *Katanga, ICC-01/04–01/07* (n 4) para 1117.

[100] See ibid, at para 1119. This interpretation is further discussed in Section 9.2.4 'An organization implementing the policy through its own actions'. However, the Chamber's reasoning is not unequivocal. It argues that an organization needs to have sufficient means and structures to 'bring about', 'carry out', or 'promote or encourage the attack'. While 'bring about' or 'promote and encourage' are broader in scope, only 'carry out' suggests that the organization has to implement the attack through its own forces. In the *Katanga* case, the organization behind the attack was 'organized within a single militia' and 'capable of conceiving and executing large-scale attacks'. Thus, it had the capacity to carry out the attack itself. ibid, at paras 1139–41.

attack to an entity behind it, it is also possible that a state or organization merely promotes and encourages attacks without being itself involved in the 'dirty work'. Following the ordinary meaning of promoting and encouraging, this would merely require the state or organization to give support and advice in order to initiate or further the progress of the attack and to persuade perpetrators to commit the crimes.[101]

If a state or quasi-governmental organization can implement a CAH policy by deliberately failing to take action, a fortiori such entities can also instigate CAH through a policy of active promotion or encouragement. In addition, a widespread attack against a civilian population could be realized if, for example, a religious, political, or otherwise important societal organization actively promotes or encourages widespread crimes against other societal groups in a situation of a weak or failing state. In such situations, the organization would instigate an attack against a civilian population, which is carried out by individuals or militias not directly forming part of the organization. It is not very difficult to imagine a religious leader using his or her moral power to actively promote widespread crimes against adherents of another religion in a situation in which no territorial authority is in a position to stop these crimes.[102] Likewise, a right-wing political party may incite crimes against foreigners, and if no authority is able to halt these crimes, acts committed by different individuals and groups pursuant to a racist policy could amount to a widespread attack against a civilian population. In such cases, the relationship between the entity behind CAH and the actual acts forming the attack would correspond with the ILC's 1996 *Draft Code of Crimes*, which suggested that large-scale crimes can amount to CAH if they are 'instigated ... by any organization or group'.[103]

The fact that perpetrators of CAH do not need to be agents of the entity behind the crime further supports this interpretation. As Werle and Jessberger assert, 'Perpetrators need not be members of the state or organization involved in the crime, but can include all persons who act to implement or support the policy of the state or organization.'[104] Likewise, Pre-Trial Chamber II argued that article 7(1) ICC Statute only requires 'knowledge of the attack' and not 'any tighter link between the person charged and the organization bearing the policy'.[105] Accordingly, if a state or organization has sufficient capacity to actively promote and encourage an attack against a civilian population without having state or organizational agents committing the underlying acts, this entity could be an organization under article 7(2)(a) ICC Statute. After all, an attack must be 'pursuant to or in furtherance of'

[101] According to Oxford Dictionaries, online version, 'promoting' means to 'support or actively encourage (a cause, venture, etc.); further the progress of', and encouraging to 'give support, confidence, or hope to (someone)' or to 'persuade (someone) to do or continue to do something by giving support and advice'.

[102] If the territorial authority would like to but is de facto unable to halt the crimes, it does not have sufficient capacity to provide a policy of tolerance for the commission of CAH.

[103] International Law Commission, *Draft Code of Crimes against the Peace and Security of Mankind (with Commentary)* (United Nations 1996) article 18.

[104] Werle and Jessberger, *Principles of International Criminal Law* (n 38); see also Cassese, *Cassese's International Criminal Law* (3rd edn, OUP 2013) 100.

[105] *Muthaura et al, ICC-01/09–02/11* (n 11) para 223; see also *Katanga, ICC-01/04–01/07* (n 4) para 1115.

a policy, which does not require the entity behind the policy to control the crimes' perpetrators.[106]

The resulting organizational threshold would be low. Most organizations—meaning groups with some structure, stability, and operating to achieve a certain purpose—have sufficient capacity to develop an organizational policy. The required organizational work would be particularly low if the policy behind CAH is understood as not requiring a 'pre-established design or plan' but as something that can be inferred from how attacks are committed.[107] In this case, the analysis would essentially need to focus on whether the organization has the factual capacity to instigate an attack against a civilian population. Realistically, in order to instigate crimes of sufficient scale without involving the organization's own members in the direct perpetration of the acts, the organization will need to have sufficient means to initiate and guide the crimes. This would likely require those who incite the crimes to have a certain societal standing, as well as the necessary means of communication to bring about a widespread or systematic attack. Moreover, it could also be required for the organization to provide certain logistical support for the perpetrators, such as weapons, funds, means of transport, or directions on where to find the targeted population. This kind of more active involvement in CAH is discussed in Section 9.2.4 'An organization implementing the policy through its own actions'.

9.2.4 An organization implementing the policy through its own actions

A third option is the most prevelant one in practice, namely that the entity behind the policy also implements the policy through its own manpower and resources. As the *Elements of Crimes* suggest, a 'policy which has a civilian population as the object of the attack would be implemented by State or organizational action'.[108] The key notion here is 'State or organizational action'. A wide interpretation could lead to a conclusion similar to the one discussed above: active promotion and encouragement, and possibly the provision of logistics, could suffice as 'State or organizational action'. In contrast, a narrower interpretation of state or organizational action to implement a CAH policy suggests that the entity behind the policy would be required to have sufficient resources—manpower, logistics, and internal structures—to commit multiple criminalized acts against a civilian population.[109] In a first step, this section shows that, in a number of cases, ICC Chambers took the view that an organization behind CAH needs to have the capacity to commit an attack against a civilian population. In a second step, it argues that the requisite degree

[106] *Katanga, ICC-01/04–01/07* (n 4) paras 1115–16.

[107] ibid, at para 1109–10. For further elaboration of such a low policy threshold, see Robinson, deGuzman, Jalloh et al, *Amicus Curiae Observations of Professors Robinson, deGuzman, Jalloh and Cryer, ICC-02/11–01/11* (n 79).

[108] *Elements of Crimes* (n 75) 9, n 6.

[109] In addition, a grey zone is likely to exist between organizations merely instigating attacks by others and those directly implementing criminal acts: attacks may involve direct organizational action as well as acts by persons encouraged and supported by it, or acts which are not perpetrated by members of the organization but enabled through the provision of necessary logistics.

of organization to commit such acts should be derived directly from the definition of 'attack' under article 7(2)(a) ICC Statute.

9.2.4.1 The capability to commit an attack

Different ICC Chambers have taken the view that an organization behind CAH needs not only to be able to actively promote or encourage an attack but to commit an attack itself against a civilian population. As stated in the 2008 *Decision on the Confirmation of Charges* in the *Katanga and Chui* case, and repeated in a number of subsequent decisions,

> a policy may be made either by groups of persons who govern a specific territory or *by any organisation with the capability to commit a widespread or systematic attack against a civilian population.*[110]

The requirement that an entity governs a specific territory might be particularly relevant with regard to CAH committed pursuant to a policy of deliberate inaction or incitement. It would effectively limit the scope of organizations to those exercising quasi-governmental power; in other words, 'state-like' organizations. If this condition is not met, the Chambers require the entity behind CAH to have itself the capability to commit a widespread or systematic attack against a civilian population. In most CAH cases before the ICC, non-state organizations behind the alleged CAH are also parties to an armed conflict. Parties to an armed conflict necessarily have the capacity to attack military or civilian targets.[111] For example, in the *Ntaganda* case, the Chamber found that the *Union des Patriotes Congolais/Forces Patriotiques pour la Libération du Congo* (UPC/FPLC) constituted an organization under article 7(2)(a) ICC Statute because it was 'formally established', possessed a structured and disciplined military wing, had a chain of command, and 'the means and the capability to carry out military operations over a prolonged period of time'.[112] As a result, it seems uncontroversial, and arguably 'inevitable',[113] that a non-state party to an armed conflict has the capacity, and thereby the requisite degree of organization, to commit an attack against a civilian population.

In contrast, in the Kenya situation, CAH were allegedly committed with the involvement of non-state entities that were not party to an armed conflict. In the aftermath of the 2007 presidential elections, groups supporting different political parties and ethnicities committed widespread crimes against perceived adversaries.[114]

[110] *Katanga and Chui, Decision on the Confirmation of Charges, 30 September 2008, Pre-Trial Chamber I, ICC-01/04–01/07,* ICC, para 396; for further references, see *Gbagbo, ICC-02/11–01/11* (n 79) para 217 (emphasis added).

[111] For a detailed discussion on when a non-state group is sufficiently organized to be party to an armed conflict, see Chapter 3 'Organized Armed Groups in Contemporary International Practice'.

[112] *Ntaganda, ICC-01/04–02/06* (n 87) paras 14–18.

[113] Pre-Trial Chamber III went as far as to conclude that because the armed group in question qualified as a party to an armed conflict, it 'inevitably it qualifies as an organisation within the context of Article 7 of the Statute'. *Situation in the Republic of Cote d'Ivoire, ICC-02/11,* para 99.

[114] See *Report of the Commission of Inquiry into Post-Election Violence* (Kenya), viii. See also *Situation in the Republic of Kenya, ICC-01/09* (n 9) paras 102–05.

A key question in Pre-Trial Chamber II's decisions to authorize investigations in this situation and to confirm charges against the accused was whether the alleged crimes were committed pursuant to or in furtherance of a state or organizational policy. In this case, the Chamber's majority held:

> Whereas some have argued that only State-like organizations may qualify, the Chamber opines that the formal nature of a group and the level of its organization should not be the defining criterion. Instead, as others have convincingly put forward, *a distinction should be drawn on whether a group has the capability to perform acts which infringe on basic human values.*[115]

In his dissenting opinion, Judge Kaul criticized this requirement as—if left unspecified—unconvincing because it expands 'the concept of crimes against humanity to any infringement of human rights'.[116] Indeed, taken literally, requiring the 'capability to perform acts which infringe on basic human values' sets a low standard and departs from the ICC's previous jurisprudence. Instead, Judge Kaul argued that owing to the historic development of CAH and the juxtaposition of the terms 'organisation' and 'State', the organization should be an 'entity which may act like a State or has quasi-State abilities', meaning an entity able to 'carry out' a policy behind CAH.[117]

Interpretations of the two suggestions differ. For example, it remains unclear what the majority meant by 'capacity to infringe on basic human values'. Initially, some considered it to have lowered the threshold 'as much as possible' and not looked at whether there was an organization behind the crimes, but rather whether crimes were committed in an organized manner.[118] The majority's proposal has been criticized as an 'uncritically "victim-focused teleological reasoning" in the international criminal law context'.[119] Following subsequent decisions on the Kenya situation, others interpreted it as referring to the previously employed standard that an organization must be one 'with the capability to commit a widespread or systematic attack against a civilian population'.[120] At the same time, requiring 'state-like' capacities can be

[115] *Situation in the Republic of Kenya, ICC-01/09* (n 9) para 90 (emphasis added). This was reiterated in *Muthaura et al, ICC-01/09–02/11* (n 11) paras 112–14; *Ruto et al, ICC-01/09–01/11* (n 10) para 184. In support of this view, the PTC cited an article by Di Fillipo, in which he argues that 'the associative element, and its inherently aggravating effect, could eventually be satisfied by purely private criminal organizations, thus not finding sufficient reasons for distinguishing the gravity of patterns of conduct directed by "territorial" entities or by private groups, given the latter's acquired capacity to infringe basic human values.' In n 84, the PTC also refers to other scholars in support of its interpretation, and in para 91 to the International Law Commission, *Draft Code of Crimes against the Peace and Security of Mankind with Commentaries* (United Nations 1991).

[116] *Situation in the Republic of Kenya (Dissent Kaul), Dissenting Opinion of Judge Hans-Peter Kaul, 31 March 2010, Pre-Trial Chamber II, ICC-01/09,* ICC, para 53.

[117] ibid, at paras 51–52. The first part of this argument has been discussed in more detail in Section 9.1.3 'A contextual interpretation of organization' above.

[118] Jalloh, 'Situation in the Republic of Kenya' (2011) 105 American Journal of International Law 545.

[119] Kress, 'On the Outer Limits of Crimes against Humanity' (n 26) 861.

[120] See Jalloh, 'What Makes Crimes against Humanity Crimes against Humanity?' (n 24) 409; Giorgou, 'State Involvement in the Perpetration of Enforced Disappearance and the Rome Statute' (n 41) 1003; International Law Commission, *First Report on Crimes against Humanity* (n 1) para 148.

criticized for different reasons: being 'state-like' is a relatively broad and undefined term;[121] it might be overly narrow to address atrocities 'in the Modern Age';[122] some consider it 'Eurocentric';[123] and it is arguably unsupported by 'the "general practice accepted as law", identified by the jurisprudence of the ad hoc tribunals'.[124]

In order to reinforce their respective arguments, the majority and Judge Kaul suggested sets of indicative criteria—not strict conditions—according to which an evaluation of whether or not a non-state entity meets the respective organizational threshold can be made.[125] These lists contain two main common factors: first, whether the group operates under a responsible command and an established hierarchy; and second, whether it has the capacity or means to commit an attack against a civilian population. In addition, the majority lists factors such as territorial control, the purpose of the group, its intentions, or whether it is part of larger group qualifying as an organization behind CAH.[126] In contrast, Judge Kaul added some basic group characteristics, as well as whether the group has 'some kind of policy level' and the capacity to impose a policy on its members. Thus, in particular with regard to key elements—a group's structure and its capacity—the majority and Judge Kaul are not so far apart.[127] It is, however, unfortunate that neither the majority—which only referred to the Additional Protocol II to the Geneva Conventions of 1949 and some scholars—nor Judge Kaul provided explanations on how they arrived at these criteria.

A convincing approach to determining the characteristics of an organization capable of realizing CAH through 'organizational action' could be to interpret the term 'organization' in its context in article 7 ICC Statute: it must be an organization with sufficient capacity to develop and implement a policy to commit a widespread or systematic attack against a civilian population.

9.2.4.2 The required degree of organization as deduced from the contextual elements of CAH

Trial Chamber II proposed the approach of deducing the requisite degree of organization of a non-state entity under article 7(2)(a) ICC Statute from the definition's

[121] Rodenhäuser, 'Beyond State Crimes: Non-State Entities and Crimes against Humanity' (n 9) 922. Jalloh, eg, argues that certain African tribes could be considered 'state-like'. Jalloh, 'What Makes Crimes against Humanity Crimes against Humanity?' (n 24) 430.

[122] Sadat, 'Emerging from the Shadow of Nuremberg' (n 6); Bartels and Fortin, 'Law, Justice and a Potential Security Gap: The "Organization" Requirement in International Humanitarian Law and International Criminal Law' (n 38).

[123] Hansen, 'The Policy Requirement in Crimes against Humanity' (n 9); Sadat, 'Emerging from the Shadow of Nuremberg' (n 6) 336.

[124] *Katanga, ICC-01/04–01/07* (n 4) para 1121. For a contrary view, see Kress, 'On the Outer Limits of Crimes against Humanity' (n 26) 869.

[125] See *Situation in the Republic of Kenya, ICC-01/09* (n 9) para 93; *Situation in the Republic of Kenya (Dissent Kaul), ICC-01/09* (n 116) para 51.

[126] For some criticism of these factors, see Kress, 'On the Outer Limits of Crimes against Humanity' (n 26) 857–61.

[127] See also Ambos, *Treatise on International Criminal Law* (n 2) 74–75.

context in the *Katanga* case.[128] Interpreting the meaning of 'organization' under article 7(2)(a) ICC Statute, it argued:

In the Chamber's view, the connection of the term 'organization' to the very existence of the attack and not to its systematic or widespread nature presupposes that the organisation has sufficient resources, means and capacity to bring about the course of conduct or the operation involving the multiple commission of acts referred to in article 7(2)(a) of the Statute. It therefore suffices that the organisation have a set of structures or mechanisms, whatever those may be, that are sufficiently efficient to ensure the coordination necessary to carry out an attack directed against a civilian population.[129]

The Chamber held that no other requirements are necessary, in particular not 'any centralised and hierarchical structure'.[130] Likewise, Werle and Jessberger contend that in order to determine whether a non-state entity qualifies as an organization under article 7(2)(a) ICC Statute,

the crucial factor is not the internal structure of the group, but its potential, in terms of both personnel and physical capacity, to commit a widespread or systematic attack on a civilian population.[131]

These approaches favour a contextual interpretation—in line with the general rules on treaty interpretation—over a rather abstract and history-based 'state-like' criterion or factors without apparent basis in article 7 ICC Statute. In the Trial Chamber's words, an organization behind CAH must be an entity 'that, by very reason of the means and resources it possesses and its membership, allow[s] an attack to be executed'.[132] The suggested approaches differ, however, in one respect. While Trial Chamber II suggests examining what is needed to execute an attack, different Pre-Trial Chambers and scholars argue that an organization needs to have sufficient capacity to commit an attack *that is widespread or systematic*.

To determine the minimum capacity of a non-state entity to qualify as an 'organization' under article 7(2)(a) ICC Statute, the following paragraphs examine what the ICC Statute requires for acts to constitute an 'attack directed against any civilian population'. Article 7(2)(a) ICC Statute defines such an attack as a 'course of conduct involving the multiple commission of acts referred to in paragraph 1 against any civilian population' which is 'pursuant to or in furtherance of a State or organizational policy to commit such attack'. This definition contains two pertinent elements, one referring to the magnitude of the crimes, the other to the collective and targeted nature of the crime, also referred to as its 'associativity'.[133] The first two

[128] Previously, this approach has been hinted at by ICC PTCs requiring an organization to have the 'capability to commit a widespread or systematic attack against a civilian population'. See n 110 above.

[129] *Katanga, ICC-01/04–01/07* (n 4) para 1119.

[130] ibid, at para 1118.

[131] Werle and Jessberger, *Principles of International Criminal Law* (n 38) 343.

[132] *Katanga, ICC-01/04–01/07* (n 4) para 1120.

[133] Robinson, 'Crimes against Humanity: A Better Policy on "Policy"' (n 19) 711. As Pre-Trial Chamber I argued in the *Gbagbo* case, 'this definition already involves—although to a lesser extent—quantitative and qualitative aspects that may also be relevant for the establishment of the "widespread" or "systematic" nature of the attack under article 7(1) of the Statute'. *Gbagbo, ICC-02/11–01/11* (n 79) para 208.

sections, 'Course of conduct involing the multiple commission of acts … against any civilian population' and 'Pursuant to and in furtherance of a … policy' examine these two elements. A third section, 'Widespread or systematic' analyses what impact the 'widespread or systematic' requirement may have on the requisite degree of organization.

'Course of conduct involving the multiple commission of acts … against any civilian population'

The requirement of a 'course of conduct involving the multiple commission of acts …against any civilian population' has been interpreted as referring to a 'campaign, an operation or a series of action directed against the civilian population'.[134] A 'campaign or operation' or a 'series of action' implies necessarily an element of scale, which distinguishes such an attack from isolated incidences of crimes.[135] This cannot, however, mean that the crimes are also widespread; otherwise, the alternative formulation that an attack must be 'widespread or systematic' would be 'rendered meaningless'.[136] Instead, a course of conduct must simply consist of the multiple commission of the listed acts against a civilian population.[137] The *Elements of Crimes* clarifies that the acts committed 'need not constitute a military attack'.[138] CAH under the Rome Statute do not require any link to an armed conflict.[139]

An organization able to commit such course of conduct against a civilian population needs to have at least the capacities to realize a campaign or operation that involves multiple commissions of crimes.[140] This requires sufficient means and resources to orchestrate either one crime of extraordinary magnitude, or a series of acts.[141] For example, in the *Katanga* case, one pertinent argument for proving that

[134] *Katanga, ICC-01/04–01/07* (n 4) para 1101.

[135] As Pre-Trial Chamber II argued in the *Bemba* case, an attack under article 7(2)(a) ICCSt requires 'more than a few' isolated crimes. *Bemba, ICC-01/05–01/08* (n 31) para 81. On the question of the scale of the attack, see also Robinson, deGuzman, Jalloh et al, *Amicus Curiae Observations of Professors Robinson, deGuzman, Jalloh and Cryer, ICC-02/11–01/11* (n 79) paras 7–13. See also Ambos, *Treatise on International Criminal Law* (n 2) 59.

[136] *Katanga, ICC-01/04–01/07* (n 4) para 1101.

[137] See Robinson, deGuzman, Jalloh et al, *Amicus Curiae Observations of Professors Robinson, deGuzman, Jalloh and Cryer, ICC-02/11–01/11* (n 79) para 10; Werle and Jessberger, *Principles of International Criminal Law* (n 38) 338.

[138] *Elements of Crimes* (n 75) 5. This is also clear from the acts listed in article 7(1): the crimes of persecution or apartheid may be carried out by adopting legislative acts or specific policies. See Schabas, *The International Criminal Court* (n 16) 153. Likewise, the ICTY Appeals Chamber argued in the *Kunarac* case that 'the attack in the context of a crime against humanity is not limited to the use of armed force; it encompasses any mistreatment of the civilian population'. *Kunarac et al, IT-96-23 & IT-96-23/1-A* (n 77) para 86.

[139] On the armed conflict nexus of CAH, see Schabas, *The International Criminal Court* (n 16) 144–47; Cassese, *International Criminal Law* (n 4) 108; *Tadić, IT-94-1-T* (n 77) para 141.

[140] *Katanga, ICC-01/04–01/07* (n 4) para 1120.

[141] See ibid, at para.1119; *Ruto et al, ICC-01/09–01/11* (n 10) para 167; *Muthaura et al, ICC-01/09–02/11* (n 11) paras 117–41; *Ntaganda, ICC-01/04–02/06* (n 87) para 26. While from the text of article 7(2)(a) Rome Statute it could be concluded that multiple distinct acts have to be committed, the 'course of conduct' requirement should be understood as also comprising single acts of an extraordinary magnitude. See *Situation in the Republic of Kenya, ICC-01/09* (n 9); *Blaškić, Judgment, 3 March 2000, IT-95-14-T*, ICTY, para 206; Ambos, *Treatise on International Criminal Law* (n 2) 59.

the 'Ngiti combatants of the *collectivité* formed an organization behind CAH was their capability of 'conceiving and executing large-scale attacks'.[142] This assessment should be factual, meaning that it suffices to prove that a group executed a course of conduct involving multiple commissions of crimes.[143] It should not matter whether this was achieved by any sophisticated strategy, or through the use of technology.[144] As these acts do not need to constitute a military attack and can be committed outside armed conflicts, an organization behind CAH does not need to have the same degree of organization as a party to an armed conflict.[145] For example, the ability to conduct military operations and act under some sort of a command and disciplinary structure are elements that armed groups must fulfil to be considered party to an armed conflict.[146] The considerations that necessitate these requirements for parties to an armed conflict, however, do not apply per se to the commission of CAH.[147]

The victims must be part of a civilian population. While their civilian character is an essential requirement of CAH, it does not influence the capacity of the entity behind the crimes.[148] Arguably, the requirement that such attacks target 'a population' reinforces the notion that the crimes need to be 'of a collective nature and thus excludes single or isolated acts'.[149] Moreover, it has been suggested that the victim population needs to have a 'distinguishing feature'—for example, nationality, ethnicity, or political affiliation.[150] While others have argued that such features are 'immaterial' and CAH can be committed against any civilian population,[151] the attack must at least be targeted towards the victims. The targeted nature of the attack suggests that the organization behind the crimes must avail of mechanisms to target or coordinate the attack; this is further discussed in the section 'Pursuant to or in furtherance of a ... policy', with regard to the policy behind the acts.[152]

'Pursuant to or in furtherance of a ... policy'

An attack committed by state or organizational action needs to be 'pursuant to or in furtherance of a ... policy'. As discussed above, the policy serves to exclude

[142] *Katanga, ICC-01/04–01/07* (n 4) para 1140.

[143] See ibid, at para 1138.

[144] No such requirements are found in article 7 ICC Statute.

[145] The required degree of organization for a non-state party to an armed conflict is examined in Part II of this book.

[146] See Chapter 3 'Organized Armed Groups in Contemporary International Practice'.

[147] eg, while a command structure enables a party to a non-international armed conflict (NIAC) to implement basic international humanitarian law (IHL), this ability is not required for non-state entities to form the organization behind CAH.

[148] For some discussion, see Ambos, *Treatise on International Criminal Law* (n 2); Werle and Jessberger, *Principles of International Criminal Law* (n 38); Cassese, *Cassese's International Criminal Law* (n 104) 101–05.

[149] *Bagilishema, Judgment, 7 June 2001, Trial Chamber, ICTR-95-1A-T,* ICTR, para 80.

[150] See *Situation in the Republic of Kenya, ICC-01/09* (n 9); *Gbagbo, ICC-02/11–01/11* (n 79) para 209.

[151] *Katanga, ICC-01/04–01/07* (n 4) para 1103.

[152] While the policy element is normally the one associated with the collective nature or 'associativity' of the attack, Pre-Trial Chamber I argued in the *Gbagbo* case, 'The expression "course of conduct" already embodies a systemic aspect as it describes a series or overall flow of events as opposed to a mere aggregate of random acts. For the chamber, course of conduct can be evidenced by the victim population, the perpetrators, the chronology/pattern of events.' *Gbagbo, ICC-02/11–01/11* (n 79) para 209.

individual or isolated acts from the attack, it interlinks the underlying acts, guides them, and also links the attack to the organization behind it.[153] While the policy element requires that 'the State or organization actively promote or encourage such an attack against a civilian population',[154] this does not mean that the organization must meticulously plan the attack.[155] As Trial Chamber II argued, it is 'relatively rare' that the entity behind CAH will 'adopt and disseminate a pre-established design or plan' setting out the attack.[156] Instead, in the Chamber's view, a policy can be inferred from 'repeated actions occurring according to a same sequence, or the existence of preparations or collective mobilisation orchestrated and coordinated by that State or organisation'.[157] In this respect, a policy may not only signify a pre-existing plan or strategy but, in the context of CAH, a policy can also be implicit and become evident from the way in which the crimes are committed.[158]

The capacity required for implementing a policy providing broader guidance for the attack varies according to the circumstances. In some cases, such policy is adopted by an organization's leadership and promulgated throughout the forces via the organization's chain of command.[159] Accordingly, a leadership able to adopt a policy and structures to promulgate it among the rank and file would be needed. In other cases, however, a policy may evolve more organically. For example, an attack might be guided by an organization's broader ideology marking the targeted population as an enemy, or as 'oppressors and potential invaders' who shall be wiped out.[160] If the organization behind the policy is an organized armed group involved in an armed conflict, it normally possess the structures and means to implement such policy.[161] Where the organization is not party to a conflict, however, Pre-Trial Chamber II found the following issues to be 'crucial for the implementation of the policy' in the *Ruto et al* case:

(i) the appointment of commanders and divisional commanders responsible for the operations on the field; (ii) the production of maps marking out the areas most densely inhabited by communities perceived to be or actually siding with the PNU [targeted

[153] See Section 9.2.1 'The policy behind CAH' above.

[154] *Elements of Crimes* (n 75) 5. See also *Ruto et al, ICC-01/09–01/11* (n 10) para 210.

[155] See also Robinson, 'The Draft Convention on Crimes against Humanity: What to Do with the Definition?' (n 3).

[156] *Katanga, ICC-01/04–01/07* (n 4) para 1109.

[157] ibid. See also *Tadić, IT-94-1-T* (n 77) para 653. For additional elements, see also jurisprudence discussed in Robinson, 'Crimes against Humanity: A Better Policy on "Policy"' (n 19) para 719.

[158] See *Katanga, ICC-01/04–01/07* (n 4) para 1110; Robinson, deGuzman, Jalloh et al, *Amicus Curiae Observations of Professors Robinson, deGuzman, Jalloh and Cryer, ICC-02/11–01/11* (n 79) paras 21–34; Werle and Jessberger, *Principles of International Criminal Law* (n 38) 342; Ambos, *Treatise on International Criminal Law* (n 2) 70.

[159] *Ntaganda, ICC-01/04–02/06* (n 87) paras 19–21. In that case, 'the UPC/FPLC adopted an organisational policy to attack civilians perceived to be non-Hema', and this 'general message [was] conveyed in the context of the attack by UPC/FPLC superiors to their troops'.

[160] *Katanga, ICC-01/04–01/07* (n 4) para 1143. In the *Katanga* case, the Chamber argued, 'It was primarily that ideology which instigated the action taken against the Hema population in Bogoro.' ibid, at para 1145. In that case, however, this ideology fed into a planned military attack against an armed group and the affiliated civilian population.

[161] See, for instance, ibid, at paras 1134–62; *Ntaganda, ICC-01/04–02/06* (n 87) paras 20–32; *Situation in the Republic of Cote d'Ivoire, ICC-02/11* (n 113) paras 93–105.

population]; (iii) the identification of houses and business premises owned by PNU supporters with a view to target them; (iv) the purchase of weapons as well as of material to produce crude weapons and their storage before the attack; (v) the transportation of the perpetrators to and from the target locations; and (vi) the establishment of a stipendiary scheme and a rewarding mechanism to motivate the perpetrators to kill and displace the largest number of persons belonging to the target communities as well as to destroy their properties.

The organization's ability to develop a policy and operate or establish a command structure as well as plans to implement an attack brings the 'policy' element close to the systematic nature of attacks. This would, however, contradict the interpretation that the ability to implement a policy behind CAH does not require an organization to implement the attack in a systematic manner, meaning that it directs the crimes to ensure they follow a similar pattern. For example, in an armed conflict an organization behind CAH may have an ideology encouraging the killing of 'enemy' civilians, which its members internalize and implement at their own discretion in the course of a military operation. This policy would not be implemented through planning and commands but through individual acts pursuant to or in furtherance of the organization's general policy or ideology. In this respect, the policy requirement alone does not necessitate the existence of sophisticated organizational structures. To implement a policy, the organization behind CAH would only need to have 'sufficient means to promote or encourage a campaign' leading to multiple commissions of crimes against a civilian population.[162]

'Widespread or systematic'

Article 7 ICC Statute defines CAH as a widespread or systematic attack directed against any civilian population. Thus, the crimes need to be either widespread or systematic.[163] According to '[a]n established line of authority',[164] 'the adjective "widespread" connotes the large-scale nature of the attack and the number of targeted persons, whereas the adjective "systematic" refers to the organised nature of the acts of violence and the improbability of their random occurrence'.[165] In more detail, a widespread attack 'should be massive, frequent, carried out collectively with considerable seriousness and directed against a multiplicity of victims'.[166] These criteria are neither exclusively quantitative nor geographical.[167] The term systematic is understood either to signify the continuous occurrence of certain crimes that follow

[162] *Katanga, ICC-01/04–01/07* (n 4) para 1117.

[163] For discussion of the alternative formulation, see International Law Commission, *First Report on Crimes against Humanity* (n 1) paras 125–27.

[164] *Katanga, ICC-01/04–01/07* (n 4) para 1123.

[165] *Katanga, Decision on the Evidence and Information Provided by the Prosecution for the Issuance of a Warrant of Arrest for Germain Katanga, 5 November 2007, Pre-Trial Chamber I, ICC-01/04-01/07*, ICC, para 33. This definition has been taken up in subsequent decisions, see *Katanga and Chui, ICC-01/04–01/07* (n 110) para 394; *Katanga, ICC-01/04–01/07* (n 4) para 1123; *Situation in the Republic of Kenya, ICC-01/09* (n 9) paras 95–96.

[166] *Bemba, ICC-01/05–01/08* (n 31) para 83; *Gbagbo, ICC-02/11–01/11* (n 79) paras 222, 224.

[167] *Situation in the Republic of Kenya, ICC-01/09* (n 9) para 95. Moreover, citing the ICTY the ICC found that the widespread nature of an attack can be derived from the 'cumulative effect of a series of inhumane acts or the singular effect of an inhumane act of extraordinary magnitude'.

a preconceived plan or policy, or as ' "patterns of crimes" such that the crimes constitute a "non-accidental repetition of similar criminal conduct on a regular basis" '.[168]

If a state or organization pursues a policy tolerating or merely promoting and encouraging an attack against a civilian population without being directly implicated in the commission of underlying acts, the attack's widespread nature would depend on how others implement the policy. Consequently, it would not affect the requisite degree of organization of the entity behind the policy. In contrast, implementing a widespread attack through organizational action in the narrow sense requires the manpower, weapons, and other logistics to commit large-scale crimes.[169] Once again, this capacity is uncontroversial with regard to parties to an armed conflict. It is more difficult to establish, however, if considering crimes by an organization operating outside armed conflicts. In the case of *Ruto et al* concerning post-election violence in Kenya, for example, Pre-Trial Chamber II established the capability to commit widespread crimes by examining the 'amount of capital, guns, crude weapons and manpower' as well as other logistics available to the perpetrators.[170] This general assessment seems apt; the exact way of implementing a large-scale attack depends on the circumstances of the crimes.

In order to commit a systematic attack against a civilian population, an organization behind CAH needs to have the capacity to develop and implement a plan or policy directing the crimes, or to coordinate crimes and to ensure that they follow a regular pattern.[171] Admittedly, however, it is difficult to imagine a coordinated attack against a civilian population following a regular pattern without an underlying plan or strategy.[172] Thus, a systematic attack 'requires more active planning and coordination'.[173] This suggests that the entity behind the crimes has some form of leadership planning the attacks and sufficient internal structures to ensure the plan's implementation. If such an organization is a party to an armed conflict, the systematic nature of the crimes is often evident from the pursuit of military tactics

[168] See *Katanga and Chui, ICC-01/04–01/07* (n 110) para 203. See also *Katanga, ICC-01/04–01/07* (n 4) para 1123, with extensive reference to ICTY and ICTR case law. Under ICTY jurisprudence, the systematic nature of a crime can be inferred from the following elements: the existence of a political objective or plan underlying the crimes; the large-scale commission of interlinked acts; the use of significant public or private resources; or the definition of the plan or policy at a high level. See also *Gbagbo, ICC-02/11–01/11* (n 79) para 223. See also International Law Commission, *First Report on Crimes against Humanity* (n 1) paras 128–32.

[169] See *Ntaganda, ICC-01/04–02/06* (n 87) para 32.

[170] *Ruto et al, ICC-01/09–01/11* (n 10) para 200.

[171] In this respect, the pattern in which systematic CAH are committed must distinguish these crimes from an accumulation of individual crimes of a large group of persons.

[172] For Ambos, eg, examination of ICC and other international case law suggests that 'the common denominator of the various definitions of a systematic attack is that such an attack "is one carried out pursuant to a preconceived policy or plan". More explicitly, what constitutes the *systematic* nature of the attack is the *guidance* provided for the individual perpetrators as to the envisaged object of the attack, namely the civilian population.'. Ambos, *Treatise on International Criminal Law* (n 2) 61. Nevertheless, the ICTY Appeals Chamber held that proof of a policy or plan is not necessarily needed for a systematic attack. *Kunarac et al, IT-96-23& IT-96-23/1-A* (n 77) para 98.

[173] Robinson, 'Crimes against Humanity: A Better Policy on "Policy" ' (n 19) 711. In Robinson's view, a systematic attack 'may also require an entity with some authority or power'. See also Werle and Jessberger, *Principles of International Criminal Law* (n 38) 340.

in their commission.[174] Parties to conflicts also have some form of command structure.[175] In the *Ntaganda* case, for example, the systematic nature of the crime was revealed in the following pattern of violence: the alleged perpetrators 'approached the targets simultaneously, in large numbers, and from different directions, they attacked villages with heavy weapons, and systematically chased the population by similar methods, hunting house by house and into the bushes, burning all properties and looting'.[176]

In contrast, non-state entities not party to an armed conflict do not necessarily operate under a command structure or are not able to implement military tactics. Nevertheless—for example, in the *Ruto et al* case—Pre-Trial Chamber II established the systematic nature on the basis of the following facts: in preparation for the attacks and in executing them, 'coordinators' were charged with identifying and directing attacks against the victim population. During the attacks, 'perpetrators approached the target locations simultaneously, in large numbers, and from different directions, by vehicles or on foot, or both'. Moreover, the perpetrators erected roadblocks to catch fleeing victims and used petrol and inflammable means to carry out their crimes.[177] Similarly, in the *Muthaura et al* case, the Chamber considered 'the precise identification of targets by the attackers [as] indicative of the planned and systematic nature of the violence'.[178] Accordingly, in order to commit a systematic attack, an organization must have the capacity to organize and coordinate an attack following a preconceived pattern. An attack that is tolerated by an entity or instigated by active promotion or encouragement without further organizational action is unlikely to meet this criterion.

9.3 Conclusions on Non-State Entity Involvement in Crimes against Humanity

The kinds of non-state entities that may constitute *the entity behind CAH* remain disputed. Neither the widely accepted definition of CAH under article 7 ICC Statute, nor any of its predecessors, nor the ICC's *Elements of Crimes* provide an unequivocal answer, except that the entity behind CAH does not need to be a state. Jurisprudence from the Yugoslavia Tribunal, the Sierra Leone Court, and the ICC further discharged the argument that non-state entities behind CAH need to have state-like characteristics, such as quasi-governmental control over territory and institutions. With the notable exception of the Kenya situation, in most cases before international courts and tribunals, non-state entities behind CAH have been party to armed conflicts. Undisputedly, these groups possess the capacity to commit widespread or systematic attacks against a civilian population, and have therefore been

[174] See *Katanga, ICC-01/04–01/07* (n 4) paras 1157–62.
[175] See Chapter 3 'Organized Armed Groups in Contemporary International Practice'.
[176] *Ntaganda, ICC-01/04–02/06* (n 87) para 31.
[177] *Ruto et al, ICC-01/09–01/11* (n 10) para 197.
[178] *Muthaura et al, ICC-01/09–02/11* (n 11) para 176.

considered sufficinently organized to commit CAH. Looking at this type of group from a conceptual or systemic point of view, it has been argued that international criminal law should address crimes committed by parties to armed conflicts because such groups either control part of a state's territory, or have otherwise destabilized the state in which they operate to an extent that the state is unlikely to be able to address these crimes.[179]

The more intriguing question is which other non-state entities—operating outside armed conflicts—may develop a relevant policy and commit CAH. Likewise, the question of whether any non-state entity could merely promote and encourage the commission of a widespread attack against a civilian population without being more directly involved in the commission of the criminal acts has not been authoritatively answered. In practical terms, these legal scenarios come down to issues such as whether certain crimes committed by small groups of persons can amount to CAH, for example if a 'terrorist cell' commits a systematic attack against a civilian population following its own policy. Likewise, considering the relation between individual crimes and the collective entity behind such acts, the question arises of whether societal actors such as political parties could incite CAH. Looking at even more complex contemporary realities such as international terrorism, an issue needing more refection is whether a widespread attack against a civilian population committed by individuals in one state, which is inspired by the policy of an organization primarily based in another state, can amount to a CAH.

Valid legal arguments exist for different positions on these questions. One commentator suggested that, ultimately, taking a position 'comes down to the personal preference or background of the respective author' or judge.[180] Accordingly, it has been suggested that 'the ICC should make a policy choice on which understanding to embrace'.[181]

Whether labelled as 'personal preference', 'policy choice', or simply 'interpretation', any conclusion on the question of which non-state groups can form the organization behind CAH should be based on legal, conceptual, and practical considerations. Conceptually, this study has shown that crimes harming humanity are best understood as heinous human rights violations targeted at a victim group or population in a societal context in which victims are deprived of effective protection by the governing authority. Consequently, the nature of the entity behind the crimes is not decisive as long as it is able to bring about a situation of large-scale violence in which the territorial state is unwilling or unable to protect the victims. While this conceptual understanding of CAH is not fully embraced in the crime's legal definition, it can provide important guidance in borderline questions. For example, it can be argued that there is no need for international criminal justice if a non-state organization commits a widespread crime against a civilian population in a state in which functioning law enforcement structures effectively respond to and

[179] See Kress, 'Actes de Terrorisme: Nouvelles Formes de Crimes contre l'Humanité?' (manuscript with the author 2016).

[180] Ambos, *Treatise on International Criminal Law* (n 2) 75.

[181] Jalloh, 'What Makes Crimes against Humanity Crimes against Humanity?' (n 24) 390.

subsequently prosecute the crimes. In contrast, similar crimes should invite an international criminal law response if the territorial state is a 'failed state', meaning that the crime is committed in a context of de facto impunity because the state is unable to respond adequately.

Following this line of argument, the rather broad legal definition of CAH in the ICC Statute has some merit. Article 7 defines CAH as a widespread or systematic attack directed against any civilian population, inter alia pursuant to or in furtherance of a state or organizational policy. The definition leaves the nature of the entity behind the crimes undefined; the decisive characteristics of the crime are the commission of widespread or systematic crimes against any civilian population. Thus, if the ICC has jurisdiction, and if the crimes are sufficiently grave and not responded to at the national level, the Court could prosecute perpetrators of large-scale or systematic crimes committed by very different types of non-state entities. Practical considerations further underline the need to focus on the crimes and their context instead of applying strict definitions of the entity behind a crime. In many parts of the world, not only states but also different types of non-state actors have the capacity to instigate or orchestrate crimes factually showing all characteristics of CAH.[182] Thus, different commentators have argued that applying a definition of the organization criterion could have positive practical results:

> In this way, we make large-scale and systematic crimes that take place in a wide variety of situations deserving of international investigation and prosecution if the concerned State fails to act or is unwilling or unable to do so.[183]

Following a broad interpretation of the entity behind CAH does not downgrade CAH, or equate it to human rights violations. Even if acts factually amounting to CAH could be committed pursuant to or in furtherance of a policy of a group with relatively limited capacities, CAH would still consist of a widespread or systematic course of conduct involving defined acts committed against a civilian population. These elements need to be proved in any case, meaning that the crime will still need to reach the 'gravity of systematic injustice'[184] as reflected in its definition, which led states to including CAH among the list of core international crimes.[185] If the objectives of international criminal law are to address heinous crimes that shock humanity's conscience, to protect world peace and well-being, and to end impunity,

[182] See also Hansen, 'The Policy Requirement in Crimes against Humanity' (n 9) 35; Sadat, 'Emerging from the Shadow of Nuremberg' (n 6); Jalloh, 'What Makes Crimes against Humanity Crimes against Humanity?' (n 24) 416–17.

[183] Jalloh, 'What Makes Crimes against Humanity Crimes against Humanity?' (n 24) 432. Jalloh refers to his, Robinson's, and Sadat's views. For contrary views, see Schabas, *Unimaginable Atrocities* (n 3) 139–40; 150. See also Chouliaras, 'A Strategic Choice: The State Policy Requirement in Core International Crimes' (2015) 28 Leiden Journal of International Law 953–75.

[184] *Situation in the Republic of Kenya, ICC-01/09* (n 9) para 69.

[185] For a number of authors, '[t]he "widespread or systematic attack" requirement is fundamental in distinguishing "crimes against humanity" from domestic crimes. It is this element that turns these crimes into attacks against humanity rather than isolated violations of the rights of a particular individual.' See, eg, Badar, 'From the Nuremberg Charterto the Rome Statute: Defining the Elements of Crimes against Humanity' (2004) 5 San Diego International Law Journal 73–144, 142.

acts meeting all other elements of CAH should not be excluded from the crime's scope only because they have not been committed by states or state-like entities. In addition, going beyond the ICC's objectives, international criminal law serves the function of universally condemning certain types of internationally unacceptable behaviour.[186] In the words of Schabas, 'The declaratory value of criminal law is probably its most important contribution to the struggle against impunity. Society declares that certain specific kinds of behaviour are wrong and anti-social.'[187] Therefore, in a world in which different non-state organizations direct or instigate large-scale human rights violations against victim populations, these crimes should be labelled as harming humanity and prosecuted accordingly.

[186] See deGuzman, 'The Road from Rome' (n 56) 34; Van der Wilt, 'Crimes against Humanity: A Category Hors Concours in (International) Criminal Law?' in Van Beers, Corrias, and Werner (eds), *Humanity across International Law and Biolaw* (CUP 2014) 28.

[187] Schabas, 'Sentencing by International Tribunals: A Human Rights Approach' (1997) 7 Duke Journal of Comparative & International Law 461–518, 516.

10

Non-State Entity Involvement in Genocide

Sometimes referred to as the 'crime of crimes',[1] genocide signifies the 'denial of the right of existence of entire human groups'.[2] The term 'genocide' was coined by the Polish law professor of Jewish descent Raphael Lemkin, who composed it 'from the ancient Greek word *genas* (race, tribe) and the Latin *cide* (killing)'.[3] Under treaty and customary international law, genocide is defined as the commission of certain criminal acts[4] 'with intent to destroy, in whole or in part, a national, ethnical, racial or religious group, as such'.[5] The distinct characteristic of genocide is the 'special' or 'ulterior' intent, meaning that the crime aims to destroy the targeted group as such, in whole or in part.[6] Accordingly, the principal objective of the criminalization of genocide is to prevent the destruction of human groups, rather than specific individuals. As the International Court of Justice put it, the denial of the right to existence of

[1] For a very complete analysis of the use of the expression 'crime of crimes' to describe the crime of genocide in its legal context, see Schabas, *Genocide in International Law: The Crime of Crimes* (2nd edn, CUP 2009) 11, n 32. For some criticism on the exaggeration of the significance of the crime of genocide as compared to crimes against humanity, see, eg, Kress, 'The ICC's First Encounter with the Crime of Genocide: The Case against Al Bashir' in Stahn (ed), *The Law and Practice of the International Criminal Court* (OUP 2014) 704.

[2] United Nations General Assembly, *The Crime of Genocide*, 1946, GA/Res 96 (I).

[3] Lemkin, *Axis Rule in Occupied Europe: Laws of Occupation, Analysis of Government, Proposals for Redress* (Carnegie Endowment for International Peace 1944) 79.

[4] These acts are exhaustively listed under article 2 of the Convention on the Prevention and Punishment of the Crime of Genocide (hereafter Genocide Convention).

[5] Article 2 Genocide Convention. This definition has been reproduced *verbatim* in the statutes of the International Criminal Tribunal for Rwanda (ICTR), the International Criminal Tribunal for the former Yugoslavia (ICTY), and the International Criminal Court (ICC), and can be considered customary international law. See *Akayesu, Judgment, 2 September 1998, ICTR-96-4-T*, ICTR, para 495; *Krstić, Judgment, 02 August 2001, IT-98-33-T*, ICTY, para 541; *Karadžić, Judgment, 24 March 2016, Trial Chamber, IT-95-5/18-T*, ICTY, para 539; International Court of Justice, *Reservations to the Convention of the Prevention and Punishment of the Crime of Genocide, International Court of Justice, Advisory Opinion, 28 May 1951, International Court of Justice*, ICJ, 12; *Vasiliauskas v Lithuania, Application no 35343/05*, ECtHR, para 172. For further analysis and references on this point, see Jessberger, 'The Defintion and the Elements of the Crime of Genocide' in Gaeta (ed), *The UN Genocide Convention: A Commentary* (OUP 2009) 87–112, 88.

[6] The terms 'special intent', or '*dolus specialis*', have been used in case law. See, eg, *Akayesu, ICTR-96-4-T* (n 5) para 498; *Jelisić, Judgment, 14 December 1999, IT-95-10-T*, ICTY, para 108; *Case concerning Application of the Convention on the Prevention and Punishment of the Crime of Genocide (Bosnia and Herzegovina v Serbia and Montenegro)*, ICJ, para 187. Some commentators, however, suggest speaking of an 'ulterior intent'. See, eg, Ambos, 'What does 'Intent to Destroy' in Genocide Mean?' (2009) 91 International Review of the Red Cross 833–58, 835; Kress, 'The ICC's First Encounter with the Crime of Genocide: The Case against Al Bashir' (n 1) 698.

entire human groups 'shocks the conscience of mankind and results in great losses to humanity, ... which is contrary to moral law and to the spirit and aims of the United Nations'.[7] Case law and literature have continuously reiterated this objective.[8]

The question of whether genocide requires involvement of a state or another collective entity has produced diametrically opposing views.[9] To some extent, this is due to a schism between genocide as a historic phenomenon and its legal definition: while Nazi Germany's extermination of European Jews is generally accepted as the 'archetypal genocide',[10] which triggered the codification of the crime under international law, no state-involvement requirement is found in the crime's legal definition.[11] Arguing from historic precedent, Schabas has suggested that 'genocide presents itself as the archetypical crime of State',[12] arguing that under international law the crime requires a policy by a state or 'State-like actors'.[13] At the other extreme, following the legal definition's wording the International Criminal Tribunal for the former Yugoslavia (ICTY) held that even individuals acting alone could commit the crime.[14] Looking at genocide's 'criminological reality'—not at its definition—Ambos suggests some sort of middle ground: 'genocide cannot be committed by a few crazy individuals alone, but needs intellectual masterminds and an organizational apparatus to implement the evil plans'.[15]

This chapter examines whether a collective entity's involvement is legally required for the crime of genocide, and, if so, what degree of organization such an entity

[7] International Court of Justice, *Reservations to the Convention of the Prevention and Punishment of the Crime of Genocide* (n 5) 12. Going one step deeper, Lemkin stressed, 'The world represents only so much culture and intellectual vigor as are created by its component national groups. .... The destruction of a nation, therefore, results in the loss of its future contributions to the world.' Lemkin, *Axis Rule in Occupied Europe: Laws of Occupation, Analysis of Government, Proposals for Redress* (n 3) 91.

[8] See, eg, *Akayesu, ICTR-96-4-T* (n 5) paras 521–22; *Jelisić, IT-95-10-T* (n 6) para 66; *Situation in Darfur, Sudan, Decision on the Prosecution's Application for a Warrant of Arrest against Omar Hassan Ahmad Al Bashir, 4 March 2009, Pre-Trial Chamber I, ICC-02/05–01/09*, ICC, para 114. See also Kress, 'The ICC's First Encounter with the Crime of Genocide: The Case against Al Bashir' (n 1) 295; Ambos, *Treatise on International Criminal Law* (OUP 2013); Werle and Jessberger, *Principles of International Criminal Law* (3rd edn, OUP 2014). For the view that genocide relates primarily to the interests of individuals in the targeted group, see May, *Genocide: A Normative Account* (CUP 2010).

[9] These views will be discussed in detail in Section 10.2 'The Perpetrator(s) of Genocide in International Jurisprudence' below.

[10] Ambos, *Treatise on International Criminal Law* (n 8) 1. See also Van der Wilt, Vervliet, Sluiter et al (eds), *The Genocide Convention: The Legacy of 60 Years* (M. Nijhoff 2012) ix.

[11] See Section 10.1 'The Definition of Genocide in International Law'.

[12] Schabas, *Genocide in International Law: The Crime of Crimes* (n 1) 244.

[13] Schabas, 'State Policy as an Element of International Crimes' (2008) 98 The Journal of Criminal Law & Criminology 953–82, 972. Accordingly, 'Bodies like the Republika Srpska, the FARC [Revolutionary Armed Forces of Columbia], the Palestinian Authority, and perhaps the government of Taiwan would be addressed in this manner, but not organizations like the Hell's Angels or the mafia.' Indeed, in the 1990s, the two cases of genocide—the one in Rwanda and the one in Srebrenica—involved either a state (Rwanda) or a state-like entity (the 'Republika Srpska').

[14] This is further discussed in Section 10.2.1 'The dismissal of a genocidal plan requirement and the lone génocidaire'.

[15] Ambos, *Treatise on International Criminal Law* (n 8) 29. So far, there has not been a conviction for genocide without the involvement of a collective entity. See Schabas, *Unimaginable Atrocities: Justice, Politics, and Rights at the War Crimes Tribunals* (OUP 2012) 131. Similar views are also found in non-legal literature. See, eg, Spencer, *Genocide since 1945* (Routledge 2012).

needs to possess. The objective is to establish whether and under what conditions non-state entities have sufficient capacity to instigate or commit genocide. In this book, the much-debated question of whether perpetrators of genocide always need to act themselves with genocidal intent ('purpose-based approach'), or whether they could also commit genocide if committing one of the underlying acts with knowledge of a collective genocidal campaign to which their act contributes ('knowledge' or 'structure-based approach') is not discussed.[16] The question of whether or not any individual committing acts of genocide needs to act with genocidal intent—which is at the heart of that debate—is not important to this study. Yet, the present analysis may add an important element to the 'intend debate'. If a knowledge- or structure-based approach is taken, a genocidal campaign is required to which an individual's act contributes and of which the perpetrator needs to have knowledge. In such cases, it is crucial to know whether a genocidal campaign needs state or state-like entity involvement or could also be instigated or committed by other non-state entities.

10.1 The Definition of Genocide in International Law

The definition of genocide as contained in article 2 of the Genocide Convention is universally accepted and forms part of customary international law.[17] It provides:

> In the present Convention, genocide means any of the following acts committed with intent to destroy, in whole or in part, a national, ethnical, racial or religious group, as such:
> (a) Killing members of the group;
> (b) Causing serious bodily or mental harm to members of the group;
> (c) Deliberately inflicting on the group conditions of life calculated to bring about its physical destruction in whole or in part;
> (d) Imposing measures intended to prevent births within the group;
> (e) Forcibly transferring children of the group to another group.

Unlike definitions of war crimes or crimes against humanity, this definition does not contain any contextual elements.[18] It does not explicitly require state or organizational involvement.[19] The definition's wording suggests that any individual can commit genocide by perpetrating one of the listed acts with the intent to destroy,

[16] For recent discussion, see, eg, *Situation in Darfur, Sudan, ICC-02/05–01/09* (n 8); Greenawalt, 'Rethinking Genocidal Intent: The Case for a Knowledge-Based Interpretation' (1999) 99 Columbia Law Review 2259–94; Gil Gil, 'Die Tatbestände der Verbrechen gegen die Menschlichkeit und des Völkermord im Römischen Statut des Internationalen Strafgerichtshofs' (2000) 112 Zeitschrift für die Gesamte Strafrechtswissenschaft 381–95; Vest, 'A Structure-Based Concept of Genocidal Intent' (2007) 5 Journal of International Criminal Justice 781–97; Ambos, *Treatise on International Criminal Law* (n 8) 21–38; Kress, 'The ICC's First Encounter with the Crime of Genocide: The Case against Al Bashir' (n 1); Schabas, *Genocide in International Law: The Crime of Crimes* (n 1) 137–38.

[17] See n 5 above.

[18] In particular, genocide does not require a nexus to an armed conflict. See article 1 Genocide Convention.

[19] This has recently been pointed out by an ICC Pre-Trial Chamber, see *Situation in Darfur, Sudan, ICC-02/05–01/09* (n 8) para 117.

in whole or in part, a protected group as such. At least the acts listed under points (a) and (b) do not require the perpetrator to have particular capacities; in contrast, acts (c)– (e) appear to require involvement of an entity with quasi-governmental capacities.[20] The Convention's paramount objective to protect groups from extermination does not contradict a literal interpretation that rejects any collective-entity involvement as one of the crime's legal elements.

Read in the wider context of the Genocide Convention, it is uncontroversial that the definition focuses on individuals and not entities.[21] Different provisions in the Convention state or imply that criminal conduct is not restricted to that of state officials but includes crimes by non-state actors. Article 4 foresees punishment for 'constitutionally responsible rulers, public officials or *private individuals*'.[22] Moreover, article 6 prescribes that alleged crimes 'shall be tried by a competent tribunal of the State in the territory of which the act was committed'.[23] If genocide was restricted to crimes with state involvement, the focus on prosecution before the territorial state's tribunal would be a major flaw in the Convention's enforcement system: a state is unlikely to prosecute crimes it committed itself.[24] The lack of an explicit requirement for state involvement combined with the explicit reference to acts by 'private individuals' and focus on national prosecution suggest that the Genocide Convention applies to any act amounting to genocide, whether committed by state or non-state actors. It does not restrict the crime to acts by state officials, or require state involvement in acts committed by non-state actors. In fact, it does not specify whether involvement of any collective entity is necessary for the commission of genocide. This conclusion is further strengthened by the travaux préparatoires.

10.1.1 The question of state involvement in the Genocide Convention's drafting history

Omitting a requirement for state involvement from the definition of genocide was a conscious decision by the Convention's drafters. The very first UN General Assembly resolution on genocide did not include such a requirement.[25] Likewise, the UN Secretary General defined a wide scope of perpetrators in the first draft

[20] This point is further discussed in Section 10.3.3 'Limitations to a functional approach' below.

[21] As an international treaty aimed at facilitating state cooperation in the prevention and punishment of genocide, the Convention defined the crime of genocide with the focus on punishing individuals responsible for any act defined in article 3. Cassese, *Cassese's International Criminal Law* (3rd edn, OUP 2013) 111.

[22] (emphasis added). However, the significance of this provision was, arguably, less the inclusion of 'private individuals' and more that of 'constitutionally responsible rulers' and 'public officials'.

[23] The article also referred to a competent 'international penal tribunal' as a forum to prosecute such crimes. Yet, at the time no such tribunal existed.

[24] In fact, states were aware that the Convention was unlikely to have effect if high-ranking state officials commit genocide. See the remarks of the United States during the *Debates in the Sixth Committee*, 1948, A/C.6/SR.93. In this respect, the Convention has been criticized as being based on the 'naïve assumption of the Convention's draughtsmen that . . . contracting states themselves would not dare to engage in genocide'. Cassese, *Cassese's International Criminal Law* (n 21) 111. See also Yale Law Journal, 'Genocide: A Commentary on the Convention' (1949) 58 Yale Law Journal 1142–60, 1147.

[25] See *The Crime of Genocide*, GA/Res 96 (I).

convention he prepared.[26] The Secretary General argued that while statesmen bear the heaviest responsibility for genocide,

> private persons, that is to say, persons who are neither rulers nor officials, can also commit acts of genocide ('public incitement to any act of genocide', Article-II-20, and propaganda-Article 3), either by collective action (through a political group, league, or clandestine or other association), or by individual action.[27]

With this formulation the Secretary General underlined that non-state individuals can be punished for acts of genocide, possibly referring to acts committed as part of a larger genocidal campaign. It did not directly address the question as to whether genocide required state or organizational involvement. With regard to a provision—which was later dropped—requiring the disbanding of groups or organizations that were involved in genocide, however, the Secretary General argued that the crime of genocide is 'of a "social" nature, in the sense that it is always, to a greater or smaller extent, organized, provoked or instigated by movements, groups or organizations'.[28] Accordingly, in the Secretary General's view, genocide did not require state involvement, but could also be committed with the involvement of non-state entities.

A majority of states shared this view and rejected a US proposal to add a strict requirement of government complicity.[29] Some states, such as France, agreed with the US proposal, arguing that if one group carried out a 'private war' against another group within a state this situation would be covered by national laws.[30] Other states partly agreed with such suggestions but opposed government involvement as a strict requirement, arguing that government involvement could also be 'indirect' or 'not obvious'.[31] Yet, for some states, such an amendment would 'unduly restrict' and 'dangerously narrow' the concept of genocide.[32] According to these states, a strict government-involvement requirement would be based on the 'false conception that government authority was always effective',[33] that governments could always prevent genocide, and would not take account of cases 'of a weak Government unable to prevent the extermination of a group occupying a distant region'.[34] Moreover, the Soviet Union underlined, 'Genocide was fundamentally the deliberate annihilation of a racial, religious or national group and the participation of a Government did not change the nature of the crime.'[35] With the rejection of the US proposal,

[26] See United Nations Economic and Social Council, *Draft Convention on the Crime of Genocide* (United Nations 1947). This first draft was prepared with the assistance of three experts on genocide, namely Mr Donnedieu de Vabres, Professor Pella, and Professor Lemkin. The Secretary General opted for this broad approach despite one expert's opinion that 'genocide should be restricted to the actions of rulers'. ibid, at 35.

[27] ibid. [28] ibid, at 44.

[29] See United Nations Economic and Social Council, *Ad Hoc Committee on Genocide: Summary Record of the Fourth Meeting*, 1948, E/AC.25/SR.4, 3 (United States).

[30] See ibid, at 4 (France). [31] ibid, at 5 (Soviet Union), 6 (China).

[32] ibid, at 6 (Poland), 7 (Venezuela). [33] ibid, at 6 (Poland).

[34] ibid, at 7 (Venezuela). While the United States found that in such situations government complicity should be assumed, France admitted the validity of these arguments and suggested abandoning the proposed limitation. ibid, at 4 (United States), 6 (France).

[35] ibid, at 5 (Soviet Union).

to the drafters the issue seemed resolved.[36] Hence, while states were aware that, in the past, genocide had been committed with a direct or indirect involvement of the territorial government, they consciously decided not to include a strict government-involvement requirement in the definition of genocide.[37] Instead, in order to prevent the 'great losses on humanity' genocide inflicts and 'to liberate mankind from such an odious scourge', states opted for a wide definition not specifically requiring any collective-entity involvement.[38]

10.1.2 Subsequent state practice and the inclusion of genocide in the Rome Statute of the International Criminal Court (ICC Statute)

Subsequent state practice did not change the definition of genocide: states have consistently used the 1948 definition in later codifications. In 1951, the first *Draft Code of Offences against the Peace and Security of Mankind* defined genocide in accordance with the Genocide Convention, stating that genocide includes 'acts by the authorities of a State or by private individuals, committed with intent to destroy, in whole or in part, a national, ethnical, racial or religious group as such'.[39] Subsequent ILC Draft Codes of Crimes included *verbatim* the Convention's definition, arguing that it has been 'widely accepted by the international community' and constitutes an 'authoritative definition of the crime'.[40] This broad acceptance is also reflected in the literal inclusion of the definition of genocide in the statutes of the ICTY, the International Criminal Tribunal for Rwanda (ICTR), and the International Criminal Court (ICC),[41] as well as in the fact that there was very little debate on the definition of genocide during the drafting of the latter.[42] This confirms that state involvement is not required as a legal element of the crime.

[36] At one point in the Sixth Committee, when Syria suggested that 'de facto rulers' including those that 'usurped authority' should be added to the scope of perpetrators of genocide, other states argued that such non-state or quasi-state actors would certainly be covered as either rulers or private individuals. United Nations General Assembly, *Debate in the Sixth Committee*, A/C.6/SR.96.

[37] See also *Jelisić, IT-95-10-T* (n 6) para 100; Kress, 'The ICC's First Encounter with the Crime of Genocide: The Case against Al Bashir' (n 1); Schabas, 'State Policy as an Element of International Crimes' (n 13) 966.

[38] Genocide Convention, preamble.

[39] International Law Commission, *Draft Code of Offences against the Peace and Security of Mankind* (United Nations 1951) article 2(9).

[40] See International Law Commission, *Draft Code of Crimes against the Peace and Security of Mankind (with Commentary)*, (United Nations 1991) article 19; and International Law Commission, *Draft Code* (n 39) article 17.

[41] This definition is also found in the statutes of the Special Panels for East Timor and of the Extraordinary Chambers for Cambodia.

[42] There seems to have been no debate on the inclusion of the definition of genocide as contained in article 2 Genocide Convention in the ICC Statute. See *Definition of Core Crimes: Chairman's Informal Texts and Compilation of Proposals and Suggestions with Regard to the Definition of Core Crimes*, UN Doc A/AC.249/CRP.9/Add.4; *Report of the Working Group on the Defintion of Crimes*, UN Doc A/AC.249/1997/L.5; *Official Records of the United Nations Diplomatic Conference of Plenipotentiaries on the Establishment of an International Criminal Court (Vol. I-III)* UN Doc A/CONF.183/13, Vol II, debates at 147 et sec. See also Robinson and von Hebel, 'Crimes within the Jurisdiction of the Court' in Lee, Institut des Nations Unies pour la formation et la Project on International et al (eds), *The International Criminal Court: The Making of the Rome Statute Issues, Negotiations, Results* (Kluwer Law International 1999) 79–126, 89.

In 2000, in the ICC's *Elements of Crimes*,[43] states expressed the view that in order to constitute genocide under the ICC Statute, alleged crimes need to have taken place 'in the context of a manifest pattern of similar conduct directed against that group or was conduct that could itself effect such destruction [of a targeted group]'.[44] The *Elements of Crimes* do not explicitly require a genocidal plan or policy behind the crimes, or the strict requirement that crimes are committed on behalf of a collective entity.[45] For the purpose of article 6 ICC Statute, an act of genocide needs to meet one of the two requirements listed in the *Elements of Crimes*: it must either be committed in the context of similar conduct, or have itself the potential to destroy a group in whole or in part. While the latter alternative could encompass genocide committed by a single individual, under the first alternative a context of a 'manifest pattern of similar conduct' is required. The *Elements of Crimes* specify that the word 'manifest', which normally requires something to be 'clear or obvious',[46] is 'an objective qualification'.[47] Moreover, the ordinary meaning of 'pattern' is a 'regular and intelligible form or sequence discernible in the way in which something happens or is done'.[48] Consequently, it can be argued that a 'manifest pattern' comes very close to requiring a plan or policy behind the crimes; otherwise, how could violence develop into an obvious sequence of similar conduct?[49] Yet, as shall be seen below, concluding that a 'manifest pattern of similar conduct' always requires a policy or plan would be premature. In any case, in light of the very general definition of genocide under international law, the *Elements of Crimes* provide a 'welcome clarification' on the definition of genocide by expressing 'a "consensus by the international community" that a certain crime should be interpreted in a certain way'.[50]

[43] Under article 9 ICC Statute, the *Elements of Crimes* 'shall assist the Court in the interpretation and application of articles 6, 7 and 8' and 'be consistent with this Statute'. On the debate to what extent the *Elements of Crimes* must be applied by the Court, see *Situation in Darfur, Sudan, ICC-02/05–01/09* (n 8) paras 125–33; *Situation in Darfur, Sudan, Decision on the Prosecution's Application for a Warrant of Arrest against Omar Hassan Ahmad Al Bashir, 4 March 2009, ICC-02/05–01/09-3*, ICC, fn 25.

[44] See Preparatory Commission for the International Criminal Court, *Elements of Crimes*, 2 November 2000, PCNICC/2000/1/Add.2, 6–8.

[45] The suggestion made by the United States that for the crime of genocide there must have existed 'a plan to destroy such group' or that the accused must have had 'intent to take part in or had knowledge of the plan to destroy such group' was eventually not included in the document. Preparatory Committee on the Establishment of an International Criminal Court, *Proposal Submitted by the United States of America: Elements of Offences for the International Criminal Court*, 1998, A/AC.249/1998/DP.11; United Nations Diplomatic Conference of Plenipotentiaries on the Establishment of an International Criminal Court, *Proposal Submitted by the United States of America: Annex on Definitional Elements for Part Two Crimes, 19 June 1998*, A/CONF.183/C.1/L.10..

[46] *Oxford Dictionary*, online version, defintion of 'manifest'.

[47] See Preparatory Commission for the International Criminal Court, *Elements of Crimes* (n 44) 6.

[48] *Oxford Dictionary*, online version, defintion of 'pattern'.

[49] See Schabas, 'State Policy as an Element of International Crimes' (n 13) 967.

[50] Kress, 'The ICC's First Encounter with the Crime of Genocide: The Case against Al Bashir' (n 1) 677. However, disagreement exists as to whether the *Elements of Crimes* contradict the definition of genocide under article 6 ICC Statute and should therefore be considered void. For arguments in favour of considering the *Elements of Crimes* void, see Ambos, *Treatise on International Criminal Law* (n 8) 17; Werle and Jessberger, *Principles of International Criminal Law* (n 8) 311. For arguments against such a conclusion, see *Situation in Darfur, Sudan, ICC-02/05–01/09* (n 8) para 128. One suggestion to resolve

To sum up, the universally accepted definition of genocide focuses on the criminalization of individual genocidal acts and does not define a specific genocidal context. The distinguishing element of the crime is the intent to destroy, in whole or in part, a particular group as such. Accordingly, the Genocide Convention provides that private individuals and public officials can be responsible for acts of genocide. Whether the crime nonetheless needs collective-entity involvement is, however, unclear. During the Convention's drafting process, states dismissed state complicity as a legal element of genocide, and subsequent codifications of the crime did not reintroduce such requirement. Yet in 1996, for example, the International Law Commission (ILC) argued that crimes such as genocide 'are of such magnitude that they often require some type of involvement on the part of high level government officials or military commanders as well as their subordinates'.[51] Under the ICC's *Elements of Crimes*, however, states defined contextual elements for the crime without requiring collective-entity involvement. As a result, a certain divide exists between, on the one hand, a fairly broad legal definition of genocide, and, on the other hand, the recognition that, in practice, genocide is normally committed with the involvement of states or other collective entities. This tension is also seen in different tribunals' case law on genocide.

10.2 The Perpetrator(s) of Genocide in International Jurisprudence

In light of the fairly broad definition of genocide under international law and conflicting views on the crime's elements, genocide jurisprudence and commentators present different interpretations as to whether the crime requires involvement of a collective entity. In essence, two approaches have emerged. The first one argues that the definition of genocide does not require involvement of any collective entity, meaning in an extreme case that individuals can commit genocide alone (the so-called 'lone génocidaire'). According to a second approach, while the crime's definition does not explicitly demand collective-entity involvement, such involvement is required in practice, is needed to prove the perpetrator's genocidal intent, or stems from states' views as expressed in the ICC's *Elements of Crimes*. These two views are considered next. Based on the analysis of how genocide can be committed, this book suggests three ways in which collective entities can be involved in the crime. Each type of involvement requires different capacities from the entity.

a possible contradiction between the well-established and clear definition of genocide and the contextual requirements suggested in the *Elements of Crimes* could be to consider the context as part of the genocidal intent. In Kress's view, the contextual requirement could constitute an 'objective point of reference' to prove a realistic genocidal intent. Kress, 'The ICC's First Encounter with the Crime of Genocide: The Case against Al Bashir' (n 1); see also Ambos, *Treatise on International Criminal Law* (n 8) 18.

[51] International Law Commission, *Draft Code of Crimes against the Peace and Security of Mankind with commentaries* (UN 1996), article 17, para 10 of the commentary.

10.2.1 The dismissal of a genocidal plan requirement and the lone génocidaire

Contrary to some national jurisprudence,[52] neither the ICTR nor the ICTY considered collective-entity involvement, or a plan or policy to be material elements of genocide. In cases before the ICTR, the existence of a state plan or policy for the Rwandan genocide was undisputed.[53] Yet, Chambers did not consider this element decisive. In the *Akayesu* case, the tribunal argued that the three constituting elements of the crime of genocide are (i) that one of the listed acts is committed; (ii) against a protected group; and (iii) with the intent to destroy the group as such.[54] For the ICTR, the distinctive element of genocide is the 'special intent' or 'dolus specialis'.[55] Likewise, in the *Kayishema* and *Ruzindana* case, an ICTR Trial Chamber argued that 'a specific plan to destroy does not constitute an element of genocide'.[56] The ICTY Appeals Chamber articulated a similar view in the *Jelisić* case by stating: 'the existence of a plan or policy is not a legal ingredient of the crime'.[57]

Following the Tribunals' legal reading, Ambos finds that while central guidance, normally in the form of a plan or policy, 'may be present in most cases, it is not *legally* required' for the crime of genocide.[58] Jessberger and Werle hold that there is a 'clear position in customary international law not to require an objective contextual element'.[59] In their opinion, '[f]rom a purely terminological point of view, therefore, even an isolated individual acting with specific intent can, through his or her individual conduct, be guilty of the crime of genocide'.[60] Likewise, Cassese argued:

> It would be incorrect to conclude that the genocidal policy or campaign is one of the legal ingredients of genocide. Even admitting that historically genocide has been perpetrated within a genocidal context, still it is theoretically possible that a lone perpetrator may realistically aim at the destruction of a targeted group in the absence of such context.[61]

The ICTY elaborated on the idea that individuals can commit genocide without collective-entity involvement in the *Jelisić* case. Goran Jelisić was a member of the

[52] eg, the German *Oberlandesgericht* Düsseldorf required 'a structurally organized central direction' as a 'precondition for the crime of genocide'. *Jorgic, Judgment, 5 January 1998, IV-26/96,* Oberlandesgericht Düsseldorf, 162 (translation by the author).

[53] See *Akayesu, ICTR-96-4-T* (n 5) paras 112–29.

[54] See ibid, at paras 498–99.

[55] See ibid, at para 498.

[56] *Kayishema et al, Judgment, 21 May 1999, ICTR-95-1-T,* ICTY, para 94. In the Chamber's view, however, 'it would appear that it is not easy to carry out a genocide without such a plan, or organisation'.

[57] *Jelisić, Judgment, 5 July 2001, Appeals Chamber, IT-95-10-A,* ICTY, para 48. This view was also maintained in subsequent case law. See, eg, *Krstić, Judgment, 19 April 2004, Appeals Chamber, IT-98-33-A,* para 225; UNGA, *Ad Hoc Committee on Genocide: Summary Record of the Fourth Meeting,* 1948 (n 29) para 705. As Schabas argues, the 'plan or policy' can only be understood as an actual plan or policy by a collective entity, because it would be contradictory to argue that the individual—required to act with special intent—would not need to actually plan the destruction of a group. Also, the term 'policy' is normally used to refer to collective entities and not to a plan or intent of an individual. See Schabas, 'State Policy as an Element of International Crimes' (n 13) 147. He emphasizes, 'Individuals have intent. States have policies.'

[58] Ambos, *Treatise on International Criminal Law* (n 8) 17. Ambos also bases this finding on many commentators' views.

[59] Werle and Jessberger, *Principles of International Criminal Law* (n 8) 310.

[60] ibid, at 309.

[61] Cassese, *Cassese's International Criminal Law* (n 21) 124.

Serbian police force in the town of Brčko. Calling himself the 'Serbian Adolf', Jelisić was charged, inter alia, with committing or aiding or abetting genocide by killing and severely mistreating Muslim detainees in a prisoner camp.[62] In this case, the Chamber could not find a 'plan to destroy the Muslim group in Brčko or elsewhere within which the murders committed by the accused would allegedly fit'.[63] Consequently, Jelisić could not have aided or abetted genocide. With regard to the question of whether Jelisić could have alone perpetrated genocide, the ICTY found that this was 'theoretically possible':

> The murders committed by the accused are sufficient to establish the material element of the crime of genocide and it is a priori possible to conceive that the accused harboured the plan to exterminate an entire group without this intent having been supported by any organisation in which other individuals participated.[64]

The Chamber, however, also noted that it would be 'very difficult in practice' to prove the genocidal intent of a perpetrator 'if the crimes committed are not widespread and if the crime charged is not backed by an organisation or a system'.[65]

The ICTY's suggestion of a lone génocidaire is in line with the view that the crime of genocide does not require a plan, policy, or other involvement of a collective entity.[66] Still, scholars have criticized it. For example, while acknowledging that the definition of genocide does not explicitly require an 'interplay between individual and collective act', Kress argued that reducing genocide to an act of an individual without connection to collective activity is:

> fundamentally misconceived because it ignores the specificity of the crime of genocide as a systemic crime, trivializes the crime's horrendous destructive potential and thus fails to capture the raison d'être of genocide's status as a crime under international law as it is clearly reflected in the Genocide Convention's *travaux préparatoires*.[67]

He asserts that genocide 'for all practical purposes, is a systematic crime' requiring collective activity.[68] Related to this argument, Schabas argues that genocide has always been committed on behalf of, or in accordance with, plans or policies of states or state-like entities, and that the idea of a lone génocidaire has not found support in

[62] See *Jelisić, IT-95-10-T* (n 6) para 109.

[63] ibid, at para 98, and at para 88.

[64] ibid.

[65] ibid, at para 101. The Trial Chamber concluded, however, that given the random manner in which Jelisić committed the crimes and his apparently 'disturbed personality', his crimes did not express 'an affirmed resolve to destroy in whole or in part a group as such' (ibid, at para 107). This factual conclusion on the evidence was, however, dismissed by the Appeals Chamber. Still, no retrial was allowed. See *Jelisić, IT-95-10-A* (n 57) paras 71–72 and 77.

[66] This view has also been supported by the International Commission of Inquiry on Darfur. See United Nations Secretary General, *Report of the International Commission of Inquiry on Darfur to the United Nations Secretary-General*, 25 January 2005, para 520.

[67] Kress, 'The Crime of Genocide under International Law' (2006) 6 International Criminal Law Review 461–502, 471. As Kress recognizes that this requirement is not found explicitly in the definition of genocide, he argues that it should be regarded as being part of the special intent, namely in the requirement that this intent 'must be *realistic* and must thus be understood to require *more than a vain hope*'. ibid, at 472.

[68] Kress, 'The Darfur Report and Genocidal Intent' (2005) 3 Journal of International Criminal Justice 562–78, 572.

subsequent case law.[69] In his view, 'The theory that an individual, acting alone, may commit genocide is little more than a sophomoric hypothèse d'école, and a distraction for international judicial institutions.'[70]

Whichever view is taken, it is difficult to completely discard the lone génocidaire theory under contemporary international law: states endorsed the possibility of a lone génocidaire in the ICC's *Elements of Crimes*.[71] In their view, acts of a single perpetrator, vested with the requisite intent, can amount to genocide if this conduct 'could itself effect' the destruction, in whole or in part, of a national, ethnical, racial or religious group.[72] Thus, in the *Elements of Crimes* of genocide states explicitly included conduct of isolated individuals in the crime of genocide. A similar view was taken by the ICTY. Possible examples of such crimes include individuals using weapons of mass destruction against a particular group, or an individual killing the leadership of a group, which realistically endangers the existence of at least part of a group.[73]

As a result, states, the ICTR, the ICTY, as well as different commentators agree that a plan or policy, normally issued by a collective entity, has historically been part of genocide but does not constitute one of the crime's legal elements under international law. Consequently, it cannot be excluded that an act of a single individual with the intent and the means to destroy a certain group in whole or in part amounts to genocide. In such cases, no involvement of any collective entity is needed.

10.2.2 The relevance of a genocidal context

Despite agreement that the definition of genocide does not require a genocidal plan or policy, tribunals have frequently invoked a genocidal context in their findings. For example, in the *Akayesu* case, the Rwanda Tribunal considered a 'general context of the perpetration of other culpable acts systematically directed against that same group' important to prove the perpetrators' intent.[74] Furthermore, in the *Kayishema* and *Ruzindana* case it held that 'it is not easy to carry out a genocide without such

[69] Schabas, 'State Policy as an Element of International Crimes' (n 13) 954 and 957; Schabas, *Unimaginable Atrocities* (n 15) 131–32 and 141; Schabas, 'Darfur and the 'Odious Scourge': The Commission of Inquiry's Findings on Genocide' (2005) 18 Leiden Journal of International Law 871–85, 877.

[70] Schabas, 'Darfur and the 'Odious Scourge': The Commission of Inquiry's Findings on Genocide' (n 69) 877.

[71] See also Kress, 'The ICC's First Encounter with the Crime of Genocide: The Case against Al Bashir' (n 1) 674; Gaeta, *Genocide* (Routledge 2011) 114. For a contrary view, see Akhavan, *Reducing Genocide to Law: Definition, Meaning, and the Ultimate Crime* (CUP 2012) 46. Likewise, Schabas considered that the *Elements of Crimes* would at least exclude perpetrators such as Jelisić. See Schabas, *Unimaginable Atrocities* (n 15) 141.

[72] Preparatory Commission for the International Criminal Court, *Elements of Crimes* (n 44) 6–8.

[73] See Cassese, *Cassese's International Criminal Law* (n 21) 124. The example of an individual with weapons of mass destruction was indeed what states discussed when developing the *Elements of Crimes*. See Rückert and Witschel, 'Genocide and Crimes against Humanity in the Elements of Crimes' in Fischer, Kress, and Lüder (eds), *International and National Prosecution of Crimes under International Law: Current Developments* (Berliner Wissenschafts-Verlag 2004) 59–93, 66.

[74] *Akayesu, ICTR-96-4-T* (n 5) para 523.

a plan, or organisation'.[75] Likewise, in the *Krstić* case, an ICTY Trial Chamber argued that '[t]he gravity and the scale of the crime of genocide ordinarily presume that several protagonists were involved in its perpetration', and suggested that the individual's genocidal intent could be deduced from the intent to destroy the group as evident in the joint action.[76] Despite the Appeals Chamber's repeated ruling that a plan is not a legal element of the crime, nonetheless it recognized that in order to prove the accused's specific intent, 'the existence of a plan or policy may become an important factor in most cases'.[77]

In these cases, the tribunals did not try to introduce a plan or the involvement of multiple perpetrators as part of the crime's actus reus. Instead, they suggested that a genocidal context is significant to establish the requisite mens rea. Indeed, the genocidal intent cannot merely be a general or vague wish, but has to be somewhat realistic. As the ICTR underlined in the *Mpambara* case, the intent must be 'genuine'.[78] Following similar logic, in the *Jelisić* case the ICTY Trial Chamber did not convict the accused as a lone génocidaire because the judges were—despite testimony that Jelisić wanted to kill all Muslims—not convinced of his 'affirmed resolve' to destroy a group.[79] This understanding of the genocidal intent is also manifest in the ICTR's finding in the *Akayesu* case—which was later taken up by the United Nations International Commission of Inquiry on Darfur—that the accused not only consciously desired the destruction of the targeted group but also 'knew or should have known that the act committed would destroy, in whole or in part, a group'.[80] This suggests that hate crimes committed with the wish to destroy at least part of a group but without any real prospect of achieving this ulterior objective do not constitute genocide. Linking the intent to the crime's context, Cassese argued that, in most cases, a genocidal policy of a collective entity 'will in fact make it possible for the perpetrator to form a "realistic" intent to attain the destruction of the group'.[81]

The idea that crimes may constitute genocide if they pose a realistic threat to the targeted population finds further support in the ICC *Elements of Crimes* and jurisprudence. Under the ICC's *Elements of Crimes*, any genocidal act as defined under article 6 ICC Statute needs to take place 'in the context of a manifest pattern of similar conduct directed against that group *or* was conduct that could itself effect

[75] *Kayishema et al, ICTR-95-1-T* (n 56) para 94. The Chamber even concurred with the view of two scholars that 'it is virtually impossible for the crime of genocide to be committed without some or indirect involvement on the part of the State given the magnitude of this crime'.

[76] *Krstić, IT-98-33-T* (n 5) para 549.

[77] *Jelisić, IT-95-10-A* (n 57) para 48. See also *Krstić, IT-98-33-A* (n 57) para 225.

[78] *Mpambara, Judgment, 11 September 2006, Trial Chamber I, ICTR-01-65-T,* ICTR, para 8.

[79] *Jelisić, IT-95-10-T* (n 6) para 107.

[80] *Akayesu, ICTR-96-4-T* (n 5) para 520; United Nations Secretary General, *Report of the International Commission of Inquiry on Darfur to the United Nations Secretary-General* (n 66) para 491.

[81] Cassese, *Cassese's International Criminal Law* (n 21) 124. Likewise, Kress finds that case law of different courts supports the view that the genocidal intent 'must be realistic and must thus be understood to require more than the vain hope of a single perpetrator of hate crimes to destroy (a part of) the hated group'. Kress, 'The ICC's First Encounter with the Crime of Genocide: The Case against Al Bashir' (n 1) 679.

such destruction'.[82] As one commentator reports from the negotiations, this contextual requirement was included to address states' concerns

> about trivializing genocide by defining it in such a way as to include an isolated hate crime—for example, where a single crazed individual formed the necessary genocidal intent in his or her own mind, and committed an isolated murder.[83]

The first and presently only case addressing the definition of genocide under article 6 ICC Statute and its *Elements of Crimes* is the Arrest Warrant decision in the case of the Sudanese president Al Bashir.[84] Pre-Trial Chamber I held that unlike in ICTR and ICTY jurisprudence, under the ICC statute the actus reus of genocide requires a context as defined in the *Elements of Crimes*. Interpreting these contextual elements, the Chamber argued that 'the crime of genocide is only completed when the relevant conduct presents a concrete threat to the existence of the targeted group, or part thereof'.[85] Such a concrete threat exists 'when the threat against the existence of the targeted group, or part thereof, becomes concrete and real, as opposed to just being latent or hypothetical'.[86] Thus, when examining alleged acts of genocide—including conduct by a single individual—in the Chamber's view, the contextual elements are designed to ensure that the threat of annihilation of the targeted group is concrete and real.[87] The Chamber did not require collective-entity involvement.

Comparing the Pre-Trial Chamber's (PTC's) reading with that of the Rwanda and Yugoslavia tribunals, it appears that the ICC Chamber considered a genocidal context as part of the crime's actus reus, whereas the tribunals considered contexts primarily to prove genocidal intent. While an obvious difference exists between these approaches, requiring a real threat for the targeted group as a material element of the crime is not too far away from the approach that a genocidal intent must be realistic, 'genuine', or an 'affirmed resolve'. In fact, commentators have suggested that the ICC should actually follow the tribunals: because contextual elements do not form part of genocide's actus reus as defined in article 6 ICC Statute, 'the contextual

82 See *Elements of Crimes* (n 44) 6–8 (emphasis added).

83 Oosterveld, 'The Elements of Genocide: Introduction' in Boas, Reid, and Bischoff (eds), *Elements of Crimes under International Law* (CUP 2008) 45.

84 In the arrest warrant decision, however, Pre-Trial Chamber I found that the evidence presented was not sufficient 'to provide reasonable grounds to believe that the GoS acted with dolus specialis/specific intent to destroy in whole or in part the Fur, Masalit and Zaghawa groups'. *Situation in Darfur, Sudan, ICC-02/05–01/09* (n 8) para 206.

85 ibid, at para 124.

86 ibid. As the *Elements of Crimes* emphasize that the genocidal context includes 'initial acts in an emerging pattern', the 'concrete threat' requirement set out by the PTC should not be interpreted narrowly in the sense of an 'immediate threat' of full destruction, which could only arise once the genocidal campaign is at full scale.

87 In Kress's view, the idea that the crime of genocide must pose a real threat and danger to the targeted population is consistent with the historic development of the crime and systematic considerations on international criminal law. Yet, he also emphasized that a 'concrete threat' should not be misunderstood as requiring a result, meaning that the crime should come close to achieving its intended objective. See Kress, 'The Crime of Genocide and Contextual Elements: A Comment on the ICC Pre-Trial Chamber's Decision in the Al Bashir Case' (2009) Journal of International Criminal Justice 4–6; Kress, 'The ICC's First Encounter with the Crime of Genocide: The Case against Al Bashir' (n 1) 681–82.

Element should not be seen as an addition to the crime's actus reus but as an *objective point of reference* of a *realistic* genocidal *intent*'.[88] In both cases, a context of a manifest pattern of similar crimes or exceptional means at the disposal of the perpetrator create circumstances in which a real threat to the targeted group exists, and in which an individual's intent to destroy the group in whole or in part becomes credible.

To sum up, the universally accepted definition of genocide and the ICC's *Elements of Crimes* leave open the possibility of a lone génocidaire. The crime's definition does not require a collective genocidal plan, or the involvement of a collective entity. In this respect, under the ICC Statute the crime of genocide is distinct from crimes against humanity, which must be committed pursuant to or in furtherance of a state or organizational policy. At the same time, it seems widely agreed that genocide requires a credible or realistic intent on the part of its perpetrators. While in exceptional cases the genocidal intent of a single individual might be realistic and sufficient, in most cases the intent is proved by reference to a collective genocidal campaign.

Having examined different ways in which individuals can commit acts of genocide—either alone or as part of a collective endeavour—at least three genocidal scenarios are conceivable:

- First, a single individual—including state or non-state actors—could commit genocide if he or she had the capacity to commit a genocidal act that can in itself effect the destruction of at least part of a protected group.
- Second, a collective of individuals—not constituting a defined group or organization—could commit genocide by spontaneously attacking a national, ethnical, racial, or religious group with the realistic intent to destroy it in whole or in part.[89] For example, an unorganized group of individuals, for instance former soldiers or fighters, could follow a collective intent and decide to attack, with the intent to destroy, a minority assembled in one part of a town or in a refugee camp.
- Third, the historically—and realistically—most relevant cases of genocide consist of situations of collective violence instigated or committed by a state or non-state entity with the intent to destroy the targeted group as such. In such situations, conduct will come closest to what *Lemkin* described as 'a coordinated plan of different actions aiming at the destruction of essential foundations of the life of national groups, with the aim of annihilating the groups themselves'.[90]

[88] Kress, 'The ICC's First Encounter with the Crime of Genocide: The Case against Al Bashir' (n 1) 674. For Ambos, the context element could be understood as a 'carrier' or 'holder' for the intent requirement, especially if a structure or knowledge-based approach is used to establish the intent. Ambos, *Treatise on International Criminal Law* (n 8) 18 and 28.

[89] See also Ambos, *Treatise on International Criminal Law* (n 8) 30.

[90] Lemkin, *Axis Rule in Occupied Europe: Laws of Occupation, Analysis of Government, Proposals for Redress* (n 3) 79.

Obviously, the lone génocidaire case does not require any collective-entity involvement. The second and third cases, however, involve groups of perpetrators.

10.3 The Involvement of Collective Entities in the Crime of Genocide

Except in lone génocidaire cases, at least under the ICC Statute, the crime of genocide requires individual acts to be committed in a context of collective violence, meaning a manifest pattern of similar conduct. Likewise, such context is practically relevant to establish genocidal intent. This part examines two possibilities of how such contexts can develop. First, it is conceivable that genocide occurs rather spontaneously without significant involvement of a pre-existing collective entity planning and directing the crimes. Second, genocide could be instigated or committed by a collective entity. In each case, the degree of organization such a group or collective entity would need in order to be involved in the commission of genocide is examined.

10.3.1 Genocide through collective action with little organization

If an individual with sufficient resources and the requisite intent can commit genocide alone, a fortiori a group of individuals sharing a genocidal intent can do similar; in other words, genocide can be committed by a group of individuals with a shared genocidal intent and means at their disposal to commit crimes that can effect the destruction of a national, ethnical, racial, or religious group. Indeed, if these individuals act collectively—yet without a pre-conceived plan or policy—and attack a specific group in order to destroy it in whole or in part, individual genocidal acts would also occur 'in the context of a manifest pattern of similar conduct directed against that group'.[91] Consequently, this conglomeration of individual genocidal acts would be likely to pose a realistic threat of destruction to the targeted group. An example of such a situation could be a societal context in which tensions and conflict between different ethnic groups have long existed and in which the state is unable or unwilling to control such tensions. If a sudden event, such as a particularly odious crime by persons belonging to a minority group, triggers collective outrage by a majority group, a dynamic could emerge in which individuals unite spontaneously, take up arms, and attack the minority that they consider responsible for their grief. In order to amount to genocide, they would need to do so with the intent to destroy this minority once and for all.

The threshold for qualifying such an attack as genocide is, however, high. The ICC and the International Court of Justice emphasized that large-scale atrocities alone are insufficient to prove genocide.[92] They need to be specifically directed against a certain group with the intent to destroy it in whole or in part. The requisite genocidal pattern

[91] Preparatory Commission for the International Criminal Court, *Elements of Crimes* (n 44) 6–8.

[92] See *Situation in Darfur, Sudan, ICC-02/05–01/09* (n 8) paras 191–96, which includes an analysis of the ICJ Genocide Judgment.

is often evident if a campaign is 'systematically directed against that same group, while excluding members of other groups'.[93] Likewise, the scale of atrocities can indicate the existence of a collective genocidal context,[94] and so do consistent patterns of crimes in which no members of the targeted group are spared.[95] As a result, while it is easy to conceive a mob turning against a victim group, it might be difficult to establish whether such a spontaneous mob operated with a shared genocidal intent unless individuals acted at the instigation or direction of some kind of leadership.

10.3.2 Genocide instigated or committed by a collective entity

As shown above, the definition of genocide does not require state involvement as a material element of the crime; the definition's drafters explicitly dismissed such requirement. Thus, acts of genocide can be committed with state or non-state entity involvement. For example, following the ICTY in the *Kristic* case,[96] the International Court of Justice found that genocide in *Srebrenica* was committed by members of *Republika Srpska*,[97] which was a non-state entity not acting under a state's effective control.[98] The requisite degree of organization of a non-state entity behind genocide is not defined anywhere, however. While some commentators argue that practice or history show that genocide requires involvement of a state or state-like entity, such finding is not supported by strong evidence in legal documents, case law, or states' opinions.[99] Instead, in line with the approach that even individuals can commit genocide, and following the crime's principal objective to protect groups from annihilation, the degree of power and organization of an entity involved in genocide should be defined functionally. This means that a collective entity involved in the commission of genocide will need to have either the capacity to incite the crimes or the organizational and material ability to direct a manifest pattern of genocidal acts against a particular group with the intent to destroy the group in whole or in part.

[93] *Akayesu, ICTR-96-4-T* (n 5) para 523. See also *Kayishema et al, ICTR-95-1-T* (n 56) para 93; *Jelisić, IT-95-10-A* (n 57) para 47; *Krstić, IT-98-33-T* (n 5) para 546; United Nations Secretary General, *Report of the International Commission of Inquiry on Darfur to the United Nations Secretary-General* (n 66) para 502. Yet, as the Appeals Chamber emphasized in the *Jelisić* case, alleged randomness of crimes committed does not necessarily negate other evidence of a special intent. *Jelisić, IT-95-10-A* (n 57) para 71.

[94] See *Akayesu, ICTR-96-4-T* (n 5) para 523; *Kayishema et al, ICTR-95-1-T* (n 56) paras 531–45; *Krstić, IT-98-33-T* (n 5) para 572.

[95] eg, in the Al Bashir Arrest Warrant Decision, the PTC emphasized that the hindrance of humanitarian and medical assistance to internally displaced person (IDP) camps varied greatly and did not provide strong evidence for genocidal intent. See *Situation in Darfur, Sudan, ICC-02/05–01/09* (n 8) para 189. In the *Jelisić* case, the Trial Chamber referred to the alleged randomness of the acts committed in order to dismiss the claim that *Jelisić* acted with genocidal intent. See *Jelisić, IT-95-10-T* (n 5) paras 106–08.

[96] *Krstić, IT-98-33-T* (n 5) paras 360–62.

[97] *Case concerning Application of the Convention on the Prevention and Punishment of the Crime of Genocide (Bosnia and Herzegovina v Serbia and Montenegro)* (n 6) para 297.

[98] See ibid, at paras 235 and 394.

[99] None of the cases discussed in Section 10.2 'The Perpetrator(s) of Genocide in International Jurisprudence' above mentions such a requirement. Neither does the ICC's *Elements of Crimes* (n 44).

The requisite degree of organization of a non-state entity to be able to instigate or commit genocide is examined next.

10.3.2.1 Entities able to instigate genocide

More likely than genocide by a spontaneous mob acting without central guidance is a genocidal campaign instigated by an influential individual, a powerful organization, or a state. A genocidal campaign does not need to be executed by members of the entity instigating it. As found by the ICTR, Rwandan armed and political forces planned and organized the genocide in Rwanda but primarily civilians—both organized in militias and ordinary civilians—executed the crimes.[100] In practice, an underlying plan or policy is crucial to instigate a pattern of individual genocidal acts against the targeted group,[101] meaning that perpetrators select individual victims on the basis of their belonging to the targeted group with genocidal intent.[102] Accordingly, a collective entity involved in genocide should have the ability to develop such a plan or policy and to promulgate it. This plan or policy must reflect the intent to destroy the victim group in whole or in part.[103] Unless such a policy is formally adopted and articulated, it is regularly inferred from the circumstances of the crimes.[104] One factor from which tribunals inferred individual special intent is utterances of the accused.[105] In analogy, a plan or policy underlying a genocidal campaign can also be inferred from an entity's announcements, or from relevant documents.[106] Unless they call 'more or less explicitly, for the commission of genocide' or the elimination of a particular group',[107] relevant indices may include

[100] See *Akayesu, ICTR-96-4-T* (n 5) para 129.

[101] The close link between a 'manifest pattern' and a policy is also evident from the drafting history of the *Elements of Crimes*, in which the formulation of 'manifest pattern' replaced the requirement of a 'widespread or systematic policy or practice' found in a previous draft. See Schabas, *The International Criminal Court: A Commentary on the Rome Statute* (2nd edn, OUP 2017) 124.

[102] See, among others, *Situation in Darfur, Sudan, ICC-02/05–01/09* (n 8) paras 134–35; *Jelisić, IT-95-10-T* (n 6) para 67; *Akayesu, ICTR-96-4-T* (n 5) paras 521–22. While individual perpetrators of genocide are normally guided by their individual genocidal intent, directing a manifest pattern of similar genocidal conduct against a particular group requires a plan or policy providing instructions for the perpetrators.

[103] As Schabas points out, states or collective entities 'do not have specific intent ... Individuals have intent. States have policies.' Thus, when looking at collective entities, the question is not one of intent but one of policy. Schabas, *Unimaginable Atrocities* (n 15) 147.

[104] See, eg, *Krstić, IT-98-33-T* (n 5) para 549.

[105] *Akayesu, ICTR-96-4-T* (n 5) para 728. As the ICTR emphasized in the *Bagilishema* case, 'intent should be determined, above all, from his words and deeds, and should be evident from patterns of purposeful action'. *Bagilishema, Judgment, 7 June 2001, ICTR-95-1A-T*, ICTR, para 63. See also *Jelisić, IT-95-10-T* (n 6) para 102.

[106] Interestingly, in the Al Bashir Arrest Warrant decision, PTC I examined whether the Government of Sudan had a special intent because Al Bashir was in full control of the government and his intent could be equated with the government's intent. See *Situation in Darfur, Sudan, ICC-02/05–01/09* (n 8) 148–51. Accordingly, the PTC examined official documents of the Government of Sudan as well as statements by its members in order to determine whether a genocidal policy existed. ibid, at paras 166–67.

[107] *Akayesu, ICTR-96-4-T* (n 5) paras 729 and 709. See also *Jelisić, IT-95-10-A* (n 57) paras 67–68.

racially motivated statements or derogatory language against the targeted group,[108] or statements calling for the killing of the elderly, mothers, and babies among the group.[109]

The instigating actor or entity would not be required to have an abstractly defined authority (such as being a political or religious actor) but the decisive fact is whether the instigation is sufficient to orchestrate the likely destruction of a group in whole or in part. The material capacity to commit genocidal acts—meaning manpower under its command, as well as the requisite weapons, logistics, and finances—would not be needed. As in the case of the spontaneously formed but leaderless mob, individual perpetrators or militias could bring their own means to commit the constituent acts. Thus, at least theoretically, a non-state actor or entity may incite genocide without otherwise participating—or having the capacity to participate—in the implementation of the crimes.[110] It is also conceivable that the entity behind the genocidal policy provides logistical support without commanding the crimes. However, in order to constitute a real threat to the existence of the targeted group, such crimes would need to be committed in a context in which the territorial state either approves or condones the crimes, or is unable to intervene.

10.3.2.2 Entities able to commit genocide

In most cases, collective entities not only instigate genocide but also commit it, meaning that perpetrators of individual genocidal acts are members of the entity and/or operate under its instructions. In addition to the capacity to develop a policy directing collective violence against a targeted group, the entity would need to have sufficient internal structures as well as the requisite means and logistics to implement the genocidal plan or policy. With regard to the entity's internal structures, it would require sufficient capacity to enforce the systematic implementation of a plan. This is normally done through command-and-control structures or disciplinary systems as found among parties to armed conflicts or other hierarchical organizations.[111] The entity must be able to commit crimes collectively and consistently against a

[108] See United Nations Secretary General, *Report of the International Commission of Inquiry on Darfur to the United Nations Secretary-General* (n 66) para 513; *Kayishema et al, ICTR-95-1-T* (n 56) para 538.

[109] *Situation in Darfur, Sudan, ICC-02/05–01/09* (n 8) para 172. For the latter, see *Kayishema et al, ICTR-95-1-T* (n 56) paras 538–42. In contrast, statements or orders that no prisoners shall be taken during an armed attack against opponents are not sufficiently strong proof for a genocidal intent. In any case, inferring intent must meet a high evidentiary threshold: evidence must show that the 'only reasonable inference' from speeches or other documents is a genocidal intent. See *Karadžić, IT-95-5/18-T* (n 5) para 2605.

[110] Public statements calling for the destruction of a protected group can amount to the criminal act of incitement of others to commit genocide. This is criminalized under article 3(c) Genocide Convention, article 4(3)(c) ICTY Statute, article 2(3)(c) ICTR Statute, and article 25(3)(e) ICC Statute. For further details on this point, see *Krstić, IT-98-33-T* (n 5) para 362; *Akayesu, ICTR-96-4-T* (n 5) para 729.

[111] In principle, these structures would not be significantly different from those needed to commit a systematic attack against a civilian population forming part of a crime against humanity. See discussion in Section 9.2.4.2 'The required degree of organization as deduced from the contextual elements of CAH'. This, eg, has been the case in *Srebrenica*, where acts of genocide were committed by members of the military wing of a well-structured collective entity. See *Krstić, IT-98-33-T* (n 5) para 362.

targeted group. Moreover, if an entity implements a genocidal plan through its own capacities, it needs to have sufficient manpower, weapons, and other logistics to do so. Exact determinants of this capacity—such as the number of persons or the kind of weapons—are, however, context-dependent. As a result, if a collective entity has the ability to develop a genocidal plan or policy, the manpower and logistics to implement it, and the internal structures to ensure that crimes are committed systematically in a way that evidences the underlying genocidal plan, the collective action qualifies as genocide.

10.3.3 Limitations to a functional approach

The above considerations apply to most cases of genocide by killing or causing serious bodily or mental harm. In principle, such acts can be committed with relatively basic means and do not require a degree of power or organization above the perpetrator(s)' ability to commit the crimes with the realistic intent to destroy the targeted group in whole or in part.[112] A collective entity behind such crimes would not need to have additional capacities, such as territorial control or governance infrastructure. In contrast, acts such as 'deliberately inflicting on the group conditions of life calculated to bring about its physical destruction', 'imposing measures intended to prevent births within the group', or 'forcibly transferring children of the group to another group' usually cannot be committed unless the perpetrator exercises authority over the targeted group or the territory in which they reside.[113] This does not mean, however, that state involvement is required. Non-state entities with quasi-governmental authority in a territory can develop sufficient capacity and infrastructure to adopt and enforce policies to deprive certain populations of resources indispensible for their survival, or to implement such 'measures designed to prevent births as prohibition of marriages, separation of the sexes, forced birth control, sterilization, large-scale sexual mutilation'.[114] It is unlikely that such acts would be committed by single individuals, spontaneously formed mobs, at the mere instigation of societal actors, or otherwise without the involvement of the territorial authority.

10.4 Conclusions on Non-State Entity Involvement in Genocide

Fortunately, cases of genocide are rather rare, and so are criminal cases against alleged perpetrators.[115] Unfortunately for a lawyer, this also means that legal practice on

[112] As Cassese pointed out, these acts require neither a collective entity behind the crime nor a policy according to which they are committed. See Cassese, 'Is Genocidal Policy a Requirement for the Crime of Genocide?' in Gaeta (ed), *The UN Genocide Convention: A Commentary* (OUP 2009) 128–36, 134–35.

[113] See ibid, at 135–36. Yet, it should not be excluded that a group without territorial control or quasi-governmental capacities could find ways to transfer children or prevent births.

[114] Cassese, *Cassese's International Criminal Law* (n 21) 125.

[115] For recent statistics on different crimes before international tribunals, see Sadat, 'Crimes against Humanity in the Modern Age' (2012) 107 American Journal of International Law 334–77, 343, 347, 350, 357.

the interpretation of the crime's definition is scarce, especially when it comes to genocide without state involvement: the Rwanda Tribunal has adjudicated crimes committed as part of a state-led genocide; the Tribunal for the former Yugoslavia found that genocide was perpetrated with the involvement of an entity with quasi-state capacities; and in the *Al Bashir* case before the ICC, genocide has allegedly been committed with the involvement of the Sudanese state.[116] Consequently, the question of whether and under which conditions genocide can be committed with the involvement of non-state entities without quasi-state capacities has not formed part of the ratio decidendi of international decisions. Nonetheless, in line with the universally accepted definition of genocide, its drafting history, and subsequent state practice, tribunals found that genocide does not require state involvement. The definition does not specify, however, whether any collective-entity involvement is required for the crime's commission. At least theoretically, individuals acting alone can commit the crime as long as they have the means to effect the destruction of a targeted group and thereby pose a real threat to the group's existence. A fortiori, groups of individuals acting with the requisite intent and capacity can do the same. If this line of argument is followed, there can be no objection to the conclusion that any collective entity can instigate or commit genocide if it has the means to do so. For genocide by killing or by causing serious bodily or mental harm, this includes the capacity to develop and promulgate a genocidal policy or plan, to have sufficient resources to realize it, and to enforce its systematic implementation.

Considering that states agreed on the definition of genocide right after the Holocaust, their foresight in not defining genocide narrowly as a state crime is remarkable.[117] Following the primary objective of protecting national, ethnical, racial, or religious groups from annihilation, the drafters did not want to exclude non-state mass-crimes in situations in which a state is unable to protect groups living under its jurisdiction effectively. In today's world, a narrow definition of genocide would be detrimental: recent allegations of genocide include crimes committed by members of different non-state armed groups. For example, since 2013, different reports have suggested that crimes by the ragtag 'Anti-Balaka' armed group in the Central African Republic could have amounted to genocide.[118] Moreover, in 2015, the Office of the High Commissioner for Human Rights found that the killing of Yezidis in Iraq by members of the 'Islamic State Group' is likely to constitute genocide.[119] If these

[116] The Extraordinary Chambers in the Court of Cambodia are likewise concerned with alleged genocide committed with state involvement.

[117] eg, a 1949 commentary on the Genocide Convention argued that to carry a genocidal programme 'to successful completion would almost necessarily require active or silent support of the State having territorial jurisdiction of the offense'. Yale Law Journal, 'Genocide: A Commentary on the Convention' (n 24) 1147.

[118] See *The International Commission of Inquiry on the Central African Republic—Final Report*, S/2014/928, paras 443–361. For some discussion, see Labuda, 'What Lies beneath the 'G' Word? Genocide-Labelling and Fact-Finding at the UN' (EJIL: *Talk!*, 28 May 2015) http://www.ejiltalk.org/what-lies-beneath-the-g-word-genocide-labelling-and-fact-finding-at-the-un/ accessed 15 November 2017.

[119] Human Rights Council, *Report of the Office of the United Nations High Commissioner for Human Rights on the Human Rights Situation in Iraq in the Light of Abuses Committed by the So-called Islamic State in Iraq and the Levant and Associated Groups*, 13 March 2015, A/HRC/28/18, paras 17, 78.

allegations are true, perpetrators must face justice. Moreover, the word genocide continues to have a 'peculiar political magic',[120] which might trigger more decisive action by the international community than war crimes or crimes against humanity. If a specific group is threatened by or faces annihilation, prosecution or political action should not be denied simply because the perpetrators lacked the support of an entity with abstractly defined state-like characteristics.

[120] Milanovic, 'European Court Tackles the Definition of Genocide' (EJIL: *Talk!*, 27 October 2015) <http://www.ejiltalk.org/european-court-tackles-the-definition-of-genocide/> accessed 15 November 2017.

Part III: Conclusion

A key characteristic distinguishing war crimes, crimes against humanity, and genocide from ordinary crimes is some form of collective-entity involvement.[1] Under international criminal law, collective-entity involvement normally creates a context in which individuals commit crimes that 'deeply shock the conscience of humanity', 'threaten the peace, security and well-being of the world', and which 'must not go unpunished'.[2] In other words, the involvement of a collective entity enables crimes of particular scale that harm key interests of the international community and are unlikely to be halted or prosecuted by national authorities. Classically, such contexts occur if a state uses its position as the territorial authority and its resources to orchestrate crimes against persons within its power. Yet, international crimes are not limited to state crimes. This book has shown that the definitions of international crimes are rather broad with regard to the nature of the collective entities involved: war crimes in non-international armed conflict require involvement of at least one organized armed group; crimes against humanity (CAH) require a 'State or organizational policy' behind the crimes; and for genocide, collective-entity involvement is not a strict requirement, but the crime needs to be committed with a realistic intent to destroy the targeted group in whole or in part. It is generally accepted that state involvement is not a strict requirement in any of these definitions.

Determining the degree of organization, power, or capacity of non-state entities to commit war crimes, CAH, or genocide, or to create a context in which these crimes can be committed, should not be done in the abstract. Requiring broadly state-like capacities, such as territorial control and governance institutions, is imprecise: while such capacities would generally enable entities to create an environment in which international crimes can be committed, the definition of a non-state party to an armed conflict, for example, does not require the armed group to exercise territorial control. Likewise, territorial control is not a prerequisite for an organization to develop and promulgate a policy underlying CAH. Instead, characteristics of collective entities behind these crimes should be derived from the crime's definition and an assessment of what is functionally needed to create the required context. In the case of war crimes, this means that the requisite degree of organization of the non-state armed group should be strictly defined by what is needed to qualify as a

[1] As emphasized in Section 10.2 'The Perpetrator(s) of Genocide in International Jurisprudence', a notable exception to this general rule is the 'lone génocidaire'.
[2] The Rome Statute of the International Criminal Court (ICC Statute), preamble.

Organizing Rebellion: Non-State Armed Groups under International Humanitarian Law, Human Rights Law, and International Criminal Law. Tilman Rodenhäuser. © Tilman Rodenhäuser, 2018. Published 2018 by Oxford University Press.

party to a non-international armed conflict. With regard to CAH and genocide, the capacity of a collective entity behind a CAH policy or a genocidal pattern depends on the relation between the collective entity and the acts constituting the international crimes in the particular circumstances. For example, if such crimes can be committed at the mere instigation of a collective entity, that entity's capacities would be different than in cases in which the entity directs the crimes and executes them through its own forces and resources.

While many of the early international criminal law cases prosecuted Nazi and thereby state crimes, the majority of situations currently investigated by the ICC involve crimes committed by different kinds of non-state armed groups.[3] If these acts factually amount to international crimes, deriving restrictions from a crime's history should not narrow their definition. Except if reflecting customary international law, states have not included the crimes' history as a source of law in the ICC Statute. Crises, conflicts, and atrocities have always been complex, changing patterns, involving new actors depending on the specific societal, political, or cultural circumstances. Interpreting international crimes as defined under the ICC Statute in accordance with their wording, context, and object and purpose leaves sufficient flexibility to address a broad variety of situations and actors in order to end impunity for unimaginable atrocities.

International Responsibility of Collective Entities

In its present form, international criminal law focuses on individual criminal responsibility and not on the responsibility of collective entities. Yet, it is similarly clear that international crimes 'are often caused by collective entities in which the individual authors of these acts are embedded'.[4] In this respect, it has been suggested that international crimes should be characterized as 'system criminality': such criminality 'serves the system, and it is caused by the system'.[5] Others have emphasized with regard to international crimes that 'the system and individual level are not mutually exclusive but rather complement each other; a one-sided focus on one or the other would not fully take into account the complexities of macro criminality'.[6] Indeed, as shown in this book, a certain degree of collective entity involvement is normally a defining and indispensible element of crimes against humanity, genocide, and war crimes. If collective entities play a decisive role in the commission of

[3] This does not necessarily mean that armed groups commit more international crimes these days than states. Situations under ICC investigation are simply those over which the court has jurisdiction. Many states that are implicated in international crimes are not parties to the ICC Statute, and other ways for the court to exercise jurisdiction are limited. See articles 13 and 14 ICC Statute.

[4] Nollkaemper, 'Introduction' in Wilt and Nollkaemper (eds), *System Criminality in International Law* (CUP 2009) 1–25, 1.

[5] Röling, 'The Significance of the Laws of War' in Cassese (ed), *Current Problems of International Law: Essays on UN Law and on the Law of Armed Conflict* (A Giuffrè 1975) 138.

[6] Ambos, 'Command Responsibility and Organsationsherrschaft: Ways of Attributing International Crimes to the "Most Responsible"' in Wilt and Nollkaemper (eds), *System Criminality in International Law* (CUP 2009) 127–57, 129.

international crimes, arguably international criminal responsibility should not only exist for individuals but also for the collective entity.

The rise and fall of the idea of state criminality has been discussed in depth in legal literature.[7] In contrast, while 'the criminalization of individual members of rebel groups under international law is now well-established . . ., the question of whether the groups as such can be said to have violated international criminal law remains, however, under explored'.[8] The present book does not analyse the current state of international criminal responsibility of non-state armed groups in detail and does not aim to establish whether such responsibility can be said to reflect an established norm or principle of international law. Instead, the following paragraphs analyse to what extent the finding that a collective entity is sufficiently organized to constitute a collective entity behind an international crime for the purposes of individual criminal responsibility also suggests that the entity in question should, as such, incur international (criminal) responsibility.

The relation between individual acts and the collective entity behind the crime

Before delving into the legal questions that are at the heart of this book, it is helpful to briefly recall the broad lines of how social scientists analyse the relation between an individual's commission of an international crime and the collective entity behind the act. For example, the social ethics professor Kelman characterizes international crimes as 'crimes of obedience' because they are committed 'under explicit instruction from the authorities to engage in these acts, or in an environment in which such acts are implicitly sponsored, expected, or at least tolerated by the authorities'.[9] Going one step further, with regard to parties to armed conflicts it has been argued that members of the parties 'are subject to group conformity phenomena such as depersonalization, loss of independence and a high degree of conformity'.[10] In such 'systems', permissible behaviour is no longer determined by the individual's own

[7] See, eg, Pellet, 'The New Draft Articles of the International Law Commission on the Responsibility of States for International Wrongful Acts: A Requiem for States' Crime?' (2001) 32 Netherlands Journal of International Law 55–79; Wyler, 'From "State Crime" to Responsibility for "Serious Breaches of Obligations under Peremptory Norms of General International Law"' (2002) 13 European Journal of International Law 1147–60; Zimmermann and Teichmann, 'State Responsibility for International Crimes' in Wilt and Nollkaemper (eds), *System Criminality in International Law* (CUP 2009) 298–313; Scobbie, 'Assumptions and Presumptions: State Responsiblity for System Crimes', in Wilt and Nollkaemper (eds), *System Criminality in International Law* (CUP 2009) 270–97.

[8] Clapham, 'Extending International Criminal Law beyond the Individual to Corporations and Armed Opposition Groups' (2008) 6 Journal of International Criminal Justice 920.

[9] Kelman, 'The Policy Context of International Crimes' in Wilt and Nollkaemper (eds), *System Criminality in International Law* (CUP 2009) 26–41, 27. This analysis corresponds, to an important extent, with the legal analysis of collective entity involvement in international crimes as presented in this book.

[10] Munoz-Rojas and Fresard, 'The Roots of Behaviour in War: Understanding and Preventing IHL Violations' (2004) 86 International Review of the Red Cross 193. This means that when operating in armed groups, individuals are likely to obey to the rules of the group and the authority of it's leader. See also discussion in Nollkaemper, 'Collective Accountability' 6.

moral or other values but by the group, meaning that in many cases international crimes conform with the norms or values promulgated by the group. Moreover, within group dynamics individuals tend to shift 'individual responsibility from themselves to their superior(s) in the chain of command'.[11] This may lead to a 'dilution of the individual responsibility of the combatant within the collective responsibility of his combat unit'.[12] Accordingly, it has been argued that 'organizations kill', in the sense that 'there are no "individuals" in organizations and that organizations commit "crimes"'.[13]

The conclusions presented in this book suggest that from a legal point of view, the relation between an armed group and international crimes committed by individuals can take different forms.[14] First, the most direct and common link between a group and international crimes exists if the perpetrators of the crimes are members of the group and act under orders by group leadership or more generally in accordance with a group's policy. Second, individuals may also commit international crimes without being members of such a group but in accordance with a group's policy that incites such acts. Likewise, individuals that are not members of the group may commit international crimes that are tolerated and thereby encouraged by the group. Third, war crimes, and in exceptional circumstances genocide, may also be committed by individuals that are not members of a group and do not act in accordance with a group policy at all.[15] In that case, such individual crimes are unlikely to engage any form of collective-entity responsibility. In contrast, in the other two cases, an international crime inviting the international criminal responsibility of individual perpetrators may—if such responsibility became accepted under international law—also engage the (criminal) responsibility of the entity to which the act is attributable. Moreover, even if individual acts are not attributable to a collective entity, the entity might be responsible for the policy that guided the crime and formed an indispensible component of the crime.

[11] Munoz-Rojas and Fresard, 'The Roots of Behaviour in War: Understanding and Preventing IHL Violations' (n 10) 194.

[12] ibid.

[13] Punch, 'Why Corporations Kill and Get Away with It: The Failure of Law to Cope with Crimes in Organizations' in Wilt and Nollkaemper (eds), *System Criminality in International Law* (CUP 2009) 42–68, 42.

[14] In a different analysis, Nollkaemper came to somewhat related conclusions: 'Collective entities can be involved in the commission of international crimes in an active or passive manner. Active involvement may take the form of ordering or encouraging international crimes to be committed, for instance by orders from military or civilian commanders, whose acts in term may be attributable to states or other collectivities. Encouragement may also take more subtle forms, as incitement and propaganda, dehumanisation of victims of violence by indoctrination, and policies directed as changing the normative climate. Passive involvement may take the form of permitting or tolerating the committing of international crimes, by systematically not acting when individuals commit international crimes which further the objectives of the state.' Nollkaemper, 'Introduction' (n 4) in Wilt and Nollkaemper (eds), *System Criminality in International Law* (CUP 2009) 1–25, 16–17.

[15] Certainly, at least two sufficiently organized collective entities need to engage in sufficently intense violence for a non-international armed conflict (NIAC) to exist. However, once the armed conflict threshold has been crossed, an individual that is otherwise not involved in the conflict may commit a war crime through a criminalized act that shows a suffcient link to the conflict as such—not to a party thereof.

Key principles that could guide collective-entity responsibility

There is no international treaty or other document, such as the ILC 'Draft articles on Responsibility of States for Internationally Wrongful Acts', setting out secondary rules for the international legal responsibility of non-state armed groups.[16] Moreover, there is very little international practice on the question. While international humanitarian law (IHL) or international human rights law (IHRL) violations by armed groups, as well as alleged international crimes, are regularly condemned in international fora and groups are called upon to end violations and to respect applicable international law, technical legal questions relating to the definition of an internationally wrongful act, the attribution of conduct, or the consequences of wrongful acts or crimes are rarely addressed in detail.[17] It seems to be generally assumed that—in analogy to one of the foundational principles of the international legal regime on the responsibility of states—non-state armed groups are responsible for internationally wrongful acts that consist of acts or omissions, which (i) constitute a breach of an international obligation of the group; that (ii) is attributable to the non-state entity.[18]

With regard to the first element of this principle, it is uncontroversial that armed groups have international legal obligations under IHL and there is an increasing international practice suggesting that different non-state entities have varying degrees of IHRL obligations. Moreover, it has been suggested that all international legal persons are bound by peremptory norms of international law, which include the prohibition of genocide and of crimes against humanity.[19] Accordingly, acts or omissions attributable to a non-state armed group that breach one of the listed obligations could potentially involve the international legal responsibility of the group. If the question is not only whether a group's international responsibility was

[16] Yet, the commentary to article 10 of the ILC's Articles on the Responsibility of States for Internationally Wrongful Acts (ARSIWA), which concerns state responsibility for the conduct of successful insurrectional movements, emphasizes that a 'further possibility is that the insurrectional movement may itself be held responsible for its own conduct under international law, for example for a breach of international humanitarian law committed by its forces'. The ILC did, however, not consider this possibility further. International Law Commission, 'Responsibility of State for Internationally Wrongful Acts (with Commentary)' *Yearbook of the International Law Commission*, 2001, Vol II, Part Two, 2001, para 16 on article 10.

[17] For an extensive analysis of relevant international reports, see Chapter 6 'A Three-Pronged Approach to Human Rights Obligations of Non-State Armed Groups'. For an analysis of additional practice by international and non-governmental organizations, see Bellal, 'Establishing the Direct Responsibility of Non-State Armed Groups for Violations of International Norms: Issues of Attribution' in Noemi Gal-Or (ed), *Responsibilities of the Non-State Actor in Armed Conflict and the Market Place* (Brill Nijhoff 2015). For further analysis of the lack of a legal framework for determining non-state armed group responsibility, see also Sassòli, 'Taking Armed Groups Seriously: Ways to Improve their Compliance with International Humanitarian Law' (2010) 1 Journal of International Humanitarian Legal Studies 44; Kleffner, 'The Collective Accountability of Organized Armed Groups for System Crimes' in H v d Wilt and A Nollkaemper (eds), *System Criminality in International Law* (CUP 2009) 238–69, 257.

[18] For the corresponding articles on state responsibility, see articles 1 and 2 ARSIWA.

[19] See International Law Commission, 'Responsibility of State for Internationally Wrongful Acts (with Commentary)' (n 16) para 5 on article 26. On the question of whether armed groups are bound by peremptory rules of international law, see Section 6.5.3.2 'Legal sources binding armed groups without control over territory and population'.

involved but also whether the group is criminally responsible for an alleged international crime, this would require an additional rule or principle that criminalizes certain acts by non-state armed groups. However, no such rule or principle exists under contemporary international law, and there is little, if any, practice suggesting international *criminal* responsibility of non-state entities.[20]

The second element of the principle, namely the question of attribution, is relevant for 'simple' international responsibility and for possible considerations on criminal responsibility. In analogy to the international responsibility of states and international organizations, a starting point could be that the conduct of an organ or agent of a non-state entity is considered an act of the entity under international law.[21] While seeming obvious at first sight, this analogy faces obstacles because of the different natures of states, international organizations, and non-state entities such as armed groups. With regard to state responsibility, an organ is defined as including 'any person or entity which has that status in accordance with the internal law of the State',[22] and for international organizations it is proposed that 'the rules of the organization apply in the determination of the functions of its organs and agents'.[23] Defining organs of, or more broadly membership in, armed groups by reference to 'internal law' or 'rules of the organization' may not only be politically very sensitive but also encounters practical hurdles.[24] There are certainly groups that organize in a manner similar to states with different organs such as police forces, intelligence forces, fighting forces, as well as different civilian components involved in the administration of territory.[25] In such cases, the roles of the different organs and membership in the group are often defined in internal documents of the group in question. Hence, the analogy to existing principle of international responsibility should be instructive.[26] In other cases, however, non-state armed groups may not have any formalized internal rules or documentation defining organs or membership.

[20] For a brief analysis with pertinent references on why the criminal responsibility for legal entities was not included on the ICC Statute, see Schabas, *The International Criminal Court: A Commentary on the Rome Statute* (2nd edn, OUP 2017) 564–66.

[21] See article 4 ARSIWA; article 6(1) International Law Commission, *Draft Articles on the Responsibility of International Organizations* (UN 2011).

[22] Article 4(1) ARSIWA.

[23] Article 6(2) *Draft Articles on the Responsibility of International Organizations* (n 21).

[24] For a discussion of some of the 'political dilemmas' that make developing a system of non-state armed group responsibility difficult, see Bílková, 'Establishing Direct Responsibility of Armed Opposition Groups for Violations of International Humanitarian Law?' in Noemi Gal-Or (ed), *Responsibilities of the Non-State Actor in Armed Conflict and the Market Place* (Brill Nijhoff 2015) 263–84, 277–78.

[25] See analysis of groups in Section 6.3 'Human Rights Obligations of Groups Exercising Quasi-Governmental Authority in Defined Territory'. See also Zegveld, *Accountability of Armed Opposition Groups in International Law* (CUP 2002) 154.

[26] See Kleffner, 'Collective Accountability' (n 17) 262–63. As Verhoeven argues, if a non-state entity succeeds in establishing quasi-governmental authority in defined territory, 'from that point in time, the rules of attribution of conduct to a State would apply, which would reflect the changing structure and activities of the insurrectional movement'. Verhoeven, 'International Responsibility of Armed Opposition Groups: Lessons from State Responsibility for Actions of Armed Opposition Groups' in Noemi Gal-Or (ed), *Responsibilities of the Non-State Actor in Armed Conflict and the Market Place* (Brill Nijhoff 2015) 285–303, 301.

In situations in which the formal criterion of referring to internal documents cannot be applied, more factual approaches have been suggested. Sassòli, for example, has argued that armed groups are responsible for acts committed by their 'members and other persons exercising elements of their authority, who act in that capacity' as well as persons over which groups exercise 'direction or control'.[27] Likewise, Kleffner has discussed different ways in which the ILC articles on state responsibility may be instructive for the collective responsibility of non-state entities.[28] Without going into further detail on the different possible analogies, in the absence of well-developed and formalized structures within armed groups and no agreed definition of who constitutes a group's membership, a reasonable bottom line to define whose acts are attributable to a group seems to be those of persons or groups of persons that are operating under the de facto control of the group. As Zegveld argued with reference to some international practice, 'attribution of acts or omissions to smaller armed opposition groups is based on their actual control over individuals, rather than on the existence of a defined state-like structure'.[29]

At least two cases should be distinguished: first, which individuals or entities might be considered de facto organs of a non-state entity; and second, the conduct of which third persons might be attributable to a collective non-state entity. Regarding the question of when persons, groups, or entities can be considered de facto organs, the ICJ has suggested a high threshold. In the Court's view, qualifying as a de facto organ would require that 'in fact the persons, groups or entities act in "complete dependence" on the State, of which they are ultimately merely the instrument'.[30] If reference to internal laws or documents of armed groups is not deemed politically appropriate or is practically not feasible, a starting point should be to include persons that completely depend on the collective entity among its de facto organs.[31]

As seen especially in Chapter 3 'Organized Armed Groups in Contemporary International Practice', however, the organizational structures of armed groups may not always be sufficiently well defined to satisfy the threshold of 'complete dependence'. Thus, a somewhat lower test may be more realistic to define persons as de facto organs. Armed groups should be considered as one collective entity if their organizational structures do not follow well-defined hierarchies but if their internal organization follows more decentralized structures. It has been suggested that if the 'complete dependence' threshold cannot be met, the overall control test based on the ICTY's *Tadić* case should be applied.[32] While interpretations differ on how

[27] Sassòli, 'Taking Armed Groups Seriously' (n 17) 45.

[28] See Kleffner, 'Collective Accountability' (n 17) 262–64.

[29] Zegveld, *Accountability of Armed Opposition Groups* (n 25) 155. However, Zegveld confines this to acts under the effective control of the group. For further support of this argument, see Kleffner, 'Collective Accountability' (n 17) 264; Sassòli, 'Taking Armed Groups Seriously' (n 17).

[30] *Case concerning Application of the Convention on the Prevention and Punishment of the Crime of Genocide (Bosnia and Herzegovina v Serbia and Montenegro), Judgment, 26 February 2007*, ICJ paras 392–93.

[31] See also Verhoeven, 'International Responsibility of Armed Opposition Groups: Lessons from State Responsibility for Actions of Armed Opposition Groups' (n 26) 300.

[32] ibid, at 301–02.

much control is actually required to satisfy this test, at least with regard to parties to armed conflicts this book concludes that in order to consider an armed group to be part of a collective entity, the collective entity's leadership needs to exercise a degree of both *operational coordination* and *strategic authority* over all parts of a group.[33] This includes an element of de facto authority exercised by the entity's leadership over its different subgroups or other components. If in such cases an armed group can be considered one collective entity for the purposes of conflict classification, the different sub-groups should also be considered as forming the de facto organs of the collective entity, and their conduct should be attributable to it. A similar threshold of control may also be instructive beyond the armed conflict context.

Moving from the group level to the individual level, individuals that form part of a collective entity are generally those that are factually subject to the entity's disciplinary system. In organized armed groups, this would include all those that operate under the group's chain of command.[34] However, a clear chain of command from top to bottom does not necessarily exist in armed groups and focus would need to be placed rather on the de facto relationship between commanders and subordinates than on formally defined structures. In decentrally organized groups, membership should also encompass all persons that are subject to the disciplinary system of a de facto organ, meaning a sub-group that operates under the *operational coordination* and *strategic authority* of the collective entity as a whole.

Beyond the question of which persons—groups or individuals—can be said to form part of a collective entity and therefore constitute its de facto organs or agents, the international legal responsibility of collective entities should also be engaged by conduct of persons that are not part of the group but 'at a certain point in time they are directed, controlled or instructed by the insurrectional movement'.[35] For such contexts, the ICJ suggests that states are responsible for the acts of persons acting under their 'effective control'.[36] When considering the attribution of possible violations or international crimes committed by individuals or groups that do not have a more structural link to the collective entity, the effective control test would require that the collective entity 'directed or enforced the perpetration of the acts', meaning that it effectively controlled the specific 'operations in the course of which the alleged violations were committed'.[37] While this test might be too demanding for being the sole test to determine which individuals or sub-groups form the de facto organs of a collective non-state entity, it could be instructive for attributing wrongful acts committed by third persons.

[33] See Section 3.2.1.2 'Decentralized command structures'.

[34] See Section 3.2.3.1 'Enforcing respect for IHL in armed groups with centralized command structures'.

[35] For a similar suggestion, see Verhoeven, 'International Responsibility of Armed Opposition Groups: Lessons from State Responsibility for Actions of Armed Opposition Groups' (n 26) 300.

[36] See *Case concerning Application of the Convention on the Prevention and Punishment of the Crime of Genocide (Bosnia and Herzegovina v Serbia and Montenegro)* (n 30) paras 400–01; *Case concerning Military and Paramilitary Activities in and against Nicaragua (Nicaragua v United States of America), Judgment, 27 June 1986*, ICJ, para 115.

[37] *Case concerning Military and Paramilitary Activities in and against Nicaragua (Nicaragua v United States of America)* (n 36) para 115.

Beyond the questions of which acts can be considered internationally wrongful when committed by armed groups and how to attribute individual acts to a collective non-state entity, proposing a regime for international legal responsibility of non-state entities would require detailed considerations of a range of questions. These would include considerations on acts committed ultra vires, circumstances precluding wrongfulness by armed groups, or the consequences of a wrongful act committed by an armed group.[38] Instead of delving further into conceptual issues regarding the possible collective responsibility of collective entities, section 'Crimes committed directly by persons whose conduct is attributable to the collective entity' considers concretely how the different types of collective entity involvement in international crimes may engage a possible collective responsibility of the entity.

Crimes committed directly by persons whose conduct is attributable to the collective entity

The most direct link between a collective entity and an international crime, or an internationally wrongful act more generally, exists if all acts constituting the crime are committed by persons attributable to the collective entity. With regard to IHL or IHRL violations, this would be the case if the person committing the crime or the wrongful act—for example, killing or torturing a captured person—is a de facto organ of the collective entity or otherwise attributable to it. In contrast, if a person commits a war crime but the person's conduct is not attributable to the collective entity in question, the collective entity will not be responsible for the act even though it created the context—the armed conflict—which is a necessary background of the crime. The situation is slightly more complex with regard to crimes against humanity or genocide. These acts are considered to be 'composite acts', meaning that the wrongful act consists of two or more 'acts or omissions defined in aggregate as wrongful'.[39] Indeed, genocide or CAH normally require more than one act, including the underlying acts (such as killing or torturing) and a contextual element, normally in the form of a policy behind the crimes. With regard to both crimes, this book has shown that the clearest and most common case is that a collective entity develops the requisite plan or policy and commits the underlying criminal acts through persons attributable to it. In such cases, the collective entity should also be responsible for the wrongful act, in addition to a possible individual criminal responsibility of the individual perpetrators.

[38] For discussion on some of these issues, see, for instance, Kleffner, 'Collective Accountability' (n 17); Sassòli, 'Taking Armed Groups Seriously' (n 17); Verhoeven, 'International Responsibility of Armed Opposition Groups: Lessons from State Responsibility for Actions of Armed Opposition Groups' (n 26); Bílková, 'Establishing Direct Responsibility of Armed Opposition Groups for Violations of International Humanitarian Law?' (n 24) 263–84, 275–83.

[39] International Law Commission, 'Responsibility of State for Internationally Wrongful Acts (with Commentary)' (n 16) para 2 on article 15.

Crimes committed following a collective entity's policy but not by persons attributable to it

Establishing collective-entity responsibility for certain wrongful acts or crimes may be less clear-cut if different components of the composite act are committed by different persons. As has been shown above, international law foresees individual criminal responsibility for CAH or genocide if the relevant acts are committed by individuals that are neither part nor under the control of a collective entity, but their crimes are pursuant to or in furtherance of a collective entity's plan or policy. In such circumstances, a policy needs to 'actively promote or encourage' an attack, which may exceptionally be done through 'a deliberate failure to take action, which is consciously aimed at encouraging such attack'.[40] Concretely, a crime against humanity could be committed if a collective entity that effectively governs a certain city incited widespread acts of rape against a civilian population, which were not committed by its members but by other civilians or militias.

If there was an international legal obligation prohibiting states or collective non-state entities to incite certain crimes, developing and promulgating a policy that actively or passively instigates international crimes would violate that obligation.[41] However, no such obligation is explicitly included in, for example, the Convention on the Prevention and Punishment of the Crime of Genocide. Nonetheless, following the reasoning presented by the International Court of Justice regarding states' implied conventional obligation not to commit genocide, it could also be argued that it would be 'paradoxical' if states were under an obligation—in line with article 3(c) of the Convention—to prevent and punish the direct and public incitement to commit genocide 'but were not forbidden to commit such acts through their own organs'.[42] Likewise, if a non-state entity had an obligation not to commit genocide or CAH under general international law, it would similarly be paradoxical if that entity was not prohibited from inciting such acts.

In addition, or if it cannot be established that a collective entity is prohibited from inciting CAH or genocide, the intriguing question arises of whether international law foresees some form of responsibility for an entity that commits one part of a composite act while another person commits the other necessary component. For example, if a collective entity promulgated a policy inciting crimes against humanity, and private individuals commit crimes as part of a widespread attack against a civilian population pursuant to that policy, would the collective entity be responsible for the resulting harm?[43] In the absence of agreed rules or principles

[40] Preparatory Commission for the International Criminal Court, *Elements of Crimes*, PCNICC/2000/1/Add.2, 9.

[41] As the ILC pointed out, 'While composite acts are made up of a series of actions or omissions defined in aggregate as wrongful, this does not exclude the possibility that every single act in the series could be wrongful in accordance with another obligation.' International Law Commission, 'Responsibility of State for Internationally Wrongful Acts (with Commentary)' (n 16) para 9 on article 15.

[42] *Case concerning Application of the Convention on the Prevention and Punishment of the Crime of Genocide (Bosnia and Herzegovina v Serbia and Montenegro)* (n 30) para 166. For some discussion on that finding, see Gaeta, 'On What Conditions can a State be Held Responsible for Genocide?' (2007) 18 European Journal of International Law 631–48.

[43] The present author is not aware of any pertinent practice or principles regarding this question.

on collective-entity responsibility under international law, no clear answer exists. One possible avenue to consider further could be collective-entity responsibility for aiding or assisting the commission of an international crime or wrongful act in analogy to article 16 ARSIWA. By promulgating a policy inciting international crimes by other actors, a collective entity would be aware of the wrongfulness of the incited act, the policy would certainly be 'given with a view to facilitating the commission of that act' and actually do so, and the incited acts would also be wrong if committed by the inciting entity itself.[44] It could even be argued that the inciting entity would not only be responsible for aiding or assisting but for the resulting crime or wrongful act as such because it would contribute 'a necessary element in the wrongful act in absence of which it could not have occurred'.[45]

[44] International Law Commission, 'Responsibility of State for Internationally Wrongful Acts (with Commentary)' (n 16) para 3 on article 16.
[45] ibid, at para 10 on article 16.

General Conclusion

When analysing violence in places such as Syria, Libya, Nigeria, Ukraine, or the Central African Republic, lawyers inevitably ask some of the following questions. Who are the actors involved? Which actors commit human rights violations? Does the situation amount to an armed conflict? Are international crimes being committed? Determining applicable law depends on a number of factors, one of which is the degree of organization and power of the non-state armed groups involved. Normally, these groups do not, from the outset, establish clear structures, train members, and subsequently engage in violence. Instead, their structures, abilities, and power change throughout their existence and in the course of a crisis. These complex realities pose important legal challenges; yet, the question of which aspects of an armed group's power and organization are legally relevant has not been subject to comprehensive legal research. Thus, the objective of this book has been to identify the degree of organization required from non-state armed groups (i) to become party to an armed conflict and thereby bound by applicable international humanitarian law (IHL); (ii) to have human rights obligations; or (iii) to commit international crimes or to create a context in which individuals commit them. While in practice determining such issues often involves significant factual or evidentiary challenges, any analysis requires a clear understanding of the legal framework.

Different Thresholds of Organization, Power, or Capacity as Identified in this Book

Part I of this book examined the degree of organization required from non-state armed groups to become party to a non-international armed conflict. It provided an analysis of the requisite degrees of organization to be eligible for recognition as belligerent, to become a party to a non-international armed conflict governed by article 3 common to the four Geneva Conventions and customary IHL, an 'organized armed group' as defined under Additional Protocol II, or a party to a conflict to which the ICC Statute applies. While the requisite degree of organization to reach these thresholds varies, three principal rationales for a strict organisational requirement exist:

- First, armed conflicts are different from situations in which groups of loosely connected individuals engage in isolated or sporadic armed violence alone

Organizing Rebellion: Non-State Armed Groups under International Humanitarian Law, Human Rights Law, and International Criminal Law. Tilman Rodenhäuser.
Published 2018 by Oxford University Press.

instead of under a group command. Thus, parties to armed conflicts must be *collective entities showing some form of vertical or horizontal command structure.*

- Second, armed conflicts are situations of intense violence in which two parties challenge each other militarily. Consequently, all conflicting parties need to have the *capacity to engage in sufficiently intense violence*, which requires manpower, logistics, and the ability to coordinate operations.
- Third, IHL provides an international legal framework designed to govern armed violence in situations in which national laws are often inadequate and rarely accepted by conflicting parties. In order to ensure that the IHL framework can be effective—and in accordance with the principle that parties to a conflict have equal rights and obligations under IHL—any party needs to *have command or disciplinary structures to implement at least basic humanitarian norms.*

These three rationales behind the organization criterion also define the minimum threshold of organization as required under Common Article 3, the ICC Statute, and customary law.

Part 2 analysed recent international practice regarding human rights violations committed by non-state armed groups. The main objective was to suggest a structured approach providing legal justifications, sources, and considerations on the scope of possible human rights obligations of non-state armed groups. The key justification of why human rights obligations for armed groups are needed is that human rights are individual rights, which are at present—if threatened by armed groups—inadequately protected under the traditional, state-centric international human rights protection system. The resulting systemic or structural need for human rights obligations of non-state armed groups, however, varies from context to context, and so do armed groups' capacities to respect, ensure, or fulfil human rights. This book suggests that the extent of possible human rights obligations of armed groups is best understood by analysing three different types of groups:

- First, if *groups exercise quasi-governmental authority in defined territory*, the de jure government is normally unable to protect or fulfil human rights of individuals living under its jurisdiction. In such cases, human rights mechanisms have demanded armed groups to respect and to ensure respect for a broad scope of human rights. Human rights obligations could bind this type of group either because the territorial state's obligations devolve to the new territorial authorities, or based on customary law.
- Second, if *groups exercise de facto control over territory and population*, the de jure government's ability to ensure and fulfil human rights is often severely restricted. While the nature and firmness of a group's territorial control, as well as its capacities, vary widely, human rights mechanisms increasingly call upon such groups to respect human rights. Indeed, any group exercising de facto control over territory and people should be expected to respect customary human rights law. In contrast, a possible obligation to ensure respect for human rights depends on the circumstances.

- Third, even if *groups do not control territory and population*, they may operate in situations in which the de jure government is unable to protect individuals. This includes situations of failed states, internal violence short of armed conflicts, or armed conflicts in which different groups use a power vacuum to pursue their own objectives. On some occasions, international mechanisms have called upon groups to respect peremptory human rights obligations. Indeed, human rights obligations qualifying as jus cogens might bind any armed group. Likewise, any group could be required to respect—meaning not to interfere with—customary human rights.

Part III engaged with the trend that, over recent decades, numerous international crimes have been committed not only by states but also by non-state armed groups. It recalls why state involvement is not a legal element of war crimes, crimes against humanity (CAH), or genocide. These crimes can be committed in contexts brought about by non-state entities. In exceptional cases, even isolated individuals might commit genocide. If collective-entity involvement is needed, this book finds that the requisite capacity of such collective entities should not be determined in the abstract but depending on the crimes' definition and on the circumstances. If the principal objectives of international criminal law (ICL) are to prosecute unimaginable atrocities that harm humanity, threaten fundamental international values, and are likely to go unpunished, no acts should be a priori excluded if, factually, they resemble an international crime.

Accordingly, *war crimes* can be committed by anyone during armed conflicts; however, the existance of an armed conflict requires at least two sufficiently organized parties, as examined in Part I of this book. Under the Rome Statute of the International Criminal Court (ICC Statute) and, arguably, customary law, *crimes against humanity* must be committed pursuant to or in furtherance of a state or organizational policy. At least three broad possibilities exist as to how such policy relates to the underlying acts, which suggest three different capacities of the organization behind the policy:

- First, the entity might encourage the attack on a civilian population by deliberately abstaining from action. While consciously abstaining from action does not require much, in order to thereby encourage CAH the abstaining entity would need to be a state or a non-state armed group otherwise obliged and able to protect the targeted population.
- Second, an entity might actively promote or encourage an attack against a civilian population without being directly involved in the commission of the underlying criminal acts. While this possibility has not yet come up in case law, theoretically it merely requires the organization to be able to instigate the crimes, meaning to initiate and guide crimes committed by individuals or groups not formally linked to the entity behind the policy.
- Third, the entity behind the policy could also implement the attack against a civilian population by organizing or directing crimes primarily committed by persons operating under its control. This has been the common case in

> jurisprudence. In such cases, the group needs sufficient capacities to implement the policy, which normally includes the means to commit large-scale crimes and an internal structure to target the crimes against a victim population.

Strictly speaking, the crime of *genocide* does not require any collective entity involvement. Yet, states emphasized in the International Criminal Court's (ICC's) *Elements of Crimes* that acts of genocide normally take place 'in the context of a manifest pattern of similar conduct'. There are at least two ways in which a non-state entity can bring about a manifest genocidal pattern: the entity may either instigate genocide committed by individuals or independent militias, or the entity may direct and implement the campaign through its own personnel and means. As in the case of CAH, the former possibility would require fewer capacities, the latter significantly more.

Comparing the Different Thresholds

As these results show, international law does not contain one single threshold of organization for non-state armed groups to become a 'subject of international law' or an 'international legal person' vested with a fixed set of international rights and obligations. Instead, the question of whether and to what extent non-state entities have international obligations or sufficient capacity to commit international crimes depends on the specificities of the field of law in question. Having obligations under one field of law, or being able to commit one sort of international crime, or to create a context in which individuals can commit such crime, does not necessarily mean that a group will also bear obligations in another field of law. Whether a non-state armed group becomes an entity that is legally relevant in different fields of law depends on whether it meets requisite thresholds explicitly or implicitly defined in the respective field with regard to a specific set of obligations, or the commission of a specific crime.

The following two tables illustrate this book's main conclusions and facilitate comparison of the identified thresholds.

Table 1 provides a list of thresholds for armed groups under IHL, international human rights law (IHRL), and ICL, and the requisite degree of organization. In order to facilitate comparison, the degree of organization is divided into four sub-categories, namely territorial control; governance infrastructure; military capacity; and internal structure/discipline. As shall be seen, not all sub-categories apply to all thresholds. For example, for the question of whether a group should have human rights obligations, its military capacity is not essential. Yet, if a group controls territory, in most cases it can be assumed that it conquered this territory by use of force and therefore possesses some military capacity.[1]

[1] Yet, this is not strictly required. A political group de facto governing certain territory, eg, can also have international human rights law (IHRL) obligations without possessing military capacity. The territory could be defended by militia not belonging to but supporting the political group. At the same time, this does not need to mean that the group is party to an armed conflict. See examples in Murray, 'Author's Response: Human Rights Obligations of Non-State Armed Groups' (EJIL: *Talk!*, 7 November 2016) <http://www.ejiltalk.org/book-discussion-human-rights-obligations-of-non-state-armed-groups-authors-response/> accessed 15 November 2017.

Table 2 illustrates how different degrees of organization correspond to different sets of obligations or capacities. Dark shading and a '+' indicates that the listed group has—or should have—certain obligations or capacities, while lighter shading and a '-' means it does not. 'N/A' indicates that a key piece of information is missing—for example, whether a group operates under a 'responsible command' or has military capacities. Table 2 is based on the assumption that groups able to control or govern territory also possess sufficient military capacity to defend it in an armed conflict. Thus, Table 2 is only indicative. Examinations of which obligations and capacities are pertinent in a given situation need to be done on a case-by-case basis.

Table 1 Overview of thresholds of organization of armed groups

Threshold	Required degree of organization/capacity			
	Territorial control	*Governance infrastructure*	*Military capacity*	*Internal structure/ discipline*
International humanitarian law				
Recognition of belligerency	Territorial control	Quasi-governmental capacities	Organized armed forces	Ability to implement IHL of IACs
'Organized armed group' as defined in APII	Territorial control	None	Ability to carry out sustained and concerted military operations	Ability to implement APII
Party to a NIAC	None	None	Ability to engage in sufficiently intense hostilities	Ability to ensure respect for basic IHL
International human rights law				
Group exercising quasi-governmental authority	Exclusive control over territory and population	Quasi-governmental capacities; ability to protect/fulfil IHRL	N/A; presumably like a party to a NIAC	Ability to respect IHRL
Group exercising de facto territorial control	Control over territory and population	None/possibly ability to protect/ fulfil IHRL	N/A; presumably like a party to a NIAC	Ability to respect IHRL
Group without territorial control	Operating beyond effective government control	None	N/A	Ability to respect applicable IHRL norms
International criminal law				
Party to an armed conflict	None	None	Ability to engage in sufficiently intense hostilities	Ability to ensure respect for basic IHL
Group able to tolerate crimes against humanity	Control over territory and population	Quasi-governmental capacities; ability to protect IHRL	N/A; Presumably like a party to a NIAC	Ability to respect IHRL
Group able to commit crimes against humanity	None	None	Sufficient means to commit large-scale crimes	Sufficient structure to implement a policy
Group able to instigate crimes against humanity	None	Ability to develop and promote a policy instigating crimes by others	N/A	None
Group able to commit genocide	None	None	Sufficient means to commit large-scale crimes	Sufficient structure to implement a genocidal plan/policy
Group able to instigate genocide	None	Ability to develop and promote a plan/ policy instigating crimes by others	N/A	None

Table 2 Possible obligations of armed groups according to their degrees of organization/capacity

Obligations/ability — threshold/degree of organization	Possible obligations in international law: Customary IHL of IAC	APII/customary IHL of NIAC	CA3/customary IHL of NIAC	Respect, protect, fulfil IHRL	Respect/protect customary IHRL	Respect IHRL/jus cogens norms	Ability to . . . Create a war crimes context	Tolerate CAH	Commit CAH	Instigate CAH	Commit genocide	Instigate genocide
a. Armed group . . . (IHL)												
Recognized as belligerent	+	+	+	+	+	+	+	+	+	+	+	+
Party to an APII NIAC	-	+	+	N/A	+	+	+	N/A	+	+	+	+
Party to a NIAC	–	–	+	–	–	+	+	–	+	+	+	+
b. Armed group exercising . . . (IHRL)												
Quasi-governmental authority	+	+	+	+	+	+	+	+	+	+	+	+
De facto territorial control	–	N/A	+	–	+	+	+	N/A	+	+	+	+
No territorial control	–	–	N/A	–	–	+	N/A	–	N/A	+	N/A	+
c. Armed group able to . . . (ICL)												
Create a context in which war crimes can be committed	–	–	+	–	–	+	+	–	+	+	+	+
Tolerate CAH	+	+	+	+	+	+	+	+	+	+	+	+
Commit CAH	–	N/A	+	–	N/A	+	+	–	+	+	+	+
Instigate CAH	–	–	–	–	–	+	–	–	-	+	-	+
Commit genocide	–	N/A	+	–	N/A	+	+	–	+	+	+	+
Instigate genocide	–	–	–	–	–	+	–	–	-	+	-	+

Comparing the different thresholds, it appears that non-state armed groups exercising territorial control and quasi-governmental authority have a comparatively high degree of legal personality: they can become party to a non-international armed conflict (NIAC) governed by different sets of rules; should be required to respect, protect, and fulfil a broad range of human rights obligations; and with their involvement different international crimes can be committed. Likewise, if an armed group exercises de facto territorial control—which normally happens by violently ousting the de jure government—the group is likely to have sufficient capacity to be party to a NIAC governed by Common Article 3, and possibly by Additional Protocol II (APII). Moreover, it should at least respect human rights of persons under its de facto control, and will normally have the capacity to instigate or commit different international crimes.

Beyond these two broad types of armed groups, situations become more complex. For example, an armed group sufficiently organized to become party to an armed conflict but not controlling territory and population might only have limited human rights obligations, if at all; yet, it normally has the capacity to instigate or commit international crimes. In contrast, an armed group without territorial control but arguably bound to respect customary human rights obligations might not be able to engage in intense military violence, or commit large-scale crimes. It would not be sufficiently organized, therefore, to become party to an armed conflict, to create a context in which war crimes can be committed, and it cannot be determined in the abstract whether such groups have sufficient capacity to commit, through their own forces, most crimes against humanity, or genocide. While an armed group with sufficient manpower and logistics to commit large-scale crimes is likely to be sufficiently organized to become party to an armed conflict and should be obliged to respect basic human rights, groups merely able to instigate but not to commit international crimes are unlikely to have a sufficient degree of organization to be party to an armed conflict.

A key finding of this book is that international law applies, or should apply—to varying degrees—to a variety of non-state entities. Beyond the basic requirement that a collective entity needs to be distinct from its members and have some form of command structure, international law does not require generic characteristics—such as territorial control or governance structures—to qualify an armed group as relevant or not. Instead, whether and to what extent a specific group has international legal personality in the sense that the group is a social entity 'relevant to the international legal system'[2] depends on the exigencies of the legal field in question. This book has shown that different kinds of non-state armed groups have, or should have, different international legal obligations and can be involved in different international crimes. The basic determinant for assessing whether or not a group is relevant under a certain field of law is whether it has a sufficient degree of organization, power, or capacity to fall under the field's scope of application.

[2] Portmann, *Legal Personality in International Law* (CUP 2010) 1.

Non-State Entities other than Armed Groups

In line with the above conclusions, in principle any collective non-state entity might be considered legally relevant under different fields of law if it meets the requisite threshold of application—including the required degree of organization—as defined in that field. The criteria identified in this study should not only be relevant to what is ordinarily considered a non-state armed group but to a broader range of actors. Under international law, it is not essential which status a non-state entity has under national law, which purpose it pursues, or what it calls itself.[3] They can be corporations, non-governmental organizations (NGOs), faith-based associations, or 'terrorist' groups. What matters is whether a non-state entity meets the legal criteria to become party to an armed conflict, to invite possible human rights obligations, or to create a context in which international crimes can be committed.

Legally speaking, there is no reason why any type of non-state entity could not become party to an armed conflict if, in fact, it is sufficiently organized as required under IHL and engages in sufficiently intense armed violence with an adversary. For example, it is neither convincing nor supported by state practice to suggest that the criteria determining the applicability of international humanitarian law to multinational forces, such as UN peacekeeping forces, would be substantially different from any other conflict situations because UN peacekeeping forces normally act on behalf of the international community.[4] The applicability of international humanitarian law does not depend on the legitimacy or illegitimacy of the use of force by a party to an armed conflict, nor on a group's name or on it status under national law. The only relevant criteria are those established in international law and practice.

Likewise, different non-state entities can be implicated in international crimes. Pertinent documents, such as the ICC Statute, do not exclude non-state actors from being relevant entities in the context of international crimes. Any non-state entity that is sufficiently organized to become party to a NIAC is necessarily also sufficiently organized to create a context in which war crimes can be committed. Likewise, as argued in this book, a variety of societal actors might have sufficient capabilities to instigate violence amounting to CAH. Apparently following the same assumption, the 2016 International Law Commission's (ILC) draft articles on crimes against humanity contain the requirement that 'each State shall take measures, where appropriate, to establish the liability of legal persons' for crimes against humanity.[5] Following an analysis of the national law of different states, the ILC argues that criminal liability for legal persons 'is typically imposed when the offence at issue was

[3] With regard to the applicability of international humanitarian law, this point was emphasized in International Committee of the Red Cross (ICRC), *International Humanitarian Law and the Challenges of Contemporary Armed Conflicts*, 'Challenges Report (2011)' (ICRC 2011) 11–12.

[4] For a discussion of different views on this subject, see Ferraro, 'The Applicability and Application of International Humanitarian Law to Multinational Forces' (2013) 95 International Review of the Red Cross 563–568.

[5] See United Nations General Assembly (UNGA), *Report of the International Law Commission*, 18 August 2016, A/71/10, 248 (article 5(7)).

committed by a natural person on behalf of or for the benefit of the legal person'.[6] Thus, the draft articles support the conclusions that a legal person as defined in national law—which certainly includes companies or NGOs—might constitute an entity behind CAH. It is indeed not very difficult to imagine a company hiring a militia to commit widespread or systematic attacks against a civilian population pursuant to a company policy. Likewise, a private security company might be responsible for CAH, for example if it operates under a policy instigating interrogation methods that amount to torture, which is systematically used against a civilian population.

Contrary to the fields of IHL and ICL, not all circumstances in which the analysis and arguments presented in this book would justify human rights obligations for armed groups are also pertinent for business enterprises or other non-state entities. For example, business enterprises are unlikely to exercise quasi-governmental authority in defined territory, or control over territory and population, without some form of agreement by the territorial state. If private entities exercise such control, in many circumstances their conduct would be attributable to a state.[7] Thus, the argument that in these situations there is a systemic need for direct human rights obligations for non-state entities because the state can no longer effectively protect human rights does not easily apply to business enterprises. Likewise, while a number of very powerful corporations exist, they may not operate beyond state control or have a degree of power justifying imposing rather broad human rights obligations as suggested for armed groups with control over territory and population.

In contrast, the rationale of the argument that any non-state actor operating beyond effective state control should at least respect basic human rights can resonate to situations involving business companies or other non-state organizations. If the territorial state is unable to prevent or to effectively address human rights violations committed by non-state entities, they should be subjected to elementary human rights obligations. A case in point would be private military and security companies. These companies provide services which easily affect human rights, such as the right to life or the rights to liberty and humane treatment. They are also actors which certainly have a sufficient degree of internal structure and organization to respect fundamental human rights. Moreover, they often operate in complex environments where state authorities are unable to provide security and to effectively regulate companies.[8] As a result, following the arguments developed in this book, such actors can and should be required to respect basic human rights obligations.

[6] ibid, at para 37 on article 5. Yet, the ILC's commentary is, admittedly, not entirely conclusive on whether or not legal persons can commit CAH without the involvement of any other entity. At some point in the commentary it states, 'The Commission decided to include a provision on liability of legal persons for crimes against humanity, given the potential involvement of legal persons in acts committed as part of a widespread or systematic attack directed against a civilian population.' ibid. This statement could also be read as assuming that legal persons might only participate in, but not be at the origin of, CAH.

[7] eg, if companies exercise 'elements of governmental authority' or carry out action 'in the absence or default of the official authorities', their conduct would be attributable to the territorial state. See articles 5 and 9 of the Articles on the Responsibility of States for Internationally Wrongful Acts (ARSIWA).

[8] This is why, eg, the International Code of Conduct for Private Security Service Provisers provides a set of human-rights based rules for companies operating in so-called complex environments.

The arguments and conclusions developed in this book to justify human rights obligations of non-state actors are somewhat narrower than some of the approaches taken in the broader field of business and human rights. For example, the UN *Guiding Principles on Business and Human Rights for implementing the UN 'Protect, Respect and Remedy' Framework* state that 'the responsibility to respect human rights is a global standard of expected conduct for all business enterprises wherever they operate. It exists independently of States' abilities and/or willingness to fulfill their own human rights obligations, and does not diminish those obligations.'[9] Thus, contrary to this book the UN *Guiding Principles* advance that any business enterprise has certain responsibilities—not obligations—irrespective of the context in which they operate. These principles have been advanced to complement states' legal obligation to protect human rights. They are based on the finding that 'enterprises can affect the human rights of their employees, their customers, workers in their supply chains or communities around their operations' and the conclusion that therefore they should have certain international human rights responsibilities.[10] Indeed, strong policy arguments may exist to call for the development of new regulatory framework for business enterprises or transnational corporations. While the legal analysis presented in this book does not affect such calls, it can complement policy arguments by showing that at a minimum, certain circumstances should invite elementary human rights obligations for any non-state entity.

Quo Vadis? Possible Next Steps in Addressing Non-State Armed Groups through Different Fields of International Law

Debates on whether and to what extent different fields of international law apply to non-state armed groups are likely to continue. In light of the sensitivity of the legal and political issues involved in the wider 'armed groups' discussion, it is difficult to predict how the law will develop in the coming years. Nonetheless, the comparative analysis developed in this book enables us to identify not only differences between how the three fields of law under examination address armed groups, but also certain commonalities. IHL, IHRL, and ICL are all part of public international law, which historically addressed, and still focuses primarily on, sovereign states. Accordingly, the laws of war originally applied to states only, most human rights treaties contain obligations for states only, and at the outset, ICL addressed only crimes committed by or with important involvement of states. Examining how these fields of law have been opening up to also address non-state armed groups shows certain patterns that could provide hints on possible next steps in these developments. Indeed, three broad stages can be observed of how international law has developed, and continues

[9] Office of the United Nations High Commissioner for Human Rights (OHCHR), *Guiding Principles on Business and Human Rights: Implementing the United Nations 'Respect, Protect, and Remedy' Framework* (OHCHR 2011), 13.

[10] OHCHR, *The Corporate Responsibility to Respect Human Rights: An Interpretive Guidance* (OHCHR 2011) 10–11.

to develop, from a states-only focus towards increasingly addressing different types of non-state armed groups.

At the first stage of the process, the formerly exclusively state-focused law opens up to address 'state-like' entities. Under IHL, this development is evident in the concept of recognition of belligerency: while the laws of war traditionally applied to wars between states, under the concept of recognition of belligerency, it became applicable to civil wars if a number of conditions were met, including that the non-state party disposed of political and military capacities akin to those of states.[11] Likewise, while in the aftermath of World War II ICL cases addressed crimes committed or condoned by states, this practice changed with the prosecution of crimes committed by entities with quasi-governmental abilities in the former Yugoslavia, such as the Republika Srpska. Professor Kress refers to this change as a shift from the first to the 'second generation of international criminal law'.[12] Likewise, in the field of human rights law, some of the earlier references to obligations of armed groups are found in documents addressing entities with quasi-governmental authority, such as the Hamas in Gaza or the Hezbollah in Lebanon.[13]

This development should not be surprising. If non-state entities factually resemble states, the pragmatic step of applying existing international law to these entities is not a very big one. With regard to human rights law, it is widely agreed that addressing human rights obligations to such entities reflects the 'spirit of both the conceptual scope of human rights and the rationale behind the international law approach to them'.[14] In a way, applying international law to entities with quasi-governmental authority addresses a factual situation in which such obligations are needed while avoiding the often politically sensitive issue of whether a particular entity represents a state under international law. At this first stage, state-like armed groups invite obligations, or can be recognized as having capacities, akin to those of states.[15]

While during the first stage international law addresses a broad set of obligations to a narrowly defined set of actors, it seems that at the second stage of opening different fields of international law to non-state armed groups, a narrower scope of obligations is applied to a broader scope of actors. This is most obviously the case regarding Common Article 3 of the four Geneva Conventions: in 1949, states

[11] See analysis in Section 1.3 'A State-Like Non-State Entity? Recognition of Belligerency' above.

[12] Kress, 'On the Outer Limits of Crimes against Humanity: The Concept of Organization within the Policy Requirement: Some Reflections on the March 2010 ICC Kenya Decision' (2010) 23 Leiden Journal of International Law 873.

[13] See, eg, Human Rights Council, *Mission to Lebanon and Israel (Report of different Special Rapporteurs)*, A/HRC/2/7, para 19; Human Rights Council, *Human Rights Situation in Palestine and other Occupied Arab Territories*, A/HRC/10/22, para 22.

[14] Rodley, 'Can Armed Opposition Groups Violate Human Rights?' in Mahoney and Mahoney (eds), *Human Rights in the Twenty-First Century: A Global Challenge* (M Nijhoff 1993) 313. See also Murray, *Human Rights Obligations of Non-State Armed Groups* (Hart 2016) chapter 5, in particular at 151; Kleffner, 'The Applicability of the Law of Armed Conflict and Human Rights Law to Organized Armed Groups' in Kleffner and De Wet (eds), *Convergence and Conflicts of Human Rights and International Humanitarian Law in Military Operations* (Pretoria University Law Press 2014) 57.

[15] Recognition of belligerency would bring customary IHL of international armed conflicts into application, and under international criminal law a state-like entity is likely to have the capacity to commit, instigate, or encourage crimes by omission. If Murray's effective control test was to be applied, these groups would also obtain human rights treaty obligations. Murray, *Non-State Armed Groups* (n 14) chapter 5.

agreed that instead of applying the four Conventions to narrowly defined state-like non-state actors, certain very basic rules should apply to a barely defined set of parties to NIACs. As seen in Chapter 2 'Parties to Non-International Armed Conflicts under International Treaty Law', the requisite degree of organization required for a group to have obligations under Common Article 3 is fairly low and far from requiring state-like political and military structures.

Tendencies leading in the same direction can be identified in international jurisprudence and expert reports regarding ICL and human rights law. For example, CAH jurisprudence at the International Criminal Tribunal for the former Yugoslavia (ICTY), the Special Court for Sierra Leone (SCSL), and notably the ICC not only recognized that a policy behind these crimes can be adopted and implemented by 'groups of persons who govern a specific territory', but also that such a policy could emanate from 'any organisation with the capability to commit a widespread or systematic attack against a civilian population'.[16] In the latter case, the scope of entities behind a policy is certainly broader than the narrow group of non-state entities with quasi-governmental authority. At the same time, this broader array of groups might only commit certain types of CAH through their own forces. For example, they do not have the capacity to encourage CAH thought deliberate inaction, or to commit CAH in the form of acts of apartheid.

While in the field of human rights law relevant treaty law and jurisprudence are largely absent, other recent international practice also shows a trend of broadening the scope of human rights addressees while at the same time limiting possible obligations. For example, at a very early stage of the Syria crisis, a UN commission of inquiry first held that all armed groups have to respect peremptory human rights norms, while shortly after asserting that armed groups have to 'respect the fundamental human rights of persons forming customary international law (CIL), in areas in which such actors exercise *de facto* control'.[17] As discussed in Chapter 6 'A Three-Pronged Approach to Human Rights Obligations of Non-State Armed Groups' above, the UN Security Council, the Human Rights Council, and notably different UN experts increasingly address an undefined—but probably rather narrow—set of fundamental human rights to a broad scope of armed groups exercising varying degrees of control over territory and population.

As a result of these developments, on the one hand highly organized armed groups invite a broad scope of obligations and can be involved in the commission of different international crimes. On the other hand, a broad variety of armed groups is subject to rather basic obligations and might be able to commit certain acts of violence amounting to international crimes. Following the analysis and arguments presented in this book, the next stage in addressing armed groups under different fields of international law would be to align the scope of obligations, or the legal

[16] *Katanga and Chui, Decision on the confirmation of charges, 30 September 2008, ICC-01/04–01/07*, ICC, para 396; for further references, see *Gbagbo, Decision on the confirmation of charges, 12 June 2014, ICC-02/11–01/11*, ICC, para 217.

[17] Human Rights Council, *Report of the Independent International Commission of Inquiry on the Syrian Arab Republic*, A/HRC/21/50, annex II, para 10. For further practice, see Sections 6.4 'Human Rights Obligations of Groups Exercising De Facto Control over Territory and Population' and 6.5 'Human Rights Obligations of Groups Not Controlling Territory and Population' above.

personality of groups, to their degree of organization, power, or capacity. To some extent, this approach was taken when negotiating Additional Protocol II to the four Geneva Conventions. While this treaty broadened the scope of applicable norms as compared to Common Article 3, it narrowed the scope of armed groups that might be bound by these rules to those that are sufficiently organized to implement the Protocol's obligations.[18] In the view of the International Committee of the Red Cross (ICRC), this approach reflected 'a degree of realism'.[19] Such an approach has also received some support in more recent reflections among government experts on the question of how to strengthen IHL protecting persons deprived of their liberty. In order to account for the 'diversity of capabilities and organization among various non-State parties to NIACs', there was reportedly 'a general trend' among experts 'in favor of baseline standards plus additional protections that should be implemented to the extent that a particular group is capable of doing so'.[20]

As this book proposes, a nuanced approach towards international obligations of armed groups is not only implicit in recent practice in the field of human rights, but it should also be the avenue that courts pursue with regard to international crimes. As argued in Part III of the book, the ICC Statute and its *Elements of Crimes* suggest that armed groups' possible involvement in international crimes depends on their capacities: while instigating CAH or genocide might require rather minimal capacities, committing such crimes through a group's own forces requires more sophisticated structures and abilities. Going one step further, it appears that only groups with quasi-governmental capacities can also encourage CAH through a deliberate failure to take action. Likewise, in Part II this book suggested a three-pronged approach to determine to what extent human rights law should address armed groups. It was shown that the scope of possible human rights obligations of armed groups should depend on the degree of organization and power of the armed groups in question. This approach would take duly into account both the different contexts in which armed groups operate and the great differences between armed groups' capacities. It has also been suggested that the approach of tailoring the scope of obligations to the capacity of armed groups—and thereby not treating them akin to states—'might ease States' worries about the process of NGOs [or UN actors] engaging with them on human rights obligations'.[21]

Pursuing such a nuanced approach might appear complex at first sight, and it reflects a lawyer's desire to legally address complex realities in a nuanced manner. However, the suggested approach would also be pragmatic in practice. Under the proposed model, basic human rights obligations would apply from a very low threshold onwards and would complement states' human rights obligations. They would provide elementary protections even at a stage when a situation has not escalated into an armed conflict, or if the classification of a situation as an

[18] See Section 2.2 'Raising the Bar? 'Organized Armed Groups' under Additional Protocol II'.

[19] Pilloud, Sandoz, Swinarski et al, *Commentary on the Additional Protocols of 8 June 1977 to the Geneva Convention of 12 August 1949* (ICRC 1987) para 4470.

[20] ICRC, *Thematic Consultation of Government Experts on Grounds and Procedures for Internment and Detainee Transfers* (ICRC 2015) 56.

[21] Geneva Call, *Positive Obligations of Armed Non-State Actors: Legal and Policy Issues—Report from the 2015 Garance Talks* (Geneva Call 2016) 10.

armed conflict is disputed. Additional obligations would become applicable in layers, corresponding with increasing degrees of power and capacity of an armed group: once an armed group is sufficiently organized to become party to an armed conflict and factually engages in sufficiently intense violence, IHL starts applying. Thus, Common Article 3 and customary IHL would add a layer of protection and responsibility. Subsequently, if non-state entities conquer territory and start controlling populations, APII may become applicable and binding on all parties to the conflict. At the same time, positively correlated to the amount of control over territory and populations a group exercises, it would also be required to respect, and at some point to also protect, human rights of populations under their control. Finally, while under international humanitarian law it is unlikely that a state will recognize belligerency and thereby render the customary laws of international armed conflict applicable, if a group firmly establishes itself as the authority governing a defined and stable part of a state's territory, it should be bound to respect, protect, and fulfil human rights. At the different stages of that development, members of armed groups could also be prosecuted for crimes that their groups instigate, commit, or tolerate.

In a time in which numerous states are involved in armed conflicts and the international discourse seems dominated by a narrative that all too easily depicts non-state armed groups as terrorists, it is unlikely that states will conclude further treaties or soft law instruments directly addressing armed groups. Thus, a variety of state and non-state actors will continue to apply, interpret, and thereby shape existing written and unwritten norms. In this environment, different push-and-pull factors may affect various actors' legal interpretations of the fields of law examined in this book. The state on whose territory a group is operating, a third state with an interest in fighting an armed group abroad, a humanitarian orgnization, a human rights expert, a tribunal, or even academics each have their own policy consideration affecting their reading of the law. In this pushing and pulling based on different backgrounds and interests, there might not always be space for deep conceptual reflections. Yet, in-depth and practice-oriented legal research and analysis is strongly needed to maintain and strengthen the international legal system.

Closing Remarks

Lack of clarity on how contemporary IHL, IHRL, and ICL regulate today's reality in which different types of non-state entities engage in human rights violations, armed conflicts, and international crimes triggered the idea of writing this book. This challenge also defined the book's overarching objectives: as an academic study, it analyses theoretical challenges of applying 'the law of nations' to non-state entities, aimes to provide new insights, and hopes to prompt further studies.[22] At the same time, this book was inspired by practice and shall be useful for practitioners. Thus, it aims to clarify legal concepts, conceptualize complex reality, and present different ways in

[22] eg, in the field of international obligations of armed groups, further studies are needed on such questions as how to attribute individual conduct to armed groups, or how principles on international responsibility apply to non-state entities.

which existing law can be interpreted. Throughout the research and writing process, my motivation was to explore the outer limits of the three fields of law, to push intellectual boundaries, and to present results in an accessible and practice-oriented manner.

Focusing on the limits of how far existing law encompasses non-state armed groups, this book—admittedly—set key parameters accordingly: it rejected the idea that an abstract and undefined 'international legal personality' needs to exist before international law could possibly address armed groups; it dismissed the idea that identifying non-state parties to armed conflicts is best done by comparing these groups to states; it looked at human rights as individual entitlements in need of international protection irrespective of whether they are violated by states or non-state entities; and it examined definitions of international crimes according to their wording, object and purpose, and in their context, without giving too much weight to the crimes' early history. All of these decisions can be challenged, yet none of them lacks support among key authorities that apply international law, such as the International Court of Justice, the ICC, different UN organs or institutions, or the ICRC. In fact, the parameters chosen for this book seem essential in order not to shield international law from changing realities and put it in danger of becoming irrelevant.

Changing interpretations and new concepts necessarily provoke counter-arguments, both in terms of substance and regarding their real-world impact. For example, interpreting IHRL as addressing a broad scope of non-state entities could be opposed by arguing that this might multiply the number of cases before human rights institutions and thereby overwhelm an already burdened enforcement system.[23] Similar concerns have been raised with regard to ICL.[24] Relatedly, it can be argued that addressing a broader scope of armed groups is somewhat fruitless if not accompanied by institutional arrangements and methods designed to address these actors effectively.[25] No doubt, such concerns are valid. However, institutional considerations should not determine the interpretation of legal texts but should be addressed by, for example, jurisdictional clauses.[26] The scope of non-state armed groups addressed by different fields of international law is not only relevant for institutions such as the ICC or regional human rights tribunals but also for national courts, as well as for a variety of inter-governmental and NGOs.[27]

[23] See, eg, Inter-American Commission on Human Rights, *Inter-American Yearbook on Human Rights* (M Nijhoff 1990) 360.

[24] See, eg, *Situation in the Republic of Kenya (Dissent Kaul), ICC-01/09*, para 10.

[25] eg, when considering how the UN human rights protection system could address armed groups' human rights violations, Rodley asked, '[A]fter all, to what office or official would the *notes verbales* containing urgent appeals or the allegations of violations be sent? At what address?' Rodley, 'Non-State Actors and Human Rights' in Sheeran and Rodley (eds), *Routledge Handbook of International Human Rights Law* (Routledge 2013) 535.

[26] See, eg, article 17 ICC Statute.

[27] With regard to international criminal law, see also Robinson, 'The Draft Convention on Crimes against Humanity: What to Do with the Definition?' in Bergsmo and Song (eds), *On the Draft Crimes against Humanity Convention* (Torkel-Opsahl Academic EPublisher 2014) 103–33. With regard to human rights law, one example of how non-state entities' human rights obligations could be important before national tribunals is the United States 'Alien Tort Statute', under which only acts 'in violation of the law of nations' can be adjudicated. For further discussion, see Clapham, 'Focussing on Armed Non-State Actors' in Clapham and Gaeta (eds), *The Oxford Handbook of International Law in Armed Conflict* (OUP 2014) 531–49.

If interpretations of international law adjust in order to address increasingly complex realities, necessary changes in implementation or enforcement mechanisms can develop accordingly, depending on political will and innovative ideas. For example, at the request of the UN Security Council, the Secretary General has developed a system to engage armed groups to respect elementary rights of children;[28] the UN Security Council has targeted sanctions at individuals and groups 'involved in planning, directing, or committing acts that violate international human rights law or international humanitarian law';[29] a number of special sessions of the Human Rights Council was called to discuss human rights violations by armed groups; the NGO Geneva Call has developed an approach to engage armed groups to sign declarations to respect basic humanitarian and human rights norms;[30] and scholars have suggested establishing a world court of human rights to address violations by state and non-state actors.[31] These examples show that if the international community recognizes the need to address non-state actors, it will also find means and methods to solve the challenge.

IHL, human rights law, and ICL address different types of non-state armed groups to different degrees. New legal instruments are not necessarily required: at least existing IHL and ICL apply comprehensively to violence involving non-state entities. However, more clarity regarding human rights obligations of armed groups is needed to address today's reality effectively. Human rights obligations should complement the state-centred international human rights protection framework. Given that most existing human rights instruments only provide state obligations, however, a treaty or an unambiguous state declaration clarifying to what extent human rights law binds armed groups would be helpful. Yet, prospects for further state agreement on politically sensitive issues, such as international legal obligations of armed groups, are rather low. Thus, it will likely be up to researchers, legal advisers, and judges to analyse contemporary practice and identify in which direction the law develops. The present book is designed to contribute to this process by providing a thorough analysis of contemporary international law and practice.

[28] See discussion in Section 6.5.2 'Contemporary international practice'.

[29] UN Security Council, Resolution 2134 (2014), S/RES/2134 (2014), para 37.

[30] See <www.genevacall.org> accessed 15 November 2017. For some discussion on Geneva Call's approach to engaging armed groups, see Somer and Bongard, 'Monitoring Armed Non-State Actor Compliance with Humanitarian Norms: A Look at International Mechanisms and the Geneva Call Deed of Commitment' (2011) 93 International Review of the Red Cross 673–706.

[31] See, eg, Nowak and Kozma, *A World Court of Human Rights* (2009) <http://www.udhr60.ch> accessed 2 November 2017; Clapham, 'Overseeing Human Rights Compliance' in Cassese (ed), *Realizing Utopia: The Future of International Law* (OUP 2012) 318–25.

Bibliography

Abi-Saab, G, 'Non-International Armed Conflicts' in UNESCO and Institut Henry-Dunant (eds), *International Dimensions of Humanitarian Law* (M Nijhoff 1988) 217–39.

Addis, CL and CM Blanchard, *Hezbollah: Background and Issues for Congress* (Congressional Research Center 2011).

African Union, 'Explanatory Note on the African Union Convention for the Protection and Assistance of Internally Displaced Persons in Africa' (African Union 2009).

Akande, D, 'Classification of Armed Conflicts: Relevant Legal Concepts' in E Wilmshurst (ed), *International Law and the Classification of Conflicts* (OUP 2012) 32–80.

Akhavan, P, *Reducing Genocide to Law: Definition, Meaning, and the Ultimate Crime* (CUP 2012).

Alston, P, 'The "Not-a-Cat" Syndrome: Can the International Human Rights Regime Accommodate Non-State Actors?' in P Alston (ed), *Non-State Actors and Human Rights* (OUP 2005) 3–36.

Alston, P, J Morgan-Foster, and W Abresch, 'The Competence of the UN Human Rights Council and its Special Procedures in Relation to Armed Conflicts: Extrajudicial Executions in the "War on Terror"' (2008) 19 European Journal of International Law 183–209.

Altman, A, 'The Persistent Fiction of Harm to Humanity' (2006) 20 Ethics & International Affairs 367–72.

Altman, A and CH Wellman, 'A Defense of International Criminal Law' (2004) 115 Ethics 35–67.

Ambos, K, 'Command Responsibility and Organsationsherrschaft: Ways of Attributing International Crimes to the "Most Responsible"' in H v d Wilt and A Nollkaemper (eds), *System Criminality in International Law* (CUP 2009) 127–57.

Ambos, K, 'What does "Intent to Destroy" in Genocide Mean?' (2009) 91 International Review of the Red Cross 833–58.

Ambos, K, 'Crimes against Humanity and the International Criminal Court' in LN Sadat (ed), *Forging a Convention for Crimes against Humanity* (CUP 2011) 279–304.

Ambos, K, *Treatise on International Criminal Law* (OUP 2013).

Ambos, K and J Alkatout, 'Has "Justice Been Done"? The Legality of Bin Laden's Killing Under International Law' (2012) 45 Israel Law Review 341–66.

Ambos, K and S Wirth, 'The Current Law of Crimes against Humanity: An Analysis of UNTAET Regulation 152000' (2002) 13 Criminal Law Forum 1–90.

Amnesty International, *'The Hands of Cruelty': Abuses by Armed Forces and Taliban in Pakistan's Tribal Areas* (Amnesty International 2012).

Andreopoulos, GJ, 'On the Accountability of Non-State Armed Groups' in GJ Andreopoulos, P Juviler, and ZF Kabasakal Arat (eds), *Non-State Actors in the Human Rights Universe* (Kumarian Press 2006) 141–63.

Aquinas, T, *The Summa Theologica* (translated by Fathers of the English Dominican Province, 2nd edn, Christian Classics 1265–74).

Arendt, H, *Eichmann in Jerusalem: A Report on the Banality of Evil* (revised and enlarged edn, Penguin Books 1994).

Arimatsu, L and M Choudhury, *The Legal Classification of the Armed Conflicts in Syria, Yemen and Libya* (Chatham House 2014).

Arnold, R, *The ICC as a New Instrument for Repressing Terrorism* (Ardsley: Transnational Publishers 2004).

Ayala, B, *De Jure et Officiis Bellicis et Disciplina Militari Libri III* (translated by Carnegie Institution, Carnegie Institution of Washington 1548–84).

Badar, ME, 'From the Nuremberg Charter to the Rome Statute: Defining the Elements of Crimes against Humanity' (2004) 5 San Diego International Law Journal 73–144.

Baderin, MA and M Ssenyonjo (eds), *International Human Rights Law: Six Decades after the UDHR and Beyond* (Ashgate 2010).

Bakke, KM, KG Cunningham, and LJM Seymour , 'The Problem with Fragmented Insurgencies', *The Washington Post* (13 May 2015).

Barnidge, RP, *Non-State Actors and Terrorism: Applying the Law of State Responsibility and the Due Diligence Principle* (TMC Asser Press 2008).

Bartels, R, 'From Jus In Bello to Jus Post Bellum: When do Non-International Armed Conflicts End?' in C Stahn, JS Easterday, and J Iverson (eds), *Jus Post Bellum: Mapping the Normative Foundations* (OUP 2014) 297–314.

Bartels, R, 'Timelines, Borderlines and Conflicts' (2009) 91 International Review of the Red Cross 35–67.

Bartels, R and K Fortin, 'Law, Justice and a Potential Security Gap: The "Organization" Requirement in International Humanitarian Law and International Criminal Law' (2015) 21 Journal of Conflict & Security Law 29–48.

Bassiouni, MC, *The Legislative History of the International Criminal Court* (Transnational Publishers 2005).

Bassiouni, MC, *Crimes against Humanity: Historical Evolution and Contemporary Application* (CUP 2011).

Bassiouni, MC, *Libya from Repression to Revolution: A Record of Armed Conflict and International Law Violations, 2011–2013* (M Nijhoff 2013).

Bates, E, 'History' in D Moeckli, S Shah, and S Sivakumaran (eds), *International Human Rights Law* (OUP 2014) 15–33.

Baxter, RR, 'The First Modern Codification of the Law of War—Francis Lieber and General Orders No. 1 00—(II)' (1963) 3 International Review of the Red Cross 234–50.

Baxter, RR, 'Ius in Bello Interno: The Present and Future Law' in JN Moore and WG Friedmann (eds), *Law and Civil War in the Modern World* (The Johns Hopkins University Press 1974) 518–36.

Baxter, RR, 'Some Existing Problems of Humanitarian Law' (1975) 14 Military Law and Law of War Review 298.

Beale, J, 'The Recognition of Cuban Belligerancy' (1896) 9 Harvard Law Journal 406–19.

Beate, R and A Eriksson, 'Women's Rights under International Human Rights Treaties: Issues of Rape, Domestic Slavery, Abortion, and Domestic Violence' (2007) 5 International Journal of Constitutional Law 507–25.

Beckett, IFW, *Modern Insurgencies and Counter-Insurgencies: Guerrillas and their Opponents since 1750* (Routledge 2001).

Bellal, A, 'Establishing the Direct Responsibility of Non-State Armed Groups for Violations of International Norms: Issues of Attribution' in C Ryngaert, M Noortmann and N Gal-Or (eds), *Responsibilities of the Non-State Actor in Armed Conflict and the Market Place* (Brill Nijhoff 2015) 304–22.

Bellal, A, G Giacca, and S Casey-Maslen, 'International Law and Armed Non-State Actors in Afghanistan' (2011) 93 International Review of the Red Cross 47–79.

Bellinger, JB and WJ Haynes, 'A US Government Response to the International Committee of the Red Cross Study Customary International Humanitarian Law' (2007) 89 International Review of the Red Cross 443–71.

Benvenisti, E, 'Customary International Law as a Judicial Tool for Promoting Efficiency' in *The Impact of International Law on International Cooperation: Theoretical Perspectives* (CUP 2004) 85–116.

Berti, B, 'Non-State Actors as Providers of Governance: The Hamas Government in Gaza between Effective Sovereignty, Centralized Authority, and Resistance' (2015) 69 Middle East Journal 9–31.

Bertram, SK, 'Authority and Hierarchy within Anonymous Internet Relay Chat Networks' (2015) 6 Journal of Terrorism Research 15–34.

Bianchi, A and Y Naqvi, *International Humanitarian Law and Terrorism* (Hart 2011).

Bílková, V, 'Establishing Direct Responsibility of Armed Opposition Groups for Violations of International Humanitarian Law?' in C Ryngaert, M Noortmann and N Gal-Or (eds), *Responsibilities of the Non-State Actor in Armed Conflict and the Market Place* (Brill Nijhoff 2015) 263–84.

Blank, LR, 'Defining the Battlefield in Contemporary Conflict and Counter-terrorism: Understanding the Parameters of the Zone of Combat' (2010) 39 Georgia Journal of International and Comparative Law 1–38.

Blank, LR and GS Corn, 'Losing the Forest for the Trees: Syria, Law, and the Pragmatics of Conflict Recognition' (2013) 46 Vanderbilt Journal of Transnational Law 693–746.

Boelaert-Suominen, S, 'Commentary: The Yugoslavia Tribunal and the Common Core of Humanitarian Law Applicable to all Armed Conflicts' (2000) 13 Leiden Journal of International Law 619–53.

Boister, N, '"Transnational Criminal Law"?' (2003) 14 European Journal of International Law 953–76.

Bond, JE, *The Rules of Riot: Internal Conflict and the Law of War* (Princeton University Press 1974).

Boothby, B, '"And for Such Time": The Time Dimension of Direct Participation of Hostilities' (2010) 42 International Law and Politics 741–68.

Bothe, M, 'War Crimes' in A Cassese, P Gaeta, and JRWD Jones (eds), *The Rome Statute of the International Criminal Court: A Commentary* (OUP 2002) 379–425.

Bothe, M, *New Rules for Victims of Armed Conflicts: Commentary on the Two 1977 Protocols Additional to the Geneva Conventions of 1949* (2nd edn, M Nijhoff 2013).

Breitegger, A, 'The Legal Framework Applicable to Insecurity and Violence Affecting the Delivery of Health Care in Armed Conflicts and Other Emergencies' (2013) 95 International Review of the Red Cross 83–127.

Brierly, JL and A Clapham, *Brierly's Law of Nations: An Introduction to the Role of International Law in International Relations* (7th edn, OUP 2012).

Brooking, ET, 'Anonymous vs The Islamic State', *Foreign Policy* (13 November 2015).

Buergenthal, T, 'The Normative and Institutional Evolution of International Human Rights' (1997) 19 Human Rights Quarterly 703–23.

Burgers, JH, 'The Road to San Francisco: The Revival of the Human Rights Idea in the Twentieth Century' (1992) 14 Human Rights Quarterly 447–77.

Burniske, J, NK Modirzadeh, and DA Lewis, *Armed Non-State Actors and International Human Rights Law: An Analysis of the Practice of the UN Security Council and UN General Assembly* (Harvard School of Law Program on Interational Law & Armed Conflict 2017).

Bussolati, N, 'The Rise of Non-State Actors in Cyberwarfare' in JD Ohlin, K Govern, and C Finkelstein (eds), *Cyberwar: Law and Ethics for Virtual Conflicts* (OUP 2015) 102–26.

Cahin, G, 'Attribution of Conduct to the State: Insurrectional Movements' in J Crawford, A Pellet, and S Olleson (eds), *The Law of International Responsibility* (OUP 2010) 247–56.

Cahin, G, 'The Responsibility of other Entities: Armed Bands and Criminal Groups, in J Crawford, A Pellet, and S Olleson (eds), *The Law of International Responsibility* (OUP 2010) 334–41.

Callimachi, R, 'ISIS Enshrines a Theology of Rape', *New York Times* (13 August 2015).

Caron, DD, 'The ILC Articles on State Responsibility: The Paradoxical Relationship between Form and Authority' (2002) 96 American Journal of International Law 857–73.

Carswell, AJ, 'Classification des Conflits: Le Dilemme du Soldat' (2009) 91 Revue internationale de la Croix-Rouge 65–85.

The Carter Center, *Syria Countrywide Conflict Report #2* (The Carter Center, 20 November 2013).

Cassese, A, 'The Spanish Civil War and Customary Law concerning Internal Armed Conflicts' in A Cassese (ed), *Current Problems of International Law* (MVLTA PAVCIS 1975) 287–318.

Cassese, A, 'The Status of Rebels under the 1977 Geneva Protocol on Non-International Armed Conflicts' (1981) 30 International & Comparative Law Quarterly 416–39.

Cassese, A, *International Law* (2nd edn, OUP 2005).

Cassese, A, *International Criminal Law* (2nd edn, OUP 2008).

Cassese, A, 'Is Genocidal Policy a Requirement for the Crime of Genocide?' in P Gaeta (ed), *The UN Genocide Convention: A Commentary* (OUP 2009) 128–36.

Cassese, A, *Cassese's International Criminal Law* (3rd edn, Oxford: OUP 2013).

Cassese, A and A Eide (eds), *The New Humanitarian Law of Non-International Armed Conflict* (Editoriale Scientifica 1979).

Cerone, J, 'Human Rights on the Battlefield' in S Lagoutte, H-O Sano, and P Scharff Smith (eds), *Human Rights in Turmoil: Facing Threats, Consolidating Achievements* (M Nijhoff 2007) 97–131.

Chatham House, *Classification of Conflicts: The Way Forward* (Chatham House 2012).

Chehtman, A, *The Philosophical Foundations of Extraterritorial Punishment* (OUP 2010).

Chehtman, A, 'Contemporary Approaches to the Philosophy of Crimes against Humanity' (2014) 14 International Criminal Law Review 813–35.

Chesney, R, 'Transatlantic Dialogue on International Law and Armed Conflict: When does LOAC Cease to Apply?' (*Lawfare*, 3 September 2014) <https://www.lawfareblog.com/transatlantic-dialogue-international-law-and-armed-conflict-when-does-loac-cease-apply> accessed 2 November 2017.

Chesney, R, 'The Global War on ISIL and its Associated Forces' (*Lawfare*, 14 November 2015) <https://www.lawfareblog.com/global-war-isil-and-its-associated-forces> accessed 2 November 2017.

Chinkin, C, 'Sources' in D Moeckli, S Shah, and S Sivakumaran (eds), *International Human Rights Law* (OUP 2010) 103–23.

Chouliaras, A, 'A Strategic Choice: The State Policy Requirement in Core International Crimes' (2015) 28 Leiden Journal of International Law 953–75.

Clapham, A, *Human Rights Obligations of Non-State Actors* (OUP 2006).

Clapham, A, 'Human Rights Obligations of Non-State Actors in Conflict Situations' (2006) 88 International Review of the Red Cross 491–523.

Clapham, A, 'Extending International Criminal Law beyond the Individual to Corporations and Armed Opposition Groups' (2008) 6 Journal of International Criminal Justice 899–926.

Clapham, A, *The Rights and Responsibilities of Armed Non-State Actors: The Legal Landscape and Issues Surrounding Engagement* (SSRN 2010).
Clapham, A, 'Overseeing Human Rights Compliance' in A Cassese (ed), *Realizing Utopia: The Future of International Law* (OUP 2012) 318–25.
Clapham, A, 'Focussing on Armed Non-State Actors' in A Clapham and P Gaeta (eds), *The Oxford Handbook of International Law in Armed Conflict* (OUP 2014) 766–810.
Clapham, A, 'Non-State Actors' in D Moeckli, S Shah, S Sivakumaran, and D Harris (eds), *International Human Rights Law* (OUP 2014) 531–49.
Clapham, A, 'The Concept of International Armed Conflict' in A Clapham, P Gaeta, and M Sassòli (eds), *The 1949 Geneva Conventions: A Commentary* (OUP 2015) 3–26.
Clapham, A, 'Human Rights Obligations for Non-State-Actors: Where are We Now?' in F Lafontaine and Fo Larocque (eds), *Doing Peace the Rights Way: Essays in International Law and Relations in Honour of Louise Arbour* (Intersentia forthcoming).
Clark, RS, 'History of Efforts to Codify Crimes against Humanity: From the Charter of Nuremberg to the Statute of Rome' in LN Sadat (ed), *Forging a Convention for Crimes against Humanity* (CUP 2011) 8–27.
Commission des Crimes de Guerre des Nations Unies, *History of the United Nations War Crimes Commission and the Development of the Laws of War* (His Majesty's Stationery Office 1948).
Constantinides, A, 'Human Rights Obligations and Accountability of Armed Opposition Groups: The Practice of the UN Security Council' (2010) 4 Human Rights & International Legal Discourse 89–110.
Cook, RJ (ed), *Human Rights of Women: National and International Perspectives* (University of Pennsylvania Press 1994).
Corn, GS and ET Jensen, 'Transnational Armed Conflict: A "Principled" Approach to the Regulation of Counter-Terror Combat Operations' (2009) 42 Israel Law Review 1–34.
Corn, GS, 'Triggering the Law of Armed Conflict?' in GSea Corn (ed), *The War on Terror and the Laws of War: A Military Perspective* (OUP 2015).
Council of Europe Parliamentary Assembly, *Accountability of International Organisations for Human Rights Violations* (Council of Europe 2013).
Crawford, J, *Brownlie's Principles of Public International Law* (8th edn, OUP 2012).
Crawford, J, *State Responsibility: The General Part* (CUP 2013).
Cryer, R, 'The Doctrinal Foundations of International Criminal Law' in MS Bassiouni (ed), *International Criminal Law* (M Nijhoff 2008) 107–28.
Cryer, R, F Hakan, D Robinson, and E Wilmshurst, *An Introduction to International Criminal Law* (CUP 2014).
Cullen, A, 'Key Developments affecting the Scope of Internal Armed Conflict in International Humanitarian Law' (2005) 183 Military Law Review 66–109.
Cullen, A, 'The Definition of Non-International Armed Conflict in the Rome Statute of the International Criminal Court: An Analysis of the Threshold of Application Contained in Article 8(2)(f)' (2007) 12 Journal of Conflict and Security Law 419–45.
Cullen, A, *The Concept of Non-International Armed Conflict in International Humanitarian Law* (CUP 2010).
Cullen, A, 'The Characterization of Armed Conflict in the Jurisprudence of the ICC' in C Stahn (ed), *The Law and Practice of the International Criminal Court* (OUP 2014) 762–77.
Cullen, A and S Wheatley, 'The Human Rights of Individuals in De Facto Regimes under the European Convention on Human Rights' (2013) 13 Human Rights Law Review 691–728.

D'Aspremont, J, 'Rebellion and State Responsibility: Wrongdoing by Democratically Elected Insurgents' (2009) 58 International and Comparative Law Quarterly 427–42.

Daes, E-IA, *Liberté de l'Individu en Droit: étude des devoirs de l'individu envers la communauté et limitations des droits et libertés de l'homme en vertu de l'article 29 de la Déclaration universelle des droits de l'homme* (Nations Unies 1990).

Dahl, AW and M Sandbu, 'The Threshold of Armed Conflict' (2006) 45 Military Law and Law of War Review 369–88.

David, E, 'Internal (Non-International) Armed Conflict' in A Clapham and P Gaeta (eds), *The Oxford Handbook of International Law in Armed Conflict* (OUP 2014) 353–62.

DeGuzman, MM, 'The Road from Rome: The Developing Law of Crimes against Humanity' (2000) 22 Human Rights Quarterly 335–403.

DeGuzman, MM, 'Crimes against Humanity' in WA Schabas and N Bernaz (eds), *Routledge Handbook of International Criminal Law* (Routledge 2011) 62–83.

Dinstein, Y, *The Interaction between Customary International Law and Treaties* (Brill 2006).

Dinstein, Y, 'Concluding Remarks on Non-International Armed Conflicts' (2012) 88 International Law Studies 399–421.

Dinstein, Y, *Non-International Armed Conflicts in International Law* (CUP 2014).

Dörmann, K, *Elements of War Crimes under the Rome Statute of the International Criminal Court: Sources and Commentary* (repr, CUP 2004).

Dörmann, K and T Rodenhäuser, 'Contemporary Challenges for International Humanitarian Law' in J Crawford, A Koroma, S Mahmoudi, and A Pellet (eds), *The International Legal Order: Current Needs and Possible Responses* (Brill 2017) 677–99.

Doswald-Beck, L, *Human Rights in Times of Conflict and Terrorism* (OUP 2011).

Doswald-Beck, L and J-M Henckaerts, *Customary International Humanitarian Law* (CUP 2005).

Draper, GIAD, *The Geneva Conventions of 1949* (M Nijhoff 1965).

Draper, GIAD, 'Humanitarian Law and Internal Armed Conflicts' (1983) 13 Georgia Journal of International and Comparative Law 253–77.

Draper, GIAD, 'The Development of International Humanitarian Law' in UNESCO and Institut Henry-Dunant (eds), *International Dimensions of Humanitarian Law* (Henry Dunant Institute; UNESCO; M Nijhoff 1988) 67–90.

Dröge, C, 'Get Off my Cloud: Cyber Warfare, International Humanitarian Law, and the Protection of Civilians' (2012) 94 International Review of the Red Cross 533–78.

Dudai, R, 'Closing the Gap: Symbolic Reparations and Armed Groups' (2011) 93 International Review of the Red Cross 783–808.

Dumberry, P, 'New State Responsibility for Internationally Wrongful Acts by an Insurrectional Movement' (2006) 17 European Journal of International Law 605–21.

Elder, DA, 'The Historical Background of Common Article 3 of the Geneva Conventions of 1949' (1979) 11 Case Western Reserve Journal of International Law 37–69.

Falk, RA, 'Janus Tormented: The International Law of Internal War' in Rosenau JN, *International Aspects of Civil Strife* (Princeton University Press 1964) 185–248.

Farwell, JP, 'How ISIS Uses Social Media' (*Politics and Strategy*, 2 October 2014) <https://www.iiss.org/en/politics%20and%20strategy/blogsections/2014-d2de/october-931b/isis-media-9d28> accessed 2 November 2017.

Ferraro, T, 'The Applicability and Application of International Humanitarian Law to Multinational Forces' (2013) 95 International Review of the Red Cross 561–612.

Ferraro, T, 'The ICRC's Legal Position on the Notion of Armed Conflict Involving Foreign Intervention and on Determining the IHL Applicable to this Type of Conflict' (2015) 97 International Review of the Red Cross 1227–52.

Ferraro, T and International Committee of the Red Cross, *Occupation and other Forms of Administraion of Foreign Territory* (ICRC 2012).
Fisher, KJ, 'The Distinct Character of International Crime: Theorizing the Domain' (2009) 8 Contemporary Political Theory 44–67.
Forsythe, DP, 'Legal Management of Internal War: The 1977 Protocol on Non-International Armed Conflicts' (1978) 72 American Journal of International Law 272–95.
Fortin, K, *The Accountability of Armed Groups under Human Rights Law* (OUP 2017).
Frésard, J-J and International Committee of the Red Cross, *The Roots of Behaviour in War: A Survey of the Literature* (ICRC 2004).
Frowein, JA, *Das de facto-Regime im Völkerrecht: Eine Untersuchung zur Rechtsstellung 'nichtanerkannter Staaten' und ähnlicher Gebilde* (C Heymann 1968).
Frowein, JA, 'De Facto Regime' in R Wolfrum and Max-Planck-Institut für Ausländisches Öffentliches Recht und Völkerrecht (Heidelberg) (eds), *The Max-Planck Encyclopedia of Public International Law* (OUP 2012).
Gaeta, P, 'On What Conditions can a State be Held Responsible for Genocide?' (2007) 18 European Journal of International Law 631–48.
Gaeta, P, 'International Criminalization of Prohibited Conduct' in A Cassese (ed), *The Oxford Companion to International Criminal Justice* (OUP 2009) 63–74.
Gaeta, P (ed), *Genocide* (Routledge 2011).
Garner, JW, 'Recognition of Belligerency' (1938) 32 American Journal of International Law 106–13.
Garraway, C, 'War and Peace: Where is the Divide?' (2012) 88 International Law Studies Series. US Naval War College 93–115.
Garraway, C, 'Armed Conflicts and Terrorist Organizations' in L v d Herik and N Schrijver (eds), *Counter-Terrorism Strategies in a Fragmented International Legal Order: Meeting the Challenges* (CUP 2015) 425–32.
Geiss, R, 'Armed Violence in Fragile States: Low-Intensity Conflicts, Spillover Conflicts, and Sporadic Law Enforcement Operations by Third Parties' (2009) 91 International Review of the Red Cross 127–42.
Geiss, R, 'Cyber Warfare: Implications for Non-International Armed Conflicts' (2013) 89 International Law Studies 627–45.
Geneva Academy of International Humanitarian Law and Human Rights, *Rules of Engagement—Protecting Civilians through Dialogue with Armed Non-State Actors* (Geneva Academy 2011).
Geneva Call, *Positive Obligations of Armed Non-State Actors: Legal and Policy Issues—Report from the 2015 Garance Talks* (Geneva Call 2016).
Gentili, A, *De Jure Belli Libri Tres* (Clarendon Press; H Milford 1589).
German Ministry of Defence, *Humanitäres Völkerrecht in bewaffneten Konflikten—Handbuch* (ZDv15/2), 2013).
Giacca, G, *Economic, Social, and Cultural Rights in Armed Conflict* (OUP 2014).
Gil Gil, A, 'Die Tatbestände der Verbrechen gegen die Menschlichkeit und des Völkermord im Römischen Statut des Internationalen Strafgerichtshofs' (2000) 112 Zeitschrift für die Gesamte Strafrechtswissenschaft 381–95.
Giorgou, I, 'State Involvement in the Perpetration of Enforced Disappearance and the Rome Statute' (2013) 11 Journal of International Criminal Justice 1001–21.
Giustiniani, FZ, 'New Hopes and Challenges for the Protection of Idps in Africa: The Kampala Convention for the Protection and Assistance of Internally Displaced Persons in Africa' (2009) 39 Denver Journal of International Law and Policy 347–70.

Goel, V, 'An Introduction to Origin, Evolution and Development of International Humanitarian Law' in L Doswald-Beck (ed), *International Humanitarian Law: An Anthology* (Lexis Nexis 2009) 1–22.
Graham, DE, 'Defining Non-International Armed Conflict: A Historically Difficult Task' (2012) 88 International Law Studies Series 44–55.
Grear, A, "Framing the Project' of International Human Rights Law: Reflections on the Dysfunctional "Family" of the Universal Declaration' in CA Gearty and C Douzinas (eds), *The Cambridge Companion to Human Rights Law* (CUP 2012) 1–35.
Green, LC, *The Contemporary Law of Armed Conflict* (3rd edn, Manchester University Press 2008).
Greenawalt, AKA, 'Rethinking Genocidal Intent: The Case for a Knowledge-Based Interpretation' (1999) 99 Columbia Law Review 2259–94.
Greenwood, C, 'Historical Development and Legal Basis' in D Fleck and M Bothe (eds), *The Handbook of International Humanitarian Law* (OUP 2008) 1–38.
Grignon, J, 'The Beginning of Application of International Humanitarian Law: A Discussion of a Few Challenges' (2014) 96 International Review of the Red Cross 139–62.
Grotius, H, *The Rights of War and Peace, including the Law of Nature and of Nations* (M Walter Dunne 1625).
Hakimi, M, 'State Bystander Responsibility' (2010) 21 The European Journal of International Law 341–85.
Hannum, H, 'The Status of the Universal Declaration of Human Rights in National and International Law' (1995) 25 Georgia Journal of International and Comparative Law 287–398.
Hansen, TO, 'The Policy Requirement in Crimes against Humanity: Lessons from and for the Case of Kenya' (2011) 43 George Washington International Law Review 1–41.
Hampson, F, 'Other Areas of Customary Law in Relation to the Study' in E Wilmshurst and S Breua (eds), *Perspectives on the ICRC Study on Customary International Humanitarian Law* (CUP 2007) 55–56.
Haque, AA, 'Group Violence and Group Vengeance: Toward a Retributivist Theory of International Criminal Law' (2005) 9 Buffalo Criminal Law Review 273–328.
Harding, I, 'The Origins and Effectiveness of the Geneva Conventions for the Protection of War Victims' (1973) 13 International Review of the Red Cross 283–90.
Hashim, A, *Insurgency and Counter-Insurgency in Iraq* (Hurst 2006).
Hasselbacher, L, 'State Obligations regarding Domestic Violence: The European Court of Human Rights, Due Diligence, and International Legal Minimums of Protection' (2010) 8 Northwestern Journal of International Human Rights 190–215.
Heintze, H-J, 'Are De Facto Regimes Bound by Human Rights?' in Institute for Peace Research and Security Policy at the University of Hamburg (ed), *Yearbook on the Organization for Security and Co-operation in Europe (OSCE)* (Nomos 2010) 267–76.
Heller, KJ, 'The Use and Abuse of Analogy in IHL' in J Ohlin (ed), *Theoretical Boundaries of Armed Conflict and Human Rights* (CUP 2016).
Hellestveit, C, *Tribes, Thugs, Terrorists and the Law: Can Non-Conventional Armed Violence be Regulated?* (Norwegian Peacebuilding Resource Centre Report, May 2015).
Henckaerts, J-M and C Wiesener, 'Human Rights Obligations of Non-State Armed Groups: A Possible Contribution from Customary International Law?' in R Kolb and G Gaggioli (eds), *Research Handbook on Human Rights and Humanitarian Law* (Edward Elgar 2013) 146–69.
Henkin, L, *The Age of Rights* (Columbia University Press 1990).

Hessbruegge, JA, 'The Historical Development of the Doctrines of Attribution and Due Diligence in International Law' (2003–2004) 36 NYU Journal of International Law and Politics 265–306.
Hessbruegge, JA, 'Human Rights Violations Arising from Conduct of Non-State Actors' (2005) 11 Buffalo Human Rights Law Review 21–88.
Higgins, R, 'International Law and Civil War' in E Luard (ed), *The International Regulation of Civil Wars* (Thames and Hudson 1972) 169–86.
Higgins, R, *Problems and Process: International Law and How We Use It* (Clarendon Press 1994).
Hobbes, T, *Hobbes's Leviathan* (Clarendon Press 1651).
Hoffman, B, *Inside Terrorism* (Columbia University Press 2006).
Hoffman, B, *The Myth of Grass-Roots Terrorism* (Foreign Affairs 2008).
Holliday, J, *Syria's Armed Opposition* (Institute for the Study of War 2012).
Howard, ME, *The Laws of War: Constraints on Warfare in the Western World* (Yale University Press 1994).
Human Rights Watch, *'You Can Still See their Blood'— Executions, Indiscriminate Shootings, and Hostage Taking by Opposition Forces in Latakia Countryside* (Human Rights Watch 2013).
ICRC, *Humanitarian Aid to the Victims of Internal Conflicts. Meeting of a Commission of Experts in Geneva* (ICRC 1962).
ICRC, *Reaffirmation and Development of the Laws and Customs Applicable in Armed Conflicts (Report Submitted to the XXIst International Conference of the Red Cross)* (ICRC 1969).
ICRC, *Report of the Work of the Conference (Conference of Government Experts on the Reaffirmation and Development of International Humanitarian Law Applicable in Armed Conflicts)* (ICRC 1971).
ICRC, *Rules Applicable in Guerrilla Warfare—Paper Submitted the Conference of Government Experts on the Reaffirmation and Development of International Humanitarian Law Applicable in Armed Conflicts* (ICRC 1971).
ICRC, *Report of the Work of the Conference (Conference of Government Experts on the Reaffirmation and Development of International Humanitarian Law Applicable in Armed Conflicts), Vol. I* (ICRC 1972).
ICRC, *International Humanitarian Law and the Challenges of Contemporary Armed Conflicts* (ICRC 2003).
ICRC, *International Humanitarian Law and the Challenges of Contemporary Armed Conflicts* (ICRC 2007).
ICRC, *How is the Term 'Armed Conflict' Defined in International Humanitarian Law? (Opinion Paper)* (ICRC 2008).
ICRC, *Increasing Respect for International Humanitarian Law in Non-International Armed Conflicts* (ICRC 2008).
ICRC, *Interpretive Guidance on the Notion of Direct Participation in Hostilities under International Humanitarian Law* (ICRC 2009).
ICRC, 'A Collection of Codes of Conduct Issued by Armed Groups' (2011) 93 International Review of the Red Cross 483–501.
ICRC, *International Humanitarian Law and the Challenges of Contemporary Armed Conflicts* (ICRC 2011).
ICRC, *International Humanitarian Law and Terrorism: Questions and Answers* (ICRC 2011).
ICRC, *Strengthening Legal Protection for Persons Deprived of their Liberty in Relation to Non-International Armed Conflict* (ICRC 2012).
ICRC, *ICRC Startegy 2015–2018* (ICRC 2014).

ICRC, *Internment in Armed Conflict: Basic Rules and Challenges (Opinion Paper, November 2014)* (ICRC 2014).
ICRC, *International Humanitarian Law and the Challenges of Contemporary Armed Conflicts* (ICRC 2015).
ICRC, *Strengthening International Humanitarian Law Protecting Persons Deprived of their Liberty—Draft Resolution and Concluding Report* (ICRC 2015).
ICRC, *Thematic Consultation of Government Experts on Grounds and Procedures for Internment and Detainee Transfers* (ICRC 2015).
ICRC, *Convention (I) for the Amelioration of the Condition of the Wounded and Sick in Armed Forces in the Field: Commentary of 2016* (ICRC 2016).
Institute de Droit International, *Droits et devoirs des Puissances étrangères, au cas de mouvement insurrectionnel, envers les gouvernements établis et reconnus qui sont aux prises avec l'insurrection* (Institute de Droit Internationale 1900).
Inter-American Commission on Human Rights, *Inter-American Yearbook on Human Rights* (M Nijhoff 1990).
International Law Association, *Final Report on the Exercise of Universal Jurisdiction in Respect of Gross Human Rights Offences* (ILA 2000).
International Law Association, *Final Report on the Meaning of Armed Conflict in International Law* (ILA 2010).
International Law Association, *The Hague Conference (2010): Non-State Actors* (ILA 2010).
International Law Association, *ILA Study Group on Due Diligence in International Law: First Report* (ILA 2014).
International Law Association, *Washington Conference (2014): Non-State Actors* (ILA 2014).
Jalloh, C, 'Situation in the Republic of Kenya' (2011) 105 American Journal of International Law 540–47.
Jalloh, C, 'What Makes Crimes against Humanity Crimes against Humanity?' (2013) 28 American University International Law Review 381–441.
Jennings, SR and SA Watts, *Oppenheim's International Law, Vol. 1* (9th edn, OUP 2008).
Jessberger, F, 'The Defintion and the Elements of the Crime of Genocide' in P Gaeta (ed), *The UN Genocide Convention: A Commentary* (OUP 2009) 87–112.
Jinks, D, *The Temporal Scope of Application of International Humanitarian Law in Contemporary Conflicts* (Program on Humanitarian Policy and Conflict Research 2003).
Jochnick, C a and R Normand, 'The Legitimation of Violence: A Critical History of the Laws of War' (1994) 35 Harvard International Law Journal 49–95.
Johnson, DHN, 'The Draft Code of Offences against the Peace and Security of Mankind' (1955) 4 International and Comparative Law Quarterly 445–68.
Johnson, JT, *Ideology, Reason, and the Limitation of War: Religious and Secular Concepts, 1200–1740* (Princeton University Press 1975).
Joscelyn, T, *Osama bin Laden's Files: Al Qaeda's Deputy General Manager in Yemen* (The Long War Journal 2015).
Joseph, H and J Beale, 'The Recognition of Cuban Belligerency' (1896) 9 Harvard Law Journal 406–19.
Joseph, S and M Castan, *The International Covenant on Civil and Political Rights: Cases, Materials, and Commentary* (3rd edn, OUP 2013).
Junod, S, 'Additional Protocol II: History and Scope' (1983–1984) 33 American University Law Review 29–40.
Justice and Equality Movement, *Statement by the Opposition Movements* (2008).
Justice and Equality Movement, *Establishment of a JEM Committee for Human Rights* (Justice and Equality Movement 2010).

Kalpouzos, I, 'The Applicability of International Law to Armed Conflicts involving Non-State Armed Groups: Between Status and Humanitarian Protection' (unpublished PhD thesis, University of Nottingham 2011).

Kamatali, J-M, 'The Application of International Human Rights Law in Non-International Armed Conflicts: From Rhetoric to Action' (2014) 4 Journal of International Humanitarian Legal Studies 220–61.

Kamminga, MT, 'State Succession in Respect of Human Rights Treaties' (1996) 7 European Journal of International Law 469–548.

Kamminga, MT, '"Due Diligence" Mania: The Misguided Introduction of an Extraneous Concept into Human Rights Discourse' (2011) Maastricht Faculty of Law Working Paper No 2011/07.

Kant, I, *On the Common Saying: That may be Correct in Theory, but it is of No Use in Practice* (CUP 1793).

Kelman, HC, 'The Policy Context of International Crimes' in H v d Wilt and A Nollkaemper (eds), *System Criminality in International Law* (CUP 2009) 26–41.

Kelsen, H, *Principles of International Law* (Rinehart & Co 1952).

Klabbers, J, *An Introduction to International Law* (CUP 2003).

Klabbers, J, '(I Can't Get No) Recognition: Subjects Doctrine and the Emergence ofNon-State Actors' in J Petman and J Klabbers (eds), *Nordic Cosmopolitanism* (M Nijhoff 2003) 351–69.

Klabbers, J, 'The Concept of Legal Personality' (2005) 11 Ius Gentium 35–66.

Kleffner, JK, 'The Collective Accountability of Organized Armed Groups for System Crimes' in H v d Wilt and A Nollkaemper (eds), *System Criminality in International Law* (CUP 2009) 238–69.

Kleffner, JK, 'The Applicability of International Humanitarian Law to Organized Armed Groups' (2011) 93 International Review of the Red Cross 443–61.

Kleffner, JK, 'The Applicability of the Law of Armed Conflict and Human Rights Law to Organised Armed Groups' in JK Kleffner and E de Wet (eds), *Convergence and Conflicts of Human Rights and International Humanitarian Law in Military Operations* (Pretoria University Law Press 2014) 49–66.

Kotzsch, L, *The Concept of War in Contemporary History and International Law* (E Droz 1956).

Krähenmann, S, 'Positive Obligations in Human Rights Treaties' (unpublished PhD thesis, Graduate Institute of International and Development Studies, Geneva, 2012).

Krähenmann, S, 'Positive Obligations in Human Rights Law during Armed Conflicts' in R Kolb and G Gaggioli (eds), *Research Handbook on Human Rights and Humanitarian Law* (Edward Elgar 2013) 170–87.

Kress, C, 'War Crimes Committed in Non-International Armed Conflict and the Emerging System of International Criminal Justice' (2001) 30 Israel Yearbook on Human Rights 103–77.

Kress, C, 'The 1999 Crisis in East Timor and the Threshold of the Law on War Crimes' (2002) 13 Criminal Law Forum 409–70.

Kress, C, 'The Darfur Report and Genocidal Intent' (2005) 3 Journal of International Criminal Justice 562–78.

Kress, C, 'The Crime of Genocide under International Law' (2006) 6 International Criminal Law Review 461–502.

Kress, C, 'The Crime of Genocide and Contextual Elements: A Comment on the ICC Pre-Trial Chamber's Decision in the Al Bashir Case' (2009) 7 Journal of International Criminal Justice 297–306.

Kress, C, 'On the Outer Limits of Crimes against Humanity: The Concept of Organization within the Policy Requirement: Some Reflections on the March 2010 ICC Kenya Decision' (2010) 23 Leiden Journal of International Law 855–73.

Kress, C, 'Some Reflections on the International Legal Framework Governing Transnational Armed Conflicts' (2010) 15 Journal of Conflict and Security Law 245–74.

Kress, C, 'The ICC's First Encounter with the Crime of Genocide: The Case against Al Bashir' in C Stahn (ed), *The Law and Practice of the International Criminal Court* (OUP 2014) 669–704.

Kress, C, 'Actes de Terrorisme: Nouvelles Formes de Crimes contre l'Humanité?' (manuscript with the author 2016).

Kretzmer, D, 'Rethinking the Application of IHL in Non-International Armed Conflicts' (2009) 42 Israel Law Review 8–45.

Kuchins, AC, M Malarkey, and S Markedonov, *The North Caucasus—Russia's Volatile Frontier* (Center for Strategic and International Studies 2011).

Kuschnik, B, 'Humaneness, Humankind and Crimes against Humanity' (2010) 2 Goettingen Journal of International Law 501–30.

La Haye, E, *War Crimes in Internal Armed Conflicts* (CUP 2008).

La Rosa, A-M and C Wuerzner, 'Armed Groups, Sanctions and the Implementation of International Humanitarian Law' (2008) 90 International Review of the Red Cross 327–41.

Labuda, P, 'Lieber Code' in R Wolfrum (ed), *The Max-Planck Encyclopedia of Public International Law* (OUP 2012).

Labuda, P, 'What Lies beneath the 'G' Word? Genocide-Labelling and Fact-Finding at the UN' (EJIL: *Talk!*, 28 May 2015) <http://www.ejiltalk.org/what-lies-beneath-the-g-word-genocide-labelling-and-fact-finding-at-the-un/> accessed 2 November 2017 accessed 2 November 2017.

Larsen, KM, '"Territorial Non-Application" of the European Convention on Human Rights' (2009) 78 Nordic Journal of International Law 73–93.

Lauterpacht, H, 'The Subjects of the Law of Nations' (1947) 45 Law Quarterly Review 438–61.

Lauterpacht, H, 'The Limits of the Operation of the Law of War' (1953) 30 British Year Book of International Law 206–43.

Lauterpacht, H, *Recognition in International Law* (CUP 2012).

Lauterpacht, H, *An International Bill of the Rights of Man* (OUP 2013).

Lemkin, R, *Axis Rule in Occupied Europe: Laws of Occupation, Analysis of Government, Proposals for Redress* (Carnegie Endowment for International Peace 1944).

Lillich, RB, 'The Growing Importance of Customary International Human Rights Law' (1996) 25 Georgia Journal of International and Comparative Law 1–30.

Lin, H, 'Cyber Conflict and International Humanitarian Law' (2012) 94 International Review of the Red Cross 515–31.

Lister, C, 'Assessing Syria's Jihad' (2014) 54 Adelphi Series 71–98.

Lister, C, 'Profiling the Islamic State'13 Bookings Doha Center Analysis Paper (Brookings Doha Centre 2014).

Locke, J, *Two Treatises of Government* (Dent 1689).

Lotsteen, YM, 'The Concept of Belligerency in International Law' (2000) 166 Military Law Review 109–41.

Luban, D, 'A Theory of Crimes against Humanity' (2004) 29 Georgetown Law Faculty Publications and other Works 85–167.

Luban, D, 'State Criminality and the Ambition of International Criminal Law' in T Isaacs and R Vernon (eds), *Accountability for Collective Wrongdoing* (CUP 2011) 61–91.

Lubell, N, 'The War (?) against Al-Qaeda' in E Wilmshurst (ed), *International Law and the Classification of Conflicts* (OUP 2012) 421–54.

Lubell, N, *Transnational Armed Conflicts* (XVIII Round Table on Current Issues of International Humanitarian Law 2015).

Lubell, N and N Derejko, 'A Global Battlefield?: Drones and the Geographical Scope of Armed Conflict' (2013) 11 Journal of International Criminal Justice 65–88.

Mackinlay, J, 'The Classification of Insurgent Forces' (2002) 42 The Adelphi Papers 41–92.

Macleod, C, 'Towards a Philosophical Account of Crimes against Humanity' (2010) 21 European Journal of International Law 281–302.

Malik, S, 'The ISIS Papers: Leaked Documents Show how ISIS is Building its State', *The Guardian* (7 December 2015).

Mampilly, ZC, *Rebel Rules—Insurgent Governance and Civilian Life during War* (Cornell University Press 2011).

Mampilly, ZC, 'Insurgent Governance in the Democratic Republic of the Congo' in H Krieger (ed), *Inducing Compliance with International Humanitarian Law—Lessons from the African Great Lakes Region* (CUP 2016) 44–78.

Mao, Z, *On Guerilla Warfare* (US Marine Corps Combat Development Command 1937).

Margulies, P and M Sinnot, 'Crossing Borders to Target Al-Qaeda and Its Affiliates: Defining Networks as Organized Armed Groups in Non-International Armed Conflicts' (2015) 16 Yearbook of International Humanitarian Law 2013 319–45.

Marrin, A (ed), *War and the Christian Conscience: From Augustine to Martine Luther Jr* (Henry Regnery Company 1971).

Marx, K, 'On the Jewish Question' in D McLellan (ed), *Karl Marx: Early Works* (Blackwell 1844).

Maslen, S (ed), *The War Report 2012* (New York: Oxford University Press 2013).

May, L, *Crimes against Humanity: A Normative Account* (CUP 2005).

May, L, 'Humanity, International Crime, and the Rights of Defendants' (2006) 20 Ethics & International Affairs 373–82.

May, L, *Genocide: A Normative Account* (CUP 2010).

McCorquodale, R, 'Overlegalizing Silences: Human Rights and Nonstate Actors' (2002) 96 Proceedings of the Annual Meeting (American Society of International Law) 384–88.

McCorquodale, R, 'Non-State Actors and International Human Rights Law' in A Clapham (ed), *Human Rights and Non-State Actors* (Edward Elgar 2013) 69–86.

McCorquodale, R and R La Forgia, 'Taking off the Blindfolds: Torture by Non-State Actors' (2001) 1 Human Rights Law Review 189–218.

McKeon, RP, 'The Philosophic Basis and Material Circumstances of the Rights of Man' in UNESCO (ed), *Human Rights: Comments and Interpretations* (UNESCO 1948) 23–34.

McLaughlin, R, 'Legal-Policy Considerations and Conflict Characterisation at the Threshold between Law Enforcement and Non-International Armed Conflict' (2012) 13 Melbourne Journal of International Law 1–28.

McNair, AD, 'Law Relating to Civil War in Spain' (1937) 53 The Law Quarterly Review 471–99.

McNair, AD, *International Law Opinions* (CUP 1956).

McNair, AD, *The Law of Treaties* (Clarendon Press 1961).

McQuinn, B, *After the Fall: Libya's Evolving Armed Groups* (Small Arms Survey 2012).

McQuinn, B and F Oliva, *Preliminary Scoping Report—Analyzing and Engaging Non-State Armed Groups in the Field* (United Nations System's Staff College 2014).

Melzer, N, *Cyberwarfare and International Law* (UNIDIR Resources 2011).

Melzer, N, 'The Principle of Distinction between Civilians and Combatants' in A Clapham and P Gaeta (eds), *The Oxford Handbook of International Law in Armed Conflict* (OUP 2014) 296–331.

Meron, T, 'On the Inadequate Reach of Humanitarian and Human Rights Law and the Need for a New Instrument' (1983) 77 American Journal of International Law 589–615.

Meron, T, *Human Rights and Humanitarian Norms as Customary Law* (Clarendon Press 1989).

Meron, T, 'Francis Lieber's Code and Principles of Humanity' (1998) 36 Columbia Journal of Transnational Law 269–81.

Meron, T, 'The Humanization of Humanitarian Law' (2000) 94 American Journal of International Law 239–78.

Meron, T, *The Humanization of International Law* (M Nijhoff 2006).

Mettraux, G, 'Crimes against Humanity in the Jurisprudence of the International Criminal Tribunals for the Former Yugoslavia and for Rwanda' (2002) 43 Harvard International Law Journal 237–316.

Mettraux, G, *International Crimes and the 'Ad Hoc' Tribunals* (OUP 2006).

Mettraux, G, 'The Definition of Crimes against Humanity and the Question of a "Policy" Element' in LN Sadat (ed), *Forging a Convention for Crimes against Humanity* (CUP 2011) 142–76.

Meyersfeld, BC, 'Opuz v Turkey: Confirming the State Obligation to Combat Domestic Violence' (2009) 5 European Human Rights Law Review 684–93.

Milanovic, M, 'European Court Tackles the Definition of Genocide' (EJIL: *Talk!*, 27 October 2015) <http://www.ejiltalk.org/european-court-tackles-the-definition-of-genocide/> accessed 2 November 2017.

Milanovic, M, 'The End of Application of International Humanitarian Law' (2014) 96 International Review of the Red Cross 163–88.

Milanovic, M and V Hadzi-Vidanovic, 'A Taxonomy of Armed Conflict' in ND White and C Henderson (eds), *Research Handbook on International Conflict and Security Law: 'Jus ad Bellum', 'Jus in Bello', and 'Jus Post Bellum'* (Edward Elgar 2013) 256–314.

Moir, L, *The Law of Internal Armed Conflict* (CUP 2002).

Moir, L, 'The Concept of Non-International Armed Conflict' in A Clapham, P Gaeta, and M Sassòli (eds), *The 1949 Geneva Conventions: A Commentary* (OUP 2015) 391–414.

Momtaz, D, *Le Droit International Humanitaire Applicable Aux Conflits Armés Non Internationaux* (M Nijhoff 2002).

Moore, J, 'From Nation State to Failed State: International Protection from Human Rights Abuses by Non-State Agents' (1999) 31 Columbia Human Rights Law *Review* 82–121.

Moore, JB and F Wharton, *A Digest of International Law: As Embodied in Diplomatic Discussions, Treaties and other International Agreements, International Awards, the Decisions of Municipal Courts, and the Writings of Jurists* (US Government Printing Office 1906).

Mowbray, AR, *The Development of Positive Obligations under the European Convention on Human Rights by the European Court of Human Rights* (Hart 2004).

Moynier, G, *La Croix-Rouge, son Passé et son Avenir* (Sandoz & Thuillier 1882).

Mukhimer, T, *Hamas Rule in Gaza* (Palgrave Macmillan 2013).

Munoz-Rojas, D and J-J Fresard, 'The Roots of Behaviour in War: Understanding and Preventing IHL Violations' (2004) 86 International Review of the Red Cross 189–206.

Murray, D, 'How International Humanitarian Law Treaties Bind Non-State Armed Groups' (2015) 20 Journal of Conflict and Security Law 101–31.

Murray, D, 'Author's Response: Human Rights Obligations of Non-State Armed Groups' (EJIL: *Talk!*, 7 November 2016) <http://www.ejiltalk.org/book-discussion-human-rights-obligations-of-non-state-armed-groups-authors-response/> accessed 2 November 2017.

Murray, D, *Human Rights Obligations of Non-State Armed Groups* (Hart 2016).
Nair, R, 'Confronting the Violence Committed by Armed Opposition Groups' (1998) 1 Yale Human Rights & Development Law Journal 1–16.
Nebehay, S, 'Some Syria Violence Amounts to Civil War: Red Cross', *Reuters* (8 May 2012).
Netherlands, *The Military Manual of the Netherlands* (Netherlands Ministry of Defence 2005).
Nijman, JE, *The Concept of International Legal Personality: An Inquiry into the History and Theory of International Law* (TMC Asser Press 2004).
Nijman, JE, 'Non-State Actors and the International Rule of Law: Revisiting the "Realist Theory" of International Legal Personality' in M Noortmann and C Ryngaert (eds), *Non-State Actor Dynamics in International Law: From Law-Takers to Law-Makers* (Ashgate 2010) 91–124.
Nollkaemper, A, 'Introduction' in H v d Wilt and A Nollkaemper (eds), *System Criminality in International Law* (CUP 2009) 1–25.
Nowak, M and KM Januszewski, 'Non-State Actors and Human Rights' in M Noortmann, A Reinisch, and C Ryngaert (eds), *Non-State Actors in International Law* (Hart 2015) 113–61.
Nowak, M and J Kozma, *A World Court of Human Rights* (2009) <http://www.udhr60.ch> accessed 2 November 2017.
Office of the Special Representative of the Secretary-General for Children in Armed Conflict, *Working Paper No. 1: Six Grave Violations against Children during Armed Conflict* (The Legal Foundation 2013).
Office of the United Nations High Commissioner for Human Rights, *Guiding Principles on Business and Human Rights: Implementing the United Nations 'Respect, Protect, and Remedy' Framework* (OHCHR 2011).
Office of the United Nations High Commissioner for Human Rights, *International Legal Protection of Human Rights in Armed Conflict* (OHCHR 2011).
Office of the United Nations High Commissioner for Human Rights, *The Corporate Responsibility to Respect Human Rights: An Interpretive Guidance* (OHCHR 2011).
Ojeda, S, 'The Kampala Convention on Internally Displaced Persons: Some International Humanitarian Law Aspects' (2010) 29 Refugee Survey Quarterly 58–66.
Oosterveld, V, 'The Elements of Genocide: Introduction' in G Boas, NL Reid, and JL Bischoff (eds), *Elements of Crimes under International Law* (CUP 2008).
Oppenheim, LFL, *International Law* (Longmans, Green & Co 1905).
Oppenheim, LFL, *International Law: A Treatise* (2nd edn, Longmans, Green & Co 1912).
Parks, WH, 'Combatants' (2009) 85 International Law Studies 248–306.
Passerin d'Entrèves, A, *Natural Law: An Introduction to Legal Philosophy* (6th edn, Hutchinson University Library 1961).
Paulus, A and M Vashakmadze, 'Asymmetrical War and the Notion of Armed Conflict: A Tentative Conceptualization' (2009) 91 International Review of the Red Cross 95–125.
Paust, J, 'The International Criminal Court does not have Complete Jurisdiction over Customary Crimes against Humanity and War Crimes' (2010) 43 John Marshall Law Review 681–713.
Paust, J, MC Bassiouni, and MP Scharf, *International Criminal Law: Cases and Materials* (4th edn, Carolina Academic Press 2012).
Pejic, J, 'Terrorist Acts and Groups: A Role for International Law?' (2005) 75 British Yearbook of International Law 71–100.
Pejic, J, 'Status of Armed Conflicts' in E Wilmshurst (ed), *Perspectives on the ICRC Study on Customary International Humanitarian Law* (CUP 2007) 77–100.
Pejic, J, 'The Protective Scope of Common Article 3: More than Meets the Eye' (2011) 93 International Review of the Red Cross 189–225.

Pejic, J, 'Conflict Classification and the Law Applicable to Detention and the Use of Force' in E Wilmshurst (ed), *International Law and the Classification of Conflicts* (OUP 2012) 80–116.

Pejic, J, 'Extraterritorial Targeting by Means of Armed Drones: Some Legal Implications' (2015) 96 International Review of the Red Cross 67–106.

Pellet, A, 'The New Draft Articles of the International Law Commission on the Responsibility of States for International Wrongful Acts: A Requiem for States' Crime?' (2001) 32 Netherlands Journal of International Law 55–79.

Pellet, A, 'Shaping the Future Of International Law: The Role of the World Court in Law-Making' in MH Arsanjani, J Cogan, R Sloane, and S Wiessner (eds), *Looking to the Future—Essays on International Law in Honor of W Michael Reisman* (M Nijhoff 2010) 1065–84.

Perna, L, *The Formation of the Treaty Law of Non-International Armed Conflicts* (M Nijhoff 2006).

Perrin, B, *Modern Warfare: Armed Groups, Private Militaries, Humanitarian Organizations, and the Law* (UBC Press 2012).

Pictet, JS, *Geneva Convention I for the Amelioration of the Condition of the Wounded and Sick in Armed Forces in the Field: Commentary* (ICRC 1952).

Pilloud, C, Y Sandoz, C Swinarski, and B Zimmermann, *Commentary on the Additional Protocols of 8 June 1977 to the Geneva Conventions of 12 August 1949* (ICRC 1987).

Pisillo-Mazzeschi, R, 'The Due Diligence Rule and the Nature of the International Responsibility of States' (1992) 35 German Yearbook of International Law 9–51.

Pisillo Mazzeschi, R, *Responsabilité de l'Etat pour Violation des Obligations Positives Relatives aux Droits de l'Homme* (Brill 2008).

Policzer, P, *Human Rights Violations and Non-State Armed Groups: A New Framework* (Centre of International Relations Working Papers 2005).

Porter, J, 'From Natural Law to Human Rights: Or, Why Rights Talk Matters' (1999) 14 Journal for Law and Religion 77–96.

Portmann, R, *Legal Personality in International Law* (CUP 2010).

Preux, J d, *Geneva Convention Relative to the Treatment of Prisoners of War: Commentary* (ICRC 1960).

Program on Humanitarian Policy and Conflict Research, *Advanced Practitioner's Handbook on Commissions of Inquiry: Monitoring, Reporting and Fact-Finding* (Harvard Humanitarian Initiative 2015).

Provost, R, *International Human Rights and Humanitarian Law* (CUP 2002).

Punch, M, 'Why Corporations Kill and Get Away with It: The Failure of Law to Cope with Crimes in Organizations' in H v d Wilt and A Nollkaemper (eds), *System Criminality in International Law* (CUP 2009) 42–68.

Quenivet, N, 'Applicability Test of Additional Protocol II and Common Article 3 for Crimes in Internal Armed Conflict' in D Jinks, J Maogoto, and S Solomon (eds), *Applying International Humanitarian Law in Judicial and Quasi-Judicial Bodies: International and Domestic Aspects* (TMC Asser Press 2014) 31–55.

Radin, S, 'Global Armed Conflict? The Threshold of Extraterritorial Non-International Armed Conflicts' (2013) 13 International Law Studies 696–743.

Randall, MH, 'The History of International Human Rights Law' in R Kolb and G Gaggioli (eds), *Research Handbook on Human Rights and Humanitarian Law* (Edward Elgar 2013) 3–34.

Rasulov, A, 'Revisiting State Succession to Humanitarian Treaties: Is there a Case for Automaticity?', (2003) 14 European Journal of International Law 141–70.

Ratner, SR and JS Abrams, *Accountability for Human Rights Atrocities in International Law: Beyond the Nuremberg Legacy* (3rd edn, OUP 2009).
Reinisch, A, 'The Changing International Legal Framework for Dealing with Non-State Actors' in P Alston (ed), *Non-State Actors and Human Rights* (OUP 2005) 37–89.
Rengger, N, 'The Jus in Bello in Historical and Philosophical Perspective' in L May and E Crookston (eds), *War: Essays in Political Philosophy* (CUP 2008) 30–46.
Renzo, M, 'A Criticism of the International Harm Principle' (2010) 4 *Criminal Law and Philosophy* 267–82.
Renzo, M, 'Crimes against Humanity and the Limits of International Criminal Law' (2012) 31 Law and Philosophy 443–76.
Roberts, S, 'Cyber Wars: Applying Conventional Laws of War to Cyber Warfare and Non-State Actors' (2014) 41 Northern Kentucky Law Review 535–72.
Robinson, D, 'Defining Crimes against Humanity at the Rome Conference' (1999) 93 American Journal of International Law 43–57.
Robinson, D, 'Crimes against Humanity: Reflections on State Sovereignty, Legal Precision and the Dictates of the Public Conscience' in F Lattanzi and W Schabas (eds), *Essays on the Rome statute of the International Criminal Court* (il Sirente 2000) 139–69.
Robinson, D, 'The Elements of Crimes against Humanity' in RS Lee (ed), *The International Criminal Court: Elements of Crimes and Rules of Procedure and Evidence* (Transnational 2001) 57–80.
Robinson, D, 'Essence of Crimes against Humanity Raised by Challenges at ICC' (EJIL: *Talk!*, 27 September 2011) <http://www.ejiltalk.org/essence-of-crimes-against-humanity-raised-by-challenges-at-icc/> accessed 2 November 2017.
Robinson, D, 'Crimes against Humanity: A Better Policy on "Policy"' in C Stahn (ed), *The Law and Practice of the International Criminal Court* (OUP 2014) 705–31.
Robinson, D, 'The Draft Convention on Crimes against Humanity: What to Do with the Definition?' in M Bergsmo and T Song (eds), *On the Draft Crimes against Humanity Convention* (Torkel Opsahl Academic EPublisher 2014) 103–33.
Robinson, D and H von Hebel, 'Crimes within the Jurisdiction of the Court' in RS Lee (ed), *The International Criminal Court: The Making of the Rome Statute Issues, Negotiations, Results* (Kluwer Law International 1999) 79–126.
Robinson, D, M deGuzman, C Jalloh, R Cryer et al, *Amicus Curiae Observations of Professors Robinson, deGuzman, Jalloh and Cryer, ICC-02/11-01/11* (ICC 2013).
Rodenhäuser, T, 'Fundamental Standards of Humanity: How International Law Regulates Internal Strife' (2013) 26 Journal for International Law of Peace and Armed Conflict 121–30.
Rodenhäuser, T, 'Human Rights Obligations of Non-State Armed Groups in other Situations of Violence: The Syria Example' (2013) 3 Journal of International Humanitarian Legal Studies 263–90.
Rodenhäuser, T, 'Beyond State Crimes: Non-State Entities and Crimes against Humanity' (2014) 27 Leiden Journal of International Law 913–28.
Rodenhäuser, T, 'International Legal Obligations of Armed Opposition Groups in Syria' (2015) 1 Review of Law 1.
Rodenhäuser, T, 'Squaring the Circle? Prosecuting Sexual Violence against Child Soldiers by their "Own Forces"' (2016) 14 Journal of International Criminal Justice 171–93.
Rodenhäuser, T, 'Armed Groups, Rebel Coalitions, and Transnational Groups: The Degree of Organization Required from Non-State Armed Groups to Become Party to a Non-International Armed Conflict' (2017) 19 Yearbook of International Humanitarian Law (forthcoming).

Rodenhäuser, T and G Giacca, 'The International Humanitarian Law Framework for Humanitarian Relief during Armed Conflicts and Complex Emergencies' in SC Breau and KLH Samuel (eds), *Research Handbook on Disasters and International Law* (Edward Elgar 2016) 132–53.

Rodley, NS, 'Can Armed Opposition Groups Violate Human Rights?' in KE Mahoney and P Mahoney (eds), *Human Rights in the Twenty-First Century: A Global Challenge* (M Nijhoff 1993) 297–318.

Rodley, NS, 'Non-State Actors and Human Rights' in S Sheeran and NS Rodley (eds), *Routledge Handbook of International Human Rights Law* (Routledge 2013) 523–44.

Rohan, G and A Oreg, 'Al Qaeda's Organizational Structure and its Evolution' (2010) 33 Studies in Conflict & Terrorism 1043–78.

Röling, BVA, 'The Significance of the Laws of War' in A Cassese (ed), *Current Problems of International Law: Essays on UN Law and on the Law of Armed Conflict* (A Giuffrè 1975) 133–55.

Ronen, Y, 'Human Rights Obligations of Territorial Non-State Actors' (2013) 46 Cornell International Law Journal 21–50.

Rosas, A, *The Legal Status of Prisoners of War: A Study in International Humanitarian Law Applicable in Armed Conflicts* (Institute for Human Rights Åbo Akademi University 2005).

Rousseau, J-J, *Du Contrat Social* (Dover Publications 1762).

Rousseau, J-J, *The Social Contract* (Hafner Publishing 1762).

Rückert, W and G Witschel, 'Genocide and Crimes against Humanity in the Elements of Crimes' in H Fischer, C Kress, and SR Lüder (eds.), *International and National Prosecution of Crimes Under International Law: Current Developments* (Berliner Wissenschafts-Verlag 2004) 59–93.

Rudolf, B, 'Non-State Actors in Areas of Limited Statehood as Addresses of Public International Law Norms on Governance' (2010) 4 Human Rights and International Legal Discourse 127–44.

Rwelamira, M, 'The Significance and Contribution of the Protocol Additional to the Geneva Conventions of August 1949' in C Swinarski, M Petitpierre, P Graber, and JS Pictet (eds), *Etudes et Sssais sur le Droit International Humanitaire et sur les Principes de la Croix-Rouge en l'Honneur de Jean Picte* (M Nijhoff 1984) 227–36.

Ryngaert, C, 'Human Rights Obligations of Armed Groups' (2008) 41 Revue Belge De Droit International 355–81.

Ryngaert, C and M Noortmann, 'New Actors in Global Governance and International Human Rights Law' (2010) 4 Human Rights & International Legal Discourse 5–14.

Sadat, LN, 'The Interpretation of the Nuremberg Principles by the French Court of Cassation: From Touvier to Barbie and Back Again' (1994) 32 Columbia Journal of Transnational Law 289–380.

Sadat, LN, 'Crimes against Humanity in the Modern Age' (2012) 107 American Journal of International Law 334–77.

Sassòli, M, *Transnational Armed Groups and International Humanitarian Law* (Humanitarian Policy and Conflict Research 2006).

Sassòli, M, 'Humanitarian Law and International Criminal Law' in A Cassese (ed), *The Oxford Companion to International Criminal Justice* (OUP 2009) 111–20.

Sassòli, M, 'Taking Armed Groups Seriously: Ways to Improve their Compliance with International Humanitarian Law' (2010) 1 Journal of International Humanitarian Legal Studies 5–51.

Sassòli, M and Y Shany, 'DEBATE: Should the Obligations of States and Armed Groups under International Humanitarian Law Really be Equal?' (2011) 93 International Review of the Red Cross 425–42.

Schabas, WA, 'Sentencing by International Tribunals: A Human Rights Approach' (1997) 7 Duke Journal of Comparative & International Law 461–518.

Schabas, WA, 'Darfur and the "Odious Scourge": The Commission of Inquiry's Findings on Genocide' (2005) 18 Leiden Journal of International Law 871–85.

Schabas, WA, 'State Policy as an Element of International Crimes' (2008) 98 The Journal of Criminal Law & Criminology 953–82.

Schabas, WA, *Genocide in International Law: The Crime of Crimes* (2nd edn, CUP 2009).

Schabas, WA, *The International Criminal Court: A Commentary on the Rome Statute* (OUP 2010).

Schabas, WA, 'London Riots: Were They Crimes Against Humanity?'(15 August 2011) <http://humanrightsdoctorate.blogspot.ch/2011/08/london-riots-were-they-crimes-against.html> accessed 2 November 2017.

Schabas, WA, *Unimaginable Atrocities: Justice, Politics, and Rights at the War Crimes Tribunals* (OUP 2012).

Schabas, WA, *The Universal Declaration of Human Rights: The 'Travaux Préparatoires'* (CUP 2013).

Schabas, WA, *The International Criminal Court: A Commentary on the Rome Statute* (2nd edn, OUP 2017).

Schindler, D, 'State of War, Belligerency, Armed Conflict' in A Cassese and A Eide (eds), *The New Humanitarian Law of Armed Conflict: Proceedings of the 1976 and 1977 Conferences* (Editoriale Scientifica 1979) 3–20.

Schindler, D, *The Different Types of Armed Conflicts According to the Geneva Conventions and Protocols* (M Nijhoff 1979).

Schmitt, MN, 'Classification of Cyber Conflict' (2012) 17 Journal of Conflict & Security Law 245–60.

Schmitt, MN, 'Charting the Legal Geography of Non-International Armed Conflict' (2014) 90 International Law Studies Series 1–19.

Schmitt, MN and NATO, *Tallinn Manual on the International Law Applicable to Cyber Warfare* (CUP 2013).

Schöberl, K, 'The Geographical Scope of Application of the Conventions' in A Clapham, P Gaeta, and M Sassòli (eds), *The 1949 Geneva Conventions: A Commentary* (OUP 2015) 68–83.

Schoiswohl, M, 'De Facto Regimes and Human Rights Obligations—The Twilight Zone of Public International Law' (2001) 9 Austrian Review of International and European Law 45–90.

Schwelb, E, 'Crimes against Humanity' (1946) 23 British Year Book of International Law 178–226.

Scobbie, I, 'Assumptions and Presumptions: State Responsiblity for System Crimes' in H v d Wilt and A Nollkaemper (eds), *System Criminality in International Law* (CUP 2009) 270–97.

Scott, JB, *Prize Cases Decided in the United State Supreme Court* (Clarendon Press 1923).

Seralvo, J, 'Government Recognition and International Humanitarian Law Applicability in Post-Gaddafi Libya' (2016) 18 Yearbook of International Humanitarian Law 2015 3–41.

Shahabuddeen, M, 'Does the Principle of Legality Stand in the Way of Progressive Development of Law?' (2004) 2 Journal of International Criminal Justice 1007–17.

Shaheen, K and C Stephen, 'From Syria to Bosnia: ISIS and its Affiliates around the World', *The Guardian* (3 July 2015).

Shestack, JJ, 'The Philosophic Foundations of Human Rights' (1998) 20 Human Rights Quarterly 201–34.

Shue, H, *Basic Rights: Subsistence, Affluence, and US Foreign Policy* (Princeton University Press 1980).

Shue, H, *Basic Rights* (2nd edn, Princeton University Press 1996).

Simma, B and P Alston, 'The Sources of Human Rights Law: Custom, Jus Cogens, and General Priniples' (1988) 12 Australian Yearbook of International Law 82–108.

Simma, B and AL Paulus, 'The Responsibility of Individuals for Human Rights Abuses in Internal Conflicts: A Positivist View' (1999) 93 American Journal of International Law 302–16.

Sinno, AH, 'Armed Groups' Organizational Structure and Their Strategic Options' (2011) 93 International Review of the Red Cross 311–32.

Sivakumaran, S, 'Binding Armed Opposition Groups' (2006) 55 International & Comparative Law Quarterly 369–94.

Sivakumaran, S, 'Courts of Armed Opposition Groups' (2009) 7 Journal of International Criminal Justice 489–513.

Sivakumaran, S, 'Identifying an Armed Conflict not of an International Character' in G Sluiter and C Stahn (eds), *The Emerging Practice of the International Criminal Court* (Brill 2009) 361–80.

Sivakumaran, S, 'Re-Envisaging the International Law of Internal Armed Conflict' (2011) 22 European Journal of International Law 219–64.

Sivakumaran, S, 'Non-International Armed Conflicts: The Applicable Law' in C d Bruges (ed), *Scope of Application of International Humanitarian Law* (College of Europe 2012) 25–33.

Sivakumaran, S, 'Command Responsibility in Irregular Groups' (2012) 10 Journal of International Criminal Justice 1129–50.

Sivakumaran, S, *The Law of Non-International Armed Conflict* (OUP 2012).

Sivakumaran, S, 'The Addressees of Common Article 3' in A Clapham, P Gaeta, and M Sassòli (eds), *The 1949 Geneva Conventions: A Commentary* (OUP 2015) 415–33.

Sivakumaran, S and A Roberts, 'Lawmaking by Non-State Actors: Engaging Armed Groups in the Creation of International Humanitarian Law' (2011) 37 Yale Journal of International Law 107–52.

Somer, J, 'Jungle Justice: Passing Sentence on the Equality of Belligerents in Non-International Armed Conflict' (2007) 89 International Review of the Red Cross 655–90.

Somer, J, *Education and Armed Non-State Actors: Towards a Comprehensive Agenda* (Protect Education in Insecurity and Conflict 2015).

Somer, J and Borgard P, 'Monitoring Armed Non-State Actor Compliance with Humanitarian Norms: a Look at International Mechanisms and the Geneva Call Deed of Commitment' (2011) 92 International Review of the Red Cross 673–706.

Spencer, P, *Genocide since 1945* (Routledge 2012).

Spieker, H, 'The International Criminal Court and Non-International Armed Conflicts' (2000) 13 Leiden Journal of International Law 395–425.

Spieker, H, 'Twenty-Five Years after the Adoption of Additional Protocol II: Breakthrough or Failure of Humanitarian Legal Protection?' (2001) 4 Yearbook of International Humanitarian Law 129–66.

Stark, W (ed), *Jeremy Bentham's Economic Writings: Critical Edition Based on his Printed Works and Unprinted Manuscripts* (transferred to digital printing, Routledge 2010).

Taki, H, 'Effectiveness' in R Wolfrum and Max-Planck-Institut für Ausländisches Öffentliches Recht und Völkerrecht (Heidelberg) (eds), *The Max-Planck Encyclopedia of Public International Law* (OUP 2012).

Talmon, S, 'Determining Customary International Law: The ICJ's Methodology between Induction, Deduction and Assertion' (2015) 26 European Journal of International Law 417–43.

Thomas, DQ and ME Beasley, 'Domestic Violence as a Human Rights Issue' (1995) 58 Alabama Law Review 1119–48.

Thürer, D, 'The "Failed State" and International Law' (1999) 81 International Review of the Red Cross 731–61.

Tomuschat, C, 'Crimes against the Peace and the Security of Mankind and the Recalcitrant Third State' in Y Dinstein and M Tabory (eds), *War Crimes in International Law* (M Nijhoff 1996).

Tomuschat, C, 'The Applicability of Human Rights Law to Insurgent Movements' in H Fischer and D Fleck (eds), *Krisensicherung und Humanitärer Schutz: Festschrift für Dieter Fleck* (BWV 2004) 573–91.

Tomuschat, C, *Human Rights: Between Idealism and Realism* (2nd edn, OUP 2008).

Tomuschat, C, 'The Responsibility of other Entities: Private Individuals' in J Crawford, A Pellet, and S Olleson (eds), *The Law of International Responsibility* (OUP 2010) 317–29.

Triffterer, O (ed), Commentary on the Rome Statute of the International Criminal Court: Observers' Notes, Article by Article (2nd edn, CH Beck 2008).

US Department of Defense, *Remarks by the General Counsel of the Department of Defense on the Legal Framework for the United States' Use of Military Force Since 9/11* (US Department of Defense, 10 April 2015).

US Department of Defense, *Statement from Pentagon Press Secretary Peter Cook on US Strike in Libya* (US Department of Defense, 14 November 2015).

Uhler, O and H Coursier, *Geneva Convention Relative to the Protection of Civilian Persons in Time of War: Commentary* (ICRC 1958).

United Kingdom Ministry of Defence, *The Joint Service Manual of the Law of Armed Conflict* (Ministry of Defence 2004).

United Nations, *Yearbook of the International Law Commission, Vol II* (United Nations 1966).

United Nations Childrens' Fund, *Guide to the Optional Protocol on the Involvement of Children in Armed Conflicts* (UNICEF 2003).

United Nations Economic and Social Council, *Draft Convention on the Crime of Genocide* (United Nations 1947).

United States National Intelligence Council, *Global Trends 2025: A Transformed World* (US National Intelligence Council 2008).

Van der Wilt, H and A Nollkaemper (eds), *System Criminality in International Law* (CUP 2009).

Van der Wilt, H, J Vervliet, G Sluiter, and JH t Cate (eds), *The Genocide Convention: The Legacy of 60 Years* (M Nijhoff 2012).

Van der Wilt, H 'Crimes against Humanity: A Category Hors Concours in (International) Criminal Law?' in B van Beers, L Corrias, and WG Werner (eds), *Humanity across International Law and Biolaw* (CUP 2014) 25–41.

Vandewiele, T, *Optional Protocol: The Involvement of Children in Armed Conflicts—A Commentary on the United Nations Convention on the Rights of the Child* (M Nijhoff 2006).

Vattel, E d, *The Law of Nations* (translation by Joseph Chitty) (T & JW Johnson & Co 1758).

Venturini, G, 'The Temporal Scope of Application of the Conventions' in A Clapham, P Gaeta, and M Sassòli (eds), *The 1949 Geneva Conventions: A Commentary* (OUP 2015) 51–66.

Verhoeven, SI, 'International Responsibility of Armed Opposition Groups: Lessons from State Responsibility for Actions of Armed Opposition Groups' in CR a MN Noemi Gal-Or (ed), *Responsibilities of the Non-State Actor in Armed Conflict and the Market Place* (Brill Nijhoff 2015) 285–303.

Vermeulen, ML, *Enforced Disappearance: Determining State Responsibility under the International Convention for the Protection of All Persons from Enforced Disappearance* (Intersentia 2012).

Vernon, R, 'What is Crime against Humanity?' (2002) 10 Journal of Political Philosophy 231–49.

Vest, H, 'A Structure-Based Concept of Genocidal Intent' (2007) 5 Journal of International Criminal Justice 781–97.

Veuthey, M, 'Guérilla et Droit Humanitaire' (1983) 65 International Review of the Red Cross 119–42.

Vité, S, 'Typology of Armed Conflicts in International Humanitarian Law: Legal Concepts and Actual Situations' (2009) 91 International Review of the Red Cross 69–94.

Watkin, K, 'Opportunity Lost: Organized Armed Groups and the ICRC Direct Participation in Hostilities Interpretive Guidance' (2009) 42 New York University Journal of International Law and Politics 641–95.

Wehberg, H, *La Guerre Civile et le Droit International* (M Nijhoff 1938).

Weinstein, JM, *Inside Rebellion: The Politics of Insurgent Violence* (CUP 2007).

Weissbrodt, D, 'Business and Human Rights' (2005) 74 University of Cincinnati Law Review 55–74.

Werle, G, *Principles of International Criminal Law* (TMC Asser Press 2005).

Werle, G, *Principles of International Criminal Law* (2nd edn, TMC Asser Press 2009).

Werle, G and B Burghardt, 'Do Crimes against Humanity Require the Participation of a State or a 'State-Like' Organization?' (2012) 10 Journal of International Criminal Justice 1151–70.

Werle, G and F Jessberger, *Principles of International Criminal Law* (3rd edn, OUP 2014).

Wheaton, H, *Elements of International Law* (Clarendon Press 1936).

Wilde, R, 'Understanding the International Territorial Administration Accountability Deficit: Trusteeship and the Legitimacy of International Organizations' (2010) 12 International Peacekeeping: The Yearbook of International Peace Operations 155–70.

Wilhelm, R-J, *Problèmes Relatifs à la Protection de la Personne Humaine par le Droit International dans les Conflits Armés ne Présentant pas un Caractère International* (Brill 1972).

Wilmshurst, E (ed), *Perspectives on the ICRC Study on Customary International Humanitarian Law* (CUP 2007).

Wilson, HA, *International Law and the Use of Force by National Liberation Movements* (Clarendon Press 1988).

Woolsey, TS, 'The Consequences of the Cuban Belligerency' (1896) 5 Yale Law Journal 182–86.

Wyler, E, 'From "State Crime" to Responsibility for "Serious Breaches of Obligations under Peremptory Norms of General International Law"' (2002) 13 European Journal of International Law 1147–60.

Xenos, D, *The Positive Obligations of the State under the European Convention of Human Rights* (Routledge 2012).

Yale Law Journal, 'Genocide: A Commentary on the Convention' (1949) 58 Yale Law Journal 1142–60.

Yun, S, 'Breaking Imaginary Barriers' (2014) 5 Journal of International Humanitarian Legal Studies 213–57.

Zappalà, S, 'Can Legality Trump Effectiveness in Today's International Law?' in A Cassese (ed), *Realizing Utopia: The Future of International Law* (OUP 2012) 105–17.
Zegveld, L, *Accountability of Armed Opposition Groups in International Law* (CUP 2002).
Zimmermann A and Teichmann M, 'State Responsibility for International Crimes' in H v d Wilt and A Nollkaemper (eds), *System Criminality in International Law* (CUP 2009) 298–313.
Zorgbibe, C, 'Sources of the Recognition of Belligerent Status' (1977) 17 International Review of the Red Cross 111–27.

Index